CENTRAL ITALY
Tuscany & Umbria

the collected traveler

ITALIA
I.P.Z.S. - ROMA
€ 0.34
650
L'VANGELI

Also in the series by Barrie Kerper

PARIS

The Collected Traveler

CENTRAL
ITALY

Tuscany & Umbria

the collected traveler

ITALIA
50
ROCCA DI CALASCIO
LAZS-ROMA

AN INSPIRED
ANTHOLOGY & TRAVEL
RESOURCE

Collected by Barrie Kerper

Three Rivers Press / NEW YORK

Additional credits appear on page 612.

Published by Three Rivers Press, New York, New York
Member of the Crown Publishing Group
Random House, Inc. New York, Toronto, London, Sydney, Auckland
www.randomhouse.com

THREE RIVERS PRESS is a registered trademark and the Three Rivers Press logo is a trademark of Random House, Inc.

Printed in the United States of America

DESIGN BY LYNNE AMFT

Library of Congress Cataloging-in-Publication Data
Central Italy, Tuscany & Umbria. The collected traveler:
an inspired anthology & travel resource / collected by Barrie Kerper.
1. Tuscany (Italy)—Guidebooks. 2. Umbria (Italy)—Guidebooks.
3. Travelers' writings. 4. Tuscany (Italy)—Description and travel—
Sources. 5. Umbria (Italy)—Description and travel—Sources.
I. Kerper, Barrie.
DG732.C46 2000
914.5'504—dc21   00-025351

ISBN 0-609-80443-X

10 9 8 7 6 5 4

acknowledgments

Publishing a book requires a staggering amount of work by a team of dedicated people. An anthology, however, requires the participation of an even greater number of people, ensuring the project will be that much more complex. It is essential, therefore, that I extend my heartfelt thanks and deep gratitude to the following colleagues and friends: Alison Gross, Anne Messitte, Bonnie Ammer, Anthony Gambino, Jessica Schulte, Kristen Wolfe, Whitney Cookman, Teresa Nicholas, Jane Searle, Jay and Kathleen Goodfriend, Maha Khalil, Vivian Fong, Ana Suffredini, Amy Myer, Florence Porrino, Patty Flynn, Steve Weissman, Darcy DiMona, and the staff at the Italian Government Tourist Office in New York. Special thanks are due to Steve Magnuson, whose enthusiasm for this project resulted in it becoming reality; each of the individual writers, agents, and permissions representatives for various publishers and periodicals—especially Leigh Montville of The Condé Nast Publications and Rose Sorvino of *The New York Times*—without whose generosity and understanding there would be nothing to publish; Shaye Areheart, my editor, who I am honored to work with and am grateful to for a million reasons, most especially for her belief in the series and her firm but guiding hand; Amy Boorstein, Mark McCauslin, and Lynne Amft of Crown's production editorial and art departments, who after many missed deadlines and an initial manuscript of over 2,000 pages, somehow figured out how to pull everything together and get the thing published; Chip Gibson, the best boss and mentor I've ever had, who allowed me to spend much of my time at the office working on this (although there were many days he questioned the wisdom of that decision); and Lorraine and Luc Paillard, *mes amis intimes* and correspondents *par excellence*, who sent more notes, restaurant and hotel tips, postcards, and invaluable observations than I can possibly count. Lastly, my sincere apologies to the many friends, relatives, and colleagues not named here—you know who you are—who never failed to inquire about my progress but with whom I was out of touch for over a year, and to my husband, Jeffrey, and daughter, Alyssa. It was perhaps inevitable that Jeff would be left with baby duty more often than he imagined, but while I'm sorry for creating the burden, I believe the effort will prove to have been worthwhile. Alyssa is too young to realize it now, but I hope our home and, by extension, this series, will inspire in her a love of reading and travel, ensuring she will grow up to be a true citizen of the world.

contents

CENTRAL ITALY
Tuscany & Umbria

The Collected Traveler

PER VIA AEREA
PAR AVION

Mod 24-R

Introduction

"A traveller without knowledge is a bird without wings."
—Sa'di, *Gulistan* (1258)

SOME YEARS AGO, MY HUSBAND and I fulfilled a dream we'd had since we first met: We put all our belongings in storage and traveled around the countries bordering the Mediterranean Sea for a year. In preparation for this journey, I did what I always do in advance of a trip, which is to consult my home archives, an extensive library of books and periodicals. I have been an obsessive clipper since I was very young, and by the time I was preparing for this trip, I had amassed an enormous number of articles from periodicals on various countries of the world. After a year of reading and organizing all this material, I created a package of articles and notes for each destination and mailed them ahead to friends we'd be staying with as well as appropriate American Express offices—although we had no schedule to speak of, we knew we would spend no less than six weeks in each place.

My husband wasted no time informing me that my research efforts were perhaps a bit over the top. He shares my passion for travel (my mother-in-law told me that when he was little he would announce to the family exactly how many months, weeks, days, hours, minutes, and seconds it was before the annual summer vacation) but not necessarily for clipping (he has accused me of being too much like the anal-retentive fisherman from an old *Saturday Night Live* skit, the one where the guy neatly puts his bait, extra line, snacks, hand towels, etc., into individual plastic sandwich bags. In my defense, I'm not *quite* that bad (although I *am* guilty of trying to improve upon pocket organizers, and I do have a wooden rack for drying rinsed plastic bags in my kitchen).

While we were traveling that year, we would occasionally meet other Americans, and I was continually amazed at how ill prepared some of them were. Information, in so many different forms, is in such abundance in the twenty-first century that it was nearly inconceivable to me that people had not taken advantage of the resources available to them. Some people we met didn't even seem to be having a very good time; they appeared to be ignorant of various customs and observances and were generally unimpressed with their experience because they had missed the significance of what they were seeing and doing. Therefore, I was surprised again when these same people—and they were of varying ages with varying wallet sizes—were genuinely interested in my little packages of notes and articles. Some people even offered to *pay* me for them, and I began to think that my collected research would perhaps appeal to other travelers. I also realized that even the most well-intentioned people were overwhelmed by trip planning or didn't have the time to put it all together. Later, friends and colleagues told me they really appreciated the packages I prepared for them, and somewhere along the line I was being referred to as a "modern-day hunter-gatherer," a sort of "one-stop information source." Each book in The Collected Traveler series provides resources and information to travelers—people I define as inquisitive, individualistic, and indefatigable in their eagerness to explore—or informs them of where they may look further to find it.

While there is much to be said for a freewheeling approach to travel—I am not an advocate of sticking to rigid schedules—I do believe that, as with most things in life, what you get out of a trip is equal only to what you put into it. I feel that learning about a place is part of the excitement of travel, and I wouldn't dream of venturing anywhere without first poring over a mountain of maps, books, and periodicals. I include cookbooks in my reading (some cookbooks reveal much historical detail as well as prepare you for the food and drink you will most likely encounter), and I also like to watch movies that have something to do with where I'm going. Additionally, I buy a blank journal and begin filling it with all sorts of notes, reminders, and entire passages from books I'm not taking along. In other words, I immerse myself in my destination before I leave. It's the most enjoyable homework assignment I've ever had.

Every destination, new or familiar, merits some attention. I don't endorse the extreme—you don't want to spend all your time in the hotel room reading books—but it most definitely pays to know before you go (just leave some room for the chance encounter or unpredictable surprise. The reward for your efforts is that you'll acquire a deeper understanding and appreciation of the place and the people who live there, and, not surprisingly, you'll have more fun.

"Every land has its own special rhythm, and unless the traveler takes the time to learn the rhythm, he or she will remain an outsider there always."
—Juliette de Baircli Levy, E n g l i s h   w r i t e r

Occasionally I meet people who are more interested in how many countries I've been to than in those I might know well or particularly like. If "well-traveled" is defined only by the number of places I've been, then I suppose I'm not. However, I feel I really *know* and have really *seen* the places I've visited, which is how *I* define well-traveled. I travel to see how people live in other parts of the world, not to check countries off a list, and to do that requires immediately adapting to the local pace and rhythm and (hopefully) sticking around for more than a few days. I am curious about the elderly man in his shoe repair shop, the fruit vendor at the Mercato Centrale who talks nonstop and greets everyone like she's known them all her life. What is life like in the beautiful apartment building off the piazza, the one the young boy has just entered carrying a purchase from the *panificio?* And, enviously, I wonder where the two office girls breaking for a cigarette bought their beautiful suits. Certainly any place you decide is worthy of your time and effort is worthy of more than a day, but you don't always need an indefinite period of time to immerse yourself in the local culture or establish a routine that allows for getting to know the merchants and residents of your adopted neighborhood. One of the fastest ways to adjust to daily life in Italy is to abandon whatever schedule you observe at home and eat when the Italians eat. Mealtimes in Italy are generally well established, and if you have not purchased provisions for a picnic or found a place to eat by one, restaurants will be full and shops closed. Likewise, dinner is not typically served at six, an hour that is entirely too early for anyone in a Mediterranean country to contemplate his or her next meal. Frances Mayes, in her justifiably popular book *Under the Tuscan Sun,* addresses this issue well in writing that many tourists make the mistake "of eating two wedges of great sausage pizza at eleven and now have no inclination to eat anything. Instead, they wander under the unbearable sun, peeking through metal grates covering shop windows, pushing at the massive doors of locked churches, sitting on the sides of fountains while squinting into miniscule guidebooks. Give it up! I've done the same thing. Then, later, it's hard to deny yourself the luscious *melone* ice cream cone at seven, when the air is still hot and your sandals have rubbed your heels raw. Those weak ones (mea culpa) who succumb possibly will have another wedge, artichoke this time, on the way to the hotel; then, when Italy begins eating at nine, the foreign stomach doesn't even mumble. That happens much later, when all the good restaurants are full." Adjust your schedule and you'll be on Italian time, doing things when the Italians do them, eliminating possible disappointment and frustration, and feeling utterly out of step.

About fifteen years ago, the former Paris bureau chief for *The New York Times,* John Vinocur, wrote a piece for the travel section entitled "Discovering the Hidden Paris." In it, he noted that the French have a word, not easily translated into English, known as *d'épaysement.* His translation of the word was "the feeling of not being assaulted by the familiarity of things, a change in surroundings where there is no immediate point of reference." He went on to quote a French journalist who once said that "Americans don't travel to be *dépaysés,* but to find a home away from home." This is unfortunate but too often true. These tourists can travel all around the world if they desire, but their unwillingness to adapt ensures they will never really leave home.

Similar are the people who endorse "adventure travel," words which make me cringe as they seem to imply that unless one partakes in kayaking, mountain climbing, biking, rock climbing, or some other physical endeavor, a travel experience is somehow invalid or unadventurous. *All* travel is an adventure, and unless adventure travel allows for plenty of time to adapt to the local rhythm, the so-called adventure is really a physically strenuous—if memorable—outdoor achievement. Occasionally I hear descriptions of a biking excursion, for example, where the participants spend the majority of each day in the same way: making biking the priority instead of working biking into the local cadence of daily life. When I ask if they joined the locals at the *caffè* for a morning capuccino or an evening *aperitivo,* shopped at the outdoor *mercato,* went to a local *festa,* or people-watched in the *piazza,* the answer is invariably no. They might have had an amazing bike trip, but they do not know Italy. One has to get off the bike a bit more often for that sort of knowledge. And if a biking experience alone is what they were seeking, they certainly didn't need to fly to Italy; there are plenty of challenging and beautiful places to bike in the United States.

I believe that every place in the world offers *something* of interest. In her magnificent book *Black Lamb and Grey Falcon*, Rebecca West recounts how in the 1930s she passed through Skopje, Yugoslavia (formerly the Yugoslav Republic of Macedonia), by train twice, without stopping, because friends had told her the town wasn't worth visiting. A third time through she did stop, and she met two wonderful people who became lasting friends. She wrote, "Now, when I go through a town of which I know nothing, a town which appears to be a waste land of uniform streets wholly without quality, I look on it in wonder and hope, since it may hold a Mehmed, a Militsa." I, too, have been richly rewarded by pausing in places (Skopje included) that first appeared quite limiting. While it's true the world is more accessible—and therefore feels smaller—I do not believe it is more homogenous. Those who think Europe, or Italy, isn't exotic enough are simply mistaken. Perhaps it's been a while since they were there; perhaps they've never been at all. Things *are* different in Italy. Everyday scenes of young women crossing a cobblestone street in stiletto heels balancing two cups of espresso, men conversing animatedly using so many unfamiliar hand and facial gestures you think you've landed on Mars, widowed women dressed head to toe in black, and merchants closing up shop simultaneously for siesta on a hot summer afternoon are just as foreign as those in Asia or Africa.

"Travel is fatal to prejudice, bigotry, and narrow-mindedness."
—Mark Twain

"The world is a book, and those who do not travel read only a page."
—St. Augustine

I am assuming if you've read this far that something compelled you to pick up this book and that you feel travel is an essential part of life. I would add to Mark Twain's quotation above one by Benjamin Disraeli (1804 1881): "Travel teaches toleration." People who travel with an open mind and are receptive to the ways of others cannot help but return with more tolerance for people and situations at home, at work, in their cities and communities. I find that travel also ensures I will not be quite the same person I was before I left. After a trip, I typically have a lot of renewed energy and bring new perspectives to my job. At home, I ask myself how I can incorporate attributes or traits I observed into my own life and share them with my husband and daughter.

The anthologies in The Collected Traveler series offer a record of people's achievements and shortcomings. It may be a lofty goal to expect that they might also offer an opportunity for us to measure our own deeds and flaws as Americans and realize that despite cultural differences between us and our hosts—in *any* country where we happen to be guests—we have much more in common than not. It is a sincere goal, however—one that I hope readers and travelers will embrace.

About This Series

The Collected Traveler editions are not guidebooks in the traditional sense. In another sense, however, they *may* be considered guidebooks in that they are books that guide readers to other sources. Each book is really the first book you should turn to when planning a trip. If you think of the individual volumes as a sort of planning package, you've got the right idea. To borrow a phrase from a reviewer who was writing about the Lonely Planet Travel Survival Kit series years ago, The Collected Traveler is for people who know how to get their luggage off the carousel. If you enjoy acquiring knowledge about where you're going, whether you plan a trip independently or with a like-minded tour organization, this series is for you. If you're looking for a guide that simply informs you of exact prices, hours, and highlights, you probably won't be interested in the depth this book offers. (That is not meant to offend, merely to say you've got the wrong book.)

A few words about me might also help you determine if this series is for you. I travel somewhat frugally, more because I choose to than out of necessity. I respect money and its value, and I'm not convinced that if I spent $600 a night on a hotel room, for example, that it would represent a good value or that I would have a better trip. I've been to some of the world's finest hotels, mostly to visit friends who are staying at them or to have a drink in the bar. With a few notable exceptions, it seems to me that the majority of these places are alike, meant to conform to a code of sameness and predictability. There's nothing about them that is particularly Italian or French or Turkish. You could be *anywhere.* The cheapest of the cheap accommodations don't represent good value either. I look for places to stay that are usually old, possibly historic, with lots of charm and character. I do not mind if my room is small; I do not need a television, telephone, or hair dryer; and I most definitely do not care for an American-style buffet breakfast, which is hardly what the locals eat. I also prefer to make my own plans, send my own letters and faxes, place telephone calls, and arrange transportation. Not because I think I can do it better than a professional agent (whose expertise I admire), but because I enjoy it and learn a lot in the process. Finally, lest readers think I do not appreciate beauty or elegance, allow me to state that I think you'll quickly ascertain that I do indeed enjoy many of life's little luxuries, when I perceive them to be of good value to me.

This series promotes the view of staying longer within a smaller area. Susan Allen Toth refers to this in her book *England as You Like It,* in which she subscribes to the "thumbprint theory of travel"—

spending at least a week in one spot no larger than her thumbprint covers on a large-scale map of England. She goes on to explain that excursions are encouraged, as long as they're about an hour's drive away. As I have discovered in my own travels, a week in one place, even a spot no bigger than my thumbprint, is rarely long enough to see and enjoy it all. The Collected Traveler focuses on one corner of the world, the countries bordering the Mediterranean Sea. I find the Mediterranean endlessly fascinating. The sea itself is the world's largest, the region is one of the world's ancient crossroads, and it is home to the most diverse humanity as it stretches from Asia to the Atlantic. As Paul Theroux has noted in his excellent book *The Pillars of Hercules*, "The Mediterranean, this simple almost tideless sea, the size of thirty Lake Superiors, had everything: prosperity, poverty, tourism, terrorism, several wars in progress, ethnic strife, fascists, pollution, drift nets, private islands owned by billionaires, Gypsies, seventeen countries, fifty languages, oil drilling platforms, sponge fishermen, religious fanatics, drug smuggling, fine art, and warfare. It had Christians, Muslims, Jews; it had the Druzes, who are a strange farrago of all three religions; it had heathens, Zoroastrians and Copts and Baha'is." Diversity aside, the great explorers in the service of Spain, Portugal, France, and Italy departed from Mediterranean ports to discover so much of the rest of the world. The Collected Traveler also focuses on cities and regions rather than entire countries (there will not be a book on all of Italy, for example), but Italy is a member of two communities, European and Mediterranean, and an understanding of both is essential to understanding Italy. This central Italy edition covers Tuscany and Umbria, two regions that can manageably be seen together. Some travelers may fly in or out of Rome or may be heading south from Emilia-Romagna, Milano, or Venezia, but each of these areas deserves to be covered in a separate book and is too far outside this particular thumbprint.

Each section of this book features a selection of articles from various periodicals and an annotated bibliography relevant to the theme of each section (the *Informazioni Pratiche* section is a bit different, with the books being a part of the A–Z listings). I have chosen the articles and books from my own files and home library, which I've maintained for over two decades. The selected writings reflect the culture, politics, history, current social issues, religion, cuisine, and arts of the people you'll be visiting. They also represent the observations and opinions of a wide variety of novelists, travel writers, and journalists. These writers are authorities on Tuscany or Umbria or Italy or all three; they either live there (as permanent or part-time residents) or visit there often for business or pleasure. I'm very discriminating in seeking opinions and recommendations, and I am not interested in the remarks of unobservant wanderers. Likewise, I don't ask someone who doesn't read much what he or she thinks of a particular book, and I don't ask someone who neither cooks nor travels for a restaurant recommendation. I am not implying that first-time visitors to Italy have nothing noteworthy or interesting to share—they very often do, and are often very keen observers; conversely, frequent travelers are often jaded and apt to miss the finer details that make Tuscany and Umbria the exceptional places they are. I am interested in the opinions of people who want to *know* central Italy, not just *see* it.

I've included numerous older articles (even though some of the specific information regarding prices, hours, etc., is no longer accurate) because they were either particularly well written, thought-provoking, or unique in some way and because the authors' views stand as a valuable record of a certain time in history. Often, even with the passage of many years, you may share the same emotions and opinions of the writer, and equally as often, *plus ca change, plus c'est la meme chose*. I have many, many more articles in my files than I was able to reprint here. Though there are a few pieces whose absence I very much regret, I believe the anthology you're holding is very good.

A word about the dining out section, *A Tavola!:* I have great respect for restaurant reviewers. Their work may seem glamorous—it sometimes is—but it is also very hard. It's an all-consuming, full-time job, and that is why I urge you to consult four very good books: *Eating in Italy* by Faith Heller Willinger, *Italy for the Gourmet Traveler* by Fred Plotkin, *Cheap Eats in Italy* by Sandra Gustafson, and *The Food Lover's Companion to Tuscany* by Carla Capalbo, all detailed in the *A Tavola biblioteca.* My files are bulging with restaurant reviews, and I could have included many, many more articles about *ristoranti* and *trattorie;* but it would be too repetitive and ultimately beside the point. I have selected a few articles that give you a feel for eating out in central Italy, alert you to some things to look for in selecting a truly worthwhile place versus a mediocre one, and highlight some dishes that are not commonplace in America. My files are also bulging with hotel recommendations, but as with dining out, I urge you to consult one or more of the great books I recommend in *Informazioni Pratiche.*

The annotated bibliography for each section is one of the most important features of this book. Reading about travel in the days before trans-Atlantic flights, I always marvel at the number of steamer trunks and amount of baggage people were accustomed to taking. If it were me traveling then, however, my bags would be filled with books, not clothes. Although I travel light and seldom check bags, I have been known to fill an entire suitcase with books, secure in the knowledge that I could have them all with me for the duration of my trip. Each *biblioteca* features titles I feel are the best available, most worth your time. I realize that "best" is subjective; readers will simply have to trust me that I have been extremely thorough in deciding which books to recommend. (I have read them all, by the way, and I own them all, with the exception of a few I borrowed.) If the lists seem long, they are, but the more I read, the more I realize there is to know, and there are an awful lot of really good books out there! I'm not suggesting you read them *all,* but I do hope you will not be content with just one. I have identified some books as *essenziale,* meaning that I consider them required reading; but I sincerely believe that *all* the books I've mentioned are important, helpful, well written, or all three. There are surely some books I've not seen, so if some of your favorites aren't included here, please write and tell me about them.

I have not hesitated to list out-of-print titles because some excellent books are declared out-of-print (and deserve to be returned to print!), and because many of these books can be found through individuals who specialize in out-of-print books, booksellers, libraries, and on-line searches. I should also mention that I believe the companion reading you bring along should be related in some way to where you're going. Therefore, the books listed in *La Bella Vita* are novels and nonfiction books that feature characters or settings in Tuscany or Umbria, or feature aspects of Italy and the Italians (such as *A Room with a View, The English Patient, Desiring Italy,* and *Italy in Mind*). Also, biographies make up most of the books in the *I Personaggi* section. The selection isn't meant to be comprehensive—there are many more I could have included—but represent a variety of books about a variety of interesting people, one or more of whom might also interest you. The *Piazze, Giardini, e Musei* section, therefore, doesn't include biographies of artists, as I thought it better to separate art-history books and museum catalogs, with their many reproductions of artworks, from memoirs and biographies.

Together, the articles and books lead you on and off the beaten path and present a reality check of sorts. Will you learn of some nontouristy things to see and do? Yes. Will you also learn more about the better-known aspects of Florence? Yes. The Ponte Vecchio and the little neighborhood *piazza* in the middle of the Oltrarno are equally representative of the city. Seeing them *both* is what makes for a memorable visit, and no one, by the way, should make you feel guilty for wanting to see some famous sites. They have become famous for a reason: They are really something to see, the Ponte Vecchio included. Readers will have no trouble finding a multitude of other travel titles offering plenty of noncontroversial viewpoints. This is my attempt at presenting a more balanced picture. Ultimately, this is the compendium of information that I wish I'd had between two covers years ago. I admit it isn't the perfect book; for that, I envision a waterproof jacket and pockets inside the front and back covers, pages and pages of accompanying maps, lots of blank pages for notes, a bookmark, mileage and size conversion charts . . . in other words, something so encyclopedic—in both weight and size—that positively no one, my editor assures me, would want to read it. That said, I am exceedingly happy with The Collected Traveler, and I believe it will prove helpful in the anticipation of your upcoming journey, in the enjoyment of your trip while it's happening, and in the remembrance of it when you're back home.

There are very good reasons why Giuseppe Verdi is known to have said, "You may have the universe if I may have Italy." I hope you will discover them. *Buon viaggio!* on all your journeys to central Italy in the new millennium.

romano

ALBERGO TOURING
VIA O. SILLA N. 7 · TELEFONO N. 22360
VERONA

VIA AEREA

2000 LIRE DUEMILA
BANCA D'ITALIA
KB 002409 N
KB 002409 N

Informazioni Pratiche
(Practical Information)

"Everything considered, the best and quickest way to get around Florence is on foot; the historic centre (centro storico) *is relatively compact. In pedestrian areas, beware of speeding bicycles and mopeds, and do not be surprised if you meet two-wheeled vehicles zooming the wrong way up a one-way street. Don't expect cars to stop instantly for a traffic light, and expect cars making right turns from side streets to ignore red lights. If you really want to take your life in your hands, hire a bicycle or scooter."*
> —*Time Out Guide,* FLORENCE & TUSCANY

A–Z Informazioni Pratiche

Accommodations

IF YOU ARRIVE IN FLORENCE without a room (which I don't recommend), booking services are available at the Consorzio Informazioni Turistiche Alberghiere (ITA) offices in the Stazione di Santa Maria Novella (train station). You'll be charged a fee, and may be asked to pay the first night in advance. If you're driving into Florence, services are also available at some of the exits into the city. Outside of Florence, accommodation services are less likely, although it has been my experience that the staff at even the smallest tourist office in the smallest town will be able to assist you in finding a place to stay. They will not usually place telephone calls for you or make reservations, but they will tell you what choices there are and give directions. *Agriturismo* (the name given to accommodations offered on farms, most of them bed-and-breakfast) is a relatively new concept in Italy. As little as a dozen years ago, it was virtually nonexistent. Accommodations range from basic to luxurious, on small working farms and larger estates. The best source for *agriturismo* accommodations throughout Italy are the directories published by three national organizations: Associazione Nazionale per l'Agriturismo (Corso Vittorio Emanuele II–101, 00186 Roma, Italia; 06.68521 / fax: 06.6852424); e-mail: agrituri@gol.grosseto.it; Turismo Verde (via Mariano Fortuny 20, 00196 Roma, Italia; 06.3611051 / fax: 06.36000294) and Terranostra (via XXIV Maggio 43, 00187 Roma, Italia; 06.4682370 / fax: 06.4682204). There is a fee for the directories, and they are in Italian; but the lack of English text is really not a problem. I have a directory from the Associazione Nazionale, titled *Guida dell'Ospitalita Rurale: agriturismo e vacanze verdi,* and it's not difficult to figure out the basic information for each listing, and there is a photograph of each one. Specific *agriturismo* information for Tuscany is available from the following organizations: Toscana Agriturismo (Piazza San Firenze 3, 50122 Florence; 055.287838); Turismo Verde Toscana (via Verdi 5, Florence; 055.2344751); Terranostra Toscana (via dei Magazzini 2, Florence; 055.280539 / fax: 055.2360288). *Agriturismo* information for Umbria is available from Terranostra Umbria (via Campo di Marte 10, 06124 Perugia, 075.5009559 / fax: 075.5092032) and Agriturist Umbria (c/o Federumbria Agricoltori, via Savonarola 38, 06121 Perugia; phone / fax: 075.32028). If you prefer that someone else do the legwork, a U.S. company that arranges *agriturismo* is Italy Farm Holidays (547 Martling Avenue, Tarrytown, New York 10591; 914-631-7880 / fax: 631-8831; e-mail: Italyfarms@aol.com. Additionally, Italy Farm Holidays offers watercolor classes at Molino le Gualchiere wine farm in Tuscany and cooking classes at Fattoria di Camporomano in Tuscany and La Cacciata in Umbria). See also the article by Bill Marsano, "Come Stay With Me," in this section, and two other articles I did not include in this book: "Farmhouse Hospitality: Tucked Away Among Vineyards and Olive Groves, Italy's Agriturismi Offer all the Comforts of Home" (Faith Heller Willinger, *Gourmet,* May 1999, which highlights special places to stay in Piedmont, Friuli-Venezia-Giulia, Tuscany, Campania, and Sicily as well as some good tips, such as, if you're fond of sleeping late, avoid farms with animals) and "Bed and Board in the Chianti Hills" (Gerald Asher, *Gourmet,* March 1995, which features twelve agritourist accommodations as well as restaurants and wine estates). Additionally, two great books to consult are *Caffelletto: High Quality Bed & Breakfast in Italy* (not widely available outside of Italy, and if you can't find it at your favorite travel bookstore, contact either Michael Kesend Publishers Ltd., 1025 Fifth Avenue, New York, New York 10028, 800-488-8040 / 212-249-5150 or Emmebi 3 s.r.l., via di Marciola 23, 50020 S. Vincenzo a Torri, Firenze, Italia, 055.730.9145 / fax: 055.768.121; www.caffelletto.it. The book is printed in both English and Italian. There are fifteen accommodations for Tuscany—including some apartments in Florence—and four for Umbria. Color photos and good descriptions accompany each very appealing place, most of which are historic *palazzi* and villas, some of which have noble lineage. Prices range from about $30 to $90 per person); and *Karen Brown's Italy: Charming Bed & Breakfasts* (Fodor's Travel Publications; a complete description of *agriturismo* is found in the introduction, which also states that 60 percent of Italy's participants in *agriturismo* are concentrated in Tuscany and Trentino—Alto Adige, so readers will have no difficulty finding a farm-stay. These lodgings are less expensive than those listed in Karen Brown's *Inns & Itineraries* book but are no less charming or special).

Apartment or Villa Rentals might be a suitable choice depending on how long you'll be in the area and the number of people traveling together. Organizations that arrange short- and long-term rentals would fill a small book, and it is not my intent here to provide a comprehensive listing. Rather, following are some sources that have either come highly recommended or with which I have had a positive experience: The Parker Company ("Italy is all we do and we do it very well" is the Parker motto) staff arranges rentals of cottages, castles, villas, farmhouses, and apartments, and they are the cherry-pickers of the industry, selecting less than 10 percent of what they see. A plus to my mind is that an agent in Italy is assigned to renters, just to make sure everything is as planned. Parker also arranges rentals of cars and cell phones, organizes wine tours and classes at its Tuscany Institute, and offers real estate (800-280-2811 / fax: 781-596-3125; www.theparkercompany.com); Vacanze in Italia (This company offers over 500 properties in a wide variety of sizes and styles ranging from simple to over-the-top luxury; prices vary according to the season; 22 Railroad Street, Great Barrington, Massachusetts 01230; 800-533-5405 or 413-528-6610; fax: 413-528-6222; www.homeabroad.com); Villas d'Italia / Tuscan Enterprises (this agency has specialized in Tuscany for sixteen years, and 30 percent of its business is from referrals; I've been impressed with its catalog since 1989 as there is a good mix of types of accommodations in a variety of price ranges; to read a firsthand account, see "Right Time for Tuscany," *Los Angeles Times,* September 20, 1998; 5578 Vista Del Amigo, Anaheim, California 92807; phone / fax: 714-998-2179; e-mail: vac2italy@aol.com); Home in Italy (relatively new company that offers villas, chateaux, apartments, and historical residences; two offices: via Adelaide 50/C, 06128 Perugia, Italy; 75.505.7865 / fax: 75.500.6127; and 343 City Road, London, EC1 1LR, England; e-mail: homeinitalyltd@edisons.it); Barclay International Group (well-established company offering worldwide rentals; Barclay also reserves car rentals, sightseeing tours, rail passes, theater tickets, cellular phones, and laptop computer rentals; the Last-Minute Specials feature of its web site is a good deal; 3 School Street, Glen Cove, New York 11542; 516-759-5100 / 800-845-6636 / fax: 516-609-0000; www.barclayweb.com); Homebase Abroad Ltd. (features rentals of fine private homes, villas, and apartments in Paris and Italy only. Its properties share "distinction, quality, and value"; searching for places in Florence, I found rates of $850 and $1,100/week; 29 Mary's Lane, Scituate, Massachusetts 02066; 781-545-5112 / fax: 545-1808; www.homebase-abroad.com); Italianvillas .com (offers rentals in Tuscany, Rome, Umbria, and the Lake District; 261 East 10th Street, New York, New York 10009; 800-700-9549; www.italianvillas.com); Ville et Village (agency offers rentals in the cities and countryside of France, Italy, Spain, and Portugal; 2124 Kittredge Street, Suite 200, Berkeley, California 94704; 510-559-8080 / fax: 559-8217); Villas and Apartments Abroad Ltd. (arranges rentals in Italy, France, and the Caribbean; I like that its web site clearly defines four seasons, low, mid, high, and peak, and gives prices for all four; many of these properties have cooks and housekeepers; 420 Madison Avenue, Suite 1003, New York, New York 10017; 800-433-3020 / fax: 212-755-8316; www.vaanyc.com). If you don't mind making arrangements yourself, or you just want some inspiration, a great book to consult is *Italian Country Hideaways: Vacationing in Tuscany's and Umbria's Private Villas, Castles, and Estates* (photography by Stefano Hunyady, text by Kelley F. Hurst, Universe Publishing, a division of Rizzoli International Publications, 1999; the thirty estates featured in this book—five in Umbria—had to meet the following criteria: the primary business of the estate must be something connected to the land, such as wine, olive oil, cheese, horse raising, etc.; accommodations must be offered, and typically the estates are not commonly known among travelers; and each estate "must possess a special intangible quality, something that truly sets it apart: a notable history, unforgettable food, spectacular views, or some other outstanding feature so compelling that it merits particular attention." Color photos of each property are provided, and all the usual contact information. Prices are quoted for the week—which is why I included this book here instead of under *agriturismo*—and range from about $225/week in low season to about $1,400 in high season. Most helpful is a good list of questions to ask the proprietors in advance, plus good tips on services offered, seasonal considerations, and transportation).

Camping (known as *campeggio* or simply *camping*): The European conception of camping is about as opposite from the American as possible. Europeans do not go camping to seek a wilderness experience, and European campgrounds are designed without much privacy in mind, offering amenities ranging from hot-water showers, facilities for washing clothes and dishes, electrical outlets, pastry and cappucino for breakfast, and flush toilets to tiled bathrooms with heat, swimming pools, cafés, bars, restaurants, telephones, televisions, and general stores. If you find yourself at a campground during the summer, you might notice that entire families have literally moved in (having reserved their spaces many months in advance) and that they return every year to spend time with their friends, the way we might return every year to a ski cabin or a house at the beach. It's quite an entertaining and lively spectacle, and camping like this is not really roughing it! There are two campgrounds in Florence: Italiani e Straniere (Viale Michelangelo 80; 055.681.1977) and Villa Camerata (Viale Augusto Righi 2-4, on the grounds of the main youth hostel; 055.600.315) but I think the campground in Fiesole is far superior to either and is in a beautiful setting (Panoramico, via Peramonda 1; 055.599.069 / fax: 055.59186). As always, the tourist offices here and in Italy have specific information. Ask for the campground directory, *Campeggiare in Italia,* or contact the Federazione Italiana del Campeggio e del Caravanning directly for a copy (Federcampeggio, Casella Postale 23, 50041 Calenzano, Firenze, Italia; fax: 55.882.5918). It's been my experience that at municipal *campeggiare* during the off-season, no one ever comes around to collect fees. The campgrounds are still open and there is running water, but the thinking seems to be that it just isn't worth it to collect money from so few campers. (This will not hold true at privately run campgrounds.) If you plan to camp for even a few nights, I recommend joining Family Campers and RVers. Annual membership (valid for one year from the time you join) is $25. FCRV is a member of the Federation Internationale de Camping et de Caravanning (FICC) and is the only organization in America authorized to issue the International Camping Carnet for camping in Europe. Only FCRV members are eligible to purchase the carnet—it cannot be purchased separately—and the membership fee is $10. The carnet is like a camping passport, and since many FICC member campgrounds in Europe are privately owned, the carnet provides entry into these member-only campsites. A carnet offers campers priority status and, occasionally, discounts. An additional benefit is that instead of keeping your passport overnight, which hotels and campgrounds are often required to do, the campground staff simply keeps your carnet, allowing you to hold on to your passport. One ICC membership is good for the entire family, parents and all children under eighteen. To receive an application and information, contact the organization at 4804 Transit Road, Building 2, Depew, New York 14043; phone / fax: 800-245-9755 / 716-668-6242.

Home Exchange might be an appealing option: I've read wildly enthusiastic reports from people who've swapped apartments/houses, and it's usually an economical alternative. Some services to contact include Vacation Exchange Club (the leading agency, which publishes multiple directories each year; P.O. Box 650, Key West, Florida 33041; phone / fax: 800-638-3841; Trading Homes International (P.O. Box 787, Hermosa Beach, California 90254; 800-877-8723 / fax: 310-798-3865); and Worldwide Home Exchange Club (806 Branford Avenue, Silver Spring, Maryland 20904; 301-680-8950). A reputable home-swapping web site is www.homeexchange.com, which started in 1996 as an Internet-only service.

Hotels and Pensione: I feel the same way about books on hotels as I do about guidebooks: the right one for you is the one whose author shares a certain sensibility or philosophy with you. It's important to select the right book(s) so you can make choices that best suit you and your style. I'd like to emphasize here that in the same way you put your trust in the author of a guidebook, put that same faith in the authors of these books. Trying to validate (or not) your choice by searching the web, for example, is not only a time-waster, but serves no good purpose. Remember, *You don't know the people writing reviews on the Internet, and you have no idea if the same things that are important to you are important to them.* The author of the book you've chosen has shared his or her standards with you and explained the criteria used in rating accommodations. Stick with them and move on to the next step in planning! Following are some books I like to use when searching for a hotel in this part of Italy. I have found that it is never difficult to learn of places to stay in either the luxury or budget categories. Harder is finding beautiful and unique places that fall in between, which is why the following titles are my favorites: *Charming Small Hotel Guides: Italy,* edited by Andrew Duncan, Duncan Petersen Publishing, London / Hunter Publishing, Edison, New Jersey. This series features the kind of places where I like to stay, and this edition is particularly useful in planning a trip to central Italy as "No other region of Italy is as rich in good small hotels as Tuscany" (there are lots of good choices for Umbria, too). Featured are 350 captivating small hotels, *pensione,* and bed-and-breakfast establishments, any one of which would make a memorable night's stay. *Cheap Sleeps in Italy: Florence, Rome, Venice* (Sandra Gustafson, Chronicle Books), a companion volume to Gustafson's *Cheap Eats in Italy,* is a great resource for best-value places to lay your head. Lest you get the wrong idea about Gustafson's aim, she states that "It is important that you know *Cheap Sleeps in Italy* is not for those travelers who are looking for a list of the cheapest beds in Florence, Rome, and Venice. It is for those who are concerned with having a better trip by saving money and not sacrificing comfort, convenience, and well-being in the bargain. Life is too short not to treat it as a grand adventure." She also wisely reminds us that value is not always equated with price. There are sixty-nine hotel, apartment, rental-agency, residence-hotel, and student-accommodation listings for Florence—some splurges included—making it a book for *everyone.* Additionally, there is a shopping section at the end of the book with listings for the best places to purchase a variety of

Florentine specialties at good prices. *Hello Italy! An Insider's Guide to Italian Hotels $50–$99 a Night for Two,* 2nd edition, Margo Classé, Wilson Publishing, Los Angeles, California, 1999: The author traveled alone to twenty-six of Italy's most popular cities and discovered this selection of clean, safe, centrally located, and inexpensive places to spend the night. There are sixty-four listings for Florence, fifteen for Siena, nine for Perugia, and four for Orvieto. *Karen Brown's Italy: Charming Inns & Itineraries* (Fodor's Travel Publications): My husband and I have found some of the most wonderful places to stay with the help of Karen Brown's guides. In addition to the thorough descriptions of lodgings (some of which are in *palazzi,* old mills, and buildings of historic significance), *my* favorite features of these guides are ones no one ever mentions: the sample Reservation Request letter (in Italian and English so readers can construct a letter or fax of their own) and the tips that appear in the introduction, such as to be aware that some hotels will accept a credit card to hold a reservation but don't allow you to pay the final bill with a credit card. The itineraries are useful for planning your route in advance and deciding if you want to travel by car or not, but the descriptions of individual towns and sites is not detailed enough to warrant taking the book along. This is really a "before you go" book. I find the organization of the guides maddeningly cumbersome. The lodgings are listed alphabetically by individual city, town, or village, but maps are at the back of the book, so you end up constantly flipping pages back and forth to evaluate all the available choices in any given region of the country. For Florence itself the listings are alphabetical, but if you're unfamiliar with some of the smaller towns of Tuscany and Umbria, you'll have to consult the maps. However, this frustration is a small price to pay for the opportunity to stay in memorable *alberghi* or *pensioni*. As this edition features over twenty places to stay in Tuscany and Umbria, it's a good guide to consult even if you don't plan on going to other parts of Italy. *Fodor's Rivages Hotels and Country Inns of Character and Charm in Italy* (Fodor's Travel Publications): The French *Rivages* guides have been popular in Europe for years, and with Fodor's exclusive English-language translation, I think they are a welcome addition to lodgings literature here in the States. All the guides feature color photographs of the properties with one-page descriptions and good road maps. There are 117 pages of listings for Tuscany and twenty-eight for Umbria, and at the back of the book is a section on restaurants. Some of the listings will be familiar to readers of other guidebooks, but many do not appear in any other books. "Character and charm" are not exclusively equated with four-star luxury, but there are lots of three- and four-star listings in this guide; however, there are a number of two-, three-, and no-star choices, even though this book will never be of interest to the serious budget traveler. By way of explanation: The Italian government's star rating system awards stars based on the comfort of a hotel and pays special attention to the number of bathrooms and toilets versus the number of rooms. Stars have nothing to do with charm or quality of hospitality, and the reason some of the listings in this guide have no stars is simply because the owners never asked the government to rate them. *Hotel Gems of Italy* (compiled by Luc Quisenaerts, written by Anne and Owen Davis, D-Publications): This is a beautiful book in the new Hotel Gems of the World series. These places are to die for, with prices to match, but still, I'd rather spend my money on one of these than on an international chain hotel. Each hotel is described in four to six pages with photos that make you want to pack your bags *immediatamente,* and practical information—prices, contact information, etc.—is at the back of the book. Featured hotels in Tuscany include Il Pellicano, Torre di Bellosguardo, Borgo San Felice, Grand Hotel Villa Cora, Castello dell'Oscano, Certosa di Maggiano, Borgo Pretale, Villa San Michele, Relais La Suvera, and the Regency. Readers may be especially interested, as I am, in an association called Abitare la Storia (Living in History), a group of beautiful, unique, small hotels throughout Italy. Each hotel—some of which also have a restaurant—is a former *palazzo,* castle, monastery, or farmhouse, and travelers can plot an entire itinerary around the thirty-member properties. There are several hotels to choose from in Tuscany and Umbria. Abitare la Storia rates range from under $100 for simple rooms to over $300 for grander quarters. For information and a catalog, contact Abitare la Storia in Italy: Località l'Amorosa, 53048 Sinalunga (Siena); 0577.632256 / fax: 0577.632160; e-mail: mailbox@abitarelastoria.it; www.abitarelastoria.it. Additionally, see "The Best Country Hotels of Tuscany" (Heather Smith MacIsaac, *Travel & Leisure,* June 1999). Seven hotels, which MacIsaac describes as "a step below a villa, a rung above a casa," are featured in Cortona, Rosia, San Casciano Val di Pesa, Monticchiello di Pienza, and Castellina and Gaiole, both in Chianti. Two good books to consult for monastic lodgings are *Bed and Blessings—Italy: A Guide to Convents and Monasteries Available for Overnight Lodging* (June Walsh and Anne Walsh, Paulist Press, 1999) and *The Guide to Lodging in Italy's Monasteries: Inexpensive Accommodations, Remarkable Historic Buildings, Unforgettable Settings* (Eileen Barish, Anacapa Press, Scottsdale, Arizona, 1999). Average prices for a room range from $20 to $80 per night, and the rooms themselves range from simple to luxurious. Note that credit cards are not uniformly accepted, there is sometimes a curfew, and foreign languages are rarely spoken (a good incentive to brush up on your Italian!). There are plenty of choices for Tuscany and Umbria in both books.

Youth Hostels (*ostelli della gioventu*) are another choice for those seeking budget accommodations (and keep in mind that hostels are not just for the under-thirty crowd). I would take back in a minute my summer of vagabonding around Europe, meeting young people from all over the world, and feeling that my life was one big endless possibility. I now prefer to share a room with my husband rather than five twenty-somethings, but hosteling remains a fun and exciting experience. Younger budget travelers need no convincing that hosteling is the way to go; however, older budget travelers should bear in mind that although some hostels offer individual rooms (mostly for couples), comparing costs reveals that they are often the same price as a room in a real (albeit inexpensive) hotel, where you can reserve a room and comfortably keep your luggage (you must pack up your luggage every day when hosteling, and you can't make a reservation); additionally, most hostels have an 11 P.M. curfew. Petty theft—of the T-shirts-stolen-off-the-clothesline variety— seems to be more prevalent than it once was, and it would be wise to sleep and shower with your money belt close at hand. There are three youth hostels in Florence, one of which, at the fifteenth-century Villa Camerata, also has space for campers. Check with the tourist offices here or in Florence for the exact locations, or contact the Associazione Italiana Alberghi per la Gioventu (AIG) headquarters (via Cavour 44, 00184 Roma; 06.487.1152 / fax: 06.488.0492) for complete hostel listings for all of Italy. There are no age limits or advance bookings, but many require membership in Hostelling International. The HI national headquarters are located at 733 15th Street, N.W., Suite 840, Washington, D.C. 20005; 202-783-6161 / fax: 783-6171. Hours are 8 A.M. to 5 P.M. Eastern Standard Time, with Customer Service staff available until 7 P.M. An HI membership card is free for anyone up to his or her eighteenth birthday. Annual fees are $25 for anyone over eighteen and $15 for anyone over fifty-five. HI also publishes several guidebooks, one of which is *Europe and the Mediterranean*. The price is either $10.95 or $13.95, depending on whether you purchase it from the main office or one of its council affiliates around the country (HI staff have addresses and phone numbers for affiliates nearest you). I think a better book to get is *Hostels France & Italy: The Only Comprehensive, Unofficial, Opinionated Guide* (Paul Karr and Martha Coombs, The Globe Pequot Press, Old Saybrook, Connecticut, 1999). This is one book that lives up to its no-nonsense title. It's a funny yet very practical guide. In "How to Use This Book," the authors state that "what you're holding in your hands is the first-ever attempt of its kind: a fairly complete listing and rating of all the hostels we could find in France and Italy." They invite you to take a quiz (What Is a Hostel?), and they don't hesitate to tell it like it is, using adjectives such as sedate, educational, hoppin', quiet, plain, dirty, chaotic, strict, okay, small. ~Note that student-dormitory accommodations are also available. Contact Casa della Studente, Gaetano Salvemini, Piazza dell'Independenza 15, Firenze; 055.438.9603. You don't need HI membership to take advantage of these rooms. Reminders: ~Florence is a noisy city! Even though a number of streets in the city center are limited or closed to cars, *motorini* (scooters) are permitted. ~Breakfast is rarely a good value taken at a hotel. Save some money—and get the same thing, often better—and join the locals at the corner caffè. ~When you first arrive at your hotel, ask to see your room first. This is a common practice in Europe, and it is understood that if a room is not to your liking, you may request a different one. This is also your opportunity to ask for a room upgrade. If the hotel is not fully booked (and it rarely will be during low season), you might end up with a significantly nicer room at the same rate.

It never hurts to ask. ~Speaking of fully booked: If you've been told that you can't get a room, call again between 4 and 6 P.M. and double-check. This is the time of day when many establishments cancel the reservations of guests who haven't shown up. ~If a hotel you choose also has a reservations office in the U.S., call both numbers. It is entirely possible that you will be quoted different rates. Also, some of the more expensive hotels offer a rate that must be prepaid in full, in advance of your trip, in U.S. dollars, but that is lower than the local rack rate. ~Useful vocabulary: *il cuscino* (pillow); *la chiave* (key); *biancheria da letto* (bed linens); *l'aschiugamano* (towel); *acqua calda* (hot water); *incluso* (included, as in, is breakfast—*la prima colazione*—included in the price?).

Airfares & Airlines

We all know that not everyone pays the same price for seats on an airplane. One of the reasons for this is that seats do not hold the same value at all times of the year, months, or even days of the week. Recently, I was researching some fares to Paris for a long weekend. One of my calls produced a particularly helpful representative who proceeded to detail all available fares for the entire month of September. There were approximately fifteen different prices, based on a seemingly endless number of variables, within that month alone. The best way, therefore, to get the deal that accommodates your needs is to check a variety of sources. If you think all the best deals are to be found on the web, you're mistaken: Airlines, agencies, charters, and consolidators offer plenty of good fares over the telephone and through advertisements. To know with certainty that you've got a good deal, you need to have fares to compare, which requires checking more than one source. I like flying a country's own airline—Alitalia, for example—and even though Alitalia fares are usually among the highest available, its off-season fares are among the lowest. Following are some sources I typically consult before I purchase anything (note that some of these have corresponding web sites mentioned below, but I prefer calling): 1-800-AIRFARE (1-800-247-3273); Cheap Tickets Inc., 800-377-1000; Lowestfare.com, 888-777-2222; 1-800-FLY4-LESS; Air Europa (New York is the only American city this airline serves), 888-238-7672. Booking travel on the web works best for people with simple requirements and lots of flexibility. If you have a lot of questions, as I always do, you can't get them answered and are setting yourself up for potential headaches. In my experience with sky auctions, I never seem to be able to find a flight scenario that works with my schedule, and I don't like that I can't alter the criteria of my initial bid if it isn't accepted. Resubmitting bids has, for me, proved to be much more time consuming than picking up the phone. But if you have no parameters to work around and are just looking for a good fare, here are some web sites to check for domestic and/or overseas tickets: www.skyauction.com, www.previewtravel.com, www.cheaptickets.com, www.priceline. com, www.expedia.msn.com, www.travelocity.com, www.economytravel. com, www.lowestfare.com, www.TRIP.com, www.travelscape.com, www.air-fare.com, www.thefarebusters.com, and www.itn.com. And if you're in Italy and want to fly somewhere else within Europe, or want to fly to Italy from another European city, check with Europe by Air, which offers great prices to over 125 cities (888-387-2479; www.europebyair.com). Reminders: ~Don't be afraid of reputable consolidators, but recognize that their lower fares come with more restrictions. If there are flight cancellations or delays, you have no recourse with the airline since it didn't sell you the ticket directly. If you want to make any changes, you have to pay a penalty. ~Reputable charter flights, too, should not be feared. I've had three good experiences on charter flights and encourage you to investigate them. The limitations are that most charters offer only coach class and tend to be completely full—in fact, a charter operator is legally allowed to cancel a flight up to ten days before departure if it doesn't fill enough seats. I wouldn't, therefore, travel with children or plan a honeymoon on a charter flight. Although I did not experience any problems on my charter flights, I understand that delays are common, and—as with consolidators—passengers don't have any recourse. However, operators who organize charter flights are required to place passengers' payments for the flight in an escrow account, so if the flight is canceled or if the operator doesn't abide by its agreement, you receive a refund. ~Flying as a courier might be the best deal of all, if you're a light packer (luggage is usually limited to one carry-on bag). Couriers also can't usually reserve a seat for more than one person, although your traveling companion could purchase a ticket on the same flight. Air couriers are cogs in international commerce; they are completely legal and legitimate, and demand for them exceeds the supply. They are a necessity simply because companies doing international business send a large number of documents overseas, and those documents can get held up in customs unless accompanied by a person. Couriers are responsible for chaperoning documents through customs and then hand-delivering them to a person waiting outside the customs area. There are several companies that arrange courier flights in the U.S., but the one I'm most familiar with is Now Voyager (74 Varick Street, New York, New York 10013; 212-431-1616). To review more options, consider joining the International Association of Air Travel Couriers (P.O. Box 1349, Lake Worth, Florida 33460; 561-582-8320). Members receive a regular bulletin with a variety of international routes being offered by air-courier companies departing from several U.S. cities. Reservation phone numbers are included so you can make inquiries and schedule your trip yourself. I have seen some *incredible* bargains, and some fares were valid for several months. ~Note that airlines are not required to offer much to passengers due to flight delays or cancellations.

If you have visions of free meals, hotel rooms, and flights, you might be in for a disappointment. Each airline has its own Conditions of Carriage, which you can request from an airline's ticket office or public-relations department, but the legalese is not identical from airline to airline. From what I can tell, the employees who stand at the gates are the ones who have the authority to grant passengers amenities, so if you *don't* ask them for something (a seat on the next flight, a long-distance phone call, a meal, whatever) you *definitely* won't get it. ~Technically, airlines no longer allow passengers to fly standby at a discount but I've been told that seats are occasionally sold at reduced prices for flights that aren't full. I've also been told that one of the best days of the year to show up at the airport without a ticket is Christmas day. I can't personally confirm this, and it's doubtful an airline employee can, either. Perhaps this is either a very well-kept secret or a myth, but if you're able to be that flexible, it would be worth trying.

Airports

Florence is served by two airports: Vespucci Airport (known as Peretola, after the suburb of the same name) and Galilei Airport (known as Pisa Airport, as it is just south of Pisa). Vespucci is about a half-hour from the center of Florence, and the most economical way to get there or back is by either the SITA bus or ATAF city bus (Florence is too small to support a subway system). Even though it costs significantly more, you might want to consider a taxi (depending on the time of day) as the airport is only about three miles from the city. From Galilei, the best way of getting to Florence is by train. However, direct service from the airport is often not timed with flight arrivals, so you might want to take a cab or city bus to Pisa Centrale (Pisa train station) and catch a train from there. The train ride to Florence's Santa Maria Novella station is about an hour. Avoid the train from the airport to Florence via Lucca, as it takes about two hours. Check at the information desk for the timetable once you land, and depending on how much luggage you're carrying, decide accordingly.

B

Biking

Biking opportunities within Florence are limited, perhaps owing to the density of the city center. Bikes can be rented at Stazione Santa Maria Novella, as well as at Motorent (Via San Zanobi 9/r; 055.490113) and Noleggio della Fortezza (107–109 Via Faenza; 55.283448). For guided tours in the city, one company, Florence by Bike (Via della Scala 12/r; 055.26403), seems to have found some routes that work and seems to be the leader in guiding cyclists around town. It is more Italian to get around in a Vespa (Motorent also rents scooters), but I feel Florence—as well as Pisa, Lucca, Perugia, and Orvieto—is small enough to simply walk around. Biking

farther afield, in the Tuscan and Umbrian countryside, is a much more sensible option. The Tuscan and Umbrian regional tourist offices have information on biking trails, as well as the Club Alpino Italiano (inquire at the Florence tourist office for contact information). Also, the Stella Alpina bookstore in Florence (14B Via Corridoni; 055.411688) carries some English-language titles on biking in Tuscany. I Bike Italy (Borgo degli Albizi 11, Firenze; 055.2342371) is a company that offers guided routes in the countryside around Florence.

Bookstores

Like the Italians (and most Europeans in general), I prefer to buy whatever goods and services I need from specialists. One-stop shopping is a nice idea in theory but has not been very appealing to me, as convenience seems to be its only virtue. Therefore, I buy fish from a fishmonger, flowers from a florist, cheese from a real cheese shop, etc. And when I'm looking for travel books, I shop at travel bookstores or independent bookstores with strong travel sections. The staff in these stores are nearly always well traveled, well read, very helpful, and knowledgeable. An aspect I don't like about chain stores is that travel guides tend to be shelved separately from travel writing and related history books, implying that guidebooks are all a traveler needs or wants. Stores specializing in travel take a wider view, understanding that travel incorporates many different dimensions. Following is a list of stores nationwide that offer exceptional travel-book departments (I've also included a few stores specializing in art books and cookbooks, as some of these titles are mentioned throughout the book). Note that all of them accept mail orders, and some publish catalogs and/or newsletters. ~Additionally, I must mention my favorite mail-order book catalog: *A Common Reader,* which is issued monthly and offers the most excellent selection of books for adults and children. The reviews are of the sort that wander here and there and make you want to read every single book in the catalog (the writing has been an inspiration to me for the annotated bibliographies in The Collected Traveler series). Not content to simply offer new books, the creators of the catalog even arrange to bring out-of-print books back into print by publishing them under its own Common Reader Editions imprint. A wide variety of travel, history, art, and cooking titles are regularly featured in the catalog (141 Tompkins Avenue, Pleasantville, New York 10570; 800-832-7323 / fax: 914-747-0778; www.commonreader.com). ~If your favorite bookseller can't find an out-of-print title you're looking for, try one of the following web sites: www.abebooks.com (American Book Exchange) or www.alibris.com. I've had the most success with ABE, and I like that you purchase titles directly from individual booksellers.

CALIFORNIA

Black Oak Books
1491 Shattuck Avenue, Berkeley
510-486-0698

Bon Voyage Travel Books & Maps
2069 W. Bullard, Fresno
800-995-9716
www.bon-voyage-travel.com

Book Passage
51 Tamal Vista Boulevard, Corte
Madera
800-999-7909 or 415-927-0960 locally
www.bookpassage.com

The Cook's Library
8373 W. Third Street, Los Angeles
323-655-3141

Distant Lands
56 South Raymond Avenue, Pasadena
626-449-3220 / 800-310-3220—
California only
www.distantlands.com

The Literate Traveller
8306 Wilshire Boulevard, Suite 591,
Beverly Hills
800-850-2665 or 310-398-8781 / fax:
5151
www.literatetraveller.com
*In addition to its regular catalog, The
Literate Traveller publishes *Around
the World in 80+ Mysteries*.

Pacific Travellers Supply
12 West Anapamu Street, Santa
Barbara
888-PAC-TRAV
pts@maplink.com

Phileas Fogg's Books, Maps & More
87 Stanford Shopping Center,
Palo Alto
800-533-3644
www.foggs.com

The Travelers Bookcase
8375 West 3rd Street, Los Angeles
323-655-0575 / fax: 655-1197
www.travelbooks.com

COLORADO

Tattered Cover
2955 East 1st Avenue, Denver
303-322-7727

WASHINGTON, D.C.

AIA/Rizzoli
1735 New York Avenue, N.W.
202-626-7541
800-52-BOOKS (catalog orders)

Travel Books & Language Center
4437 Wisconsin Avenue, N.W.
202-237-1322 / fax: 237-6022
800-220-2665 (mail orders)
e-mail: travelbks@aol.com

ILLINOIS

The Savvy Traveller
310 Michigan Avenue, Chicago
888-666-6200
www.thesavvytraveller.com

Rizzoli
Water Tower Place, Chicago
312-642-3500
800-52-BOOKS (catalog orders)

MASSACHUSETTS

Brattle Book Shop
9 West Street, Boston
617-542-0210 / fax: 617-338-1467
800-447-9595 (mail orders)
*Brattle's specialty is art books, but it also stocks over 250,000 used, rare, and out-of-print books.

Globe Corner Bookstore
500 Boylston Street, Boston
800-358-6013 / 617-859-8008

Rizzoli
Copley Place, Boston
617-437-0700

MINNESOTA

Books For Travel, Etc.
857 Grand Avenue, St. Paul
888-668-8006

NEW YORK

Archivia: The Decorative Arts Book Shop
944 Madison Avenue, New York
212-439-9194
*beautiful store with a beautiful selection of decorating, garden, style, history, and art titles, some in Italian.

The Complete Traveller
199 Madison Avenue (35th Street), New York
212-685-9007
*In addition to a great selection of current books, a separate room is reserved for rare and out-of-print travel books. Owners Harriet and Arnold Greenberg and their superb staff will do their very best to track down your most obscure request.

Hacker Art Books
45 West 57th Street, New York
212-688-7600 / fax: 754-2554
e-mail:
hackerartbooks@infohouse.com / www.hackerartbooks.com
*John Russell, former art critic of *The New York Times,* has written of Hacker that "For an all-round art bookstore, this one is something near to ideal."

Kitchen Arts & Letters
1435 Lexington Avenue (between 93rd and 94th), New York
212-876-5550 / fax: 3584

Strand Book Store
828 Broadway (at 12th Street), New York
212-473-1452 / fax: 473-2591
800-366-3664 (mail orders)
e-mail: strand@strandbooks.com

Strand Book Annex
95 Fulton Street, New York
212-732-6070 / fax: 406-1654

Rizzoli—five locations:
Manhattan:
31 W. 57th Street
212-759-2424
3 World Financial Center
212-385-1400
454 West Broadway
212-674-1616
1334 York Avenue
212-606-7434

Manhasset:
The Americana
516-365-9393
800-52-BOOKS (catalog orders for all)

NORTH CAROLINA

Omni Resources
10004 South Mebane Street,
Burlington
800-742-2677
www.omnimap.com

OKLAHOMA

Traveler's Pack LTD
9427 North May Avenue, Oklahoma
City
405-755-2924
www.travelerspack.com

OREGON

Powell's City of Books
1005 West Burnside, Portland
800-878-7323 / 503-228-4651—locally
www.powells.portland.or.us

Powell's Travel Store
701 SW Sixth Avenue, Portland
800-546-5025
www.powells.com

PENNSYLVANIA

Franklin Maps
333 S. Henderson Road, King of
Prussia
610-265-6277 / fax: 337-1575
*Extraordinary selection of foreign

and domestic maps as well as books.
One journalist wrote, "What travelers
will find at the 15,000-square-feet
Franklin Map store are maps, charts,
and books covering almost every
square inch of earth and universe."

VERMONT

Adventurous Traveler Bookstore
P.O. Box 64769 (for mail orders)
245 South Champlain Street (for
visiting), Burlington
800-282-3963 or 802-860-6776—locally
www.adventuroustraveler.com

VIRGINIA

Rizzoli
Merchants Square, Williamsburg
757-229-9821

WASHINGTON

Wide World Books & Maps
4411A Wallingford Avenue, North,
Seattle
206-634-3453
www.travelbooksandmaps.com

And, because some books I recommend
are British publications, I include two
excellent stores in London: The Travel
Bookshop (13-15 Blenheim Crescent,
W11 2EE, 44.171.229.5260 / fax:
243.1552) and Books for Cooks (a few
doors down from The Travel
Bookshop at 4 Blenheim Crescent,
44.171.221.1992 / fax: 221.1517).

BM, Borgo Ognissanti 4/r, not an exclusive English-language bookstore, but there are a lot of English and American titles.

Feltrinelli International, Via Cavour 12/r, again not exclusively English, but there is a rather large English-language section.

Paperback Exchange, via Fiesolana 31/r.

Libreria della Signoria, Via dei Magazzini 3/r, specializing in graphic arts and posters.

Libreria Il Viaggio, Borgo degli Albizi, 41/r, specializing in travel books and maps for Tuscany and Italy.

Salimbeni, Via Matteo Palmiere 14-16/r, specializing in art and antiquarian books. *Salimbeni* is also a prestigious publisher, specializing in Italian and Tuscan history and culture.

Buon Viaggio: A Bouquet of Reminders

This is actually the title of the final chapter of Kate Simon's wonderful book *Italy: The Places in Between* (see Guidebooks for description). The chapter is nothing more than a list of reminders, but it is so good and so appropriate to the spirit of The Collected Traveler that I feel it is indispensable to this volume: "Remember that everything is subject to change—museum hours, and prices, which are rising steadily. If there were rigidity it wouldn't be Italy. Don't fret; don't set tight limits of time or lire, don't eat your heart out if some art goal or other is closed on your day, or most days, for lack of personnel. Normally, closing days are either Monday or Tuesday and safe times are 9:30–12:30, 3:00–5:30. Remember that no one ever has any change. When you pay a gas attendant, he will ask you for *spiccioli* (coins). The girl in the small chain department store will leave her register and a group of customers to run from one co-worker to another for change from the 100-lire you have given her for a 75-lire purchase. She returns with 10-lire pieces—no 5's—after a long absence, and one or the other of you has to be sporting about the difference between 20 and 30 lire. Remember that Italians find standing in line an absurdity: Learn to push and an advantageous spot conquered, gyrate in it like an animal marking out its territory. Remember that the recoil on a salesgirl's face doesn't mean that she dislikes you, she is afraid to cope with your English—or worse still, your Italian. Remember, when you ask directions, that one of the national characteristics is to point right as one says left (*sinistra*) and to point left when speaking of right (*destra*). Make sure whether it is gesture or word that counts. Remember that a little learning can be a pleasant thing. Italy gives much, in beauty, gaiety, diversity of arts and landscapes, good humor and energy—willingly, without having to be coaxed or courted. Paradoxically, she requires (as do other countries, probably more so) and deserves some preparation as background to enhance her pleasures. It is almost impossible to read a total history of Italy. There was no united country until a hundred years ago, no single line of power, no concerted developments. It is useful, however, to know something about what made Siena run and stop, to become acquainted with the Estes and the Gonzagas, the Medicis, and the Borgias, the names that *were* the local history. It helps to know something about the conflicts of the medieval church with the Holy Roman Empire, of the French, Spanish, and early German kings who marked out large chunks of Italy for themselves or were invited by a nervous Italian power. Above all, it helps to turn the pages of a few art and architecture books to become reacquainted with names other than those of the luminous giants. The informed visitor will not allow himself to be cowed by the deluge of art. See what interests you. There is no Italian Secret Service that reports on whether you have seen *everything*. If you try to see it all except as a possible professional task, you may come to resist it all. Relax, know what you like and don't like, and let the rest go. By moving ruminatively, all antennae out and receptive, you may learn—in the gesture of an old woman's finger stroking the arm of a baby as if he were the Infant Jesus, in the warmth and pleasure of friends meeting on a street, in the loud rumble of angry café voices when a father boxes his young son's ears, in the infinite bounty of concern among the members of a family, in the working-class coins that drop into the cap of a beggar—more about living, and Italy, than in miles of magniloquent buildings and seas of paint." (Excerpt, as submitted from *Italy: the Places in Between,* Revised and Expanded Edition by Kate Simon. Copyright © 1970, 1984 by Kate Simon. Reprinted by permission of HarperCollins Publishers, Inc.) Everything about this excerpt remains true, to a degree, all over Italy.

Buses

I can count on one hand the times I've ridden a bus anywhere in Tuscany or Umbria. Certainly within city and town centers, it is seldom necessary, even in Florence. A potentially confusing aspect about bus travel in Italy is that in addition to SITA, the state-owned company, there are a great number of privately owned services. Lazzi is the name of the company that offers long-distance service around Italy and beyond. It therefore serves Tuscany and Umbria, as do CLAP, CAP, CAT, COPIT, TRA-IN, APT, and RAMA. Within Florence and other cities, there are several different types of bus tickets available in addition to a monthly pass: *biglietto 60 minuti* (valid for an hour of travel on all buses); *biglietto multiplo* (four single tickets, each one good for an hour); *biglietto 3 ore* (valid for three hours); and *biglietto 24 ore* (valid for 24 hours). You must purchase tickets before you board, and these are available at the ATAF office in Florence's Piazza Stazione, newsstands, bars, some automatic machines near the bigger stops, and, of course, at *tabacchi* (as in other European countries, nearly anything can be purchased at the corner tobacco shop). As tickets are to be purchased in advance, some people try to avoid paying since the driver doesn't check; but inspectors do come around, and they are not forgiving. As you board, you must stamp your ticket in one of the machines at the front or back of the bus. Riders should also get on the bus by either the front or back doors and get off the bus using the center doors. ATAF in Florence offers one all-night bus that makes a circular route from Stazione Santa Maria Novella. This is the only bus where you can purchase a ticket on board, but it's about double the price of a regular daytime ticket. Inquire at the tourist office for schedules and routes for both local and long-distance service.

C

Car Rental

My favorite feature of travel publications is the section featuring reader's letters. I have probably learned more from these letters than any other source, and the largest number of complaints seem to be about problems encountered when renting a car. No matter what you read, hear, or assume, the only word that counts is the one from your policy administrator, be it a credit-card or insurance company. If you have any questions about renting a car overseas and what is and isn't covered on your existing policy (including collision damage waiver), contact your provider in advance. Request documentation in writing, if necessary. It is your responsibility to learn about your coverage *before* you rent a car. I have never encountered any rental-car problems, but I make it a habit to state to the company representative, "When I return the car to you, I will not pay anything more than this amount" while pointing to the total on my receipt. I highly recommend renting a car to see the Tuscan and Umbrian countryside. Public transportation schedules can foil even the most determined visitors. I am not referring to *service*—trains serve most places, and the various buses reach almost everywhere else—but the *schedules* do not always accommodate tourists, making it necessary to choose between seeing a small village in an hour or two or spending the night there in order to catch the bus out the next morning. Reminders: ~Gas prices in Italy are the highest in Europe. Years ago, visitors crossing into Italy by car were eligible for discount gas coupons by the Touring Club Italiano. Unfortunately, these are no longer available, so budget accordingly. ~Tolls in Italy, as elsewhere in Europe, are extremely expensive. It's a good idea to purchase a Via Card if you'll be driving a lot on the *autostrade*. The Via Card is like a debit card. You purchase it in units of either 20,000 or 50,000 lire and amounts are then deducted from the card. It can be purchased at tollgates. ~Hertz offers a competitive rate with its prepaid car-rental voucher. The conditions are that you pay in U.S. dollars in advance of your trip, and vouchers are faxed to a U.S. fax number or mailed to a U.S. address. The prepaid rate does not include things such as drop charges, car seats, collision damage waiver, or gas, and these must be paid for in local currency at the time you pick up the car. ~Maggiore, a Budget Car Rental partner, is the largest car-rental company in Italy. By making arrangements with Central Holidays in the U.S. in advance of your trip, rates are discounted as much as 50 percent: 800-935-5000. ~You don't need an International Driver's License in Italy. Save the $10 fee for driving in less developed countries, where the absence of the license could open the door for bribery to cross a border, etc. ~For information on leasing a car (as well as rentals), contact Europe by Car (1 Rockefeller Plaza, New York, New York 10020; 800-223-1516 / in New York: 212-581-3040 / 9000 Sunset Boulevard, Los Angeles, California 90069; 800-252-9401 / in California: 323-272-0424; www.europebycar.com). Factory-direct new cars from Peugeot, Citroen, and Renault are available for low daily rates, with special rates for faculty members and students. ~If you'll be driving around the Tuscan and Umbrian countryside, it's helpful to begin thinking in kilometers instead of miles. I jot down sample distances to use as a ready reference as I'm motoring along the *strade principali* or speeding along the *autostrade:* 1 mile = 1.6 kilometers, so 12 km = 7½ miles; 16 km = 10 miles; 40 km = 25 miles; 80 km = 50 miles; 160 km = 100 miles; 320 km = 200 miles, etc. ~Driving in the fast lane on European roads can be a bit disconcerting as any car suddenly looming up behind you is closing in at a *much* faster speed than we're accustomed to in the U.S. These drivers usually have no patience for your slowness and will tailgate you and flash their lights until you get out of the way. So if you're going to pass, step on the gas and go, and return quickly to the right lane. ~The Automobile Club d'Italia (ACI) has a 24-hour hotline in English (06.44.77), and although its services aren't free, rates are reasonable. If you'll be living in Italy for any length of time, you might want to become a member. ~I've read conflicting advice on parking tickets, so I would not recommend taking a chance if you're in doubt. Rental agencies do have your credit-card number, and it seems to me they can eventually bill you for any tickets you've received and add a service charge if they're so inclined. ~Gas stations offer full service on weekdays (from 7:00–12:30 and 3:00–7:30), but be prepared to see no one about at night and on weekends. However, most stations have automatic self-serve pumps that accept 10,000 and 50,000 paper lire. You might also find someone there on weekends who is not employed by the station but who will service your car for a tip, anywhere from L500 to 1,000. (Ordinarily, gas station attendants do not receive tips.) Service is guaranteed 24 hours a day on autostrade. ~A great book to get if you'll be driving at all in Tuscany or Umbria is *Italy's Best-Loved Driving Tours: 25 Unforgettable Itineraries* (Paul Duncan, Frommer's). Of particular interest are tours nine (Treasures of Tuscany), ten (The Cradle of the Renaissance) and eleven (The Green Heart of Italy). ~Useful vocabulary: *autonoleggio* (car rental), *gasolio* (diesel gas), *super* (regular gas), *senza piombo* (unleaded gas), *senso unico* (one way), *senso vietato* (no entry), *polizia stradale* (highway police), *divieto di sosta / sosta vietata* (no parking), *uscita* (exit), *accostare a destra* (merge to the right) or *accostare a sinistra* (left), *rallentare* (slow down), *pedaggio* (toll), *pericolo* (danger), *guasto* (breakdown), *sempre diritto* (straight ahead), *vicino* (near), and *lontano* (far).

Children

Although I have been unable to find a book devoted to traveling with children in Italy, some guidebooks—including many of those mentioned below under Guidebooks—offer excellent suggestions for things to see and do with kids. Something parents will be sure to notice is that in Italy, as in most other Mediterranean countries, young children stay up late at night, even at restaurants and *trattorie*. Do not be surprised if it's midnight and there are lots of kids running around. I've never seen the children looking unhappy or tired, and it seems to make sense in a country with a tradition of an afternoon siesta. There is not an abundance of books available on traveling with children in general (the most I've ever seen in one store is three), but even if there were a lot more I still think the best one would be *Have Kid, Will Travel: 101 Survival Strategies for Vacationing With Babies and Young Children* (Claire Tristram with Lucille Tristram, Andrews McMeel Publishing, Kansas City, Missouri, 1997). It's loaded with good, concrete suggestions and tips, and I wish I'd discovered it before we took our ten-month-old on her first plane flight, from New York to Seattle. Claire Tristram has visited all 50 states and 30 countries, and Lucille, her daughter, has been named "the best baby in the world" by several strangers sitting next to her on long-distance flights (a great recommendation for reading this book!). Among the best words of advice: "Above all, don't let a bad moment become a bad day, and don't let a bad day become a bad week."

Clothing

The way I see it, you can hardly talk about clothing without talking about packing, but I have included a separate Packing entry under P. I pack light and, unless I have plans to be at fancy places, I pack double-duty items (stuff that can go from daytime to evening) in low-key colors that also mix and match so I can wear garments more than once. Remember that the Italians tend to dress up a bit more than Americans, so reserve your jeans for casual daytime wear and the most casual of places at night, and leave the color-coordinated jogging suits at home. Italians also remain conservative when it comes to visiting their houses of worship. Visitors will earn respect and goodwill by refraining from wearing sleeveless shirts and short skirts and shorts, no matter how hot it is. You may find this odd in a country where topless sunbathing is permitted on the beaches, but make no mistake about it: It is still frowned upon, especially in smaller villages, to dress inappropriately around town and in churches. Suits and ties are necessary only at the finest restaurants, and polo shirts and khakis will always serve men well. Although comfortable shoes are of the utmost importance, I never, ever take sneakers—my husband is also forbidden to take them—and you might not either once you realize that they scream "American." I prefer Arche, a line of French walking shoes and sandals for men and women, but there are several other lines available that are stylish *and* comfortable. The following mail-order catalogs offer some practical clothes and gadgets for travelers: L. L. Bean Traveler (800-221-4221 / www.llbean.com); Magellan's (800-962-4943 /www.magellans.com); TravelSmith (800-950-1600 / www.travelsmith.com; one of the best items in the catalog is a lightweight, waterproof, attractive raincoat, available as a jacket or trench-coat for men and women. Each folds up inside a small pouch, and you can purchase Thermolite liners for extra warmth—the jacket liner can also be worn as a casual vest); The Territory Ahead (800-686-8212 / www.territoryahead.com); and Travel 2000 (800-903-8728 / www.travel2k.com).

Coins

If you have leftover lire in the form of coins, you can always save them for a future trip. But perhaps a better idea is to give them to a great cause: UNICEF's Change for Good program. A number of airlines pass out envelopes to passengers on flights back to the U.S., but if you've never received one and want to contribute, contact the U.S. Committee for UNICEF (333 East 38th Street, 6th floor, New York, New York 10016; 212-824-6972 / fax: 824-6969).

Cooking Schools

The best single source for cooking schools in Italy—and the entire world—is *The Guide to Cooking Schools: Cooking Schools, Courses, Vacations, Apprenticeships, and Wine Instruction Throughout the World* (ShawGuides, Inc., New York, 2000). Programs that might be familiar to cooking enthusiasts—such as Badia a Coltibuono, Tenuta di Capezzana, and La Cucina al Focolare—are listed as well as lesser-known classes, and interested food-lovers can also view updates to the guide at its Web site: www.shawguides.com. See also the articles in the *La Toscana* section to read of some firsthand experiences, and EMI International below—under Studying in Italy—for one of the cooking classes offered in Perugia at a beautiful *pensione*.

Customs

There seems to be a lot of confusion over what items can and positively cannot be brought into the U.S.—and not only on the part of travelers but customs agents, too. The rules, apparently, are not as confusing as they might seem, but sometimes neither customs staff nor travelers are up to date on what they are. Some examples of what's legal and what's not include: olive oil, yes, but olives, no (unless they're vacuum-packed); fruit jams and preserves, yes, but fresh fruit, no; hard cheeses, yes, but soft, runny cheeses, no; commercially canned meat, yes (if the inspector can determine that the meat was cooked in the can after it was sealed), but fresh and dried meats and meat products, no; nuts, yes, but chestnuts and acorns, no; coffee, yes, but roasted beans only; dried spices, yes, but not curry leaves; fresh and dried flowers, yes, but not eucalyptus or any variety with roots. If you think all this is unnecessary bother, remember that it was quite likely a tourist who carried in the wormy fruit that brought the Mediterranean fruit fly to California in 1979. Fighting this pest cost more than $100 million. For more details, call the U.S. Department of Agriculture's Animal and Plant Health Inspection Service at 301-734-8645 or view its Web site: www.aphis.usda.gov (click on Travelers' Tips).

E

Eating In and Taking Away

As in other European countries, the price for food and drink is different depending on where you sit. You'll notice that Italians mostly stand at the bar, especially in the morning, when they down little cups of espresso. If you sit at a table, you can expect to pay up to twice as much (although you can also expect to remain in your seat for as long as you like). In most bars and *caffès* it's customary to pay the cashier first and then take your *scontrino* (receipt) to the counter, where you usually repeat your order. It is also customary to give a tip of 100 or 200 lire to the person who hands you your food or drink. ~Don't let the words *menu turistico* turn you away from a potentially great meal. Just like the *menu del dia* in Spain or the *prix fixe* meal in France, the *menu turistico* in Italy is usually a good value and nearly always includes a carafe or half bottle of wine. Reminders: ~Some good words of advice from *Cheap Eats in Italy* by Sandra Gustafson: "Italians believe that God keeps an Italian kitchen, and so everyone should enjoy *la cucina italiana*. . . . Dealing with Italian waiters is similar to crossing Italian streets: You can do it if you are brazen enough, showing skill and courage and looking all the time as though you own the place. A good waiter should explain the dishes on the menu and help you select the wine. But if you order coffee or tea during the meal, ask for the ketchup bottle, or request a doggie bag . . . watch out, you will be in big trouble." ~Useful vocabulary: *da porta via* is how you say you'll be taking food away, like when you're ordering a *panino* (sandwich) from an *alimentare* (combination store/deli also known as a *salsamentario* or *salumeria*). Often, *alimentari* are located next door to a *fornaio* (bakery), so you can count on the bread being good and fresh. Order the filling for your sandwich in two ways: either by the *fette* (number of slices) or by the *etto* (weight, an *etto* being about four ounces).

Elderly Travel

The two best-known organizations for elderly travelers are Elderhostel (75 Federal Street, 3rd floor, Boston, Massachusetts 02110; 877-426-8056 / fax: 426-2166) and

Interhostel (University of New Hampshire, 6 Garrison Avenue, Durham, New Hampshire 03824; 800-733-9753 / fax: 603-862-1113; www.learn.unh.edu). I've listed them here instead of under tour operators because I wanted them to stand apart from the more general travel companies. For some good articles about these two educational companies and others, see "Senior Classes" and "Catering to Older Travelers," both of which appeared in *The New York Times* travel section, August 25, 1991.

Etruscans

Though most of Italy's Etruscan sites are closer to Rome, there are a few in Tuscany and Umbria. (I have to admit, however, that Rome is a logical place to begin or end a trip exploring Etruria, for its excellent Etruscan collections at the Villa Giulia and Museo Gregoriano Etrusco in the Vatican are what inspired my own interest in the Etruscans.) Visitors should be aware that without a car it is a bit of an effort to reach the Etruscan villages. There is no train service, so you'll have to rely on the bus, and you might have to make a connection or two. I would recommend renting a car and setting out early in the day, perhaps including Livorno in the journey.

An excellent companion article to read which I was unable to include here is "The Glory That Was Not Rome" (Robert Hughes, *Condé Nast Traveler,* May 1991).

F

Film

I'm aware that the FAA maintains film less than 1,000-speed sent through X-ray scanners won't harm picture developing; but my friend Peggy, a freelance photographer, maintains that multiple trips through the scanner will, indeed, harm the film. Also, if you pack your film in checked bags, the scanners that inspect them are stronger than those for carry-on bags and should definitely be avoided. ~I always keep rolls of film, no matter what speed, accessible and hand them to the security inspectors before I walk through the scanner (remember to retrieve them after you pass, however!). ~If you take a lot of photos, you might want to buy some lead-lined pouches from a camera store. They're inexpensive and will even protect film in checked bags. ~Professional film (which is very sensitive and must be kept refrigerated until used and developed a day later) aside, a guideline for us amateurs is that the higher the film speed, the faster the film—and fast film requires less light. So, think about the situations in which you anticipate taking pictures: if it's off-season and overcast in Florence, select 200; if it's summer with bright sunlight, select 400; for indoor gatherings in restaurants, try 800 or higher (unless you want to employ the flash); if you'll be in Siena for the *Palio,* select 400 or higher; for approaching dusk and sunsets, select 400. ~I happen to be very fond of black-and-white photos, so I always include a roll or two in my bag.

Firenze (Florence)

One of my favorite books—and not just for cooking—is *A Taste of Tuscany* by Leslie Forbes (see *La Cucina Italiana* for more details). The following passage is one of my favorites about Florence, and offers a good word of advice for summertime visitors: "Just when you think you have cracked the system, everything shuts at one o'clock for lunch. Grey steel shutters clang down abruptly to cover all the tempting displays of goodies, leaving formerly lively shopping streets bare and bleak. For four hours nothing moves except the occasional fly and in the summer heat of Florence (one of the hottest and most humid cities in Italy) even the flies can be a little sluggish. The only solution is to follow the Florentine example. Rise early to shop and see the staggering variety of museums and churches and save the afternoon for a long, lazy lunch in a cool restaurant. Or picnic and siesta in the huge formal Boboli gardens behind the Pitti Palace. If you can cope with the heat, explore the narrow streets lined with medieval and Renaissance palaces in the precious quiet hours between one and five o'clock. During the rest of the day, whining mopeds are a constant hazard, whizzing merrily down so-called "pedestrian only" thoroughfares and missing tourists and Florentines alike only by centimetres. The city is not now and never has been a restful place to visit. Exhilarating, yes. Restful, no."

Fly Fishing

There are wonderful opportunities in central Italy for trout-fishing enthusiasts. A good article to read is "The Catch of the Day Wasn't Always Fish" (Alan Cowell, *The New York Times,* April 9, 1995), which details Cowell's experiences on the Burano and Sangro rivers. As with other activities in Italy, fishing requires a bewildering array of permits. Cowell recommends the services of a guide, and he provides the names and contact information for several.

Frequent Flier Miles

From what I've read, airlines wish they'd never created mileage programs, and there are now fewer and fewer seats reserved for frequent fliers, *and* you need even more miles to earn these seats. Should you happen to have enough miles and want to fly to Florence, plan to redeem those miles about six months to a year ahead *or* plan to fly in the off-season (it's also possible that airlines will reduce the miles needed for the flight in the off-season). Don't immediately give up if your initial request can't be confirmed. Apparently, the airlines fiddle with frequent-flier seats every day as they monitor the demand for paying customers. If the number of paying travelers is low as the departure date approaches, more frequent-flyer awards might be honored. Also, try to reserve your mileage for expensive flights rather than those that you can get for a good price anytime.

G

General Travel

Here are some good books to consult about trip planning in general: *The New York Times Practical Traveler Handbook: An A–Z Guide to Getting There and Back,* Betsy Wade, Times Books, 1994; and *Wendy Perrin's Secrets Every Smart Traveler Should Know:* Condé Nast Traveler*'s Consumer Travel Expert Tells All,* Fodor's Travel Publications, 1997. It might seem like these two books cover the same ground, but in fact there is very little overlap and I refer to both of them all the time. The Practical Traveler book really is an A–Z guide, organized alphabetically and covering topics such as airline code sharing, customs, hotel tipping, and closing up the house. Perrin's book is divided into eight sections plus an appendix, and the anecdotes featured were all previously published in the Ombudsman column of the magazine. She covers the fine art of complaining; what to do if your luggage is damaged or pilfered; travel agents and tour operators, car rentals, shopping and cruises, etc., as well as the ten commandments of trouble-free travel, which I think should be given to every traveler before he or she boards the plane. In a similar vein, I highly recommend *Traveler's Tool Kit: How to Travel Absolutely Anywhere!,* Rob Sangster, Menasha Ridge Press, Birmingham, Alabama, 1996. "Tool kit" really is the best description of this travel bible, which addresses *everything* having to do with planning, packing, and departing. Who is this book for? Everyone, really, or at least people who are curious about the rest of the world; people who are thinking about their very first foreign trip; budget travelers; business travelers; people who want to travel more independently; and people who know "that life offers more than a two-week vacation once a year." It's a *great* book, with lots of great ideas, tips, and advice. I've found Sangster's checklists at the back of the book particularly helpful.

Guidebooks

Choosing which guidebooks to use can be bewildering and frustrating. I have yet to find the perfect book that offers all the features I need and want, so I consult a variety of books, gleaning tips and advice from each. Then I buy a blank journal and fill it with notes from all these books (leaving some pages blank) and end up with what is the perfect package for me: the journal plus two or three guidebooks I determine to be indispensable (I don't carry them around at the same time). In the end, the right guidebook is the one that speaks to you. Place yourself in front of the Italy section of a bookstore and take some time to read through the various guides. If you feel the author shares a certain sensibility with you, and you think his or her credentials are respectable, then you're probably holding the right book. Recommendations from friends and colleagues are fine only if they travel in the same way you do and seek the same qualities as you in a guidebook. Also, if you discover an older guide that appeals to you, don't immediately dismiss it. Background information doesn't change—use it in combination with an updated guide to create your own perfect package. Keep in mind, too, that guidebooks within the same series are not always consistent, as they aren't always written by the same authors. The following books, listed alphabetically, are those I typically peruse before a trip to Tuscany and Umbria. Note that I do not recommend books on all of Italy—unless one is traveling extensively throughout the country, the Tuscany and Umbria sections in these books is entirely too condensed. I have also indicated which books are essential to bring along:

Access Florence & Venice, Plus Tuscany and the Veneto, Richard Saul Wurman, Access Press (a registered trademark of HarperCollins Publishers, Inc.). There's not enough historical background for me in Access Guides, and descriptions are too brief, but the beauty of Access is that it enables you to *really* get to know neighborhoods. The Florence section features maps and details for the Oltrarno, Santa Croce, San Lorenzo, Santa Maria Movella, Colli, and Centro Storico neighborhoods. Things to see and do are listed numerically, corresponding to the numbers on the maps. Entries are color-coded, blue for hotels, red for cuisine, green for special finds, and black for cultural and historic sights. Lots of unique stores are listed in each neighborhood, and there's a good section on "The Treasures of Tuscany" day-trips. I also especially like the "Eat, Drink and Be Merry at Florence's Wine Bars." My favorite feature of the Access Guides is the "Bests" suggestions, which are a wide variety of recommendations contributed by noteworthy personalities. I've discovered some great tips and ideas here. A bring-along.

Baedeker's Tuscany, Baedeker Stuttgart (distributed in the U.S. by Fodor's Travel Publications). No book sums up the excitement and romance of travel to me like an old hardcover Baedeker guide (if you're a nut for them like me, The Complete Traveller in New York always seems to have a good assortment—see Bookstores for address and phone). The first Baedeker guide appeared in 1844, and the series has been the authoritative leader ever since. Current guides are paperback, with color photos and an easy-to-read format. The best feature of a Baedeker is the foldout map (in the old editions this was glued to the back cover; in the updated guides the map is completely separate from the book itself and is housed in a plastic sleeve at the back of the package). The book is divided into three color-coded sections: Nature, Culture, History (blue); Sights from A to Z (pink); and

Practical Information from A to Z (yellow). In keeping with Baedeker tradition, sites are described in alphabetical order and are rated with one star (especially worth attention) or two (outstanding). The features I like best are "Baedeker Specials," essays on subjects such as "A Culinary Phenomenon—Extra Virgin Olive Oil," "Lovers Ride Vespas," and "Tuscan Dreams," and the practical information section, which includes more complete information than found in other guides.

Blue Guide: Tuscany and *Blue Guide: Florence,* published by A & C Black Publishers, London; distributed in the U.S. by W. W. Norton. Perhaps because it is so authoritative, like Baedeker, I always feel like I *have* to check in with the Blue Guide. In fact, the Blue Guide series has been around since 1918, and the founders were the editors of Baedeker's English-language editions. Blue Guides are very straightforward and practical with a no-nonsense approach that sets the series apart from so many others. I did not realize until I read the Tuscany guide that the region has more museums than any other in Italy. I was similarly enlightened reading about explanations of place names in Italian towns and cities. Many place names have ancient origins, others date from the Middle Ages, but most are from the nineteenth century, when local patriotism determined the names to celebrate local history, and political, literary, religious, and scientific figures. "But," as author Alta Macadam writes, "the choice of place names can reflect wider issues, and events and figures from Italian national history are prominently represented. Thus a united republican Italy can be celebrated in terms of concepts (e.g., Via della Repubblica, della Liberta, della Vittoria), events (e.g., Via del Plebiscito recalling the vote that preceded a region uniting with the kingdom of Italy in the nineteenth century), or by drawing on the gazetteer of Italian rivers, mountains, seas, and cities." A good feature of the Tuscany guide is a list of prominent people and historic events from recent Italian history that travelers are likely to encounter often. The *Florence* guide is equally good, and although I wouldn't use a Blue Guide exclusively, I would recommend one as a bring-along.

Cadogan: Tuscany, Umbria & The Marches, Dana Facaros and Michael Pauls, Cadogan Books plc, London; distributed in the U.S. by Globe Pequot Press, Old Saybrook, Connecticut. Cadogan (rhymes with toboggan) Guides are almost all written by the Facaros-Pauls team (they've written over twenty now), and I consider them to be of the bring-along variety. They're discriminating and honest, witty, and interesting without being snooty. The authors are not very easily impressed, so when they enthuse about something, I pay attention. I'm most especially fond of the History and Topics sections in the front of each book, which reveal how perceptive the authors are and introduce the reader to their style. They may have special affection for this edition since they lived for three years in an Umbrian hilltop village. There are lodging and dining recommendations for all budgets, and good commentary on sights famous and little known. The walking tours are good, and there are the usual maps, menu vocabulary, glossary, bibliography, and list of architectural, artistic, and historical terms. At the front of this book is a new feature: The Best of Tuscany, Umbria and The Marches, which is a listing of the authors' recommendations for things such as antiquities, beaches, best-kept secrets, coastal scenery, ceramic towns, restaurants, etc. Definitely my favorite all-around guidebook. ~Companions to this guide are *Cadogan Florence, Siena, Pisa, Lucca* (which comes in a smaller size, although it's still chunky) and *Cadogan Gourmet Guides: Lazy Days Out in Tuscany* (Ros Belford, Dana Facaros, and Michael Pauls). The gourmet guide is a little paperback featuring twenty restaurants the authors enthusiastically recommend. Maps, recipes, some touring information, and a culinary glossary make it a must-have.

Central Italy: Trip Planner & Guide, Fiona Duncan and Peter Greene, Passport Books, a division of NTC/Contemporary Publishing Group, Chicago. I wasn't at all sure I would like this slender paperback, but I was surprised at how thorough it is. The book covers Tuscany, Umbria, the Marche, and northern Lazio, and features coordinated itineraries and suggested routes for the region as well as local explorations. Some of its other features I think are particularly noteworthy include the Something for Everyone themes, such as City Sights, Rugged Uplands for Walkers, Sun and Sand, Lakeside Idylls, Wine Tours, Hidden Central Italy, etc.; an A–Z of artists and architects; suggested walks and driving detours in the cities and countryside; color photos and maps; and dozens of good tips and details, such as museums open on a Monday in Florence, spots throughout the region with great views, and the following advice about bus service in Florence: "If you want a bus, but you don't know its route, head for the terminus at Santa Maria Novella station; most buses stop at either Piazza del Duomo or Piazza di San Marco as well. Bus No. 7 goes from the station to the Duomo to Fiesole; bus No. 10 goes from the station to the Duomo to San Marco to Settignano; bus No. 13 goes from the station to Piazzale Michelangelo and San Miniato." I am very impressed with the overall quality and portability of this guide, and think that it would cover every base if used in conjunction with Cadogan.

Eyewitness Travel Guides: Florence & Tuscany, DK (Dorling Kindersley) Publishing. Like the Knopf Guides, the Eyewitness series features bold graphics, full color photos, maps, and illustrations. Unlike Knopf Guides, there are lots of bird's-eye views of historic buildings, street-by-street maps, and a timeline from prehistoric times to the present day. Overall, Eyewitness guides are visually appealing more than they are substantive, but the most useful features of this guide are for me the beginning section (with topics such as A Portrait of Tuscany, Understanding Art in Tuscany, a Tuscan Town Square, The Landscape of Tuscany, etc.), the Florence Street Finder (with three double-page spreads of maps), and the Florence Area by Area section, which divides the city up into City Center North, West, East, and the

Oltrarno. For each area there are about ten pages of sights and streets, and it's easy for visitors to grasp what's where. The writers of this edition prove to have a sense of humor, as when they offer advice for crossing busy streets: a green Avanti light they translate as meaning marginally less dangerous to cross, which in theory gives pedestrians the right of way, but you should never expect drivers to recognize this. "Seize your opportunity and walk out slowly and confidently, glaring at the traffic and maintaining a determined pace. The traffic should stop or at least swerve." For a red ALT light they advise, "Stay on the pavement at all costs."

Fodor's Florence, Tuscany and Umbria, Fodor's Travel Publications. I typically crave more information than Fodor's guides seek to provide. I think, however, that the entire line of Fodor's guides just keeps getting better and better every year. I *always* read them before I go and *always* discover a handful of useful tips. Once, my husband and I planned on having dinner at a particular restaurant in Antibes, on the Cote d'Azur in France, which was recommended in numerous books. Only the Fodor's guide stated that coat-and-tie attire was required for men. This is a small but important piece of information that I consider crucial for business and holiday travelers alike. It would not only be disappointing but embarrassing—and potentially offensive—to appear at a restaurant improperly dressed, all the more so if you had arranged to meet friends or colleagues there. The Rand McNally map at the back of the book, the wider range of choices for lodging and dining, color photos, the boxed "Close-Up" essays, and the Off the Beaten Path suggestions throughout the book make this gold guide for central Italy more valuable than it's ever been. ~Also worth perusing is *Fodor's Exploring: Florence & Tuscany,* which is filled with color photographs. I'm fond of the suggested walks and drives and the "Florence Was, Florence Is" section in the front of this guide.

Fodor's UpClose Italy, Fodor's Travel Publication. The UpClose series is aimed at travelers on limited budgets, but not necessarily the *Let's Go* crowd. There are lots of money-saving tips throughout the book as well as information on rail passes, youth hostels, and studying in Italy, but there is a also a wealth of practical information for *all* types of travelers, not just students. The range of options for transportation, lodging, and dining is wide, there are numerous maps, and—my favorite feature—there are interesting "trivia boxes" all through the book (some of these in the Italy guide are Lucky Black Rooster, This Ain't No Rodeo, and Wine-Snob Etiquette). Historical background is too thin for my taste, but this series is particularly welcome because I believe this audience—intelligent travelers who want an authentic experience on a modest budget—more accurately reflects the majority of people traveling today. There is one chapter on Florence and Tuscany, and another on Umbria and the Marche.

The Heritage Guides to Italy: Florence and Umbria, Touring Club Italiano. It was good news last year when Abbeville Press began distributing these TCI guides in English. TCI maps are the equivalent of IGN maps in France and

Ordnance Survey in England, so it's no surprise that this edition includes a twenty-seven-page city atlas and twenty-six walking and driving tours with detailed maps. Although I prefer even more historical information, The Heritage Guides provide better, more thorough details than nearly any other guidebook. The gray pages at the back of each book is a section of listings for hotels, restaurants, and places of interest, including shops, crafts, and fine art. The Florence book also covers the surrounding countryside and Chianti region. Highly recommended—a bring-along.

Insight Guides: Tuscany and *Insight Guides: Florence,* APA Publications, Singapore (distributed by Houghton Mifflin). I have been an enormous fan of the Insight Guides for years. When they first appeared, about twenty years ago, they were the only books to provide outstanding color photographs matched with perceptive text. The guiding philosophy of the series has been to provide genuine insight into the history, culture, institutions, and people of a particular place. The editors search for writers with a firm knowledge of each city or region who are also experts in their fields. I do not think that recent editions are quite as good as they used to be; however, as I mentioned above, some guidebooks in a series are better than others, and I think the Tuscany and Florence editions are very good. The introduction (which has always been the best section, in my opinion, in *all* the books), is a series of magazine-style essays on architecture, food, markets, the people, history, arts, and politics. Some of the essays in the Tuscany book are "The Tuscan Miracle," "Foreign Writers in Tuscany," "The Medici," "The Etruscans," "The Roman Legacy," "Feuds of the City-States," "Defining the Renaissance," and "Tuscany Today." There are practical tips at the back of the book, plus very helpful floor plans of the Uffizi, Duomo, and Church of San Lorenzo.

Italy: The Places in Between, Kate Simon, Harper & Row, 1970. Sadly, this wonderful, wonderful book is out-of-print, but it does occasionally turn up. If you ever run across a copy, buy it without hesitation. There are no more travel writers quite like Kate Simon, except perhaps Jan Morris and Barbara Grizzuti Harrison. A quotation from the jacket reads, "How splendid is Kate Simon, the incomparable Kate Simon, whom no one has ever rivaled in the long, long history of guidebooks." This is, just as her books on Paris, Mexico, and New York are, an uncommon guidebook, and indeed is like no other guidebook ever published. At the end of each chapter (and there is a separate one for Tuscany) is an essay, such as "The Subject Is Eating," "Knowing the People and the Language," etc. These essays are brilliant observations that make this book unique. Simon does not approach things to see and do in a predictable fashion, which I think encourages travelers to approach Tuscany and Umbria in an unpredictable manner. This is a special, inspiring book. *Essenziale.*

Knopf Guides: Florence, Alfred A. Knopf, originally published in France by Nouveaux-Loisirs, a subsidiary of Gallimard, Paris. I'm fond of the Knopf Guides in general, and the Florence edition is no exception. I like the bold design and the various sections in the front of the book (Florence as Seen by Painters, The Iris and the Olive Tree, The Arno, The Stones of Florence, City Defenses and Fortified Dwellings, etc.). I also like the foldout page for the Corridoio Vasariano. Surprisingly, for such a *luxe* book, there are listings for budget hotels, plus youth hostels and campsites. Additionally, there is a chapter on the outskirts of Florence. As visually appealing and chunky as Knopf Guides are, they are actually surprisingly short on in-depth information. I wouldn't use this Florence edition exclusively, but it's a good companion to a more substantial guidebook.

Let's Go: Italy, including Tunisia, Bruce F. McKinnon, editor, St. Martin's Press. "The World's Bestselling Budget Travel Series" is the *Let's Go* slogan, which is hardly debatable. *Let's Go* is still the bible, and if you haven't looked at a copy since your salad days, you might be surprised: Now each edition contains color maps, advertisements, and an appendix that features a wealth of great practical information. A team of Harvard student interns still offers the same thorough coverage of places to eat and sleep, and things to see and do, and true to *Let's Go* tradition, rock-bottom budget travelers can find suggestions for places to sleep under $10 a night (sometimes it's the roof), and travelers with more means can find clean, cozy, and sometimes downright fancy accommodations. The inside back cover of this Italy guide features important phrases, phone numbers, Italian symbols, a Celsius/Fahrenheit chart, and a ruler with inches and meters, providing a quick reference that's easy to read. The color maps at both the front and back of the book are repeated, which I found baffling, especially since there are several maps of Rome and only one for Florence. It seems to me that travelers don't need maps in duplicate but rather an assortment, which would allow for more than one for Florence and its surrounding suburbs. I think the presentation of facts and history is quite substantive in *Let's Go,* and I would eagerly press a copy into the hands of anyone under a certain age (thirty-five?) bound for Italy.

Living, Studying, and Working in Italy: Everything You Need to Know to Fulfill Your Dreams of Living Abroad, Travis Neighbor, Monica Larner, Henry Holt, 1998. Just as the title indicates, here's the book you need to inspire and prepare you to go. The authors lived in Italy, separately and in different cities, for a combined total of more than ten years, and they wrote this book because they couldn't find one that addressed the practical side of living in Italy. Readers will find great information on looking for a job, including over 900 addresses and Internet sites; freelance, seasonal, part- and full-time employment options, language schools, American colleges and Italian universities; tips on money and banking; and a great appendix with telephone and mail, times, measurements, etc. Obviously useful for long-term visitors, but short-term visitors with a serious interest in Italy will be glad to have it.

Lonely Planet: Italy, Helen Gillman, Damien Simonis, Stefano Cavedoni. Lonely Planet guides have been among my favorite for many years. Tony and Maureen Wheeler founded the series in Australia in 1973. Originally, the series focused solely on Asia; but about a dozen years ago they realized that the Lonely Planet approach to travel was not exclusive to any geographic area of the world. The series is aimed at independent travelers, and each book is organized by chapters such as Facts for the Visitor (covering everything from health and gay and lesbian travelers, to pickpockets and legal matters), Getting Around, Things to See & Do, Places to Stay, and Places to Eat. I am fondest of the opening chapters covering history, politics, ecology, religion, economy, and practical facts. The information on sites to see is not nearly detailed enough. I like that hotels and restaurants are presented least expensive to most expensive, and I like the candid opinions of the contributing authors. Though I never like books on all of Italy, *Lonely Planet* doesn't (yet) publish an individual guide to Florence, Tuscany, or Umbria. This Italy edition features a section on Italian art and architecture with color photographs. A percentage of each book's income is donated to various causes such as Greenpeace's efforts to stop French nuclear testing in the Pacific, Amnesty International, and agricultural projects in Central America.

Michelin Green Guide: Tuscany. A Michelin guide might be more trustworthy than your best friend. Its famous star-rating system and "worth a detour" slogan may have become a bit too formulaic, but it's a formula that works. The series was created in 1900 by Andre Michelin, who compiled a little red book of hotels and restaurants, which today is the Michelin Red Guide famous for the stars it awards to restaurants. The green tourist guides first made their appearance in 1926. Each guide is jam-packed with information and is easy to pack. It will come as no surprise to readers that I prefer even more detail than Michelin offers, but I find it an excellent series, and each guide I've used has proven to be exceptionally helpful. Florence occupies most of the pages in this guide, but a good portion is devoted to the Tuscan countryside. Each Michelin guide is complemented by a Michelin map, of course, and this edition is meant to be used in conjunction with Map 430 Central Italy, Map 988 Italy, as well as the Motoring Atlas 465 Italy. A new route-planner service, which I happen to think takes much of the joy out of trip planning, is available by visiting www.michelin-travel.com. Viewers type in start and finish points and are provided with a suggested route, travel time, distances, road numbers, and any tolls.

The Rough Guides: Tuscany & Umbria, Jonathan Buckley, Mark Ellingham, and Tim Jepson, distributed in the U.S. by Penguin Books. When the Rough Guides first appeared, in the early eighties, they had limited distribution in the U.S. Then the guides were sort of but not quite the British equivalent of *Let's Go.* I sought them out because I found the British viewpoint refreshing and felt the writers imparted more knowledge about a place than was currently available in U.S. guidebooks. Mark Ellingham was inspired to create the Rough Guides series because at the time current guidebooks were all lacking in some way. They were either strong on ruins and museums but short on bars, clubs, and inexpensive eating places or so conscious of the need to save money that they lost sight of things of cultural and historical significance. None of the books mentioned anything about contemporary life, politics, culture, the people and how they lived. Now, since the Rough Guides opened a New York office in the late nineties, the series has evolved into one that is broader-based but still appealing to independent-minded travelers who appreciate the Rough Guides' honest assessments and historical and political backgrounds (these last are found in the Contexts section of each guide, and my only complaint is that I think this section should appear at the beginning of each book instead of at the end). Like its cousin *Let's Go*, readers will find specifics on working and studying in Italy, gay and lesbian life, and hotels that are frequented both by the backpacking crowd and those who carry luggage with their hands. Some of the features of the Tuscany and Umbria guide I like are checklists for particular food and wines unique to each region, a directory of artists and architects, and charts for the descendants of Cosimo Il Vecchio and Lorenzo de'Medici. On-line updates to Rough Guides can be found at www.roughguides.com for those who feel this is essential. All in all, each edition in the Rough Guides series is dependable and informative. ~There is also a Mini Rough Guide edition for Florence, a pocket-size book I recommend if you like the Rough Guides style.

Time Out Guide: Florence & Tuscany, Penguin Books. Published by the same hip folks who brought London's *Time Out* magazine to some of our U.S. cities, Time Out guidebooks are compact, well written, and jammed with information. The style and tone are similar to the Rough Guides and Lonely Planet, but the books are a little more glossy and are visually more appealing, with good design and both color and black-and-white photos. This Florence and Tuscany guide features good information on history (including two pieces on Medici Who's Who and Tuscany in the Risorgimento) and contemporary life. The Florence in Focus section is particularly good, as is the Italian vocabulary section: In addition to the usual useful stuff, you can learn to say idiot (*stronzo*), what the hell are you doing? (*che cazzo fai?*), and *merda* and *vaffanculo* (both of which I think you can figure out). There are seven color maps at the back of the book, plenty of black-and-white maps throughout the book, and a plethora of recommendations for music, film, dance, theater, nightlife, sports, and fitness, etc. Also, for those who need weekly updated information, Time Out guides can be accessed via the Internet at www.timeout.co.uk.

Italy's Finest, Bona Frescobaldi, Edizioni del Titano, Republic of San Marino. Published annually in both Italian and English and written by marchesa Frescobaldi (of the wine-making family), this unique and personal guide is unavailable in the U.S. All of Italy is covered, but Frescobaldi is a native Florentine, and she knows Tuscany perhaps better than anyone. *Essenziale,* both for those who can afford the finest, and for anyone who appreciates the inside scoop. The guide can be purchased in Florence at International Bookshop Seeber, via Tornabuoni, 70r; 055.215697.

H

Health

Staying healthy while traveling in Italy should not be a challenge, but things do happen. Outside of Rome, I don't drink tap water, including to brush my teeth. A good general reference book is *Travelers' Health: How to Stay Healthy All Over the World* (Richard Dawood, M.D.—former medical editor for *Condé Nast Traveler*—foreword by Paul Theroux, Random House, 1994). This thick, 600-plus page book isn't for taking along—it's for consulting before you go. In addition to Dr. Dawood, sixty-seven other medical experts contributed to this volume, which covers everything from insect bites, water filters, and sun effects on the skin to gynecological problems, altitude sickness, children abroad, immunizations, and the diabetic traveler. It also features essays on topics like "The Economy-Class Syndrome" and "Being an Expatriate."

Hiking

There are lots of opportunities for hiking in Tuscany and Umbria. Two different mountain ranges, the Apennine Alps and the Apuan Alps, offer two different experiences: the Apennines are more like rolling hills, round and bald at the top, and the Apuans are more of a classic range with jagged peaks, cliffs, and valleys. An important point to keep in mind about hiking in Italy is that often what you walk on is more of a pathway, not a well-groomed trail. Paths weren't created at random; they connect old footpaths that have existed for a long, long time. Routes wind through the middle of villages, sometimes cross private property where you have to open and close a gate, and are often farm tracks where you'll encounter shepherds and farmers. Walking in Italy is generally not a wilderness experience, but there are very few places in Europe where you can backpack into completely isolated places and not encounter roads, people, or towns. Conversely, there are few, if any, places in the U.S. where you can backpack and be assured of finding a place to sleep in a bed plus a meal with wine or beer at the end of the day. ~The best book I've seen on hiking in Italy is *The Independent Walker's Guide to Italy* (Frank Booth, Interlink Books, Brooklyn, New York, 1996). I took an immediate liking to Booth because he explains that although he has written a guide about walking in Italy, his book is also about escaping and avoiding the DROPS (Dreaded Other People). "Even with this book in hand," he writes, "you will not always be able to completely avoid the DROPS, but you will have a strategy to retain your independence and sanity." This is your clue that he has lots of surprises in store for the visitor who wants to escape from the beaten path from time to time. There are thirty-five great walks in Tuscany and Umbria: Fiesole to Ponte a Mensola; Monteaperto to Siena; Zona di Foci to San Gimignano; Monte Capanne to Marciano on Elba; Parco Naturale della Maremma; Lago Trasemino; Monte Ingino to Gubbio; Eremo delle Carceri to Assisi; Monteluco to Spoleto. In addition to these, there are ten thematic itineraries: Ancient Ruins; Great Castles and Walls; Famous Cathedrals, Churches, and

Abbeys; Fabulous Feasts; High Hills and Massive Mountains; Captivating Coasts and Beaches; Inland Waterways; Great Art Centers; the Must-See Itinerary: All the Greatest Sights; and Author's Favorite Walks (three out of ten are in Tuscany and Umbria). For those inspired to embark on a more serious hike, Booth recommends the Grand Tour, which is simply all the walks in the book in order, which he calls "peerless as a vehicle for an in-depth discovery of Italy." A map and trail notes accompany each walk, and the book is a small paperback meant to be a bring-along. ~The *Lonely Planet Walking in Italy* guide is another good book (by Helen Gillman, Sandra Bardwell, Stefano Cavedoni, and Nick Tapp, 1998). There are no walks featured in Umbria, but there are two for Tuscany, plus a variety of long-distance walks. There is a helpful chart in the front of the book with a description of each walk, duration, best season to do it, and the level of difficulty, and there are a few color photos. ~A third book, with more color photographs, is *Wild Italy: The Sierra Club Natural Traveler,* Tim Jepson, Sierra Club Books, San Francisco, 1994. This is one edition in the Wild Guides Series (others include France and Spain), and author Jepson has a particular interest in Tuscany and Umbria. The areas for naturalists and hikers that he covers in this book include Alpi Apuane, Migliarino-San Rossore-Massa Ciucoli, Bolgheri, Maremma, Monte Argentario, Laguna di Orbetello, Lago di Burano, Parco Nazionale d'Arcipelago Toscano, Monte Cucco, and Valnerina. Jepson notes that in the Maremma, "Tuscany can claim the finest piece of untouched coastline in the country: a pristine tract of maquis, hills, dune and coastal pine woods (or *pinete*) that enjoys fierce protection and is one of only two proposed national parks in the region." Umbria, he notes, is equally as beautiful and pastoral as Tuscany; but, strangely, though native Saint Francis of Assisi was noted for his love of nature, birds in particular, the Umbrians regularly kill local birds. Despite a campaign to try and stop them, nothing's been done. Some fauna unique to these regions that naturalists are likely to encounter are the bee-eater bird, Hermann's tortoise, osprey, crested porcupine, and the black-winged stilt. ~There is a new park near Orvieto in Umbria called Parco Fluviale del Tevere with a network of hiking paths. The park borders the Tiber, and even in cold weather there are plenty of good days for walking.

I

Internet Access

I'm including this here for business travelers. If you're traveling for pleasure and feel you need to surf the Web, perhaps you should save your money and stay home. (I take the view that vacations are for removing yourself from your daily grind; visiting another country is about doing *different* things and putting yourself in unfamiliar situations.) Overseas telephone services are not as reliable as those in the U.S., ensuring that connecting to the Internet is also not as easy or inexpensive.

Business travelers who need to check in with the office via e-mail should consider what it will cost for a laptop, power adapter, disk and/or CD-ROM drives, plus any other related accessories, as well as how heavy it will be to carry. You might conclude that cybercafes (or Internet cafes) are more economical (and easier on your back). Fees for access to the Internet vary, but when you compare a hotel's charges for the same access, often at slower speeds, cybercafes represent good value. I found over ten cybercafes in Florence, Lucca, and Siena by searching in www.cybercaptive.com and www.netcafes.com. Additionally, I've noticed that some public telephone booths at airports are equipped for Internet access.

Istituto Italiano di Cultura

The Italian Cultural Institute is a great organization to help keep you immersed in all things Italian, both before you leave and when you return. I have attended some truly memorable events at the Institute here in New York, and the center has a great library and offers Italian classes. Readers far from New York might find the center's Web site (www.italcultny.org) a useful resource as it offers a forum for Italian teachers, a bulletin board for a wide variety of inquiries, Italian government grants for translations, and a calendar of events. The Istituto is located at 686 Park Avenue, New York, New York 10021; events hotline: 212-879-4242, extension 89.

J

Jewish History in Italy

Rome is home to the second-oldest continuous Jewish community in the world (after Jerusalem), and Tuscany has a great number of things of Jewish interest. The best book to consult is *Tuscany Jewish Itineraries: Places, History and Art* (edited by Dora Liscia Bemporad and Annamarcella Tedeschi Falco, Marsilio Regione Toscana / Marsilio Publishers, New York, 1997). One volume in the Jewish Itineraries Series (others cover Emilia-Romagna, Piemonte, Lombardia, and Venice), this paperback guide is small enough to pack and highlights Jewish cultural heritage in Tuscany. The historic roots of a Jewish presence in Tuscany extend back a long way, at least to the sixth century. Color and black-and-white photographs, a bibliography, and glossary are included, as well as three selected itineraries with maps. *Italy: Jewish Travel Guide* (Annie Sacerdoti and Luca Fiorentino, Israelowitz Publishing, Brooklyn, New York, 1993) is another good book, but covers all of Italy. However, history and sites in Tuscany (Florence, Livorno, Marina di Massa, Monte San Savino, Pisa, Pitigliaono, Siena, Sorano, Viareggio) and Umbria (Perugia, Spoleto) are covered well. A bigger book is *A Travel Guide to Jewish Europe* (Ben Frank, Pelican Publishing Company, Gretna, Louisiana, 1996), which includes Florence, Tuscany, and Umbria. An excellent article I was unable to include here is "A Turreted Corner of Tuscany" (William

Whitman, *The New York Times,* March 12, 1989), which presents a history of Pitigliano in the Maremma, where a Jewish community thrived since 1569.

L

Language

I do not speak Italian, but I do know some key words and phrases that rarely fail to bring a big smile to the faces of my hosts. The natives of *any* country love it when visitors try to speak their language. Italian might not be as widely spoken around the world as French, for example, but that doesn't mean you shouldn't attempt to learn some Italian vocabulary. It's a beautiful language, and if you studied Latin, you'll learn it in a snap. The Tuscan dialect is considered "standard" Italian, and though there are local dialects spoken in every part of Italy, almost everyone will recognize the Tuscan variety when you speak it and will most likely be happy to converse in it as well. You might notice that Florentines tend to turn the letter *c* into *h* and that each area of Tuscany and Umbria has its own similar quirk; but essentially the dialect is the same across the region. ~The best language-course program I've used is Living Language. There are others—Berlitz, Barron's, Language/30, etc.—but Living Language has been around longer (since 1946), the courses are continually updated and revised, and in terms of variety, practicality, and originality, I prefer it. Italian courses are available for beginner, intermediate, and advanced levels, in either audiocassette or CD editions. The Fast & Easy course (referred to as "virtually foolproof" by the New York *Daily News*) is for beginner business or leisure travelers and is a sixty-minute survival program with a cassette and pocketsize pronunciation guide. The Ultimate Course is for serious language learners and is the equivalent of two years of college-level study. In a copublishing venture with Fodor's, Living Language also offers the pocketsize *Italian for Travelers,* which is a handy book/cassette reference, designed for business and leisure travelers, with words and phrases for dozens of situations, including exchanging money, using ATMs, finding a hotel room, etc., and also includes a two-way dictionary. And to help build excitement for young children coming along, there's the *Learn in the Kitchen* and *Learn Together: for the Car* series. These book/cassette kits are for children ages four to eight, and include a sixty-minute bilingual tape; sixteen songs, games, and activities; a forty-eight-page illustrated activity book with color stickers; and tips for parents on how to vary the activities for repeated use. For readers who already have a foundation in Italian and want to maintain proficiency, I highly recommend *Acquerello italiano,* a monthly audiomagazine available by subscription only. I subscribe to the French version, *Champs-Elysées,* and have found it thoroughly enjoyable, practical, and timely. Subscribers choose cassette or CD, and can also select a study guide for an additional fee. Current events, culture (including music), cuisine, and business are profiled in each monthly edition. To subscribe: *Acquerello italiano*, P.O. Box 158067, Nashville, Tennessee 37215-8067; 800-824-0829; www.champs-elysees.com. A five-month cassette subscription is about $79, one year, $129. ~An essential book to have is *501 Italian Verbs* (Barron's). In addition to really good descriptions of the various tenses, a full page is allotted to each verb, showing all the tenses fully conjugated, plus the definition and a useful selection of Words and Expressions Related to This Verb at the bottom of each page. As if this weren't enough, there are also chapters on Verbs Used in Idiomatic Expressions, Verbs With Prepositions, Verbs Used in Weather Expressions, Thirty Practical Situations for Tourists and Popular Phrases, Words and Expressions for Tourists. If you're serious about learning or brushing up on Italian, I really can't see doing it without this book. ~Some related books for language lovers are *Latina pro Populo* (*Latin for People*) (Alexander and Nicholas Humez, Little, Brown and Company, 1978) and *Le Mot Juste: A Dictionnary of Classical and Foreign Words and Phrases* (Vintage Books, 1991), which includes classical languages, French, German, Italian, Spanish, and a smattering of other languages around the world. It's a great reference book that I use all the time, and what I'm reminded of each time I consult the Italian pages is the great number of words we use for music and art that derive from Italian.

Luggage

I've read of a syndrome—really—called B.S.A. (Baggage Separation Anxiety), which you might at first be inclined to laugh at. But as reports of lost luggage have escalated in the last few years, I'm not at all surprised (all the more reason, I say, not to check bags, and *definitely* the reason to at least pack some essentials in a carry-on bag). Even if you are the sort of traveler who cannot lighten your load, you will still probably take a carry-on. As I write this, the standard limit for carry-on luggage is 9″ × 14″ × 22″, otherwise known as 45 linear inches to the airlines. Although not all airlines enforce this policy, it seems foolish not to comply. Storage space is limited, and less baggage means more on-time schedules and better passenger safety. Some airlines have even installed sized templates at the security X-ray machines, so if your bag doesn't fit, you don't walk through. Many luggage manufacturers, including Tumi and Samsonite, have responded, turning out a variety of bags at varying prices, which are meant to hold enough stuff for about three days of traveling—about the time it takes for a misrouted bag to show up, assuming it isn't lost altogether!

M

Maps

Getting lost is usually a part of everyone's travels, but it isn't always a bonus. Happily, there are maps, and no shortage of good ones. *For Italy:* a terrific map is one produced by the National Geographic Society. It's unusual in that it's a double-sided map, with a full depiction in relief on one side and historical themes (the Etruscans, Papal States, the Renaissance, Napoleon in Italy, etc.) on the other. NGS doesn't publish two-sided maps often, and this one is shipped flat, and is suitable for framing. Dimensions are 34″ × 23″ and costs about $11 plus shipping. Contact NG Maps, P.O. Box 4357, Evergreen, Colorado 80437; 800-962-1643 / 303-670-3457; www.nationalgeographic.com (viewers can request a map catalog or purchase NGS maps by browsing the on-line store). *For Florence: Tutto Citta* is the map all the locals use, but I have no idea where to obtain one. My first encounter with it was in a hotel lobby, and I've not seen it for sale in bookstores. Florence—and all the other cities of any size in Tuscany and Umbria—is small enough that you really don't need a super-duper map. But if you're planning on staying for a while, a comprehensive map is necessary, so ask someone at the tourist office where to get one. Some maps I've seen here in the States that I think are good include *Insight* (the guidebook publisher), which is laminated and also includes an enlargement for Fiesole and a map of Pisa, a general map of Tuscany, and 10 Sights You Shouldn't Miss; and *Artwise Florence: The Museum Map* (published by Streetwise Maps, Amagansett, New York), which is in some ways better than a street map for short-term visitors. This, too, is laminated and there's a map on one side with a brief description of thirty-four museums on the reverse. *For driving in Tuscany and Umbria:* the best choices are the large, bound edition of *Atlante stradale d'Italia* published by Touring Club Italiano, and the foldout *Carta turistica stradale,* also published by TCI, for Italia centrale, foglio 2, at a scale of 1:4000,000. This volume, at a scale of 1:200,000, is available in three editions: Nord, Centro, and Sud. You might want to consider using the TCI map in conjunction with *Streetwise Tuscany* (also published by Streetwise Maps), a foldout, laminated map that shows the relief features of Tuscany better. And as anyone who has ever driven in Tuscany knows, driving across it—that is, against the grain, so to speak—takes a *lot* longer than appears on a map. Always a lot more time than you think you'll need when setting out on a driving adventure because, well, you'll probably need it. And don't be alarmed if the paved road suddenly turns into gravel and potholes. The ride might occasionally be bumpy, but it is almost always beautiful.

Mercate (Markets)

Outdoor markets are one of the great pleasures of Italy. Even if you have no intention of purchasing anything, visitors should not miss walking around an outdoor (or indoor) market. Florence's Mercato Centrale (San Lorenzo), designed by Giuseppe Mengoni (who also designed the magnificent Galleria Vittorio Emanuele II in Milan), is world-famous, and its covered food market is the largest in Europe. Prices for food seem to be displayed and fixed in Italy, but for other things bargaining is the accepted method of doing business (merchants will tell you if it's not); therefore, a visit to the market should not be an activity you try to do in a hurry. Take your time, remember to stop for something to eat or drink so your stomach (or companion) doesn't grumble, and enjoy searching for a unique *ricordo* (souvenir) or soaking up the atmosphere. While most of my own bargaining efforts have been practiced in Turkey and Egypt, here are some tips that work well for me in Italy, too: ~Walk around first and survey the scene. Identify the vendors you want to come back to, and if prices are not marked, try to ascertain what they are for the items you're interested in. If you don't have any idea what the general price range is, you won't have any idea if you're paying a fair price or too much. Even better is if you learn the prices of what items (such as leather gloves, handbags, and jewelry) sell for here in the States before you leave home, then you'll also know whether savings are being offered. ~If you do spy an item you're interested in, try not to reveal your interest. Act as nonchalant as you possibly can, and remember to be ready to start walking away. ~It's considered rude to begin serious bargaining if you're not interested in making a purchase. This doesn't mean you should refrain from asking the price on an item, but to then begin naming numbers is an indication to the vendor that you're a serious customer and that a sale will likely be made. ~You'll get the best price if you pay with cash, and Italy isn't in the vanguard of credit-card acceptance anyway. I prepare an assortment of paper lire and coins in advance so I can always pull them out and indicate that it's all I have. It doesn't seem right to bargain hard for something and pay for it with a 100,000L note. ~Occasionally, I feign interest in one particular item when it's a different item I *really* want. The tactic here is to begin the bargaining process and let the vendor think I'm about to make a deal. Then I pretend to get cold feet and indicate that the price is just too much for me. The vendor thinks all is lost, and at that moment I point to the item I've wanted all along, sigh, and say I'll take that one, naming the lowest price from my previous negotiation. Usually, the vendor will immediately agree to it as it means a done deal. ~Other times, I will plead poverty and say to the vendor that I had *so* wanted to take back a gift for my mother from "your beautiful country . . . won't you please reconsider?" This, too, usually works. ~Finally, remember that a deal is supposed to end with both parties satisfied. If, after much back and forth, you encounter a vendor who won't budge below a certain price, it's likely that it's not posturing but a way of letting you know that anything lower will no longer be advantageous to him or her.

Money

The best way to travel is with a combination of local cash, American Express traveler's checks (other types are not universally accepted), and credit cards. If you have all three, you will never have a problem, and note that you should not rely on wide acceptance of credit cards, especially in the countryside. How you divide this up depends on how long you'll be traveling and on what day of the week you arrive.

Banks, which of course offer the best exchange rate, aren't generally open on the weekends and, in Italy, aren't open all day during the week. If you rely solely on your ATM card and you encounter a problem, you can't fix it until Monday, when the banks reopen. Overseas ATMs may also limit the number of daily transactions you can make, as well as place a ceiling on the total amount you can withdraw. ~Make sure your password is compatible with Italian ATMs (if you have too many digits, you'll have to change it) and if, like me, you have memorized your password as a series of letters rather than numbers, write down the numerical equivalent before you leave. Most European cash machines do not display letters, and even if they did, they do not always appear in the same sequence as we know it in the U.S. ~Call your bank and inquire about fees for withdrawals, and ask if there is a fee for overseas transactions (there shouldn't be, but ask anyway). As there is a charge per transaction, plan to make a few big withdrawals rather than lots of small ones; inquire if you can withdraw money from both your checking and savings accounts or only one; and ask if you can transfer money between accounts. ~Though I think this is a bit anal-retentive even for me, it's possible to view in advance the exact street locations of ATM machines in Italy on-line. To see where Plus systems are, type in www.visa.com; for the Cirrus network, type www.mastercard.com/atm. Once in, select ATM Locator, and you'll be given an opportunity to select a country, city, street address, and postal code (not essential but helpful if you have it). I found over ninety locations for Florence, over fifty for Perugia, over forty for Pisa, and over thirty for Siena. ~Savvy travelers always arrive with some local currency in their possession (I feel most comfortable with about $50–$100). While the rates of exchange and fees charged obviously vary, it is far more important not to arrive empty-handed. We are, after all, talking about a small sum of money, and it will be money well spent when you get off the plane with the ability to quickly make your way to wherever you're going. After a long flight, who wants to then exchange money, especially while looking after luggage and/or children? And keep in mind that there are very often long lines at the exchange counters and cash machines, and that cash machines are sometimes out of order or out of cash. (Once, I even had the admittedly unusual experience of going directly to a large bank only to find a posted sign stating that the bank was closed because it had *run out of money!*) Smart travelers arrive prepared to pay for transportation, tips, snacks, personal items, or unanticipated expenses. If you're too busy to get the cash yourself, call International Currency Express and request its Currency Rush mail-order service. With two offices, in Los Angeles and Washington, D.C., the company offers excellent rates. Call 888-278-6628 and request either UPS second-day or overnight service. ~Traveler's checks should be cashed at banks as vendors prefer not to deal with them. This is not a reflection of a dim view of traveler's checks, but a reflection that Italy remains very much a cash economy. ~Refrain from wearing one of those ubiquitous waist bags, or, as my friend Carl says, "Make our country proud and don't wear one of those fanny packs!" A tourist + fanny pack = magnet for pickpockets. I know of more people than I can count who've had valuables stolen from these ridiculous pouches. Keep large bills, credit cards, and passport hidden from view in a money belt worn under your clothes, in a pouch that hangs from your neck, or in an interior coat or blazer pocket. And for the person who balks at the suggestion of a money belt in a fine restaurant, it is a simple matter to excuse yourself from the table, head for the W.C., and retrieve your money in the privacy of a stall. It is doubtful you'll be robbed walking from the bathroom back to your table. ~If possible, don't keep everything in the same place, and keep a separate piece of paper with telephone numbers of companies to contact in case of emergency. ~Useful vocabulary: *monete* or *spiccioli* (coins), *denaro* (money), *assegni di viaggio / per viaggiatori* (traveler's checks).

Movies

Plan a meal from one or more of the cookbooks mentioned in the *La Cucina Italiana biblioteca* and invite some friends and family over for dinner and a movie. Some suggestions: *A Room with a View, Stealing Beauty, La Vita È Bella* (*Life Is Beautiful*), *The English Patient,* and *In Search of Tuscany with John Guerrasio* and *The Power of the Past: Florence with Bill Moyers* (both PBS home videos). And while you're cooking, get in the mood by listening to some appropriate music: *Viva Italia!: Festive Italian Classics* (RCA), *Mob Hits* (Triage Entertainment), and *Italy After Dark* (EMI) are all great choices that will have you ready to say *cin-cin* (pronounced *cheen-cheen,* the Italian equivalent of "cheers!") when your guests arrive.

Museums and Monuments

Italy's art treasures face an unfair number of obstacles to their survival: pollution, earthquakes, fires, floods, terrorist bombs, theft (over 500,000 works have been stolen since 1970 and only about one third have been recovered), enormous numbers of tourists, lack of money, and even apathy. However, when Walter Veltroni became culture minister of Italy in 1995, he brought a completely new approach to the arts and how they should be viewed, funded, and maintained. Veltroni began a new lottery in 1997 that has generated a sum more than twice the amount the government previously earmarked for restorations. In addition, he instituted a policy of stricter adherence to posted hours of operation at museums. Not only are haphazard hours and three-hour lunches discouraged, but a number of museums remain open until 10 P.M., later even than museums in France, which has a long tradition of caring for its *patrimoine*. Museum hours used to be somewhat of a joke in Italy, but this is changing. In 1998, sixteen of Italy's major museums standardized their hours and are now open all day long, without a three-hour break for lunch, and some have bookstores and cafes. ~Remember that many museums in Florence and the rest of Italy are closed on Monday. Some of the smaller museums and monuments are open, however, as well as churches. Be sure to check in advance to avoid disappointment. ~Lines can be long, especially in Florence. Firenze Musei in Florence offers a service that allows visitors to reserve tickets for some sites, including the Uffizi, Boboli Gardens, Vasari Corridor, Pitti Palace, etc. This booking service is open Monday through Saturday, and the telephone number is 055.5294883. There is a small fee charged on top of the admission price, and a set time is selected for your visit. Tickets are then picked up at the museum or site no earlier than thirty minutes before your appointment. ~For the Uffizi only, reservations can be made through the Informazioni Turistiche Alberghiere office, by either calling (055.471960) or faxing (055.2478232) ahead, or showing up in person (9/A viale Gramsci or the tourist-information office in the Santa Maria Novella train station). As with the booking service above, you need to agree to a set time on a given date.

Nightlife in Florence
A good tip from the Time Out guide: "The opening times and closing days of bars and clubs in Florence are notoriously vague and erratic, and change without warning. Phones that are actually answered are a rarity, so be prepared to take a chance."

Orario continuato (Continuous hours)
In other words, open all day, as more and more businesses in Italy are these days.

P

Packing
Most people, whether they travel for business or pleasure, view packing as a stressful chore. It doesn't have to be, and a great book filled with excellent suggestions and tips is *Fodor's How to Pack: Experts Share Their Secrets* (Laurel Cardone, Fodor's Travel Publications, 1997). You might think it silly to consult a book on how to pack a suitcase, but this is eminently practical and worthwhile. Cardone is a travel journalist who's on the road a lot, and she meets a lot of fellow travelers with plenty of packing wisdom to share. How to buy luggage, how to fill almost any suitcase, nearly crease-free folding, the right wardrobe for the right trip, and how to pack for the way back home are all thoroughly covered. ~Some pointers that work for me include selecting clothing that isn't prone to wrinkling, like cotton and wool knits. When I *am* concerned about limiting wrinkles, I lay out a large, plastic dry-cleaning bag, place the garment on top of it, place *another* bag on top of that, and fold the item up between the two bags. The key here is that the plastic must be layered in with the clothing, otherwise it doesn't really work. ~If I'm packing items with buttons, I button them up before I fold them—the same with zippers and snaps. ~If I'm carrying a bag with more than one separate compartment, I use

one for shoes; otherwise, I put shoes at the bottom (or back) of the bag opposite the handle so they'll remain there while I'm carrying the bag. ~Transfer shampoo and lotions to plastic, travel-size bottles, which can be purchased at pharmacies— and then put these inside a Ziploc bag to prevent leaks. ~Don't skimp on under-wear—it's lightweight, takes up next to no room in your bag, and it's never a mistake to have more than you think you need. ~Belts can be either rolled up and stuffed into shoes or fastened together along the inside edge of your suitcase. ~Ties should be rolled, not folded, and stuffed into shoes or pockets. ~Some handy things to take along that are often overlooked: a pocket flashlight, for looking into ill-lit corners of old buildings, reading in bed at night (the lights are often not bright enough), or, if you're staying at a hotel where the bathroom is down the hall, for navigating the dark hallways at night (the light is usually on a timer and typically runs out before you've made it to either end of the hallway); binoculars, for look-ing up at architectural details; small travel umbrella; penknife/corkscrew; if I'm camping, plastic shoes—referred to in the U.S. as jellies, which the Italians have been wearing on some of their rocky *spiaggi* (beaches) for years and years—for campground showers; an empty, lightweight duffel bag, which I fold up and pack and then use as a carry-on bag for gifts and breakable items on the way home; copies of any current prescriptions in case I need to have a medicine refilled; pho-tocopies of my passport and airline tickets (which should also be left with someone at home).

Pane e coperto

About four years ago, there was a movement to try and stop Italian *ristoranti* and *trattorie* from charging a *pane e coperta* fee (supposedly for the bread and linens), which ranged from about $2–$6. Although *pane e coperta* is no longer ubiquitous (I even encountered it at campground restaurants), I have it on good authority from the Italian Tourist Office that, regrettably, some establishments still charge it. It's not really a big deal, but if you're just stopping for a plate of pasta and a glass of wine, the *coperta* could cost half as much as your meal.

Passports

For last-minute crises, it *is* possible to obtain a new passport, renew an old one, or get necessary visas (not required for Italy). Two companies that can meet the chal-lenge: Travisa (2122 P Street, N.W., Washington, D.C. 20037; 800-222-2589) and Express Visa Service, Inc. (353 Lexington Avenue, Suite 1200, New York, New York 10016; 212-679-5650 / fax: 679-4691)

Pazienza (Patience)

Kate Simon, in her book *Italy: The Places in Between*, defines this as "the capacity to endure with serenity." Very much worth remembering when traveling in Italy.

Periodicals

Following are some newsletters and periodicals, a few of which are not available at newsstands, that you might want to consider subscribing to in advance of your trip or upon your return if you decide you want to keep up with goings-on in Italy:

The Art of Eating: Named "Most Nourishing Food Quarterly" by *Saveur* in 1999 and, in my opinion, one of the very best publications ever, of any kind—see *La Cucina Italiana biblioteca* for more details and my enthusiastic endorsement. Back issues pertaining to various aspects of Italian food include No. 33 ("Olive Oil"), No. 41 ("In Tuscany," which covers the Sangiovese grape, Chianti, *vin santo,* saltless bread, olive oil, etc.), and No. 52 ("Restaurants in Northern Italy," which includes an excellent essay entitled "What Is Italian Food?"—essential for anyone interested in the current state of *la cucina italiana*). Back issues are $9 each or $7.50 each for any four or more. To order on-line, visit www.artofeating.com or write to Box 242, Peacham, Vermont 05862.

Dove Dossier: This monthly magazine is in Italian and is devoted to *"vacanze e tempo libero"* (vacation and free time). The June 1999 issue was devoted to Umbria, and although I do not speak or read Italian, I could still decipher some of the basic words and found the magazine useful for the names and addresses of restaurants, places to stay, things to do, etc., and the maps and color photos were great. *Dove Dossier* can be found at bigger newsstands that offer a variety of international periodicals; or, to subscribe, contact the magazine at De Agostini—Rizzoli Periodici, via Montefeltro 6/A, 20156 Milano; 02.380781 / fax: 02.38003497.

Events in Italy: This bimonthly magazine is published in Florence but is in English and features art, music, and museum events going on all over Italy as well as sections on places to stay, news and culture, travel, fashion, food and restaurants, and classified ads. It's available on some of the bigger U.S. newsstands, or you can subscribe by contacting the magazine directly: Lungarno Corsini 6, Firenze, 50123; 055.215613; www.events-italy.it.

Gambero Rosso: This quarterly magazine, devoted to wine, travel, and food in Italy, is among my favorite publications. I can't describe it better than its own promotional motto: "A magazine for intelligent travelers, gourmets on a budget, value-conscious buyers of nothing but the best." I anxiously await for each issue to appear in my mailbox, but *Gambero Rosso* can also be found at better newsstands; to subscribe, contact the magazine's U.S. distributor: Speedimpex USA Inc., 35-02 48th Avenue, Long Island City, New York 11101; 800-969-1258 / fax: 718-361-0815; to subscribe to the Italian version of the magazine, contact the main office in Rome: 53 via Arenula, 00186, Roma, Italia; (39) 06.68300741 / fax: 39.06.6877217; e-mail: gambero@gamberorosso.it; www.gamberorosso.it.

Italy Italy: "A Guide to All Its Best" is this bi-monthly magazine's motto, and each issue offers a variety of articles pertaining to history, contemporary events, travel, personalities, and the arts. It's available at some of the larger newsstands, but to subscribe, contact IAM Italian American Multimedia Corporation, P.O. Box 1255, New York, New York 10116-1255; 800-98-ITALY / fax: 212-982-3852; www.italyitaly.com.

Per piacere, per favore, permesso?, piu lentamente, and prego

Some good Italian *p* words to know. *Per piacere* and *per favore* mean "please," *permesso* means "permission" (a polite way to ask if you may enter, sit down, take something, ask a question, etc.). *Piu lentamente* is useful to remember when you want to say "please speak more slowly," and *prego* is an all-purpose word used to mean "please," "you're welcome," "okay," "of course, go ahead."

Photography

I would rather have one great photo of a place than a dozen mediocre shots, so I like to page through photography books for ideas and suggestions on maximizing my picture-taking efforts. Some books I've particularly enjoyed include: *The Traveler's Eye: A Guide to Still and Video Travel Photography* (Lisl Dennis, Clarkson Potter, 1996). Dennis, who began her career in photography at the *Boston Globe,* writes the "Traveler's Eye" column for *Outdoor Photographer.* I like her sensitive approach to travel photography and find her images and suggestions in this book inspiring. After chapters covering topics such as travel photojournalism, shooting special events, and landscape photography, she provides an especially useful chapter on technical considerations, with advice on equipment, film, packing, the ethics of tipping, and outsmarting airport X-ray machines. *Focus on Travel: Photographing Memorable Pictures of Journeys to New Places* (text by Anne Millman and Allen Rokach, photographs by Allen Rokach, Abbeville Press, 1992). More of a tome than *The Traveler's Eye,* although this doesn't cover video cameras. The authors offer much more information on lenses, filters, films, and accessories, and there are separate chapters on photographing architecture, shooting subjects in action, and taking pictures in a variety of weather conditions. The appendix covers selecting and preparing your photos after the trip, fill-in flash guidelines, color correction chart, and a page-by-page reference to all the photos in the book. *Kodak Guide to Shooting Great Travel Pictures: How to Take Travel Pictures Like a Pro* (Jeff Wignall, Fodor's Travel Publications, 1995). Unlike the books above, which should be consulted before you go, this is a very handy, small paperback good for taking along as a reference. Six chapters present specific photographic challenges—such as city vistas, stained-glass windows, close-ups of faces, mountain scenery, motion, lights at night, and taking pictures through frames—and each is dealt with in one page with accompanying photos. Note that this guide is meant for experienced *and* point-and-shoot photographers, and many of the images featured in the book are from the Eastman Kodak archives, a great number of which were taken by amateurs.

La Posta (mail)

If you'll be traveling on to Rome, mail all your postcards, letters, or packages from a *ufficio postale* (post office) in the Citta del Vaticano (Vatican City) as it's the only place in Italy with reliable mail service. Your postcards (*cartolini*) will actually arrive at their destinations if you mail them from here. Postcards mailed from Florence *might* arrive, just don't be surprised if they don't. I have never had a problem on the occasions I was mailing items home to myself, but the utter disarray inside a typical Italian post office—especially in smaller towns—led me to think many times that I would never see the items again. If you're mailing anything of value or if it's very large, you might want to consider a packing and shipping service. I don't recommend trying to pack and mail something yourself unless you have an *abbondanza* of patience, because Italian postal requirements are so complex your head will hurt. Much better to employ a service, one that is familiar with the proper way to wrap and the proper stamps, seals, and paperwork. One very reliable service is offered by Fracassi (Massimo Fracassi, Via Santo Spirito 11, Florence; 055.283597). He speaks English, will come and fetch your goods, and will ensure your packages arrive in good condition. ~As in other European countries, *francobolli* (stamps) are also sold at *tabacchi* (tobacco shops).

R

Real Estate

If you find Tuscany and Umbria *bella* and want to stay for the rest of your life—or if you're a student or have been transferred overseas—two good books to consult are *Living in Italy: The Essential Guide for Property Purchasers and Residents* (Yve Menzies, Robert Hale Limited, London, 1999) and *Buying a Home in Italy* (David Hampshire, 1999). Both books address identity cards, banking, insurance, Italian taxes, etc., and if you can't find them in your favorite bookstore, they can be ordered direct from Seven Hills Book Distributors (1531 Tremont Street, Cincinnati, Ohio 45214; 800-545-2005 / fax: 888-777-7799; www.sevenhillsbooks.com).

Riposo settimanale

A good Italian phrase to know, as it refers to a regular day of the week an establishment is closed. You'll often see this posted on a sign, and the day is often Monday.

S

Saint Days

Nearly every day of the year is a saint day somewhere in Italy, at either the national or local level. National saints' days fall on November 1 (*Tutti Santi*, All Saints' Day) and December 26 (*Santo Stefano,* for Saint Stephen). Offices and stores are typically closed on national saints' days, as well as on feast days, which honor local patron saints. In Florence, this day is June 24, for St. John the Baptist. ~Public holidays are known as *giorni festivi,* and *chiusu per ferie* (closed for the holidays) is a phrase you'll hear often in the month of August, when Italians (and most Europeans) are on vacation, and many stores and restaurants are closed for much of the month. A *ponte* (bridge) is the equivalent of our long weekend, when a holiday falls on Thursday, Friday, Monday, or Tuesday. Most Italians take advantage of a *ponte.*

Scusi (excuse me)
Another good Italian word you'll hear often, meaning "excuse me." It's used to make your way through a crowd, on public transportation, or to get someone's attention.

Single Travelers
Those traveling alone (not necessarily looking for romance) might be interested in a great book: *Traveling Solo: Advice and Ideas for More Than 250 Great Vacations* (Eleanor Berman, Globe Pequot Press, 1997). Berman offers the names of tour operators for different age groups and different types of trips and asks all the right questions in determining if a proposed vacation is right for you. ~Female *and* male solo travelers should beware of revealing too many personal details about their travels. If you admit that you're traveling for an indefinite period of time, for example, the perception is that you are probably carrying a lot of money. I met an Australian man who had the bulk of his money stolen from a youth hostel safe, and he was certain it was taken by a fellow hosteler he had befriended (but who had disappeared by the time the discovery was made).

Slow Food
Although Slow Food is an international movement, it's based in Italy, and so I felt it would not be out of place to mention it here. Slow Food is for food and wine enthusiasts who care about and promote traditional foodstuffs from around the world and who "share the snail's wise slowitude." ~Readers of Frances Mayes may remember that she and her husband are members of Slow Food, which she mentions in *Bella Tuscany.* Members meet regularly for lively (and delicious) meals and receive the quarterly review, *Slow,* published in Italian, German, English, French, and Spanish. *Slow* is also found in selected stores in the U.S., such as Kitchen Arts & Letters in New York. To join, contact Slow Food, via Mendicità Istruita 14, 12042 Bra (Cn) Italy; 0172.419611 / fax: 0172.421293; e-mail: international@slowfood.com.

Stendhal Syndrome
Named for the sick, physical feeling that afflicted French novelist Stendhal after he visited Santa Croce in Florence, this syndrome is synonymous with being com-

pletely overwhelmed by your surroundings (my translation: seeing and doing way too much). Visitors to Florence who arrive with too long a list of must-sees are prime candidates for the syndrome. My advice is the same as Kate Simon's as quoted in "Buon Viaggio": Organize your days, factor in how long it takes to get from place to place, and see what you want. There will be no quiz.

Storage

If you plan on traveling around Italy or beyond for extended periods of time (say, a month or longer) and want to store some baggage or other belongings, you should first investigate the left luggage facilities at Santa Maria Novella train station in Florence or at the *stazione* in other towns of Tuscany and Umbria. A locker at one of the stations might prove to be the ideal location if you'll be traveling by train anyway. Otherwise, check with the tourist office and ask for recommendations of storage companies.

Strade (streets)

Streets in Florence have two numbering systems: Blue numbers are reserved for hotels and residences; red numbers are for businesses. The problem is that there is seemingly no rhyme or reason to the order in which they appear on any given street. Good luck, and allow yourself plenty of time to get where you're going.

Studying in Italy

Dozens and dozens of American colleges and universities sponsor study abroad programs in central Italy. I am partial to those that have had schools there for a long time (these include Georgetown University, Middlebury College, New York University, Rutgers University, Syracuse University, and Sarah Lawrence College). My advice is to select a program that allows you to stay a year or even longer. And if you have to change your major to go, do it—you won't regret it! Alternatively, investigate attending an Italian college or university, and remember that studying in Italy isn't limited to language (courses are also offered in the fine arts, photography, painting, business, literature, etc.) or age (plenty of programs welcome adults, and plenty of adults attend). *The* guide to get is the *Directory of Italian Schools and Universities* by Michael Giammarella (EMI International, P.O. Box 640713, Oakland Gardens, New York 11364-0713; 718-631-0096 / fax: 631-0316). The guide, $19 + $3 for first-class shipping, details a wide variety of programs—not just language—in Italy. Giammarella also handles the bookings for the programs and publishes directories for Spain, France, and England. ~Other organizations that offer programs and classes in Tuscany and Umbria include the British Institute of Florence (Piazza Strozzi 2, 50123, Firenze; 055.284031 / fax: 055.287071: a nonprofit organization founded in 1917 whose mission is to promote British culture in Italy and Italian culture to

English-speaking visitors and to maintain a library of English books in Florence; courses are offered in language and culture—some of which are intensive for the benefit of short-stay visitors—and its library is housed in Palazzo Lanfredini, which it inherited from Sir Harold Acton); Centro Lingua Italiana Calvino (viale Fratelli Rosselli 74, 50123 Florence; 055.288081 / fax: 055.288125; offers language, art history, literature, cooking, economic and fashion courses); Accademia del Giglio (via Ghibellina 116, 50122 Firenze; 055.2302467 / fax: 055.2302467; e-mail: giglio@mail.cosmos.it; offers language, culture, and studio art courses); Istituto di Lingua e Cultura Italiana Michelangelo (via Ghibellina 88, 50122 Firenze; 055.240975 / fax: 055.240997; e-mail: michelangelo@dada.it; offers course in language and culture, and organizes activities such as trips into the Tuscan countryside and visits to museums, Italian cinemas, and concerts, etc.); Scuola Leonardo da Vinci (contact Michael Giammarella above at EMI International, P.O. Box 640713, Oakland Gardens, New York 11364; offers courses in language, art, cuisine, wine, studio art, business, and hotel industry in Florence, Siena, and Rome); and The Language Center (via S. Arcangelo 32, 06059 Todi, Umbria; 0758948364 / fax: 075.8949049; www.icom.it/language; *"la lingua, la vita"*—"to communicate is to live"—is The Language Center's motto, and the staff believes that language is an expression of a country, its people and traditions. In addition to language, there are courses on cooking, ceramics, and painting). Toscana Photographic Workshops (055.1636.0519 / fax: 055.1399626; www.tpw.it; offers week and weekend courses, and students are housed in Tuscan estates; workshops are based in Buonconvento, near Montalcino). ~Remember that the tourist offices here in the States and the Istituto Italiano di Cultura in New York have numerous brochures on language and cultural programs in Italy.

T

Telephones

Remember that Italy is six hours ahead of Eastern Standard Time, seven ahead of Central Time, eight ahead of Mountain Time, and nine ahead of Pacific Standard Time. To call Italy from the U.S., dial 011 + 39 + local number (011 = the overseas line, 39 = country code for Italy, and the local number includes the appropriate city code). The city code for Florence is 055, Siena is 0577, and Perugia is 075. Note that when calling any city or town in Italy from the U.S. it is no longer necessary to omit the intial 0. You must include it, and all phone numbers in this book include the 0. To call the U.S. from Italy, dial 00 + 1 + area code + number. To make a local call in Italy you must include the local prefix of the area you're in (for example, it you're in Florence and want to call a restaurant, you must dial 055 then the number of the restaurant). Within Italy, to reach an Italian operator for local assistance, dial 12. To reach an operator for assistance outside of the local area, dial 175. To reach an English-speaking operator, dial 176. For tourist information, dial 110. In an emergency (the equivalent of 911 in the U.S.), dial 113. ~Do not be alarmed that some Italian phone numbers have more digits than others. I can't explain it, but it's just Italy. ~Remember that almost all public phones in Italy no longer accept *gettoni* (tokens). A *carta telefonica* (phone card) is the way of the future, and is available in three denominations: 5, 10, and 15,000 lire. *Carte telefoniche* can be purchased at Telecom Italia offices and *tabacchi* (tobacconist shops). You can also place calls at Telecom Italia offices, where there are individual cabins and you pay after you make the call. Inquire at the tourist office about the least expensive times of day to call— it's usually after 6:30 P.M. during the week, from 10:00 P.M. to 8:00 A.M. on weekends and holidays, and after 1:30 P.M. on Saturday. ~Useful vocabulary: *Elenco Telefonico* (telephone directory); *una telefonata* (a telephone call); *aspetti un momento, per piacere* (hold on, don't hang up); *scatti* (units used on the telephone card).

Theft

Whether of the pickpocket variety or something more serious, theft can happen anywhere, in the finest neighborhoods, on the bus, in a park, on a street corner. As stated in *The Central Italy Trip Planner & Guide,* "Florence is a safe city compared with Rome or Naples, but don't relax completely. Wherever tourists are found *en masse,* there too are pickpockets and bag-snatchers—including the Vespa thieves known as *scippatori.*" I met an American woman at the Florence *sinagoga* who had her arm in a sling because she decided to hold on to her handbag as it was being pulled from her shoulder by a guy on a Vespa. It's a personal decision whether you want to attempt to hold on to your bag, but you can certainly be injured in the process. It bears repeating not to wear a waist pack, which is nothing but a neon magnet for thieves. I read about a lot of incidences that could so easily have been avoided. In 1998 I read a lengthy piece in the travel section of *The Philadelphia Inquirer* about a husband and wife traveling in France who had a pouch with all their valuables in it stolen. What made this story remarkable was that they were shocked the pouch was stolen. *I* was shocked reading their tale because they seemed to think it was a good idea to *strap their pouch under the driver's seat of their rental car.* This couple had apparently traveled all over Europe and North America every year for twelve years, so they weren't exactly novices. I think it's a miracle, however, that they hadn't been robbed earlier. ~Some pointers: Rental cars are easily identified by their license plates and other markings that might not be so obvious to you and me but signify pay dirt to thieves. Do not leave anything, anything at all, in the car, even if you're parking it in a secure garage. My husband and I strictly follow one rule when we rent a car, which is that we never even put items in the trunk unless we're immediately getting in the car and driving away, as anyone watching us will then know there's something of value there. Also, hatchback-type cars are good to rent because you can back into spots against walls or trees, making it impossible to open the trunk. ~Do not leave your passport, money, credit cards, important documents, or expensive camera equipment in your room (yes, American passports are still very much a hot commodity). The hotel safe? If the letters I read are any indication, hotel safes—whether in your room or in the main office—are only slightly more reliable than leaving your belongings out in plain view. Sometimes I hear that valuable jewelry was taken from a hotel safe, which I find baffling as there really is only one safe place for valuable jewelry: your home. No occasion, meeting, or celebration, no matter how important or festive, requires bringing valuable jewelry. *Leave it at home.* I happen to also find it offensive to display such wealth. ~Pickpockets employ a number of tactics to prey on unaware travelers. Even if you travel often, live in a big city, and think you're savvy, professional thieves can usually pick you out immediately (and they'll also identify you as American if you're wearing the trademark sneakers and fanny pack). Beware the breastfeeding mother who begs you for money (while her other children surround you looking for a way into your pockets), the arguing couple who make a scene (while their accomplices work the crowd of onlookers), the tap on your shoulder at the baggage-security checkpoint (when you turn around, someone's made off with your bags after they've passed through the X-ray machine), . . . anything at all that looks or feels like a setup. For a look at some common tricks, you might want to see *Traveler Beware!,* a video directed by a seventeen-year undercover cop, Kevin Coffey. This is a real eye-opening program with all the scams used to target business and holiday travelers. Coffey was founder of the Airport Crimes Detail and investigated literally thousands of crimes against tourists. He's been a guest on *Oprah!* and *20/20* and has been featured in *The Wall Street Journal* and *USA Today.* The seventy-minute cassette is available from Penton Overseas, Inc. (800-748-5804; e-mail: info@pentonoverseas.com) and is $14.95. ~If, despite your best efforts, your valuables are stolen, go to the local police. You'll have to fill out an official police report, but this is what helps later when you need to prove you were really robbed. Also, reporting thefts to the police alerts them that there is a persistent problem. You need to call your credit-card companies (which is why you have written down these numbers in a separate place), make a trip to the American Express office if you've purchased traveler's checks, and go to the U.S. embassy to replace your passport.

Tipping

Tipping in Italy is not the mystery some people perceive it to be. At many restaurants, *caffès,* and *trattorie,* the tip—known as *Servizio Compreso*—is included in the total. You'll see this amount (usually about 15 percent) as a line item on your receipt. It is common to round up the bill, leaving anywhere from one L2–10,000;

however, you are not obligated to do so. If you're in a three-star restaurant and the wine steward has chosen a special wine for you or the host has been especially attentive, it's considered appropriate to give him or her about L5,000 or L10,000. At family-run *trattorie,* tips are not expected, but, again, if you feel the waiter has been especially helpful, leave an extra L1,000. If you stand at the counter in a *caffè,* a tip is not included in the bill, so you should leave some change, about L100 or L200. At fancy hotel bars, however, it's expected to leave more, about L1,000. If you receive exceptional service at any establishment or you want to return and be remembered, you should of course feel comfortable leaving a larger tip. Other tipping guidelines: taxis—Italians tip very little or not at all, but it's expected for visitors to give 10 percent; bathroom attendants—L200; cloakroom attendants—L500 per coat; tour guides—L2,000 or a little more if they've given an exceptional or very long tour; porters—L1,500 per bag; hotel doormen who call you a cab—L500; parking attendants who fetch your car—L2,000; concierges who obtain reservations or tickets—L3,000 per day for overall helpfulness or between L5–10,000 for special, one-time-only tasks; chambermaids—L1,000 per night; room service (if it's not already included)—L1,000; valet—L1,000; barbers and hairdressers—about L2–8,000 depending on the cut and type of salon; theater and movie ushers—L500. ~For the above estimates relating to hotels, double the amounts if you're in a very expensive place. ~Be prepared to tip by putting some small change in your pocket in advance, before you arrive at the hotel, for example, or before you go to the theater.

Toilet Paper

As in, never set out each day without stuffing some in your pockets or your bag. Public toilets—and even those in some of the nicest places—can be abominable and often do not have toilet paper, which is *carta igienica* in Italian. I have always found good, American-style toilet paper in the bathrooms at the American Express office in Florence (via Dante Alighiere 22/r).

Tourist

Whether you travel often for business or are making a trip for the first time, let's face it: We're all tourists, and there's nothing shameful about that fact. Yes, it's true that you feel a real part of daily life when you blend in and are mistaken for a native. But since that's not likely to happen unless you live there, it's far better to just get on with it and have a good time.

Tourist Office (Azienda di Promozione Turistica—APT—or Ente Nazionale Italiano per il Turismo—ENIT)

I cannot stress enough how helpful it is to contact the Italian Government Tourist Board as soon as you learn you're going to Italy. Think of it as the ultimate resource. All the information you need is there, or the staff will know how to direct you elsewhere. At the New York office, I have never stumped anyone with my questions or requests, and I think readers have observed that I ask a lot of questions about a lot of little details. A word of advice for dealing with tourist offices in general: It is not very helpful to say you're going to Florence and would like "some information." Allow the staff to help you by providing them with as many details about your visit as you can. Is it your first trip? Do you only need information about hotels? The offices are stocked with mountains of material, but unless you ask for something specific, it will not automatically all be given to you. Sometimes I am amazed at what's available, at no charge—but you have to ask. Some particularly noteworthy booklets available in the U.S. offices are "Planning Your Trip to Italy," which is published annually; "Art Itineraries: Prato, Pistoia, Lucca, Pisa"; "Touring Club Italiano: Regione Toscana"; "Florence Map and Tour Itineraries," a foldout brochure detailing five walks around the city; "Le Piu Belle Chiese del Comuni del Territorio Pisano," detailing Pisa and the surrounding area; "Thermal Regions Italia"; and "Walking Around Perugia." There are three tourist offices in the States: 630 Fifth Avenue, Suite 1565, New York, New York 10111; 212-245-5618 / fax: 586-9249; brochure hotline: 212-245-4822; 500 North Michigan Avenue, Suite 2240, Chicago, Illinois 60611; 312-644-0996 / fax: 644-3019; brochure hotline: 312-644-0990; 12400 Wilshire Boulevard, Los Angeles, California 90025; 310-820-1898 / fax: 820-6357; brochure hotline: 310.820.0098. Travelers can also visit the Web site: www.italiantourism.com. *APT or ENIT:* ENIT refers to the national tourist network of Italy, and APT refers to each local tourist office. Just to make things more Italian, there is also the Ufficio Informazione Turistiche, the municipally-run office, and the Azienda Turistica office for each region of Italy (the Tuscany and Umbria offices are listed below). No matter what the offices are called, look for the little 'i' sign. The main tourist office in Florence is at via Cavour 1/r; 055.290832 / fax: 055.2760383. Other offices are at Piazza Stazione (Santa Maria Novella train station; 055.212245); via Manzoni 16; 055.23320 / fax: 055.2346286; and at Aeroporto Vespucci; 055.315874 / fax: 055.315874. The regional tourist board offices are in Florence and Perugia: Tuscany (via Novoli 26, 50127 Florence; 055.4383657 / fax: 055.4383049; www.regione.toscana.it) and Umbria (via Mazzini 21, 06128 Perugia; 075.575951 / fax: 075.5736828; www.regione.umbria.it).

Tours

For tours of Florence in English, contact Associazione Guide Turistiche di Firenze, the largest and best-known guide association (055.210612). The tours are approximately three hours in length and are about $34 per person. Advance reservations are advised. The Florence tourist office should also be able to recommend other organizations that offer walking tours. A list of full-service tour companies would fill a separate book, and it is not my intent to promote only one company or one type of trip. Following are some companies which have appealed to me and offer an authentic experience:

Alternative Travel Group (69-71 Banbury Road, Oxford, OX2 6PE, England, 011.44.1865.315678 / fax: 011.44.1865.315697; e-mail: info@alternative-travel.co.uk). "The best way to see a country is on foot" is the ATG motto. Recent trips in Italy included a variety of walks throughout Tuscany and Umbria, including some with unusual themes: "Flowers of the Monti Sibillini" in eastern Umbria, "Piero della Francesca," "Routes of the Medieval via Francigena," and "Walking and Italian Landscape Painting." ATG also offers walking and cycling tours, and a variety of less expensive walking tours along continuous routes. I have been very impressed with this group's philosophy and lengthy catalogs.

Altritalia (10 Mt. Vernon Street, Suite #21, Winchester, Massachusetts 01890; 877-721-9071 / fax: 781-729-9288; e-mail: info@altritalia.com). "Discovering the Other Italy!" is Altritalia's motto, and in addition to customized tours, sports, archaeology, art, gastronomical, and architecture itineraries, language and cooking lessons and summer camps are offered.

Caravella Italia (2112 Walnut Street, Philadelphia, Pennsylvania 19103; 888-665-2112 or 215-665-1233; www.seeitaly.com). Offers small escorted trips throughout Italy, including Tuscany and Umbria, as well as custom tours for four people or more.

Cross-Culture: Foreign Travel Programs Designed for Travelers Rather Than Tourists (52 High Point Drive, Amherst, Massachusetts 01002; 413-256-6303 / fax: 253-2303; e-mail: xculture@javanet.com; www.javanet.com). Its trips to Italy include Florence and the Tuscan Hilltowns.

Esperienze Italiane: Unparalled Experiences of Italian Food, Wine and Culture (c/o Felidia Ristorante, 243 East 58th Street, New York, New York 10022; 800-480-2426 or 212-758-1488; www.lidiasitaly.com; Founded by Lidia Bastianich, author of *La Cucina di Lidia* (Doubleday, 1990) and *Lidia's Italian Table: Companion to the National Public Television Series* (Morrow, 1998) and co-owner of Felidia Ristorante, Becco and Frico Bar in New York. Esperienze allows travelers to explore Italy with leading experts in food, wine, art, and history. In addition to Tuscany and Umbria, there are trips to Friuli-Venezia-Giulia, where Bastianich grew up, Piedmont, and Sicily.

Essence of Tuscany (Katlin Travel Group, The Mall at Lincoln Station, Lincoln, Massachusetts, 01773; 781-259-3100 / fax 1310; attention: Cynthia Hill; e-mail: linctrar@aol.com). This new trip was developed by cookbook author Nancy Harmon Jenkins, who is joined by fellow foodies Carla Capalbo and Burton Anderson in leading visitors to wineries, cheesemakers, bakeries, olive mills, butchers, and other food producers.

France in Your Glass (814 35th Avenue, Seattle, Washington 98122; 800-578-0903 / fax: 7069; www.inyourglass.com). Despite the fact that most of these wine vacations are in France, there is one trip, Pleasures of Tuscany, that explores Italian wine, food, and culture in the Chianti hills.

R. Crusoe & Son (566 W. Adams Street No. 505, Chicago, Illinois 60661; 888-490-8047 / fax: 312-980-8100; www.rcrusoe.com). The price of its The Essential Tuscany trip seems high, but these folks are definitely doing things the right way. To quote from a brochure, "Our definition of a traveler (vs. a tourist) is someone who *likes* getting away from the familiar. There is no more engaging way of finding out who you are, who you might be. Travelers, by nature, want to see *inside stuff*, go *behind the scenes,* come home with good stories that are *actually true* (and that their friends haven't already heard)."

Stay & Visit Italy (its U.S. representative is Great Travels, Inc., 5506 Connecticut Avenue, NW, Suite 23, Washington, D.C. 20015; 800-411-3728 / fax: 202-966-6972; e-mail: gtravels@erols.com; in Italy: Giorgio, Fabio and Luca Orofino, via F. Caracciolo 14, 80122 Napoli; 081.5980511 / fax: 081.5980531; www.stayandvisit.com). Offers trips all around Italy, including one to Tuscany and Umbria and two others that include the Cinque Terre in Liguria. Group size is limited to eighteen people. The Wayfarers (172 Bellevue Avenue, Newport, Rhode Island, 02840; 800.249.4620 or 401.849.5087 / fax: .5878). Two Tuscan walking tours are offered, one of which is "Gourmet Tuscany" and includes hands-on cooking lessons with local chefs. ~If you select a tour operator, ask a lot of questions so you get what you expect. For starters, ask if the operator employs its own staff or if it contracts with another company to run its trips. Remember, however, that standards differ around the world, and operators don't have control over every detail. For example, many beautiful old villas and inns do not have screens in the windows, and many first-class hotels don't have air conditioning. The price you pay for accommodations might not be the same as the posted rates, but you have to accept that you're paying for the convenience of someone else booking your trip. Tour operators also reserve the right to change itineraries, thus changing modes of transportation as well as hotels. If you have special needs, talk about them with the company in advance.

Trains (Ferrovie dello Stato [FS])

The Italian train network offers some reduced fares to riders in addition to rail passes, but there is not quite the bewildering choice as in France, for example. There is a *Carta d'Argento* (silver card) for seniors (men over sixty-five, women over sixty) and a *Carta Verde* (green card) for those 26 and under. Families traveling together are eligible for a discount, and there is also a *Biglietto Chilometrico,* which is valid for 3,000 kilometers and can be used by up to five adults. The Flexi Card Pass is available three ways: four days of unlimited travel within a nine-day period, eight days of travel within twenty-one days, and twelve days of travel within thirty days. The best rail pass for those planning on lots of train travel is the *Biglietto Chilometrico Libera Circolazione,* which allows for unlimited travel in either first or second class and is only available to nonresidents, so you must show your passport when purchasing it. A *Carta Blu* is a reduced price ticket for the disabled. Depending on what type of ticket you have, you may be required to purchase supplements on the Super Rapido, Rapido, and Intercity trains. Remember to buy the supplement when you purchase your ticket or you'll be charged extra for it once on the train. Also, remember to stamp your ticket in the machines at the head of each platform. These aren't always so noticeable, so allow some extra time for finding them. Unstamped tickets usually result in a fine. No one wants to waste money, but I do not find train fares in Italy prohibitively expensive. One or two short trips might cost less at the regular fare. Make sure you will get the most out of a special discount, and make sure the option you're considering isn't simply a discount for first-class travel, which you might not have wanted in the first place. In addition to different types of tickets, there are also different types of trains: *pendolino* (intercity, first-class only service); *eurocity* (international express service); *intercity* (national express train); *espressi* (long-distance express trains within Italy but not as fast as intercity); *diretti* or *interregionali* (slower than *espressi,* and making most stops); *locali* or *regionali* (local service making all stops, no matter how small). Individual cars are labeled with a number one or two indicating first or second class, and there are also symbols indicating where smokers can sit. Some trains have bar and dining cars. The FS publishes two timetables twice a year: the *Pozzorario* (pocketsize, for all of Italy; a smaller version called *Pozzarario: Nord e Centro* is for everything above Rome), and the *Orario delle FS* (which is in two volumes, *Nord Centro Italia* and *Sud Centro Italia*). These are, of course, indispensable bibles. A good book for planning train trips around Tuscany and Umbria (and all of Italy) is *Italy by Train: 50 Unforgettable Trips and All the Sights Along the Way* (Tim Jepson, Fodor's Travel Publications, 1994). This is not a book of train schedules, so the fact that it dates from 1994 is not a deterrent—even if the book were brand new, train arrivals and departures would still have to be confirmed. The FS network, like train networks in most other European countries, is quite extensive and there are very few corners of Italy one can't get to by train. For each destination, Jepson provides information about the number of trains per day, the duration of the trip (not likely to have changed drastically), brief descriptions of noteworthy sites to see, and a "Practicalities" section that includes specifics on the tourist office, railway station, buses, hiking possibilities, youth hostels, markets, festivals, hotels, and restaurants. There is a chapter on Tuscany and Umbria with suggested routes. ~You can purchase some rail passes in advance from CIT Tours (800-CIT-RAIL; fax: 888-2-FAX-CIT; www.cit-tours.com). Both the Italy Rail Card and Italy Flexi

Rail Card are available for a variety of time periods, as well as the Eurailpass and Europass, which is valid in Italy, France, Germany, Spain, and Switzerland and the associated countries of Portugal, Benelux, Austria, Hungary, and Greece. ~Useful vocabulary: *un biglietto andata* (one-way ticket); *andata e ritorno* (round trip); *binario* (platform); *diretto* and *locale* (refer to local trains making stops at all the small places along the route); *deposito bagaglio* (left luggage locker); *biglietteria* (ticket office or window); *orario* (timetable); *prima classe* (first class); *seconda classe* (second class); *una prenotazione* (a reservation); *fumatore* (smoking); *non fumatore* (no smoking); *la porta* (door); *la finestra* (window).

Travel Insurance

I have never purchased travel insurance because I have never determined that I need it, but it's worth considering if you think the risks to you are greater without it. Ask yourself what it would cost if you needed to cancel or interrupt your trip, and how expensive it would be to replace any stolen possessions. If you have a medical condition or if a relative is ill, insurance might be a wise investment. First, check to see if your existing health or homeowner's policies offer some protection. If you decide you need to purchase additional insurance, read all the fine print and make sure you understand it; compare deductibles; ask how your provider defines preexisting condition and inquire if there are situations in which it would be waived; and check to see if the ceiling on medical expenses is adequate for your needs.

V

VAT (Value-Added Tax)

VAT or IVA (Imposta Valore Aggiunto) is the tax amount that visitors to Italy (except from EEC member countries) are entitled to receive as a reimbursement. I have an entire file on conflicting information about the VAT, so even if you meet the eligibility requirements, be prepared for a potentially confusing procedure. Frankly, I think the procedure seems to be a lot of bother unless visitors are making a significant purchase, and I think it would be worth asking the retailer to simply not charge any tax; but for those who are determined, you must produce your passport at the time of the purchase, spend at least 300,000 lire at one store (but retailers are not required to participate in the program nor to match the dollar amount, so ask first), and produce receipts *and* merchandise for inspection at customs. Note that some shops don't have the necessary forms and that the paperwork must be stamped by customs officials *before* you enter the U.S. Problems seem to arise when the customs desk is closed, although if you'll be in any other country before you return to the States, a customs stamp from that country is also valid (if the officials are willing to validate your forms). Also, it seems customs officials are rather lax at some borders, vigilant at others. ~For a 20 percent fee, Global Refund will handle your refund through the Europe Tax-Free Shopping (ETS) network, and many stores in Italy are now affiliates. The ETS refund form is known as a Shopping Cheque. Once your forms are stamped, you're able to receive a refund—in the form of cash, check (in *lire*), or charge-card credit—right away at an ETS counter (or you can mail the forms from home). ~If you have attempted to have your forms validated in Italy and were thwarted in your efforts, or if it has been more than three months since you applied for a refund, contact Global Refund (707 Summer Street, Stamford, Connecticut 06901; 800-566-9828 / fax: 203-674-8709; www.taxfree.se).

Villa I Tatti

Visiting the Villa I Tatti, just outside of Florence in Settignano, remains one of the highlights of my life. Even the drive there was memorably beautiful. I Tatti was the home for fifty-two years of art historian Bernard Berenson, who died at the age of ninety-four in 1959. Berenson's will left the villa to his alma mater, and today it is the Harvard University Center for Italian Renaissance Studies. I have a number of interesting articles in my files about Berenson, and I tried very hard to include at least one of them in this book, to no avail. Readers who want to learn more about Berenson should see the *I Personaggi biblioteca* for a good biography recommendation and the *Piazze, Giardini, e Musei biblioteca* for books authored by Berenson. Guided tours of the villa (not including the library) and its gardens are available for scholars, students, Harvard alumni, and those with ties to Harvard or a special interest in the Renaissance. Tours are offered only a few days a week and are one hour in length. Readers who would like to try to arrange a visit are encouraged to write a letter well in advance: The Secretary, Villa I Tatti, Harvard University, 124 Mt. Auburn Street, Cambridge, Massachusetts 02138. I recommend viewing the I Tatti Web site first for all details: www.vit.firenze.it. A wonderful book you might want to see before you go is *A Legacy of Excellence: The Story of Villa I Tatti* (William Weaver, photographs by David Finn, Abrams, 1997). Aside from the fact that it's a beautiful book, there are photos of the library and other outstanding features of the property that are off-limits on the tour, so it is really the only access one can have to such a treasure.

W

Weather

Central Italy is perhaps most beautiful in the fall (many places in the world are at that time of year), but each season offers its own delights. Picking the perfect time of year is subjective. When it's rainy and cold—and it does get quite cold in the winter months—you don't have the pleasure of picnicking and hiking outdoors, but prices drop and you'll have little trouble securing reservations at hotels and restaurants. Go when you have the opportunity and that will be your experience, your Italy. It's true that peak season means higher prices and more people, but if you've determined you want to be in Umbria in July, then the cost and the crowds don't matter. I've visited Florence in the middle of summer twice, and I never once wished it was another season of the year. If you're a weather maven, you'll love *Fodor's World Weather Guide* (E. A. Pierce and C. G. Smith, 1998; published in 1998 in Great Britain as *The Hutchinson World Weather Guide, New Edition* by Helicon Publishing Ltd., Oxford). As frequent business or pleasure travelers know, average daily temperatures are only a small part of what you need to know about the weather. Humidity, number of wet days, and hours of sunshine are all factors affecting travelers. Tuscany and Umbria have changeable weather conditions in every season of the year except summer, which is predictably sunny. This guide features weather specifics for over 200 countries and territories and also includes a map of the world's climate regions, humidity and wind chill charts, a centigrade and Fahrenheit conversion table, rainfall conversion table, and a bibliography pointing interested readers to other sources.

Web Sites

Personally, I don't find a single one of the following Web sites better than the tourist office or the appropriate books, but a few offer some good features:

www.beniculturali.it: In Italian (I couldn't open the British flag icon for English), this site represents the Ministero Per I Beni E Le Attività Culturali.

www.italyemb.org: The official site of the Italian Embassy in the U.S. Provides up-to-date information on Italy in general and Italian activities in the U.S. The "Tips for Travelers" section is very good.

www.borsaitalia.it: Official site of the Italian Stock Exchange, and there is an icon for English.

www.initaly.com: This is for searching Italian ancestry and is the world's best Italian genealogy web club.

www.fionline.it: Firenze online, which allows you to select tourism, arts, dance, music, jobs, health, Internet train, media, etc.

www.spoletoarts.com: The place to look for the Spoleto Arts Symposia, which in 1999 included writing workshops, a cooking school, creativity workshop, and vocal-arts symposium.

Women Travelers

Whether traveling solo or not, lots of great advice is offered in *Travelers' Tales Gutsy Women: Travel Tips and Wisdom for the Road* (Marybeth Bond, Travelers' Tales, Inc., San Francisco, distributed by O'Reilly & Associates, 1996). This packable little book is filled with dozens and dozens of useful tips for women of all ages who want to travel or already travel a lot. Bond has traveled all over the world, much of it alone, and she shares a multitude of advice from her own journeys as well as those of other female travelers. Chapters address safety and security; health and hygiene; romance and unwelcome advances; money, bargaining, and tipping; traveling solo; mother–daughter travel; travel with children, etc. ~Also, the Women's Travel Club might be of interest. Founded by Phyllis Stoller, this organization plans numerous domestic and international trips a year and guarantees everyone a roommate. Its great list of travel-safety tips was featured on NBC's *Today* as well as in *Travel & Leisure* (August 1999). Member-ship is $35 a year, and members receive a newsletter. 800-480-4448; e-mail: Womantrip@aol.com; www.womenstravelclub.com.

Y

Yellow Pages

Sometimes, you just need the Yellow Pages, and the English Yellow Pages is what you need for Italy. There is an indispensable section on Florence, and though I've never seen the book for sale in the U.S., you can find it easily in both Italian- and English-language bookshops in Florence.

Come Stay With Me

BY BILL MARSANO

editor's note

This is one of the first articles I read about *agriturismo,* and I still think it is the most inspirational and encouraging for travelers considering this type of accommodation. Note that although this piece was originally written in 1994, the author, Bill Marsano, kindly agreed to update prices and contact information.

BILL MARSANO is a freelance writer who won the 1999 James Beard Award for his writing on wine and spirits in *Hemispheres,* the in-flight magazine of United Airlines. Issue no. 9 of *Saveur* featured his article on Italian sparkling wines.

I have never seen anything more pleasing." So said Saint Francis, returned to Umbria after travels and travails abroad. You may well say the same: This is a landscape of painters, poets, and saints, of low mountains and green hills. There is a strange quality to the light, and a low silvery haze. An Umbrian farmhouse on its sentinel hill, picked out against the evening sky, will make you wish powerfully to live there.

And you *can* live there, at least for a while, because of *agriturismo*—the Italian version of a grassroots enterprise that has spread through Europe in various guises. *Agriturismo* extends throughout Italy and yet remains partly secret. Long practiced informally in varying ways, *agriturismo* was sanctioned in 1985 by a law permitting family-run farms to provide lodgings and meals. It is partly secret because although the nearly seven thousand *agriturismo* properties were visited by some seven million people last year, only three percent of those visitors were foreigners.

Agriturismo makes farming more profitable and provides jobs while making more accessible the hill towns that flit by the windows of your car as you make time on the autostrada. It lets visitors see Italy as Italians see it, and there is nothing an Italian loves better than *il paese*—the countryside. Rural *agriturismo* properties also deliver cheaper rates than city hotels, which means you won't find snappy five-star service—but you'd be missing the point if you were inclined to complain.

Other rates of exchange tend to favor *il paese* too: You'll swap wake-up calls from desk clerks for crowing cocks or the sun through your window; a concierge who briefly knows your name for a *contadino* full of peasant lore; linen tablecloths and too-civilized ceremony for country cooking with wine made on the property and served in the generous spirit of *abbondanza*.

Italy is a compact country, and even a remote farm is seldom far from art or archaeological sites worth seeking. Help yourself, but after a little while the landscape itself may slow you down, turn you toward country matters. Instead of searching churches for Giottos, you may search Ligurian forests for chestnuts or gather mushrooms in Tuscany, where old women in the kitchen will separate them into two piles—the small pile edible, the large, poisonous.

You can pick grapes, as I did once, in a late harvest, when the student help had fled back to school in Perugia. I was purple and sore for three days, but by noon of the second they had stopped sending a child behind me to collect the clusters I'd missed, and the following June I was shipped a case of "my vintage" as thanks.

You can seek summer truffles in Umbria ("the tastiest I know," wrote Waverley Root), where you will find three *agriturismo* farms at the end of this piece.

Fattoria di Vibio, near Todi, has stone buildings, a lovely lawn, and a swimming pool edged with patio tables under yellow umbrellas. Signora Gabriella Moscati retired four years ago to run this *fat-*

toria, and she requires only a small staff to see to the ten rooms and one suite that are let to guests year-round. The farm continues to yield a harvest that appears on your plate at dinner—the tomatoes on your gnocchi, the onions with your slice of venison roast, and, over ice cream, sweet cherries from the trees by the pool. The simple rooms have iron beds and stucco walls, and some have panoramic views that let in floods of sunlight when you throw open the windows. Within walking distance of the farm, up a steep hill, one crosses paths with Saint Francis at a tiny, dank chapel where spiders spin webs between pews and a fresco is fading above the altar. A statue of the saint presides over the oratory, and along the walls family portraits hang like antiques among dusty plastic flowers.

Outside Assisi, you find the Umbria that Saint Francis loved, a landscape that is coarse and rustic—adjectives which also apply to Malvarina, an *agriturismo* farm standing amid trees and wildflowers under the shadow of Mount Subasio. The rooms at Malvarina are modest, some only large enough to contain double beds, and the grounds are overgrown rather than groomed, thick with vines and shrubs. The yield of its olive groves and vineyards finds its way, of course, to the kitchen and then to the stucco dining room, where Signora Maria Maurillo and her son Claudio Fabrizi reign with great generosity—the wine flows as reliably at Malvarina as it did at Cana.

I passed one afternoon in Umbria shelling a dinner's peas in the sun with an old woman of the old school who was scandalized to learn that I could cook my own dinner (what could be wrong with my wife?). She told me how to find Umbrian truffles without a dog (look for bare spots on the ground; almost nothing grows above truffles). She spoke no English but didn't mind if I practiced my bad Italian on her, so I learned that "very seldom" in Italian is *ogni morte di papa* ("every death of a pope") and that "to give birth" is *dare alla luce* ("to give to the light"). *Dare alla luce* is not a verb but a poem. *Il paese* is a poem, too.

~

Agricultural tourism has spread throughout Europe in different forms but it is perhaps nowhere as deeply embedded as in Italy. For Italians the countryside is more a place to be than to do; they picnic or walk in the hills, seek wildflowers, songbirds, and butterflies. *Agriturismo* indulges guests in all of that, and may include pools, tennis courts, golf, and horseback excursions as well. The properties are also usually within reach of notable towns and art or archaeological sites that are dauntingly distant from major cities.

Agriturismo is not standardized travel, so smart travelers ask questions to avoid *agri*vation. The properties may be villas, farms with livestock, or wine estates with vineyards and olive groves (sometimes combined, in the system happily called *coltiva promiscua*—promiscuous cultivation). Accommodations plain and fancy include rooms, suites, and apartments; some meals or a kitchen may be provided. There are scheduling peculiarities (e.g., some "weeks" run Wednesday to Wednesday).

Most properties are near tiny villages or are entirely rusticated; you'll need a good local map (1:200,000 scale or larger), and the narrow roads suggest a small car. For maps and guidebooks: The Complete Traveler, New York (212-685-9007) or Book Passage, California (800-999-7909).

In Italy, properties are best booked directly and, unless you speak Italian, by fax: If there are English-speaking employees at the farm, a fax will find them. The properties listed below can be contacted directly. You can also order *agriturismo* guides—which are in Italian—by mail from three competing organizations in Italy. Send a money order—prices include postage—for 43,000 lire (about $26) to Terranostra, Via Magazzini 2, 50122 Florence; 35,000 lire ($21) to Agriturist, Corso Vittorio Emanuele 101, 00186 Rome; or 18,000 lire ($11) to Turismo Verde, Viale Ettore Franceschini 89, 00155 Rome.

You can also inquire about *agriturismo* properties through such U.S. booking agents as Barclay International in New York (800-845-6636 or 212-832-3777; fax: 753-1139) and Katlin Travel Group, Lexington, Massachusetts (800-552-8546 or 781-862-6229; fax: 674-2080).

Tuscany

Borgo Trerose is a functioning medieval hill town on the Tuscany-Umbria border. Per week for four persons, $500 to $1,550; for two persons, $430 to $1,166. Rates vary significantly according to seven seasonal periods; each residence can accommodate two additional persons in day beds. Access to the Montepulciano, Chianti, and Brunello wine regions.

Castello di Volpaia is a superb winery built into the ancient stone houses of Volpaia, a hamlet on a tall forested hill north of Siena. Five apartments available, one to three bedrooms, $485 to $880 a week ($700 to $1,100 July–September); all have modern baths and kitchen equipment; most have gardens for al fresco dining. Rental includes one-day course in cooking, herbalism or watercolors (0577.738.066 / fax: 738.619). Dinners can be arranged—and should be: the splendid Nuccia reigns in the kitchen. Just outside Volpaia are the villas La Pozza (for eleven persons, with guest house) and Il Casetto (for eight; both have pool and staff). Book through Salogi in Lucca (0583.48717 / fax: 48727).

Castello La Leccia is a medieval hamlet south of Castellina in Chianti, complete with its own church. It stands at the end of a cypress-lined drive and gives long valley views of oaks, chestnuts, and vines. There are four modern apartments: the owner, Dr. Lorenzo Daddi, speaks excellent English and makes memorable wine on the property (Barclay International: from $900 per week).

Fattoria Nittardi makes "the wine of Michelangelo," one of its former owners, although the sprawling property is more woods than vines. Quiet but not isolated; the small town of Castellina in Chianti is just a few miles away. The week-long Momenti Toscani program ($975–$1,060 per person) includes lessons in spoken Italian, painting, Tuscan crafts and cooking, plus art excursions. The Gourmet Week programs in July and August ($1,425–$1,510 per person) include wine tastings, all meals, and tickets to the Palio, that famous horse race in Siena.

Poggerino lies north of Siena near the small town of Radda in Chianti. This wine estate, owned by Floriana Ginori Conti, is informal yet gracious, after her manner. Four homey, small apartments have comfortable rustic furniture in two typically Tuscan fifteenth-century stone buildings with private entrances and gardens. (577.738.232 / fax: 738.051; e-mail: poggerin@chianti.it; per week for four persons: $400–$600; for two, $350–$400. Higher figures are June–August prices).

Stagioni del Chianti is a consortium of a dozen Chianti Classico wine estates (including the splendid Castello di Fonterutoli and Castello di Brolio) as well as farms and villas located in the hills between Florence and Siena. All accommodations have been recently and handsomely renovated and include modern plumbing and pool access. Rates for the six wine estates (two to ten persons): $455 to $2,850, low season; $515 to $3,200, high season. For the villas and farms (two to nineteen persons): $395 to $3,400, low season; $485 to $4,600, high season. Book through Katlin Travel Group, 800.552.8546.

Vignamaggio, in the Chianti hills south of Florence, near the wine town of Greve, is where Mona Lisa was born and *Much Ado About Nothing* was filmed. Ten handsome suites are spread among the fifteenth-century main house and restored farm buildings (Barclay International: $143 per night for two, with a two-night minimum).

Oasi Verde Mengara, on the scenic road between Perugia and Gubbio, has spectacular views and a kitchen to match. *Gastonomia* is the draw here, with Umbrian specialties well prepared and generously served. The rooms are less welcoming—motel plain—but even high-season rates are very low. Per person, double room: $26 with breakfast; the same including dinner, $46; all meals, $58. Rates in low season (which is, here, most of the year except for major holidays) are reduced by a little more than 10 percent. (075.922.7004 / fax: 075.920.049).

Poggio delle Vigne, the first agriturismo venture of the famous Lungarotti winery, is almost brand-new. Ten apartments for two to six persons ($505 to $750 weekly, low season; $705 to $945, high season) have been carved out of an old stone *casa colonica,* or farmhouse, near Torgiano. The views are of the vineyards that provide Lungarotti's grapes and of the distant outlines of Perugia and Assisi (075.982.994 / fax: 075.988.7014; e-mail: poggiovigne@lungarotti.it).

Pomurlo Vecchio, on Lake Corbara and near a national park, is *agriturismo* at its purest—and least luxe. Guests are free to help with the chores, and should if they expect to do justice to the hearty country cooking. But even the most sated might say the *un*restored rooms dispel any romantic notions of country life. The exception is the suite in the twelfth-century tower; the price is unreasonably reasonable: $45 per person, all meals included (744.950.190 or -475 / fax: 744.950.500).

Pistoia - Cattedrale e Campanile

GIORNALI DI GUERRA

PER VIA AEREA
PAR AVION
Mod. 24-R

La Cronaca Mondana

(The Daily News— Points of View)

"Italians live in a land with many layers of history. They walk on stones worn smooth by the feet of Etruscans, Romans and Saracens who came before them. They think nothing of it. The live with centuries of history piled up visibly in the walls and stone cathedrals of every little town."

—Carol Field, *Celebrating Italy*

My Italy

BY ERICA JONG

∿

editor's note

....

ERICA JONG is the author of *Fear of Flying* (Holt, Rinehart & Winston, 1973; Signet paperback reissue, 1996), *Fear of Fifty* (Houghton Mifflin Company, 1994), *Serenissima* (Houghton Mifflin, 1987), and *What Do Women Want?* (Bloomsbury, 2000), among others, and five volumes of poetry.

Whenever I go anywhere but Italy for a vacation, I always feel as if I have made a mistake. All too often I have changed my plans and left—from a ski resort in the French Alps, a mountain town in Switzerland, a country house in Provence—to get to Italy as soon as possible. Once across the border I can breathe again. Why bother to go anywhere, I think in those first ecstatic moments of reentry, but Italy?

What do we find in Italy that can be found nowhere else? I believe it is a certain permission to be human that other countries lost long ago. Not only is Italy one of the few places left where fantasy runs unfettered (as Luigi Barzini said in *The Italians,* "even instruments of precision like speedometers and clocks are made to lie in Italy for your happiness"); it is also one of the few places that tolerate human nature with all its faults. Italy is the past, but it is also the future. It is pagan, but it is also Christian and Jewish. It is grand and tawdry, imperishable and decayed. Italy has seen marauding armies, Fascists and Communists, fashions and fripperies come and go. And it is still, for all its layers of musty history, a place that enhances existence, burnishes the moment.

Consider the Italian art of making the small transactions of life more pleasant. On my first visit to Italy, when I was nineteen, I was mistakenly riding in a second-class carriage with a third-class ticket. Upon discovering this, the train conductor refused to accept the *supplemento* I readily proffered. He said (in Italian it sounds even better than in English), "Signorina, you have given Italy the gift of your beauty. Now let Italy give this small gift to you." The conductor wasn't coming on to me; rather, it was Italian charm at work. And Italian charm is often a delicious combination of rule-bending and harmless flirtation.

The seven deadly sins seem somewhat less deadly in Italy; the Ten Commandments slightly more malleable. This is a country that not only accepts contradictions; it positively encourages them. The Italian shrug embodies this philosophy. It says, "Things have been this way forever and always will be this way. Why buck *la forza del destino?*"

And even the rigid northern Italian relaxes and has another glass of wine.

Your trip here will never quite go as planned. This is part of the *avventura*. There may be strikes, mixed-up reservations, maddening *imbrogli* of all sorts. But they will be charming *imbrogli* because the Italian people are charming, down to the whimsical tone of their language. A lost reservation in Germany is a Walpurgisnacht; in Italy it is an opera buffa.

Being in Italy is rather like being in love. So what if people have been in love before? So what if Italy has been a tourist trap for at least a thousand years? So what if everything you say in criticism—or praise—of Italy has already been said? Writers and travelers yet unborn will say it all again, blissfully unaware that anyone has uttered the same thoughts before.

The first place I knew in Italy was Florence—or, more specifically, Bellosguardo, a lovely hilltop section of the city looking down on the Duomo from a yew-studded prominence. As a college junior, I lived in the Torre di Bellosguardo, a thirteenth-century tower adjoining a fifteenth-century villa. I studied Italian and Italians and fell in love with Italy.

The moon was brighter in Italy. The geraniums were pinker and more pungent. The wine was more intoxicating. The men were handsomer. Italian had more rhymes than English. It was the language of love, the language of poetry.

I thought my impressions were original. I filled notebooks, aerograms, and sheets and sheets of something we then called "onionskin" with my banal musings. If I had known at nineteen what I know now—that a thousand years of similar musings by similar young musers had preceded me—I would have felt diminished. Thank God I *didn't* know. I felt special, chosen. Italy has the power to confer this sense of chosenness.

I went back to Bellosguardo a few years ago and stayed in the same villa (now a lovely small hotel owned by the erudite Amerigo Franchetti). I was with my daughter, Molly, who was at the *least* charming age of teenage daughters: thirteen going on fourteen. Because she knew I had wonderful memories of this part of Italy, Molly whined in the car from Arezzo to Florence, whined while passing through beautiful hill towns, whined at gas stations, whined as we threaded our way past the congestion of a procession in honor of Nostra Signora del Autostrada. She hated Florence, our room in Bellosguardo, the swimming pool, the restaurant, and of course her mother—until I had the inspiration to empty a bottle of icy San Pellegrino on her head. Whereupon she threw her arms around me and said, "Mommy, I love you!"

Trips like that have taught me a lesson. For me, the secret of being happy in Italy now is to live life *all'italiana:* to stay in one place and follow the eminently sensible Italian schedule, walking in the morning and evening, eating and resting in the middle of the day.

During the last few years, I have concentrated on two particular sections of Italy: Lucca, in Tuscany, and Venice and the Veneto.

Don't Miss:

Bicycling along the fortified walls of Lucca while admiring the town's Renaissance architecture.

Strolling in Marostica, with its chessboard square, and climbing the fortifications above town.

Wandering through the ghetto of Venice and visiting the ancient Jewish cemetery on the Lido.

A visit to the Villa Barbaro at Masèr—the fountains and Veronese frescoes here are spectacular.

A stroll across the covered bridge at Bassano del Grappa, the gateway to the Tyrolean Alps (this is where much of Italy's grappa is made).

I discovered Lucca almost by accident. My friends Ken and Barbara Follett had rented a place called Villa Michaela, outside Lucca in the town of Vorno, and they invited us to stay. Since the Follett clan never goes on summer holidays without having room for their five grown daughters and sons, various pals and partners, cousins, siblings, and work colleagues, they have to rent enormous houses. Molly and I joined this happy throng; later my husband sprang himself from New York and met us.

To reach Lucca you drive west of Florence on the autostrada, past Montecatini, the spa town, and stop just east of Pisa and Livorno. Lucca is a walled and gated city; you first see it from a ring road, with bicyclists cruising the wide parapets and cars parked outside the impressive walls of the town's historic center. There is a lovely restaurant on the walls called Antico Caffè delle Mura; a Roman colosseum turned into a honeycomb of dwellings during the Middle Ages; medieval streets; a glorious duomo. Nearby is a cluster of small country towns with some delightful places to stay, from modest pensiones to entire twelve-bedroom villas, such as the one the Folletts rented that summer.

Villa Michaela is entered through narrow gates. It's a sprawling eighteenth-century villa, once a ruin, with gorgeous views and an ample swimming pool. Hills covered with vineyards rise around it.

The joy of vacationing in Italy is in *far niente:* doing nothing. The teenagers slept till noon every day; the grown-ups—if you can call us that—wrote, faxed, and telephoned in the morning, then lazed by the pool after lunch. If we went to Lucca to bike around the walls or shop or see works of art, it was never until three-thirty or four. I remember one lunch that ended at six in the evening. I remember passionate political discussions while we all sat topless around the pool. I finished a chapter of *Fear of Fifty,* called "Becoming Venetian," while sitting near that pool with a yellow legal pad balanced on my knee. I remember a cruise we took to snorkel and swim in the Golfo dei Poeti. When we stopped for lunch at Portovenere we looked out over Carrara, where Michelangelo's white marble was quarried. The joy of Italy often consists of doing ordinary things in extraordinary settings.

Lucca has the layers of history characteristic of Rome and Verona. It was founded in 180 B.C. as a Roman encampment; it evolved into a medieval village and then a Renaissance city. The arches of its colosseum were long ago filled in with houses; the central stage remains as a vast piazza. Lucca reached its zenith as a trading town during the eleventh, twelfth, and thirteenth centuries. Between the fourteenth and eighteenth centuries it remained an independent city-state like Venice—until Napoleon conquered them both.

Perhaps the most beautiful thing in Lucca is the white Carrara marble sepulchre, in the duomo, of Ilaria del Carretto, done by Jacopo della Quercia in 1408. Ilaria was the young wife of Paolo Guinigi, one of the fifteenth-century bosses of Lucca. I forget how she died; I'm sure I deliberately blank out her story because I loathe tales of women who die at tender ages. I would rather see monuments to women who survived their first loves and went on to have several more.

Lucca has a taste for luxury. The food is excellent even in little *pizzerie*. Posh jewelry shops, displaying antique and modern treasures, seem to be everywhere. And there are wonderful shoemakers—one of whom, Porselli, makes slippers for the dancers of La Scala; I never leave without ballerina flats in half a dozen colors. How can you go wrong in a town with good shoe shops?

We enjoyed that first time with the Folletts so much that the next summer we rented a house up on a promontory just outside Lucca, in a town called San Macario al Monte. Molly and I both invited friends to stay with us. It was a comfortable farmhouse rather than a *palazzo,* but it was spacious, with lots of bedrooms and dazzling sunrise and sunset views. (I've found that such houses are often reached by spectacularly tricky roads, and this one was no exception. The road fell away in places to resemble the corniche along the Dalmatian coast—after the shelling.)

The grounds held a swimming pool beside a vine-shaded pergola, silvery olive trees, and dark cypresses. It was a ten-minute drive to Lucca, fifteen minutes to the Folletts at Villa Michaela, and half an hour to Pisa.

Between Lucca and Pisa, there are sweet country inns, restaurants in gardens, restaurants on terraces both splendid and modest. The jolliest meal we had was at a hilltop trattoria whose kitchen had closed when we arrived. With great panache, the obliging *padrone* laid out cheeses and salami and prosciutto for us. This out-of-the-way trattoria is nowhere near as famous as Vipore or Il Giglio or the other starred restaurants around Lucca—again, it was the kindness of the people that made it so exceptional.

～

Molly is a Leo, born on August 19, so she has spent almost every birthday in Italy. Her fifteenth summer was one of our best times; we celebrated with the Folletts, their guests, and our guests at Villa La Principessa, a beautiful country hotel with a garden restaurant surrounded by huge chestnut trees. We sat at a horseshoe-shaped table: the teenagers captured the middle and the grown-ups commanded the ends.

Surrounded by our crowd of friends, we rarely stirred without twenty people. Fortunately, Italians find that normal: they, too, rarely stir without twenty people. Parties of family, friends, big kids, little kids, are not only tolerated, they are considered simpatico—which makes Italy the ideal spot for a family vacation. There are few places where children are not treated as full-fledged guests.

A villa on a hill about five minutes from ours sold excellent local wine; the simple meals we made at home were as memorable as the ones in restaurants. Sitting on our terrace under the rising moon, eating prosciutto and *melone* and grilled local fish, drinking inexpensive wine, playing charades—this was as magical as any evening out.

What is this fatal charm of Italy? Why does it reflect us like a mirror that obliterates wrinkles, subtracts pounds, and gives our eyes a devil-may-care sparkle? Why does Italy remain the country of the Saturnalia—the feast when everything was permitted? Is it because the pagan past is still alive in Italy and Christianity is just a thin veneer that scarcely covers?

To wake up on a Sunday morning in Italy, to hear the roosters crowing and the bells pealing, is one of life's greatest pleasures. To take a walk or a run in that tintinnabulation is even better. The mornings are cool, the birds swoop from hill to hill, and the bells seem to have been created not to draw worshipers to church but—like so many things here—for your particular pleasure.

If you stay long enough to transform yourself from tourist to habitué, the headwaiters will also call you *maestro* or *contessa* or *dot-*

tore or perhaps even *commendatore*. To Italians, this flattery is almost meaningless; only Americans take it semi-seriously. Typically, we at first fall madly in love with this overstatement; somewhat later we pronounce Italians liars and fakes when we discover it is only a form of social lubrication. Actually, both reactions are wrong. Naked truth, the Italians believe, can always do with some enhancement.

The Facts: Italy

To find a villa to rent in Italy, contact Vacanze in Italia (22 Railroad St., Great Barrington, Massachusetts 01230; 800-533-5405 or 413-528-6610 / fax: 413-528-6222; www.homeabroad.com). The company handles a wide variety of over 500 properties; prices vary according to the season.

Hotels

Torre di Bellosguardo, 2 Via Roti Michelozzi, Florence; 39-55/229-8145; Fax: 39-82/229-008.

Villa La Principessa, Massa Pisana, S.S. 12, Lucca; 39-583/370-037; Fax: 39-583/379-136.

Restaurants

Al Ringraziamento, 107 Via Santo Pio, Cavasso del Tomba; 39-423/543-271.

Antico Caffé della Mura, 2 Via Vittorio Emanuele, Lucca; 39-583/479-62.

Il Giglio, Piazza del Giglio, Lucca; 39-583/494-058.

Vipore, Via Pieve Santo Stefano, Lucca; 39-583/59245.

Italy Writhes in Revolution
Against Corruption

BY RAY MOSELEY

editor's note

Since World War II, the average length of time Italy's fifty-one various governments have lasted is eleven months. It used to be that all Italians knew whose palm to grease to obtain a favor, knew how to avoid paying a fine, or how to get a job even if they weren't entirely qualified. Some of this corruption still exists in Italy—perhaps it always will—but in the early nineties nothing short of a revolution swept through the country. Though revolutionary ideas and changes are still occurring, nothing has been as shattering as the initial Tangentopoli scandal, which revealed that enormous bribes had been paid to political parties for a number of years by construction companies seeking contracts.

I have many articles in my files reporting on the scandal and its results, but I've always felt this one, from *The Chicago Tribune,* explained it especially well. Since its appearance in 1993, the Northern League has grown in power (under the leadership of Umberto Bossi it has tried to gather support to secede from Italy and form a new state called Padania); the Italian Social Movement, a neo-Fascist party, was formed in 1994 (and Mussolini's granddaughter, Alessandra, became a legislator); Italy has become a home for greater numbers of immigrants (Denny Mendez, originally from the Dominican Republic, was crowned Miss Italy in 1996); and, perhaps most noticeable to tourists, public services have been completely reformed. Now, government workers can actually be fired for poor performance, and longtime visitors to Italy will notice an improvement in the areas of public transportation, postal service, and health care. (One reason for this reform, of course, is the Northern League's accusations of inefficient services.) In 1998, Italy and many of its European neighbors formally joined the European Monetary Union. For years, however, Italy was widely considered one of the least likely candidates: A huge public debt, a legacy of corruption, and overall fiscal irresponsibility nearly prevented Italy from qualifying. But the government of Prime Minister Romano Prodi managed to get a firm grip on inflation and make fiscal discipline a reality without too much turmoil

(Georgio Benvenuto, Finance Committee President in Parliament, was quoted as saying in 1998 that "We Italians have had to go without dessert a few times, but we have not yet had to miss a meal"). It of course remains to be seen if Italy can continue on this course, but most Italians feel to be left out of the Monetary Union is equivalent to third-world status.

Italy has made great strides and is changing so rapidly it's difficult to keep up with political figures and parties and all the ways in which it has redefined business as usual. Here's how it all began:

Former Prime Minister Bettino Craxi recently strolled over from the hotel where he lives to meet a friend in Rome's Piazza Navona. He never quite made it.

A crowd of people in the square spotted him and drove him back. "Thief!" they shouted. "Shame!"

Former Foreign Minister Gianni De Michelis tried to slip out the back door of the public prosecutor's office in Venice after he was interrogated, but a crowd waiting for him spotted his white raincoat and mobbed him.

As he tried to flee, insults rained down on him: "Thief, buffoon, bandit, criminal, shame, shame!" The crowd chased him across a bridge spanning a canal. De Michelis escaped in a water taxi, leaving his constituents shaking their fists as he sped away.

It is a brave Italian politician who goes out in public these days. Roman restaurants that once were gathering places for members of parliament have lost that part of their clientele.

Members who ostentatiously had paraded the aisles of the Rome-Milan express train now furtively show their passes to ticket collectors.

A corruption scandal reminiscent of the decadence that marked the dying days of the Roman Empire continues to unfold and is churning up what some liken to a peaceful revolution. One French historian says it is not a revolution but is the disintegration of the Italian republic.

Whatever it is, it is certain to change Italy profoundly. A country that has been wedded to a venal and outmoded political system of Mediterranean and Byzantine complexion is about to transform itself, painfully but surely, into a modern Western democracy.

More than 800 politicians and industrialists, a veritable Who's Who of Italian public life, have been arrested, and scores remain in jail. Seven people who were to be questioned have committed suicide. At least fifty members of parliament are under investigation. Three leading figures are on the run. Four cabinet members have resigned, three of them under criminal suspicion. And worse is yet to come.

So far the investigation has focused on Socialist politicians and has been directed principally from Milan. When it develops further in Rome and the south, prosecutors are expected to uncover evidence of the ties long believed to exist between the dominant Christian Democrats and the Mafia. Leading Communist politicians in the south also are likely to be targeted by the *mani pulite* (clean hands) investigation.

De Michelis, who professes to be unruffled by his recent encounter with Venetian voters, predicts that Italy's entire ruling class is about to be swept away.

"I don't think most of us will be in politics in the future," he said. "We will have a whole new political class, probably with more women. This is one of the positive aspects of a confused situation. It will accelerate change."

Change is something that has been missing from Italian political life for forty-eight years. The country has had fifty-one governments since World War II, but in a sense it has had only one.

Every government has been dominated by Christian Democrats, and as governments fell most ministers did not leave office—they simply played a game of musical chairs, swapping one ministry for another.

Backed by the Vatican and at one time by CIA money, the

Christian Democrats were seen as the bulwark against a takeover of Italy by the Western world's most powerful Communist Party.

Over time the Christian Democrats, their Socialist coalition allies and even the Communists devised a cozy system of political patronage that was all-encompassing. Each party controlled its own television network and the thousands of jobs that go with that. Each also has its fiefdoms in state-owned industry, which represents more than 30 percent of all industry in the country. Each controls its share of central government, provincial and municipal administration.

Two years ago a Milan prosecutor named Antonio Di Pietro, who has since become a national hero, discovered that a Socialist politician, Mario Chiesa, was heavily involved in collecting bribes from an undertaker who had the funeral concession at a city-owned old people's home.

Di Pietro's investigation led to Chiesa's arrest, and then it snowballed. As he learned more and arrested a growing number of politicians, bureaucrats and businessmen, those who fell into his net began to implicate others.

By now Di Pietro and his fellow prosecutors in Milan have produced evidence that businessmen, especially from the state sector and from the construction industry, have been paying billions of dollars in bribes to the leading political parties over the years. By some estimates, the bribes amount to $7 billion a year. Italians now refer to the scandal as *Tangentopoli*—Bribesville.

Odd as it may seem, the exposure of this gigantic scandal is a direct outgrowth of the collapse of the Soviet Union.

Before the fall of communism, everyone in Italy knew the political system was rotten. They were well aware of freeways built in the poor south that ended abruptly in the midst of nowhere. They knew of earthquake victims who spent years living in tents even though hundreds of millions of dollars had been allocated to rebuild their villages. And they knew that political parties operated on a lavish scale that could not be explained by their public financing.

But no one would have dreamed of disturbing this web of corruption, because to do so could have undermined the Christian Democrats and let the Communists into power. Even the Vatican kept silent.

"The East-West confrontation acted like a thermostat, an element of control," De Michelis said. "It was impossible in Italy to go outside a certain range of action."

With the breakup of the Soviet Union, the rules of the game no longer applied but, as Francesco D'Onofrio of the Christian Democrats observes, the old political parties were slow to recognize this.

"We didn't make any changes," he said. "We kept the same faces, the same language. We became ossified."

D'Onofrio and others say it is no accident that the scandal was exposed in Milan. Milan is the most European of Italian cities, the country's industrial and commercial capital and a bastion of free-market values.

The Milanese have long resented the drain of funds to the poor south, the inefficient bureaucracy centered in Rome and payments to politicians. Since the fall of communism, this resentment has given rise to a new party, the Northern League, which has advocated the secession of the rich north from the south. Today the league has displaced the Christian Democrats as the leading party in two regions—Lombardy and the Veneto—and possibly in Piedmont.

The league has been helped by moves toward European integration. Franco Ferrarotti, a sociologist at Rome University, says the Milanese and other northerners recognized, more than Romans did, that Italy would be at a competitive disadvantage with other European countries unless it mended its ways.

"The Milanese realized that we had a ruling class that was absolutely mediocre," Ferrarotti said. "Why should we be represented by this bunch of *dummkopfs?*"

Antonio Preiti, of the Rome research center Censis, said, "If we have a revolution, it's a Milanese revolution. The industrialists, and above all small businessmen, denounced the system. It is a rebellion of the middle class."

The rebellion is proving costly to the Italian economy. It has engendered a loss of confidence and has resulted in a virtual freeze on major infrastructure projects, since everyone is afraid of signing a contract with the state.

The lira has been repeatedly devalued, and prices have plummeted on the stock exchange. The mammoth Italian budget deficit remains out of control.

Where the rebellion will end is not clear. Prime Minister Giuliano Amato, a Socialist, tried to temper its effects last week by drawing up a bill that would have amounted to an amnesty for guilty politicians if they paid back triple the amount of money they stole.

"It was like turning a homicide into a traffic violation," said Ferrarotti.

A public outcry stifled Amato's attempt and almost forced his resignation. He is expected to quit after an April 18 referendum that could pave the way for a reform of political party financing and abolition of the proportional representation system for holding elections.

But these reforms will have to grind through a slow-moving parliament, and this could take many months.

To put its economy back on course, Italy needs to hold new elections.

But if elections were called in the next few months, as some opposition parties are demanding, they would have to be held under the old laws and therefore would leave the current political lineup little changed.

So elections probably will be delayed until the spring of 1994, after reforms are in effect. Then Italy will have gone over to a new electoral system, probably a combination of American-style majority voting and some remnant of proportional representation.

This should bring about the disappearance of some small parties and leave about three major contenders for power—the Christian Democrats, the former Communists (now called the Party of the Democratic Left) and the Northern League.

But the first two of these parties seems certain to undergo radical change, and the Christian Democrats are even thinking of going back to their old name, *Partito Populare* (Peoples Party).

To the extent that the old parties remain on the scene, then it could seem that there has been no revolution.

But what is happening implies a complete break with the way politics has been conducted in Italy for a half-century, the emergence of a new political class and a shift toward a more market-oriented economic system.

D'Onofrio of the Christian Democrats likens the current development to what happened in Eastern Europe in 1989–90. "It's the dismantling of the *nomenklatura*," he said. "It's like a volcano."

Nadio Delai, president of Censis, argued that none of the surviving parties is likely to command a major share of the vote, and therefore the new system could be "much more unstable than in the past."

The future is unclear because there never has been a revolution conducted by prosecutors. But what is clear is that, after *Tangentopoli,* nothing in Italy will ever be quite the same again.

Biblioteca

Mediterranean

Italy is often the first country people think of when they hear the word Mediterranean, and with good reason: Italy has long held a dominant position in the region, and, more so than some of the other Mediterranean countries, her history and continued existence is inextricably entwined with the Sea; indeed, she utterly depends upon it. Here are some books I highly recommend about the history, culture, natural history, architecture, and uniqueness of the Mediterranean. Italy is featured in each title.

The Mediterranean, Fernand Braudel, first published in France, 1949. English translation of second revised edition, HarperCollins Publishers, 1972. Abridged edition, HarperCollins, 1992. The definitive classic. *Essenziale.*

The Mediterranean: Lands of the Olive Tree, Culture & Civilizations, text and photographs by Alain Cheneviere, Konecky & Konecky, New York, 1997. This is that rare coffee-table book that has both perceptive text and gorgeous photos.

Mediterranean: A Cultural Landscape, Predrag Matvejevic, translated by Michael Henry Heim, University of California Press, Berkeley, 1999; previously published as *Mediteranski brevijar,* Zagreb, 1987; *Breviaire mediterraneen,* Paris, 1992; and *Mediterraneo: Un nuovo breviario,* Milan, 1993. A beautiful, unusual book in that it combines personal observations with history, maps, maritime details, people, and language. Matvejevic, a leading European intellectual originally from Mostar, Herzegovina, is a wonderful, imaginative writer.

The Inner Sea: The Mediterranean and Its People, Robert Fox, Alfred A. Knopf, 1993.

The Pillars of Hercules: A Grand Tour of the Mediterranean, Paul Theroux, G. P. Putnam's Sons, 1995.

On the Shores of the Mediterranean, Eric Newby, first published in 1984 by the Harvill Press, London; Picador, 1985, paperback.

Mediterranean: Portrait of a Sea, Ernle Bradford, Harcourt Brace Jovanovich, 1971.

Mediterranean Vernacular, V. I. Atroshenko, Milton Grundy, Rizzoli, 1991.

Villages in the Sun: Mediterranean Community Architecture, Myron Goldfinger, Rizzoli, 1993.

Mediterranean Color: Italy, France, Spain, Portugal, Morocco, Greece, photographs and text by Jeffrey Becom, foreword by Paul Goldberger, Abbeville Press, 1990.

World War II in the Mediterranean, 1942–1945, Carlo d'Este, Algonguin Books, 1990; one of the only books to deal exclusively with the war in the

Mediterranean; events in Italy—on Sicily and at Anzio, Rome, and Monte Cassino—are all well documented.

The First Eden, Sir David Attenborough, William Collins Sons & Co. Ltd., London, 1987.

The Spirit of Mediterranean Places, Michel Butor, The Marlboro Press, 1986.

Mediterranean, photography by Mimmo Jodice, essays by George Hersey and Predrag Matvejević, Aperture, 1995.

Playing Away: Roman Holidays and Other Mediterranean Encounters, Michael Mewshaw, Atheneum, 1988.

The Sun at Midday: Tales of a Mediterranean Family, Gini Alhadeff, Pantheon, 1997. I considered including this memoir in *I Personaggi,* but even though Alhadeff's life was and remains partly Italian (see her "Coming Home to Chianti" piece in *La Toscana*), this is a full Mediterranean story. Neither her mother's or father's families were very religious, but she was raised Catholic, not discovering until she was almost twenty that her family was Sephardic (she was raised Catholic because her father decided it would be a good idea, shortly after his brother was taken by the Germans in Rome). This is a beautifully written, cosmopolitan memoir with a unique Italian touch; as Alhadeff writes: "It is one of the effects of Italy that even people who have been transplanted as often as Jews have, tend to feel Italian before they feel Jewish. And to feel Italian is to feel a little Catholic, after all."

The Phoenicians, edited by Sabatino Moscati, Rizzoli, 1999. The Phoenician civilization remains mysterious, but this beautiful and fascinating paperback reveals a treasure trove of information, in the form of essays contributed by a number of scholars. I include it here simply because any discussion of the Mediterranean without it would be a glaring omission.

Italy

A Traveller's History of Italy, Valerio Lintner, Series Editor, Denis Judd, Interlink Books, Brooklyn, New York, 1994. This edition is one in a great series for which I have much enthusiasm. I'm not sure what the editors' vision for the series is, but *my* idea of it is to give readers a compact, historical overview of each place, highlighting the significant events and people with which every visitor should be familiar. Each edition is a mini What You Should Know guide, a minimum of milestones to help you really appreciate what you're seeing. The eight chapters in this volume cover the major periods in Italian history, from the Stone Age, the Etruscan civilization, and the Rinascimento to fascism and postwar and contemporary Italy. Additionally, there are charts of emperors, popes, Venetian doges, Italian artists, and prime ministers; a chart of the Chamber of Deputies, 1946–1992 and 1994–1996; and an A to Z historical gazetteer that can be used to cross-reference towns, sites, and buildings of historical importance.

Out of Italy: 1450–1650, Fernand Braudel, translated by Sian Reynolds, *Editions Arthaud, 1989*; English translation © 1991, Flammarion. I had only known Braudel as the author of *The Identity of France* and *The Mediterranean* before I ran across this beautiful and fascinating book, illustrated with color reproductions by Michelangelo, Raphael, Titian, Ghirlandaio, Van Eyck, Rubens, Poussin, etc. Braudel examines Italy's dominant position in Europe and around the Mediterranean and analyzes the interaction between art, science, politics, and commerce in terms of how they contributed to Italy's influence abroad during the two centuries of the Renaissance, Mannerism, and the Baroque periods. This is Braudel's specialty—looking at history simultaneously with other social studies—and readers will find this to be *essenziale*.

A Traveller in Italy, H. V. Morton, Dodd, Mead & Company, 1964. Morton has been described as "a fine traveling companion," and I would agree that it would be difficult to find a better one. His books on Rome, Spain, and Southern Italy are among the best ever published, although they're all, including this one, out of print. Chapters 10, 11, and 12 cover Florence and a number of hill towns in Tuscany and Umbria. Wonderful and *essenziale*.

Image of Italy, special issue of *The Texas Quarterly*, Summer 1961, volume IV, No. 2, edited by William Arrowsmith, photographs by Russell Lee, © The University of Texas, Austin. Although it's an edition of *The Texas Quarterly*, this is actually a hardbound book with unforgettable photos and superb text. The fact that it was published in 1961 is irrelevant. Today's image of Italy is just as varied and complex as it was then. As stated in the foreword, our image of Italy is occasionally distorted in part because of Italy's "staggering diversity" of people and landscape. "Her politics have been polarized by the Cold War, her Communist party is proportionally the largest in Europe, while her economic policies vacillate between state socialism and uncontrolled laissez-faire capitalism. Add to this war (and the civil war which was its consequence), overpopulation, underemployment, a growing gap between rich and poor and South and North, the flight of the peasantry from unproductive farms to cities, continual emigration, the desuetude of old ways and old customs, and the violent alterations in landscape and living, and the impression is utterly variety and change. In a half hour's drive out of almost any city in Italy you can pass through three or four successive centuries, all of them simultaneously alive and even competitive, each one with its distinctive way of being Italian, and its Italian hunger for change." This is not a record of contemporary Italian culture, nor a venue for representative Italian writing. Rather, it suggests how the ideas of Italy and of being Italian are formed and how they are shaped by the work of Italian writers and thinkers. Some of the contributors are Carlo

Cassola, Cesare Pavese, Carlo Levi, Paolo Volponi, Gabriella Parca, and Elena Croce. An outstanding collection.

The Italians and the Holocaust, Susan Zuccotti, Basic Books, 1987; *Benevolence and Betrayal: Five Italian Jewish Families Under Facism,* Alexander Stille, Summit Books, 1991; and *The Garden of the Finzi-Continis,* Giorgio Bassani, Atheneum, 1965, and MJF Books, "Library of the Holocaust" series, translated by William Weaver, 1996. Unlike the body of published works on France during World War II, there is comparatively much less on Italy during these years, and less still on the fate of the Italian Jewish population. Zuccotti's book is, I think, the best overall history of Italy and the Holocaust; but Stille's and Bassani's books are the best at conveying what the experience was like for ordinary people. As Stille notes, "the complexity of individual experience, with all its rough, solid three-dimensionality, can be a useful touchstone for the abstract linear theories of history." I include them not only because they are among the very few books of their kind but because they relate a significant period in *every* Italian's history.

Modern Italy: A Political History, Denis Mack Smith, The University of Michigan Press, 1997; first published in the U.S. as *Italy: A Modern History* by The University of Michigan Press in 1959, revised 1969. This is *the* volume to read on Italy from just before 1861 to 1996. Smith, a Fellow of the British Academy, has been awarded a dozen literary prizes in Italy and is a *Commendatore* of the Italian Order of Merit. "The best starting point for a political history of modern Italy," he notes, "is March 1861 when, at long last, Count Cavour was able to proclaim that a united Italian kingdom was in existence." From this point, Smith takes readers up to the confusing political mess of recent years, and his final chapter is the best summation I've read on this transitional period.

The Italians: A Full-Length Portrait Featuring Their Manners and Morals, Luigi Barzini, Atheneum, 1964. *Still* the classic, *still* the best book of its kind. If I were to recommend only one book, this would be it. Don't bother trying to understand Italy or grasp the Italian character without reading this, or rereading it if it's been a while since you picked it up. Each chapter is well written and thought-provoking, but a few that really stand apart are "The Problema del Mezzogiorno," "Illusion and Cagliostro," and "Sicily and the Mafia," which might be the best essay I've ever read on the history and influence of both the mafia (defined by Barzini as a state of mind, a philosophy of life, a conception of society, and a moral code, prevalent among *all* Sicilians) and the Mafia (the illegal organization that makes headlines). *Essenziale.*

Culture Shock! Italy: A Guide to Customs and Etiquette, Raymond Flower, Alessandro Falassi, Graphic Arts Publishing Company, Portland, Oregon, 1990. Each Culture Shock! edition is authored by a different writer(s) and each is eminently enlightening. The Italy edition covers such topics as language (including the enormous variety of hand gestures), the pervasiveness of Christianity in daily life (and a helpful hint to be mindful of is that in Italy, the week begins on Monday and ends on Sunday; you'll see that Italian calendars are printed this way), home life and attitudes, doing business in Italy, superstitions, gifts and tips, art and literature, and do's and don'ts in a restaurant. Although some of the information is directed at people who plan to be in Italy for an extended stay, this is a useful, basic guide that I consider to be *essenziale,* even for a short visit.

The Italian Way: Aspects of Behavior, Attitudes, and Customs of the Italians, Mario Costantino, Lawrence Gambella, Passport Books, an imprint of NTC/Contemporary Publishing Company, 1996. One of my favorite books, this is a slim, handy A to Z guide to a multitude of key traits of the Italians. Costantino and Gambella have compiled an interesting and useful list including abbreviations and acronyms tourists will need to recognize; the numerous ways the Italians have of attracting attention; the finer points of compliments, appreciation, criticism, and gallantry; a brief history of Carnevale; Italian films, *Il Malocchio, Il Palio,* and *La Vendemmia; Lo Sciopero,* pro loco; sports; ways of conveying information; and women. *Assolutamente essenizale.*

The Italians: History, Art, and the Genius of a People, edited by John Julius Norwich, Thames and Hudson, London, 1983; 1989 edition published by Portland House, A wonderful, wonderful book I include in the *essenziale* category. Norwich is an engaging historian and is also the distinguished author of A History of Venice, The Normans in Sicily, and a three-volume history of Byzantium. He has gathered an impressive bunch of authors to answer the question, how did the qualities of "Italianness" that make Italy unique arise in history? With an equally impressive collection of color and black-and-white illustrations.

Italian Days, Barbara Grizzuti Harrison, Ticknor & Fields, 1989. My enthusiasm for this beautifully written and superb book, no matter how many times I reread it, is endless. I am incapable of praising it sufficiently. In an endorsement from *The Washington Post Book World,* a reviewer wrote that it "Will be the companion of visitors for years to come." I hope this has become true since it was published, over a decade ago, and hope that it remains true. I cannot imagine going to Italy without reading it, can't imagine anyone with a serious interest in Italy not reading it, can't imagine my life without having read it. Only one chapter, the third, is relevant to this book, "Lovely Florence" and "San Gimignano: City of Fine Towers." But don't let that stand in your way from reading the entire book. You won't regret it. *Essenziale.*

Italians First!: An A-to-Z of Everything First Achieved by Italians, Arturo Barone, third edition, Renaissance Books (an imprint of Global Books, Ltd.),

Folkestone, Kent, United Kingdom, 1999. The only book of its kind I've ever seen, this is a handy and truly amazing cross-indexed listing of Italians and the areas in which they achieved "firsts," such as: Giorgio Vasari became the first art historian in 1550. The first newspaper was published in Venice in 1563. In 1871, Antonio Meucci applied for a telephone patent (Alexander Graham Bell's application came in 1876). In 1889, Giuseppe Pirelli made the first motor car tire. In 1350, gold wire was first made in Italy. Venice established the first coffee house in the western world in 1645. The list is endless (or least over 800 entries). Barone also provides commentaries for some topics that provide an interesting diversion from the entries.

Cento Città: A Guide to the "Hundred Cities & Towns" of Italy, Paul Hofmann, Henry Holt, 1988, hardcover; Owl, 1990, paperback. This is one of the most treasured books in my Italy library, and Hofmann, for many years *The New York Times* bureau chief in Rome, is one of my favorite writers. The 100 *città* (a word that is both singular and plural—one of the exceptions in Italian grammar—for city or town) featured in this book are his personal favorites, and it would be ridiculous to disagree with his selections. They are sensational. The Heartlands section, which is devoted to Emilia, Romagna, and Tuscany, highlights Arezzo, Chiusi, Cortona, Fiesole, Lucca, Montepulciano, Pienza, Pisa, Pistoia, Porto Ferraio, San Gimignano, Sansepolcro, Siena, and Volterra. The bigger cities—Rome, Florence, Venice, Milan, etc.—are not included. This is a book for those who want to get off the predictable circuit and better understand *regions* of Italy. The appendix contains practical information, such as postal and telephone codes, recommended hotels and restaurants, museums, etc., much of which might be outdated, but the distances and traveling times by car or train are still applicable. With seventy-four black-and-white photographs. *Essenziale.*

Italian Hilltowns, Norman F. Carver, Jr., Documan Press, Ltd., Kalamazoo, Michigan, hardcover and paperback, © 1979, 1995. I cherish this book. Carver, an architect, has also spent a considerable number of years photographing folk architecture in the Mediterranean region as well as Japan and Mexico. It's not only that these color and black-and-white photographs are exquisite, but that Carver is passionately concerned with preserving Italy's hilltowns and sharing what we can learn from them. He highlights many towns throughout Italy that are hardly mentioned in guidebooks: Pierele, Grisolia, Sorano, Caprancia, Archidosso, Postignano (which is featured on the cover), Castelvecchio Calviso, and the Val di Fafora, a valley west of Florence where there are seven tiny villages perched on hilltops, none of which overwhelm the environment. He writes in the preface, "Though I have included a few of the larger and more famous towns, such as Siena and San Gimignano, which have adapted well to modern life, most photographs are of small anonymous towns that retain most of their original character. To convey as much as possible the original ambiance of these medieval places, the photographs lie a little by what they leave out. You will see few contemporary signs, shops, electrical poles, though TV antennas appear with rather more frequency that I would have liked." He adds that cars posed less of a problem for his photography as the narrow streets are not suitable for motor vehicles, which are parked and used on the outskirts of each village. There is a map at the back of the book indicating the whereabouts of each hilltown, and a great number are in Tuscany and Umbria. *Essenziale.*

That Fine Italian Hand—What Makes the Italians Italian: A Wry Close-up of a Resourceful People, Paul Hofmann, Henry Holt and Company, 1990. Another wonderful book by Hofmann (see above). This title covers topics such as pasta, pizza, and espresso; red tape and anarchy; the Mafia; the two Italies; the carabinieri; the family; etc. . . . all subjects that are referred to as having that "fine Italian hand," which "has long meant the particular way Italians like to do things, preferring adroitness to sheer force." *Essenziale.*

Letters from Italy, J. W. von Goethe, various publishers, around 1900. Even more so than Henry James and D. H. Lawrence, Goethe and his writings on Italy are *essenziale* in any library of Italian books. Readers will notice that Goethe's letters are referenced in a great number of sources, and with good reason: they are a delight to read, filled with the sort of observations and insights that make such good quotations.

Italian Hours, Henry James, The Ecco Press; originally published by Houghton Mifflin Company, 1909. There are twenty-two essays in this wonderful book, which James wrote during the 1870s. Those pertaining to Tuscany and Umbria include "A Chain of Cities," "Siena Early and Late," "The Autumn in Florence," "Tuscan Cities," and "Other Tuscan Cities." *Essenziale.*

Henry James on Italy, Barrie & Jenkins, Ltd., London, 1988; published in the U.S. by Weidenfeld & Nicolson, New York. A handsome hardcover package with color reproductions of period paintings matched with text from James's *Italian Hours.* I am not typically fond of book excerpts, and certainly *Italian Hours* deserves to be read in its entirety; but this is such an appealing collection and I have enjoyed it so much that I am happy to include it here. Relevant to Tuscany are three chapters and Umbrian towns featured include Perugia, Narni, Spoleto, and Assisi. Great to keep or give as a gift.

D. H. Lawrence and Italy, Penguin Travel Library, 1985; first published in the U.S. in a hardbound and paperback edition by Viking Penguin, 1972. None of the three essays that make up this volume ("Twilight in Italy," "Sea and Sardinia," "Etruscan Places") are exclusively about Tuscany or Umbria, but I include this collection here for "Etruscan Places," as Volterra, one of the Etruscan places featured, is in Tuscany. Anthony Burgess, in his introduction, notes that the Etruscan tombs have not changed much over the years; but the

Italy that Lawrence knew, in the first decades of the 1900s, "is different in so many respects from the Italy of today that, entering his books, we enter a remote world which, to use a paradox, touches modernity only through its perennial antiquities." Burgess also tell us that Lawrence originally envisioned a larger Etruscan book, but he recognized that he couldn't compete with the authoritative works by D. Randall-MacIver (*Villanovans and Early Etruscans*), Pericles Ducati (*Etruria Antica*), and a major survey by George Dennis. No matter. I have felt for many years that this piece is one of the best ever written about the Etruscans, and I consider it *essenziale*.

Italian Journeys, W. D. Howells, with illustrations by Joseph Pennell, The Marlboro Press/Northwestern University Press, Evanston, Illinois, 1999; first published in 1867. Howells (1837–1920) was the American consul in Venice for four years and was also editor of *The Atlantic Monthly* and *Harper's*. His travels in Italy took him throughout the country, but Pisa is the only town in central Italy in this book (it was raining too hard while he was in Bologna to cross the Apennines to Florence). However, this is such an insightful book that I felt I should include it here.

The Civilization of the Renaissance in Italy, Jacob Burckhardt, introduction by Hajo Holborn, Modern Library, 1954. In his introduction, Holborn refers to this definitive and much-quoted work as "the greatest single book ever on the history of Italy between 1350 and 1550." If the title sounds dry, it's misleading. This is an endlessly fascinating and brilliant book, *essenziale* for *all* visitors to Italy.

Towns of the Renaissance: Travellers in Northern Italy, David D. Hume, J. N. Townsend Publishing, Exeter, New Hampshire, 1995. I am very fond of this book although it is not written by someone who is a noted historian or scholar in Italian studies. Hume has one quality, however, that is equally important: a sincere love and enjoyment of Italy, which translates into an insatiable curiosity about things Italian. He writes about Italy and travel, very much in the spirit of The Collected Traveler, and I immediately liked him when I read his "Author's Note," in which he writes, "My wife Cathy and I learned a lot about that wonderful country while we were there and perhaps twice as much by reading about it both before and after we went on these visits." He presents a good bibliography at the end of the book, offers lots of practical tips for traveling, and quite a lot of interesting observations and thoughts. The book features Renaissance towns from Venice to Rome, but there are individual chapters on Cortona, Siena, Florence, and Orvieto. The chapter titled "Understanding Italian and Italians" is worth reproducing in full, as it is an excellent encouragement for *anyone,* of any age, to learn a foreign language. Very highly recommended.

When Courage Was Stronger Than Fear: Remarkable Stories of Christians Who Saved Jews from the Holocaust, Peter Hellman, Marlowe & Company (Balliett

& Fitzgerald, Inc.), distributed by Publishers Group West, 1999; originally published as *Avenue of the Righteous,* Atheneum, 1980. In 1968, Hellman visited Yad Vashem, the National Holocaust Memorial in Jerusalem. He was struck by the simplicity of the Avenue des Justes, better known as Avenue of the Righteous in English. The avenue is really a path lined with carob—and more recently, olive—trees, and under each tree is a small plaque displaying the name of a Christian (and in some cases a Moslem) who saved one or more Jews from Nazi persecution. Hellman recognized that this simplicity was deceiving, that there was a dramatic story behind each and every one of these plaques. He decided that very day that he wanted to learn more about these remarkable people. In this book he profiles five documented cases of the Righteous, each representing a different country—Italy, France, Belgium, Holland, and Poland. His only criterion was that the Righteous person still be living and accessible. I include Hellman's work here both because it is inspiring and significant, and because the first chapter, on Monsignor Schivo (tree number 1580), gives a very good account of life in Italy from June 1940 until July 1944. The woman whose life Schivo saved, Ursula Kovn Selig (known as Uschi), is also a remarkable person; that's her as a young girl in the photo at bottom left on the cover. I consider this wonderful book *essenziale* reading for everyone, but it comes with a warning: avoid reading it on any form of public transportation unless you don't mind others seeing your tears.

Italian Dreams, photographs by Steven Rothfeld, introduction by Franco Zeffirelli, Collins Publishers, 1995. With writings about Italy and the Italians to accompany the dreamy photographs by Rothfeld, this is a special treat to buy for yourself (but it also makes a nice gift for your favorite Italophile). The images—handmade Polaroid transfers—are not the Predictable Pictures of Italy one sees in so many other books. A beautiful package for those who appreciate beautiful things.

La Storia: Five Centuries of the Italian American Experience, Jerre Mangione and Ben Morreale, HarperCollins Publishers, 1992. I've included this title here because of the significant number of Italians who have emigrated to the U.S., and because of this line in a review of the book from *The New York Times Book Review:* "And it is a book that should be read by all Americans interested in what binds us together, despite our different backgrounds and histories." The authors focus on three historical periods, including the years 1880 to 1920, when the largest number of Italians arrived, the overwhelming majority from the *mezzogiorno.* There is and has been for a long, long time a unique Italy–America (or "La Merica," as many Italians called it) bond, which may become readily apparent to you while traveling in Italy.

La Cucina Italiana
(The Italian Kitchen)

"Flavor is what I miss whenever I leave Italy and what I seek as soon as I come back. It is a hard thing to describe; still, when something tastes the way it ought to, you recognize it instantly—authenticity always being a self-defining experience. Arugula and olive oil, cherries and figs, prosciutto di Parma *sliced into transparent sheets, then draped over a wedge of melon: such foods announce themselves quietly, with assurance; then, just as quietly, they amaze the tongue. Even the Italian flag pays homage to this principle, for what do the red, green, and white stripes represent, if not tomato, basil, and mozzarella?"*

—David Leavitt, from "Flavor,"
Italian Pleasures

Italy's Original Garlic Bread

BY S. IRENE VIRBILA

~

editor's note

True Italian "garlic bread" is perfection. The American predilection for slathering copious amounts of butter and minced garlic on poor-quality bread misses the point. *Bruschetta* (one of the most mispronounced words in America; for some reason, we want to make it French and come out with *broo-SHetta,* when in fact it is pronounced *broo-SKetta*), *fett'unta,* and *soma d'aj,* in all their variations, are most delicious and satisfying *antipasti,* and easy to make at home. Although not mentioned in this piece, *panunto* is another name for a similar *antipasto* found in Tuscany. Readers should note that the phone numbers at the restaurants and frantoio recommended may have changed, and should be confirmed with the tourist office.

S. IRENE VIRBILA, restaurant critic of the *Los Angeles Times,* writes frequently about food, wine, and travel for a number of newspapers and magazines, including the *San Francisco Chronicle, San Francisco Examiner, Saveur,* and *Departures.* Virbila won the James Beard Award for newspaper restaurant criticism in 1997, and has lived in San Francisco, Paris, northern Italy, and Los Angeles.

Wherever olive oil is produced in Italy, it's traditional to celebrate the olive harvest and the pungent new oil with a feast of bruschetta. This is the original garlic bread, made with thick slices toasted over a fire, rubbed with fresh garlic and saturated with intense green olive oil. This simple yet superb dish is known by various names all over Italy—*bruschetta, fett'unta, soma d'aj*—depending on the region.

Alfredo Mancianti, a producer of cru olive oils in Umbria, said "*bruschetta* was born in Umbria, and from there diffused first to neighboring Tuscany and Lazio, and then to other regions of Italy that produce olive oil." Until relatively recently, he explained, fuel was scarce and bread was baked just once a week in the countryside, so country people developed a repertory of dishes to use bread that was no longer fresh.

Thick vegetable soups ladled over a slice of toasted bread at the bottom of the soup bowl was one solution. Another was the toasted, thick slices of bread, vigorously rubbed with garlic.

"But the true *bruschetta*," Mr. Mancianti said, "was a little different than they make now. Instead of pouring the oil from a cruet or bottle over the toasted bread, originally, the bread was actually immersed in the oil." And it was especially good during the winter toasted over an open fire, and immersed in new oil, just as it came from the *frantoio,* or olive mill.

Each year during the olive oil season (November and December), there is a celebration at Mr. Mancianti's cold-press mill in San Feliciano, on Lake Trasimeno near Perugia. Everyone who helped with the picking—all their workers, clients and friends—are invited to a feast of *bruschetta* made with the new oil. The *bruschetta* is accompanied by the year's new young wine, scarcely out of the cask, and simple grilled food such as sausages or *spiedini de fegato,* laurel leaves and pieces of pork liver threaded on skewers.

Romans will tell you the name *bruschetta* is derived from *bruschato,* which is Roman dialect for the Italian word *bruciato:* scorched or burned. To prepare in the old way, you take a *pagnotta,* or big loaf of country-style bread (preferably baked in a wood-fired oven to give it a thick, chewy crust) and, cut it into inch-thick slices. Then you toast it in the fireplace or over charcoal. It should be a little scorched or blistered. While the bread is still hot, you rub it with a cut clove of garlic, pour the best olive oil available over it, and sprinkle it with salt.

Romans and southern Italians are also fond of a summer version called *bruschetta al pomodoro.* It's made the same way, and topped with chopped, ripe tomatoes. Sometimes the tomatoes are marinated with a little garlic and oil, or chopped fresh basil.

In Lazio, the region around Rome, the dish is eaten as an appetizer, washed down with one of the fresh white wines from the region. Often you don't even have to order it: *bruschetta* will show up on the table as part of the standard antipasto, along with sausage, *prosciutto* and olives. Pizzerias generally offer it at night with their full panoply of pizza and calzone. And this is where you might find untraditional toppings such as minced porcini or fried eggplant. The place to get Roman *bruschetta* is not in the city, but in one of the many *trattorias* on the periphery of Rome, on the road to towns like Frascati and Nemi. These are down-to-earth places with open fireplaces, where you can eat outside in warm weather or inside at long tables covered with paper. At such restaurants they bring *bruschetta* throughout the meal, which might include specialties such as pasta with tomato sauce or roast lamb with rosemary.

Without ever having tasted an authentic *bruschetta,* it may be hard to understand just how delicious such seemingly meager fare can be. *Bruschetta* has its passionate devotees, in the United States and in Italy.

The San Francisco chef Carlo Middione includes *bruschetta* in *The Cooking of Southern Italy,* published by William Morrow. Mr. Middione's favorite variation is chopped tomatoes, fresh basil, oil and vinegar. In his view, *bruschetta* is an unrecognized delicacy: "If you have good bread and good olive oil and good tomatoes, what could be simpler than this to show off the quality of those ingredients?"

In Tuscany and Lazio, it turns up all through the year as a first course or as a snack. Tuscan schoolchildren like *bruschetta* (sometimes dribbled with a little vinegar, too) at their mid-morning or afternoon break. In Tuscany, where some of Italy's most prized olive oils are produced, it's called *fett'unta,* slang for anointed or oiled slice. At the Chianti estate Badia a Coltibuono, the food writer and cooking teacher Lorenza de' Medici, who, with her husband Piero Stucchi-Prinetti, produces estate-bottled olive oil, explained how they make *fett'unta.* She starts with day-old country-style bread. "It should be sliced quite thickly, generally an inch to an inch and a half, so that when the bread is grilled it will be crusty outside, yet remain soft inside." Traditionally, the bread is grilled over the embers in the fireplace. She also said that in the Tuscan countryside bread is baked from an unsalted dough so that the bread keeps longer. She sprinkles a little coarse salt over the toasted bread, then takes a peppery, sharp green olive oil and pours it lavishly over the *bruschetta.*

That's the classic, but variations abound. When tomatoes are in season, Miss de Medici might top the *bruschetta* with a slice or two of ripe tomato—an idea borrowed from country people, she said, who rub a tomato into stale bread in order to soften it. In yet another variation, *fagioli,* stewed white beans, are heaped on top. In still another version very typical of Chianti, the toasted bread is topped with boiled *cavolo nero,* the black cabbage of the region.

While *bruschetta* is more common in central and southern Italy, where much olive oil is produced, you can find it in northern Italy as well. In Piedmont, home of white truffles and red wines from Nebbiolo grapes, Barolo and Barbaresco, the dish is known as *soma d'aj.*

The name means brushed with garlic in the local dialect, according to Luciana Vietti Currado of Cantina Vietti, a wine producer in Castiglione Falletto. Though it can be made with thick slices of bread, as in Tuscany and Lazio, in Piedmont, bread sticks, or *grissini,* are often used. These are not the typical yard-long *grissini* that arrive at your table as soon as you sit down in a restaurant, but a fatter, shorter bread stick called *rubata.*

In this case, the bread won't be sliced or toasted since the stick is already crisp. A plate with a generous pool of virgin olive oil is set out for each diner, who takes a clove of peeled garlic, dips it in the oil and rubs the bread stick with the oil-impregnated garlic.

Mrs. Currado's husband, Alfredo, explained that in Piedmont they'll even eat *soma d'aj* for breakfast. Because the farm workers leave at five or six in the morning to go to the fields, they take a loaf of bread, a flask of oil and a clove of garlic with them. At about eight, they'll break for *soma d'aj*. Out in the fields, they don't usually make a fire. They simply rub the crust of the bread with garlic, and garnish with oil and salt. And they eat it with grapes from the vineyard and drink a little Barbera.

A Sampler's Guide to Bruschetta

Country restaurants in Tuscany or Umbria might offer it as a first course, even if it's not on the menu, and an order of *bruschetta* usually costs less than $5.

Badia a Coltibuono, Gaiole in Chianti (17 miles northwest of Siena); tel. 0577.749498. The restaurant at this wine estate features *fett'unta* made with Badia's olive oil, as well as ravioli with butter and sage, *stracotto,* or beef stew with dried, wild mushrooms, white beans with a drizzle of deep green olive oil, and other Chiantigiana specialties. A good selection of Badia a Coltibuono wines is available by the glass as well as by the bottle.

Cantinetta Antinori, Palazzo Antinori, 3 Piazza degli Antinori (at the foot of Via Tornabuoni), Florence; tel. 055.29.22.34. The menu of simple Tuscan fare at this restaurant featuring Antinori wines includes *fett'unta*. In the summer one can order it topped with tomato; other specialties are *ribollita,* a kind of minestrone; *trippa Fiorentina,* tripe stewed in fresh tomato sauce, and *panzanella,* a salad of torn bread, sweet onions, tomato and cucumber, tossed with sweet basil and mint, and olive oil.

Frantoio Faliero Mancianti, San Feliciano, near Lago Trasimeno and Perugia; tel. 06.70.65. Mornings, you can visit this Umbrian olive oil mill where they'll explain (in Italian) how the *artisanal frantoio* works, and if they're not too busy, they may offer you *bruschetta* so you can taste their olive oils from specific microclimates and types of olives. Call first.

If no *bruschetta* is forthcoming, you can repair to Settimio (telephone 84.91.04), also in San Feliciano, for lunch where the proprietors will make you *bruschetta* with Mancianti oil.

Ordering Coffee Irregular

BY ALAN COWELL

ᣟ

editor's note

Visitors to Italy may be baffled by the lingo used to order coffee, but Italian visitors to the U.S. are equally baffled by the bewildering array of coffee drinks to be found at some of our nationwide coffee bars. Regardless of how one orders coffee in the States, be assured that there is no such concoction in Italy as a double-tall-decaf-skinny cappuccino dusted with cinnamon. And the beans in Italy will not be overroasted or burnt (as they most always are at fancy U.S. coffee bars), and Italians will never drink a caffè latte or cappuccino after lunch or dinner (so much dairy after a full meal is not helpful for the digestion, and frankly just doesn't complement the meal).

If, as my friend Chris W. learned, you want to order coffee black, note that there is not an equivalent in Italy to American-style brewed coffee without milk (the only coffee taken black in Italy is espresso). Both caffè lungo and caffè Americano are diluted expressos, but if you ask for an Americano, do not be surprised if you are given a package of instant coffee (usually Nescafé) and a cup of hot water. There is not an exact equivalent for iced coffee, either. It might seem logical to simply ask for coffee *freddo* (cold), but you will not receive ice in your glass (it's typically strained out). This piece, which originally appeared in the travel section of *The New York Times* on August 9, 1992, explains many more mysteries of coffee.

ALAN COWELL, formerly Rome bureau chief for *The New York Times,* is now at the newspaper's London bureau.

I f there is one question that confronts the stranger grappling with a new language in a foreign land, it is: how much is enough? Where, in other words, is the invisible linguistic threshold between hermetic isolation and communication? In Beirut, in the very earliest days of the civil war, it was regarded as the absolute, irreducible core for American correspondents to be able to master the Arabic for "Don't shoot, I am an American journalist." Over the years, in places like Beirut and Baghdad, this changed to "Don't shoot, I am *not* an American journalist." But the point was the same: how much knowledge of a complex, new language will guard against peril and pitfall?

I have been pondering this question anew in the contemplation of Italian and coffee. Coffee—*un caffè*—might sound simple enough, but its inherent linguistic risks were brought home to me when a friend recounted the following story. For weeks after her arrival in Italy to take up residence, she would go to her local bar each morning to be greeted by many smiling men as she ordered what she thought was a milky coffee and a croissant. Only after many such orders did she realize the reason for the big grins. Instead of saying "*Un cappuccino e un cornetto, per favore*"—a coffee and a croissant, please—she had been ordering "*Un cappuccino e un cornuto, per favore*"—a coffee and a cuckold, please.

The further you get away from the basic American choice (regular or decaf) the more coffee becomes a verbal challenge. France is easy enough, with a simple café getting confusing only when it's a *café complet,* or what non-French people call a Continental (i.e., small) breakfast, as opposed to an American (i.e., cholesterol-laden) breakfast. It's when you reach countries where coffee is brewed by anything other than filter or freeze-dried granule that things get tricky.

In Turkey, coffee is *kahve,* but that must then be qualified as *sekerli* (literally, sugary sweet), *sade* (sugarless, or unsweet), or *orta* (medium buzz). The same distinctions apply in any place where the coffee is brewed in a single, small pot in which coffee, sugar and water are brewed up together.

In the Arabic-speaking world, though, the differences between each Arab nation's version of Arabic provoke their own variants. What's *mazbut* to an Egyptian seeking a middling dose of sugar is *wessed* to a Syrian, though both are *orta* to the Turks, whose Ottoman forebears claim to have introduced the stuff from North Africa to the Balkans.

The same dense brew in a small cup, also known as Turkish coffee, becomes Arabic coffee in countries that remain resentful of the Ottoman Empire. That, according to Webster's, is fair enough: the Turks took their *kahve* from the Arabic *qahwah,* meaning coffee or wine, and passed it on to the Italians as caffè.

Nomenclature also creates linguistic and nationalistic minefields. Turks call their coffee plain *kahve* and thereby distinguish it from American coffee—a common regional usage for all coffee brewed by sachet or filter. During the Persian Gulf war, in anti-American Arab countries, however, it was diplomatic to ask scowling waiters for a "filter coffee" rather than an American coffee.

When the Gulf war ended, the waiters themselves returned to smiling and offering American coffee, even if what you got was Nescafé.

Greeks, predictably, tune their coffee to their perennial dispute with the Turks. My Greek phrase book translates Turkish coffee as *caffè ellenico*—Greek coffee.

It is in Italy, however, that coffee demands an entire vocabulary of its own, complete with Latin roots for those who really want to know the difference between a flaky bread roll in the shape of a crescent and a betrayed husband.

My guide through this linguistic maze is Alberto Tarquini, a highly proficient teacher of IFI (Italian for Idiots), whose skills have been honed on many foreign correspondents and who cites as his references the Zanichelli etymological dictionary and Castiglioni e Mariotti's Latin Dictionary.

The basic unit of coffee is *un caffè* (what non-Italians but no Italians call an espresso): that high-voltage jolt-in-a-thimble that is consumed on the run, if only because it costs twice as much to drink it sitting down. That is where simplicity ends.

A caffè with only half the amount of water squeezed through the espresso machine, but through the same amount of coffee grounds, becomes a *caffè ristretto,* from the verb *restringere,* to squeeze or tighten, as in such Anglicisms of its Indo-European origins as the nautical term straits, or the disciplinary notion, strict.

A caffè with double the water of an ordinary caffè is a *caffè lungo*—a long coffee—that is, one that fills three-quarters of the thimble—instead of a third, which is what you get with an espresso. This is not to be confused with a *caffè doppio*—a double espresso with twice the amounts of water and coffee grounds.

Add a drop of milk to a regular caffè, however, and it becomes a *caffè macchiato*—a stained coffee, from the same Latin root, *macula,* as in the English word *immaculate.*

Milk, however, adds not only stains but also enormous linguistic complexities. The origin of cappuccino, the dictionaries say, was that its hue resembled the color of a Capuchin friar's habit, the friar himself having taken his order's title from the cappuccio, or hood, he wore, derived from the Latin *caput,* meaning head. So far so good. But there are subdivisions of the same coffee.

If you thought a cappuccino by definition was hooded with milky foam, it does not need to be so constructed. A cappuccino *senza schiuma* is literally a cappuccino without foam. Even the color of the venerable friar's habit is not sacrosanct, because you can also order a cappuccino *chiaro*—a light-colored cappuccino with less coffee and more milk—or a cappuccino *scuro*—a darker brew with more coffee and less milk, whose title, appropriately at this stage, has a lot in common with the English word obscure, going back to the Latin *obscurus.*

All that is without going into caffè *e latte*—a milky coffee with more milk than any cappuccino and certainly no froth—or a *latte macchiato,* a lot of milk with a stain of coffee. And if you should choose to drink your coffee from a small glass instead of a thimble-size cup, and with or without milk, it becomes a *caffè al vetro,* from the same root as brought us vitreous china.

At this stage, there is probably only one desperate solution—a *caffè corretto,* usually a normal caffè with a generous lacing of grappa or any other liquor of your choice. *Corretto* is from the verb *correggere,* meaning to correct in the sense of eliminating error and thereby improving things, as some people think *grappa* does, at least until the following morning.

Shaping Up the Pasta

BY RAFFAELA PRANDI

~

editor's note

....

Regardless of what shape it is, the best way to taste-test pasta is to cook it *al dente* and eat it adorned with only a little olive oil or butter and perhaps a grating of *Parmigiano-Reggiano*. You might be surprised to discover how much flavor there is in good pasta (and how little flavor there is in inferior pasta).

Pasta comes in almost as many shapes as humans do: long, short, grooved, smooth, round, square. Everyone has a favorite, and Italians get worked up about the correct sauce, size, and cooking time for a bucatino or a fusillo, a subject which often arouses hometown chauvinism. Each village on the peninsula has its own recipes for sauces based on local, seasonal ingredients. The infinite variety of enticing pasta forms came from the imagination of creative artisans. Today, with everything available in such profusion, the pairing of sauce and pasta is a question of personal pride tempered by iron-clad tradition. No one in Italy, for example, would dream of putting clam sauce on rigatoni or Bolognese meat sauce on spaghetti.

Montoni, one of the oldest manufacturers of *trafile,* the dies that determine the form of the pasta, is located in Pistoia in northern Tuscany. Forty superspecialized workers oversee a high-tech product that depends on millimeters, maniacal detail, and the world's ever-growing admiration for the Italian national dish. The firm provides 80 percent of the dies used by Barilla, one of the most important pasta manufacturers in the country, and sends *trafile* all over the world.

But what are these *trafile* and why do they matter? Instead of pasta, think about meat. Picture a meat grinder and the little interchangeable perforated disks (related to those in a food mill) from which long strands of chopped meat emerge. This is a *trafila* in its simplest form. Imagine that in each small hole you fit an insert with an opening—curvy, grooved, rectangular, star-shaped—the designs of these are myriad. This insert bestows its design on the pasta.

The first *trafile* in bronze were handmade at the end of the nineteenth century. They were applied to presses like those used for wine. A dough of flour and water went into the press and was forced out of the shaped openings of the *trafile*. A rotating blade cut the forms to the desired length. These bronze *trafile* permitted the manufacture of long pasta. Today the *trafile* are made of bronze, stainless steel, or a combination of bronze and aluminum. The inserts can be of bronze or Teflon. Teflon inserts are gentler on the dough than bronze. The bronze inserts create more friction and therefore the machines must go more slowly. Teflon permits higher speeds, and the machines produce more pasta. Teflon has other advantages: it is more easily cleaned and the pasta emerges shiny, smooth, yellow, almost glassy, with the familiar appearance of commercial pasta. There are advantages to bronze: the pasta it produces is opaque and rough, the look of prewar pasta. Roughness is a much sought after virtue since it helps the pasta absorb the sauce and its flavor. There are many Italian firms that opt for bronze, sacrificing quantity in order to satisfy a growing nostalgia, a longing for the past. Marketing does what it has to do, and takes advantage of the consumer's mood.

It's become the job of the *trafile* to evoke the pasta of yesteryear although ingredients and technology have changed. The grain produced in Italy's best durum wheat districts, Puglia and Sicily, has been modified over the decades and contains less gluten than it once did. Pasta used to be dried much more slowly. Originally, it was hung outdoors, like laundry. In the interests of efficiency, drying time for commercial pasta has been reduced since the beginning of the century from thirty-six hours to one. Manufacturers translate into technology, formula and design whatever the consumer demands. One reason so many different shapes are on the supermarket shelves is to amuse the consumer with architecture for the mouth. If the Americans want pasta that reproduces Homer Simpson and family, *trafile* designers will find a way to make that possible. If the English want Goofy and Mickey Mouse, the computer sends orders to the die cutting machines. Loris Zanon deals with Montoni's foreign orders. His fax machine spits out bizarre requests that must ultimately be transformed into entertaining mouthfuls, many destined for children who want to eat what they've seen on TV. Eighty percent of these novelty formats, such as parachutes, flying saucers, and sombreros, are destined for consumption outside Italy. Cowboys and Indians, Ninja Turtles, and even Saint Valentine's Day hearts are translated into pasta for those who don't love the food itself. The English want words and slogans. Mexico is always seeking novelty shapes for soup. Italians favor the traditional: spaghetti, fusilli, penne.

Many countries, including Japan, have studied the possibility of manufacturing their own Italian-style pasta, but have finally given it up. The product may require only water and flour, but getting it right is harder than it looks. For example, the shape of a *trafila* cannot be calculated theoretically. Even though the design is computerized, it is the manual labor of a few workers that is ultimately decisive. To make this clearer, think again about the meat grinder and the disks that are inserted to determine the texture of the meat. An insert that shapes the pasta is placed in each hole. Montoni has 2,000 of these forms, designed first by computer, then manufactured. Tiny die cutters do the job, but the *trafile* are each finished by hand. Once the inserts are mounted in the holes (the rectangular *trafile* for making long pasta can have from eight to twelve thousand openings) infinitesimal defects are visible to the naked eye of the expert. The slightest imperfection means that the pasta emerges with variations and irregularities in thickness, causing annoying inconsistencies in texture when cooked. The construction of the *trafila* can also affect the appearance, color, cooking time, and consistency of pasta. This is why workers touch up each hole, filing down, enlarging, smoothing. Yet another reason for regarding each forkful of pasta with respect.

This article originally appeared in *Gambero Rosso* #7, 1996. Reprinted by permission.

Tuscan Olive Oils

BY FAITH HELLER WILLINGER

∾

editor's note

Nearly a third of the world's olive oil is produced and consumed in Italy (Spain is the next biggest producer, followed by Greece). Olive oil differs, of course, throughout Italy, and each one pairs perfectly with each region's local specialties. Extra-virgin Tuscan oils, for example, tend to be green and peppery, which complement traditional Tuscan dishes. Umbria is equally endowed with olive trees, and its oil is bold and assertive, which pairs especially well with one of its local delicacies, truffles. Perhaps surprisingly, some elements of producing high-quality olive oil in Italy haven't changed much in centuries. Chemicals aren't used in the processing, and olives are still picked by hand.

There are dozens of Tuscan and Umbrian oils that never leave the region. Just one that I've read about is from *Il Picciolo,* near Siena, and is produced by an American named Ruth McVey. According to an article in *Saveur* No. 8, McVey's harvest doesn't produce more than about 800 liters in a good year, too little to export. She was quoted in the article as saying, "Olive oil for me isn't about making money. It's about quality, and whether that still matters anymore," a statement that could have been made by any number of Tuscans who believe, as I do, that quality does indeed still matter. (Interested visitors might be happy to know that *Il Picciolo* oil may be purchased at the estate, and McVey also rents an apartment in the villa. Phone / fax: 0577.824057). Burton Anderson, in his wonderful book *Treasures of the Italian Table,* notes that making extra-virgin olive oil is so labor intensive that "even the most expensive oils are in a sense under-priced." Quality oils like these are an obvious choice to bring back home—for gifts, but also for yourself.

It's my observation that American cooks are often disappointed when they attempt to re-create a dish they enjoyed in central Italy, not only because they don't use good-quality olive oil, but because they don't use *enough* of it. It doesn't take much to give a dish a certain flavor that makes it unmistakably Italian, and that flavor usually comes from olive oil.

FAITH HELLER WILLINGER is a contributing editor of *Gourmet* and is the author of *Red, White & Greens: The Italian Way with Vegetables* (HarperCollins Publishers, 1996) and *Eating in Italy: A Traveler's Guide to the Hidden Gastronomic Pleasures of Northern Italy* (William Morrow, 1998). Her new book, *Ingredienti,* a handbook with recipes focusing on about thirty key ingredients in Italian cooking and what to do with them when you are fortunate enough to get them, will be published next year by HarperCollins.

I grew up thinking that olive oil—transparent, yellowish, and labeled "pure"—was used only by sophisticated Americans in salad dressings, by Europeans in cooking. Then I moved to Italy and met and married a Florentine who brainwashed me about superior Tuscan oil—green, cloudy, peppery, and tasting of olives. My husband informed me that butter, too sweet and too fatty, was for unevolved palates. I learned that first-rate extra-virgin olive oil is the reason food tastes so terrific in Tuscany, adding a lusty vegetal flavor to everything it encounters. Listening to locals, I noticed that no one bothered to say *"extra-vergine"* or even *"oliva,"* just *"olio nuovo"* (when the oil is first pressed and at its most piquant), then *"olio"* (after a month or two, when flavors calm down). I began to try oils from all over Tuscany, each with its own complex taste, and was hooked. I attended *degustazioni* (learning how to "schlurp" alongside the professionals) and went to nurseries, groves, mills, and seminars, meeting professors and producers. The olive oil story is complicated—almost as complicated as the process of making a great oil.

In a good year only 5 to 7 percent of the olive oil consumed in Italy is produced in Tuscany, which amounts to around 20 million liters (think of a liquid liter as roughly a quart), most of it extra-virgin but not all *super-Tuscan*—my term for top quality—extra-virgin. Local demand for quality oil exceeds the supply, and so the quantity of great estate oil that is exported amounts to a drop in the bucket compared to Tuscany's total yield.

Super-Tuscan extra-virgins are the Maseratis of lipids. Ordinary extra-virgin olive oil is defined by law as having no serious defects and an acidity of less than 1 percent. What I call super-Tuscan extra-virgins are more virtuous, with acidity of less than 0.5 percent and bigger, spicier flavors. In the marketplace, producers of small-quantity, high-quality oils compete against industrial giants who bottle extra-virgins and what used to be labeled "pure" from elsewhere (Spain, North Africa, Greece, or southern Italy); political attempts to define the best zones of Tuscan olive-oil production have met with little success due to the financial clout of the industrial bottlers.

Many factors contribute to the production of a super-Tuscan extra-virgin olive oil, and any one of a minefield of disasters—from the dreaded oil fly to freezing weather—can destroy an entire year's efforts or, worse, the trees themselves. (Every twenty-five to thirty years, freezes kill Tuscany's olive trees; in 1985, 17 million of 22 million were leveled.) Each grower deals with the risks as well as the unique circumstances of olive variety, soil, and climate, producing an oil that expresses a particular *terroir*—a term usually applied to wine, meaning a combination of soil and site—and possesses its own particular taste.

Over a hundred different olive varieties thrive in Italy's central, southern, and coastal regions, but the Tuscan hills are dominated by *frantoio, moraiolo, leccino, pendolino,* and *coreggiolo.* With the approach of winter about mid-November, these olives—ranging in color from just-beginning-to-ripen green to purply-black—are harvested, destined to become fruity oils with zesty flavors and low acidity (the latter a protection against rancidity). An olive oil made only of ripe olives may have a more delicate flavor and a higher yield, but it also has higher acidity and, besides, only regions with temperate climates can wait long enough for all their olives to ripen. The danger of frost in the Tuscan hills dictates an earlier harvest.

At harvesttime, pickers on ladders strip the branches of their fruit with hand-held rakes so that the olives fall into nets spread under the trees. Each tree yields enough olives for one to three liters of oil. The olives are then hurried to the mill, or *frantoio,* to be stored in well-aerated crates—not sacks, in which fermentation could occur, ruining the oil before it's made—and pressed within a day or two. For anyone curious to see the oil-making process close up, mills are open at least sixteen hours a day during the November–December pressing season, but appointments are essential (see "Milling Around").

All the mills I visited begin by washing the olives and removing the leaves. Typically they crush around 600 pounds of olives at a time with *molazze,* or rolling granite wheels, in a large granite tub for thirty to forty-five minutes, then knead the resulting pulp for up to an hour and a half.

Three main techniques are used to extract oil from this pulp, each method having its adherents. Outside Castelnuovo Berar-denga, east of Siena, the mill at San Felice, which presses for Castello di Ama, still follows traditional practice. First an inch of olive pulp is piped onto circular woven mats interspersed with metal plates for reinforcement. Stacked on a spindle, the mats are then pressed, yielding a brownish mixture of oil and vegetable water, called *mosto*, which is lightly centrifuged to separate them.

The mill at Tenuta di Capezzana, twenty-four kilometers west of Florence, uses what is known as the continuous method of extraction: Traditional granite wheels still do the crushing, but the pulp is then passed directly into a horizontal centrifuge that separates the oil and the residual water from the *sansa* of leftover solids. The mats of the old method are bypassed entirely. At some mills—but rarely artisanal operations—stainless-steel hammers or rollers do the crushing, but they can heat the paste, and heat is the great enemy of an excellent olive oil. Any procedure that warms the pulp will diminish the flavor; this is the reason first-rate oils are always "cold-pressed." At Capezzana, flavor is additionally protected by the estate's practice of filling its centrifuge with only half the amount of pulp allowed by law at a single time and *no* yield-boosting hot water.

Super-Tuscan expert Maurizio Castelli works at the mill of Castello di Volpaia, south of Florence in Radda in Chianti, employing the new extraction technique known as *sinolea*. The equipment is expensive and therefore not widely used, but it is said that this method produces the finest oil. Why? Because no pressure is applied to the fruit. Instead, thousands of stainless-steel blades are plunged into the olive pulp, and the oil that adheres to them is then scraped off with a kind of rubber comb.

As much as 80 percent of the olive's oil is collected off the blades alone; then the paste that's left is centrifuged to extract the remaining oil. The bright green centrifuged oil has desirably low acidity but is not as fine as the first extraction; some producers blend the two, some allocate the centrifuged oil for cooking. The pulp residue is sold to large-scale industrial producers, who add solvents to it to extract the last of the oil, which is so unpalatable that it must be deodorized and deacidified. This final extract, virtually stripped of all flavor and color, is then mixed with a small amount of extra-virgin oil to put back some taste and create what is called olive pomace oil—a product of no worth whatsoever to any serious cook.

Whichever oil-extraction technique is favored at a given *frantoio,* cleanliness in the mill is of the utmost importance. Traditional mills such as the one at San Felice must press constantly because their oil-impregnated mats acidify with prolonged air contact. Defective olives—overripe or damaged by disease or hail—are another danger: They not only make poor oil but can also contaminate succeeding oils when machines or mats are not carefully washed.

Before bottling, the oil is stored in a cool, dark room, as exposure to light (which provokes oxidation) can be as damaging to oil as heat. Traditionally the storage receptacles of choice have been large terra-cotta urns called *orci,* although nowadays many producers prefer stainless-steel tanks. Most oil is filtered prior to bottling to remove any sediment that might harm the oil as it ages.

What I like to call home care for a fine oil is another, often overlooked consideration. Just as a cool, dark environment is key before bottling, so too is it important at home. Do not keep your prized Tuscan oil in a cupboard above the stove in the kitchen! Super-Tuscans are capable of lasting for two years or more if stored correctly—as you would a fine wine; that is, in a cellar or closet, not the refrigerator—although they taste best within a year of production.

Tasting all the subtleties of an olive oil isn't easy. Professional tasters take their oil neat, without distractions. They begin with a spoonful and, like a wine taster, a few noisy schlurps, a motion that aerates the oil while coating the taste buds on the back of the tongue and palate. Harmonious fruity aromas and flavors, green color, and density are the qualities desired in a super-Tuscan extra-virgin oil. Tasters look especially for such merits as freshness, spiciness, and balance; such flavors as artichoke, almond, apple, or freshly cut grass. Serious defects in an oil include persistent bitterness, excess fattiness, yellow-to-orange color (which denotes rancidity), and flavors of ripe melon, tropical fruit, metal, or mud.

Each year's release of super-Tuscan *olio nuovo,* or just-pressed oil, is a cause for rejoicing in Tuscany. Served uncooked as a condiment to enhance the appreciation of its unique properties, this "new oil" is almost luminescent, green with chlorophyll, peppery and aggressive, with some slightly bitter overtones. After a few months the flavors soften and the oil becomes, simply, "*olio,*" ready for cooking, including deep-frying, and continued use as a condiment.

The best super-Tuscan extra-virgins come from the hills in the province of Florence, extending to the Chianti Classico, Montalbano, Rufina, Pratomagno, and Arezzo-Cortona zones. Dedicated high-quality producers exist elsewhere, but they're in the minority. Industrial bottlers in Lucca have attained a position of prominence in the marketplace, but it's not easy to find fine artisanal oils from the area. Look for super-Tuscans made by Capezzana, in the Montalbano region; Castello di Ama, Castello di Volpaia, Jiachi, Podere Le Boncie, and Castellare in the Chianti Classico zone; Selvapiana from Rufina; I Bonsi and Frantoio di Santa Tea from Pratomagno; Grattamacco, from the hills near the coast between Livorno and Grosetto; and Tenuta di Valgiano, in the hills above Lucca; Grappolini from the Arezzo-Cortona district; and Castello Banfi and Col d'Orcia from Montalcino.

Tuscany's regional government hasn't been able to agree about where to draw the lines for the official zones of quality olive oil, but eventually a DOC status (a controlled appellation of origin designation, as is now applied to wine) will probably cover all of Tuscany without distinguishing the best areas. For now, the only guarantee of quality on the label is the phrase "*prodotto e imbottigliato*" (produced and bottled), which means that the oil comes from an estate's own olives. (Equivalent phrases are "*imbottigliato all'origine*" and "*prodotto e confezionato.*") The word "*prodotto*" or "*imbottigliato*" alone offers no guarantee of origin; it means only that the oil was bottled at an estate—any estate anywhere. Super-Tuscans will proudly display their year of harvest on the label.

The finest olive oils are never inexpensive. Bulk oil in Tuscany sells for around $10 a liter. Add to that the cost of bottling, shipping, and profits for producer, importer, distributor, and retailer—and the purchase price of a super-Tuscan can rise to at least $25 for a 0.75-liter bottle. A difficult harvest can mean higher prices still. If used sparingly, a bottle of excellent oil can last for weeks, a shortcut to enhancing many foods. Cheap oil is never a bargain, ruining everything it comes into contact with.

Note: Top-quality Tuscan extra-virgin olive oils can be purchased in New York City at Dean & DeLuca, tel. 800-221-7714 or 212-431-1691; Balducci's, tel. 800-BALDUCCI or 212-673-2600; and Agata & Valentina, tel. 212-452-0690, as well as Zingerman's in Ann Arbor, Michigan, tel. 313-769-1625; and Pasta Shop (in Rockridge Market Hall) in Oakland, California, tel. 510-547-4005. Many of these stores also offer mail-order services.

Milling Around

Readers who would like to stop by a working *frantoio* on their next visit to Italy—and possibly purchase oil at the source—are welcome at the following mills, though it is essential to be in contact a few weeks in advance to request an appointment. Accompanying the list of mills are suggestions of nearby hotels and restaurants for travelers who want to linger in the countryside rather than merely pass through.

Frantoio di Castello di Volpaia

Località Volpaia, 53017 Radda in Chianti (SI); tel. 0577.738.066; fax 0577.738.619.

Hotel Vescine, Il Relais del Chianti, Route 429.

Vescine, 53017 Radda in Chianti (SI); tel. 0577.741.144; fax 0577.740.263.

Il Vescovino, Via Ciamiolo da Panzano, 9, 50020 Panzano (SI); tel. 055.852.464.

Traditional dishes and innovative cooking share space on the menu at Il Vescovino, but super-Tuscan extra-virgin oils are an integral part of almost everything. The wine list is stellar and well-priced, inviting diners to drink big as they settle in on the terrace overlooking the countryside of olive trees, vineyards, villas, and farmhouses.

Frantoio di San Felice, San Gusme, Località San Felice, 53019 Castelnuovo Berardenga (SI), tel. 0577.359.087; fax: 0577.359.223.

Relais Borgo San Felice, Castelnuovo Berardenga, Località San Felice; tel. 0577.359.260; fax: 0577.359.089.

Comfortable, rustic gentrification is the style of this Relais & Châteaux hotel and its restaurant, Poggio Rosso. Some dishes are quite elaborate, while others remain simple, and all are beautifully prepared and presented. Atypically for Tuscany, desserts receive much attention here.

Frantoio della Tenuta di Capezzana, Via di Capezzana, 100, 50042 Carmignano (PO); tel. 055.870.6005; fax: 055.870.6673.

Hotel Paggeria Medicea, Viale Papa Giovanni XXIII, 3, 50040 Artimino (PO); tel. 055.871.8081; fax: 055.871.8080.

Da Delfina, Via della Chiesa, 1, 50400 Artimino (PO); tel. 055.871.8074.

In the 1940s and 1950s Delfina was the cook at the nearby hunting lodge of the Artimino Medici villa. Her son, Carlo Cioni, has moved her now-legendary reputation and recipes to his restaurant on the confines of the village, where his passion for the best local ingredients—wild greens, herbs, mushrooms in season—gets full play. His super-Tuscan oil (from the Montalbano area) is, however, used parsimoniously: "I serve peasant food, and oil has always been precious to people who live and work in the country," Carlo explains. His version of ribollita is the best I've ever encountered, the *ghirighio* (an unsweetened chestnut-flour tart) is worth the voyage, and the wine selection is wonderful.

The Noble Wine
of Montepulciano

BY GERALD ASHER

~

editor's note

Frank Prial, wine columnist for *The New York Times,* has written that Gerald Asher is "one of the few writers on wine whose timely pieces are a delight to read long after they first appeared." Asher has been writing about wine for *Gourmet,* where this piece initially appeared in December 1991, for many years. I am particularly fond of his writing on wine because he takes readers off on various tangents but always returns to some simple, elemental point about wine, and about life.

GERALD ASHER is also the author of *On Wine* (Random House, 1986) and *Vineyard Tales* (Chronicle Books, 1996). He has contributed to several

UK publications, including *Decanter, The Sunday Times,* and *Punch,* and for some years wrote a monthly *Letter From America* column for *Wines and Spirits.* Among the numerous honors he's received are the 1998 James Beard Award for articles on wines and spirits, and the *Merite Agricole,* an award rarely given to foreigners, with which he was decorated in 1974. Additionally, Asher received the Barbi Colombini international award for wine journalism for his "Brunello: Pride of Montalcino," which appeared in the March 1996 issue of *Gourmet.*

Paola de Ferrari's father, Egidio Corradi, was born in Cervognano, a Tuscan village tucked into hills that start at the very walls of Montepulciano, southeast of Siena, and descend in a great rolling spread to the floor of the Valdichiana, many hundred feet below. The upper reaches of the slopes are covered with a patchwork of olive groves, wheat fields, and vineyards—the customary Mediterranean trinity of oil, bread, and wine—stitched together by seams of tall cypresses that shade the cart tracks leading to farmhouses hidden from the unpaved roads. Both tracks and roads are banked, in spring and summer, by a profusion of yellow broom and sweet-smelling acacia blossoms. By autumn the vines are mottled with russet and brown, the wheat fields are no more than a dusty stubble, and a pungent aroma of fermenting grapes drifts among the trees.

From his home in Genoa, Egidio Corradi used to go back to Cervognano every year to buy a supply of the local wine, tasting his way from vat to vat and from cellar to cellar to find the right Vino Nobile di Montepulciano. "His enthusiasm for Vino Nobile was really a symptom of his nostalgia for Cervognano itself," says Signora de Ferrari. "Every year he used to complain that the wine was no longer as he remembered it.

"But a wine from Cervognano, even when it was not as good as he thought it could be, was still, in his opinion, the best Vino Nobile, better than the wine from the other villages around Montepulciano. He said it had always been that way. Eventually, to be near the village, he bought two small adjoining farms and combined them to make what is now our Boscarelli property."

Paola de Ferrari and her late husband, Ippolito, inherited Boscarelli. "We restored one of the farmhouses—it was in ruin—and then, starting in 1964, we put in two or three acres of vines. We planted them in rows, as a true vineyard should be, not mixed with fruit trees. We intended to grow just enough grapes to make some good wine for ourselves and our friends.

"But then, almost in spite of ourselves, we gradually expanded the vineyard, selling the grapes we didn't need. Some new vats and barrels increased our capacity, and one thing led to another. In the seventies we decided to keep all our grapes, and by the mid-eighties we were producing wine on a commercial scale—2,000 to 3,000 cases a year. We now have thirty acres of vines and are producing about 5,000 cases of wine a year, half of it Chianti Colli Senesi and half Vino Nobile di Montepulciano."

What Signora de Ferrari didn't, and probably wouldn't, say was that their Vino Nobile had been so lavishly praised by the Italian press that for a time there was a trough of mutual embarrassment between the De Ferraris, as beginners, and neighbors who had been making wine for generations, even centuries, with little public acknowledgment. The family kept a low profile locally—though invited, the De Ferraris did not even join Montepulciano's *consorzio* of growers—and looked for markets away from Tuscany to avoid possible comparison and confrontation. For a time, more than two thirds of Boscarelli's tiny production was being shipped out of Italy, mostly to the United States and to Germany. The rest went south to Rome or north to Genoa and Milan.

"Neither my husband nor I had had any training for what we were doing," Paola de Ferrari says. "But we managed, and Boscarelli became a passion for us and for our two sons. It so took over our lives that, contrary to what we had intended, we were eventually spending our workweeks in Tuscany and weekends at our home in Genoa just to be away from the constant demands of the vineyard."

Vino Nobile di Montepulciano is essentially a variant of Chianti. The vineyards that produce it lie within both the commune of Montepulciano and the limits of Chianti Colli Senesi (Chianti of the Hills of Siena), one of the eight zones that make up the Chianti region of Tuscany. Montepulciano has long enjoyed a high reputation for its wine. Many of its well-worn endorsements by popes, poets, and physicians in centuries past might have been prompted by politics or local chauvinism as much as judgment, but that can hardly be said of Thomas Jefferson, who claimed, in 1804, that no wine pleased him more. In a letter of January 14, 1816, to his wine agent in Genoa, Thomas Appleton, Jefferson referred to it as "a very favorite wine"; and the following year, advising the newly elected James Monroe on wines with which to stock the White House cellar, he urged the purchase of Montepulciano. He passed along Appleton's name and said, "I have imported it through him annually ten or twelve years."

It was not until 1932 that a government commission appointed to establish boundaries for Italy's tangled Chianti region recognized the special southeast exposure of Montepulciano's vineyards and confirmed the use of its name as an appellation for wine produced in them. At the time, concepts of legally defined appellations of origin were still hazy, and it was not until 1942 that a *consorzio* of Montepulciano growers was given the formal responsibility of monitoring their wines' geographic authenticity. Another twenty-five years (and World War II) went by before Italy had a body of law establishing *denominazioni di origine controllata*—often referred to as DOCs—for its wines. Vino Nobile di Montepulciano and

Chianti were among the first to be defined and regulated under decrees issued in 1966 and 1967, respectively.

The first regulations—they have since been twice modified—made clear how closely the two appellations were related. Both wines were to be made principally from Sangiovese (called Prugnolo Gentile in Montepulciano, where it exists as a clone specific to the area), the variety that emerged triumphant in Tuscany as part of the nineteenth century's quest for red wines of deep color and solid construction. Canaiolo Nero, the grape that once dominated the region, took a lesser, supportive role, lending suppleness to Sangiovese's tannic rigidity and extending the narrow limits of its aroma and flavor.

A few growers have clung to what has survived of other local black-grape varieties as well. Mammolo, one of the most persistent of these survivors, brings a particularly appealing fragrance to a wine. (The Italian word *mammola,* obviously related, means "violet.") Though the regulations make no specific reference to Mammolo, it can be used in both Chianti and Vino Nobile di Montepulciano as part of a tolerated percentage of "other," optional grape varieties. In addition, a long tradition of mixing a proportion of white grapes with the black to give these wines a silky finish was at first underscored by a regulatory obligation, but at Montepulciano, at least, the practice is now left to each grower's discretion.

The origin of the expression Vino Nobile remains obscure. Some suggest that it came into use as an honorific to distinguish wines from vineyards—usually with the best exposures—owned by the town's patrician families. Others say it was intended to indicate wines of high quality, those good enough for a nobleman's table.

Curiously the many early published references to Montepulciano wine never included the words Vino Nobile. But a passage from Alexander Hamilton's *History of Ancient and Modern Wines* (1824) might shed light on how and why the term came to be used in the nineteenth century:

> In the description of Tuscan wines, much confusion has arisen from not attending to their different qualities. As the press is [used lightly] and the grapes have, in general . . . dried for six or seven weeks within doors before they are trodden, the first juice . . . necessarily abounds in saccharine matter, and the wine procured from it will consequently belong to the sweet class. But when this is drawn off, it is customary to add a quantity of water to the murk, which, after a short fermentation, yields a very tolerable wine. . . . In this way, a great proportion of the ordinary wines of the country are made; but all the choicest growths . . . are more or less sweet. When a late traveller, therefore, describes the Montepulciano wine as the most esteemed in the Tuscan states, and at the same time compares it to "a weak claret, with little flavour," it is evident that he cannot be speaking of that "manna of Montepulciano, which gladdens the heart" . . . but must mean the common wine of the place.

Montepulciano was also celebrated at the time for a sweet red wine made from Aleatico grapes partially dried before crushing. If Alexander Hamilton was referring to that wine— his emphasis on sweetness suggests this—then it is more than likely that the term Vino Nobile evolved to distinguish its first pressing described by Hamilton, quoting an earlier, Italian author, as the "manna of Montepulciano." Aleatico has disappeared from many areas, including Montepulciano. It was probably more than coincidence that the term Vino Nobile disappeared from Montepulciano along with Aleatico late in the nineteenth century.

The term reappeared in 1933 when Adamo Fanetti, owner of the Sant'Agnese estate at Montepulciano, emblazoned the words "Vino Nobile di Montepulciano" on the labels of his best red wines—the timing possibly a consequence of the 1932 Chianti commission's recommendation with regard to use of the Montepulciano appellation. Fanetti's wines were made from the usual Chianti varieties, not from Aleatico, but he could easily have persuaded himself that, if any wines were entitled to be so described, they had to be those he had just exhibited to great acclaim at a wine fair in Siena. (His pride was probably justified: One of those Fanetti wines went on to take a gold medal in Paris in 1937.) Where Fanetti led, others followed. By the time the DOC regulations were issued, in 1966, Vino Nobile di Montepulciano had already become its accepted name.

The presidential decree establishing the Montepulciano *denominazione* did not, however, usher in an era of glory. If the wines of two or three notable producers are excepted, Vino Nobile di Montepulciano in the sixties and seventies hardly lived up to its grandiose name. All the more reason, then, for general astonishment when, in 1980, the Ministry of Agriculture declared Vino Nobile di Montepulciano raised to the status of a *denominazione di origine controllata e garantita* (DOCG), a new category of appellation introduced that year for Italian wines of the highest quality and prestige, an honor that Vino Nobile di Montepulciano was to share with only Barolo, Barbaresco, and Brunello di Montalcino, three of Italy's most distinguished wines. In the ensuing uproar, the ministry defended its action with references to the antiquity of Vino Nobile di Montepulciano, ignoring, perhaps even ignorant of, Vino Nobile's uncertain genealogy. The Italian wine community was less concerned with viticultural history than with the generally poor quality of most Vino Nobile di Montepulciano, which could attract ridicule and compromise the entire DOCG program. While some improvement had begun at Montepulciano by 1980, there was little yet to show for it. To many the ministry's move seemed at best premature.

Fortunately, Montepulciano's growers grabbed their chance. Inspired by neighbors who had been making good and even excellent wine for years—the De Ferraris and the Contuccis eminent among them—and encouraged by the very new and very glossy success of the Falvo brothers at Avignonesi, they took to their vats.

"The competitiveness among us, the obsessive drive to be best, became nothing less than a shared neurosis," Fernando Cattani of La Calonica said when I visited his estate recently. Neurotic or not, the results soon defused all opposition; each producer not only changed gear—restricting yields in favor of quality, using fruit from only the best sites for Vino Nobile, and allowing the parallel production of Chianti Colli Senesi to absorb the rest—but developed, over the course of the eighties, an individual style largely based on a manipulation of varietal options. In arriving at these separate interpretations of the wine, the growers were prompted not only by differences of temperament but also by what they perceived as the dictates of the variable terrain within the communal boundaries of Montepulciano.

Many growers have chosen to exclude all white grapes from their blends, for example, while others exercise their right to include a small percentage of them. Some use more and some less Canaiolo Nero, as allowed by upper and lower limits set by statute; some do and some don't include a modest proportion of Mammolo. And a few are experimenting with vats made of French oak rather than the milder Slovenian oak traditional to the region.

As a result, each producer's wine is distinct and, on acquaintance, easily recognized. Avignonesi's Vino Nobile, for instance, is particularly lean, even austere, compared to others. Ettore, Leonardo, and Alberto Falvo assumed management of the Avignonesi estate—one of the oldest of Montepulciano—when Ettore Falvo married Adriana Avignonesi. Educated as a classicist, Ettore Falvo claims, tongue only slightly in cheek, to have acquired his knowledge of winemaking from Columella's *Rei Rusticae,* a Latin treatise on agriculture written in the first century. Clearly, he has also been influenced by the new school of Chianti producers who have boosted Sangiovese, thrown out white grapes, and toyed with both Cabernet Sauvignon and French oak barrels. And he seems to have been inspired, too, by Angelo Gaia of Piemonte, an intensely twentieth-century grower whose international reputation for a purity of style sets his wines apart. Ettore Falvo dramatizes the structure of his Vino Nobile by using 80 percent Sangiovese (Prugnolo Gentile), the maximum allowed by law, giving it an etched precision by excluding white grapes from the blend. He reinforces both body and color by aging the wine in a battery of vats of new oak—both French and Slovenian—recently installed on Avignonesi's new property, Le Cappezzine.

Since the Falvo brothers took control of Avignonesi they have emphasized its name rather than the Vino Nobile di Montepulciano appellation, extending the estate's range of wines to include blends with some regional associations (Grifi, for example, is half Sangiovese and half Cabernet Sauvignon) as well as others, like varietal Pinot Noir, Merlot, and barrel-fermented Chardonnay, with none. Matured in French oak barrels (Ettore Falvo goes to France each year to choose the wood personally), these varietal wines are impeccably made to international standards and tastes and are clearly intended to help Avignonesi penetrate the *beau monde* of wine beyond Italy's borders. They are distinguished and follow successfully Gaia's example of stylistic clarity. Nevertheless, perhaps because they are *too* carefully made, they miss some inner warmth. They are, as writer Norman Douglas once said of Tuscan speech, emphatic rather than profound.

Avignonesi's performance has been monitored by others. Both Antinori—whose technical director, Giacomo Tachis, has been Avignonesi's chief winemaking consultant—and Ruffino, two major Chianti producers, recently acquired vineyards within the production zone of Vino Nobile di Montepulciano. The Italian insurance company SAI bought the extensive Fattoria del Cerro in 1978; and the Swiss, early admirers of the improved Montepulciano who presently buy seventy-five percent of the appellation's Vino Nobile, have begun to acquire estates there.

SAI's new winery at Fattoria del Cerro, purpose-built in 1986, is a modern, no-nonsense structure; but if Avignonesi's wines can be boldly angular, Frattoria del Cerro's are always round, even floridly rococo at times, with their bouquet of dried fruits and lively flavors long and deep enough to recall many a summer past.

Poliziano's wines, too, are richly flavored, but they are also fleshier, more powerful, lordly—qualities that give them a *grandezza* altogether appropriate for a Vino Nobile, one might think. "I'm not trying to make impressive wines," counters volubly articulate owner and winemaker Federico Carletti. "I just want them to be enjoyable." They are both, and are easily the most broadly appreciated of the appellation. When someone familiar with Vino Nobile di Montepulciano is asked to name three favorite producers, Poliziano is invariably one of them.

Carletti's consulting enologist is Maurizio Castelli, the man responsible for some of the most impressive transformations in Chianti Classico during the last fifteen years. Together they make limited quantities of two single-vineyard wines with the Vino Nobile *denominazione* as well as ten thousand cases annually of the principal *cuvée*.

La Calonica's wines are different again. They are particularly scented—doubtless because Fernando Cattani uses Canaiolo Nero to the permitted limits (and, as he seemed rather vague in telling me what he thought those limits were, possibly a shade beyond them). In May I sat with him and his wife, Esther, on the brick porch in front of their house, pleasantly distracted by a fluttering pattern of shadow cast by the leaves of a great rambling wisteria above our heads. We were comparing La Calonica's 1987 and 1988 Vino Nobile and tasting the 1989 Rosso di Montepulciano. The Rosso, the first vintage possible of this separate, new DOC, is made in accordance with regulations that do not require wood aging prior to its early release—recognition that not all wines, sometimes not even an entire vintage, are suitable for aging in wood. Some growers are now selecting lots each year for designation as Rosso di Montepulciano; others, whole sections of their vineyards. Cattani's 1989 Rosso di Montepulciano is as aromatic as all his wines are. It is also vigorously fruity and full. Paradoxically, though, La Calonica's perfumed style is seen to greatest advantage in vintages less remarkable than 1989, as was clear from comparing his 1988 and 1987 Vino Nobile di Montepulciano. The former is an excellent example of that vintage in Tuscany (the wines are expected to equal those of 1985, the best vintage currently available). The 1987 gave elegant but light wines of moderate quality—some of them, in fact, showing a jagged edge, even a little bitterness. But the aromatic style typical of La Calonica (helped, perhaps, by Cattani's abstemious use of Sangiovese in favor of Canaiolo Nero) gives the estate's 1987 Vino Nobile di Montepulciano Riserva breadth and a semblance of fullness. It's a style that diverts attention from any minor imbalances and leaves an impression of harmony that other 1987s lack.

Harmony should be essential to any wine, of course, but is often rejected for the sake of impact. That cannot be said of the wines of Alamanno Contucci, whose watchwords are balance and discretion—qualities appropriate to his standing both as president of the growers' *consorzio* and as the active director of a family estate now in its eighth century of wine production. Contucci—bespectacled, scholarly, unpretentious, and as good-humored as any well-fed gentleman farmer anywhere—has his cellars beneath the family *palazzo*, built in the sixteenth century on Montepulciano's main square by Sangallo the Elder, one of the architects of Saint Peter's in Rome.

Montepulciano has more than its share of such palaces, and of splendid churches, too. Its Church of Madonna di San Biago, one of the glories of the Renaissance, was begun by Sangallo on a grassy terrace overlooking vineyards and meadows and still separated from the town by an avenue of cypresses. It is one of the most exquisitely serene buildings in Italy. The magnificence of the town's architecture, out of all proportion to its size or relative commercial importance, is a result of wealth accumulated in the fifteenth and sixteenth centuries through marriages between Montepulciano's leading families and the great banking houses of Florence. They were shrewdly arranged to suit both the interests of the *poliziani* (as inhabitants of Montepulciano are called), who lived in constant fear of Siena, their powerful neighbor, and the interests of the *fiorentini* themselves. The alliance armed Florence with a valuable ally below Siena, its arch-rival, and provided her with a listening post on the border of the dangerously expansionist Papal States. Florence did everything possible to bind the relationship, and the splendor of Montepulciano's few streets and squares still bears witness to the generosity of Florentine fathers-in-law.

Contucci talks freely and knowledgeably about the recent changes in Vino Nobile di Montepulciano and agrees that the 1980 DOCG degree did not coincide with the wine's highest quality mark. "But the new *denominazione* was granted to acknowledge Montepulciano's past and to guarantee its future. It deferred to the historic fame of the wine, not to some temporary phase," he says with the assurance of one whose family has seen both worse and better since the first Contucci planted vines at Montepulciano in the thirteenth century. He welcomes the newcomers. "We don't always do things in the same way," he says diplomatically, "but one learns from dialogue, and the competition is very stimulating. After all, everyone has something to contribute."

Contucci has decided for himself which traditions he will keep and which of the new ideas he will adopt. He adheres to the mingling of white grapes with black—necessary in his view for a classic Vino Nobile. Rather than turning to the more usual Malvasia or Trebbiano of Tuscany, however, he uses the Umbrian Grechetto, or "little Greek," commonly known in Montepulciano as Pulcinculo.

"We crush the white and black grapes and let them ferment together in the same vat. The proportions vary with the vintage," he says, "and in some years the wine is indeed better with no white grapes at all. But in most years, if we use red grapes alone, we risk making a wine that is more like Brunello di Montalcino [the wine made one valley away] than Vino Nobile. The newcomers were all against white grapes. They wanted the regulations rewritten to prohibit their use absolutely. Those already here insisted on tolerance. We told them that if they didn't want to use white grapes no one would compel them to."

But Contucci is receptive to change, too. "I tried the wine of one of my colleagues who had used oak from the Allier, in central France, rather than the Slovenian oak we usually use, and I thought it had some good qualities. So we are introducing just a few vats of Allier wood, and we shall see."

Under Contucci's presidency the *consorzio* is dynamically active. It now employs two qualified graduates in viticulture and enology, who visit all growers regularly to inspect their vineyards for pruning and treatment practices and their cellars for cleanliness and for timely racking of their wines from the lees. They taste the wines while they are aging and again before they are bottled. "We are as scrupulous as we can be to protect and strengthen the reputation of the wine," Contucci told me.

He seemed proud, too, of the *consorzio*'s contribution to local research conducted under the supervision of the institutes of agriculture and geology of the universities of Siena, Florence, and Trentino. But then his family has a long tradition of improving the region's agricultural potential. His ancestor Giuseppe di Contucci had drained the swamps of the Valdichiana at the end of the eighteenth century, opening the region up for the cultivation of grains and the raising of cattle. (The Valdichiana breed developed there appears most familiarly off the hoof in the form of the huge *bistecche alla fiorentina* that are a specialty of Tuscany.)

The newcomers Contucci referred to were not just the Swiss and the insurance companies but also those from much closer to home, like the Falvo brothers from Cortona, across the valley, and the Dei family of Siena, who acquired its Montepulciano property just below the town in 1970. The Deis sold their grapes to the local cooperative until 1985 and have really hit their stride only since 1988 under their present manager, Lorenzo Scian, who studied philosophy and quips about neo-positivism, pragmatism, and analytical empiricism before getting down to serious matters like oak and malolactic fermentation. Scian's intensely flavored, remarkably "neo-positive" wines of the 1988 and 1989 vintages are still in big puncheons of new Yugoslav oak (he is against French oak on grounds it can distort his idea of the traditional style of Vino Nobile). They are superb wines, and for the very likable Scian's sake one hopes they will eventually arrive at the "sober elegance" he foresees.

During the entire week of my Montepulciano visit, there wasn't one wine I didn't either enjoy or learn something from—and usually I profited in both regards. But my favorite wines from this appellation are still those of the Boscarelli estate. I don't suggest that Paola de Ferrari and her sons are producing the "best" wine of the region— there is already confusion enough between subjective preference and objective judgment without my adding to it—but their wines reflect the most suitable balance between tradition and evolution. There is no doubt that their ideas, and probably much of their practice, have changed since they first planted vines in 1964. Like Contucci, they usually, but not always, include some white grapes in their blends. On the other hand there is a little Cabernet Sauvignon in their glorious 1988. Their flawless 1985 Vino Nobile di Montepulciano is a lesson in all that wine should be. They have allowed neither their intent nor their vineyard's identity to be blurred by every passing theory. And although their sales are international they have not tried to make of their Vino Nobile an "international" wine. Its path from vineyard to bottle follows an inherent logic, and I suppose that's why it can be relied on for a consistency of character unfailingly tempered by an engaging grace. It is indeed a Vino Nobile, in every sense. Egidio Corradi, were he still with us, would be both satisfied and vindicated.

Wine Talk: Inspired to Reconsider the Whites From Orvieto

BY FRANK J. PRIAL

∾

editor's note

White wines from Orvieto do not immediately come to mind when I think of my favorites. However, I believe that food and wine that grow together go together. It's not accidental that the foods unique to Tuscany and Umbria taste so good with the grapes grown on the same land. That other wines from other parts of the world might also taste good with this food is irrelevant. Many of us get stuck in wine ruts where we drink the same merlot, sauvignon blanc, or chardonnay in much the same way we reach for the same clothes hanging in our closets. An Orvieto white is the perfect complement to a number of good central-Italian recipes, and you don't need to be on vacation to enjoy one.

FRANK J. PRIAL has been writing about wine for many years and is the wine columnist for *The New York Times* as well as an author (*Wine Talk*, Times Books, 1978, and *The Companion to Wine*, which he co-authored with Rosemary George and Michael Edwards, Prentice-Hall, 1992).

I'd always taken Orvieto for granted. Another pleasant, inconsequential Italian white wine. But one day I was gazing with awe at the south wall of the Sistine Chapel in Rome, on which the life of Moses is depicted in a series of frescoes or panels. The last of them, *The Testament and Death of Moses*, was painted by the Umbrian master, Luca Signorelli. The name clicked. He was the painter who, sixteen years after his work on the chapel when he came to do his masterpieces, the frescoes in the cathedral at Orvieto, asked for part of his payment in wine.

Would a great Renaissance master permit himself to be paid off in a wimpy wine? It seemed worth the sixty-mile trip up the Autostrada from Rome to find out.

Orvieto is a popular day trip for Romans, who trudge through the hill town's stone streets, buy pottery of dubious provenance, lunch in the vine-covered trattorias and lug home a few bottles of the local white wine, which may or may not resemble what Signorelli took in kind 494 years ago.

Orvieto, or whatever it happened to be called at any particular time, was a very old wine community by the time Signorelli came here to work. Burton Anderson, a writer who lives in Tuscany, said the Etruscans made wine here, and it was probably white, like almost all the wine made in the region today.

Every so often in California, where a sense of history is not mandatory, a winery announces that it has developed a gravity system for making wine: grapes come in at the top and wine flows out at the bottom without ever having undergone harsh pumping. The Etruscans started at ground level, dug fermenting rooms out of the rock one level down and then made aging rooms at an even lower level where cool temperatures never changed.

For most of its history—including Signorelli's time, the end of the fifteenth century—Orvieto was an *abboccato* wine, that is, slightly sweet, soft and golden in color. *Abboccato* means mouth-filling.

Then came the 1950s and the beginning of a new, worldwide middle-class interest in wines, particularly white wines. For the next two decades, Italy led the world in innovative white-winemaking. California had pioneered in devising ways to make light, crisp white wines in relatively hot climates. But it was the Italians who took the technology and, so to speak, ran with it.

What was lost in the process was character; the wines were often overprocessed, making them clean, correct and boring. Orvieto, which was bypassed by Charles VIII on his way to sack Rome, didn't escape this time; its new dry white wines were as bland as everyone else's.

Soon a few producers set about, once more, to change Orvieto's image. One of the leading wine and image makers was Piero Antinori, scion of an ancient Florentine Chianti house.

The Antinoris had long been active in the Orvieto region from their base at the Castello della Sala, a fourteenth-century fortified castle that Piero's father, Niccolo, had purchased, along with about 1,200 of acres of land, just before World War II.

So I drove over the mountains to Sala, a wide spot in the road about twenty minutes north of Orvieto on the road to Arrezzo. There at the Castello della Sala, under the watchful eye of Renzo Cotarella, one of the Antinori's key wine makers, a fascinating variety of white wines take on life.

Orvieto secco, the dry version of the wine, is traditionally composed of up to 65 percent procanico, the local name for trebbiano, Italy's ubiquitous white grape, and up to 25 percent grechetto, a local variety. Three others—verdello, drupeggio and malvasia—make up the rest, depending on the winemaker's whim.

Neither Mr. Antinori nor Mr. Cotarella was satisfied with the traditional formula, although they used it in their estate-grown Orvieto Classico bearing the Castello della Sala name until 1992, when chardonnay grapes from the estate were added to make up 15 percent of the blend. A lesser Orvieto Classico, made in part from purchased grapes, adheres to the original blend.

The important Orvieto grapes grow in the Castello della Sala's vineyards, but so do chardonnay, riesling, gewürztraminer, sauvignon blanc and sémillon. There are three red varieties—pinot noir, cabernet sauvignon and merlot—but this is essentially a white-wine operation.

Borro della Sala is a blend of 70 percent sauvignon blanc and 30 percent procanico. Cervaro della Sala is composed of about 75 percent chardonnay and 25 percent grechetto. This wine is both fermented and aged in oak, with the time in wood—even the age of the barrels—varying from vintage to vintage.

Because of the procanico and the grechetto, both the Borro and the Cervaro have a distinctly local flavor. "There are technical and philosophical reasons for using the local grapes," Mr. Cotarella said. "In warm vintages, like 1988 and 1990, chardonnay alone was too flat; we needed the grechetto. In cold years, we might go from 30 down to 10 percent grechetto. But beyond that, using the old local grapes preserves some of the local culture. Piero Antinori firmly believes that it's important to preserve, as much as possible, these regional characteristics.

"Besides, anyone can make a chardonnay, but one with an Umbrian flavor is something very special."

Would old Luca Signorelli like the new style wines? Probably, but perhaps not as much as his colleague, Bernadino di Betto, who called himself Pinturicchio. Mr. Anderson said Pinturicchio was dismissed from his job at the Orvieto cathedral after some clerical bookkeeper decided he'd consumed too much azure, too much gold and too much wine.

Italy's Vin Santo: A Sip of Hospitality

BY S. IRENE VIRBILA

～

editor's note

Biscotti dipped in vin santo is divine, and as vin santo is not widely available in the U.S., it makes a good choice for a *ricorda* (souvenir). It's also, as the writer notes in this piece, a *ricorda* unique to Tuscany and Umbria. As always, readers should double-check addresses and phone numbers before setting out to the wine estates, shops, and museum the author recommends.

S. IRENE VIRBILA has been the restaurant critic of *The Los Angeles Times* since 1993, and has contributed articles about food, wine, and travel to *Saveur, Departures, Wine Spectator,* and *Metropolitan Home,* among others. Virbila trained as a sommelier in Paris, worked as a restaurant cook, wine buyer, and cookbook editor, and won the James Beard Award for newspaper restaurant criticism in 1997. She is the author of *Cook's Marketplace San Francisco* (1982), co-author of *Cook's Marketplace Los Angeles* (1984), and is currently finishing a book on the food and wines of Piedmont.

I n Tuscany and neighboring Umbria, vin santo is the wine of hospitality. Whatever the time of day, a guest is offered a small glass of the amber dessert wine. "It's the wine of hospitality, the wine of friendship and of courtesy," explains Giacomo Tachis, winemaker for the 650-year-old Tuscan firm Antinori. At one time, every family in the Tuscan countryside made some vin santo and had a prized barrel or two squirreled away in the attic. Chianti they made for sale, but vin santo was strictly for family use.

Though the tradition in Tuscany goes back for centuries, no one seems to agree on how vin santo got its name. Some say it's because the grapes are sometimes not pressed until Christmas or as late as Holy Week.

Others insist the wine is "holy" because it was often used in the mass. But the more generally held theory is that the name dates from the Ecumenical Council held in Florence in 1349, when a Greek bishop commented that the wine served tasted like the sweet wine made on the Greek island of Xantos—and the name vin santo stuck.

Every farm and estate has a slightly different system of making vin santo, which produces wines in distinctly different styles. One may be rich and honeyed, tasting of dried apricots, figs and prunes. Another is almost dry on the palate, with an aroma of hazelnuts and almonds. Whatever the style, the wine is generally 14 to 17 percent alcohol. The wine is made from partially dried grapes that are slowly pressed to yield a thick, concentrated juice. The must (unfermented grape juice) is sealed in small barrels, and then left, contrary to all normal winemaking practice, to weather extremes of hot and cold in an attic or other uninsulated structure for a minimum of three years. The fermentation can continue on and off for two or three years, starting up with the warm weather in spring, and shutting down in the cold.

Every winemaker creates a variation on the theme. The grape bunches may be strung in dramatic cascades from the rafters, or the grapes may be laid out to dry on cane mats stacked from floor to ceiling (with space between for the air to circulate). The grapes are usually local white wine varieties, but vin santo can also be made partly with red grapes. And the shriveled raisinlike grapes may be pressed anytime from late November to as late as February or March. Once the grapes are pressed, the wine is aged in barrels ranging from the traditional fifty-liter casks called caratelle to standard French oak barriques or old whisky barrels. The casks can be sealed with cement or sealing wax for three to six or more years before they are opened and the wine is bottled.

Until recently, most vin santo was made only for family consumption and to present as gifts. Now a growing number of wine estates in Tuscany are making vin santo for sale in limited quantities. One outstanding example is produced by Avignonesi, a Montepulciano firm known for its red Vino Nobile di Montepulciano. When the winemaker Ettore Falvo first tasted his father-in-law's vin santo, he was astounded. Aged twelve years, "it was dark and thick as tamarind syrup with a perfume so intense it lasted a week in an empty glass, . . . and so concentrated, a forty-liter barrel might yield only five or six liters of vin santo." It was not something he could make in any quantity.

For Mr. Falvo, Avignonesi's real treasure was the ancient madre, or mother, the dark, mucilaginous concentration of wild yeasts that had developed in the vin santo barrels through the generations the family had been making it. Carefully nurturing and dividing the mother at most by half each year, after twenty years he can now produce about fifty barrels a year, which he ages six, rather than twelve years. His vin santo is lush and concentrated with a perfume of toasted almonds, plums, prunes and dried fruit.

At his estate in Valiano, a few miles from Cortona, he has just finished building and restoring a vinsantaia (the place where vin santo is made and aged). Opening the door with a fist-sized key, he showed off the rows of cane mats covered with grape bunches to make a tapestry in shades of pale green and rose. Farther back were carpets of red and purple grapes for the rare vin santo called occhio di pernice (eye of the partridge). Windows on either side of the room help the drying process. In damp weather ingenious wooden shutters close tight.

As Mr. Falvo explained, only the handsome, healthy grape bunches are selected for vin santo. Here they are mainly Grechetto (a local white grape) with a little Malvasia. As the grapes dry, water evaporates, and the sugar, extracts and flavor become more and more concentrated. By mid-February, the sugar content is high enough that Mr. Falvo decides to press. Meanwhile he opens the barrels of wine sealed six years before, empties them and prepares them for this year's wine. He fills each of the caratelle with a small quantity of mother and pours in the thick, syrupy must to within a few inches from the top. The bunghole is closed with red sealing wax. Here they'll stay, stacked four high in the uninsulated vin santeria for six years.

Because each barrel develops on its own, there can be remarkable differences in perfume, sweetness and concentration, but in the end the barrels are blended to produce that year's wine, just 1,800 half bottles and about 400 half bottles of occhio di pernice. Most of it is shipped to top wine shops and restaurants in Italy.

Fontodi, a Chianti estate in Panzano, produces an excellent vin santo in half bottles in very limited quantities. This one is half Malvasia and half red Sangiovese grapes, dried on mats until Christmas and aged four years in four different kinds of wood: oak, chestnut, cherry and juniper. The deep golden wine is vinified dry and has an appealing perfume of honey and hazelnuts.

Another good example in the drier style is Badia a Coltibuono's vin santo with subtle overtones of apricot and hazelnut. Made from Trebbiano and Malvasia grapes pressed in early December, this one is aged in 200-liter former whisky barrels in a room over the estate's olive press. A restaurant on the grounds of the thousand-year-old abbey offers vin santo after a typical country meal. And the small retail shop sells the estate's chianti classico and other wines, plus vin santo, and its own vinegar, extra-virgin olive oil and honeys.

Another very good producer in Gaiole is Francesco Martini di Cigala at San Giusto a Rentennano. The small vin santeria in the villa's attic looks much as it did a hundred years ago, with grapes hanging from the beams to dry and the old chestnut caratelle set all in a row. Fine and complex, with layers of flavor, this vin santo is made from Trebbiano and Malvasia, and aged five years before bottling.

Northwest of Florence, in the historic red wine region called Carmignano, Count Ugo Contini Bonacossi is an old hand at vin santo. His family has been making vin santo at Tenuta di Capezzana for five generations, but the mother they inherited with the centuries-old estate is much older. The blend of Trebbiano, Malvasia and San Colombano grapes now includes a small amount of Chardonnay, and is aged four to five years in French oak barriques. His father and his father's father set aside a good quantity of wine, so Count Bonacossi is able to open bottles from the forties and fifties to prove that vin santo can age.

While vin santo is also made in the regions of Trentino and Alto Adige, it is most characteristic of Tuscany and parts of Umbria.

People from Umbria, the tiny region in the heart of Italy halfway between Rome and Florence, are proud of their vin santo tradition. Teresa Lungarotti, enologist in Torgiano for Lungarotti, Umbria's best known winery, explained that in the region vin santo is almost always sweet and made entirely with Grechetto grapes dried until February. The wine is aged four or five years in very old chestnut barrels and, just before bottling, it is fortified by adding a mistela, a concentrate of must and alcohol made from grapes.

Here, too, she says, vin santo is usually served with torcolo di San Costanzo, a dry ring-shaped cake studded with raisins and candied fruit named for the protector of Perugia; the flat cookies called mostaccioli, or the hard little almond cookies known as brutti ma buoni (ugly, but good).

One room of the Lungarotti wine museum in Torgiano is devoted to vin santo. Here you can see baskets, presses and barrels used in its production. Most interesting are the ornate cialde irons, used to cook round anise-scented wafers from a flour and egg batter moistened with vin santo. They're supposed to cook in the time it took to say an Ave Maria. And among the museum's collection of medieval and Renaissance faience is a seventeenth-century jar decorated with grape bunches, vines and birds, once used to store vin santo.

Around the corner is Le Tre Vaselle, the country inn where the Lungarotti family offers regional dishes like frittata alla menta (with mint), risotto cooked in Rubesco wine, pappardelle (wide ribbon noodles) with black truffle sauce, and grilled wild boar, followed by vin santo served with pastries, cookies and anise-scented cialde.

Order a glass of vin santo at a Tuscan restaurant and it is likely to show up at the table with a small plate of biscotti, crunchy "twice-cooked" cookies studded with toasted almonds. The shape is an elongated oval, flat on one side, and perfect for dipping in the narrow glass of dessert wine. Aficionados say that one particular type of biscotti—cantuccini di Prato—from the Mattei bakery in Prato, ten miles northwest of Florence, makes the best match.

At Cantinetta Antinori in Palazzo Antinori at the foot of Via Tornabuoni, in Florence, you can finish off a meal of simple Tuscan food with a glass of Antinori vin santo and a plate of authentic cantuccini and brutti ma buoni from Mattei.

Winemakers have discovered lots of uses for vin santo in cooking, too, from dousing roasted chestnuts along with a little sugar or deglazing the pan when making a pork roast. Contessa Lisa Contini Bonacossi adds a little vin santo to the chestnut purée for her Monte Bianco, a dessert composed of mounded chestnut purée topped with softly whipped cream to resemble the Alpine peak.

And at Badia a Coltibuono, Lorenza de' Medici, who teaches cooking at the Chianti estate she owns with her husband, Piero Stucchi-Prinetti, makes a soup with vin santo, pouring beaten egg mixed with lemon juice, lemon rind and a glass of vin santo into a rich broth. When she roasts pigeons, she stuffs them with bread crumbs, prosciutto and their livers, and glazes the birds with honey and vin santo.

The Wine of Hospitality

Wine Estates

Most wine estates in Tuscany and Umbria produce their own vin santo and may have limited quantities for sale. Several estates have restaurants where their vin santo can be sampled following a meal.

Cantinetta Antinori, Palazzo Antinori, 3 Piazza degli Antinori, Florence; tel. 055.292234. Closed in August. Rustic Tuscan specialties are featured, among them fettunta (toasted bread anointed with garlic and olive oil), tripa alla fiorentina (tripe simmered in beef broth and tomatoes) and arista (pork loin laced with garlic, rosemary, and black pepper). Vin santo Santa Cristina is served.

Le Tre Vaselle, 48 Via Garibaldi, Torgiano (Umbria); tel. 075.982447. Open daily. Typical Umbrian dishes are offered, such as pappardelle (wide ribbon noodles) with black truffle sauce, fish from Lake Trasimeno and grilled wild boar steak with rosemary, followed by Lungarotti's vin santo.

Ristorante Badia a Coltibuono, Gaiole in Chianti; tel. 055.749424. Closed Monday. Tuscan country food is served in a rustic trattoria that features dishes like ravioli stuffed with spinach and ricotta, and stracotto (beef stew) with porcini mushrooms, the Badia's wines, and, of course, their vin santo.

Shops

These wine shops have impressive collections of vin santo for sale from $5 to $20 or more a bottle. Very cheap vin santos are rarely a good bet; true vin santo is costly to make.

Enoteca del Gallo Nero, 8 Piazzetta Santa Croce, Greve (Chianti), tel. 055.853297. Over two dozen vin santos from Chianti Classico producers.

Enoteca la Fortezza, Piazzale Fortezza, Montalcino; tel. 055.849211. Closed Monday. Vin santo from producers of Brunello di Montalcino, the wine region just southwest of Siena, can be tasted by the glass (about $3 each).

Enoteca Italica Permanente, Fortezza Medicea, Siena; tel. 055.288497. This enoteca, the first in Italy, collects wines from all over Italy. Order a bottle of vin santo to enjoy with on the outdoor terrace or a room beneath a sixteenth-century fortress.

Wine Museum

Musseo del Vino, Torgiano (Umbria); tel. 075.982348. Open in summer 9 A.M. to 12:30 P.M. and 3:30 to 8 P.M.; in winter, 9 A.M. to 12:30 P.M. and 2:30 to 6 P.M.

Biblioteca

It seems to me that one cannot separate Italian food from Italian history. Really good cookbooks—ones that offer tried-and-true, authentic recipes, as well as detailed commentary on the food traditions of the country or region and the history behind the recipes and the ingredients unique to the cuisine—are just as essential to travel as guidebooks. I read these cookbooks the way other people read novels; therefore, the authors have to be more than just good cooks, and the books have to be more than just cookbooks. All of the authors and books listed below fit the bill. Rather than provide lengthy descriptions of these titles, I think it is enough to state that they are definitive, and stand quite apart from the multitude of Mediterranean and Italian cookbooks crowding bookstore shelves. I have included a few titles that aren't strictly cookbooks but are equally as interesting and relevant.

Mediterranean

A Book of Mediterranean Food, Elizabeth David, Penguin, 1988.

From Tapas to Meze, Joanna Weir, Crown, 1994.

Invitation to Mediterranean Cooking: 150 Vegetarian and Seafood Recipes, Claudia Roden, Rizzoli, 1997.

Mediterranean: The Beautiful Cookbook, Joyce Goldstein, Collins (produced by Welden Owen), 1994.

Mediterranean Cookery, Claudia Roden, Knopf, 1987.

Mediterranean Cooking, Paula Wolfert, HarperCollins, 1994.

The Mediterranean Diet Cookbook, Nancy Harmon Jenkins, Bantam Books, 1994.

A Mediterranean Feast: The Story of the Birth of the Celebrated Cuisines of the Mediterranean, From the Merchants of Venice to the Barbary Corsairs, Clifford A. Wright, William Morrow and Company, 1999. An outstanding and exhaustively researched book. *Essenziale.*

Mediterranean Light, Martha Rose Shulman, Bantam, 1989.

The Mediterranean Kitchen, Joyce Goldstein, Morrow, 1989. A unique feature of this book is that Goldstein indicates how, by changing only an ingredient or two, recipes can go from being Italian, say, to French or Portuguese, which illustrates the core ingredients each country in the region shares and also allows for more mileage out of nearly every recipe.

The Mediterranean Pantry: Creating and Using Condiments and Seasonings, Aglaia Kremezi, photographs by Martin Brigdale, Artisan, 1994.

Mostly Mediterranean, Paula Wolfert, Penguin, 1988.

The Feast of the Olive, Maggie Blyth Klein, Aris Books (Addison-Wesley), 1983; Chronicle Books, revised and updated edition, 1994.

Olives: The Life and Love of a Noble Fruit, Mort Rosenblum, North Point Press, 1996. One chapter is "Top-of-the-Line Tuscan."

Cod: A Biography of the Fish That Changed the World, Mark Kurlansky, Walker and Company, 1999. I include this wonderful book here because, as Kurlansky notes in one of the chapters, "From the Middle Ages to the present, the most demanding cod market has always been the Mediterranean." Fresh or dried salt cod is a Mediterranean staple (except in the Muslim countries), making an appearance in dishes such as *sonhos de bacalhau* in Portugal, *brandade de morue* in France, *baccala in umido* in Tuscany, and *filetti di baccala all'arancia* in Sicily. The fascinating story of cod crisscrosses the globe from Newfoundland, New England, the Basque coast of Spain, Brazil, West Africa, Scandinavia, etc., but the Mediterranean is never very far from the thread.

Italian

Dictionary of Italian Cuisine, Maureen B. Fant and Howard M. Isaacs, The Ecco Press, 1998. This is a brilliant and practical achievement. As Fant and Isaacs inform us, there are many good books on Italian cooking in English that are aimed at *either* cooks or travelers—rarely both—and are still not quite comprehensive enough for those looking at a regional restaurant menu. As they note, "In Italy, all cooking, like politics, is local." There are some shapes of pasta not known in a town only an hour away, and some vegetables are known by two or three different names throughout the country, which is why it's necessary to have this book of 6,000 entries. Not only are there words for things to eat, but also for cooking techniques, utensils, important place names, etc. One *could* take this along to restaurants, but that's not really the purpose for which it was created. For those who are serious about Italian food and drink, this is *essenziale.*

The Food of Italy, Waverly Root, Vintage Books, 1992; originally published in hardcover by Atheneum, 1971. The best summation of this excellent work comes from Samuel Chamberlain's introduction, in which he says, "This is destined to become a classic work on the subject of Italian food and wine, and a reference book that will retain its value through decades to come. The enthusiasm that has been lavished on this book can be matched only by the depth and accuracy of the author's research. Its place in gastronomic lore is already assured." The first chapter, "The Domain of the Etruscans," covers Tuscany, Umbria, Lazio, The Marches, and Emilia-Romagna. *Essenziale.*

The Cooking of Italy, Waverly Root and the editors of Time-Life Books, photographed by Fred Lyon, 1968. The collaborative effort to produce this book (one of the volumes in the Foods of the World series) was extraordinary, the likes of which we'll probably never see again (a separate, spiral-bound recipe booklet accompanied each hardbound volume). Some of the best commentary on Italian food I've ever read is presented by Luigi Barzini, who contributed the foreword: ". . . the apparently simple cooking of the Italians is, in fact, more difficult at times to achieve than the more elaborate and refined French cuisine. Things have to be good in themselves, without aid, to be exposed naked. In other words, a pleasant French dish can sometimes be made successfully even with very ordinary ingredients, while the excellence of many Italian dishes depends on the excellence of the things that go into them. The old saying that good cooking begins in the market is truer in Italy than in France." Barzini goes on to point out that "Fruit and vegetables must be picked at the right time, neither one day too early nor too late. They must not travel far, must not be preserved beyond their allotted season by chemicals or refrigeration." One chapter is devoted to Florence and Tuscany, and though this is, obviously, long out-of-print and hard to find, it does turn up at tag sales and in used bookstores. *Essenziale.*

Treasures of the Italian Table: Italy's Celebrated Foods and the Artisans Who Make Them, Burton Anderson, William Morrow, 1994. Not a cookbook, but something better: profiles of people—true culinary artisans—who continue to produce food by traditional methods, eschewing the ways of mass production. Anderson has been called "the world's greatest expert on Italian wine," and the Italian foods he has chosen to highlight in this book are *tartufi bianchi d'Alba* (white truffles of Alba), *pane Toscano* (Tuscan bread, saltless because Tuscans believe salt detracts from the flavors of food and wine), *pasta, olio extra vergine di oliva* (extra-virgin olive oil), *pizza Napoletana* (Neopolitan-style pizza), *Parmigiano Reggiano* (the one and only Parmesan), *vino* (wine), *culatello* (a pork specialty from a pig's buttocks), *risotto, bistecca alla Fiorentina* (beef from the white cattle of Chianina, cut in a certain way by Florentine butchers), *aceto balsamico tradizionale* (true balsamic vinegar from Modena), and *caffè espresso.* Obviously, not all of these specialties are Tuscan or Umbrian, but visitors are likely to find nearly all of them on menus or in shops. Anderson also recommends the names of favorite restaurants and retailers where these delicacies are available. *Essenziale.*

Savoring Italy: A Celebration of the Food, Landscape, and People of Italy, Robert Freson, HarperCollins Publishers/Callaway Editions, 1992. The successor to Freson's *The Taste of France,* this is my favorite book on Italian food. Twenty regions of Italy are featured, with essays contributed by noted Italian authorities such as Carol Field, Leslie Forbes, Barbara Grizzuti Harrison, Nadia Stancioff, and Louis Inturrisi. There is a separate chapter on Tuscany, while Umbria is included in a chapter with Lazio and Le Marche. As with the France book, Freson was interested in recording, "while it was still possible, the relationship between regional resources, climate, produce, and people . . ." This wonderful volume is inexplicably out-of-print but is *essenziale* and worth a great effort to find.

The Art of Eating Well: Italy's Most Treasured Cookbook, Pellegrino Artusi, 1820–1911, translated by Kyle M. Phillips III, Random House, 1996.

The following four cookbooks by Marcella Hazan: *The Classic Italian Cook Book* (1976), *More Classic Italian Cooking* (1978), *Marcella's Italian Kitchen* (1986), and *Essentials of Classic Italian Cooking* (1992), all published by Alfred A. Knopf in hardcover; some are available in paperback editions.

Italian Cooking: An Illustrated Guide to Classic Italian Cooking, Elizabeth David, Smithmark Publishers, 1996; previous editions published in 1954 and 1987. Among the many observations in this book is the following: "'Italian' cooking is a concept of foreigners—to Italians, there is Florentine cooking, Venetian cooking, the cooking of Genoa, Rome, Naples, Sicily, Lombardy and the Adriatic coast. Not only have the provinces retained their own traditions of cookery, but many of their products remain localized."

Celebrating Italy: The Tastes and Traditions of Italy as Revealed Through its Feasts, Festivals, and Sumptuous Foods, Carol Field, HarperPerennial, 1997; originally published in hardcover by William Morrow, 1990. About a dozen celebrations from Tuscany and Umbria are included. With dozens of period engravings and drawings and a serious, eleven-page bibliography.

Italian Festival Food: Recipes and Traditions From Italy's Regional Country Food Fairs, Anne Bianchi, Macmillan, 1999. Similar to Carol Field's book above, but not as all-encompassing, and with black-and-white photographs.

The Italian Country Table: Home Cooking from Italy's Farmhouse Kitchens, Lynne Rosetto Kasper, Scribner, 1999.

In Nonna's Kitchen: Recipes and Traditions From Italy's Grandmothers, Carol Field, HarperCollins, 1997.

Giuliano Bugialli's Foods of Italy, photographs by John Dominis, Stewart, Tabori & Chang, 1984.

Italy, The Beautiful Cookbook: Authentic Recipes from the Regions of Italy, recipes by Lorenza De' Medici, text by Patrizia Passigli (1996) and *Italy Today: The Beautiful Cookbook,* recipes by Lorenza De' Medici, text by Fred Plotkin (1997), both published by HarperCollins Publishers and produced by Weldon Owen.

Mario Batali, Simple Italian Food: Recipes From My Two Villages, Clarkson Potter, 1998. The "villages" are Borgo Capanne, on the border of Tuscany, and Emilia-Romagna, where he spent several years cooking at a *trattoria,* as well as New York City's Greenwich Village, where he has two renowned restaurants, Pò and Babbo.

Red, White & Greens: The Italian Way with Vegetables, Faith Heller Willinger,

HarperCollins Publishers, 1996. Each of these recipes is a winner, but I have to enthuse about one in particular: "Francesca's Zucchini Carpaccio," which receives raves every time I make it.

Pasta Classica: The Art of Italian Pasta Cooking, Julia della Croce, Chronicle Books, 1987.

Tuscan Cooking

The Tuscan Year: Life and Food in an Italian Valley, Elizabeth Romer, North Point Press, 1989; first published in the U.S. in 1985 by Atheneum; original © 1984. This wonderful book appeared years before *A Year in Provence* or *Under the Tuscan Sun* but, for reasons that I can't fathom, is not nearly as popular. I had a hard time deciding where to include it. It's not technically a food book, so originally I had it in *La Toscana* with the other memoirs. But after much thought, I brought it back here, since it is mostly about food. Filled with the seasonal recipes of Romer's neighbors, the Cerotti family, in a "green and secret valley joining Umbria and Tuscany," Romer takes readers through the calendar year relating each month's typical tasks and activities, nearly all of which have to do with food. As she notes, "Tuscan cuisine is inextricably bound to the culture and personality of Tuscany and its people. I do not mean by Tuscan cuisine the elaborate food that one might eat in one of the region's many grand and elegant restaurants; I mean the sort of food that the waiter will eat when he goes home, the recipes that the grandmother of the chef might cook every day." Silvana Cerotti's recipes emphasize the single most important tenet of Italian cooking in general and Tuscan cooking in particular: fresh ingredients, in their season, which ensures they will be of the best quality (and this includes cheese and olive oil, both of which have seasons). This remains an essential element of cooking that most Americans seem to ignore. Some of Silvana's recipes couldn't be simpler to make, but their success is wholly dependent on the quality of each ingredient. I was reminded of this wisdom last year while reading a newsletter from Zingerman's, the wonderful food emporium in Ann Arbor, Michigan. This particular issue featured an article titled "Want to Improve the Enjoyment of Your Eating? Start by Buying Better Ingredients." The piece reinforced that "the finished food you prepare will never be better than the *quality of the stuff you put in*," and what followed was a list of ten ingredients to buy that would immediately improve the overall quality of our meals. The list included items that any Tuscan cook would insist upon, such as better olive oil, better bread, better pasta, better Parmesan, and better fruit and vegetables. (If you don't already receive the *Zingerman's Mail Order Catalog for Food Lovers* and periodic newsletters, call or write and ask to be put on the mailing list: 422 Detroit Street, Ann Arbor, Michigan 48104; 888-

636-8162 / fax: 734-769-1260; e-mail: zing@chamber.ann-arbor.mi.us. Both the catalog and the newsletter are incredibly informative and are filled with incredibly tempting stuff.) If you try to replicate Tuscan recipes at home and try to cut corners with out-of-season produce and second-rate olive oil, you'll wonder what all the fuss is about. Another attribute of this book that makes it valuable for travelers is the thorough explanation of all sorts of unfamiliar Tuscan produce. For example, Romer explains that *cicoria,* which we might think is the equivalent to our chicory, isn't at all. Nor is it like *endivia del Belgo* or *radicchio rosso.* If, while in Tuscany, you ask for *cicoria* in a restaurant, "inevitably a plate of cooked greenery will arrive. If you want a salad of the beautiful red leaves that run from palest pink to deep porphyry then it is safer to ask for an *insalata di radicchio rosso.* However, just to make things more complicated, if you order *radicchio* without qualifying it with the word *rosso,* you will receive yet another cooked green leaf, albeit of the *radicchio* (chicory) family, which is also served as a salad in summer. The delicious green *cicoria* makes another diversion in the confusing question of endive versus *chicory.* In general if you order a plate of *verdura cotta,* cooked greenstuff, in a Tuscan restaurant, you are likely to receive a portion of one of these many sorts of delicious leaves, probably cooked in the manner I have described." *The Tuscan Year* remains one of my favorite books and deserves more admirers.

A Taste of Tuscany: Classic Recipes from the Heart of Italy, Leslie Forbes, Little, Brown and Company, 1985, hardcover; Chronicle Books, 1991, paperback. Forbes provides an abundance of folklore, historical background, restaurant notes, authentic recipes, and colorful drawings, all of which adds up to a travelogue for travelers who love food. The Chronicle Books edition is nice, but the handwritten text was abandoned for typeset words, which I think completely robs the work of its spirit.

Flavors of Tuscany: Traditional Recipes From the Italian Countryside, Nancy Harmon Jenkins, Broadway Books, 1998. The following passage from this excellent book is one of the best I've ever read to describe the central place of food in the homes of Tuscan *contadini:* "I keep speaking of the Tuscan kitchen as if it were a discrete room, set apart from the rest of the house, as kitchens are in North America even when they're the heart of the home. In the Tuscan farmhouses I know, the kitchen is not just the heart, it *is* the home, almost in its entirety, one large room that extends end to end across the front of the farmhouse. In this room all family activities take place, except for sleeping, giving birth, and dying, and sometimes even those have taken place in the kitchen. Here food is prepared and consumed, both the food of the day and that to be stored for winter; here the family enjoys its social life, guests are received, largesse is dispensed. Even the most casual visitor, a neighbor at midmorning, say, on his way down to the stream to fish, is offered, in an ancient gesture of civility, a sweet biscuit and a glass of wine to dip it in. Here, too, the family television is kept—and kept on, constantly, a flickering background of silly stuff that no one ever seems actually to watch except in the evening. The kitchen *is* the casa, and to say that a person is *in casa* is to say that he is, yes, in the house, but more specifically in the kitchen and not in one of the adjacent bedrooms or storerooms." *Essenziale*.

A Tuscan in the Kitchen: Recipes and Tales From my Home, Pino Luongo, Clarkson Potter, 1988.

Giuliano Bugialli's Foods of Tuscany, photographs by John Dominis, Stewart, Tabori & Chang, 1992 (hardcover) and 1996 (paperback).

From the Tables of Tuscan Women, Anne Bianchi, The Ecco Press, 1995. The tables are all actually in Lucca, where Bianchi lives part of the year.

Zuppa! Soups from the Italian Countryside, Anne Bianchi, photographs by Douglas Hatschek, The Ecco Press, 1996. The title might give the impression that the recipes are from all across Italy, but in fact Bianchi focuses on the Garfagnane, a largely undiscovered corner of Tuscany in between the Apuan Alps and the Apennines. I only recently discovered this book, but the few recipes I've tried have been delicious.

Solo Verdura: The Complete Guide to Cooking Tuscan Vegetables, Anne Bianchi, The Ecco Press, 1997.

The Italian Baker, Carol Field, HarperCollins, 1985.

Dolci Toscani: The Book of Tuscan Desserts, Anne Bianchi and Sandra Lotti, The Ecco Press, 1998.

In Tuscany: The Sangiovese Grape, Bread without Salt, A Pot Like a Bottle, The Veneration of Olive Oil. Not a book but issue #41 of *The Art of Eating,* of which I must make special note. Some readers might already know of this absolutely excellent, critical, and superbly written quarterly newsletter by Edward Behr. Although not exclusively about Italy, Behr has devoted several issues to various aspects of Italian food and restaurants over the years, and each of them is worth the effort to special order. Of this Tuscany issue, I would say: Don't go without it. It contains some of the best writing on Tuscan food anywhere. In addition to the individual essays noted above, there are some recipes and cookbook recommendations and names and addresses of selected wine producers, restaurants, bakeries, *enotechi*, and shops. *The Art of Eating* is really *essenziale* reading, so don't wait until the last minute to order back issues ($9 each, $7.50 each for four or more). Further, if you really want to learn about the food traditions of Italy and other countries and care about the food you eat and its future, you'll definitely want to subscribe to this stellar periodical, which has been described as "One of the most respected publications in the food world" by *Chef's Edition* on National Public Radio. Some better cookbook and cookware stores sell individual issues of *The Art of Eating* (Kitchen Arts & Letters in New York stocks it regularly), but to receive it in your mailbox you should subscribe: Box 242, Peacham, Vermont 05862; 800-495-3944; www.artofeating.com

"The Flavor of Autumn," Lori Zimring De Mori, *Saveur*, No. 37, 1999. Another article to read, about that most Tuscan of vegetables, *finocchio* (fennel).

Of Related Interest

Cheese Primer, Steven Jenkins, Workman Publishing Co., 1996. Though not exclusively about Italian cheeses, cheeses from Italy figure large in this excellent cheese bible. Jenkins, the first American to be awarded France's *Chevalier du Taste-Fromage,* created and/or revitalized the cheese counters at such New York food emporiums as Dean & DeLuca and Fairway. In addition to presenting the cheeses of Italy, and twelve other regions of the world, he explains how cheese is made, the basics of butterfat, and the seasons that are best for making and eating cheese (yes, most cheeses have a season, which is determined by pasturage—vegetation that cows, goats, and sheep have been eating at the time of milking). Jenkins also offers great suggestions for buying and serving cheese and creating cheese plates. And for travelers, he provides the names of cheeses—most never exported—to look for in various regions. This is the most comprehensive book on cheese I've ever seen.

The Joy of Coffee: The Essential Guide to Buying, Brewing and Enjoying, Corby Kummer, 1995, hardcover; 1999, paperback, both Chapters Publishing (Houghton Mifflin Company). A comment I hear often from people who visit Italy is that the coffee is so much better there. It's my opinion that it's not the coffee that's better but the quality of the dairy products. Coffee, after all, isn't grown in Italy, and roasters and vendors can buy excellent beans as easily as anybody else around the world. Anyway, if you're a coffee drinker, you can judge for yourself, and I've included this book here for those who want to know more about the elixir they love. I find this to be the best volume on coffee ever published. Kummer, who is a well-known food journalist, is a senior editor of *The Atlantic Monthly* and has also contributed to *Martha Stewart Living, New York, Food & Wine,* etc. He covers coffee plantations, cupping, roasting, grinding, storing (the best place, if you drink it every day, is not in the freezer, as many people mistakenly believe), and brewing, plus separate chapters on espresso, caffeine versus decaf, and a country-by-country guide. There are also recipes for baked goods that pair particularly well with coffee (I've made almost all of them and can vouch that they are especially yummy; the Unbeatable Biscotti are definitely the best ones ever, and I've baked a *lot* of biscotti).

About Wine in General

The Oxford Companion to Wine, edited by Jancis Robinson, Oxford University Press, 1994.

Jancis Robinson's Wine Course, BBC Books, London, 1995.

Tasting Pleasure: Confessions of a Wine Lover, Jancis Robinson, Viking, 1997. Italy and some Italian wines are mentioned or featured throughout the twenty-four essays. Robinson began her wine education in 1968, when she took a summer job as a chambermaid on the Tuscan coast in Porto Ercole at Il Pellicano, then the most expensive hotel in Italy (it is still frightfully expensive, but is also stunningly beautiful).

Vineyard Tales: Reflections on Wine, Gerald Asher, Chronicle Books, 1996. Two of the twenty-nine essays are about Italian wines.

Making Sense of Wine, Matt Kramer, Quill (an imprint of William Morrow & Co.), 1989.

The Wall Street Journal Guide to Wine, Dorothy J. Gaiter and John Brecher, Broadway Books, 1999. There is a chapter on Italian whites and one each on Barolo and Dolcetto.

About Italian Wine

The first two books on Italian wine (the best ones, in my opinion) are out-of-print but are positively worth an effort to find:

Vino: The Wines and Winemakers of Italy, Burton Anderson, Little, Brown and Company, 1980.

Italian Wine, Victor Hazan, Alfred A. Knopf, 1982. Victor is as passionate about Italian wines as his wife, Marcella, is about Italian cuisine. Do not be put off by the fact that this edition is almost twenty years old. The general information about Italian wines and wine appreciation is excellent, and the results are a joy to read.

Italian Wines 2000, Gambero Rosso Editore / Slow Food Editore. This is an annual paperback jointly published by the esteemed magazine *Gambero Rosso* and the Slow Food group. It's the English-language version of *Vini d'Italia*, an annual publication in Italy now in its thirteenth year. For both professionals and enthusiasts, to my mind there is no better guide to current Italian wines. Over 10,000 wines are evaluated and ranked in categories ranging from a simple mention to the highest award, *Tre Bicchiere* (three glasses). What I especially like is that the guide is filled with little-known wines I would otherwise never learn of, and while some of these prove difficult to find here in the U.S., they end up on my shopping list when I go (or someone I know goes) to Italy.

VINO—Italian Wines: The Quality of Life, Burton Anderson, Italian Trade Commission, 1992. This is actually a small paperback booklet (104 pages) that is a very good overall reference guide to the twenty wine regions of Italy. Anderson explains the Italian wine label, and there are maps for DOC white and red wines and a good glossary. Most helpful is a food-and-wine pairing chart at the back. This is the booklet I read when I was first learning about Italian wine. Inquire about copies available from the Italian Trade Commission (Italian Wine Center, 499 Park Avenue, 6th floor, New York, New York 10022; 212-980-1500; fax: 758-1050).

The Italian Wine Guide: Where to Go and What to See, Drink, and Eat, Touring Club of Italy, 1999. A comprehensive, well-designed companion published by the respected Touring Club of Italy, covering the twenty Italian wine-growing regions. There are separate chapters on Tuscany and Umbria, each including DOC zones, descriptions of the wines, maps, suggestions for hotels, restaurants, antiques fairs, golf courses, wine stores, farmhouse holidays, and driving directions for wine routes. I'm surprised there isn't a general description of Italian wine labels, but there are explanantions of IGT, DOC, and DOCG terms. In all, 744 wineries offering guided tours and tastings are featured. *Essenziale.*

"Tuscan Eldorado: Maremma's New Magic," *Gambero Rosso,* #20, 1999. A good article about the wines (a few whites, but mostly red) from Tuscany's up-and-coming Maremma region.

Firenze
(Florence)

"It is popular to admire the Arno. It is a great historical creek, with four feet in the channel and some scows floating around. It would be a very plausible river if they would pump some water into it. They call it a river, and they honestly think it is a river, do these dark and bloody Florentines. They even help out the delusion by building bridges over it."
— Mark Twain, *The Innocents Abroad*, 1869

The First Time I Saw Florence

BY SALLIE TISDALE

～

editor's note

SALLIE TISDALE is the author of numerous books, including *The Best Thing I've Ever Tasted: The Secret of Food* (Riverhead, 2000), *Talk Dirty to Me: An Intimate Philosophy of Sex* (Doubleday, 1995), and *Stepping Westward: The Long Search for Home in the Pacific Northwest* (Henry Holt, 1991). She also writes for *Condé Nast Traveler,* where this piece was featured in March 1997.

When I tell people I am going to Florence soon, I hear two things in reply. The first is always said a little wistfully, quietly: "I went to Florence once." And after a pause, comes the gleam in the eye, and the list: "You must do . . ." You must do/go/see—this and this and that. The tone of that second sentence is a little aggrieved. Do it for me, is the unspoken phrase—because I'm not there to do it for myself.

I have an armchair quarterback's knowledge of Florence. When I was seventeen, without warning, I became infatuated with Michelangelo. I collected copies of his work and read some of the history of his place and time, of that particular Florence, resilient and enduring in the mind: the Florence of the Medicis, Savonarola, intrigue, genius, and war. Florence is a place I know only through the wistful memories of friends, and through reading. My images are of old photographs and engravings, and I see the city filled with sober palaces, casually great museums, magnificent churches; a city of neighborhoods and alleyways; and, in my mind's eye, a labyrinth of empty, echoing avenues free of urban fuss.

I know better, of course. Stendhal, in 1817, called Florence "nothing better than a vast museum full of foreign tourists." John Ruskin was bitter about the number of hackney coaches crowding the squares. Henry James, a few years later, complained about the "crush" of winter traffic along the Cascine, the public park that skirts the Arno. Mary McCarthy, who lived in Florence in the 1950s, called it "a terrible city, in many ways, uncomfortable and dangerous to live in, a city of drama, argument, and struggle." When I came across this last quote, I shut the book. Firenze is believed to be from the Italian *fiore,* for flower; one of the city symbols is the lily; it has a bloody, brilliant, unmistakably urban history; it has always been densely populated and heavily visited; the surrounding Tuscan hillsides are famously green and bucolic. Yet to me, Florence remains canvas and stone, a monotype all shades of white and gray, a grave and silent place, a private dream. My first view of the city is by way of a careening taxi ride through busy, narrow streets; my first, jet-lagged impression is a mess of noise and cars. For what seems a long time for such a small city, the taciturn driver (who speaks only English obscenities) screeches and squeals through dim alleys, past scooters and cars parked every which way, without an inch to spare.

He leaves me on a narrow sidewalk in front of my unprepossessing hotel; through its dark foyer is a happy maze of common rooms and winding stairways, dark paintings and plush armchairs. The shuttered windows of my tiny clean room look out over a courtyard full of blooming shrubs and birdsong and mosquitoes that have had a lot of experience with shutters. I fall into linen sheets until my traveling companion arrives.

She has come to join me in Florence on her way from Rome to Venice. She is rested, cheerful, acclimated; I am in a fragile, dazed state of sleep deprivation. We walk though the crowded twilight streets, dodging bellicose scooters and manic cars, heading vaguely west through dimming stone-walled ways. There is no logic to the streets that I can see; the lingerie and shoe and clothing and paper and music shops all seem to be ten feet square with seven individual items for sale, all jumbled up with trattorias, *pizzicherie,* pastry shops, tiny bars, newsstands, pharmacies. Coffee and liquor are for sale everywhere; so are postcards of Michelangelo's *David* with sunglasses on.

Then my companion nudges me, says, "Look," and I turn to see above me the sweep of the Duomo, its rust red dome looming over the narrow walk in maternal splendor. Henry James knew this fractured view, the way the cathedral is seen "from the deep street as you greet the side of a mountain when you move in the gorge . . . content with the minor accidents." Any number of visitors have noted, with varying degrees of complaint, that there is no other way to see it. The Duomo anchors the city; it is buried in the city, and only a portion can be seen at a time—one gets little glimpses of a corner, a gable, an arch, or a sidelong look at the wedding cake facade. It seems altogether less a whole object than the sum of its highly fantasized parts, a gigantic sum for that, a continual, impossible, surprise.

We walk under the mild, delicate twilight sky, with crescent moon and clouds in a pink vault, across the Arno River. Above us rise towering cypress trees. As we cross back across the Ponte alle Grazie, I lean over the sluggish, turbid water and see giant rodents below—sleek, dark rodents, several feet long, swimming contentedly along in the midst of my imaginary city.

The next day, we set out into the daytime chaos. The streets are ravines of stone and fluttering laundry, winding just enough to confuse, slipping shyly between battlemented medieval buildings and the somber cliffside walls of palazzi. The avenues are crammed with traffic: with scooters, taxis, cars, buses, bicycles; with mobs of people trying simply to cross the road. One short stretch of road is suddenly, disconcertingly, empty, and then a single turn reveals a honking, screeching river of cars. Every corner echoes with horns and the squeal of brakes, with rapid, argumentative conversation and the unmuffled roar of the internal combustion engine, with heels ticking on cobblestones and radios bursting from behind shutters.

We pedestrians are routinely forced off the narrow walks into the streets, taking turns letting each other pass; walking becomes a rhythm of stepping up and down, looking forward and back, listening, double-checking at corners, waiting an extra beat for safety's sake. The drivers seem quite mad. I begin to see Mary McCarthy's point.

In the center of the city, near the Duomo, where cars and scooters are limited or prohibited at different times of the day, the wide avenues stream with people: half a million Florentines, dressed breathtakingly well, and visitors—Italians from out of town, Japanese in large groups and Germans in small ones, Australians in pairs and South Asians in extended families, Irish and Filipino and Ethiopian and Mexican. I see two young Hawaiians, dressed to surf. Many Americans, alone and in pairs, pushing baby strollers, folding and unfolding maps, in groups, taking pictures, holding hands, looking lost. The steps of the Duomo are covered with people, the steps on every building around the Duomo are covered with people, people line the sidewalks, lean against the walls. People walk with purpose, stand without reason, hawk cheap jewelry, smoke, read the paper, eat, talk, talk, talk. A well-dressed man carefully brushes his teeth; a carabiniere chats up three girls; a waiter walks up the center of the pavement carrying a silver tray, two fizzing glasses of champagne upon it.

We walk east through the crowd to the Church of Santa Croce, skirting bleachers in its piazza, which is filled with sand for a beach-volleyball tournament. Inside the door of the grand church is a big white arrow with the word MICHELANGELO, pointing to his tomb, where a sad angel perches, chin in hand. Next to Michelangelo is a memorial to Dante, another to Machiavelli; across the center of the church, which is filled with enormous scaffolding like a metal cobweb, is the tomb of Galileo.

Pure Gothic, this echoing space of distant arches and delicate tracery. The chancel, with its stained glass, giant crucifix, and elaborate altar, seems to wait at the end of a tall tunnel in which I am as small as a mouse, as quiet as a mouse. Chapels on both sides rest in darkness; I find a 200-lira coin for the "illumination" machine in a far corner and buy one minute of light on the frothy gold leaf decor of devotion. Heavy pews are lined up on a floor of tombs, the status symbols of wealthy patrons. The stone figures underfoot are so old and worn in places that their features are gone; they are marble ghosts.

I pass among large, milling groups, hearing snatches of tour lectures in four languages, watching the coordinated movement of faces gazing roofward all at once. The illumination machines click on, people turn and look upon Giotto, the lecture ends, the machine clicks off again. Outside, I watch people in shorts walk in past the sign saying NO SHORTS. The bare-chested volleyball players jump and slap and grunt by pairs, in the blare of speakers playing old American rock and roll.

In midafternoon, the shops and restaurants and museums close with a definitive bang and the city is almost quiet. I go to my hotel and watch *Matlock,* for the subtle pleasure of Andy Griffith dubbed by a young Italian on too much espresso.

The outdoor marketplace by the Church of San Lorenzo is a rabble of intense shoppers, full of deals and Whitney Houston yodeling out of powerful speakers. We are going up Via Cavour to the Galleria dell' Accademia so I can see *David,* a central player in my dream time. I enter with a playful sense of anticipation. "When you go to see the *David*," my friend Nancy wrote to me a few weeks ago, "wear cotton panties."

And yet I'm not prepared. I turn the first corner, and there is *David,* awash in soft light at the end of a long, vaulted hallway, with people swirling about his enormous feet. The four unfinished *Slaves* line the wall of the long gallery like guests at a wedding.

Behind me, alone and by twos and threes, other visitors turn the corner. A few gasp or murmur, surprised, suddenly whispering, in a half-dozen languages.

I take my time getting there, examining the strange, accidental *Slaves*. They are largely ignored. One can get quite close to them, and quite close to the enormous *David,* too. Close enough to stare straight up his smooth torso, close enough to see the obvious repair marks on the left forearm, the right middle finger. Close enough to see the carved MN on his right calf and the tiny white sticker on his bottom. I am startled to see that *David* is dusty. *David* has not been washed in a long time. *David,* in fact, has cobwebs.

I stand back awhile, looking at the immensely pleasing lines of this sculpture I've longed to see, soaking up the subtle color of the marble and the complexity of expression in the face. Next to me, a stout British matron in a shocking-pink suit stares too, in a long silence, and finally says, without turning her head to her friend, "His chest is just super."

We find, at La Maremmana on Via de' Macci, a polite oasis of quiet and an antipasto buffet that haunts me for weeks afterward— pickled eggplant, juicy anchovies, roasted peppers, grilled zucchini, slabs of whitefish in an oily peppercorn marinade. At Maremmana I begin to see just how hard it can be to get a cup of plain black tea in Italy. *"Tè caldo, per favore." "Tè caldo? Freddo?" "No, caldo."* The waiter is dubious, shakes his head. *"Con latte? Zucchero?" "No, niente."* I have only phrasebook Italian, and he clearly thinks I've got the wrong words. *"Niente." "Con pesca, o limone?" "No, niente, per favore."* When my tea arrives, it is lukewarm, pale, and filled with lemon. I repeat this conversation many times, in many cafés, with the same result.

The evening is gelato time in the busy, bright tile of Vivoli's. We choose between strange flavors—mascarpone and white rice and rum crisp. Strolling away from Vivoli, through the small groups with their tiny cups and tiny white plastic spoons, I see so many stunned foreigners, so many subdued Italians from down south, so many teenagers with their golden brows and restless feet, that I know I'm watching the gates of the famous Florentine summer season swing open wide.

I wake early, a few days after my arrival, to the joyful noise of low thunder, and lie drowsily in the dark for some time while the rain waxes and wanes against the shutters. The bass shout of thunder in the valley is so abrupt and demanding it makes the heart sit up and take notice; it makes me want to stand on the bed and sing. Its echoes roll down the streets even as the next bolt flashes by above.

Rest and motion—so much to do: The Museo di Storia della Scienza, with room after room of polished brass armillary spheres and painted globes and strange machines for measuring electro-magnetics, and the bones of Galileo's left middle finger. *Farmacie* and herbalists selling everything from incense and perfume to restorative unguents. The museum at the Pietre Dure Workshop, celebrating the half-forgotten and slightly weird art of painting with colored stones. The Boboli Gardens, a bit dusty and ragged, with feral cats darting from hedge to hedge.

On one corner of the ugliest piazza in town, the ill-begotten parking lot of the Mercato Centrale, we find a tiny trattoria called, simply, Mario. It has the typical trattoria's stadium seating, cramped tables of strangers keeping track of their water and wine and ignoring each other's conversations. We order bowls of an exquisite ravioli and tart mixed salads. In the ordered chaos, the food comes quickly, brought by stout, middle-aged waitresses in white aprons and little soft white caps and red lipstick; they remember everything, write nothing down. We rest, and eat, without room to cross our legs, and in the dull roar of conversation overhead is the constant murmur of the staff skirting by, *"Permesso, permesso,"* balancing bowls of soup and pasta, whispering, *"Permesso."*

The Campanile, the frosted bell tower of Giotto, stands with the Duomo like a soaring cliff beside the mountain's dignified peak. In Florence, much is lovely that needn't be lovely; much is breathtaking when lovely would do. The grand loggia of the Uffizi—the Uffizi, with its absurd wealth of art—is far grander than required. Its stairs are preposterously wide, the corridors ridiculously long. Even the Bargello, the old prison, with its history of torture and executions, is filled now with fine ivory carving, tapestries, armor, the resting bronze birds of Giambologna. And from every angle, the exquisite marblework and soaring lines of the Campanile beckon the eye upward.

Dire warnings about the effect of the climb on the ill and the weak are posted at the ticket window, where the plump, despairing guard sits in judgment on us all. We who climb become spelunkers, following the wavering bottoms of strangers up worn, narrow, and spiraling stairs, balancing against dank walls covered with cosmopolitan graffiti. At the top, winded travelers catch their breath in several languages and linger over the grand view—the sea of red tile roofs and television antennas, the cavernous streets, the distant hills of pine and olive. People take each other's pictures, trading cameras.

In the evening, we find our way to Osteria dei Cento Poveri, west of Santa Maria Novella. We scrutinize its fancy, handwritten menu, lost in the elaborate colloquialisms of Tuscan cuisine, and the fussy, baby-faced waiter finally brings us a basket of dead fish, insisting we pick our favorite. With a flourish, with distant curiosity, he brings us spaghetti with raw tomatoes and green beans and shreds of hard ricotta, good Tuscan wine, the grilled fish, and shot glasses of *vin santo* in which to dip hard almond cookies. The room is narrow, dim, and fragrant, and over the slow, intoxicating dinner we listen to Michael Jackson and bad British pop. Eventually our dimpled waiter, who speaks no English, brings a plate of pasta to our table and joins us without waiting to be invited, and we scribble on the tablecloth with pencils, drawing our conversation back and forth.

We buy gelato, quite late at night—kiwi, and *torroncino,* a kind of nougat, hazelnut and banana, and chocolate—and walk through the deserted square of San Lorenzo, by the silent, dark, comfortable church, with cups of ice cream in our hands. It begins quite suddenly to rain. We stop in a lighted shoe store doorway to wait, under the narrow roof and up against the glass, halos of light and shoes around our heads. The rain falls in white streaks through the empty dark, and four people run toward us, laughing, darting vainly, and when they reach the pedestrian rails by the empty street, they simply leap over them like so many gazelles and run on.

When we pass the Duomo, people are streaming in and out, and we enter to find a choir singing, lit only by a hundred candles burning in the shadowy space.

The next day my companion leaves for Venice; I take my happy solitude for an early morning hike to the Piazzale Michelangelo. Swifts dart like little dark arrowheads in the pale, fragrant sky, in front of fluffy bits of cloud. I cross the Arno, seeking giant rodents. In one of my city guides I have found a terse and curious reference to escaped coypu, and nothing more. The water is empty; there is nothing there.

I expect the *piazzale* to be a little park with a famously good view. The short, steep climb up Poggi's pretty steps brings me to a big parking lot filled with a sickly green copy of *David,* tour buses and souvenir carts, street artists, and flocks of people gazing at the skyline. The city's repeating tints of red and rust, dry yellow, and dark, wet green are like quiet water with only a few stark waves to break the surface. Florence is an uncompromisingly horizontal place these days; it's safer this way. In medieval Florence, every major family had a tower from which to toss pitch and garbage on their enemies.

I ask a woman from Washington, D.C., to take my picture. She tells me that her daughter studied here and has brought the whole family over to show them her adopted home. I stand before the Duomo, of course, and smile. Yes, I'm alone, I tell her; my traveling companion has gone to Venice for a few days. I wanted to stay.

"Venice is nice," she agrees. "But this place has class."

Casa Buonarroti is an unassuming, almost anonymous building on the corner of Via Ghibellina and Via Michelangelo Buonarroti. The airy, nourishing space was owned by Michelangelo and is now his museum—all small, tall, whitewashed rooms opening one into the other, with long windows and slim arches. His earliest sculptures are here, the *Madonna of the Steps* and the *Battle of the Centaurs*. A small group of lovely Italian teenagers with hardly any clothes on are carefully copying into big artists' pads; they lean against each other and whisper. One room is filled with the memorabilia of anniversary celebrations, the pomp and circumstance of intense civic pride. An entire wing of the house consists of rococo tribute rooms done by Michelangelo's nephew after his death. I feel a funny melancholy here, missing a man dead almost five hundred years, a man famously unpleasant, with little regard for women. Wandering the overdecorated memorial rooms, finding his cup, his brush, his shoes, all encased and labeled, I begin to see that there is nothing untoward in my feeling for Michelangelo. It is only reasonable here. It is simply Italian, peculiarly Florentine. For the frantic lunchtime rush, for the *spaghettini* with shellfish, for the *panzanella*—and because it is near the *David*.

This time, I wait in line for forty minutes, snaking down the sidewalk past the Senegalese poster and belt and necklace salesmen working the crowd, pushing pictures of *David*, on special today. *David* is everywhere in the city—on postcards, T-shirts, neckties, watch bands, handbags, miniaturized by the thousands. Botticelli's *Venus* is everywhere too, and certain sappy cupids, an occasional *Mona Lisa*, fragments of the Sistine. One never sees copies of the subtle, decrepit *Bacchus,* though, or the stunning *Rape of the Sabines,* or Donatello's creepy *Maddalena.* Faith in tourists is a conservative religion.

The multiple repetitions of *David* have no lasting impact; the real thing is beyond imitation. He stands there, his mind on other things, and one expects to look away for a moment and turn back to find he has changed position—to find him looking at you, serene, arrogant. To wander in *David*'s shadow is to wander in a crowd of cheerful neophytes, people frankly amazed, moved without having expected to be moved. I feel completely contented here for a long time.

The crowds ebb and flow, festive, pleased. Two Irishmen sit beside me in the gallery. "Don't bother with the camera," says one. "The postcards are better." But the thickset, balding man continues to adjust his focus. "I want it in me photo album," he says, and takes the picture.

So much to do. The paper shops, glassmakers, shoe stores. The Santa Croce cloister, with its surprise Henry Moore. Maremmana again, for the much-desired antipasto buffet, the same tepid, pale tea. The Cappella dei Principi, a kind of Mad Hatter's fever dream of precious stone—oversize, overwrought, the giant crypts like big boats of crusted jewels, the dome florid with the Greatest Hits of the Bible.

The New Sacristy, containing the tombs of Lorenzo de' Medici and his hapless son and grandson, is a small room of monochromatic intensity. Michelangelo wrote, as he worked on these statues, "here we still are crushed/by doubt of joy." There is no color but the varied grays and creams and off-whites of Carrara marble, *pietra dura, pietra serena.* On two sides are the representations of time. They are not to everyone's liking, large and naked and preoccupied as they are. *Dawn* is drowsy, and her belly and thighs are full of possibility; her bluntly erotic lines disconcert on a grave. *Dusk* is rough and entwined in the rock, at ease, disdainful. *Night* ignores us, lost in memory. *Day* is monstrous, all back and thigh and benign command. They rest among the simplest angles and most perfect curves, promising and melancholy, more the Florence of my imagination than anything I've seen. It is a room resigned to loss, to the slow descent into self-examination. A room destined for solitude.

Four downy, slouching Italian teenagers perch on the crypt railing, talking, their backs to the marble. A Paraguayan couple repeatedly shoo people away from their examination of the statues to take long, involved photographs. A guard chases the teenagers off the rail, and then berates a woman to the point of tears for using a flashbulb. A large Italian tour group arrives and piles themselves up against the simple altar, listening halfheartedly to a lecture. An American woman behind me says to her friends, over and over, "We've got to keep moving."

In Florence, Mary McCarthy wrote, the past is "near and indifferently real." The grand and rare is an everyday thing; the things of everyday are treated with the same offhand manner as the grand and the rare. This is my great surprise: not that my grave and silent Florence, my dreamed Florence, is a riot of human beings, or that it smells of exhaust and sweat and sewage, or that it rumbles with noise night and day. The surprise is that I like this peopled Florence so much more than the dream; the multitudes animate the ghostly past with their fleshy presence. Like the city's history, they—we—are dignified and cruel, cynical and innocent, full of misery and of cheer. This human swell, this rolling, mammalian river of people, is the same swell, the same people, that has been here for centuries of contentious civic debate, assassinations, festivals, plague, flood, and massacre, Raphael and Botticelli and Masaccio, olive groves and wine so good it seems to spring from the well of soil.

What better response to the noble disregard of *Dawn* and *Dusk* than to sit on their rail and talk? How else to react, confronted with Brunelleschi's improbable Dome, than to stand and stare with craning neck? And what better thing to do next than eat?

I can barely resist the Chinese restaurants scattered around town, especially after seeing a large Japanese tour group march into one, silent and single file. Hard to resist, for that matter, the lone Japanese restaurant, called Eido, off the Piazza della Signoria, which offers, among other things, "*zuppa di miso*." There is an Indian curry joint, a Brazilian disco club, an Irish pub. But I choose Sasso di Dante, near Dante's putative house, a rectangular room full of French people. I am the only person alone. The Florentines, I've decided, are mad behind the wheel because they are alone then; being alone makes them uncomfortable; driving is the tense and serious affair of getting as quickly as possible to the company of others. The handsome men at Sasso di Dante bring *spaghetti alla puttanesca* and grilled vegetables and water and wine to my little table under the kitchen window, where they seated me so I wouldn't feel lonesome.

Zubin Mehta is coming to give a free concert in the Piazza della Signoria, a spacious square filled with riotously varied sculpture: Cellini's bronze *Perseus*, Giambologna's *Hercules and the Centaur* and his magnificent *Rape of the Sabines*, a lumbering *Neptune*, another copy of *David*, a loggia of distant, writhing figures. Tiered steps of the Palazzo Vecchio were the traditional site of Florence's innumerable public debates—*arringare*, from which we get our word *harangue*. Here the fanatic Savonarola burned books and paintings on the Bonfire of the Vanities; here he was burned himself. Here, Mary McCarthy relates in a long catalog of horrors, a man was eaten by an angry crowd. Here, wrote D. H. Lawrence, is "the perfect center of the human world."

The thunderstorms have passed, and the famous summer heat of the Arno valley is pouring in. For two days, I've watched the orchestra stage go up, the sound and television trucks come in, the electrical cables being connected. The scene is attended by self-conscious, chain-smoking classical music roadies, and even more people have arrived. All over town the mood just says, "Holiday!"

The steps of the Palazzo Vecchio are covered with tired travelers politely watching the show they put on for each other. The square is sunny and fresh and crowded and loud, the roadies do a sound check—"*Uno, due, tre.*" The square swells with violins, with the roll of timpani, filling the air and startling the pigeons.

I have done what Stendhal did when he came here—"grown incapable of rational thought . . . surrendered to the sweet turbulence." When you go to Florence, you must see . . . this and this and that. You must hear a Rachmaninoff sound check on a sunny day. See a midnight choir in the Duomo. Eat gelato by a shoe store late at night, in the rain.

I return for dinner at a terrace restaurant in the piazza. The breeze is cool; my wine and water is, too. Behind me the waiters jabber like a flock of big, deep-voiced birds. The square is a slow simmer of people and pigeons, streams going every which way, shifting, sifting, changing direction, changing their mind. The bell of the Palazzo Vecchio begins to ring—a tenor gong tolling the hour for a long time, fading very slowly, sliding its sound invisibly into my dreams, into the myth I am making of Florence.

Divertimento

The list of must-see sights in Florence is exclusively artistic and historical, with a single exception. A friend said I mustn't miss a little-known museum called La Specola, which means "observatory." No casual visitor would stumble upon the place, located on a side road south of the Pitti Palace, through a dark, dirty courtyard, and up three flights of stairs. The museum is open mornings a few days a week, and, from day to day, certain floors and rooms are closed.

The surpassingly weird La Specola is the best antidote in town to an overdose of gorgeous Crucifixions. It is part of the University of Florence's Natural History Museum and contains a tribute room to Galileo, though its main attraction is zoology. La Specola is not for the squeamish or for small children, but it is not to be missed by the curious.

The zoological floor is divided into two sections—natural history and waxworks. The natural history rooms have everything from a hollowed-out elephant foot to a disconcertingly long tapeworm and a ratty-looking gorilla. Room after windowless room form a maze of brightly lit glass display cases containing hundreds of taxidermied specimens: corals and insects, sharks and land tortoises, emus and quetzals and eagles, a white rhinoceros, a hippopotamus, a Tasmanian wolf, an echidna. I wandered these eerie, hypnotic rooms, which smell faintly and constantly of preservative, in solitude; the only other visitors I saw in two hours were a mother with her two small, wide-eyed children.

But those who go to La Specola do so for the human corpses most of all. Passing out of the animal rooms and into the waxwork section is a step through the looking glass, from natural history to nightmare. In perfect realism, chickens and turtles, human fetuses and pregnant women, spinal cords and skulls, genitalia and whole bodies, fill the rooms. Each is dissected in a different way—for these are teaching models. Grand Duke Pietro Leopoldo of Lorraine, who founded the museum, and Felice Fontana, the first director, wanted to find a way to teach anatomy without the distasteful use of human corpses. An elaborate series of models was developed, from 1771 until the mid-1800s, into a collection of more than 1,400 pieces.

The Grand Duke's plan misfired dramatically. The effect of the models is one of continual vivisection; a walk through these strange rooms is a walk through a disturbingly violent fantasy world. The brilliant waxwork artists weren't content to make body parts according to drawings. They created sculpture, and all the models look alive in the midst of their evisceration. A young woman, gazing serenely, reclines on a soft bed, holding her braid in her hand, her chest and abdomen exploded into Technicolor butchery. Half-dissected heads in cases have their eyes open and a bit of goatee showing. A large man made to demonstrate the lymph system seems to rise in agony off his pallet, eyes wide and shocked by the brutality of his torture; he is called by local people *lo scorticato,* "the skinned." One room contains the life-work of a modeler famous in his time, Gaetano Zumbo—four brilliant dioramas of macabre plague scenes, a series depicting the effects of syphilis, and a decomposing head.

I mentioned my visit to the desk clerk at my hotel. He looked wistful and smiled in memory. "Ah, La Specola," he said. "I have not been to La Specola since I was a child."

Personal Best

My ideal travel guide to a city I've not visited before has a little of the historical and cultural context, the best hours to get into the most interesting museum, how to make a telephone call and where to get my linen trousers dry-cleaned, the location of every public toilet in town, how to buy a bus ticket, and a number of useful phrases for restaurants, shops, and getting around. ("I'll be 33 years old on July 16, 1967," is not a useful phrase. Neither is "I would like to buy a can of balls." Both of these are in my Italian phrase book.) My imaginary guidebook also has a complete and logical index and a good map. It does not exist.

As an experiment, I took four guides to Florence: *Knopf Guides: Florence;* Dorling Kindersley's *Eyewitness: Florence & Tuscany;* Fodor's *Exploring Florence & Tuscany;* and *Insight Guides: Florence.* Although the soberingly thorough 300-page *Blue Guide: Florence* (Norton) is *the* definitive paperback reference to art and culture, I do not include it because it has only twelve pages of practical advice.

I was immediately taken with the **Knopf** guide, one of the Gallimard series published in France and only recently translated into English. These are smartly packaged, almost gorgeous books filled with slick color prints, cutaway drawings, innumerable photographs, and even architectural plans. The explosion of information in collage form has an obvious hypertext influence, and the result is quite seductive.

The honeymoon was over once I started using it. Written by Europeans, the Gallimard books presume a certain Continental familiarity and are light on pragmatic information. The historical and cultural information is strong and authoritative, but the emphasis here is on esoteric facts and small details rather than fundamentals, and the visually inspired graphics are actually rather confusing. After a few days with this book, I felt myself to be in the presence of a densely educated and somewhat bombastic uncle with a tendency to meander; eventually he gets to the point, but there are a lot of little diversions along the way.

Whether it's the competition from Gallimard or simply the continuing trend in media, **Eyewitness** also suffers from the trendy cut-and-paste graphics design. This is a useful and practical guide with a cheerful tone, but it's trying much too hard to be visually entertaining. Of the four guides, Eyewitness easily has the best city maps—a central series dividing the city into useful sections. There is a also a street finder, vital for Florence, and map codes are given for restaurants, shops, and museums. However, I skimmed through the book's endless annotated drawings and photographs and scanned the index for two days before I figured any of this out.

Fodor's has long been determinedly middlebrow and, in consequence, boring. Less successfully than Eyewitness, it's taken on the cut-and-paste graphics approach, too. While Fodor's is less confusingly dotted with detail, it's not as well written, though the description of major artworks avoids some of the insider's snootiness of the Knopf guides.

The **Insight** guide is simply a puzzle. I can't imagine who the target audience for this glum and clunky book could be. It's basically a collection of essays on aspects of Florentine history and life, but they seem to be written for a college textbook. In spite of the academic tone, information is presented in a maddeningly nonlinear fashion. For example, the index entry for the Palazzo Vecchio sends me to single references in different chapters scattered throughout the book on everything from city planning to politics to rulers of history; there is no single description of the Palazzo itself. Restaurant addresses are given with no clue to what section of the city the addresses are in. References to museums don't list opening and closing times—that information is in a section at the back of the book.

A city like Florence, with its complex and dramatic history and immense wealth of art, really requires more than one guide. Although both require a certain amount of patient sifting, I would recommend taking the Knopf guide (for its art history) and the Eyewitness (for its cheerful information). Don't go without a phrase book, as well—you may need to say "Please forward my mail to Venice."

Devouring a Classic

BY JEAN BOND RAFFERTY

editor's note

Sometimes it seems that Florence's beauty and success have conspired against her—with over two million visitors a year, almost everything's crowded, almost all the time. It's noisy, and tour groups abound. Despite all this, however, *Firenze* is irresistible, and the presence of lots of tourists is not a reason to deter you from visiting what is still one of the most special cities in the world. Even on cloudy days (and there *are* gray and rainy days in Florence), "the warm colors many of the buildings are painted—cream, mustard, saffron, butterscotch, egg yolk, zabaglione—give the impression of sun upon them," as Mark Mitchell has noted in *Italian Pleasures*.

In a special issue of *Wine Spectator* (February 28, 1995), writer Thomas Matthews presented some sensible approaches to visiting the city in an essay titled "Why Visit Florence?" His first rule is to avoid large groups: "Florence has always been a city of brilliant individuals" and is therefore "best appreciated the same way, one on one, or with a few kindred souls." Secondly, he believes one should be prepared, and although Florence is a small city, it's dense with significant things to see: "Most visitors budget only two or three days to explore its treasures; unless you focus your attention, the city will go by in a blur." Lastly, he notes that the cuisine of Tuscany is equally noteworthy, and he recommends planning your meals with as much care as the rest of your itinerary. Matthews then suggests that a good way to incorporate all of the above is to concentrate on a particular theme or neighborhood. Having a theme "helps put the city's treasures in context, gives you a way to link and interpret what you see. And there's almost always a *trattoria* or wine bar nearby that will satisfy your hunger and soothe your tired feet. All it takes is planning." I couldn't agree more.

JEAN BOND RAFFERTY has lived in Paris for over twenty-five years and writes about a wide variety of topics for a wide variety of publications, including *Town & Country, Departures,* and the former *European Travel & Life,* where this piece originally appeared.

Florence is like a very intricate trompe l'oeil painting. Just when you think you've mastered its meaning, you notice another angle that throws everything back into question. The solution? Surrender. And no matter how many times you return to Florence, its romantic beauty comes as a shock. Soaring domes and slender towers cradled between gentle green hills, graceful colonnades marking off a peaceful square, the jumble of ocher houses with green shutters and red-tiled roofs across the silvery Arno on the Ponte Vecchio, impossibly beautiful frescoes, the perfection of human forms frozen in marble: Florence is the world's greatest celebration of the triumph of the human spirit, and one is still fortunate to be invited in.

Some celebrants always overdo, of course. The French writer Stendhal gave his name to the syndrome that continues to afflict the overindulgent in the Renaissance magnificence that, despite wars and floods, still dazzles on every side. Stendhal simply swooned at the splendor of Santa Croce. Modern manifestations range from dizzy spells to a sensory overload requiring bed rest. The Florence hospital regularly reports such cases. Contemporary sculptor Marino Marini had a fainting spell on his first childhood sight of the Baptistery, the Duomo, and Giotto's bell tower in the Piazza San Giovanni. Afterward, he would walk along the *lungarno* and sneak up on the Piazza della Signoria from behind, peeping around the corner to lighten the impact of the full frontal view that made his head spin.

The youthful strategy seems to be to take the city in tandem. Paris has the reputation for romance. Florence has the reality. Everywhere one looks, couples—nestled in a niche of a marbled facade, hidden in a thicket in the Boboli Gardens, silhouetted against the moonlit Arno, or even bicycling nose to nose in a death-defying glide across the Piazza della Santissima Annunziata—are clasped in close embrace.

"Florence is impossible to describe," says Marchese Emilio Pucci, who, as war hero, politician, philosopher, and sportsman as well as couturier, is a modern Renaissance man. "If you look at an Etruscan museum, you're flabbergasted by the beauty of things made three or four thousand years ago," he says. "It's impossible to understand how they did these things that cannot be done today."

The mysterious people who settled the Fiesole hills above Florence and gave their name to Tuscany predated the Romans and rivaled the Greeks and Phoenicians. They are vital to understanding why the Florentines are a race apart. Their language and origins are still enigmas, and the beauty of their art, exemplified by the *Chimera of Arezzo*, the mythical monster in the Archaeological Museum, astonished even the Renaissance. Florentines consider themselves the Etruscans' rightful heirs, so much so that the Italian government has failed to convince many of them that Etruscan relics, which are uncovered from time to time, belong to the state.

Florentines, refreshingly, make no bones about the role of money in their remarkable achievements. "We were the biggest thieves in history," one quips. "We invented banks." The extraordinary concentration of magnificent art and architecture that was the Renaissance owes much to a brand of capitalism that would be saluted on Wall Street today. The Renaissance was paid for, COD, by the powerful Florentine establishment in banking, like the Medicis, and the wool and silk traders who, fortunately for posterity, translated their power into enduring art.

"Florentine nobility was built on money, unlike the French, who go on about being *chevaleresque,*" says American-born Helen de Saint-Anthost, who with husband Jean and five children has split her time between homes in Paris and Florence for the last thirty years. "Florence was the bank of Europe. People like to separate art and money, but that's ridiculous."

French kings dispensed with any snobbery when it came to making matches with Medici merchant heiresses. Florentines like to say the French were still eating with their hands when Caterina de' Medici brought civilization to the French court on her marriage to the future Henry II. She gave birth to three more French kings, Francis II, Charles IX, and Henry III.

"Florence is very international," adds Saint-Anthost, "and Florentine society is more open than French society. Having intermarried with English and Americans, Florentines are used to foreigners, and for an American it's much nicer. But it's also a small town with an *esprit de province.* You always run into everyone you know when you're in town. My sister-in-law said it reminded her of Charleston."

The story of her family in Florence could be right out of the pages of Henry James or E. M. Forster, whose chronicles of

Americans and English in Italy were literary lures for the grand tour. "My grandfather was an artist, and he went to Florence every year for two months. When my father bought a villa here in 1956, it was the most wonderful place in the world to live."

Few Florentines feel that way today. Other European cities have revitalized and revamped, but Florence's permanent population of 450,000 has a trying time living in a city that resembles a Renaissance film set, with waves of tourists surging on and off stage like so many Greek choruses. From taxi drivers to marchesi, they complain about the government's inability to come to grips with such pressing problems as the pollution that is eating away at the statues and darkening the marble facades; the traffic, which, despite a daytime limitation on cars in the center of town, is nightmarish; the total inadequacy of parking; and the tourist buses that shoulder their way through narrow medieval streets, sometimes knocking off a piece or two of a Renaissance palazzo.

And, while walking across the tarmac to a propeller plane at the city's tiny airport may bring visitors a rush of nostalgia for the last scene in *Casablanca,* residents find it a rankling reminder of their small-town status. "It's easier to get to Anchorage," says Alessandro Pucci, Emilio's son, who frequently flies abroad to promote his antique silk manufacture. Most international flights leave from Pisa, which has a direct train connection with Florence, taking about an hour. The entrepreneurial excitement has moved west to the town of Prato, known as the Manchester of Tuscany. Florentines admit the city has been outdistanced by a community of wealthy and successful textile industrialists, the "pirates of Prato."

"In this city, there is generalized decay," says Alessandro. "After ten years of discussion, you get a new bus stop." But there are rumblings of revival, and the Puccis are in the forefront. The new wave of Puccimania, the big fashion renaissance of the nineties, is being orchestrated by the Marchese's twenty-nine-year-old daughter,

Laudomia. "People my age didn't know Pucci," she says. "Madonna and Paloma Picasso discovered the leggings Papa designed in 1954. Now it means something to this generation." After a year in Paris working for Hubert de Givenchy, Laudomia came back to work with her father, streamlining the staff, adding her own team of multinational young women her own age, and rediscovering the colors in the bold shades of blue, violet, pink, and yellow that had made her father the prince of prints, while adding new shapes, like a bomber jacket. She plunged into a very un-Florentine lifestyle of "working day and night to keep it going," commuting between Florence, Paris, New York, and London. When Bergdorf Goodman sold out its first order in three days and Pucci was splashed across the covers of all the fashion magazines, she knew she was on the right track.

Alessandro, thirty-one, is reviving the Antico Setificio Fiorentino, the family's silk factory, where silk is handwoven in the techniques of the Renaissance on antique machines. (The showroom is open to the public.) Because this silk is so phenomenally pricey (up to $1,200 a meter), he has used modern technology to produce a similar silk made on looms in the north of Italy. He has teamed up with London designer Scott Crolla to turn remnants into a line of classic jackets, shirts, pants, and shoes, and there are plans to open a boutique in Milan's Brera.

Making your mark while young is not easy here even if you bear one of the city's famous names. "In Florence, they don't give you responsibility until you are ready to die," says Alessandro. Laudomia had her own solution to not being taken seriously. "When you have a university degree in Italy, you are called Dottore, so I call myself Dottoressa. It works much better than Marchesa or Signorina."

The Pucci palazzo, on the Via dei Pucci, steps from the Duomo, brims with new energy. Everything is handmade in the palazzo, and, along with the family wine, truffles, and olive oil from the country estates, is on sale in the palazzo boutiques. Both young Puccis still live at home, in separate apartments at the top of the house with terraces and splendid views of the Duomo and green hills of Fiesole. Alessandro's bachelor penthouse was designed by Gae Aulenti in the sixties; Laudomia's is deliberately minimalist in homage to the view. She says, "We are very backward here. You live with your family until you have your own. The patriarchal system continues all through life."

In the heart of Chianti country, it was almost sacrilege when Marchese Lodovico Antinori, of the famous wine family, bucked the patriarchal pattern to create his own Bordeaux-style wine in what he calls "the wild west of Tuscany." Florentine eyebrows arched when he built an architecturally avant-garde, high-tech winery near the sea in the non-wine-producing Maremma, known as the Italian Camargue. When the 1986 vintage of his hearty, fruity Ornellaia was named one of the ten best Italian wines by *The Wine Spectator* it caused even more Florentine furor. "Everything new disturbs the establishment. They might have to change, and that is boring for them," he laughs.

"Too-cultured people have problems inventing things," says Israeli-born architect and designer David Palterer, who stayed on after architecture school and has lived here for the last twenty years. "They see everything with criticism." He is currently designing a contemporary tower for a theater restoration in San Casciano and is working on the extension of Florence's airport. "At forty-two in Italy," he says, "you finally begin to do architecture."

"You have to think in Chinese generations here. It's not New York," says Italo-American Amerigo Franchetti, who gave up his job as head of an advertising agency in Milan to transform the thirteenth-century tower and fifteenth-century villa of Torre di Bellosguardo, inherited from his grandmother, into a pampering country inn in the Florentine hills. "It's like committing suicide. You don't think about it, you do it," he jokes. "It took two years to get permission for the conversion. I went to the offices every day. Then ten years to get the money and restore it. We opened on April Fool's Day, 1988."

The restoration is ongoing, but already the lily pond has become a swimming pool, the former ballroom with frescoed ceiling is now the reception area, and the spacious rooms have views of Florence to stun the most demanding E. M. Forster heroine.

Florentine inertia is connected to Florentine pride, Franchetti says. "They're convinced Florence is the only beautiful city in the world. They spent eight to ten years talking about what color stones or bricks to use for the repaving of the Piazza della Signoria; even a crystal pavement was proposed so one could see the Roman ruins beneath. Then it took three or four years to dig it up. With the World Cup match coming up last year, the minister of culture had to step in, and finally the decision was made: to keep the original stones. By then, they had been stolen or sold. So they put the worst stones in."

But with the piazza repaved, you can again sip a sumptuous hot chocolate on the terrace of Rivoire and watch the best free show in town. Picturesque fiacres take tourists for a scenic spin; tiny tots race through the pigeons to a ripple of wings; and virtually everyone in town seems to pass on parade. Or you can contemplate the very spot where, in 1497, the militantly puritanical monk Savonarola ordered repentant Florentines to cast all their finery, mirrors, and frivolous books onto the original Bonfire of the Vanities. After a year of all piety and no play, fed-up Florentines found new fodder for the fire, and Savonarola himself was executed. Zeal has not been popular since.

Former mayor Massimo Bogiankino has his own idea as to why the city lags behind Milan and Rome. "Florentines are intelligent and honest, but while they talk, others produce," he has been known to say. Says Roman-born Marchesa Cristina Pucci, Emilio's wife,

"Everyone feels very artistic whether they are artists or not. They like to discuss very much and not to work so much. It's like living in the country."

Florentines are indeed world-class talkers, a characteristic noticed about five hundred years ago by the city's first historian, Francesco Guicciardini, who wrote, "Florence is a city accustomed to the greatest freedom of speech, full of the most volatile and restless spirits." Even earlier, in *The Decameron*, Boccaccio's idea of how to sit out the plague was by telling tales. Today, the natives are equally witty and virtuosic, on intimate terms with the glittering cast of the Renaissance: Ghirlandaio and Gozzoli, Masaccio and Masolino, Fra Filippo Lippi and his son Filippino, Donatello and Dante, Machiavelli and Michelangelo, Brunelleschi and Botticelli, Ghiberti and Galileo, and Medicis and more Medicis.

For Florentines, the eighteenth, nineteenth, and twentieth centuries are but a stitch in the tangled tapestry of their glorious past. "Maybe we're not the best, but we definitely were the best," says Alessandro Pucci. "Athens, Rome, Constantinople, then Florence. Venice is a detail. Paris, London, and New York." Though he is too polite to spell it out, it's plain the first three were a buildup and the last three a decline. If it didn't invent civilization, Florence was its perfection.

Along with their eloquence, Florentines are renowned among their countrymen for their arrogance. "Never call a Florentine an Italian," warns Sharon Odson, Canadian wife of Giuliano Gargani (a.k.a. Garga), owner, cook, and catalyst of the Trattoria Garga, where artists and writers and *tutta Firenze* come to philosophize.

To prove Florentines are not all talk, Garga gave up his moped as his own contribution to alleviating the city's pollution and embarked on a personal civic beautification project by planting a garden on the banks of the Arno, just below Harry's Bar. In an apparent fit of pique, the council bulldozed it, but, undaunted,

Garga planted another. "The Arno is so dirty, we are showing the politicians it can be beautiful," he explains.

Even Florentine craftsmen, still patronized by the great families, are not just simple artisans. Florence's most famous silversmith, Brandimarte, whose face is straight from the Masaccio frescoes in the Brancacci Chapel, is the author of over a dozen novels and known as the philosopher of silver. His atelier on Via L. Bartolini might be taken for an automotive body shop as the silver is flamed into tarnish and hammered in ringing cacophony. But the results—from the slender sheaves of silver wheat to silver cups embossed with flower motifs and a witty silver mirror that sports two silver swallows—have earned him the sobriquet of "the new Cellini."

Most of the ateliers are in the Oltrarno quarter, in a small court-yard or in a potter's shed in a patch of garden. They are fascinating to visit. On the Via Bronzino, for example, Bruno Massini creates Della Robbia "compositions" in glazed terra-cotta that are de rigueur decorations on fifteenth-century colonnades and adorn innumerable palazzo terraces in town and villas in Chianti. On the Borgo San Jacopo, Giorgio Chilleri, who has designed jewelry for Bulgari, likes to gamble on innovative designs in both precious and semiprecious stones set in gold and platinum. His gold rings with lapis balloons are famous. He couldn't, he says, work anywhere else. "I'm in love with Florence, the extraordinary streets with each window and door different from another. It shows the fantasy of the people. Even poor people have tried to do something different."

Working part-time at nine, full-time at twelve, embroidering and fashioning the lovely linens and lingerie that are a Florentine art, Loretta Caponi might have stepped from the pages of the Florentine classic *Le Sorelle Materassi*. Her two shops on the Borgognissanti are as much a beacon to a top-drawer international clientele as nearby Harry's Bar. She sells the finest hand-embroidered linens, romantic nightdresses, pillows in silk and satin, and children's clothes.

Florence is a city of contrast, where piazzas are thronged with people whose faces come straight from paintings and suddenly snap into focus amid the blur of tourists, and where courtyards are drenched in sun and serenity. Despite the crowds, museums can be empty. On a sunny morning, you might find yourself in solitude enjoying the uniquely Florentine blend of simplicity and splendor, the Fra Angelico frescoes in the monks' cells of San Marco.

With opening hours eccentric even by Italian standards—most are open only in the morning—and with many masterpieces locked away for restoration, trying to stick to a rigid museum program will drive you mad. Branch out instead to some of the Florentines' lesser-known favorites: on Via degli Alfani, for example, the Museo dell' Opticio delle Pietre Dure, with its marquetry in marble and semi-precious stones. As you round the corner into the Brancacci Chapel in the Santa Maria del Carmine church, the first sight of the newly restored frescoes by Masaccio, Filippino Lippi, and Masolino takes your breath away. One connoisseur calls the vivid Gozzoli fresco, the *Procession of the Magi,* in the chapel of the Palazzo Medici-Riccardi "one of Florence's best-kept secrets." At the moment, it is an inviolable one, as the chapel is closed for restoration. Though there is a steady stream of churchgoers, most tourists never go inside the church of Santissima Annunziata. Do and you'll be greeted by an explosion of Baroque in total contrast to the simplicity of the square. Finally, there is San Miniato al Monte, a Romanesque church with delicate geometrical marble marquetry and ravishing jewel-toned frescoes in the sacristy: a sum of the best for many natives.

Having fed the spirit, you will no doubt be in quest of more earthly sustenance. Florentine finesse is as evident in cuisine as in art, and many find eating in the city's restaurants a spiritual experience in itself. When your footsteps start to flag, make for the new Monkey Business. Though it's only steps from the Piazza della Signoria, down a tiny alley, not many tourists have discovered it. The decor is jungle exotic with a full-size elephant at the entrance, but the food is deliciously Florentine. Everyone raves over the parmesan soufflé, and the risotto Brunelleschi with asparagus and the *filletto del fiaccheraio* (fillet of beef, cooked in young red wine) are no less satisfying.

At lunchtime, the chic crowd eats alfresco under large cream parasols at Giorgio Armani's new Doney on the Piazza Strozzi, or gossips over carpaccio and the Antinori's superb wines in the Cantinetta Antinori, an elegant wine bar restaurant in the family's palazzo at the end of the Via Tornabuoni. Travelers sensitive to the dollar squeeze will brighten at the insider's belief that the best food is the least ostentatious. "The less you spend, the better you eat," says Amerigo Franchetti, so tuck a list of tried and true trattorias into your address book. Franchetti recommends Sostanza on the Via della Porcellana and Alla Vecchia Bettola on Viale L. Ariosto. After dinner, the Vespa set speeds off for a drink at Dolce Vita, an island of contemporary design in the Piazza del Carmine.

For travelers who want to stay right in town, there is news on the hotel scene. The Grand, sister hotel to the Excelsior, has been lavishly redecorated. The Helvetia & Bristol's sumptuous decor and impeccable service is attracting the panama-hat-and-navy-blazer tourist to this newly renovated hotel near the Piazza della Repubblica. The Loggiato dei Serviti, revamped by Rodolfo and Roberto Budini Gattai with much of their family furniture, is one of the most charming hotels in town. Located on what many Florentines consider the most beautiful square, the Piazza della Santissima Annunziata, it offers views of Brunelleschi's foundling hospital, with its graceful colonnade and Della Robbia medallions of babies in swaddling clothes.

In the combat against cultural overdose, avoiding action may be necessary. To clear the head: a luxe and leisurely stroll through the bucolic Boboli Gardens, across the Ponte Vecchio and down the Via

Tornabuoni, Florence's premier shopping street (home of Gucci, Ferragamo, and Enrico Coveri), with breaks for truffled rolls at Proccacci, cappuccino at Giacosa, and ice cream at Vivoli, or a search for the most original hand-marbled papers in town at Ditta A Cozzi, down the narrow Via Parione near Santa Trinita. In case of acute attack, go right out of town to La Biscondola, an open-air restaurant in the woods near San Casciano, south of the city. After a few hours spent concentrating on *crespelle* crepes filled with truffles and parmesan, and arguably the best *bistecca alla Fiorentina* in Florence, with perhaps a short siesta to follow, you'll be back in shape.

Overwhelming, even infuriating, but irresistible, Florence makes you want to return. Those who stave off Stendhal's syndrome may fall victim to a complaint that affects only ardent Florentine aficionados. "It's called 'Florentite,' and it means you are addicted to Florence," explains Lodovico Antinori. "I have friends who are not happy anywhere but here. It's a *maladie d'amour.*"

The City Across the Arno

BY JANE SHAPIRO

༄

editor's note

No matter which bridge you cross to get there, the Oltrarno *is* different, bustling yet less frenetic, quieter, and less touristy. I was fortunate to see the Masaccio frescoes in the Brancacci Chapel in the summer of 1990, shortly after the chapel was reopened to the public, but they are only one of the neighborhood's riches.

Jane Shapiro is the author of *The Dangerous Husband* (Little, Brown and Company, 1999) and *After Moondog* (Warner Books, 1992, hardcover; 1993, paperback).

I am in the complicated museum that is Florence, avoiding the sights. To take a break, I'm going to hang out on the Oltrarno, the other side of the river, in the Santo Spirito quarter; it's a small world of artisans and shopkeepers, real carpenters and real shoe-makers: people actually live there. I plan to visit another Florence that lives its life, while the Duomo and Santa Croce and David live theirs, under our noses.

Many people I meet agree to help me think about Santo Spirito. Simone, a thirty-year-old man who has returned home after living in New York, working for Goldman, Sachs: "Oltrarno is the little side. So we feel a little inferior and we feel competitive. And we're very strong." Simone lays his hand on his black leather jacket, above his heart. "Oltrarno is really the heart of Florence. It's the only part that's not for rich people or tourists. Dante said Florentines are like a dog that bow-wows but doesn't bite. But in Santo Spirito, they bite!"

To get there, as we know, you just step across the green River Arno. You might approach by the most common route, the Ponte Vecchio, bridge of gold for more than 500 years, past the familiar wall of windows crammed with emerald-winged butterfly brooches, gold chains and braids and bangles, a pavé-diamond spotted leopard, a green enamel snake with diamond markings and a ruby eye. Past the caricaturist, who didn't charge an aggressively peppy Margaret Thatcher or a distraught and hunted Woody Allen the $10 or so he'll charge you to produce, in four minutes, a likeness of your worst self. But maybe this is not the choice route: you arrive in the Oltrarno in a cloud of other tourists, at Left-Bankish Borgo San Jacopo, where you can be tempted to stagger in and out of trendy stores until you're completely psychically lost.

Or you cross the river at Ponte alla Carraia, downstream, a route simpler and quieter (not literally quiet, of course, because of the mopeds, but uncrowded and visually calm), and that way you'll experience an immediate economic plummet, descending from standard-issue Florentine luxe into real life: suddenly there are hardware stores, places to buy bargain steak knives and plastic gooseneck lamps, modest bar-tabacchis and clothing shops with names in the wrong languages—Wall Street, Très Jolie.

From my hotel, the Berchielli, a beautifully run establishment, glossy but cozy, on the Lungarno near the foot of hilariously expensive Via Tornabuoni—insistent Versace, constant Gucci, "timeless" Yves Saint Laurent—I take the best route, the Ponte Santa Trinità. Santa Trinità has been rebuilt in several centuries, after several floods; built again by Ammanati in the 1560s (with lovely arches after a design by Michelangelo); destroyed by German mines in 1944 and restored; left without the head of its "Primavera" statue—which head was found in 1961 and reunited with her torso, and so Primavera too was restored.

A fine Oltrarno subject, restoration. Fabio Vegni, from a family of restorers here, tells me the Santo Spirito quarter was traditionally very poor and that, "since ancient times, always, always," it has been the home of artisans. In the small workshops lining these narrow streets, Fabio says, restorers work on paintings, silver, gold leaf, porcelain and lacquer. It sounds as if they've been restoring antique furniture here almost since the furniture was new. (In Florence, any piece older than fifty years can legally be called an antique; but many of the pieces, of course, have been around for several centuries.) Afterward, in the antiques stores on Via Maggio—once the broadest street in Europe, now certainly one of the noisiest—the beautifully restored stuff, buffed back to a sheen, is sold.

On a warm rainy evening, I stop in (with my daughter, Amy,

who lives in Florence, nearby, and who can translate) to see the Vegni brothers, Fabio and Luca; their father, Paolo; and their grand-father, Mario, at their workroom on Via Santo Spirito. The Vegnis were born a couple of blocks away, in Borgo Tegolaio, where father and sons still live, and they think they're the only three-generation restorers' family still at work in the quarter. (Upon reflection, they recall another family, but it involves nephews, not sons.) They figure to have been in the business for seventy-two years, since, after an early apprenticeship, Grandpa Mario started in earnest at twelve.

Here's Mario Vegni, eighty-four years old, maybe five feet tall, at 7 o'clock in the evening, nearing the end of his customary long day in his customary six-day week, mixing a paste to fill a scatter of tiny holes peppering a chair. He is talking to my daughter, Amy, occasionally nodding my way: "This is how I began: when I was five, I started going to a carpenter in the piazza and I helped him pound the pegs—in those days, we used wooden pegs. And since I was the best, I became the boss. Just because I'm small doesn't mean I can't be a boss. Look at this chair! They criticize us for the holes; but it's not our fault, it's the fault of the termites." How old is the chair? "Ehhhh, maybe 1800s."

The Vegnis have worked in Via Santo Spirito since 1954, selling some of the furniture they restore (along with paintings, porcelain and figurines they buy from dealers) in their shop next door. Here you can buy, if you feel like dropping, say, five million lire (about $3,000), a pair of nineteenth-century stained-glass panels, which it took the Vegnis two months to repair and which have been waiting a year for you to arrive with your hefty wallet.

Or a chest from a sacristy, about $15,000, waiting three years. Or, for about the same price, a painted corner cupboard, sea green, gray-green, turquoise-green; when the Vegnis bought it, the cup-board was a lovely gray, underneath which, when they started clean-ing it, they found the several even lovelier greens.

The most famous recent restoration in Florence, of course, has also been done in this quarter—the Brancacci Chapel frescoes in the Santa Maria del Carmine Church. No article about Florence can be complete without quoting Bernard Berenson. Let's take a walk over to the Carmine, and I shall quote him on the frescoes of Masaccio, painted between 1423 and 1428: "In later painting we shall easily find greater science, greater craft and greater perfection of detail, but greater reality, greater significance, I venture to say, never. . . . Compared with his figures, those in the same chapel by his precursor, Masolino, are childish, and those by his follower, Filippino Lippi, unconvincing and without significance, because without tactile values. . . . Masaccio's Adam and Eve stride away from Eden heartbroken with shame and grief, hearing, perhaps, but not seeing, the angel hovering high overhead who directs their exiled footsteps."

But before we can see the frescoes, Masaccio's *Expulsion From Paradise* and *Tribute Money* and the 10 other panels (visitors these days must enter the chapel in small numbers, at regular appointed moments, and leave after fifteen minutes), we must wait. A sign tells us it is not permitted to loiter in the cloister (still, if you go, take a moment; it's a cloister, after all). As we wait, a tour group tries to join us, but they're too many. An American woman with backpack, part of our small band growing, like cows at the gate, ever physically closer behind the velvet rope, speaks for us all: "Kick the group out!"

While we continue to stand here in the anteroom, I shall also quote the British man just behind me, breathing into my hair and instructing his young woman companion in a low and penetrating voice: "It's been restored so they make a big fuss about it. It's extraordinary. Before, nobody used to come here though it was just as important. That's because it was free. The average tourist has twenty-four hours to spend and it's enough to go to a leather shop, see the Uffizi and that's about it." Now at last we're admitted to the chapel, and he and I stand, unbeknown to him, together, and are deeply impressed by Masaccio's powerfully affecting figures and chuckle in tandem at poor Masolino's effete and sugary charm.

Gazing longingly back at the *Expulsion,* while being expelled from the Carmine after fifteen minutes, I decide to go straight to the Piazza Santo Spirito, the heart of this quarter, that tree-filled and rustling square uniquely beloved of Florentines. Lately it has been swept of most of the drug dealers who have plagued it for years. (I asked a few young people how they thought about the square; they think of it as the place they bought hashish at eighteen.) These days, the piazza, with its stone benches and modest fountain, is being returned to the quarter.

Visitors are most familiar with this piazza, of course, because of the Santo Spirito church and its Brunelleschi interior. The church's blank seventeenth-century facade, which dominates one end of the square, was in 1980 the subject of a contest, organized by the city: design a new face. Night after night that summer, spectators filled the piazza to view the designs being projected, life-size, on the facade itself. Amy and I hear about the contest from the barman in Ricchi, the piazza's comfortable bar, whose back room is a bright cave lined with suede banquettes. The walls of the bar are hung with photographs, taken that summer, of the designs being projected on the facade, and with the original drawings. Thus, as we sip our cappuccino, we can see Chiesa Santo Spirito as Marilyn Monroe, a giant frog, a Christmas tree, a Gucci motif, a huge fried egg, or a glowing expanse of dark and starry sky. There's an image of the Brunelleschi interior projected onto the exterior, and there's an apple orchard under a sun with a face. "What a great contest!" Amy says, and a second man behind the bar says jovially, "It was my idea!" The first barman, firmly: "No. It was not your idea. It was the idea of an architect in San Frediano."

After Ricchi, I stop at Trattoria Borgo Antico, but it's too early in the evening to see Pippo Boze, the Elvis impersonator who is often here playing his guitar while lying on his back, feet pedaling. I stop to take a look at Pensione Sorelle Bandini, the piazza's ten-room pensione, a modest, immaculate, engaging place filled with scarred antique furniture. The pensione's elevator is in No. 9, but the pensione also occupies two floors of No. 10, Palazzo Guadagni, and its flowery sixteenth-century loggia on the fourth floor looks out over terra-cotta rooftops and the piazza's trees.

I leave the square—it's the heart of the quarter, and I'll be back tomorrow. For the moment, I'll head down Via Maggio, that street of glossy antiques for sale. Here are Persian and Chinese carpets, architectural etchings and drawings, complicated jewel boxes, carved ivory, silver candlesticks, candelabra with bases of malachite; ancient furniture gorgeously displayed; small inlaid tables lighted like paintings; and, down the side streets, clotheslines out the upper windows.

At the San Felice end of Via Maggio, Daniele Boralevi displays antique carpets on the polished herringbone floors of some big empty rooms. (Daniele is third generation in rugs, of course.) Here are early nineteenth-century Aubussons; a small fuzzy, eighteenth-century Swedish carpet (bought, actually, in the United States); a lovely Tibetan carpet designed to wrap around a column, and, in the safe, a lot of rugs you wouldn't consider walking on. On the way back up the street, I revisit No. 26, rebuilt in 1570–74 for Bianca Cappello, the mistress and future wife of Francesco I. The facade is all much restored sgraffiti—human torsos, sea creatures out of water, scenes of violence, a riot of what look like black-and-white dogs and putti and cranes and angels.

Near the Santa Trinità end of the street, Bruno Gallori-Turchi, with his brother Giovanni, sells sculpture, arms and armor, and fourteenth- to eighteenth-century furniture and paintings, nothing newer. His father opened the shop in 1938; Bruno, who has been in the business for thirty years, hopes that his son, now fourteen, will be too.

In the shop these days Bruno has a massive, early-seventeenth-century sacristy credenza from Tuscany or Latium. "How much?" I ask. Bruno looks shocked. He would rather not say. Rather sorrowfully, he quotes a truly huge sum. There are always two questions Bruno would prefer not to answer: How much? and Where'd you get it? "Where'd you get it?" I ask. He thinks a while. Bruno says sweetly: "A church."

Leaving Bruno's shop, I'm faintly reeling with antique sickness, a species of tourist's disease, an accumulated queasiness from looking at too many ravishing objects. I stand awhile on Via Maggio in the blaze of traffic shooting off the bridge, to settle down, staring into the window of Fasone next door, which displays a small painting that looks restored to a shine—it looks new. That night, Amy and I go to Da Cambi, a modest, bustling, festive trattoria for pappa al pomodoro; then we look for the Elvis impersonator, who isn't there again; and then I feel much better.

The next day, as on every day this week, I revisit the piazza, stop at the morning outdoor market, watch the men in an open workshop sanding wooden cowboy hats. Then I sit, feeling at home, inside Brunelleschi's serene church. A long reverie. But at last I realize a bell has been ringing. Suddenly I get it—a priest blows past, shooing me; but when I reach the front doors they're locked. Far behind me, now, I hear the echoing shouts of an old man, and I turn to see him, framed by the heavy gray columns and pale light, calling furiously. He leans on a metal walking cane and wears a black crocheted shawl against the chill, but he's not too frail to bawl me out as I approach. He's ferociously angry at me for remaining behind, and he tries to get me to sit on a chair, but I imagine myself like a small girl dangling my feet and waiting for hours, so I refuse to sit. *"Non parlo Italiano,"* I point out. This enrages my enemy. "She doesn't speak Italian," he tells himself and the calmly soaring ceiling. I employ what Italian I do speak to insist on exiting. He repeats that I have been a fool to remain and must wait. "Exit me!" "You sit!" He pounds his cane, I stamp my foot—we are simpatico, the language barrier no barrier at all. In the end I understand this scrap developed as entertainment for both of us, to pass time interestingly. For at last I'm handed off to the merely blandly annoyed sacristan, the guy with the keys, who unlocks the side door and practically shoves me out as I practically shove him back in.

Lovely to be back in the peace of the streets after the violence of the sanctuary. And, amazingly enough, Piazza Santa Spirito is a genuinely pacific place. Even at 7 o'clock, that most frantic evening hour in always intense Florence, when all the squares of the city swarm with people and all the vespinas and Fiat Unos are smashing through the streets, you can still step into Piazza Santo Spirito and find yourself in rustling silence. A few stylish young people stand at the bar in the pink glow of Cabiria Cafe; three couples sit at the outside tables in sexy, soulful, inaudible colloquy; two old women walk by at a measured pace—that's about it. The trees cast shadow. It's quiet here. From blocks—from miles—around, you can hear all the rest of Florence, roaring.

A Musician's Florence

BY HARVEY SACHS

~~

editor's note
....

> Though hardly mentioned in guidebooks, Florence's rich musical heritage is as significant as the works of Botticelli or Brunelleschi.

HARVEY SACHS lives near Florence and is the author of *Toscanini* (J. B. Lippincott, 1978), *Music in Fascist Italy* (W. W. Norton, 1988), *Reflections on Toscanini* (Grove Weidenfeld, 1991, hardcover; Prima Publishing, 1993, paperback), and *Rubenstein—A Life* (Grove Press, 1995). He has also written for *The New Yorker, The Wall Street Journal,* and a number of other periodicals in North America and Europe. Sachs is currently preparing *The Letters of Arturo Toscanini*—the first major selection of the conductor's correspondence—for publication by Knopf in 2002.

Florence's art treasures make an extraordinarily strong claim on travelers' attention, but few visitors realize that the city played as great a role in the history of music as in the history of art and architecture. Opera and the piano were invented in Florence, and the city has for five centuries been home, haven or source of inspiration to many outstanding musicians, Italian and foreign.

Lully and Cherubini were born here, Josquin Desprès and John Dowland passed through, Rossini lived here for a time, Donizetti and Verdi wrote operas for Florence, Brahms and Tchaikovsky loved the city, Mozart and Wagner both considered moving here and the conductor Hans von Bülow—having lost his wife to Wagner—came to the banks of the Arno "to forget and to be born again." Said Berlioz: "Everything about Florence pleases me, its name, its sky, its river, its setting and surroundings—I love it all." Mendelssohn concurred: "Everything here is beautiful and glorious."

The city abounds with points of musical interest, many of them identical with points of artistic interest. Take, for instance, Florence's most imposing monument—the Duomo. The cathedral's celebrated dome was consecrated in 1436 to the accompaniment of a motet written for the occasion by Guillaume Dufay. The French composer, who was in town at the right moment, exercised as great an influence on fifteenth-century music as the dome's designer, Filippo Brunelleschi, exercised on fifteenth-century architecture.

Music's importance at the Duomo, as indeed in the whole Renaissance concept of universal order, is indicated by the prominence of Jubal the Musician in the series of biblical bas-reliefs sculptured by Andrea Pisano for the monumental bell tower. The panels now visible on the tower are copies; to see the originals, visit the adjacent Museo dell'Opera del Duomo (Cathedral Works Museum), which also houses two of the most significant "musical" artworks ever made: the relief panels sculpted by Luca della Robbia and Donatello for the Duomo's choir lofts. These pieces show children and angels singing, dancing, playing instruments and generally making a tremendous ruckus.

The guidebooks say that Dante was baptized at the Baptistery, opposite the Duomo, but they do not point out that Girolamo Frescobaldi, one of the greatest keyboard composers of all time, was organist here in 1630, or that this ancient building once housed an outstanding vocal ensemble whose most illustrious member was the Flemish composer Heinrich Isaac. Isaac entered the service of Florence's ruling Medici family in the 1480s and probably gave music lessons to Lorenzo the Magnificent's children at the Palazzo Medici-Riccardi on Via de' Martelli, one block north of the Duomo.

The great church of San Lorenzo, a block west of the Medici-Riccardi Palace, contains the tomb of one of the most important composers of the fourteenth century, the native Florentine Francesco Landini (second chapel on the right as you enter). And half a block north of the Medici-Riccardi Palace, at 13 Via Cavour, stands the building that was Rossini's home during the 1850s. Rossini spent many an evening across the street at the Capponi Palace, now the local headquarters of the Bank of Naples. At that time it was the home of the Poniatowskis, a family of noble Polish musicians whose salon was a focal point of Florentine musical society.

Donizetti, another of the Poniatowskis' friends, wrote his *Parisina* while staying with them. The opera had its world premiere in 1833 at the seventeenth-century Teatro della Pergola, in Via della Pergola, four blocks from the Capponi Palace. Ten years later the theater was the site of the first Italian production of Weber's *Der Freischütz,* and in 1847 Verdi's *Macbeth* was given its world premiere here under the composer's supervision. According to the first Lady Macbeth, Marianna Barbieri-Nini, just as the dress rehearsal was about to begin Verdi dragged her and the baritone Felice Varesi to a piano in the foyer for a run-through of one of their difficult duets.

"But for God's sake," said Varesi, "we've already rehearsed it 150 times."

"I wouldn't say that if I were you," replied Verdi, "for within half an hour it will be 151."

At the Pergola, Berlioz attended performances of *I Capuleti e I Montecchi* and *La Sonnambula,* both by Bellini. He stayed at a nearby hotel, where he composed his *King Lear* overture and began to think about writing an opera based on the life of a celebrated Florentine artist and rapscallion, Benvenuto Cellini. Although the Pergola is now mainly used for spoken drama, it still hosts recitals by the world's best-known artists, under the auspices of the Amici della Musica association.

Older still than the Pergola, the Teatro Niccolini—formerly Teatro del Cocomero—was built in 1650 in the shadow of the Duomo, at the bottom of Via Ricasoli. The first Florentine production of Gluck's *Orfeo*, which had a profound influence on opera by stressing the dramatic importance of the text, took place at the Niccolini in 1771, and Liszt played here in 1838. Two blocks north, at the corner of via Ricasoli and Via degli Alfani, stands the Florence Conservatory, alma mater of such important Italian musicians as the composers Luigi Dallapiccola and Mario Castelnuovo-Tedesco. The conservatory's library, which owns precious manuscripts of early Italian and Flemish composers, codices of fifteenth- and sixteenth-century madrigals and compositions and letters of Monteverdi and Rossini, was a shambles for decades; only the most intrepid and fortunate of visitors were able to see any of the treasures. It is said to have improved in recent years.

The conservatory now bears the name of the composer Luigi Cherubini, who was born in 1760 in Via Fiesolana, behind the Pergola. As you walk south on this street, its name changes to Via Verdi and then, after Piazza Santa Croce, to Via de' Benci. Have a look at the plaque on the facade of the building at 5 Via de' Benci; it proclaims that Giovanni de' Bardi, Count of Vernio, played host here, late in the sixteenth century, to "the celebrated Camerata, whose intention was to bring the art of music, which had been barbarized by Flemish peculiarities, back to the sublimity of Greek melody." And indeed it was here, in this unarresting palazzo designed by Brunelleschi in his youth, that Florentines made their most enduring contribution to music: opera.

Count Bardi's Camerata consisted of poets and musicians who attempted, as the plaque suggests, to create a form of musical theater that would resemble ancient Greek drama as they believed it had been performed. They rejected the increasingly complex harmonies favored by influential northern European composers since the days of Dufay and Isaac—thus the inscription's nasty reference to "Flemish peculiarities"—and replaced the northerners' thick musical textures with what they called "singing recitation." Their experiments led to transformations in the realms of vocal technique, ensemble playing and harmonic language, that have influenced the history of European music to our own day.

You would do well to cross the street now, and walk along the diagonal Borgo Santa Croce to the great church of Santa Croce, where Rossini is entombed close by Michelangelo, Machiavelli and other celebrated Italians connected in some way with Florence. A block from the church, facing the Arno, is the Biblioteca Nazionale (National Library), which contains an even richer collection of early musical manuscripts than the conservatory's, including the *Fronimo Dialogo*—works by Lassus, Palestrina and others, copied by Vincenzo Galilei, father of Galileo and a member of the Camerata.

From the library, the nearest bridge over the Arno is the Ponte alle Grazie; cross it and continue up Piazza de' Mozzi, then turn left on Via San Niccolò. The building at No. 94 was for many years the home of the Austrian contralto Caroline Unger, who had sung in the first performance of Beethoven's Ninth Symphony under the composer's direction. On the same street, the church of San Niccolò contains an organ built by Dionigi di Agostino Romani in 1581 and restored in the 1980s by Pier Paolo Donati and his assistants at the Gabinetto Restauro Organi, which is based in the nearby Pitti Palace. Donati's team, one of the finest in the world, is responsible for resuscitating several other Florentine organs, all made by Onofrio Zeffirini of Cortona between 1550 and 1571; they are in the Badia (opposite the Bargello Palace), in San Giorgio sulla Costa (on the hill behind the Pitti Palace) and in Santa Trinita (on the other side of the bridge of the same name).

If you visit San Giorgio, and if you feel like taking a long walk, much of it uphill, continue along the Costa di San Giorgio, past Fort Belvedere, and down Via San Leonardo to No. 64, at the corner of Viale Galileo. This is the Villa Bonciani, where Tchaikovsky wrote his Third Suite for Orchestra and parts of *Capriccio Italien* and the opera *The Maid of Orleans.* Like a modern tourist, he may have found the uphill hike too strenuous, because when he next visited the city he rented rooms overlooking the Arno—and there worked on *The Queen of Spades* and his string sextet, *Souvenir de Florence.* Tchaikovsky's patroness, Nadezhda von Meck, lived in the Villa Oppenheim (now called Villa Cora) on Viale Machiavelli, which is near Via San Leonardo. In 1880, she invited the eighteen-year-old Debussy to stay there, to give music lessons to her daughter, but when he fell in love with the girl his services were dispensed with.

The massive Pitti Palace, back at the bottom of the hill, is almost as rich in musical memories as in works of art. Its great Sala Bianca, for instance, was the site, in 1600, of the first performance of the first known opera, *Euridice,* composed by Jacopo Peri to a text by Ottavio Rinuccini, and created for Maria de' Medici's wedding. (The bridegroom, Henri IV of France, was too busy to attend; he had himself represented by proxy.) In the following centuries, works by Gluck, Paisiello and many other composers were performed in the Sala Bianca, and in 1923 Arnold Schoenberg conducted his *Pierrot Lunaire* there before an audience that included Giacomo Puccini. Behind the Pitti Palace, the Boboli Gardens, too, have hosted many a musical extravaganza from the Medicis' day on—including a spectacular version of Purcell's *Faerie Queene,* staged by Luca Ronconi for the 1987 Maggio Musicale festival.

Re-cross the river on the Ponte Vecchio and head for the nearby town hall—Palazzo della Signoria, also called Palazzo Vecchio. Its Great Hall of the Five Hundred has often been used for musical performances, despite its inadequate acoustics; in the nineteenth century, such major choral-orchestral works as Haydn's *Creation* and Mendelssohn's *St. Paul* had their Florentine premieres here. Today, the Signoria houses the Medicis' magnificent musical instrument collection, which includes string instruments by

Stradivari, Amati and Ruggeri, an ancient Jewish shofar and an ancient Roman tibia (an ancestor of the flute) found at Pompeii. The first curator of this collection was Bartolomeo Cristofori, who invented the piano at the Medici court in 1709. No examples of his work have remained in Florence, but the Signoria's collection contains an early (1739) upright piano by Domenico del Mela.

The Uffizi Palace, opposite the Signoria, is no longer a site of musical interest, for the theater built within it 400 years ago by the Medicis was demolished during the nineteenth century. It was there that the twenty-two-year-old Handel first achieved international success as an opera composer, when his *Rodrigo* was performed before an enthusiastic public in 1707; the Grand Duke of Tuscany rewarded him with 100 sequins and a silver service.

A three-minute walk will take you from Piazza della Signoria through Piazza della Repubblica to the corner of the elegant Via Tornabuoni and Villa della Vigna Nuova. Verdi used to stay at what is now the Hotel Esplanade (Hotel Suisse in those days), and one wonders whether he ever bumped into the music-loving George Eliot, who lived at the Suisse while gathering material for her Florentine novel, *Romola*.

It is a good idea to proceed along Via della Vigna Nuova. If you're hungry—and most people who are interested in music seem to be uncommonly interested in food—turn right on the narrow Via Palchetti and stop at the boisterously informal Latini for excellent, traditional Florentine fare.

Via della Vigna Nuova ends at Piazza Goldoni, and Borgo Ognissanti begins on the other side of the piazza. One of the first buildings—no one seems sure exactly which one—on the north side of the borgo used to be a well-known hotel, the Aquila Nera (Black Eagle). The fourteen-year-old Mozart and his father stayed here in 1770, and so, a few months later, did the English musician and traveler Charles Burney. "The rooms are very lofty," noted

Burney in his diary, "so that the bedrooms, which are up two pair of stairs, seem nel mondo della luna." The Mozarts were impressed by the city, and Leopold Mozart wrote to his wife in Salzburg, "I should like you to see Florence itself and the surrounding country and the situation of the town, for you would say that one should live and die here."

From Piazza Ognissanti a walk of four blocks will lead you past the United States Consulate on Corso Italia to the Teatro Comunale, hub of modern Florentine musical life. New and old operas, symphony concerts, ballets and chamber music are presented here by leading Italian and foreign performers throughout the fall and winter and during the Maggio Musicale festival, which runs from early May through June. An evening at the Comunale is surely a logical way to end a musical tour of Florence.

Learning to Live With Arrivederci

BY SUSAN JACOBY

~∍

editor's note

Freelance writer SUSAN JACOBY is the author of a number of books, including *Half-Jew: A Daughter's Search for Her Family's Buried Past* (Scribner, 2000), *The Possible She* (Farrar, Straus & Giroux, 1979), *The Friendship Barrier: Ten Russian Encounters* (The Bodley Head, London, 1972), and the co-author, with Yelena Khanga, of *Soul to Soul: A Black*

Russian American Family 1865–1992 (W. W. Norton, 1994). This piece originally appeared as the back-page essay in the travel section of *The New York Times* on October 12, 1997.

It has been exactly six weeks since I closed the door of my small rented apartment in Florence and headed home to New York. I know that because my final memento of the trip—a majolica jar adorned with a gaily dancing putto—arrived intact, meticulously packaged, in today's mail. For twenty-five years, on each visit to Florence, I have been buying china in the same small, utterly reliable shop on the Via Guicciardini. And each time, as if there were no postal, airport or customs snafus on either side of the Atlantic, my purchases have arrived, give or take a day, in six weeks. Now, once again, I must come to terms with the fact that I am truly here and won't see Florence again for a span of time I cannot bear to estimate or contemplate.

Travel books never discuss the end of the journey. People are always trying to convince themselves, and everyone else, that "it was great to get away but it's great to be home." I've even felt that way myself, after trips to places I don't love as much as I love Tuscany.

But Florence feels like home, or rather, like what might have been home had I chosen a very different life when I was young. I know Florence well enough to know where to buy paper towels and cheap flowers, well enough to face a dental emergency with equanimity, well enough to be greeted with recognition (or feigned recognition, which amounts to the same thing) by certain shopkeepers and restaurant proprietors. I have never spent an uninteresting day in this city, never experienced small vicissitudes or deeper sorrows that could not be ameliorated by contact with the noble civilization of these stony streets.

In the past, each return from Florence followed a predictable, dispiriting pattern. I would unpack immediately. (Out of sight, out of mind?) Reverting to a modus operandi best suited to the after-math of a love affair, I then plunged straight back into work—more work than I really needed to accomplish during the first few weeks of readjustment. I rarely talked about my trip, reminding myself that there is no worse bore than a travel bore.

Above all, I stayed away from museums, on the premise that they would only arouse a most painful longing for the feast that had been mine for the gorging only a few weeks earlier. No more statues of David, in either Donatello's or Michelangelo's version. No Giottos, no Masaccios, no Leonardos. I also avoided my art books because their reproductions only made me yearn more intensely for the real masterpieces I had left behind.

When these avoidance tactics failed—as they inevitably did—I would succumb to tears, self-pity and something approaching gen-uine depression.

This year, I tried to handle my homecoming in a different and less dour manner. First, I told everyone I wouldn't be back until two days after I really intended to arrive. The white lie gave me time to catch up on my sleep and set my house in order before anyone could reasonably expect me to return a phone call or answer a fax. More important, it gave me breathing room to think about how to incor-porate some of the small, portable pleasures of Florence into my New York life. I decided to follow the advice of a new friend acquired on the journey, who told me she always tries to bring back at least one new foreign habit from each trip abroad.

During this stay in Florence, I developed a taste for something I never used to like: biscotti dipped in vin santo. Not the assortment of weirdly flavored, oversized American biscotti (cousins to those humongous breakfast muffins), but the trim, plain almond Italian version. On my second day back, I scoured my neighborhood for the right sort of biscotti and, this being New York, found them in only the second gourmet store I tried. There sat distinctive orange-colored boxes of cookies, labeled i famosi, made in Florence itself and selling for a fraction (these are, after all, the Oreos of Italy) of what the same store was charging for its mutant American-made monsters.

I easily slipped back into the vacation habit of finishing dinner by dipping five or six (or ten or twelve) of the crusty cookies into a double shot glass of vin santo. Drinking down the dregs with the crumbs is the best part, now an everyday routine rather than a memory of a no-longer-attainable treat.

I made a more significant change by spending a considerable sum enlarging and framing some of the best photographs I took on the trip. Instead of stowing them away in a box, I made room for them on the walls in spots that catch my eye several times a day. I used to tell myself that putting away the photos was part of not boring others with vacation tales, but I now realize that I was trying to lock away my own yearning for everything Florence represents.

The presence of these new pictures on my walls may mean that I am ready to pay more attention to the part of me that comes alive most fully in the golden-ocher light reflecting off the facades along the Arno. To that end, I have been devoting more time, not less, to the pursuit of art in New York.

I had seen the Metropolitan's dazzling exhibit on the art of Byzantium before I went away, but it took on new meaning when I discovered its riches for the second time after my return. I focused on certain connections I had marked only in passing the first time around, felt the full power of the Byzantine influence in the West.

Gazing for the second time upon the remarkable icon from the Egyptian Monastery of Saint Catherine, with demons gloating over souls losing their precarious footing on a ladder to heaven, I found myself mentally comparing them to assorted Florentine devils lurking and cavorting in the Church of Santo Spirito, the Baptistry and the museum of the Duomo.

In that moment, I realized I was no longer struggling to contain my beloved Florentine apparitions in a box.

I am learning to let the images breathe, as Charles Dickens advised in his own "Pictures From Italy." How exceptionally horrid it must have been to return from the Mediterranean world to the dank London of the 1840s! "What light is shed upon the world, at this day," Dickens wrote, "from amidst these rugged Palaces of Florence! . . . Here, the imperishable part of noble minds survives, placid and equal, when strongholds of assault and defence are overthrown; when the tyranny of the many, or the few, or both, is but a tale; when Pride and Power are so much cloistered dust. . . . Let us look back on Florence while we may, and when its shining Dome is seen no more, go travelling through cheerful Tuscany, with a bright remembrance of it; for Italy will be the fairer for the recollection."

Let me look back on Florence while I may, for New York will only be the fairer for it.

Biblioteca

The Stones of Florence, Mary McCarthy, photographs by Evelyn Hofer, Harcourt Brace Jovanovich, Publishers, 1959. Even in 1959, McCarthy wrote: "Everyone complains of the noise; with windows open, no one can sleep. . . . In truth, short of leaving Florence, there is nothing to be done until fall comes and the windows can be shut again." Anyone who has ever visited Florence in the summer knows this to be unequivocally true (to say nothing of the mosquitos!). Absolutely *essenziale,* and you positively must get the large, 8½-by-11-inch edition with the superb photos (128 black-and-white images with twelve color plates). Do not even *think* of reading the significantly smaller edition. I would never have been inspired to visit the wonderful Tuscan town of Pistoia were it not for the photos in the large edition, and I would not really have understood the Guelph–Ghibelline conflict without the opportunity to see how architecture was defined by politics. A parting passage: "The Florentines, in fact, invented the Renaissance, which is the same as saying that they invented the modern world—not, of course, an unmixed good. Florence was a turning-point, and this is what often troubles the reflective sort of visitor today—the feeling that a terrible mistake was committed here, at some point between Giotto and Michelangelo, a mistake that had to do with power and megalomania or gigantism of the human ego. You can see, if you wish, the handwriting on the walls of Palazzo Pitti or Palazzo Strozzi, those formidable creations in bristling prepotent stone, or in the cold, vain stare of Michelangelo's *David,* in love with his own strength and beauty. This feeling that Florence was the scene of the original crime or error was hard to avoid just after the last World War, when power and technology had reduced so much to rubble."

Florence: The Biography of a City, Christopher Hibbert, W. W. Norton & Company, 1993. Historian Hibbert, who is also the author of over twenty-five books—including *Rome: The Biography of a City* and *Venice: The Biography of a City*—is a British authority on Italy. This book is as much a guidebook as a lively history book, and also includes hundreds of black-and-white photos, engravings, and line drawings and sixteen color reproductions. *Essenziale.*

The City of Florence: Historical Vistas & Personal Sightings, R.W.B. Lewis, Farrar, Straus & Giroux, 1995, hardcover; Holt, 1996, paperback. A very special, wholly enjoyable and engaging book by award-winning writer and biographer Lewis, who has lived in Florence much of the year for over fifty years. Though a personal story of Florence, Lewis includes much historical material, and whether he is pondering the Via Lamarmore or how he was trapped behind enemy lines in 1943, you never want it to end. It's also a beautiful book, with numerous black-and-white reproductions and photographs. At the end of the book there are very helpful and fascinating notes on the maps and illustrations, some scholarly and literary sources, and a contemporary bibliography.

Florence Explored, Rupert Scott, New Amsterdam Books, 1987; first American edition published in 1988. This is one of my favorite books. It's very much of a companion volume to *Venice for Pleasure* by J. G. Links; the books are the same size and shape and follow the same format. Scott notes that "Florence is and always has been a city that gives most pleasure to those who take their pleasures seriously. The single most compelling reason for coming here is to see Florentine Art. Thus it is in galleries and churches that users of this guide will spend the greater part of their days. Since Florence has possibly a denser concentration of beautiful works of art than any other city in the world, this can hardly be seen as an insupportable burden." There is a thought-provoking passage on nearly every page, such as this one: "Though untouched by the First World War, Florence suffered badly in the Second. It is ironic that one of Hitler's few recorded acts of cultural clemency—a personal order that the Ponte Vecchio, which he had seen and admired in 1938, be spared—should have resulted in a much worse loss, the destruction of the borghi at its either end, which were mined in order to block its access roads. Appalling disaster though this was, permanently scarring the core of the city, and transforming its most beautiful streets into its worst eyesores, Florence was fortunate not to be damaged more badly and has been just as fortunate since then in having a local government that has rebuilt the Ponte S. Trinita as a perfect facsimile and preserved most of the wonderful country immediately to the south from speculative building. The contado still sweeps right up to the walls of Forte del Belvedere and S. Miniato, which permits the delectable and rare sensation of being able to move in a single step from the city gates to the country, as if in a medieval town." This small paperback fits easily into a small bag and is organized by neighborhoods, more or less. With lots of black-and-white illustrations, photos, and maps. *Essenziale*.

Florence: A Traveller's Companion, selected and introduced by Harold Acton and Edward Chanery; first published in Great Britain by Constable and Company, Ltd., London, 1986. I received this book as a gift from my friends, Jesse and Barbara, who bought it at one of the English-language bookshops in Florence. My husband and I visited them one summer when they were renting an apartment in the Oltrarno, and with the help of this wonderful book, we made daily in-depth discoveries in Florence. The selected essays include topics such as "A pro-Brunelleschian view of how Lorenzo Ghiberti won the competition to produce the bronze reliefs on the north doors of the Baptistery," "The 21-year-old Ruskin climbs the Campanile for the first time in November 1840," "The colours of the Lungarno," "The Mercato Vecchio in the fourteenth century," "An eye-witness account of the installation of the 'David' outside the Palazzo Vecchio in 1504," "The courtyard of Palazzo Pitti in the summer of 1944," and they are extracted from books, letters, diaries, and memoirs. In his introduction, Sir Harold Acton writes that rivers of ink have flowed on the subject of Florence so that it is difficult to say anything new, "but from the majority who have recorded their impressions and opinions we have selected those extracts which form a mosaic of its long history and illustrate changes of taste. It is still intensely alive as a capital of the arts and crafts." With black-and-white, contemporary and period drawings, photographs, and engravings.

"Why Visit Florence?" (*Wine Spectator,* February 28, 1995) is a good article to read that was too lengthy for me to include here. With essays by Thomas Hoving, Harvey Steiman and David Rosengarten, among others, this special issue features hotels, restaurants, *gelato,* wine bars, markets, specialty groceries, art masterpieces, jewelry and leather goods, and profiles of Burton Andersen and Faith Heller Willinger. Unfortunately, back issues of *Wine Spectator* only date back to 1996, but check your library—this is still a great issue.

Piazze, Giardini, e Monumenti

(Piazzas, Gardens, and Monuments of Note)

"Aaron looked and looked at the three great naked men. David so much whiter, and standing forward, self-conscious: then at the great splendid front of the Palazzo Vecchio: and at the fountain splashing water upon its wet, wet figures; and the stone-flaged space of the grim square. And he felt that here he was in one of the world's living centres, here, in the Piazza della Signoria. The sense of having arrived—of having reached a perfect centre of the human world: this he had."

—D. H. Lawrence, *Aaron's Rod*

Where City and Country Connect

BY LOUIS INTURRISI

᳐

editor's note

....

Seeing the gardens described here in bloom seems a worthy excuse for a springtime trip to Florence.

LOUIS INTURRISI, whose work is featured elsewhere in this section, lived in Rome for many years.

Although the model of Renaissance urbanity, Florence has always had a close rapport with nature and the surrounding countryside. No better artistic testimony to this connection exists than Botticelli's *Primavera,* in which the Florentine spring is depicted as a goddess sweeping into a typical Tuscan meadow full of wildflowers and ripe fruit. Every year Florence celebrates the arrival of spring with music—notably the Maggio Musicale—and with displays of spring flowers in its parks, villas and public gardens, the most famous of which is of course the Boboli Gardens. At this time of year, a visit to the Uffizi to see the Primavera is not complete without a stroll in the gardens where many of the flowers in that painting can be seen.

The flower on the Florentine coats-of-arms is not a lily, as is commonly thought, but an iris, like the one in the bottom right-hand corner of the *Primavera*. Every May, on a tranquil hillside half hidden under the belvedere of Piazzale Michelangelo, Florence celebrates its heraldic red iris with an international competition sponsored by the Italian Iris Society. Not widely publicized, the show lasts only two weeks, but I never miss the opportunity to visit it in the six-acre Iris Garden, which has more than 2,500 varieties and is only open for this show.

The garden is divided into sections corresponding to past years of the competition. A map and a guide in English are available at the entrance. Starting with the early years, the 1950s, one can observe the changes the hybridizers have wrought. Tags on each plant tell the name and nationality of the grower, the title given the iris (my favorite last year was a satiny deep purple blossom called "Shadow of Dracula") and the award, if any, the plant received. In section A1 all the first- and second-prize winners from 1957 to 1994 have been placed together. Professional and amateur iris growers from all over the world send their rhizomes to Florence three years in advance to climatize them.

The competition is open only to the tall bearded iris, which has three outer petals, called falls, that can be either smooth or ruffled, and three smaller inner petals that stand erect and form a dome. The "beard" refers to the brushlike row of hairs running down the center of each fall.

Because it can assume a wide range of colors from deep purple through apricot to pure white, the iris is named after the Greek goddess of the rainbow. In medieval times the Florentine standard was a white iris on a vermilion field, but after the banishment of the Ghibellines in 1266, the Guelfs reversed the colors. In addition to the Iris Society awards, the city council gives a special prize to the iris that comes closest to matching the red one in the city crest. So far, the hybridizers have been unable to create a truly red iris, but their efforts can be viewed in section B3, where the "rosso fiorentino" are grouped.

I usually spend a couple of hours in the Iris Garden, following the flagstone paths that weave in and out of the flowerbeds, and gradually descend the hill, at the bottom of which is a gold fish pond where elegant yellow and white aquatic iris grow in clumps. From this vantage point the hillside looks as if it has been covered with a floral tapestry.

Only minutes away, at the opposite end of Piazzale Michelangelo, is the Rose Garden, which I also visit every spring. But before leaving the piazzale, I always stop to look over the balustrade at the splendid view of the city dominated by Brunelleschi's cupola, the winding Arno with its bridges and the bumpy line of purple mountains in the distance. At a break in the railing are stairs leading to a small outdoor cafe, Le Lance, surrounded by huge pots of multicolored pansies where I have my second cappuccino of the day.

The Rose Garden is just below the cafe on the street descending the hill. An open iron gate on the left marks the entrance. Once inside, the noise of the traffic fades and the buzzing of bees and the unmistakable fragrance of wild roses remind me that I am approaching one of my favorite places in all of Florence.

Here, too, one can look for connections with Botticelli; roses figure prominently in many of his paintings. In the *Primavera,* the goddess Flora has gathered a mass of red, pink and white roses in her dress; in the *Birth of Venus,* the wind gods, the Zephyrs, are blowing a shower of yellow roses with gold centers onto the newly born Venus. Another Botticelli in the Uffizi is the *Madonna of the Rose Garden.*

The Florence Roseto is built on terraces, bordered with rose bushes, that trace the hillside and are punctuated at intervals by pergolas and tiny gold fish ponds. Here, too, I always start at the top and make my way down, stopping to check on the progress of a bower of porcelain white trailers or sitting for a while in an alcove of gold floribundas. The Florence of 20,000 tourists a day is only ten minutes away, yet I seem to be in a rustic paradise.

The presence of the caretaker's house in the middle of the two-and-a-half acre garden adds to the rural scene. On one visit, I saw the caretaker working on a fan-shaped lattice, while his wife hung the wash from below. Nature, however, rather than any premeditated human plan, has had the upper hand here. The serious rosarian, in fact, may find the collection wanting: there aren't any rare specimens or unusual hybrids; no tortured topiaries and no annual competitions. Instead, the Florence Rose Garden is a simple collection, lovingly maintained, the closest thing the city has to the medieval secret gardens Boccaccio praised and Botticelli painted.

On the benches, which have been placed to catch the first cheerful rays of warm sun, elderly visitors nod off or lovers embrace; some read newspapers; others contemplate the view. In the distance the ancient stone walls wind up to the Fortezza through fields of black-green cypress, silvery green olive trees and newly sprouting grape vines, while in the foreground is the Duomo—elegantly framed in a trellis of tiny pink tea roses.

Another ideal visit in spring is to the gardens of the Medici villas. Of the half dozen summer residences the Medici built in the hills around Florence, Villa di Castello and Villa della Petraia, both in the suburb of Castello, are a convenient half-hour bus ride from the city center.

In 1575 the grand-duke of Tuscany, Cardinal Ferdinando de' Medici, commissioned Bountalenti to transform a medieval castle into an elegant villa where he could escape the summer heat of Florence. La Petraia is approached, in typical Tuscan fashion, by a long avenue of cypress trees leading to a double tiered garden. The upper garden is arranged around a central fountain from which geometrically shaped parterres extend in all directions. On the lower terrace are groupings of miniature lemon and orange trees and a belvedere that looks out over olive groves to the city and across the Arno to Piazzale Michelangelo and the Iris Garden. A double staircase leads to the terrace and moat, now a carp pool, in front of the entrance.

The present layout dates from the seventeenth century. Paths weave in and out of the parterres, which by the fifteenth century had already become a developed form in Italy. Elaborate interlacing circles and knots were executed in box, myrtle or scented herbs, their contrasting tones of green decorative in winter and a frame for flowers in summer.

Florence developed a passion for the tulip when it was introduced to Europe from central Asia in the second half of the sixteenth century. It is difficult to comprehend today how exotic the tulip—named after a Turkish turban—was when it first appeared or how people like the grand duke of Tuscany became ardent collectors. This part of La Petraia's past is recalled each spring when the upper garden, a dull monochromatic dark green all winter, becomes an enormous abstract painting as the parterres fill with the brilliant colors of hundreds of tulips.

When Florence became the capital of Italy in 1861, the house of Savoy chose La Petraia for its royal palace and the king's former apartments are open to the public.

Many of the estimated 150 specimens of flowering plants in the meadow at the base of Botticelli's *Primavera* can be seen in spring in La Petraia's 44.5-acre park; the villa's gardeners make a special effort to cultivate and preserve Renaissance wildflowers. Signs at the entrance to the park list the plants, including forget-me-nots, narcissus, grape hyacinths, cornflowers, periwinkles, wild gladioluses, wood anemones and violets.

A pleasant half-mile walk down Via di Castello will bring you to another former Medici residence, Villa di Castello. Although its garden is not as impressive as La Petraia's, it is worth stopping briefly to see the place where, according to Vasari, both the *Birth of Venus* and the *Primavera* hung before they were moved to the Uffizi in 1815.

The oldest of the Medici villas, the Villa di Castello was built in 1477 for Lorenzo Pierfrancesco de' Medici, Botticelli's patron and the envious cousin of Lorenzo the Magnificent. Only the garden and park behind it are open to the public.

The garden is walled in on three sides and has a single avenue interrupted by a fountain running down the middle. Buontalenti, Ammannati and Giambologna all worked on it after it was laid out by Tribolo in 1540. When it was finished in 1592 it became one of the most renowned gardens in Europe and the model for both La Petraia and the Boboli Gardens. Like the *Primavera,* it was meant to be a grandiose allegorical conceit alluding to themes of nature, love and the cycle of the seasons. A maze of clipped box hedges followed precise perspective ratios, the trees formed arches and tunnels, and hidden paths led to grottoes in the walls.

Unfortunately, centuries of neglect have largely ruined most of these effects. But there are still enough traces of the statues, fountains, grottoes, box mazes and secret gardens to suggest its former glory. Above the wall at the far end is a terrace backed by a forest of ilex trees. This is now a park, threaded with meandering paths; in its center is a large pool containing a moss encrusted island.

The path through the park descends the hill along the side of the villa and eventually leads back to the entrance. Just before it ends, a round grassy field opens up, dotted with tiny white daisies and other wildflowers in spring. Flower-filled thickets like this are common to the Tuscan countryside. Early in May, before the planting begins, they appear much as the quattrocento painters depicted them: thick carpets of grass dotted with red poppies and blue irises, deep pink gladioluses and lavender anemones. In *The Stones of Florence,* Mary McCarthy compares these teeming meadows full of daisies and buttercups to the starry firmament; the wildflowers in them, she writes, seem to have been "spilled out onto the earth—just as in Botticelli's Primavera."

The **Iris Garden** (Il Giardino dell'Iris) is on the west side of Piazzale Michelangelo, the panoramic belvedere across the Arno from the Uffizi. An iron gate to the right of the piazzale leads to the garden.

The **Florence Rose Garden** (Il Giardino delle Rose), 2 Viale Poggio, 055.2342426, is on the opposite side of Piazzale Michelangelo from the Iris Garden. Free.

The gardens of both the **Villa di Castello** and **Villa della Petraia** are in the suburb of Castello, less than two miles northwest of Florence and about a thirty-minute bus ride from the center. Take bus 28A, 28B or 28C from the side of the train station. Get off at the Castello stop. Walk up Via Collodi; turn left onto Via Giuliani and then right onto Via Quercino until the cross street. To the right is Villa La Petraia; to the left, Villa di Castello. One ticket for both gardens. Telephone 055.454791 (Castello); 055.452691 (Petraia).

The Piazza della Signoria

BY ROBERT BARNARD

~

editor's note

I have stood in many a piazza, place, plaza, and praça, and while each of them may have been beautiful or grand or harmonious or all three, none except the Piazza della Signoria gave me a profound sense of standing where so much history took place.

Writer ROBERT BARNARD lives in England.

To travel, as we did, from Venice direct to Florence is to experience the Time Machine at its most devastating. Venice, still recognizably the city of Canaletto and Guardi, is the world's largest pedestrian precinct; Florence is a gigantic toyshop with malignant, destructive boys in little vehicles tearing up and down the aisles, bent on raising havoc. In Venice the loudest noise we heard was that of the pigeons eating themselves silly in the Piazza San Marco; in Florence there is hardly a moment's relief from the hideous clamor of the internal-combustion engine in one or another of its forms.

Down the narrow streets we edge our way, clutching to the grudged pavements, our ankles grazed by the inevitable Vespas weaving maniacally in and out between the cars; drivers accelerate, then slam on their brakes and hoot to assert their manhood; buses emit hideous hisses as they open doors to let passengers out; lorries lumber by, the Pavarottis of the traffic scene. Galleries and churches are in present-day Florence not so much places of spiritual refreshment as literally places of refuge—from the incredible noise and the actual danger of the streets.

To come to Florence after Venice is to appreciate the terrible damage the motor vehicle has inflicted on our environment, and on the tenor of our lives. But the Piazza della Signoria is a safe haven; the Piazza is traffic-free—bar the occasional Vespa and the occasional police car, both a law unto themselves. Here the city traffic becomes a dull background roar, and one can sit over a spremuta and watch the mix of tourists, scurrying local citizens and city officials, the representative mix that reflects the Florence of today.

"The piazza of exclusive bars and restaurants," someone said to me before I left. Perhaps, up to a point. Rivoire's, certainly, is expensive—but exclusive? How could it be exclusive when its function is to cater for the mass of tourists, single and in troops, who are the lifeblood of Florence? If you sit outside Rivoire's expecting Jacqueline Onassis or Princess Caroline to drop in, you will be disappointed. You will only hear the English at the next table complaining about the prices, or the Germans complaining about the service. On the other hand, for meeting your wife, or for watching the Florentines go by, it is ideal.

In the Piazza, a couple are reunited. They run joyously across the wide open space, and the girl buries her head, laughing and babbling, in the boy's chest. "How I love you!" her whole body says. The boy's eyes stray round to the watchers: "How she loves me!" his expression says.

The Italian male, at least in public, seems determined to illustrate all the qualities that feminists have ever attributed to men in general. This behavior is not endearing, but in Florence it is not out of place. For Florence is a male city. Not for nothing is it dominated by Michelangelo's *David*—glorious of body, noble of head, and peacock-pleased with himself. Florence in its period of preeminence seems a place of men, going about men's business, complete in themselves only when they are with other men. The Piazza is a male place—martial, sturdy, open.

There is no city square in Europe that is more definitively the heart of a city, the epitome of its history, its art and its present. There is a gloriously absurd stage-direction in Max Beerbohm's mock-poetic drama in his short story " 'Savonarola' Brown": "Enter Michael Angelo. Andrea del Sarto appears for a moment at a window. . . . Enter Boccaccio, Benvenuto Cellini and many others, making remarks highly characteristic of themselves." Absurd, yes, but it contains a certain grain of truth. The fourteenth-century giants of Florence were men of the city, who lived in the city and mingled with each other and with the working people—even the most humble—in a way that would have been inconceivable in most other cities of that time, or of any time. To sit in Trafalgar Square and to people it in the mind's eye with Gladstone, Queen Victoria and George Eliot would be absurd. To sit in the Piazza della Signoria and imagine Cosimo the Elder, Brunelleschi and Donatello, is to place them and their city in a proper relationship.

At the entrance to the Uffizi a guided tour swells the queue, until its tail reaches into the Square. One imagines them trooping past masterpieces with all the dogged inevitability of Napoleon's armies, until they stop for edification before an approved chef-d'ocuvre. What happens, one wonders, if someone's eye is caught by some other painting, and he stops to look? Is he crushed under culture-hungry boots?

The modern tourist, in comparison with his Edwardian predecessors, lacks stamina. In the works of Forster and his contemporaries, there scuttle through the Square culture-hungry ladies, en route from a minor esthetic frisson in Sant' Angelo delle Tagliatelle to a serious artistic confrontation in Santa Maria della Chipolata. Now, after one gallery or church, they flop down for a cappuccino or a beer, and quite soon after noon start filling up the tables outside Cavallino's, the best of the unpretentious restaurants in the Piazza. Here the atmosphere is friendly and unhurried, the proprietor benevolent, and the pappardelle con lepre (thickly cut pasta with hare sauce) is delicious. Couples of all nationalities relax over wine and, under its influence, wonder whether they dare admit that they found the Chapel of the Medici Princes quite hideous. Over their second glass they do. Well, it's only fair, isn't it, that Florence too, like any other city, should have its share of architectural clinkers.

A German approaches the queue to the Uffizi. He sees friends some way down the line, hails them loudly, then, tapping the shoulders of the intervening queuers with an authoritative *"Bitte!"* he makes his way past them until he has reached his friends.

It is nice for the British and the Americans that they are no longer everybody's least favorite tourists.

The middle-aged Englishwoman drifts past Rivoire's into the Piazza. She gazes round in disappointment. "They seem to be doing it up," she says.

They do indeed, for the reign of the motorcar is taking its toll. Scaffolding mantles the Palazzo Vecchio, the Uffizi and the Loggia della Signoria—so thickly in the last case that the statues are unviewable. It is the same at the Duomo, and at many of the churches. Only the Pitti Palace, all the commentators' least favorite building in Florence, seems not to be in danger of falling down.

And they are not only doing it up. A large rectangle in front of the Vecchio has been fenced off for archeological excavation. Fascinated Florentines mingle with the tourists to watch their own past being uncovered before their eyes. These were the palaces of the Ghibelline nobility, perennially locked in incomprehensible conflict with the Guelph faction in the high Middle Ages. Their dwellings were razed and paved over to make the Vecchio more easily defensible, and to form that essentially Florentine concept: a meeting-place for all its citizens.

But it was also Florence and its people who taught men to reverence their own past. Today, no native of any other city feels so passionately that his home city's buildings are part of his birthright: the Florentine who bustles past the Cathedral daily, and gives it not a second glance, yearns for its dome when he is abroad. In his mind's eye it is part of his picture of himself. Whether, to save it, he would give up driving his car around it is another matter. Perhaps if we are being optimistic, we can regard the Piazza della Signoria not as an oasis, but as a start.

This piece originally appeared in "The Sophisticated Traveler" edition of *The New York Times Magazine* on March 13, 1988. Copyright © 1988 by Robert Barnard. Reprinted with permission of the author.

The Cloisters of Florence

BY LOUIS INTURRISI

editor's note

The Metropolitan Museum of Art has in its possession not only one of the treasures of New York but of the entire country: the Cloisters, a collection of medieval art that incorporates sections of actual European cloisters. While there, it's possible to feel a million miles away from a major metropolis, even though the Cloisters lies nearly at the tip of Manhattan.

As Louis Inturrisi notes in this piece, which was featured in the November 1995 issue of *Gourmet*, the majority of the cloisters in Florence date from the Renaissance, but no matter what their architectural style, they're all serene spots for reflection and repose.

LOUIS INTURRISI was a freelance writer and professor who lived in Rome. He wrote often about Italian culture and food for a variety of publications, including *Gourmet*, *HG*, and *The New York Times*.

Cloisters have always seemed to me the least intimidating of architectural forms. Their classical rhythms never take getting used to, and experiencing their comforting repetitions always feels like coming home to rest among the familiar folds of a mother's skirt. Moreover, because cloisters strike just the right balance between confinement and freedom, they invite lingering and encourage a childlike tendency toward indolence that is difficult to resist.

The cloisters attached to the great churches of Florence are no exception. They are blessed islands of repose amid the hurly-burly of open markets, whirlwind tours, and the noise and frustration of rush-hour traffic. And with their cool fountains, covered loggias, and open centers, cloisters make perfect places in which to curl up and while away the afternoon. Especially on sunlit days, I find it

hard not to stay put and let myself be cradled by the soothing harmony of a cloister such as the Chiostro Grande (Great Cloister) at Santa Croce, with its elegant gray-and-white loggia echoing Brunelleschi's Pazzi Chapel around the corner.

The Great Cloister is the more remote of two cloisters at Santa Croce and is almost hidden away behind a beautifully sculpted portal by Benedetto da Maiano. Few tourists ever venture this far, so it is one of the most tranquil public places in Florence. Birds chirp, bees hum, and the monastic simplicity here is the opposite of the sensual onslaught one experiences in the church and chapel next door. Finished in the mid-fifteenth century by a disciple of Brunelleschi, the Great Cloister is a fine example of Renaissance harmony. All its measurements were worked out so that, for example, the span between the arches marching in stately procession around the center is one-and-a-half times the height of the pillars.

Nothing detracts from these careful calculations. A few curly acanthus leaves atop the smooth columns and some floral medallions in the white spandrels between the arches are the only frills in this soberly peaceful place. It's the pleasant predictability of column and arch—repeated in their silhouettes along the pavement—that holds the attention here and makes it impossible not to stop and note how the sky framed above a cloister always seems brighter and clearer than it would otherwise.

Cloisters, of course, are nothing new. They are descendants of the Roman atrium—the heart of patrician houses at the time of the empire. The ruins at Ostia Antica and Pompeii show that the model for this type of dwelling was a series of rooms set around a large rectangle open to the sky to provide light as well as a basin for collecting rainwater.

The culmination of this plan is the House of the Vestals in the Roman Forum. There the celibate order of women lived around an open courtyard in much the same way Europe's religious orders would in the Middle Ages. The Dominican, Franciscan, and Benedictine monks and nuns adopted the Roman atrium for their abbeys and monasteries because it provided a covered walkway between sleeping quarters and chapel. This closed-in space, or *claustrum* in Latin, represented the boundaries beyond which they did not venture: Outside was chaos, war, and the plague, but inside was a corner of life safely tucked away.

The impression one gets when viewing the world from the second story of the austerely simple cloister of Florence's San Lorenzo, near the Mercato Centrale and the neighborhood's street market, is almost Zen-like. Everything here is reduced to the essential: The arcade is a sweeping unadorned surface; the pillars are slender sticks; and the colors —ochre, brown, and terra-cotta—are the humble tones of the Tuscan hills. Silence is part of the architecture. You realize it whenever it is broken—by the birds hopping about the roof tiles or by the bells in Santa Maria del Fiore's campanile, its striated green-and-white marble soaring incongruously over the adjacent rooftops. In the garden below, rows of sharp-edged boxwood hedges converge on a miniature orange grove.

In Renaissance cloisters, which predominate in Florence, elements of the medieval cloister were modified. Before the fifteenth century, for example, the second storys of most cloisters were merely open passageways covered by roof tiles, like the one at San Lorenzo. But during the Renaissance these passageways were often walled up, windows added, and the whole converted into monks' cells. In addition, the open centers of many medieval cloisters were obscured from view by an exterior wall. In the fourteenth and fifteenth centuries this wall was gradually diminished and eventually disappeared.

Both these changes are evident in the beautiful cloister of Santa Maria Maddalena dei Pazzi in Borgo Pinti (at number 58), where the second-story loggia has been "filled in" and the dividing wall reduced to a base for a portico of Ionic columns. Moreover, instead of continuing uninterrupted around the square as it would have in a medieval cloister, the portico is broken at opposite ends by tall arches that cut into the second story and point toward the kind of monumental grandeur that typifies the Renaissance cloister.

Designed by Giuliano da Sangallo in 1480, Santa Maria Maddalena's cloister is among the most serene in Florence. Apart from the few tourists who come to see Perugino's well-preserved *Crucifixion and Saints* fresco in the lower church, this is a place where you can be alone for long periods of time, accompanied only by the sunlight and by the gray-green elegance of *pietra serena,* or "serene stone," which here, more than anywhere else in Florence, demonstrates the merit of its name.

The most refined of the Renaissance cloisters in Florence is perhaps the one called the Chiostro degli Uomini (Men's Cloister) inside the Spedale degli Innocenti (Hospital of the Innocents), in Piazza della Santissima Annunziata. Named for the biblical incident in which Herod, reacting to the birth of Christ, ordered the deaths of hundreds of innocent children, this was the first (1421) foundlings' hospital in Europe. Its cloister (visible through the gateway) is one of the wonders of Renaissance art. The noble colonnade of wide arches and smooth *pietra serena* columns echoes the elegant geometry of Brunelleschi's design for the surrounding piazza, which many Florentines consider their most beautiful square.

But there is something new here. Unlike Brunelleschi's other cloisters, where refinement and satisfaction are derived mostly from a careful consideration of "order, measure, and rule," the hospital's main cloister has a bit of decoration as well. Large white circles enclosing emblems of the other foundlings' hospitals in Florence cover the surface of the low-lying second story. And, because these were executed in white lime sgraffito against a terra-cotta background, they also give the surface depth. In addition, in the spaces where the arches meet, delicately incised medallions repeat the touching motif of babes in swaddling clothes, which Andrea della Robbia created in the 1480s for the blue-and-white porcelain tondos that grace the portico in the piazza.

There are a few benches here, among the potted lemon trees, where I make a customary stop. Beyond the arches the sound of children playing can often be heard because this is still a hospital and an orphanage. The babes above the arches backed by the sound of real children reinforce my conviction that cloisters are a most motherly invention. Before leaving, I always go through the little doorway on the right that leads to a second cloister—the graceful, oblong Chiostro delle Donne (Women's Cloister), also by Brunelleschi— where slender Ionic columns support a tiny cream colored loggia like the ones so often seen in early Renaissance paintings.

The problem with cloisters, of course, is the corners. The number of arches and the span between them have to follow a precise canon or an unharmonious bunching up of columns will occur in the corners (as at the cloister at San Matteo) or a jump from columns to pilasters (as at Santa Maria Maddalena). One of the things that makes the Men's Cloister at the Innocents' Hospital so satisfying is that nothing interrupts the solemn procession of column and arch around the perfect square.

Though the hospital's main cloister is unmatchable in its serene classicism, for my money the most impressive of the Renaissance cloisters in Florence is the *chiostrino,* or "little cloister," next to the Church of San Giovanni Battista dello Scalzo on Via Cavour (at number 69). Built in 1511 for a medieval confraternity of barefoot (*scalzi*) brothers, the *chiostrino* is unique. Instead of the usual single columns, here are pairs of beautifully sculpted Corinthian columns. And they do not rest on the ground or on a wall, as in other cloisters, but are raised on pedestals, which makes them more like sculptures than mere supports. (If you look carefully at these pedestals, you will see that they are decorated with skulls and crossbones, alluding to the group's avowed mission during the Middle Ages of collecting and burying the dead from plagues and wars.)

A terra-cotta walkway surrounds the *chiostrino* and along the walls are Andrea del Sarto's hauntingly lovely scenes from the life of Saint John the Baptist, painted in pale grisaille against a dark green background. The center of this cloister is glassed over to protect the frescoes, and this feature makes it a good place to visit in the rain.

Many charming cloisters in Florence are worth visiting, yet these are my favorites. Others not to miss if you can help it, however, are the cloister next to the Church of the Carmine, with its tall cypresses so typical of Tuscany; the cloister of the Ognissanti (All Saints) along the Arno, which has an impressive *Last Supper* by Ghirlandaio; and the beautiful cloister by Michelozzo at San Marco. And Santa Maria Novella has six cloisters!

There are sixty-two cloisters in Florence in all, and it is enough to note that visitors who have strayed into any one of them know the tug to postpone tasks, stay put a while, and let themselves be nourished by this most compassionate of buildings—which shuts the world out and lets it in at the same time.

Biblioteca

General Art Reference

History of Art, H. W. Janson, Anthony F. Janson, fifth revised edition, Harry N. Abrams, 1997. Still enormous, still a classic, and still a great source for Italian arts, Etruscan to modern.

The Story of Art, E. H. Gombrich, Phaidon Press Ltd., London, sixteenth edition, 1995. Although Sir Ernst Gombrich has authored numerous volumes on art, this is the one that really established his reputation. To quote from the jacket, "*The Story of Art* is one of the most famous and popular books on art ever published. For 45 years it has remained unrivalled as an introduction to the whole subject. . . ." Though a comprehensive book, Italian artists are well represented.

The Oxford Companion to Christian Art and Architecture: The Key to Western Art's Most Potent Symbolism, Peter and Linda Murray, Oxford University Press, 1998. A thorough reference guide with color plates; general background to the Old and New Testaments and Christian beliefs; a glossary of architectural terms; and a detailed bibliography.

From Abacus to Zeus: A Handbook of Art History, James Smith Pierce, Prentice-Hall, 1977. Pierce has keyed the entries in this guide to the second edition of H. W. Janson's *History of Art,* which illustrates the extent this is a thorough and indispensable reference. Entries are presented A to Z within five chapters: Art Terms, Processes, and Principles; Gods, Heroes, and Monsters; Christian Subjects; Saints and Their Attributes; and Christian Signs and Symbols.

Angels A to Z: A Who's Who of the Heavenly Host, Matthew Bunson, Three Rivers Press, 1996. This is *not* just another angel book. It's a fascinating and useful reference you'll be glad to have. From "abaddon" to "zutu'el" and with numerous black-and-white reproductions of major and minor art works, this is really a great resource for looking at art. In his foreword, Bunson gives several reasons for the popularity of angels, and he states that "Finally, and perhaps most important, throughout history one thought has proven powerfully constant and nearly universally accepted by Jewish writers, Christian saints, Muslim scholars, and followers of the New Age: The angel is one of the most beautiful expressions of the concern of God for all of his creations, an idea beautifully expressed by Tobias Palmer in *An Angel in My House:* 'The very presence of an angel is a communication. Even when an angel crosses our path in silence, God has said to us, "I am here. I am present in your life." ' "

Italian Art and Architecture

Lives of the Painters, Sculptors and Architects, in two volumes, Giorgio Vasari, Everyman's Library, translated by Gaston du C. de Vere, with an introduction and notes by David Ekserdjian, translation by de Vere first published in 1912. The opening line of the introduction is the only recommendation one need ever read or hear on this masterpiece, originally published in 1550: "Giorgio Vasari's *Lives of the Painters, Sculptors and Architects* is the Bible of Italian Renaissance—if not all—art history." *Essenziale.* And a wonderful companion volume is *The Great Masters* (Beaux Arts Editions, Hugh Lauter Levin Associates, 1986), which pairs Vasari's biographies on Giotto, Botticelli, da Vinci, Raphael, Michelangelo, and Titian with related paintings, sculptures, drawings, and architecture in 120 color plates and 127 black-and-white illustrations. There are also twenty gatefolds of selected works, including Botticelli's *Primavera:* An oversized, beautiful book worthy of your diligent efforts to find.

The Splendors of Italy, translated by Geoffrey Braithwaite, G. P. Putnam's Sons; originally published by Librairie Hachette as *L'Italie et ses Merveilles,* 1964. Inexplicably out-of-print (but worth an enormous effort to find), this is a definitive, gorgeous, heavy (an oversized hardcover at about 350 pages) volume with hundreds of black-and-white and color reproductions and photographs of Italy's artworks and architectural masterpieces. With dozens of tip-ons, good text, some maps, and a chart of the three great schools of Italian painting (Siena, Florence, and Venice/Padua/Verona), this is a must-have, and I've not seen any other book quite like it in either quality or scope. They just don't make books like this anymore.

Italian Gothic Sculpture, Italian Renaissance Sculpture, Italian High Renaissance & Baroque Sculpture, John Pope-Hennessy, three-volume boxed set, Phaidon; original publication dates for the individual volumes date from the late 1950s and early 1960s. An absolutely gorgeous, incomparable set.

The Arts of the Italian Renaissance: Painting, Sculpture, Architecture, Walter Paatz, Prentice-Hall and Harry N. Abrams, 1974. This is still my favorite book on the *quattrocentro.* I believe it was intended to be a textbook, and it is long out-of-print, but it remains my favorite single volume. With 301 illustrations, including sixty-one in color. A very comprehensive edition, with an excellent bibliography.

The Art of the Italian Renaissance: Architecture, Sculpture, Painting, Drawing, edited by Rolf Toman, Konemann, 1995. Also a good volume, with many color reproductions and lineage charts for the Sforza, Este, and Gonzaga families, the Popes, and Doges of Venice.

Architecture of the Renaissance: From Brunelleschi to Palladio, Bertr and Jestaz, Harry N. Abrams and Thames and Hudson, 1996. This is an edition in the "Discoveries" series, originally published in France by Gallimard Discoveries paperbacks, and is a terrific value: It's jammed with information; the quality of the reproductions is good; it's lightweight and easy to pack (approximately 5-by-

7 inches); and the price is right (about $12.95). At the time of this writing, this is the only edition in the series applicable to central Italy (there are, however, editions on *The Search for Ancient Rome* and *Pompeii: The Day a City Died*).

The Italian Painters of the Renaissance, Bernard Berenson, Phaidon Press, Ltd., London, 1952. To my mind, this is without doubt the single best book on the subject of Italian Renaissance painters. There are, of course, hundreds of other titles, and this one is out-of-print; but I urge readers to check in your library or used bookstores for this edition. Berenson presents the Venetian, Florentine, central Italian, and north Italian Renaissance painters in separate chapters, which contain some color tip-ons of various works. Following a chapter on "The Decline of Art," there are over 200 pages of black-and-white reproductions. One of the reasons I, and many others, are so fond of Berenson is perhaps best explained by this excerpt from the preface: "Yet too much time should not be wasted in reading about pictures instead of looking at them. Reading will help little towards the enjoyment and appreciation and understanding of the work of art. It is enough to know when and where an artist was born and what older artist shaped and inspired him, rarely, as it happens, the master or teacher who first put pen, pencil and brush into his hands. Least profit is to be got from the writings of the metaphysical and psychoanalytical kind. If read one must, let it be the literature and history of the time and place to which the paintings belong." *Essenziale.*

Looking at Pictures with Bernard Berenson, selected and with an introduction by Hanna Kiel, with a personal reminiscence by J. Carter Brown, Harry N. Abrams, 1974. Kiel, who translated several of Berenson's works into German and prepared the bibliography at the end of this book, here combines text from Berenson's books, diaries, and letters with 150 great Italian paintings from museums and private collections in Europe and America. I wouldn't qualify this as *essenziale,* unless, like me, you really enjoy Berenson.

The Passionate Sightseer—Bernard Berenson, From the Diaries 1947–56, preface by Raymond Mortimer, Simon & Schuster/Harry N. Abrams, 1960. Similar to *Looking at Pictures* above, this book pairs 168 works of art with Berenson's diary entries. Chapters are on various cities or regions—mostly Italian but also North Africa—the last one devoted to Florence and dated June to July 1956. Nearly every page in the book features a black-and-white photo or reproduction, and there are three full-page color plates. Also not *essenziale,* but Berenson fans will be glad to have it.

The Renaissance, Walter Pater, Oxford World's Classics, Oxford University Press, 1986, originally published in 1873. Pater's classic—and infamous—work is a collection of essays on those artists who to him best expressed the spirit of the Renaissance: Pico della Mirandola, Sandro Botticelli, Luca della Robbia,

Michelangelo, Leonardo da Vinci, Giorgione, Joachim du Bellay, and Johann Winckelmann. No reproductions, unfortunately.

Florentine and Tuscan Art

The Art of Florence, Glenn Andres, John Hunisak, and A. Richard Turner, principal photography by Takashi Okamura, Abbeville Press, 1988, in two enormous, hardcover volumes almost as heavy as a coffee table. You do not need to read any other books except these, which are among the most beautiful and outstanding the publishing world has ever seen. The quality of the reproductions and photographs is breathtaking, and the text is equally as superb—and it's not only about art. Volume I sets the historical stage with chapters on "Prelude to Greatness, 59 BC–AD 1200" and "Civic Pride and Prosperity, 1200–1340." Last year, Abbeville announced a significant reduction in the price for this slipcased set—it was originally published at around $395—to around $135. It's an awful lot of money to spend on books, but I think it's a very good value for what's between the covers. *Essenziale.*

The Architecture of the Italian Renaissance, Peter Murray, Schocken Books, 1986; originally published in different form as *The Architecture of the Renaissance* in Great Britain by B. T. Batsford, Ltd., London, 1963. This paperback reprint of one of the classic volumes on one of the most pivotal periods in art and architectural history contains a revised bibliography and some new illustrations. Usually such definitive books are too heavy to take along, but this one will fit easily in a handbag (252 pages, approximately 8¼″ by 5¾″). Though there are a few chapters on Milan, Rome, and the Veneto, the majority of the book deals with Florence and Tuscany.

Painting and Illumination in Early Renaissance Florence: 1300–1450, the Metropolitan Museum of Art/Harry N. Abrams, published in conjunction with the exhibit held at the Metropolitan November 17, 1994, through February 26, 1995.

The Brancacci Chapel, Florence, Andrew Ladis, George Braziller, 1993. This is one volume in The Great Fresco Cycles of the Renaissance series, meant to highlight the frescoes painted in chapels and town halls across Italy. The frescoes were commissioned by both private patrons and the Church and together represent one of the greatest achievements of Renaissance art. Each volume in the series is written by a leading scholar in the field who sets the frescoes in their artistic and historical context.

Painting in Renaissance Siena: 1420–1500, Keith Christiansen, The Metropolitan Museum of Art/Harry N. Abrams, 1988. This is the catalog that accompanied the exhibition of the same name. Not only was this show one of the best I've ever seen, but the catalog is fascinating. As Christiansen states, "This is not mainstream Italian art, but neither is it provincial. It is, for the most part, distinctly anti-Florentine, and I truly believe it is also among the most seductive schools of painting ever created."

The Basilica of St. Francis in Assisi, Elvio Lunghi, SCALA, Istituto Fotografico Editoriale/Riverside Book Company, 1996. A good paperback volume with color reproductions of the basilica, some views of the surrounding countryside, the frescoes, and artistic and architectural details. Also included are chapters on Brother Francis, the construction of the church, and the decline of Assisi, and an index of artists—including Giotto, Simone Martini, and Pietro Lorenzetti—whose works are featured in the basilica.

Single Artist Books and Museum Catalogs

The following are definitive volumes (some are comprehensive catalogs that accompanied museum exhibitions) and are worth a special effort to track down. I've only included titles that represent an artist's full *oeuvre* as opposed to specialized subjects or periods (unless the subject or period is inseparable from the artist's style or are related to Tuscany or Umbria in some way).

Botticelli: Images of Love and Spring, Frank Zöllner, Pegasus Library, Prestel, 1998. This is one volume in the Pegasus Library series, a hardcover imprint (only a handful of editions are available in paperback) similar to Discoveries but a little more scholarly. The books are not pocket-size but are still slender, lightweight, and packable. Highly recommended.

De Chirico and the Mediterranean, edited by Jole de Sanna, Rizzoli, 1998.

Giorgio de Chirico: Il mito, le armi e l'eroe, Domenico Guzzi, Edizione Bora, Bologne, 1998. In Italian but very comprehensive with hundreds of color and black-and-white reproductions.

Piero della Francesca, Marilyn Aronberg Levin, George Braziller, 1994. Another great volume in the brilliant Great Fresco Cycles of the Renaissance series.

Piero della Francesca, Maurizio Calvesi, Rizzoli, 1998.

Fra Angelico at San Marco, William Hood, Yale University Press, 1993.

Fra Filippo Lippi: Life and Work, Jeffrey Ruda, Phaidon, 1993.

Fra Filippo Lippi: The Carmelite Painter, Megan Holmes, Yale University Press, 1999.

Alberto Giacometti: Sculpture, Paintings, Drawings, edited by Angela Schneider, Prestel, 1994.

Andrea Mantegna, edited by Jane Martineau, The Metropolitan Museum of Art, 1992. First published on the occasion of the exhibition of the same name held at the Royal Academy of Arts, London (January 17 through April 5, 1992) and The Metropolitan Museum of Art (May 5 through July 12).

Simone Martini, The Library of Great Masters, SCALA, Istituto Fotografico Editoriale S.p.A/Riverside Book Company, 1989.

Michelangelo: Paintings, Sculpture, Architecture—Complete Edition, Ludwig Goldscheider, Phaidon, 1953, reprinted 1997, 1998, 1999. Excellent quality paperback with mostly black-and-white reproductions and twelve pages of color in the front of the book.

The World of Michelangelo: 1475–1564, Robert Coughlan, H. W. Janson, consulting editor, Time-Life Books, 1966. This volume in the Time-Life Library of Art is out-of-print but can, with other editions in this wonderful series, be found often in used bookstores. I have found each edition in this series to be very comprehensive and well illustrated with color and black-and-white photos, drawings, and reproductions. Included in this edition is a chronology of artists, other works of Michelangelo, a catalogue of illustrations, and a bibliography.

Amadeo Modigliani: Portraits and Nudes, Anette Kruszynski, Pegasus Library, Prestel, 1996. Another volume in the Pegasus Library.

Modigliani, collector's edition published in 1985 by Harry N. Abrams for the Easton Press, Norwalk, Connecticut. This is the concise edition of Alfred Werner's *Modigliani* originally published in 1966.

Pietro Perugino: Master of the Italian Renaissance, Joseph Antenucci Becherer, Rizzoli/The Grand Rapids Art Museum. Published in conjunction with the exhibition of the same name organized by The Grand Rapids Art Museum, November 16, 1997, through February 1, 1998.

The Sculptures of Andrea Del Verrocchio, Andrew Butterfield, Yale University Press, 1997.

Giardini

Italian Villas and Their Gardens, Edith Wharton, with pictures by Maxfield Parrish, Da Capo Press, originally published by The Century Co., 1904. This paperback reprint is an unabridged republication in Da Capo's Classical America Series in Art and Architecture. As Arthur Ross states in the foreword, *Italian Villas and Their Gardens* "has stood the test of time since its original publication in 1904." The first chapters feature Florentine and Sienese villas, and the remaining cover Roman, Genoese, Lombard, and Venetian villas. Most of the Parrish illustrations in this edition are black-and-white, but happily there is a thirteen-page insert in the center of the book with a selection of color reproductions. Wharton has provided a bibliography of books mentioned in the text, as well as an alphabetical listing of architects and landscape-gardeners. *Essenziale.*

Italian Gardens of the Renaissance, J. C. Shepherd and G. A. Jellicoe, Princeton Architectural Press, 1993; originally published in 1925 by E. Benn, London. In much the same way that Wharton's book is a classic, this work is, too. Shepherd and Jellicoe were fifth-year students of London's Architectural Association when they set off on a grand tour of Europe. While in Italy, they studied in great detail selected gardens dating from the fifteenth to seventeenth centuries and produced this masterful project as a result. Reuben Rainey notes in the foreword that the gardens appear in a general chronological order, but readers are not told the criteria for the gardens chosen for inclusion. They are all significant examples, but the majority of them are in the areas around Rome, Florence, and Lucca. No matter. Serious garden and Renaissance lovers will rejoice at this collection. With black-and-white watercolors, line drawings, and photographs of twenty-six major Italian villas.

The Garden Lover's Guide to Italy, Penelope Hobhouse, Princeton Architectural Press, 1998; first published in Great Britain in 1998 by Mitchell Beazley, an imprint of Reed Consumer Books, Ltd., London. Hobhouse is a world-renowned gardener and writer, and she has a special affection for Italian gardens. This edition, one in the Garden Lover's Guide series, is divided into five regional chapters, and twenty-six gardens are highlighted for Tuscany (there are, unfortunately, none for Umbria). I was especially happy to find that Iris Origo's garden at Villa La Foce, near Montepulciano was included, as I hadn't known it was open to the public. Many of these Tuscan gardens, including the one at La Foce, are open by appointment only, so interested readers should plan on obtaining permission well in advance. Addresses, fax, and telephone numbers, hours, and brief directions are provided, as well as color photos and a map at the beginning of each chapter. A glossary of Italian gardening terms and a good selection of related biographies are found at the back of the book.

"The Back Roads of Tuscany," William Sertl, *Garden Design,* October/ November 1996. A highly recommended article describing nine Tuscan *giardini:* Venzano, Villa La Foce, Villa Massei, Centinale, Gamberaia, Roseto Botanico di Cavriglia Carla Fineschi, Torrigiani, Vignamaggio, and Villa Medici. As a travel editor, Sertl is often asked for his favorite places in Tuscany. His reply is that he has too many. "I love this part of Italy," he notes, "and while I'm not one to clip coupons, my Tuscany scrapbook is stuffed with old menus, maps heavy with annotation, and the elegant receipts doled out by garden gatekeepers. It's not the great cities of Florence or Siena that lure me. My Tuscany is more about being set free in a civilized wilderness." With color photos, recommendations, and practical tips.

A Tavola!

(To the Table—Let's Eat!)

"No, Italy's idiosyncratic ways of cooking shouldn't be muddled in generic stews. It's worth recalling that Italian peoples, historically separated by mountain ranges and expanses of water, never supported monolithic rule long enough or strongly enough to forsake their parochial identities. Even now, long after former kingdoms, principalities, duchies, and lilliputian republics metamorphosed into twenty regions comprising nearly a hundred provinces, ethnic peculiarities remain in customs, speech, and cooking. The local flavors of Italy's trattorie, osterie, locande, taverne, pizzerie, pasticcerie, botteghe, *and* mercati *are often imitated but rarely duplicated elsewhere. In more than thirty years of dining in the country, the meals I've most savored invariably told a story of a people and a place."*

—Burton Anderson, from the introduction to
Treasures of the Italian Table

Where Every Meal Is a
Fabulous Feast

BY RUTH REICHL

~

editor's note

....

As I emphasized in the introduction, specific restaurant recommendations are not the province of The Collected Traveler series. In my opinion, travelers will be better served by reading about the food and drink unique to Tuscany and Umbria and how these are prepared and served. Some specialties to look for include *pasta fagioli* (a souplike pasta with cannellini beans and rosemary), *bistecca alla fiorentina* (thick steak from Chianina cows, usually grilled), *ricciarelli* (soft, chewy almond cookies), *acquacotta* (a simple bread-and-garlic soup, usually with a lightly poached egg added at the last moment), *pollo al mattone* (chicken cooked under a brick), *ribollita* (a bread, bean, and vegetable soup), *schiacciata* (flatbread topped simply with salt and olive oil or more elaborately with grapes and sugar), *porchetta* (spit-roasted suckling pig), *panzanella* (a salad of bread mixed with tomatoes, onions, basil, and olive oil), and *crostini* (an appetizer of crisp bread spread with a chicken-liver paste). When you know about a particular dish, you will know when you come across an authentic version of it, which is most likely a sign that the kitchen prepares its dishes with care.

Though I remain reluctant to feature many articles about restaurants, I admit that some guidance from respected authorities is very welcome. I do not wish to deny anyone the experience of eating at either Cibreo or Il Latini, where I had a *pappa al pomodoro* I still dream about, and by checking several sources you'll begin to see a few of the same names, usually with good reason. But the point is, you should know what kind of food to expect at a *trattoria* versus a restaurant, and if one place or another has closed its doors, rest assured you'll have a good meal somewhere else, or you might discover a favorite of your own. I am happy to include the following three articles for two reasons: Because the reviewers, Ruth Reichl, Faith Heller Willinger, and Nancy Harmon Jenkins, write about food and the people who prepare it, not just about the pleasures of dining out, and because it has been my observation that restaurants in Florence do not open and close, or rise and decline, with the frequency found in other cities. Therefore, older articles are not to be disregarded. Some items might no longer be found on restaurant menus, and some establishments might have undergone a renovation, but generally the places held in high regard still are.

Unlike Ruth Reichl, I have never had a bad meal in France—some meals have been disappointing, but never bad. It is equally true that I've never had a bad meal in Italy, and it is worth repeating that, even if in the two years since Reichl wrote this piece the specific restaurants she mentions have closed their doors, it matters not. You will eat just as well at numerous other places, some of which you might discover quite by accident. And it is indeed telling that Reichl did not see a single McDonald's in Umbria, reason alone to cross the Tuscan border.

RUTH REICHL, former restaurant critic for *The New York Times,* is now the editor in chief of *Gourmet.* Her adventures in the food world are related in her own book *Tender at the Bone* (Random House, 1998, hardcover; Broadway Books, 1999, paperback) and *Dining Out* (Andrew Dornenburg and Karen Page, Wiley, 1998).

There is no bad food in Italy. That may be an exaggeration, but after three weeks of traveling there, I have come to believe it is true. In small towns and big cities, in tiny trattorias and even tourist restaurants, we ate well everywhere.

It was not what I expected. When I told friends I was heading to Italy in the month of August they were all incredulous. August, they assured me, was a stupid time to go. The whole country would be closed; the place would be packed with tourists. Indeed, my best Italian friend was planning to spend the month in Bali.

"I don't care," I said. Defiantly, I did not take a single restaurant guidebook and made no reservations. We would eat wherever we happened to be when we got hungry; if we ate badly for a few weeks we would certainly survive.

I have learned, the hard way, that you can no longer count on serendipity in France; although it is still home to many of the world's greatest restaurants, if you leave your meals to chance, you may end up eating terribly. I expected Italy to be the same.

But it was not. Italy is still what France used to be: a fabulous feast, a place where good food is always just around the corner.

We started out in a rented house in Umbria, the pastoral region just south of Tuscany. The brochure had made it sound so splendid that I had allowed myself to fantasize an elegant palazzo high on a hill. There was a hill all right, and the house was very pretty, surrounded by fruit and olive trees, with an extraordinary view. There was a pool and a large outdoor oven. The romance, however, ended at the gate—the town beyond it was a jumble of ugly new buildings.

It took a while to find a grocery store, but we finally discovered that the supermarket was in the middle of the housing project near the railroad station. It did not look promising. When the electric doors opened I nearly gasped: the shelves were lined with artisanal pastas, the cheese and prosciutto looked terrific, the butcher was friendly, and the fruits and vegetables that winked and glistened beneath the fluorescent lights were as fresh as anything you find in New York's Greenmarkets. I bought melons and prosciutto, I bought an entire loin of pork, I bought local potatoes, tomatoes and arugula. Our first dinner, cooked in the outdoor oven, was splendid.

The next day I headed for Narni, a nearby hill town that seems to have been slumbering since the twelfth century. Cobbled streets twisted up to the fortress at the top of the village, and the morning market was in a covered loggia.

Everything—from the melons casually tossing their fragrance into the air to the glowing peaches—was at the perfect point of ripeness.

"Where should we eat?" I asked the old lady who sold us figs. She pointed a gnarled finger up the hill to the Hotel dei Priori, where we had a wonderful lunch on the terrace of manfrigoli, the thick square-cut strands of local pasta, with a fresh wine that tasted like cherries.

And so it went, everywhere. Italians still eat simply, locally and very well. It is telling, I think, that in two weeks in Umbria I did not stumble upon a single McDonald's. I did, however, stumble upon a great many unforgettable meals.

In Todi, desperately trying to find a place to park, I got stuck at the end of a cobbled dead-end street. As I tried to back up the 45-degree incline, the car stalled. The proprietor of the nearest restaurant watched me, shook his head and then motioned for me to get out of the car. He backed it all the way up to the top of the street and handed it back, without a word. The least I could do, I thought, was patronize his restaurant.

Ristorante Umbria turned out to have a romantic grape-shaded terrace overlooking the valley. We ate a thick, powerful soup of local lentils and sweet little lamb chops grilled over a roaring fire. It was beautiful there, and by the time I had finished the better part of a bottle of Orvieto I had gathered the courage to thank the owner for rescuing me from my car. "It was nothing," he said graciously. "But how did you like the food?"

Two days later, in Spoleto, I happened into a small dusty grocery store with shelves that stretched all the way up to the ceiling. "How long has this store been here?" I asked the cheerful proprietor. "Oh," he replied, "since 1620."

I bought cheese, local salami made of boar, and a bottle of thick, old balsamic vinegar. "Is it good?" I asked. The proprietor shook his head.

"It's not good," he replied. "It is extraordinary."

And so was the restaurant we found in nearby Pigge, on the road to Assisi. From the outside, the Taverna del Pescatore doesn't look like much; its beauty unfolds so slowly that it has an almost magical quality. Bit by bit, you discover a terrace overlooking a clear stream and then the island in the center of it. Only when you are seated do you hear the chirping of birds and the droning of bees. But the moment you open the menu you discover how truly fortunate you are to be there.

It is filled with local specialties like strangozzi di magro, homemade pasta tossed with tomatoes and peppers, and salads of wild greens topped with smoked trout. Crayfish are steamed simply with local olive oil and peppers, and goose is cooked with local chestnuts. The vegetables come from the garden, the fish from the stream. But the real treat here is the beef; the local Chianina cattle, fed on grass, produce lean and flavorful meat.

The wine list is extraordinary, too. And very reasonably priced. We began with grechetto, a pleasant, light white Umbrian wine that is perfect in the summer, and went on to a riserva Montefalco rosso, a powerful red regional wine made from sagrantino, sangiovese and trebbiano grapes.

Lunch took a long time, and when it was done we lingered in the shade of the terrace, eating biscotti and fruit and watching children playing in the water. It was a perfectly languid Umbrian afternoon.

After such peace, Florence was traumatic. It was, as promised, packed with tourists. And all the famous restaurants, were, as promised, closed for the month. When I asked a shopkeeper where we should eat, he said: "Try Il Latini. Tourists seem to like it."

It wasn't much of a recommendation, but we were hungry. The room, with its rustic communal tables set beneath hanging prosciuttos, was certainly attractive. It was also filled with Florentines, so when the man on my right asked the waiter for a recommendation, I leaned in to hear his response.

"Have the bean soup," the waiter said. So I did. It was big, thick, filling and served with a cruet of good olive oil. It was impressive. He recommended the veal chop even more highly, and no wonder; the oven-roasted chop turned out to be the best piece of veal I had ever tasted. With a simple salad of greens, tomatoes and the grated carrots that all Italians seem to put on insalata mista, it made an extremely satisfying meal.

I had been having amazing luck, but when I got to Venice I lowered my expectations. I had never eaten particularly well there, and I certainly did not expect to do so at the height of the tourist season. But after spending a morning rambling through the fish market by the Rialto I was suddenly very hungry. There was not one fish that was not gorgeous, and I was eager to find a restaurant that cooked seafood with style.

I went to Corte Sconta, a former working-class trattoria. Since my first visit, thirteen years ago, it has become very popular with Americans. My Venetian friends assured me that it was no longer very good. They were wrong.

We began with the house appetizer, which arrives in many small courses. The first consisted of fillets of marinated salmon topped with chopped arugula and fresh red currants. It was a beautiful plate, but it tasted even better than it looked. Then there were steamed vongole verace—clams so delicious I scooped up every drop of sauce. They were followed by sardines in saor—the sweet and sour sauce that is typical of Venice.

Then the waitress set down freshly picked spider crab, in the shell, with herbs, olive oil and lemon. And finally, a platter covered with squid, sea snails, anchovies, octopus, scallops and a variety of shrimp, from tiny sea crickets to giant gamberi. We went on to pasta tossed with fresh sardines and a single, exquisitely grilled sole.

It was my last day, and I felt sated and happy. More than that, I felt optimistic. Italy is a thoroughly modern country, despite its government's instability, which has moved forward without sacrificing all the good things of the past. At its highest level the country's cuisine is not as imaginative as that of France, but at every level it has remained true to itself.

Italian cooking sticks to its basic principles: you can count on finding excellent ingredients that are treated with enormous respect. Sipping my espresso and munching on lemony little biscotti, I thought what a pleasure it was to be in a country where it is still possible to eat well, without reservations.

La Loggia-Hotel dei Priori, Vicolo del Commune 4, Narni; tel. 0744.726.843.

Ristorante Umbria, Via San Bonaventura 13, Todi; 075.894.2737.

Taverna del Pescatore, Strada Statale Flaminia, Pigge; 0742.780.920. Fax: 0742.381.599.

Il Latini, Via dei Panchetti 6r, Florence; 055.210.916.

Corte Sconta, Calle del Pestrin, Castello 3886, Venice; 041.522.7024. Fax: 041.522.7513.

Florentine Trattorias

BY FAITH HELLER WILLINGER

~

editor's note

FAITH HELLER WILLINGER is the author of *Red, White, & Greens: The Italian Way With Vegetables* (HarperCollins Publishers, 1996) and *Eating in Italy: A Traveler's Guide to the Hidden Gastronomic Pleasures of Northern Italy* (William Morrow and Co., 1998). She is also a contributing editor of *Gourmet* and is working on a new book, *Ingredienti*, which will be published next year by HarperCollins.

I live in Florence. So in order to write about *trattorie* in my adopted hometown I spoke to a lot of friends, noted down their suggestions, revisited places I hadn't been in years, and checked out a couple of new ones. And I looked for a good definition of *trattoria*. Webster's says it's "a small, inexpensive restaurant in Italy." Not exactly. My Italian dictionary comes closer because it includes "a synonym of *osteria*," a derivation of the word for host.

Notice that neither décor, cuisine, nor service is mentioned in either definition. A *trattoria*, more often than not a family-run establishment, is presided over by a host or hostess acting as a link between the kitchen and the dining room, or cook and diner, and has as its most important aspect its sense of neighborhood: Locals dine there daily, or at least weekly, and are treated with familiarity.

Trattoria menus are composed of regional specialties and classic Italian dishes that highlight fresh ingredients and spare, unadorned preparations—the kind of cooking people eat at home (or wish they did). In other words, don't expect culinary fireworks or the showy artistry of a celebrity chef.

Meals in Florentine *trattorie* frequently begin with chicken liver–spread *crostini* (toasts) or thinly sliced *salumi*—salt-cured pork products such as prosciutto, fennel-flavored *finocchiona,* or *salame toscano* (with garlic and peppercorns). Bread, baked in wood-fired ovens, is rustic, dense, and saltless—an acquired taste for most.

Typical winter *primi,* or first courses, are hearty vegetable soups such as *ribollita* (a reboiled bread, bean, and cabbage combination), *pappa al pomodoro* (a porridge-like mixture of onion, garlic, tomatoes, basil, and local olive oil thickened with bread), and *pasta e ceci* (with chick-peas), or rich, meaty sauces served on the broad, flat noodles known as *pappardelle.* Summer diners can count on *panzanella,* a refreshing salad made from tomatoes, bread, onion, and fresh basil, and on pasta sauced with vine-ripened tomatoes and basil. A few nontraditional dishes centered around seasonal ingredients generally share space on the menu with such classics as pasta with meat sauce; *bollito misto* (mixed boiled meats); and breaded and fried *cotoletta* (pork, lamb, or veal chop).

Main-course meats include chops and *bistecca alla fiorentina,* a thick grilled T-bone that's served with a lemon wedge (particularly good are those from the local Chianina breed of cattle). Poultry and rabbit are deep-fried or oven- or spit-roasted. *Arista,* roast pork loin with rosemary and garlic, is another *trattoria* favorite. On Fridays, fish lovers can look forward to *baccalà*—salt cod, which is either cooked in tomato sauce, stewed with leeks, or served with chickpeas—and to spicy *calamari in inzimino,* squid braised in red wine with tomatoes, spinach, and Swiss chard. Vegetables get minimalist preparations: Most arrive pristine, accompanied only by a cruet of a fruity, murky local extra-virgin olive oil that's called simply *olio*— a world-class ingredient that is used here not just as a cooking medium but as an everyday condiment.

The cheese of Tuscany is Pecorino Toscano, not hard but a pungent product made from sheep's milk. Pecorino can be eaten *fresco* (up to a month old), *semi-stagionato* (aged one month or so), or up to six months later, when it is fully *stagionato* and thus drier and sharper in flavor. Look also for fresh sheep's-milk ricotta, which is far richer and more flavorful than the cow's-milk variety. And, finally, the classic conclusion to a *trattoria* meal are *biscotti di prato,* golden, eggy, hard almond cookies that are best dipped in a glass of *vin santo,* the region's dried grape-based dessert wine. Old-fashioned *torta della nonna* (a custard-and-nut-stuffed pastry), *tiramisù* (originally from the Veneto), and *panna cotta* (cooked cream) also can be found.

The wine served in Florentine *trattorie* is usually red and probably from the zones Chianti Classico, Chianti Rufina, Chianti Colli Fiorentini, or Chianti Montalbano. Only in the hot summer months will white wine appear on the tables. Those *trattoria* proprietors who have graduated from offering simply the *vino della casa* or from pointing at one or another of their displayed bottles to actually printing up a wine list probably will feature nonregional or nontraditional whites as well as a wider selection of well-respected Tuscan reds.

Florence's Santa Croce neighborhood is home to the Sant'Ambrogio market, a magnet for both farmers and retailers and a prime source for two of my favorite establishments. Cibrèo, named after an old-fashioned chicken-innards dish reputed to be an aphrodisiac, comprises both a formal restaurant and, in a back room, a casual *trattoria.* Chef-owner Fabio Picchi carefully controls each pot on the stove and takes full advantage of local ingredients such as the hot red peppers known in Tuscan dialect as *zenzero* (his are homegrown by his dad). The *trattoria* décor—tiled walls, wooden tables set with paper place mats, short-stemmed glasses— is decidedly more casual than that of the restaurant. In addition, the menu is shorter, the service swift, and the seating communal. Reservations are not accepted, and lingering is discouraged. Still, prices are less than half those at the restaurant, and the food comes from the same kitchen.

A starter—usually the spicy tomato aspic or the *sformato di ricotta* (ricotta flan)—is followed by one of the four or five first courses, including the signature yellow bell pepper soup and the polenta topped with butter and Parmigiano-Reggiano. There are ten or so main-course selections, among them chicken meatballs in tomato sauce, eggplant alla Parmigiana, sausage with Tuscan white beans, and spicy *calamari in inzimino*. Several vegetable sides—stewed potatoes, braised artichoke wedges, a cooked vegetable salad brilliantly red with beets—also are offered. A slim wedge of flourless chocolate cake or a serving of the house *panna cotta,* which is like a super-rich *crème caramel,* makes for a sweet finish. Bargain hunters should head to Cibrèo after 10 P.M., when leftover front-room items (herb-and-lemon-marinated lamb chops and squab stuffed with *mostarda,* a piquant candied fruit) are served in the *trattoria.*

Only the front room of the brand-new Osteria del Caffè Italiano, also in the Santa Croce neighborhood, feels like a real *trattoria:* The décor looks as though it hasn't been touched in years. The room behind it is another story. This softly lit space features terra-cotta floors, vaulted ceilings, and grand chandeliers. Black-vested waiters sporting long white aprons scurry about with an air of formality that is a bit extreme for a typical *trattoria,* though the menu is a standard one. The front room, on the other hand, with its dark-wood cabinets, shelves of wine bottles and glasses, display of *salumi,* and simple, place mat–covered wooden tables, feels just right. People stop in here throughout the day and into the evening for an espresso or a glass of wine, some first-rate *salumi* or equally impressive Pecorino. A blackboard lists an ample selection of red wines by the glass or by the smaller, less-expensive *degustazione,* or "taste." In addition, there's a much more extensive, much pricier, written list. The lunch menu is short—three first- and three main-course choices—and inexpensive. I always enjoy a walk through the dining room, with its tablecloths and brass candlesticks, to the kitchen for a glimpse of its large charcoal grill and imposing deep-red enamel stove.

The aptly named La Casalinga ("the housewife") is my neighborhood hangout in the Oltrarno (beyond the Arno) district. The food is ultra home-style and the ambiance, no-frills: The two dining rooms feature white-paper tablecloths, varnished pale-pine wainscotting, prepoured carafes of wine, and bright lights. Daily specials are written all over the menu, which is posted just outside the door. Begin with *fettunta* (garlic-rubbed toast, here topped with beans); *bruschetta* with fresh tomato; *salumi;* or herring fillets. Or skip the *antipasti* altogether and start with a seasonal vegetable soup, salad, or pasta. Main dishes include *bollito,* or boiled meats, served with *salsa verde* (herbs and olive oil); stewed meats; (slightly over-roasted) guinea hen; rabbit; and veal. Raw vegetables are served *pinzimonio* style, with a little bowl of extra-virgin oil and salt for dipping. Look for such *contorni* (side dishes) as stewed beans, mixed boiled vegetables, tuna salad, and sliced tomatoes. For dessert, there's usually *panna cotta, tiramisù,* or a selection of fresh fruit. The house wine is inexpensive (and unfortunate); for more discriminating palates, a few bottles are available behind the bar in the front dining room.

There's always a crowd waiting to be seated at Ruggero, the inviting domain of Ruggero Corsi, near the Boboli Gardens in the neighborhood outside Porta Romana. Though Ruggero stays in the kitchen, his wife, Anna, and his son and daughter, Riccardo and Paola, are dynamic presences in the dining room, amid the display of seasonal produce, the homemade desserts, and the hissing espresso machine. Such Tuscan classics as chicken-liver *crostini, salumi,* and hearty soups always tempt me, but I can never pass up the perfectly cooked, spicy, tomato-sauced spaghetti *alla carrettiera* (literally "teamster-style," or prepared with garlic and parsley). Other options include roast pork loin, grilled beef, and *bollito misto* with *salsa verde*. Desserts are a letdown, but no one seems to mind. And the wine selection is small, though thoughtfully chosen and well priced.

Omero, located in the gentrified countryside ten minutes from the heart of the city, may seem more like a fancy restaurant than a *trattoria*, but it is a popular local hangout, with the friendly ambiance of a casual eatery. Fronted by a general store where you can pick up everything from cheese, *salumi*, and bread to cigarettes and bus tickets, it also has two large dining rooms and a terrace, all with splendid views of the city below. Walk past the huge terra-cotta *orcio*—urn of extra-virgin olive oil—and settle in at one of the comfortable tables for some *fettunta*, dipped, in the fall and winter months, in just-pressed extra-virgin. Delicious *crostini* of chicken liver or artichoke purée keep impatient diners content as they wait for such *primi* as *pasta e ceci, ribollita, pappardelle* with rabbit or hare, and spinach-and-ricotta–filled ravioli. Main-course options include grilled steak Florentine; veal or pork chops; and deep-fried chicken, rabbit, and squab. Among the perfectly prepared deep-fried seasonal vegetables are irresistibly light, batterless artichoke wedges. The dessert cart tempts with (nontraditional) cheesecake and chocolate tart, as well as with such classics as pears cooked with prunes and marinated whole oranges. The wine list, with lots of unusual choices, also is guaranteed to please.

My favorite *trattoria* in the San Lorenzo neighborhood is Mario, with a tiny dining room that looks in on a glassed-in kitchen dominated by a pot-covered stove and by Romeo Colzi, the chef. His wife, Patrizia, waits on the customers, and his brother, Fabio, totals up the bills at the register. To avoid crowds at this popular lunch spot, arrive at noon; after 12:30 there's always a line of students and market workers waiting for a space at one of the paper-covered tables. Romeo stops ladling out food at around 3 P.M. The menu, displayed outside by the door as well as alongside the kitchen, features such regional classics as *ribollita,* vegetable soup, and (fantastic) pasta with hen or rabbit sauce. Regulars know there's tripe on Mondays, rabbit on Thursdays, fish on Fridays, and the town's least-expensive steak Florentine every day of the week. Romeo is wild about wine and offers, in addition to the decent house Chianti, an amazing selection of heavy hitters at bargain prices. For dessert, there's *biscotti* and *vin santo.*

Da Sergio is the favorite *trattoria* of a friend of mine who lives in the San Lorenzo area. Tucked behind market stalls selling souvenirs, it is easy to miss. Two large, rather unattractive dining rooms hung with diplomas, awards, ceramics, and a Florentine soccer-squad scarf are lit by enormous iron chandeliers festooned with ugly energy-saving bulbs. This, too, is a family affair: Sergio Gozzi is in the kitchen; his wife, Grazia, is posted behind the entryway bar, where she slices bread, pours wine, and hands off the plates to her sons, Andrea and Alessandro. Seating is open, so expect to share a table with locals or tourists. My friend raved about the pasta with tomato sauce, with good reason—I no longer think of ordering anything else (though the bean-and-grain *zuppa di farro* always looks delicious). Boiled meats, tripe, breaded and fried meatballs, and *baccalà alla livornese* (salt cod with tomato sauce) are among Sergio's mainstays. Fresh fruit or *biscotti* are the only dessert selections; the wine list is equally spare.

Knowing the addresses and star dishes of a handful of Florence *trattorie* is just the first step to fully appreciating the peculiar dynamic of this city's warm, down-to-earth eating establishments. How can you, as a visitor, have the same—or at least a similar— experience to that of the locals? Seek out a *trattoria* that seems to have some promise. Dine there three times. On your first visit you'll be a tourist. On your second, your face will be recognized and your presence acknowledged. By your third visit, they'll begin to treat you like a regular.

Cibrèo Trattoria, Piazza Ghiberti, 35; tel. 234.1100. Closed Sundays and Mondays.

Da Sergio, Piazza San Lorenzo, 8r; tel. 281.941. Lunch only; closed Sundays; no credit cards.

Omero, Via Pian dè Giullari, 11r; tel. 220.053. Closed Tuesdays.

Osteria del Caffè Italiano, Via Isola delle Stinche, 11/13r; tel. 289.368. Closed Mondays.

Ruggero, Via Senese, 89r; tel. 220.542. Closed Tuesdays and Wednesdays.

Trattoria La Casalinga, Via dei Michelozzi, 9r; tel. 218.624. Closed Sundays.

Trattoria Mario, Via della Rosina, 2r; tel. 218.550. Lunch only; closed Sundays; no credit cards.

Florence: A Restaurant Renaissance

BY FAITH HELLER WILLINGER

~

I am lucky: I live in Florence. Built on Roman ruins in the heart of Etruscan country and the birthplace of the Renaissance, this onetime capital of Italy is home to world-class art, architecture, and artisans. Local archives are jammed with manuscripts, ledgers, etchings, paintings, and sculpture: twenty-five centuries of Florentine documentation of almost everything, notably food and wine. The Tuscan table has been chronicled in a long-gone sixth century B.C. fresco of honey-glazed grape flatbread, a four-teenth-century recipe for ravioli, Michelangelo's sketched grocery list, Bartolommeo Bimbi's more-than-just-botanical paintings of long-lost fruit cultivars, Jacopo Chimenti's still-life pantries, and Ardengo Soffici's memoirs of spit roasting. Even the Mannerist architect Bernardo Buontalenti is honored not with a stone memo-rial but with a silky rich custard flavor of *gelato* called, appropri-ately, *buontalenti* (he invented the dessert). And many of these preparations—barely changed with the passage of time—still appear on modern menus.

Tuscan austerity is reflected in simple, unadorned dishes made with the best ingredients. The visitor to Florence should not look for formality or fussiness but should focus instead on the kind of food eaten in the home, which recently—and happily—has been appearing in restaurants. The one luxury on every table has always been local extra-virgin olive oil—usually fruity and a murky, almost phosphorescent green, with an exuberant peppery bite when first pressed in early winter. Its flavors calm down after a few months of aging, and it contributes a suave, cholesterol-free richness essential to the Florentine *cucina*. Such olive oil should be thought of as a condiment, not just a cooking medium. I've found that Vino e Olio, on Via dei Serragli, has the best selection.

Bread is another fundamental element in the Florentine diet: saltless, dense, and baked in a wood-fired oven. (Mine comes from a bakery called Vera on the Piazza Frescobaldi.) It is consumed fresh, toasted, or stale and is paired with *salumi* (salt-cured meats), Pecorino (sheep's milk cheese), walnuts, dried figs, or even chocolate. *Fettunta*—the minimalist garlic-rubbed toasted bread drenched in extra-virgin olive oil that was and is the snack of Tuscan olive-oil pressers—is almost always available, even if it's not listed on a menu. First-course soups such as bean and vegetable *ribollita* and tomato *pappa al pomodoro* are thickened to the consistency of oatmeal with stale bread; refreshing *panzanella* is a summery salad mixed with moist bread. All are far more delicious than they might sound.

Fresh pastas—wide strips of *pappardelle*, cheese- and greens-filled ravioli, meat-sauced *tortelli*—are often found on menus. Traditional *penne strascicate* (quill-shaped pasta "dragged" through meat sauce), spicy spaghetti *alla carrettiera* ("teamster-style"), or other creatively colored and dressed pastas are served as starters. Unfortunately, restaurants rarely get risotto or pizza right. Locals eat little seafood; what fish dishes there are—including *baccalà* (salt cod) and *inzimino* (a stew made with tomatoes, Swiss chard, and cuttlefish or squid)—are generally found on Fridays. Although sturgeons from the Arno are said to have once provided caviar with which to top white beans, this world-class dish is now executed with costly imported roe.

"Bean-eater" may not sound terribly offensive, but the term has been pejoratively applied to Florentines for centuries. And beaneaters they are. White *cannellini* beans are still a favorite, boiled and then dressed with olive oil or served *all'uccelletto*, stewed "like little birds" with garlic, sage, and a touch of tomato. In the summer natives become addicted to the thin-skinned, pale beans known as *fagioli sgranati*. A vegetable of note is winter's *cavolo nero* (curly kale), and spring or fall brings *porcini* mushrooms. Best of all is the *pinzimonio* medley of raw fennel, artichokes, celery, or other seasonal *verdure* accompanied by a do-it-yourself sauce of olive oil, salt, and pepper.

Above all else, however, Florence is a town for carnivores. Don't miss the *fiorentina*, a large, lean, but well-marbled steak, optimally Chianina beef, cut at least two inches thick, grilled rare over charcoal, and dressed with salt, pepper, and a wedge of lemon. Pork products include fennel-spiked salami and fresh sausage, salt-cured *pancetta* (bacon), skewered livers, and *arista* (roast pork loin with rosemary).

Some of Italy's best red wines happen to be the local beverage of choice and include Chianti Classico, Carmignano, Vino Nobile di Montepulciano, and Brunello di Montalcino. Those worth seeking out include Chiantis from Castello di Ama, Fattoria di Felsina, Castello dei Rampolla, Selvapiana, San Felice, Castello di Volpaia, Isole e Olena, and Monte Vertine; Carmignanos from Tenuta di Capezzana; Vino Nobiles from Avignonesi, Poliziano, and Contucci; and Brunellos from Tenuta Caparzo, Poggio Antico, and Col d'Orcia. (Many of these fine wineries also produce top-drawer extra-virgin olive oils.)

Meals most often conclude with fresh fruit or *gelato* (both Badiani, on Viale dei Mille, and Cavini, on the Piazza delle Cure, make wonderful *buontalenti gelato*). Many restaurants, however, now serve sweets more special than the city's not-always-easy-to-love native desserts. Smoky, unleavened *castagnacci* (chestnut tarts), *schiacciata con l'uva* (grape flatbread), and the rock-hard almond *biscotti di Prato* or *cantucci* cookies tend to be acquired tastes.

For an overview of Florentine fare I recommend a visit to one of the city's food markets. Clothing and souvenir stands surround architect Giuseppe Mengoni's cast-iron-and-glass Mercato di San Lorenzo (also known as the Mercato Centrale), one of three neighborhood markets built for the city's low-rent *camaldoli* districts during an 1864 urban renewal project. Inside, ground-floor stalls are populated by vendors of bread, meat, poultry, game, fish, cheese, *salumi,* pasta, cookies, and imported out-of-season vegetables.

I can never resist stopping at the market's culinary highlight, Da Nerbone, founded in 1872 and located on Via di San Casciano (all aisles in the market are named after nearby villages) on the periphery of the ground floor. A throng of locals waits first to pay and then to hand a receipt to Alessandro Stagi while his able sandwich chef chops, seasons, and stuffs boiled beef or tripe into crispy rolls dipped in broth and dressed with *salsa verde* (herbs and olive oil). A simple menu is chalked on the blackboard—pasta, soup, a hot or cold meat dish, and a few vegetables. I usually eat at one of the marble and wrought-iron tables across the aisle. The house wine is Chianti Classico, the service nonexistent, and the ambiance pure marketplace. The boiled beef sandwich is one of the city's great gastronomic experiences and a bargain in overpriced Italy. Then, it's up the escalator (if it's working) for a look at produce stands selling wares that still smell like the country, casually piled in crates yet looking like perfect still lifes.

The Mercato di Sant'Ambrogio, on Piazza Ghiberti and also constructed in 1864, is the vegetable market for the Santa Croce neighborhood. Vendors indoors sell perishables, and those outside hustle clothing, plants, and produce. Farmers in a row at the back of the market peddle their own seasonal wares, supplying some of the area's finest restaurants. Of these dining spots, my favorite is

Cibrèo, named after an old-fashioned chicken innards dish reputed to be an aphrodisiac. This culinary fiefdom was founded about twenty years ago, when Fabio Picchi and Benedetta Vitali dropped out of college to prove a point about family-style food. They opened a trattoria and a restaurant connected by a common kitchen that specializes in the *cucina* of a Tuscan granny—Florentine comfort food rarely, until that time, found outside the home. Ristorante Cibrèo, which opens onto Via dei Macci, has a classic dining room with white tablecloths and sparkling stemware.

Eating at the tiny Cibrèo Trattoria, on the other hand, is like eating in a friend's kitchen. It's crowded, has communal seating, and there are no place mats. It also takes no reservations, allows no lingering, and charges far lower prices for what is, except for a few exceptions, the same food served in the restaurant. (Starters such as Pecorino and raw fava bean salad; flan-like *sformati* of ricotta or vegetables; chicken liver spread on toasts, or *crostini;* and tripe salad are available only in the restaurant.) Pasta is never featured (it's not really Florentine, insists Picchi), but it isn't missed with such flavorful offerings as delicate yellow bell pepper or woodsy *porcini* mushroom soups, classic *pappa al pomodoro, ribollita,* polenta with herbs, or summery tomato aspic. Stuffed duck, baked liver, pigs' feet, fish steamed in its own juices, and mussels in butter are often on the menu, as is the city's best *calamari*-and-chard *inzimino. Palombo* (a small member of the shark family, it is also known as "veal of the sea") is prepared *alla livornese:* It is cooked in a sauce of tomatoes, garlic, chili peppers, and parsley. Beans are on the menu year round, joined by side dishes that include beet salad, stewed potatoes, and cauliflower with sausage. Wines are well-chosen although somewhat pricey. And the desserts—all made by Vitali—are tempting, especially the intense, fudge-like flat chocolate wedge and the Neapolitan *pastiera* (ricotta tart).

Cibrèo Caffè, across the street, is perfect for sipping a glass of wine while waiting for a table at the restaurant or the trattoria or for having a sandwich, snack, cocktail, or an espresso. The menu is limited but appealing and includes fresh mozzarella (when available) and all of Vitali's desserts. The tables are cramped, but the prices are the lowest of any of the Cibrèo eateries. When the weather is warm, outdoor seating is at a premium.

La Baraonda serves homestyle Florentine food with the same sense of whimsy that prompted the choice of its name, which is Italian for "convivial chaos." There's a handsome marble butcher's counter in the front room; three small connecting dining rooms lie beyond. For non-Italian speakers, owner Duccio Magni will expound on the unusual menu in rapid-fire English with a Scottish accent. After the decisions have been made, *crostini* spread with black olive paste or goat cheese are offered to the suddenly starving diners waiting for their first courses. I rarely can resist chef Riccardo Fiora's *risolata* (romaine risotto). Second courses—veal meat loaf served with *salsa verde,* for example, and grilled *tomino* cheese with cooked field greens—on the menu are supplemented by daily specials. Magni's wine of the month is usually Tuscan and always interesting. Dinner concludes with pine nut *gelato* with chocolate sauce; caramelized apple tart; or a few attractive, colorful fruit-shaped candies, an old-fashioned Tuscan treat. Goblets of *crema pasticciera* (pastry cream) are mixed with strawberries in the summer and with "shattered" chocolate, hazelnuts, and almonds in the winter.

With its vaulted ceilings, subdued décor, dark wood tables topped with white linen place mats, and the ambiance of the noble Antinori family (Tuscan winemakers for more than 600 years), the Cantinetta Antinori resembles a private Florentine club. Majordomo-like Gianfranco Stoppa presides. The menu includes classic dishes and a few concessions to regulars tired of the same old *pappa,* as predictable cuisine is described in Florence. One can choose from traditional soups, fresh pastas, stewed meats, simple salads, vegetable combinations, and delicious *cannellini*. The extra-virgin olive oil and sheep and goat cheeses are from the family estates. All of the Antinori wines are served by the glass as well as the bottle, a thrill for avid tasters. The desserts are unexciting, but the *biscotti di Prato* and *brutti e buoni* cookies from the Mattei bakery are the best of their kind.

Alla Vecchia Bettola ("the old dive") hasn't really been around for all that long, and it isn't really shabby enough to be a dive. There's one dining room, with benches and stools, marble tables, paper place mats, and rustic *cucina*. The extensive, hard-to-decipher handwritten menu of homey dishes changes daily. I look for simple starters: tomato-and-vodka-sauced *penne alla Bettola*, *topini* (potato *gnocchi*), and soups. Meats are the main attraction: Braised boned rabbit, herbed roast pork loin, grilled chops, and *fiorentina* steak are the stars. Except for the excellent *fagioli all'uccelletto*, vegetables and other side dishes are almost an afterthought, but desserts are homemade and always include the restaurant's lovely *tiramisù*. Most customers drink the house wine, although the list offers many Tuscan gems.

Trattoria Garga, with its low lighting, large plants, and an international clientele, epitomizes new-wave Florentine. A series of intimate dining rooms is adorned with swirling modern murals in muted Renaissance colors painted in part by Canadian pastry chef-hostess Sharon Gargani and her Florentine husband, chef/ex-butcher Giuliano Gargani, who sings of love as he cooks. The cuisine, unconventional and yet Tuscan in spirit, relies on the flavors of garlic, hot *peperoncino* peppers, fruity local olive oil, and fresh vegetables. Large oval platters of *"il magnifico"* pasta (the sauce is made of cream, lemon zest, orange zest, Parmesan, and mint) or piquant *vigliacca* (tomato-sauced *tagliatelle*) keep sophisticated diners twirling their forks. I'm always eager for spaghetti with garlic, olive oil, and barely cooked, crunchy artichokes, surrounded with a corolla of the pointy outer leaves. Veal scallops, peppery lamb, the finest *baccalà* in the city, and the house salad are good options. Mrs. Gargani's cheesecake and chocolate *torta* both win raves from dessert fans.

In 1633, Galileo was exiled to Pian dei Giullari–Arcetri. Now part of the rural but long-gentrified suburbs of Florence and only a five-minute cab ride from the city, this village is still worth a visit to check out the restaurant Omero. Its entrance-*cum*-grocery assaults the senses with marvelous Tuscan ingredients. Counterman Enzo trades gossip; sells bus tickets, stamps, cigarettes, and salt to locals; and slices prosciutto, *salumi,* and Pecorino for restaurant diners. Host Roberto Viviani leads clients past a terra-cotta *orcio* (olive oil urn; the oil is for sale by the liter during the early winter months) and a display of Tuscan wines to the dining rooms—upstairs, downstairs, and the summer terrace, each with a view. Many diners are regulars and know exactly what to expect from this purists' menu that has barely budged from the Florentine canon. In cold months bread is toasted in the fireplace for *fettunta,* but *salumi* and chicken liver *crostini* are fine meal openers for the rest of the year. Chick-pea and pasta soup, *ribollita,* and fresh ricotta- and greens-stuffed ravioli are also first-rate. Chicken is flattened under a brick and grilled, or it is deep-fried Florentine-style with fried vegetables such as crispy artichoke wedges or zucchini flowers. Of course, beans are always on the menu. A dessert cart laden with the classics—among them a golden meringue-topped *zuppa inglese* (trifle)—invites indulgence; and the wine list, focusing on Tuscany and, more specifically, on the Chianti Classico region south of Florence, is a pleasure.

Palates weary of unrelievedly Tuscan cookery should hurry to Florence's Ristorante alle Murate. The logo, an empty birdcage, evokes not only a defunct nearby prison of the same name but also liberation from local tradition in all aspects. The décor is modern without a hint of rusticity, and jazz plays softly in the background.

Multilingual owner Umberto Montano betrays his Campanian heritage with a warm welcome and hints of southern sunshine on the innovative menu. The cooking is light-handed, vegetables are treated with respect, and the homemade pasta is stuffed and sauced creatively. Not to be missed are the *orecchiette* ("little ears" of pasta) with greens and broccoli or the *farfalle* (pasta bow ties) with Robiola cheese, zucchini, and a raw tomato sauce. Chocolate-chip-cookie fans should conclude with the signature dessert called the Armstrong (named after Louis), a monster cookie served with unsweetened whipped cream. A limited menu is available in the jazz club-wine bar in the back; customers frequently stop in for a quick meal, glass of wine, or dessert. Oenophiles should ask to visit Umberto's small but packed cellar—a lovely personal selection of bottles.

Dining in Italy in the nineties can be a costly, as well as time-consuming, experience. Travelers looking for less expensive possibilities will be pleased by the many easygoing, no-frills establishments packed with locals who recognize good food even without the fine appointments. (The wine choices, however, may be unfortunate.) One should remember to bring cash to these places because credit cards are rarely accepted. Budget dining on Sundays, when Florentines fulfill family obligations or escape to *trattorie* in the countryside, is difficult as most of the city's more modest eateries are closed.

Trattoria le Belle Donne's entrance is so nondescript that it's easy to miss, although at peak lunch hours a small crowd may be waiting outside for tables. The cozy one-room trattoria is decorated with postcards from clients and an overwhelming countertop display of fruits and vegetables. Regulars—a mixture of designers, nobles, bankers, clerks, students, and shoppers—rub elbows at rustic marble tables set with paper place mats and tumblers. The service is speedy but sometimes surly. The menu (it's easiest to check out the blackboard under the window *before* sitting down) changes daily, offering traditional yet surprisingly innovative cooking. Raw mushroom salad and marinated herring starters, vegetable pastas or soups, hearty meat or poultry stews, *Carpaccio* (paper-thin slices of raw beef), and homemade desserts like chestnut pudding or creamy *panna cotta* are frequently on the board. Vegetarians will have an easy time ordering, and there's no pressure to consume a complete meal.

Trattoria la Casalinga, "the homestyle trattoria," delivers just what it promises. It's like eating at Mamma's and is frequented by a neighborhood crowd—artists, workers in overalls, artisans, businessmen in ties, elderly women in slippers, youths in designer jackets, and students who turn up daily for the hearty food dished up in massive portions for a low price. There are no food stylists in the kitchen, just Graziella and Feruccio. Oliviero at the counter fills wine carafes while Cristina and Andrea and Paolo wait on tables. The menu offers classic first courses, traditional soups, pastas with meat or tomato sauce, a large selection of stewed and roasted meats, a few simple vegetables, and homemade *tiramisù* and "*crem caramel*." Specials are always a good choice.

Tranvai must surely be the city's tiniest trattoria, roughly the size of the old-fashioned Florentine cable car for which it's named. Diners may be charmed by framed pictures of trams of the past, the headlight on the bar, metal flooring, intimate seating (expanded in summer with outdoor tables surrounded by potted hedges), and swift service. Low prices keep the locals loyal. Nanda Vanni prepares those hard-to-find Florentine favorites like pasta sauced with leeks, boiled beef and onions, and stuffed cabbage and fish on Fridays. Her specialties, however (*trippa, lampredotto,* and *budellino*—different kinds of tripe and intestine), aren't for everyone.

The most intrepid gastronomes will want to visit Il Trippaio di Porta Romana, near the Boboli Gardens, not the most central nor the oldest tripe stand in the city but part of a growing trend that applies new treatments to tripe. Classic stands serve *trippa* or *lampredotto* boiled and then stuffed in a roll. But this new-wave tripe stall substitutes strips of tripe for cuttlefish in *inzimino* or for fish in *cacciucco;* it cooks tripe with beans, potatoes, and artichokes; and it also serves tripe in classic Florentine style—tomato-sauced and Parmigiano-topped. Mixed cuts of boiled beef with *salsa verde* or stewed *guancia* (cheek) are available for those with an aversion to tripe. There's no written menu, and the selection changes daily. All preparations are sold in *panino* (sandwich) form or with a plastic fork. The open-air dining options range from standing at the nearby Totocalcio soccer betting counter, sitting on a bench outside the Fine Arts Institute, or strolling, sandwich in hand, through the Boboli Gardens. Fine food and fine art are, after all, a legacy bestowed upon everyone who lives in, or visits, Florence.

Restaurants and Trattorie

La Baraonda, Via Ghibellina, 67r; tel. 234.1171.

Cantinetta Antinori, Piazza Antinori, 3; tel. 292.234.

Cibrèo Caffè, Via Andrea del Verrocchio, 5r; tel. 234.5853.

Cibrèo Trattoria, Piazza Ghiberti, 35; tel. 234.1100.

Da Nerbone, Mercato di San Lorenzo; tel. 219.949.

Omero, Via Pian dei Giullari, 11r, Pian dei Giullari-Arcetri; tel. 220.053.

Ristorante alle Murate, Via Ghibellina, 52r; tel. 240.618.

Ristorante Cibrèo, Via dei Macci, 118r; tel. 234.1100.

Tranvai, Piazza Tasso, 14; tel. 225.197.

Trattoria Garga, Via del Moro, 48r; tel. 239.8898.

When You Go to Tuscany:
Restaurants

BY NANCY HARMON JENKINS

∽

editor's note

Although this is an excerpt from a book, *Flavors of Tuscany,* I feel it is
appropriate for this collection because it's somewhat difficult to learn of recommended places to eat outside of Tuscany's larger cities and towns, and
Nancy Harmon Jenkins is a most worthy guide. Remember that if you're
staying in the countryside on a *fattoria* (a farm or agricultural estate), your
hosts might very well offer excellent meals, and don't be shy about asking
them for recommendations of local places.

NANCY HARMON JENKINS is also the author of *Flavors of Puglia:
Traditional Recipes From the Heel of Italy's Boot* (Broadway Books, 1997)
and *The Mediterranean Diet Cookbook* (Bantam Books, 1994). She is a contributing editor of *Food & Wine* and writes frequently for *The New York
Times.*

M any Tuscan restaurants are internationally famous, and with
good reason. Others are barely known even to the writers
of guidebooks. Here are a few where I've enjoyed the food, but this
is by no means an exhaustive list. Do call ahead to be sure the restaurant is open when you want to go. And note that some of these
places also have a few rooms, usually quite delightful, by the night
or the week.

Anghiari: Castello dei Sorci, tel. 0575.789.066. The walled town of Anghiari sits conveniently between Sansepolcro and Monterchi, two imperative stops for admirers of Piero della Francesca. Castello dei Sorci, outside the town, is a fine place for lunch, offering a copious set menu of rustic food for a fixed price each day. Very inexpensive and crowded on Sundays.

Castelfranco di Sopra: Vicolo del Contento, loc. Mandri 38; tel. 055.914.9277; fax 914.9906. Mandri is a hamlet just outside Castelfranco, one of the main towns in the Pratomagno north of Arezzo. Angelo Redditi is the chef, and his wife, Lina, runs the comfortable dining room. The menu is a fine example of how country dishes can become elegant in the hands of a gifted cook. Unusually, fish is a specialty. A first-rate wine list completes the attractions. Expensive.

Chiusi della Verna: Corazzesi, loc. Corezzo; tel. 0575.518.012. Corezzo is a wide place in the road near Chiusi della Verna (not to be confused with Etruscan Chiusi in the south of Tuscany), the monastery founded by St. Francis and where he received the stigmata. Corazzesi specializes in tortelli di patate, big ravioli-like pasta stuffed with potatoes and either fried or toasted on the grill. Inexpensive.

Cortona: Il Falconiere, loc. San Martino; tel. 0575.612.616; fax 617. 927. Located in the *limonaia,* the lemon-house, of a handsome seventeenth-century villa, Silvia and Riccardo Barrachi's Il Falconiere provides an elegant menu as well as delightful views of the massive Etruscan walls of Cortona, a hill town south of Arezzo.

The cantina offers a good selection of Italian, French, and California wines; there are nine rooms and three suites in the adjacent villa. Moderate to expensive.

Ponte Buriano: Trattoria del Pescatore; tel. 0575.364.096. A famous Roman bridge arches over the Arno, north of Arezzo at Ponte Buriano. The trattoria is one of those workingmen's places that people like me are always hoping to discover, with simple, honest, local cooking. The decor is a curious assemblage of electric heaters, coffeemakers, teapots, and radios, displayed with a carefree hand. Inexpensive.

Pratovecchio: I 4 Cantoni, v. Dante Alighieri 31a; tel. 0575.58.26.96. In the heart of the Casentino, this humble truck stop serves fine hand-rolled pasta, ably turned out under the direction of Marta Goretti, who also makes a splendid, thick acquacotta casentinese, with lots of onions and country bread. But call a day ahead to order it if you want to try the acquacotta. Inexpensive.

In Siena Province

Castelnuovo Berardenga: Da Antonio, via Fiorita 38; tel. 0577.35.53.21. Curiously for Tuscany, where except on the coast, fish is not held in high esteem, this restaurant, in the heart of Castelnuovo at the southern tip of the Chianti hills, specializes in seafood and does an exemplary job. In fact, seafood is all that's served here, and Chef Antonio goes far and wide for the very best offerings, which he prepares simply and with great taste.

Chiusi: La Solita Zuppa, via Porsenna, 21; tel. 0578.21.006. Chiusi is ancient Clusium, an Etruscan capital (whence Lars Porsenna summoned his array for the Etruscan attack on Rome). After a visit to the Museo Nazionale Etrusco and the local Etruscan tombs, a stop for lunch at La Solita Zuppa ("the usual soup") will introduce you to the cooking of southern Tuscany. Hearty soups are a specialty, but there are many other items on the menu, including pici, the hand-rolled pasta from the region, and buglione, a rich stew. Moderate.

Gaiole: Trattoria della Badia a Coltibuono; tel. 0577.749.031. Badia a Coltibuono is a thirteenth-century abbey that is now home to the Stucchi Prinetti family whose best-known member is Lorenza de' Medici, noted Tuscan food authority. The trattoria on the grounds is a fine place to sample Tuscan country cuisine, though chef Maurizio Fenino is actually from Milano. Boned stuffed rabbit is one of many specialties. The exemplary wines, olive oil, honey, and other products of the estate are also sold here. Moderate.

Montalcino: Trattoria Il Pozzo; S. Angelo in Colle; tel. 0577.86.40.15. Montalcino is home to one of Italy's great wines, Brunello di Montalcino. At S. Angelo, a village in the midst of the vineyards, Laura Bindocci of Il Pozzo is a first-rate cook of regional fare, and her wine list includes many notable Brunellos as well as Vino Rosso di Montalcino, a lesser but nonetheless delicious local red. Moderate.

Montalcino: Taverna dei Barbi, Fattoria dei Barbi, loc. Podernone; tel. 0577.84.93.57. Fattoria dei Barbi is one of the important producers of Brunello di Montalcino and other fine wines. Taverna dei Barbi, on the winery estate, is a good place for simple, rustic food, including the cheeses and salumi (preserved pork products) made on the estate.

Montalcino: Ristorante Poggio Antico; tel. 0577.849.200. Roberto and Patrizia Minnetti, after many years at the helm of one of Rome's most interesting restaurants, moved up here a few years ago to bring Roberto's fine cooking closer to its country origins. The Minettis are rigorous in their devotion to local products, and the wine list includes Poggio Antico Brunello and many other fine wines from the region. Reservations recommended. Expensive.

Montefollonico: Fattoria La Chiusa; tel. 0577.669.668. Dania Luccherini, chef and owner of this elegantly rustic restaurant in a handsomely vaulted old barn, was one of the first Tuscan chefs to adapt strictly local cooking to the disciplined exigencies of fine cuisine. The result is what many consider one of Tuscany's, if not Italy's, finest restaurants. Warning: Lunch at La Chiusa can occupy most of an afternoon, but it will be time happily spent. The wine list is strong, with both Tuscan and international wines. La Chiusa also has beautifully restored rooms and suites, by the night or the week. Reservations recommended. Very expensive.

Montepulciano: Ristorante Diva; tel. 0578.716.951. Right on the main street leading up into this ancient city overlooking the Valdichiana, Ristorante Diva serves a traditional local cuisine to a devoted local clientele. It's always crowded at lunchtime but worth waiting for a table—the sense of being part of the local scene is almost as rewarding as the food itself. The wine list includes most of the great producers of Vino Nobile di Montepulciano, and you can buy wines, local sheep's milk cheeses, and other products in nearby shops. Moderate.

Montevarchi: Osteria di Rendola, loc. Rendola; tel. 055.970.7491. In a restored stone barn on a small winery outside Montevarchi, Francesco Berardinelli brings an assured and gifted hand to traditional cuisine; his presentations, such as a richly filling zampe alla fiorentina, are as pleasurable to the eye as they are to the palate. There's a small but well-thought-out selection of wines, mostly from the region. Moderate.

Murlo: La Befa, loc. La Befa; tel. 0577.806.255. Call ahead for directions. This trattoria, located deep in the countryside on a *strada bianca,* a cart track, off the main road, is hard to find but worth the effort. La Befa is the epitome of a Tuscan country eating place, with a local bar and grocery shop in front. The cooking, prepared by various members of the Marchetti family, is robust and rigorously unrefined, with excellent pastas and grilled meats, especially game when it's in season. Inexpensive.

An excursion to La Befa might begin with a visit to the small but exquisite Etruscan museum in Murlo, of which La Befa is a hamlet. The museum's holdings all come from excavations at Poggio Civitate, a fascinating Etruscan site. Each year in early September, Murlo holds an open-air "Etruscan" banquet to benefit the museum in the main square of the little town.

Santa Fiora: Il Barilotto, via Carolina 24; tel. 0564.977.089. In the heart of Santa Fiora, a village perched on the slopes of Monte Amiata, Il Barilotto serves a rigorously local cuisine, including traditional acquacotta with a dollop of local sheep's milk ricotta, and ravioli 'gnudi or strozzapreti, soft, plump, airy dumplings of spinach and ricotta. Inexpensive.

In Firenze Province

Artimino: Ristorante da Delfina, via della Chiesa 1; tel. 055.87.18.074. Carlo Cioni, chef and owner of this charming restaurant on a bluff overlooking the Arno below Florence, is an engaging authority on Tuscan country traditions. Cioni's grandmother Delfina, now in her nineties and apt to be shelling fava beans in a corner of the kitchen, is the honored source of much of his knowledge. It was she who founded the restaurant, with its surrounding vegetable gardens and handsome outdoor dining terrace, but her grandson is a worthy heir. Ribollita is a great specialty, as are many types of wild game grilled over wood embers. Reservations recommended. Moderate to expensive.

Firenze: Cibrèo, via dei Macci 118r; tel. 055.234.1100. With Fabbio Picchi in charge of the kitchen and his wife, Benedetta, overseeing the restaurant and making desserts, this small but elegant restaurant has achieved a well-deserved international reputation for strict adherence to Florentine traditions. No pasta is served, but you won't miss it when you taste the satiny richness of the chef's passato di peperoni gialli, a cream of yellow peppers that is as flavorful as a sunny garden. In the adjacent Bottega del Cibrèo, you can find a gamut of specialty food products, not just from Tuscany but from all over Italy. Reservations are a must. Moderate to expensive.

Firenze: Trattoria La Baraonda, via Ghibellina 67r; 055.234.1171. My personal favorite of perhaps half a dozen of these homey, rather old-fashioned Florentine trattorias where the food has all the honesty and direct simplicity that characterizes Tuscan cuisine. At the same time, the youthful owners of La Baraonda are not afraid of an occasional experiment with updated, modern ideas, and the results are delightful. Moderate.

Vicchio del Mugello: La Casa di Caccia, loc. Roti Molezzano; tel. 055.840.7629. Telephone ahead for instructions or, better yet, persuade a local driver to lead you up to this wonderfully rustic hideaway on a hillside overlooking the Mugello. La Casa di Caccia is in the midst of a hunting reserve, and Mirella Settori is gifted at preparing the fruits of the chase. When she's not doing that, however, she turns out magnificent tortelli di patate, stuffed with potatoes and served with a rich meat ragù. Her panna cotta is an elegantly simple sweet to end the meal. Reservations recommended. Moderate to expensive.

In Livorno Province

Cecina: Trattoria Senese, v. Diaz 34; tel. 0586.68.0335. Cecina, bombed in World War II, is not much of a town architecturally speaking, though the Saturday market is vast and interesting and with a good fish section. The real reason to come to Cecina, however, is the Trattoria Senese, where Piero Falorno turns out one of the finest examples of cacciucco, the rich, tomato-y fish stew typical of the Tuscan coast, that I've ever tasted. Call at least a day ahead to order. It's best to have at least four people, though the more the merrier, since more fish makes an even richer broth. Expensive—like all good fish restaurants.

In Lucca Province

Camporgiano: Mulin del Rancone; tel. 0583.61.86.70. On the banks of the Sérchio River, twelve kilometers from Castelnuovo Garfagnana, and incorporating parts of an old grist mill, Mulin del Rancone serves traditional cuisine of the Garfagnana—farro, dried mushrooms, river fish, chestnuts—and also has both an inn and a campground. Inexpensive.

Lucca: Buca di Sant'Antonio, via della Cervia 1/3; tel. 0583.55.881. In the heart of this delightful, rose-walled city, Buca di Sant'Antonio has been in existence for more than two hundred years. Often this indicates an eating establishment frequented only by tourists, where the waiters wear some version of local peasant costume. Here, at least in part because it is still a great local favorite, the cooking is genuine and delicious. Because of its popularity, reservations are a must, especially at lunch. Moderate to expensive.

Lucca: Locanda Buatino, v. Borgo Giannotti 508; tel. 0583.343.207. Just outside the city walls, Locanda Buatino is an unprepossessing place with delicious food. It's very popular, and you'll see bankers and telephone linemen side by side scarfing up the offerings. Inexpensive.

Lucca: La Mora, loc. Ponte a Moriano; tel. 0583.406.402. Just up the Sérchio River from Lucca, on the edge of the Garfagnana, La Mora is a stylish restaurant with a copious menu of regional specialties such as zuppa frantoiana, bean soup dressed with sweet local oil, and farro, the ancient strain of wheat that's still grown in the region. Service is elegant, and there's a first-rate wine list. Moderate to expensive.

In the Province of Massa Carrara

Bagnone: da Lina, Piazza Marconi, 1; tel. 0187.42.90.69. The place to go for testaroli, the boiled pancakes that are a delicious regional specialty.

Carrara: Venanzio, Colonnata; tel. 0585.73617. Follow the narrow winding road up into the marble mountains that tower like alabaster cliffs above, carefully skirting huge trucks laden with blocks of pure white Carrara marble. At the end of the road is the marble-dusted village of Colonnata, renowned in Tuscany less for marble than for *lardo,* a type of pork back fat that's cured in marble boxes called *concie.* As an antipasta, you'll be served thin slices of lightly seasoned, faintly herbal lardo atop crisply toasted country bread so hot the lardo melts slightly and oozes over the surface. It's a unique and extraordinary experience, one no food lover should miss. Nor should you miss the *pecorino al fosso,* sheep's milk cheese that's been aged underground, served at the end of the meal. There are other good things on the menu here too, but it's for the lardo and Pecorino that one makes the pilgrimage to this strange and wonderful spot. Moderate.

In Prato Province

Quarrata: Albergo La Bussola, Ristorante da Gino, loc. Catena; tel. 0573.743.128. Though the official name is Da Gino, everyone calls this place La Bussola. The pasta is first rate and the grilled meats are excellent too. Moderate to expensive.

Biblioteca

Eating in Italy: A Traveler's Guide to the Hidden Gastronomic Pleasures of Northern Italy, Faith Heller Willinger, William Morrow and Co., 1998, and *Italy for the Gourmet Traveler,* Fred Plotkin, Little, Brown and Company, 1996. Both of these books are good, authoritative editions, and both writers are respected cookbook authors, and I really would find it impossible to recommend one over the other. Personally, I couldn't imagine not having them *both,* so I encourage you to take a close look at each of them and decide which is for you (if you find yourself buying or borrowing them both, you'll join the large club of us who can't live without either one). Willinger's book does not stray below The Marches, and is not too heavy to take along. Plotkin's book, which covers *all* of Italy in over 700 pages, is definitely too heavy to take along, unless one was planning on an extended stay in Italy. He includes restaurants, *trattorie,* food fairs, festivals, bakeries, coffee bars, wine bars, bookstores, gourmet shops, markets, vineyards, farms, wineries, olive-oil producers, cooking schools, and some recipes. The Tuscany and Umbria sections equal fifty-five pages.

Eating and Drinking in Italy, Andy Herbach and Michael Dillon, Capra Press, Santa Barbara, 1999. This is one edition in the What Kind of Food Am I? Series (others are on Spain and France), and I *love* it. First of all, the book—a paperback, approximately 6½" by 4"—fits easily in a pocket so you won't look like a nerd in a restaurant as you look up a word. More importantly, it's *really* thorough: sixty-nine pages of Italian menu words and *methods and styles of cooking* (which as we all know is what trips people up the most), such as *affumicato* (smoked), *affettato* (sliced), *cannelloni alla Barbaroux* (pasta stuffed with ham, veal, and cheese), and *crostini Fiorentina* (toast with liver pâte). Plus, these guys are funny: After the entry for *ceche* (baby eels), they write "no thanks," and after *trippa alla fiorentina* (braised tripe and minced beef with tomato sauce and cheese), they write "you can put all the 'alla's you want on *trippa* and it's still TRIPE." There is also a list of their favorite restaurants around Italy (six in Florence and a few in Orvieto, Pisa, Perugia, San Gimignano, Siena) and an English-to-Italian pronunciation guide with other useful phrases: *I want to reserve a table, the day after tomorrow, near the window, on the patio, do you accept credit cards?, undercooked,* and *this is not what I ordered.*

Cheap Eats in Italy: Florence, Rome, Venice, Sandra Gustafson, Chronicle Books. A word about the title: Gustafson's goal is to find good-value restaurants, not to provide a listing of the cheapest places to eat. In addition to a good list of fifteen tips for eating well and economically, she recommends seventy-one restaurants, bars, cafes, and *trattorie* in Florence, plus indoor and outdoor markets, supermarkets, and a health food store.

The Food Lover's Companion to Tuscany, Carla Capalbo, Chronicle Books, 1998. Capalbo leads readers through the various parts of Tuscany and recommends restaurants, bars, wine bars, specialty food shops, bakeries, kitchen shops, pastry shops, *trattorie,* olive and flour mills, food festivals, etc. It's really a bible, for visitors and residents. Best of all there is a section on Tuscan market days, indicating weekly and monthly markets for each town. She also includes a glossary and maps at the beginning of each chapter.

Ristoranti d'Italia, Gambero Rosso/Slow Food editore. This is the restaurant companion guide to *Gambero Rosso*'s Italian wines guide, both published annually. Though the text is in Italian, there are over 200 city maps indicating the precise location of each restaurant, and there is also a separate map for all of Italy. Better bookstores carry this guide, or you can order it from *Gambero Rosso* (Speedimpex USA Inc., 35-02 48th Avenue, Long Island City, New York 11101; 800-969-1258 / fax: 718-361-0815; e-mail: gambero@gamberorosso.it; www.gamberorosso.it). For the 1999 edition, reviewers visited 3,000 eating establishments and awarded *tre forchette* (three forks) to those achieving scores of ninety and up. Visitors to Tuscany will be happy to know that in first place was Gambero Rosso (no connection to the magazine) in San Vincenzo, 40 km. south of Livorno. In 1997, *Gambero Rosso* (the magazine) featured a lengthy article on the top twelve restaurants of that year, and four of the twelve were in Tuscany: La Tenda Rossa (piazza del Monumento 9/14, San Casciano in Val di Pesa; 055.826132); Enoteca Pinchiorri (via Ghibellina 87, Florence; 055.242777); Arnolfo (via XX Settembre 50.52; Colle di Val d'Elsa, near Siena; 0577.920549); and of course Gambero Rosso (piazza della Vittoria 13, San Vincenzo; 0565.701021).

~"Cucina Rustica: Five Restaurants in the Italian Countryside" by Faith Heller Willinger (*Gourmet,* October 1997) is a good article to read. I didn't include it here because it features restaurants all over Italy, but the one restaurant she recommends for Tuscany is Da Delfina in Artimino.

--"The Italian Countryside" (May 1997) and "The Soul of Tuscany" (May 2000) are two Special Collector's Editions of *Bon Appétit,* which are great reads. A number of well-known food writers contributed pieces to each issue, and included recipes and restaurant suggestions. To order back issues, contact the magazine at Condé Nast Publications, P.O. Box 57781, Boulder, Colorado 80322; 800-765-9419. Back issues are $5.50 for second-class mail and $7.50 for first-class delivery.

I Personaggi

(Natives, Expatriates, and Passionate Visitors)

"Love and understand the Italians, for the people are more marvelous than the land."
—E. M. Forster, *Where Angels Fear to Tread*

"Close your eyes and pronounce the word Tuscany. It summons up associations of earthly perfection, of images sprinkled with happiness, daubed with ocher and marble (white from Carrara, green from Prato, pink from the Maremma), and a cyprus-lined path that leads nowhere, an infinity of hills bathed in clear light blessed by the gods, a honey-colored villa glimpsed from a baroque garden, the perfume of olive oil, faded frescoes in silent cloisters—and a long procession of great men: Leonardo da Vinci, Machiavelli, Galileo, Michelangelo, Lorenzo de' Medici, Giotto, Petrarch, Dante, Pinocchio."
—Sonja Bullaty and Angelo Lomeo, *Tuscany*

Brother Angel

BY ROBERT WERNICK

~

editor's note

At the end of a tour at Villa I Tatti, we asked our guide what some of her favorite places to visit were in Florence. The two she named were Casa Buonarotti (Michelangelo's home) and the Museo di San Marco (a convent now dedicated to the art of Fra Angelico). Although I had visited Michelangelo's home—and enjoyed it—on a previous trip to Florence, I had never felt compelled to go to San Marco. But on the recommendation of our excellent guide, I set off to the Museo on a hot day in July. Not only did I have the place practically all to myself, but I was completely amazed by the beauty and emotion of Angelico's work.

Of Angelico's magnificent *Last Judgment* painting, Robert Wernick wrote to me that though Fra Angelico was required to follow the barbarous format of all previous treatments of this theme (see Luca Signorelli's *The End of the World* frescoes in the Orvieto cathedral for an extreme example of this), he did his best to tone down its sadistic qualities, such as portraying the Devil as an imbecilic old man who simultaneously swallows and excretes naked sinners, which "wowed the populace in the Middle Ages but is now considered to be of questionable taste and is not talked about, even by the guides who boastfully show you the paintings." Wernick became somewhat of an expert in this matter while researching a piece on Satan ("Who the Devil is the Devil?" *Smithsonian,* October 1999), and he discovered a distinct change in the manner in which the Devil was depicted in art. Wernick also informed me of the contract Angelico signed with the linen-weavers guild of Florence in 1433, containing a clause that must be unparalleled in the history of art. In exchange for a triptych, Angelico fixed his remuneration at "190 florins or as much less as he might deem proper" if he found that the work consumed less time and materials than he had estimated.

ROBERT WERNICK, who lives in Paris and Georgia, travels around the world writing magazine articles on an enormous variety of subjects that interest him, including goats, megaliths, Salvador Dali, and the gin rummy championship of the world.

He grew up in a time in many ways like our own, a time of material progress and economic development, of small wars, intellectual and artistic ferment, and a growing sentiment among educated people that the world was going breakneck to hell. The Latin church itself was torn in two. One pope was in France and another in Italy. The two pontiffs held court, appointed cardinals and excommunicated anyone who followed the other. It took a strong faith to survive, and his faith was rewarded: when he was about seventeen, the Latin church was reunited, the rival popes were swept away and new hopes for reform spread over Europe.

He was born around the year 1400 and named Guido, son of Piero, who was probably a farmer near the village of Vicchio in Tuscany, about ten miles from Florence. When he took holy orders in his early twenties in a Dominican convent in Fiesole, he chose the name of Fra Giovanni, Brother John, of Fiesole. It was only after his death in 1455 that he became generally known, "because of his utmost modesty and his religious life," as Fra Angelico ("the angelic brother").

Nothing at all is known of his early life. He must have started as a boy learning the arts of manuscript illumination and of painting in tempera on wood. He would naturally have gravitated toward the effervescent artistic community of Florence, where there were forty-one painters officially registered, each with his workshop and his staff of assistants, 138 sculptors and stonecutters, forty-four goldsmiths—as against seventy butchers. Florence was a great city for its day, but it was small enough, fifty to seventy thousand souls, so that every one of any consequence could share in the excitement of the intellectual and esthetic upheaval beginning there.

His name first appears in the records when he was paid twelve florins for an altarpiece for the church of San Stefano al Ponte when he was about eighteen. Vasari in his *Lives of the Painters,* written about 125 years later, says that his talents were recognized as exceptional at a very early age and that he could have made a fortune from his paintings as a layman. He preferred to become a friar, of the order of Preaching Friars, or Dominicans, whose six hundred houses were spread throughout Europe. He might have been expected to enter the large and prestigious monastery of Santa Maria Novella in Florence. Instead he went to San Domenico in Fiesole to join the Observantines there, the strictest and most ascetic friars of all, observing to the letter the original Rule of the Order and striving to re-create the all-consuming religious fervor of the primitive Church. All his life, brother John was to be a faithful member of this house, in Fiesole and later in Florence when it took over the convent of San Marco.

Although one of the great painters of all time, he was first and above all a Dominican friar. His calling was his life, and his life, totally devoid of external dramatic incidents, was spent in being a good Dominican, bound by his vows of poverty, chastity and obedience. He never allowed his painting to interfere with the regular schedule of his ecclesiastical duties. He prayed and read sacred texts and meditated night and day, he succored the poor and the ailing, and he was quite capable, when called upon, of handling practical affairs as well. He held various posts in his community—vicar, procurator, administrator of financial affairs of the convent and, for a couple of years prior, the man running the whole community.

Biographers have found it hard to construct a life out of the surviving documents: receipts for paintings, legal papers regarding convent property. So quiet and even was his existence that Vasari, a great collector of gossip who interviewed later generations involved in the convent, could find hardly any anecdotes to record about him. According to one, tears would flow from his eyes whenever he painted a Crucifixion; skeptical modern critics say this is unlikely because he needed clear eyes to paint the way he did. Another relates that when invited to dine at the pope's table, he refused to eat meat because he had not asked for the necessary dispensation from his prior. A third, which has been called a fable, too, but which is corroborated by other sources, is that when Pope Eugenius IV had occasion to appoint a new Archbishop of Florence, he was dissatisfied with all the distinguished names submitted to him. He turned instead to the quiet friar whom he had summoned to Rome to decorate a chapel in the Vatican and offered the post to him. Angelico respectfully pointed out that there was a much better qualified man in his monastery, Antonino Pierozzi. The pope took his advice, and it was sound advice, for Antonino was to become a great defender of Florentine liberty and a saint of the Catholic Church.

Eugenius, who had learned to admire Angelico and his work during the ten years he spent in exile in Florence, when he was driven out of Rome by riots and conspiracies, was one of the first of the Renaissance popes who were to play such a great role in making Italy the world center of the arts. The early part of the fifteenth century was the springtime of the Renaissance, when the air was charged with the excitement of novelty and experimentation. Fra Angelico may have spent most of his time shut up in a cloister, but he shared in all that enthusiasm. Some art historians like Berenson have described him as a painter who stuck to a medieval vision while revolutionaries like Masaccio and Brunelleschi were pioneering new ways of looking at the world. A visit to the newly cleaned frescoes at the convent of San Marco can demonstrate at a glance how much of a pioneer he was, too.

He has been luckier than most of his contemporaries, or most Old Masters for that matter, in that the bulk of his work is concentrated in this one place. Some of it has suffered the common fate and been cannibalized; paintings that were meant to stand together to form a harmonious whole are scattered in museums from Leningrad to Detroit. But most of his masterpieces, the ones that have made him among the most familiar and most popular of all artists, are here in the fifteenth-century setting for which they were intended.

They are surprisingly well preserved. Angelico was a thoroughly professional painter who insisted on the best materials. He used the hardest woods for his panels, the most permanent pigments. He had a well-trained group of assistants, and they could cover big stretches of plaster in an unusually short time. Vasari says that once he started painting, he never changed a line or a color.

Six years of patient cleaning, begun in 1977, have removed the dirt of the centuries and the unfortunate coats of muddy red and gray put on by well-intentioned restorers in the nineteenth century. Except for the loss of some blue, the frescoes on the convent walls have reappeared, as fresh and radiant as the day they were put down. The color harmonies are both delicate and bold. The design is sure and smooth and sometimes startling. This is also true of the panel painting, *The Last Judgment,* where open graves are a jumble of geometric forms, serving dramatically to mark the absolute separation between the world of good and the world of evil. Above all, there is that air of suave serenity that is Angelico's hallmark, the deep emotion that he can pack so tightly into a gesture.

In the San Marco convent, which is now an Angelico museum, you can follow him as he kept up with the times. Like the other artists of his day, he had moved away from the rigidities of traditional painting. The bright young men of Florence had grown tired of the stiff, hieratical figures inherited from Byzantium and wanted to replace them with graceful, moving ones drawn directly from life. They studied the human body, they studied the configurations of objects in space. With the new science of perspective introduced by Brunelleschi they could paint scenes so skillfully that—for the first time in the history of art—a surveyor seeing the painting could draw a plan show-ing the precise position of every figure or building or tree.

The Human Side of Saints

This was more than a matter of showing off technical skill. The the-ologians of that day taught—as they had before and have since—that in Paradise the blessed are granted a sharper and more complete vision than they possessed as mere men and women. For an artist of Fra Angelico's temperament, creating a clear rational representation of space was like a foretaste of heaven, and he plunged into it with joy.

His style, his vision, hardly changed over the years. But he was constantly sharpening his technique in the direction of more natu-ralistic effects. There was a form that we now call the Sacred Conversation (*sacra conversazione*) in which on each side of a scene from sacred history, there are a number of saints presumed to be commenting on the scene. In the old paintings these are stiff, star-ing figures, perhaps with a pointed arch over their heads to frame them. As Angelico and his contemporaries painted more and more of these Conversations, the arches become doorways to rooms, the rooms fill out with walls and windows, landscape flowers through the windows, the saints become animated, their feet are firmly fixed on the floor, they make natural gestures.

A figure like the executioner swinging his sword to cut off a saint's head in *The Martyrdom of Saints Cosmas and Damian* shows how conscientiously Angelico had studied the muscles of the human body in motion. A scene like the *Massacre of the Innocents* shows how skillful he became in handling a crowd of people packed into a restricted space.

The new techniques implied a new vision of reality. The Virgin in medieval art is always a majestic figure, the Queen of Heaven; Angelico's Virgins are more like girls he might have seen in Florence.

The church was not always happy with the increasingly natural look of figures in works of art. There were those who pointed out that if you painted the Holy Family as peasants, you might end up displaying mere peasants without a trace of holiness.

A Certain Grandeur for the Gospels

The problem did not exist for Angelico. No one would ever mistake his Annunciations and Visitations and other biblical scenes for slices of everyday life. It is clear that something of transcendent importance is taking place in these humble settings. They have the same kind of grandeur as the Gospel stories which he loved to illustrate, and that is what has ensured his immense popularity over the centuries. In the Gospels, the ordinary and the extraordinary are mixed without self-consciousness, simple country people go about their lives getting married and dying, fishing and growing grain, paying taxes and speaking in peasant accents, yet there is never any doubt in the minds of the authors that they are living through important events. Angelico's outlook was precisely the same.

For while his techniques were up-to-date, and his eye was ever ready to see new things, the mind behind the eye remained thoroughly orthodox. Later painters of the fifteenth century whom he could have known might fill their works with gods, nymphs and satyrs. They might adopt openly pagan ways, worship sensual pleasure, glorify the nude body. They might, like Fra Filippo Lippi, also a friar, though one of a different stamp, use their mistresses as models for their Madonnas.

This side of the Renaissance was wholly foreign to Angelico. He was one of the highest paid painters of his day—when he was about 34 the guild of flaxworkers signed a contract with him for the considerable sum of 190 gold florins "or as much less as his conscience may deem right to charge"—but all the money he earned went to the convent of San Dominico. He never painted anything but sacred subjects: Holy Families, episodes from the Bible, the lives of the saints. And his choice was strictly according to the rules, drawn only from sources approved by the Church. Angelico was a model Dominican. His art was never for art's sake; it was gentle propaganda. He was, as a Spanish priest has put it, a propagandist of Paradise.

Ineffable bliss, the peace of God, was Angelico's natural element. The hell which occupies the right side of his *Last Judgment* is a dull and dingy place where seedy sinners sit lugubriously in big pots waiting to be boiled. In heaven on the left, on the other hand, whether the angels are singing or blowing trumpets and the blessed are dancing or basking in the divine effulgence, everyone is having a good time. "This man," said Michelangelo after seeing an Angelico painting, "must have found his model in paradise."

Every detail in an Angelico painting, however simple and straightforward it may look to the uninitiated eye, carries a heavy weight of theological symbolism. If there is a rose in the Virgin's garden, it is because she is called the Rose of Sharon. If there is a candlestick from the Jewish temple beside a figure representing the Church, it is because its seven branches were meant to prefigure the seven Christian sacraments.

A Fra Angelico painting can be taken as a visible sermon, sometimes with the appropriate biblical texts written right into it. The first of the thirty-five panels on the silver chest from the church of the Santissima Annunziata in Florence is a whole theological treatise packed into a space thirty-nine centimeters square. It is a commentary on the vision of a wheel within a wheel in the book of the prophet Ezekiel, and it is devoted to an intertwining of the Old and New Testaments, with Ezekiel sitting on one side of the river Chebar and Pope Gregory the Great, who wrote commentaries on him, on the other, with Hebrew prophets and Christian evangelists in circular patterns amid a flow of texts from Genesis and the Gospel of St. John.

These sermons were framed carefully for the audience that was to receive them. All but two of the forty-five cells of the monastery of San Marco contain a fresco (the experts debate on how many of these come entirely from his own hand—their estimates range from six to forty-one—but there is no doubt that he was responsible for the general design of all of them) and each fresco comprises a single striking image, the sole decoration of a room where a solitary friar would spend most of his hours day and night working, meditating and praying. They were painted on the darkest wall of the cell, beside the window, where they could be viewed by friars walking down the corridors. As aids to meditation, they might remind the friar that just as he could look through the window and see an external light streaming down from the sun, he could look through the painting to another, inner light illuminating his soul.

The paintings are quintessential Angelico, austerely graceful, a single concentrated image of one of the central scenes of sacred history in glowing colors and economical form. There are few figures, the backgrounds are stripped to their bare essentials, there is a quiet intensity that even today can sometimes make the herds of tourists catch their breath when they push into these narrow cells and catch sight of the image glowing on the bare white wall.

When he did a painting that was to be seen in church, Angelico used a less austere treatment. In the altarpiece he did for the church of San Marco commissioned by Cosimo de' Medici, the Virgin sits enthroned with her child in her arms, surrounded by angels and saints in various poses of adoration. This is the most famous of all Sacred Conversations and has a depth and naturalness in the placement of the figures that made it seem revolutionary in its time and the model for all future variations on the same theme.

Beneath this altarpiece are a series of small panel paintings, called predellas: only two of them remain in San Marco; most are in Munich and one is in Washington. They are bright and lively, full of dramatic incident; as in the scene where the two holy physicians appear by the hospital bedside of the sleeping deacon Justinian and, in a curious anticipation of twentieth-century surgical techniques, replace the leg he has lost with that of an Ethiopian who has just died in the next room.

An Eye for Detail as Well as the Monumental

When he was painting predellas, Angelico would let himself go in the direction of arresting detail, as in the flax-workers tabernacle where a Roman soldier raises his shield to protect himself from the hailstorm that accompanied the martyrdom of St. Mark. When he was painting frescoes of the lives of Saints Stephen and Lawrence for the chapel of Pope Nicholas V in the Vatican, he adopted a more formal style, placing his solemn figures against a background of the Roman monuments. When he was painting the giant Christ in majesty for the Orvieto cathedral, he aimed at a noble monumentality. Whatever the task, he came to it with the words of his fellow Dominican Thomas Aquinas firm in his mind, giving the criteria for beauty in art: *integritas, consonantia, claritas,* which James Joyce translated as wholeness, harmony, radiance.

It has been said of the painters of the early Renaissance that they looked on the world as if it were the first day of Creation. For Angelico, this was almost literally true. He had no sense of history as moderns understand it, a horizontal process of one thing following another, effect proceeding from cause, over endless centuries. For Angelico as for the medieval mystics who inspired him, it was rather a vertical pattern in which events are significant only in the way they relate to the unique central event, which is the redemption of Man through Christ. From this point of view, everything takes place in a timeless present; the world is being created, Christ is being crucified, Man is being offered the choice of salvation or damnation, all the time. What look like anachronisms to modern eyes were perfectly natural to Angelico. On one of the panels of the silver chest, he had the angel Gabriel appear to Mary in a room like one designed by his friend, the architect Michelozzo, and he put Michelozzo himself on a ladder helping to lower Christ from the cross on Calvary in a painting in the San Marco museum. The pope ordaining St. Lawrence as a priest in third-century Rome in the Vatican chapel is none other than Angelico's patron Nicholas V.

Pope, saint, Michelozzo and the crucified Christ—each is bathed in a kind of triumphant serenity. The serenity has not sat too well with some critics who would have preferred a little more spice, a little more *Angst,* in their Angelico. Berenson speaks of his "childlike simplicity" and says he was constitutionally incapable of seeing or understanding evil. Angelico would probably have disagreed. He was quite aware of the malice, cruelty and suffering in the world outside his monastic walls. He himself, according to the doctors who examined his bones when they were dug up (while a street was being widened for a tramway line) in 1915, must have suffered horribly from arthritis, but despite the pain in his hands from working in plaster, it is believed that he continued to paint in fresco up to a year before his death. He did not try to whitewash reality: the blood runs in torrents of bright red down his crucifixes, and rises in fountains from the severed veins in the necks of his decapitated saints.

Still, horror was only part of the whole, and the whole in the end was happy. Suffering and evil disappeared when the saints went dancing into Paradise.

Time Only for the Essentials

So he carried his message singlemindedly to the world till the day he could no longer pick up a brush. He never had time for anything but the essentials. There is nothing extraneous in an Angelico painting; everything is in its proper appointed place.

People were gossiping about his saintliness during his life, and took to venerating him after his death. He was always a particular favorite of the Florentines, and they soon took to calling him *beato,* or blessed—in the Catholic hierarchy, one step short of being a saint. For five hundred years the Church ignored repeated requests to give him formal recognition, on the grounds that there is no record of any miracle performed through his agency. To this, his latter-day admirers have generally replied by quoting the words of Pope John XXIII when the same comment was made about Thomas Aquinas: *Quot articulos scripsit, tot miraculos fecit,* meaning everything he wrote was a miracle. The groundswell of appeal at last broke through the Vatican walls and in October 1982 Pope John Paul II signed the decree allowing his date of death, February 18, to be celebrated, obligatorily in the liturgy of the church of Santa Maria sopra Minerva in Rome, where he was buried, and optionally in other Dominican churches throughout the world, giving official sanction to the term which had been applied to him by the public for the previous five hundred years: *beato.*

Dinners With G. de Chirico

BY FRANÇOISE GILOT

∽

editor's note

Painter and writer FRANÇOISE GILOT was Pablo Picasso's companion for many years and is the author of *Life With Picasso* (McGraw-Hill, 1964, hardcover; Doubleday, 1989, paperback) and *Matisse and Picasso: A*

Friendship in Art (Doubleday, 1990). Gilot is also an accomplished artist in her own right. For a complete look at her printmaking *oeuvre,* see *Stone Echoes: Original Prints by Françoise Gilot—A Catalogue Raisonné* by Mel Yoakum (Philip and Muriel Berman Museum of Art at Ursinus College, Collegeville, Pennsylvania, 1995).

Foreigners tend to view Italy as a romantic fantasy of song and dance—soft hilly landscapes, ancient monuments, idyllic blue coves. But having often visited Italy as a child in the 1930s (my parents owned a house on Lake Como), I would always paint it in much darker colors. The southern Mediterranean countries may appear to have received a special blessing, but under the sun's merciless eye there is a foreboding too, a sense of ominous hubris, a calm presentiment of inevitable tragedy. The very name Italy means soot, smoke. When most people still lived in the Bronze Age, the Etruscans there were already manufacturing iron tools and weapons; the merchant ships that came to the Italian shores recognized the land from afar by the somber fumes of smelting furnaces. Later—throughout history, in fact—periods of Italian greatness have alternated with times of decay and stagnation.

Once in Italy, one was always surrounded with beauty, that's true; but for me as a child there was something sinister about the repetitive slogans stenciled with tar on the walls by the blackshirts, the Fascist followers of Mussolini. Those were the Depression years, and to be sure there was a lot of poverty, but a latent desire for self-destruction also haunted the empty colonnaded piazzas, the grandiloquent arcades, the majestic porticos of Turin, or, in Rome, lurked around the monument to Victor Emmanuel, the one derisively nicknamed the *Sugar Cube* for its marmoreal whiteness. There was a desperation in the way the motto *Credere, Obedire, Combattere* ("Believe, Obey, Fight") was printed everywhere, as if to exorcise a general mood of paralysis and powerlessness.

When, a little later, during World War II, I discovered reproductions of Giorgio de Chirico's early work from 1911 to the twenties in old issues of *Cahiers d'Art,* I was transfixed by the prophetic veracity of his images. I felt that this painter had captured not only his own subjective drama but also the dilemma of a people permanently confronted by their several past ascents into greatness and retrospectively dwarfed by the Roman ruins or the memories of the efflorescence of the city-states during the Renaissance. Yes, the columns were still there, but what did they support? Where were the beliefs that could uplift and lead to positive action? Where were the people? Didn't they resemble mannequins endorsing one ideology or another more than human beings attempting to find a meaning in their own existence?

All this surged from de Chirico's paintings and their agoraphobia-inducing piazzas: a deep melancholy, an alienation, a disarray of reason in front of a senseless world, an emptiness, the vertigo of the sleepwalker who wakes up to find himself at the edge of a cornice overhanging an abyss.

Later still, I had a few conversations with Pablo Picasso about de Chirico's art. Of course, Picasso and I did not see eye to eye. I extolled the arresting qualities of the dreamlike images in de Chirico's early "metaphysical" paintings; to me he was *italianissimo,* he had aristocratic coolness and distance in the manner of his compositions, he knew the absurdity of human existence, the helplessness before destiny, even the vanity of desire. His Venuses wore dark glasses to hide their blindness. He showed the triviality of modern technology as well as the unattainable quality of Victorian stereotypes, which set goals too lofty to be reached. De Chirico had detachment and above all *morbidezza,* a sense of the futility of existence.

Picasso, who must have been mighty jealous when his dear poet-friend Guillaume Apollinaire started to praise the young de Chirico to the heavens before World War I, was somber. "So, you too like his early works, when he was part of the avant-garde," he said to me. "But later he betrayed himself and the avant-garde by falling back into neoclassicism."

"But didn't you fall back into neoclassicism yourself," I asked, "after your trip to Pompeii and a visit to the Museum of Naples?"

"For me it was not the same," he said. "I was just a temporary victim of my love for Olga, the Russian ballerina. Ah! Those Russian women! They have their share of the Slav charm, but for some reason, they all crave caviar, champagne, marriage, columns, and neoclassical art! They come along as sylphids and then they become dictators. That's why I painted all those monstrous statuesque giants in the 1920s. By the way, I have here a copy of *Hebdomeros,* a book by de Chirico. You can read it—it's excellent—but a painter shouldn't engage in literary pursuits."

"Strange, you say that in the same voice as if you were reciting the Ten Commandments," I said.

I loved *Hebdomeros.* It was a "surrealistic" novel de Chirico wrote in 1929, after he'd rejected his own early surrealist pictures (he'd even tried to destroy some of them) and been expelled by André Breton from the surrealist movement for the "abdication and apostasy" of his turn to neoclassical art. As de Chirico in his youthful metaphysical paintings made ordinary objects such as a single rubber glove seem suddenly significant, so Hebdomeros, the protagonist of his novel (a prodigal son whose "theories of life varied according to the sum of his experiences"), has the knack of seeing everyday things as if for the first time. As I was attempting to achieve a dreamlike mood in my own work (through altogether different means) the mysteriousness of this strange novel appealed to me deeply.

I separated from Pablo Picasso in 1954 and my book *Life with Picasso* was published in 1964 in the U.S. and in 1965 in many other countries including Italy. In 1966, I had an exhibition in Milan that traveled to the Galleria Santo Stefano in Venice during the Biennale. Giorgio and Uccia Zamberlan were de Chirico's dealers as well as my own. Since I intended to spend the summer in Venice with my mother and two daughters while the Zamberlans were busy preparing a show of de Chirico's recent works for September, it was inevitable that we should meet. And when indeed we did, it was a case of friendship at first sight.

Isa, de Chirico's wife (one more Russian muse!), was intelligent, charming, and soft. She did not seem to crave columns, dictatorship, or champagne. We got along very well and soon discovered that we had a number of mutual friends in Paris, particularly among the talented women of the Russian intelligentsia.

I think that the de Chiricos were staying at the Danielli, but he worked in a studio on Campo Santo Stefano and almost every day at dusk we would meet either at the gallery or directly at an outdoor café to sip Campari soda and chat about art—what else!

These were exquisite moments of repose. The maestro was relaxed and inclined to discuss the different facets of his work. He talked about the reason why he had wanted to explore not only the primitivism of his metaphysical period (which, by the way, was still strongly present in many of his new archaic compositions and original lithographs of the 1960s) but also why he had succumbed to the fascination of Raphael, Michelangelo, Dosso Dossi, and the Italian mannerists of the seventeenth century. He felt that a lot of modernistic theorizing was quite shallow, and he would set no such arbitrary limits to his own inquiries.

I thought to myself that for us artists of the twentieth century, Raphael and the other masters of the Italian Renaissance were great vampires and petrifying medusas to be avoided at all cost. Painters must be both the composers and the virtuosos of their productions. But the composer should always have the upper hand and the virtuoso should be kept under control. Uccello, Giotto, or Piero della

Francesca had been good masters in that regard, but with and after Raphael too much virtuosity had been expected of the artist.

I simply answered that most painters do not proceed in a linear fashion. That way of doing exists only in the critic's mind. At times the artist's imagination is far ahead, it reaches out to themes that will be developed only later or by a sudden increase in technical abilities, opening the path to a vast array of new solutions for which there is not yet a context.

De Chirico agreed. He was of the opinion that the artist should be able to gravitate back and forth according to subjective moods, subconscious pulsions, like a soothsayer. "After all, we are poets, not grammarians; philosophers, not cobblers or simple logicians." He told me that he had read and enjoyed *Life with Picasso* and added, "I bet that Picasso does not like or comprehend what I am after. For me, the years 1911 to 1919 were just a first phase in the unveiling of my own universe. My revolt in front of the fundamental absurdity of all things is individualistic and I am damned right to do as I please. I have always been misunderstood." He then pursed his lower lip and began to look peevish and disgruntled. His pale complexion became paler still, his silky silver hair still whiter. He became silent, self-absorbed, sad.

Isa came to the rescue by asking where he would like to have dinner that evening. A new vitality seemed to suffuse the artist and, regaining composure, he reentered the conversation to argue the diverse merits of different restaurants. This was for him a respite, a moment of pleasant expectation. He usually excluded La Fenice, L'Angelo, Montin, Cipriani, and a few others to settle for La Colomba or another place near the Rialto where there were also a lot of modern paintings on the walls and where one could find not only soft-shell crabs but also rather awful-looking crawfishlike animals called *cigalas*. But wherever we went and whatever we ordered almost never measured up to de Chirico's high standards of gourmet dining and his hypochondria would manifest itself. He would eat very little or not at all, to the great discomfort of the maître d' and the restaurant owner.

After he had expressed his displeasure to those responsible for it, he would once more resume the conversation, being very amiable to us all; especially to my daughter Paloma, who always sat to his left as I sat to his right, and whom he treated with quasi-paternal affection. Paloma, then seventeen, was beaming; she fully enjoyed his graciousness and dressed up in her nicest numbers from Jacques Heim to appear more grown-up. She also had a sweet tooth at the time and de Chirico insisted on lavishing her with the best desserts possible.

De Chirico was a man of medium height, a bit stocky, always well dressed with impeccable manners. He had a melodious voice, unctuous, almost ecclesiastical, gestures, and magnificent eyes. Above all, he had poise, allure, a great charm. He was very generous, quite likable despite his moody disposition. Isa, rather petite, most often wore outfits of a refined simplicity that flowed along the lines of her elegant silhouette. Apart from the Zamberlans and ourselves, there were usually other guests at the table; in particular I remember Mr. Giglio, the assistant director of the gallery, and Maestro Marcello Guidone, a lawyer who specialized in obtaining annulments at the Vatican for Catholic spouses who wanted to separate yet remain on good terms with God. He told rather indiscreet stories about his clients, which used to have a very positive effect on de Chirico's ever-present potential boredom. In fact, we all tried to humor the maestro and help him spend a pleasant evening. Whether in Spain, Italy, or Greece, the importance of people is measured by the number and status of the friends who surround them at all times. So around the Great White Elephant we were usually about twelve. (Because of his white hair, white complexion, and white silk outfits, Paloma and I referred to him as the *Great White Elephant*. He also had a superb aquiline nose.)

The evening of the opening of de Chirico's show went well. The critics did not attack him mercilessly about his many changes of heart and therefore he remained composed and did not become aggressive. I think that Paloma's and my presence was like a balm, since his old rival and foe Picasso would certainly be told by some friendly spies or read in the newspapers about our presence as supporters of the Italian master. In more ways than one, the two artists resembled each other in temperament and that certainly explains why they got on each other's nerves. Yet, in human terms, de Chirico was softer, and if he was cruel, he was only cruel to himself by taking bizarre stands or by making untimely declarations. That was his neurotic, self-destructive side. It was also his aristocratic side. He certainly did not take care of his publicity by catering to the press as Picasso did.

Anyway, the evening ended peacefully. Isa, Uccia, and Giorgio breathed a sigh of relief, and together planned to organize an expedition to a famous restaurant in Mestre for the next day.

It was an expedition indeed, since about twenty-five people were invited. We used gondolas or *motorscafi* to reach the famous parking lot outside Venice, get our cars, and drive to Mestre, a quite unattractive industrial city on the coast. It was the antithesis of Venice. There were the chimneys of fast-expanding industries, the trains and railroads, and the fast tempo of productive activity and business. Out of the beautiful past we had suddenly emerged into a relentless, dizzying future.

De Chirico seemed rather pleased with his friends' choice of an unseemly place for dinner. I must say the chef outdid himself to satisfy his anorectic and illustrious guest. Everyone was talking, talking, talking, so I don't remember just what we ate, merely that it was good. Yet something went wrong round the dessert and de Chirico became despondent once more. Something had not quite measured up to his standards and he was disappointed and lonely among our joyous crowd. So we left and emerged onto the piazza outside, a fugitive vision of all the artist's foreboding, hallucinatory, empty piazzas, the shortened perspectives, the arcades, the statues, the ghostly shadows, the inaccessible towers, the last train rushing in the distance forever out of reach, because it is a distance measured in time and not in space.

For a moment, I shared the sadness, the nostalgia of the hour. Night had fallen, distant stars were twinkling indifferent to human fate. Yes, the dice are loaded, man cannot escape his fate, his loneliness. A deep anxiety grabbed me. For an instant, I identified with de Chirico's deep anxiety, with his morbid obsessiveness, with his aversion to the mediocre, with his absence of desire, with his genius and his contradictions, with the tragedy of serenity.

Then I shook my head, the vision disappeared; it was only the end of a pleasant evening that was to be followed by other dinners at La Colomba and forays to Torcello, to Burano, in the now utopian hope of satisfying the Great White Elephant.

But since perfection remained out of reach, the quest remained open-ended. It went on and so did our friendship for many summers. As I recollect all this now that Giorgio de Chirico is no longer among us, thinking about the complexity, the equivocal ambiguity of the painter's actions and pronouncements, I am glad to see that the positive largely supersedes the critical restrictions we might make.

Giorgio de Chirico included the unknown in an equation with the truth. He gave his contemporaries omens, riddles, and enigmas; he gazed into the unfathomable depths of the human psyche. "Our minds are haunted by visions," he once wrote. "In public squares shadows lengthen their mathematical enigmas. Over the walls rise nonsensical towers, decked with multicolored flags; infinitude is everywhere, and everywhere is mystery. One thing remains immutable, as if its roots were frozen in the entrails of eternity: our will as creative artists." De Chirico was and remains a champion of the creative imagination, a model for other artists, encouraging them to remain individualistic, subjective, and above all free to make their own mistakes.

He had an enormous influence on Max Ernst, René Magritte, Salvador Dali, Yves Tanguy, and Paul Delvaux, and can also be called the father of the newer Italian school of Sandro Chia and Francesco Clemente.

In our century, a time torn apart by conflicting ideologies, a period of growing disappointment with the purely rational and technological ethos, when we are groping in the ruins of humanistic culture for philosophical guidelines sufficiently valid to be brought into the next millennium, Giorgio de Chirico has led us through the maze of *Paradise Lost,* perhaps to the gates of a new *Divine Comedy.*

This piece originally appeared in the September 1990 issue of *Art & Antiques.* Reprinted by permission of Françoise Gilot and the Watkins/Loomis Agency.

Lorenzo the Magnificent

BY DEREK WILSON

∾

editor's note

In the collection of the Metropolitan Museum of Art in New York there is a splendid *desco da parto* (birth tray) celebrating the birth of Lorenzo de' Medici, better known to the world as Lorenzo the Magnificent, a name synonymous with the Italian Renaissance. The tradition of commemorative birth trays is derived from the custom of presenting sweetmeats to new mothers, and the tray in the Metropolitan's collection was painted by Giovanni di Ser Giovanni, the younger brother of Masaccio. "The Triumph of Fame" image featured on the front of the tray is taken from Boccaccio's *L'Amorosa visione* and Petrarch's *Trionfi.* The painting shows knights on horseback with their arms extended in salute to a figure of Fame, who holds a sword and a cupid while standing on a globe with winged trumpets. On the reverse side are the coats of arms of the Medici and Tornabuoni families (Piero de' Medici married Lucrezia Tornabuoni in 1444, and Lorenzo was their first son). This stunning tray is an object of unique historical importance, as befits the star subject of the Renaissance: Lorenzo kept it in his private quarters in the Medici palace in Florence, and it is believed to be the largest and most opulent birth tray known to survive.

When I first saw the tray, I was in awe, for its beauty, yes, but also because the imagery suggests such a promising life for a little boy who would indeed fulfill such enormous expectations.

DEREK WILSON lives in Rome and contributes frequently to *ItalyItaly*.

Too many people mistake the inner sanctum of the Italian Renaissance for a police station and hurry on. And if you venture into what seems a massive fortress of rough-hewn stone in the heart of Florence, burly policemen carrying guns do indeed glare at you from a guardroom.

Ignore them. They are protecting tedious government offices, not the gem that you are after, which is secreted away upstairs. You have stepped into Palazzo Medici, no less, home of the banking dynasty which, through lavish patronage, virtually set in motion the Renaissance, Italy's great cultural revolution. In doing so, during the dazzling fifteenth century, they transformed medieval Florence into the artistic fulcrum of the world. The most illustrious Medici of them all lived here—Lorenzo the Magnificent, the very personification of the Renaissance, of Florence at its height of achievement.

The palazzo is, itself, a symbol of the change of taste that the Medici ushered in, a breakaway from the then usual defensive tower-house. Once clear the dour lower parts, you climb into a realm of refined simplicity, delicately Gothic windows and slender classical columns. It was the advent of a more civilized look, of comfort.

The sought-after gem, recently restored, is in the family's tiny chapel, a unique masterpiece, one of the marvels of Florence. It is a stupendous fresco by a brilliant social observer, Benozzo Gozzoli, showing in meticulous detail and color the entire Medici clan with retinue. It unfolds around the walls like a scroll, depicting a galaxy of faces taking part in a cavalcade, on a would-be Journey of the Wise Men to Bethlehem—through a rocky Tuscan landscape. To admirers, it is a family album that captures the very air of the early Italian Renaissance, its sumptuous pageantry, its solemnity and gaiety, its smug enjoyment of opulence, power and wit.

One figure that stands out is Lorenzo's black-gowned grandfather, Cosimo the Elder, the Rothschild of his day, pioneer of the Medici's prodigious patronage, a role he could assume thanks to an immense fortune built up by his shrewd father, Giovanni di Bicci de' Medici, founder of the family's banking empire. Kings and popes were his clients. Cosimo rides a mule rather than a horse—in keeping with his father's cunning precept, then passed on to Lorenzo, that in order to hang on to wealth and power, you had better not show it. Riding next to him is his son, Lorenzo's ever-ailing, seemingly ineffectual father, known as Piero the Gouty, the commissioner of the grandiose fresco. Then, leading a whole throng on a splendid white charger, richly clad, is Lorenzo himself, depicted as a comely lad of fourteen with tumbling locks.

An example it is of a paid artist's flattery for, as portrayed by others, Lorenzo was thoroughly ugly, with the long flattened nose of a prizefighter, a jutting jaw, square face and a squint. He spoke in a high-pitched, nasal voice, too, yet when he spoke, he became, it seems, so animated and infectiously eager that his looks ceased to matter. He was said to be cheerful and kind. He liked animals, insisting on personally feeding his horse, Morello. He was dogged, clever and ambitious too, and it was in this palazzo that he beavered away at expanding the family bank. His dwelling witnessed overflowing banquets he laid on for the arrival in Florence of his bride, Clarice, of Rome's powerful Orsini family. He had married her by proxy. Under his roof, she bore him ten children. Under it, too, for four years, Lorenzo the patron with a quick eye for talent, Lorenzo the discerning man of letters and poet in his own right, lodged and treated as one of the family an unknown young artist he had spotted. His name was Michelangelo.

The great man discovered the future genius in an academy for fledgling artists that he had founded. He was astonished at the perfection with which the youth had sculpted a copy of an old faun, adding to the creature, though, a mouthful of teeth. Lorenzo laughed. "Don't you know old men never have all their teeth?" As soon as his back was turned, the moody youth broke one off.

Michelangelo was but one of the artists Lorenzo drew about him and encouraged. They were all to become the magic household names of the Renaissance—the young Leonardo da Vinci, Sandro Botticelli, Filippo Lippi, Domenico Ghirlandaio and Andrea del Verrocchio, to single out a happy few.

Then there was Lorenzo the astute politician, who in the footsteps of his father and grandfather governed supposedly "republican" Florence apparently purely through popular consensus, with never any real legal title to do so. For only a few very brief periods did he agree reluctantly, or so he made it seem, to hold public office. The Medici recipe for power, which was his, too, consisted in outwardly playing the egalitarian—dressing simply, for instance—and refraining from ruffling touchy Florentine susceptibilities with any ostentation, while discreetly wielding invisible family clout to manipulate the city's political machinery. He would quietly see to it, for instance, that only Medici supporters, who were traditionally among the workers, were candidates in elections of the city's nine ruling priors. He would "fix" the voters, too.

Florence, in fact, was about big, rival families. A gory assassination attempt on Lorenzo's life, the so-called Pazzi Conspiracy, proved that the situation bred enemies. Egging on the plotters, led by the rival Pazzi banking family, was no less than the pope himself, Sixtus IV, incensed with Lorenzo for having tried to block papal territorial ambitions. Lorenzo was meant to be slain during mass inside Florence's great striped cathedral. The signal was to be the ringing of the bell at the elevation of the host. Two priests lunged for Lorenzo with daggers, but he quickly drew his sword and barricaded himself in the sacristy, wounded only slightly. Francesco de' Pazzi, however, savagely hacked Lorenzo's younger brother Giuliano to death. The ringleaders, including an archbishop, were flung naked out of high windows with ropes around their necks.

Crisis followed for Lorenzo and for Florence. The pope, furious at the botched plot, had armies sent against the city spearheaded by the troops of the Kingdom of Naples. They seized Tuscan towns. Warfare dragged on. Then Lorenzo, to rescue Florence from a menacing plight, sailed off to Naples, into the jaws of his foe, to plead for peace. After ten weeks of parleying, the ruler of Naples, King Ferrante, gave way, though exacting a crushing tribute.

It was a diplomatic triumph. Lorenzo, only twenty-nine, overnight became the undisputed master of Florence. He was quickly recognized, too, as a statesman of European stature whose negotiating skills, together with a spot of luck, obtained for Italy as a whole an unprecedented period of rejuvenating peace, cemented by a boon alliance between Naples, the papacy, Florence and Milan. He was hailed as "the needle of the Italian compass."

But, to judge from fulsome witnesses, the life Lorenzo far preferred, and for which he is best known today, was another one. His predilection was the literary life, spent not in Florence but in Medici family country villas in the company of fellow scholars—Humanists dedicated to the passionate exhumation of forgotten Greek and Latin literature. This was an activity at the very core of the Italian Renaissance, essentially a liberation from the mental mold of the Middle Ages that derived from the church, and a joyful reintroduction to the lay world of the individual. His companions included the poet Angelo Poliziano, his closest friend, and such prominent Renaissance intellectuals as Pico della Mirandola and Marsilio Ficino.

It does not seem that they were able to spend much time in his remote, fortified villa at Cafaggiolo, in the verdant Mugello region north of Florence, where he was born and to which he packed off his family after the Pazzi Conspiracy. You can visit a fairer villa, Lorenzo's favorite, at Poggio a Caiano, near Prato, a dwelling of sleek Renaissance elegance, built for Lorenzo by famed architect Giuliano da Sangallo and still adorned with splendid frescoes by Andrea del Sarto and Jacopo Pontormo. He also entertained his scholarly friends at another villa, amid olives and umbrella pines on the steep hill overlooking Florence that is surmounted by Etruscan Fiesole. But where the learned circle most often gathered was at the foot of the hills, in the family villa of Careggi, still resembling a medieval castle with battlements. Here, every November 7, Lorenzo threw a banquet for his friends to celebrate the birth of Plato.

He would stand before them to read aloud his poetry, which includes arrestingly humane and realistic tales of peasant life, at the time a quixotic theme. And one of his lyrics is on the lips of millions of Italians to this day:

Quanta bell giovinezza / Che si fugge tuttavia! /
Chi vuol esser lieto, sia: / Di doman non c'è certezza.

"Youth is beautiful, but it flies away! Who would be cheerful, let him be; for of the morrow there is no certainty" (translation by Jacob Burkhardt).

The poem could be the epitaph of Florence too. Catastrophe followed Lorenzo's death in the Careggi villa in 1492. Invading foreigners shattered Italy's peace. Lorenzo's son, Piero, was hounded out of Florence for having come to terms with the French King Charles VIII. After being twice re-instated, the Medici were to rule Florence until the eighteenth century. But the city was never again to taste the excitement of its heyday under Lorenzo the Magnificent.

Some Medici Homes

Palazzo Medici-Riccardi: Via Cavour 1, Florence.

Poggio a Caiano: Twelve miles northwest of Florence; by car, take SS 66, the Florence-Pistoia highway.

Careggi: Viale Pieraccini 17, Careggi. Now a public medical center (USL), it can be seen by appointment. Tel.: 055.4279981. Take ATAF bus 14 from Florence.

Fiesole: The gardens of the villa may be visited by appointment. Tel.: Signora Mazzini, 055.59417. Take ATAF bus 7 from Florence.

Medici Sites in Florence

Many sites in Florence are indelibly associated with the Medici dynasty, among them Palazzo Medici-Riccardi and Palazzo Vecchio, both of which served as family residences. In 1549 Cosimo I bought Palazzo Pitti, across the Arno, and had the Vasari Corridor, a covered passageway over Ponte Vecchio, built to connect Palazzo Pitti directly with the Uffizi, which housed the duchy's administrative offices. The Medici Chapels behind the church of San Lorenzo hold some monumental Medici tombs; the most famous of all are those in the so-called New Sacristy, where Michelangelo created extraordinary sculptural monuments for Giuliano, son of Lorenzo the Magnificent, and Lorenzo II, his grandson.

Florentine Master

BY SHUSHA GUPPY

∾

editor's note

To go to Tuscany and not know of Sir Harold Acton is like going to Rome without having heard of the Pope. It's common knowledge that many British and Americans come to Florence with the ambition of becoming Anglo-Florentine. It's also common knowledge that this usually takes about ten years, but it can take only a month if one is rich, beautiful, or famous—or related, in some way, to Sir Harold.

Acton passed away in 1994 at age eighty-nine, but his legacy lives on in his books and the magnificent Acton family home, Villa la Pietra, which his parents purchased in 1903. The fifteenth-century estate (with five villas, fifty-seven acres of olive groves and gardens overlooking Florence, and a renowned art collection) is now the property of New York University. Acton's gift may be the most expensive ever received by an American college or university. Though primarily for scholars and NYU students, La Pietra does welcome visitors to tour the gardens although they are currently closed for renovation.

Two other articles that I was unable to include in this collection are "Villa la Pietra" (Sir Harold Acton, *Architectural Digest,* January 1990, with color photos of the interior) and "A Last Fantasy in Florence" (David Plante, *The New Yorker,* July 10, 1995).

SHUSHA GUPPY lives in London and writes for a number of international publications.

A mile from one of the gates of old Florence, on the road to Bologna, there once stood a milestone, *una pietra.* Today the area is absorbed by urban expansion, but Villa la Pietra, on Via Bolognese, is as familiar to taxi drivers as any one of the city's famous sites. For it is the splendid Renaissance home of Sir Harold Acton—author, scholar, historian and aesthete.

I ring the bell. An ancient face peers down from the upper window of the gatehouse. Upon hearing my name he closes the window, and after what seems an age, the huge wooden gates, set back from the busy road, swing silently open. A mile-long avenue of tall cypresses, bordering olive groves and fields, leads to the house, its honey-colored walls glowing in the sun. An elderly retainer wearing a white jacket and gloves guides me through cool halls, replete with works of art, to the grand drawing room, where Sir Harold greets me with a firm handshake, a welcoming smile and a gentle bow.

Tall, elegant, wearing a light suit, he looks much younger than his eighty-five years. His charm, courtly manners and graciousness suggest an era of which he is one of the few survivors. His life and experiences span several continents and are the stuff of legend. He has been a friend to some of the most remarkable men and women of this century, and although he complains about his "octogenarian memory," he recalls them all vividly; he also knows the names, dates and provenance of thousands of works of art. He has a young man's curiosity about people and events—"Gossip is the food of history," he believes—but his anecdotes are always enlightening, never malicious.

A butler serves tea as we sit in a corner of his vast salon to chat, and Sir Harold apologizes profusely for the biscuits. "I'm afraid the cook has been on holiday; these are bought from a shop," he says. He speaks as he writes, in exquisite English heightened by dramatic inflections and seasoned with Italian and French words. Although he is the author of such classics of history as *The Last Medici* and *The Bourbons of Naples,* he is chiefly known to the general public for his best-selling *Memoirs of an Aesthete* (1948), one of the most popular postwar autobiographies. Since its publication, he is often referred to as "the last aesthete," while his wealth and way of life have won him the title of "dilettante." He accepts both charges despite their connotations of amateurism. "An aesthete is a lover of beauty, which I am," he says. "And although I'm much too special-ized to be a real dilettante, the original meaning of the word applies to me: a lover of art. The Society of Dilettanti was founded in England in the eighteenth century by a group of art lovers." Today Sir Harold is one of the most distinguished members of the society.

Born during the reign of Edward VII, in 1904, to an American mother and an English father, Harold Acton is one of a long line of English romantics, starting with Byron and Shelley, to settle in Florence and the surrounding countryside. "The Actons, who came originally from Shropshire, settled in the eighteenth century in the Kingdom of Naples, where some of them achieved high ranks," he says. "One Sir John Acton served Naples' Queen Marie Caroline and King Ferdinand IV; he reformed the Neapolitan army and navy and became prime minister. He was evidently a colorful character, because at sixty he sought Papal dispensation to marry his own fourteen-year-old niece. There are still Actons in Naples; they own Palazzo Cellamare. But I'm not a fanatic of family history. I'm a selfish bachelor entirely devoted to the arts."

If his ancestors evoke the swashbuckling eighteenth century, his own parents belong to the world of Henry James. Indeed, the quiet grandeur of La Pietra, the wealth of its art collection and the life story of its charismatic present owner remind me of *The Aspern Papers*. Sir Harold's mother, Hortense Mitchell, was the daughter of a rich banker in Chicago: "Her brother Guy was an art student in Paris, where he became friends with my father, a fellow student, and invited him to America for a holiday. My parents met, fell in love and married. They decided to come and live in Florence and eventually bought this property, which has four other villas beside this house. As a child I was often taken to America to spend holidays with my grandfather in his summer house by Lake Geneva, in Wisconsin. I remember it vividly—the beauty of the scenery, the warmth of the atmosphere, the fun and games. . . ."

Acton *père* was an amateur painter, and both he and his wife were avid collectors. La Pietra contains their rich and varied collection of paintings, sculptures, tapestries and *objets d'art* from the thirteenth to nineteenth centuries, to which Sir Harold has added a few exotic pieces from his own wide travels. "My father was a gifted artist and he had an instinct for works that very few cared for at the time. For example, he collected thirteenth- and fourteenth-century paintings when many others were keen on seventeenth century. There was a thriving international community in Florence, and many artists and art historians did some dealing on the side. So I was born and brought up surrounded by beauty."

He grew up speaking English and Italian, and studied French. "My English teacher introduced me to Shelley and Keats. I read the French poets—Racine, Verlaine, Rimbaud. Every French word was a delight, like cutting a cameo." He started writing poetry at an early age. "Living in Italy you are drawn to poetry, are you not? My mother used to take me to Comtesse d'Orsay's salon, where D'Annunzio often recited his poems. There were other artists, including Marinetti, the leader of the Futuristi, and De Chirico. It was inspiring for a ten-year-old, and I wanted to be a poet."

Following family tradition, his father sent Harold to boarding school in England, first in Wixenford and then to Eton: "It was an alien world. At first I was considered strange because I had white truffles for tea, which my mother sent from Florence. But gradually I made many good friends—David Cecil, Oliver Messel, Eddy Sackville-West, who was a musician and played Debussy on the piano—and life became more tolerable." He contributed poems to a school magazine, helped found the *Eton Candle* and "even sent a poem to *The Spectator.* To my astonishment, they published it and sent me a check for a few shillings. I was thrilled and encouraged to continue."

From Eton he went to Christ Church, Oxford, where, in the words of his contemporary A. L. Rowse, "he was an exotic bird of brilliant plumage." His charm and flamboyance made him famous overnight and won him a number of lifelong friends, Evelyn Waugh and Graham Greene among them. In fact, he is generally supposed to be one of the models for the decadent Anthony Blanche in Waugh's novel *Brideshead Revisited.*

"It was a caricature based more on Brian Howard than me. But it was my room he depicted as Sebastian Flyte's, with a harmonium and an elephant's foot. And I did read poetry from my balcony. Once I recited the whole of *The Waste Land* through a megaphone at a League of Nations garden party."

While at Oxford Harold Acton published a volume of poetry, then switched to the novel. After graduation he went to live in London, where he got involved with various literary groups, though he was often away in Florence and remained somewhat aloof, a charming outsider. One coterie was centered around the poet Edith Sitwell and her brothers Osbert and Sacheverell. "The Sitwells were partly Florentine and had a house in Tuscany, Castle Montegufoni, where they spent part of the year," he remembers. "Edith edited *Wheels,* a poetry anthology where some of the writers and poets who later became famous were first published. She lived in a gloomy flat where I often went to have tea with her. T. S. Eliot was a frequent visitor. I had a profound admiration for his poetry, but found him a cold fish—a very courteous cold fish."

By the late 1920s Harold Acton had decided to move to Paris for awhile. "I loved Paris and French culture," he says, "and there was in those days a tremendous intellectual and artistic ferment in Paris. Writers and artists from America and Europe converged there, and created an electric atmosphere of creativity. I took a flat in L'Isle St. Louis, 'round the corner from my friend Nancy Cunard, who ran the *Hours Press,* where she published many writers, known and unknown, both in English and French. She held her salon in cafés, and the Surrealists gathered 'round her. Gertrude Stein presided over a literary salon in her flat, which was crammed with pictures by Picasso, Matisse, Braque. . . ."

In 1932 he left Europe and went to China, where he stayed till the outbreak of the war. "It was the happiest time of my whole life! I had fallen in love with Chinese art and got to know Chinese poetry through Arthur Waley, who was a genius at translating and interpreting it. I got a job as a professor of English literature at the University of Peking, but that was an excuse for being in China. I lived in a most beautiful house. It had three courtyards and a garden; I studied painting with a charming prince, Prince P'u Ju, who was a cousin of the last emperor, P'ui. My students and colleagues were delightful."

There he learned Mandarin and published two volumes of translations of modern Chinese plays and poems. (He still speaks Chinese, although he fears he has lost his fluency, having had no opportunity to practice.) When war broke out he went back to England and joined the Royal Air Force, hoping to be sent back to China, where his experience and knowledge of the language would be useful. But in a secret file he found a reference to himself as "a scandalous debauchee who should on no account return to China!"

"I was bitterly hurt," he now says, "but it was the Anthony Blanche smear: my own life was remarkably unsensational." Partly to dispel that misunderstanding he wrote *Memoirs of an Aesthete* after the war. "When Evelyn heard I was writing it he said 'Goodbye! We shall never speak again!' He thought I was going to say nasty things about him. But I didn't, and our friendship lasted till the end. Poor Evelyn! A great writer—original, charming, but often so disagreeable!"

Before leaving China, Sir Harold had managed to build up a collection of Chinese art and artifacts: "In those days you could buy a Ming vase for a few dollars." Because he had planned to return to Peking, he had left his art collection behind. "Luckily an American friend managed to save some of my best pieces and take them to the States. They are now in Kansas City at the Nelson Atkins Museum of Art, which has a marvelous Chinese collection." (A large cloisonné incense burner on a stand, which now sits in his salon, was one of the few pieces he kept.)

During the war his parents were briefly imprisoned, with La Pietra occupied first by German and then Allied officers. Inevitably, some works of art were lost. "My mother was dressed for a party when they came to arrest her. She refused to change her dress, and sat in a chair for three days. Eventually my parents were released and spent the rest of the war in Switzerland." Toward the end of the war his brother William, two years his junior, was killed in action, and Acton went back to Florence to be with his parents. "William was a very gifted painter and, I think, my parents' favorite. My mother was devastated, and I tried to make her life less unhappy."

After the war came two decades of intense creativity. He wrote his *Memoirs, The Bourbons of Naples* and *Tuscan Villas,* and a great many reviews, articles and lectures. "At the center of the art world in Florence was the American art historian Bernard Berenson, and people came from all over the world to his villa, I Tatti, to work, study and listen. He was a friend of my parents, and as a boy I had the run of his vast library. He used to say, 'I live in a library with a few rooms attached to it.' When I came back to live here I saw him frequently and met many visiting American writers and scholars with him."

Berenson left I Tatti to Harvard University, which now administers it as a center of Italian Renaissance studies. Perhaps following his example, Sir Harold has bequeathed La Pietra and its collection to New York University. "I first intended to leave it to my old college, Christ Church, Oxford, but they refused it," he says. "It is a tricky business administering such properties abroad. Berenson had to *coax* Harvard to accept I Tatti! In a sense it is right that La Pietra should go to an American university, since the original money came from America, from my mother's family." By chance I met John Brademas, the president of N.Y.U., shortly after my visit to Sir Harold, and asked him what its plans were for the collection. "We have many projects for La Pietra. For example, it could be a place where Italian specialists in American studies could exchange views with American specialists in Italian studies. It would contribute to Italian-American cultural relations."

In the meantime, the most distinguished member of the international community in Florence is Sir Harold Acton, and it is to La Pietra that a stream of pilgrims comes throughout the year—scholars, students, writers and friends. Among the latter recently was H.R.H. The Prince of Wales, for whom Sir Harold has a deep admiration and affection. "The prince and princess have graced this house with their presences. They are a charming couple and a blessing on the nation. We are so lucky to have an heir to the throne who is intelligent, sensitive, talented. Here he spent his free time painting in the garden. He is very acute, listens to what one says, and understands things."

Harold Acton was knighted by the queen in 1966 for his services to the arts—he is supposed to have saved Florence single-handedly from having a Hilton Hotel—and to the British Institute in Florence, of which he was the vice-chairman.

After tea Sir Harold took me for a stroll through his gardens: green acres divided by hedges, rose parterres, stony steps, arches and columns, with the city of Florence shimmering in the distance. Centenarian cypresses, pines, ilexes and cedars cast their shadows over some one hundred statues from Northern Italy, collected by Sir Harold's father. Small lotus-covered pools around mossy fountains shelter goldfish and aquatic plants, and in a clearing stands a giant figure. "You can see it's a Bacchus—he looks a bit tiddly!" There is an open-air theater—two levels of grass bordered with hedges, where during the war the Diaghilev Ballets Russes, stranded in Florence, gave performances. Today local theater groups stage plays here every summer.

Sir Harold guided me back to the house through the central hall, a round domed space with a fountain in the center and a flight of stairs curving up on the side. "The tapestries on the walls are Flemish, made in the fifteenth century for the Medici, but the frescoes depicting the rape of Sabines are by an eighteenth-century Venetian artist."

He then showed me the dining room, large enough for state banquets, with a Donatello relief of Virgin and Child at the center of the east wall surrounded by various eighteenth-century masters' works. One marvels at the passion with which the Actons have collected art. Every wall is covered with pictures or tapestries; every niche harbors a sculpture.

Sir Harold writes in a small library adjoining the drawing room. He writes longhand in ink and has a secretary "to take care of chores like household bills." He still regularly reviews books, and is finishing a volume of short stories as well as working (with writer Edward Chaney) on an edition of his collected works. But much of his time is spent receiving visitors. Could he be the victim of his own courtesy and generosity? "It is hard to say no when one has something that can give pleasure—and I hope more than pleasure."

With such a remarkably rich life, is there anything he still wishes to do? "Oh yes! A thousand things!" he said, smiling. "I would like to see the new Musée d'Orsay in Paris, and I always look forward to London and seeing my friends. Many of my old friends are gone, alas, but one does make new friends all the time, doesn't one?"

The Funniest Italian You've Probably Never Heard Of

BY ALESSANDRA STANLEY

∽

editor's note

The subtitle for this piece, which appeared in 1998, read "Roberto Benigni is Italy's Robin Williams, but he has never caught on big in America. Maybe his new comedy, set in the Holocaust, will do the trick." The comedy was *La Vita È Bella,* which most definitely caught on big, winning the Oscar for Best Foreign Language Film.

I think the film is brilliant, and beautiful. I was heartened to read in a *New York Times* editorial by Abraham Foxman—national director of the Anti-Defamation League and a Holocaust survivor—that, although initially skeptical, he enjoyed it also. Foxman stated that Benigni "created something special—and very important. The comedy in the film actually heightens the anxiety the viewer has about the horror that is occurring, humanizing the tragedy in ways that a more direct depiction may not."

ALESSANDRA STANLEY is the Rome bureau chief of *The New York Times*.

The funniest man in Italy appeared to be talking, quite solemnly, about American dentistry. "Mandelbaum," Roberto Benigni said, breathing the name reverently. "Some of the best dentists in the world are American." Few would argue the point, but it seemed an odd topic for an Italian comic whose knowledge of the United States is limited. His teeth, moreover, are even and unblemished.

"American dentists are extremely important," Benigni continued in rapid-fire Italian, sitting in a hotel garden in Rome. "They have influenced contemporary poetry a lot. They have a perspective that is very fresh and modern compared to the older texts."

Not "dentista." *Dantista*. The Italian word for "Dante scholar." Mandelbaum is Allen Mandelbaum, a poet whose translation of *The Divine Comedy* is widely used in American universities, and Benigni is a passionate *Dantista* who, as a youth in Tuscany, could recite the entire *Divine Comedy* by heart. He recently gave an outdoor recital in Florence of the Fifth Canto of the *Inferno* before a rapt audience of 16,000.

Benigni looked a bit reproachful when told of the initial confusion, then laughed delightedly. Dumb misunderstandings, after all, have been at the core of some of his most popular movies, hugely successful slapstick farces like *Il Mostro* (*The Monster*) and *Johnny Stecchino*—movies confected around Benigni's naïve, hapless and hopelessly bumbling screen persona.

Until now, that is. His latest movie, *La Vita È Bella* (*Life Is Beautiful*), is about as abrupt a departure from his previous movies as can be imagined. It is a comedy set during the Holocaust. Benigni, who also directed and co-wrote the film, plays Guido, an assimilated Italian Jew in Arezzo who is deported, along with his five-year-old son, to a German concentration camp. To hide and protect the boy, Guido playfully works to convince him that the horrors of their concentration camp are all part of an elaborate game.

It is as risky a premise as a popular comic can undertake. So far, however, the gamble has paid off. Despite initial grumbling from some critics, the movie instantly became a hit in Italy. *Titanic* sold more tickets, but an Italian polling firm found that 30 percent of Italian women would like to take a trip with Roberto Benigni; only 20 percent preferred Leonardo DiCaprio.

Elsewhere, *La Vita È Bella* was something of a sleeper. It was accepted only at the last minute by the Cannes Film Festival, then astonished everyone by winning the Prix du Jury. At the presentation ceremony, Benigni shed all piety and reverted to his usual manic, bubbling self, sprawling on the floor in front of a startled Martin Scorsese, who led the jury, kissing his feet, then leaping up to kiss every member of the jury.

Benigni has since shown his film in Israel, where it was so acclaimed that Ehud Olmert, the mayor of Jerusalem, awarded him a medal of recognition that was roughly akin to the keys to the city. In the United States, where the film opens next week, it is likely to be an Oscar contender for best foreign language film.

At forty-five Benigni has bounced from one success in Italy to another since he first began drawing crowds to his risqué one-man shows in small experimental theaters in Rome in the early 1970s. The Italian film business has been in an artistic and commercial slump these past several years, overshadowed by the popular American imports—except for Benigni, who is the country's biggest star and top moneymaker. His 1991 movie, *Johnny Stecchino,* grossed more than $30 million, outselling *Robin Hood* and *Terminator II.* In 1994, *Il Mostro* outdrew *The Lion King* and *Forrest Gump.*

But with the American release of *La Vita È Bella,* it is not at all clear whether Benigni can make the leap to success in a country that only a handful of European actors have conquered. And this film is not Benigni's first attempt to seduce American audiences. He appeared in Jim Jarmusch's 1986 cult film *Down by Law* and, in

1993, *Son of the Pink Panther,* a limp eighth sequel to the Peter Sellers classic. *Johnny Stecchino,* a farce about a doltish school-bus driver who is the uncanny double of a murderous Mafia don, was heavily promoted in the United States but fell flat.

As Benigni works to recast himself as a more serious comic, he seems both tempted and bemused by Hollywood. "After the Jarmusch movie, I got a lot of offers from Hollywood," he says. "Americans are generous. Disney asked me to stay and write for them. They took me around the studio, showed me early drawings of Pinocchio, but what could I do there?" He starts laughing. "Even Warner Brothers came after me. A studio executive wearing a lapel pin with Bugs Bunny and Daffy Duck pointed to it and said that if I wrote for them, my face would be on the pin right next to Daffy Duck."

Still, Benigni says, "I would love to do great things in America." He admits, though, that his shaky English sometimes gets in his way. Tim Burton sent him the script for *Beetlejuice,* which he rejected after he heard the title translated. "They said it meant *spremuta di scarafaggi,* and I said, 'Yuck, no thanks.'" He beams with mock grandeur and adds: "Look what that film did for Michael Keaton. I could have been Batman." He pauses. "Well, maybe Robin."

Sometimes compared to Woody Allen (mostly because he stars in and directs his own movies, is slight, reads highbrow books and wears glasses off-camera), Benigni is actually the un-Allen—there is no detectable angst or self-loathing in either his comic persona or personal psyche. He is not insecure, neurotic or even overly neat. Happily married to Nicoletta Braschi, thirty-eight, the actress who stars opposite him in all his films, Benigni is the rare example of a comedian who seems genuinely content behind the performance mask.

"On the outside he could appear insecure, but inside he was always enormously confident," says Giuseppe Bertolucci, one of Benigni's early mentors and collaborators, who is a filmmaker and younger brother of Bernardo Bertolucci. "The great gift of all actors is the capacity to like themselves, a certain narcissism that the rest of us don't have. He had an extraordinary sense of what he should and shouldn't do."

At first, even Benigni wasn't sure he should take on the Holocaust. "You never know how ideas come, but I had this strong desire to put myself, my comic persona, in an extreme situation," Benigni says. He and his co-writer, Vincenzo Cerami, were brainstorming one winter day in 1995 at the small, melancholy working-class trattoria in Rome that is their preferred hangout. "I said, 'Well, the ultimate extreme situation is the extermination camp, almost the symbol of our century, the negative one, the worst thing imaginable.'" As soon as he said it, Benigni recalls, both men recoiled in horror.

Benigni then stood up and improvised a scene of a father trying to reassure his son by extravagantly ridiculing the idea that Germans would make buttons or soap from the remains of prisoners. From that first sketch, which ended up in the film, the rest of the story flowed.

It took them another year to summon the confidence to proceed. They read Holocaust books and studied documentaries, as well as *Schindler's List* and *The Great Dictator*. (Benigni, who is increasingly described as Chaplin-esque, is openly in Chaplin's debt: the number he wears on his concentration camp uniform in the film is the same one Chaplin wore when playing the Jewish barber in *The Great Dictator*.) Benigni also sought the counsel of Jewish historians and Holocaust experts, seeking to lend his film historical authenticity and himself moral support for a project that could easily strike audiences as sacrilege in the worst possible taste.

The risk of career-crushing failure was, after all, quite real. *The Great Dictator*, Chaplin's 1940 satire of Hitler, may well have been a masterpiece, but that was Chaplin. Then there was Jerry Lewis.

In 1971, when Lewis's career was at a nadir, he filmed *The Day the Clown Cried*, about a German clown enlisted by the Nazis to distract wailing children destined for the gas chamber. Lewis's performance was reportedly ghastly and the movie was never released. According to Shawn Levy, a Lewis biographer, the sole complete copy is in a vault in Lewis's home.

"I know about this," Benigni says quietly. "But still I would so much like to see it, because Jerry Lewis is, he is, well, *bello*."

The concept for Benigni's movie did not fall entirely from thin air. Over the past several years, the Jewish experience has become a hot topic in Italy. Memoirs by Italian Holocaust survivors are in every bookstore, as are books about Yiddish humor and culture; there are numerous conferences and exhibitions about the Holocaust and Jewish life. Benigni, who is not Jewish, had already steeped himself in the works of Primo Levi and Isaac Bashevis Singer. (Years ago, he wooed his wife by telling her Singer stories.) As he cast about for a new film subject, he could hardly help absorbing the *Zeitgeist*.

Part of the inspiration was more personal. Benigni's father was a poor Tuscan farm worker who served in the Italian cavalry in Albania during World War II and ended up in a German labor camp when Italy changed sides in 1943. For two years, Luigi Benigni was nearly worked and starved to death, and weighed 80 pounds when he was released.

What shaped Benigni's thinking about *La Vita È Bella* was not just his father's experience but the way he described it. "Night and day, fellow prisoners were dying all around him," he says. "He told us about it, but as if to protect me and my sisters, he told it in an almost funny way—saying tragic, painful things, but finally his way of telling them was really very particular. Sometimes we laughed at the stories he told."

Now seventy-nine, Luigi Benigni still tells those stories, still mixes the chilling details with whimsical ones. "We were forbidden to talk to women," he recalls. "There were Czechs, Poles, Russians in there with us, but the sign over the door that said 'Those who attempt to speak to women will be severely punished' was written only in Italian." He smiles slyly. "The Germans knew how much Italians like to [expletive]."

Benigni's parents live in the small town of Vergaio, one block from the modest stucco house his father built in 1960; they now have a larger house, which Benigni bought them in 1992 so his mother, Isolina, could have a garden. His childhood friends never left home, and Benigni returns often to see his parents and play cards with his old cronies. "If there were anger in Roberto, it would be the atavistic rage of the hungry peasant, but actually, there is no anger in him," says Franco Casaglieri, forty-six, who has known Benigni since elementary school. "He is not unhappy. He is a channel of joy. I don't know where it comes from, but he transmits it."

He was the only boy in the family, baby brother to three doting older sisters, growing up in a rural community united by postwar poverty. In their first house, near Arezzo, the medieval town where *La Vita È Bella* is set, the family didn't have running water, a toilet or electricity. Even when they moved to Vergaio, when Benigni was a child, there was no television or pocket money. In the summers, he and his closest sister, Anna, could not afford movie tickets, so they would sneak onto the field behind the town's outdoor movie screen and watch westerns and gladiator films backward.

Gifted in school, Benigni was a precocious performer who at age five would climb on top of the bandstand during a break in summer outdoor dances and tell jokes. The Benignis, like everyone else in town, voted for the left; social life revolved around the Communist Party clubhouse. Urged on by his father, the teen-age Benigni quickly mastered a local pastime, competitions in *ottava rima,* in which two people debate while improvising the eight-line rhyming verse that has been a Tuscan tradition since the thirteenth century. The whole village would gather to watch their favorites compete. "The audience would throw them a theme," Benigni recalls. "America versus Russia. The guy who played the American would always let the Russian win to get more applause."

Benigni went to a rural elementary school until a local priest took note of the boy's intelligence and enrolled him in a Jesuit school in Florence. The 1966 floods closed the school and he dropped out to work as a magician's apprentice in a traveling circus. He ended his education in an all-female secretarial school and, in 1972, made his way to Rome, falling in with actors trying to make their mark on experimental theater. Giuseppe Bertolucci saw he had a raw talent and helped tame it, transforming Benigni's funny stories about Vergaio into a monologue. In 1977, they made a satiric coming-of-age movie that took Benigni's boyhood to comic extremes—it is heavy on political message and puerile masturbation jokes.

An autodidact, Benigni absorbed the classics out of love—and, as Bertolucci points out, to lend legitimacy to his extremely lewd monologues. It didn't always work: he was repeatedly threatened with obscenity charges, and was fined and given a one-year suspended sentence in 1980 after mocking Pope John Paul II.

As dangerous as his stand-up comedy may have seemed at one time, Benigni is, in person, almost alarmingly good-natured and eager to please. When explaining why he agreed to star in Blake Edwards's *Son of the Pink Panther,* Benigni praised Edwards as the equal of Billy Wilder, then swiftly backtracked after the interviewer smiled skeptically at the analogy. "O.K., yes, there is a difference," he said. "I say Billy Wilder because he is the greatest of all, but in the American school, Edwards is a great comedic director."

His favorite adjective is *bellissimo,* which he applies with equal relish to describe Fellini, Cary Grant in *North by Northwest,* Robert Frost's poetry, gin rummy and the extravagant catering trucks on the set of *Astérix et Obélix,* a new French film in which he plays a small part opposite Gerard Depardieu.

Most often, he applies the adjective to his wife. "What I love best about her is that she is a woman who really knows how to laugh," he says. "It sounds banal—'she has a great smile'—but no, but no, it's her laugh, it's different, she really knows how to laugh."

It is the perfect encomium for a comedian's spouse, of course. Their romance began when he cast her in 1983 as the Virgin Mary in the first film he directed, *Tu Mi Turbi (You Move Me).* They married in 1991 and now live in a spacious apartment in the Aventino, a lush, exclusive residential neighborhood near the center of Rome.

In his spare time, the restless Benigni is a passionate, ruthlessly competitive card player. He is also addicted to other games of skill. Among his playmates he counts the Italian novelist and semiotics professor Umberto Eco, whom he befriended fifteen years ago when they engaged in a fierce *ottava rima* competition that lasted for weeks. They still trade complicated riddles and recondite guessing games by mail.

Benigni, whose merciless ridicule of the former conservative Prime Minister Silvio Berlusconi is credited with contributing to his political demise, has long been a darling of the left. But now that Italy has a center-left government led by a down-to-earth economist, leftist intellectuals are suffering from post-ideological angst; they accuse the government of *buonismo*—"goody-goodyism." And because Benigni has not attacked the current government, he, too, has been tarred with the same brush.

Some of his critics complain that *La Vita È Bella* is the triumph of *buonismo*. "Benigni is very simpatico, but he is self-indulgent and so politically correct," complains Giuliano Ferrara, the editor of *Il Foglio,* a maverick conservative Roman newspaper that has led a relentless campaign against Benigni. "There is this tendency to make the Holocaust banal with easy tears and narcissism. There is no intellectual rigor, just sentimentality." Benigni, Ferrara says, has overstepped his talent. "It's like Bill Cosby trying to do Off Broadway. Benigni is a good entertainer, and that is what he should stick to."

Benigni is certainly one of Italy's most ambidextrous entertainers, one who boasts the rubbery physical agility of a silent movie actor and the verbal pyrotechnics of a young and wired Robin Williams.

In his most popular movies, the gags are mostly physical: one of the memorable moments in *Il Mostro,* in which he plays a working-class loner mistaken by homicide detectives for a serial killer, is quite literally a seltzer-down-the-pants joke: he drops a lighted cigarette down his pants, and manically tries to put out the fire with Perrier. Through the lens of grainy black-and-white police surveillance cameras, Benigni battling with his crotch looks suspiciously like a sex maniac unbound.

Until now, his Italian comedies have all been quite similar, and it seemed as if Benigni had reached a plateau. That creative restlessness led to *La Vita È Bella.*

Flush with the attendant acclaim, Benigni has begun to express an almost messianic belief in his movie. "I didn't want to make a movie about the Holocaust—I wanted to make a beautiful film," he says. "But if this film has even in a tiny way helped get people to talk about this subject, to feel the absurdity and the incomprehensible folly. . . ." Benigni pauses, searching for his words. "And if we can talk about it and also even smile about it, not sneeringly, but to naturally make fun of it, to smile at the Holocaust, we will be able to get over it, even though I can't say if it is wrong or right to get over it, but it has to be done somehow."

Biblioteca

Renaissance Profiles, edited by J. H. Plumb, Harper & Row, 1965; first published in *The Horizon Book of the Renaissance* in 1961 by American Heritage Publishing Company. This book might be hard to find, but I include it here because it is so very good. The Italians profiled are Machiavelli, Michelangelo, Lorenzo de' Medici, Leonardo da Vinci, Pope Pius II, Doge Francesco Foscari, Federigo da Montefeltro, Petrarch, and Beatrice and Isabella d'Este. Some of the contributors are nearly as famous as their subjects: Kenneth Clark, Iris Origo, H. R. Trevor-Roper, and Denis Mack Smith. This is an excellent idea for a book and worth searching diligently to find. It's also a slender paperback, perfect for stuffing into your carry-on bag.

The Autobiography of Benvenuto Cellini, Penguin Classics, translated and with an introduction by George Bull, this translation first published in 1956; reprinted 1961, 1964, 1966, 1969, 1970, 1973, 1974, 1976, 1977. To those unfamiliar with this autobiography, Cellini is probably best known for his talents as a goldsmith (the gold salt cellar he made for Francis I is one of the prized attractions in Vienna's Kunsthistorisches Museum) and secondly as a sculptor (the statue of Perseus in the Loggia dei Lanzi in Florence). Despite the high opinion he had of himself, Cellini's autobiography is an excellent account of sixteenth- and seventeenth-century Florence and Rome and their inhabitants. Cellini knew *everyone,* so we learn the perspectives of nobility, prostitutes, musicians, soldiers, writers, merchants, and everyone in between. It is impossible to separate his life from Florence, and for that reason alone his story is essential reading. But it also happens that his life was extraordinarily interesting, and George Bull notes in the introduction that Cellini's work "has taken its place as the most famous, or notorious, of all autobiographies."

Of the countless biographies written on the Medici family—possibly the most famous family in history—these are the volumes I prefer above all others:

The House of Medici: Its Rise and Fall, Christopher Hibbert, Morrow Quill Paperbacks, 1974; originally published in Great Britain in 1974 under the title *The Rise and Fall of the House of Medici.* Hibbert, who has been described as "a pearl of biographers," is not only a leading biographer, but a historian as well, and Italy seems to hold special interest for him (some of his other books include *Benito Mussolini, Garibaldi and His Enemies,* and *Florence: Biography of a City*). This volume is widely considered to be one of the best overall histories of the Medici family, which ruled, influenced, and shaped

Florence and far beyond for over 300 years. This edition is well written, easy to read, and fabulously absorbing and entertaining with twenty-four pages of black-and-white photographs and illustrations, an excellent bibliography, and two maps, one of Italy circa 1490 and the other of the Florentine Dominions.

The Medici, Ferdinand Schevill, Konecky & Konecky, New York, 1949. Historian Schevill covers a period from 1434, when Cosimo de' Medici came to power, to 1537, when his last direct heir, Alessandro, was murdered. One of the reasons I like this book is because Schevill takes what remains a controversial viewpoint: that the Medici actually added less to the stature of Florence than the Florentines themselves. As he writes in the introduction, "The Florentine society of Cosimo's day owed the extraordinary empire it wielded over its members to its brilliant achievements preceding two to three hundred years. Many of these achievements belong to the sociopolitical sphere and embrace signal improvements in government and definitely startling innovations in trade and industry. Their combined operation explains the eminence among the cities of the world attained by Florence long before the name of the Medici was ever bruited in its busy streets and squares . . . The view, still not infrequently aired, that the Florentine greatness and, particularly, its cultural greatness stem from the ruling family is completely lacking in foundation. What the Medici did, and what in the nature of the case was all they could do, was to make a contribution to that greatness in their time." It is a most convincing idea, and a most interesting read. With sixteen pages of black-and-white photos and reproductions.

The Last Medici, Harold Acton, Thames & Hudson, 1980; first published in 1932 by Faber and Faber, revised edition 1958. This is an illustrated edition—with dozens of black-and-white and color photos and reproductions—of Sir Harold's classic work, hailed by no less an expert than Bernard Berenson (the Sage of Settignano, as Acton referred to him), who wrote that "it is a work of art and not a mere chronicle of irrelevant facts." Acton chose to deal specifically with the decline of the Medici, and his book is, in fact, the only single volume I know of to focus on this one aspect of the family. Sir Harold had a gift for writing as if we were reading a gossip column, noting the smallest detail. Not that the story of the Medici needs embellishment, but readers will find this to be an exceptional portrait. (Also of related interest by Acton: *The Pazzi Conspiracy: The Plot Against the Medici,* Thames & Hudson, 1979).

Caravaggio: A Life, Helen Langdon, Farrar, Straus & Giroux, 1998, and *Caravaggio: A Passionate Life,* Desmond Seward, William Morrow, 1998. Michelangelo Merisi da Caravaggio (1573–1610) is not a painter we associate with Tuscany or Umbria, but as there are several of his paintings in the Uffizi—

including the spectacular *Young Bacchus*—and these two biographies were published in the same year (and it wasn't an anniversary year that I'm aware of), I decided to include them. I enjoyed both of these books. Reviews I read tended to prefer the longer, much more comprehensive edition by Helen Langdon, but I leave that for you to decide. Both books include color reproductions.

There is a very large body of work by and about Bernard Berenson, who, before he passed away in 1959, was internationally known as the foremost authority on Italian Renaissance art. We are fortunate in America to have the beautiful Isabella Stewart Gardner Museum in Boston, as Berenson is responsible for much of the collection there, which includes one of my favorite paintings in the world, Titian's *The Rape of Europa*. The following two titles are those which I would single out, one about and the other by Berenson: *Bernard Berenson: The Making of a Connoisseur,* Ernest Samuels, The Belknap Press of Harvard University Press, Cambridge, Massachusetts, 1979. What sets this biography apart from others, besides that it is well written, is that Nicky Mariano, Berenson's literary executor, invited Samuels to write of Berenson's life "from the inside, so to speak, and as he truly was, a gifted human being, neither wholly saint nor sinner, a man who made what peace he could with himself and with a world not notable for understanding or compassion." I would have liked more photos and reproductions, but they are, after all, to be found aplenty in other books. *Rumor and Reflection,* Bernard Berenson, Simon & Schuster, 1952. This is a wartime diary kept by Berenson from January 1, 1941, to November 12, 1944, and as such it reveals more of Berenson the man rather than Berenson the art historian.

Galileo's Daughter: A Historical Memoir of Science, Faith, and Love, Dava Sobel, Walker & Company, 1999. A wonderfully woven biography about Galileo Galilei and his daughter, Virginia, who later became Suor Maria Celeste. By incorporating letters written by Galileo's daughter (which Sobel translated from their original Italian), a fascinating story of Florence during the Medicis, Catholic doctrine, heresy, and the Cosmos is revealed. With black-and-white illustrations.

Primo Levi: Tragedy of an Optimist, Myriam Anissimov, The Overlook Press, Peter Mayer Publishers, Inc., Woodstock, New York, 1999; first published as *Primo Levi ou la tragedie d'un optimiste, editions Jean-Claude Lattes,* 1996; English translation 1998 by Steve Cox; published with the help of the French Ministry of Culture / Centre Nationale du Livre. Writer and chemist Primo Levi was not native to Tuscany or Umbria (he was born in Turin), but due to his national and international reputation and the fact that he is probably the best-known Italian to write of his experiences as a Holocaust survivor, his biography is applicable here. Not all of his works have been translated into

English, but *The Periodic Table* (Schocken Books, 1984) and *If Not Now, When?* (Summit Books, 1985) are the most widely known in the States. Levi had stated about his Auschwitz experience that "My time there did not destroy me physically or morally, as was the case with other people. I did not lose my family, my country, or my home." So it did not seem inaccurate for the general public to assume Levi had been able to reconcile that hell with himself. Yet his fall down the stairwell of his home in 1987 has been widely perceived as suicide. In 1998, I attended a lecture series, "Primo Levi and Italian Jewish Heritage," at the Istituto Italiano di Cultura in New York. The speaker, Dr. Massimo Giuliani, said that "by reading the entire work of Primo Levi, it is possible to recognize many elements of Jewishness that cannot be separated from Italian Jewish history." Italian Jewry is unique in Judaism, is indeed more like a "Judaism of the conscience," to again quote Giuliani. Levi spoke for several generations of Italian Jews, and his biography speaks for them, too. With eight pages of black-and-white photographs, and a bibliography of Levi's published works.

Love and War in the Apennines (Eric Newby, Picador, 1983; first published by Hodder and Stoughton, London, 1971) and *War in Val D'Orcia, An Italian War Diary: 1943–1944* (Iris Origo, introduction by Denis Mack Smith, David R. Godine, Publisher, Boston, 1984; original copyright 1947). These two titles are *essenziale,* and are not only among the best recommended in this book, but are also among the best books I've ever read. I've placed them together here because there is much overlap in the time period of the Second World War they relate (1942 to 1944), and although their experiences were quite different (Newby was a captured officer of the British Army, Origo an Anglo-American married to an Italian landowner), they shared a desire to write about the Italian peasants who repeatedly, in the face of danger we can hardly imagine today, helped them and countless others survive the war. Newby states that he finally decided to write his book because "I felt that comparatively little had been written about the ordinary Italian people who helped prisoners of war at great personal risk and without thought of personal gain, purely out of kindness of heart. The sort of people one can still see today working in the fields as one whizzes down the Autostrada del Sole and on any mountain road in the Apennines." For her part, Marchesa Origo says that it will be obvious to readers that she loves Italy and its people, but ultimately she believes in individuals "and in the relationship of individuals to one another. When I look back upon these years of tension and expectation, of destruction and sorrow, it is individual acts of kindness, courage or faith that illuminate them; it is in them that I trust. I remember a British prisoner of war in the Val d'Orcia helping the peasant's wife to draw water from the well, with a ragged, beaming small child at his heels. I remember the peasant's wife mending his socks, knitting him a sweater, and baking her best cake for him, in tears, on the day of his departure. These—the shared, simple acts of everyday life—are the realities on which international understanding can be built. In these, and in the realization that has come to many thousands, that people of other nations are, after all, just like themselves, we may, perhaps, place our hopes." I was moved to tears at both the cruelty and benevolence that human beings bestowed upon one another in these years. Both books depict ways of life in the mountains and valleys of Tuscany now much changed. Actually, life changed right after the war, politically, economically, socially—in every way, really. The *mezzadria* system (a method of working the land—more like a partnership between landowners and farmers—which had been in use in Tuscany since the thirteenth century) disappeared, and the Apennine villages became easier to reach when the roads were paved. The books are therefore valuable historical records. They are also exceptional, even though both authors emphasize that their experiences are not. It's true that thousands of other Italians and Allied soldiers have similar memoirs, but the majority of them were not written down, let alone published. We are fortunate to have these wonderfully written, tragic accounts of an ugly, dark time in Italy.

Peace and War: Growing Up in Fascist Italy, Wanda Newby, Picador, 1992; originally published by William Collins Sons & Co. Ltd., London, 1991. Wanda is of course mostly known as the wife of travel writer Eric Newby, but the story of her life before she met him deserves to be better known. She was born Wanda Skof in a small Slovenian village near Trieste, but in the early 1930s, Mussolini issued an order that civil servants of Yugoslav origin who were employed in parts of the country ceded to Italy after 1918 must be removed from their posts and relocated to live among Italians in other parts of Italy, as he did not trust their loyalty. As Wanda's father was a schoolteacher, the Skof family had to move, and they ended up in a village called Fontanellato, near Parma. Although her life during this period did not take her to Tuscany or Umbria, she did marry Eric in Santa Croce in Florence after the war, and I think readers will still find her story an important and endearing one.

Giacometti: A Biography, James Lord, Farrar, Straus & Giroux, 1986. An excellent biography of Giacometti, by someone who had the great fortune to know the artist. Lord has been acquainted with a number of the most prominent modern European artists. As with some of his other biographies (*Picasso and Dora, Six Exceptional Women,* and *Some Remarkable Men*), I could not put this down. Highly recommended.

POSTE ITALIANE

1100

№ 18481

CASA
BVONARROTI

BIGLIETTO D'INGRESSO
L. 300

La Toscana
(Tuscany)

"In this part of Italy, 'perspective' entered the vocabulary, and Tuscany still gives a special perspective on life. To us, one of the enduring legacies of Tuscany is the hope of becoming a Renaissance person. When the mind is challenged, and the senses are engaged, this development seems possible."

—Sonja Bullaty and Angelo Lomeo, from the preface to *Tuscany*

". . . But whatever the style, bichromatism was prevalent throughout Tuscany in the Romanesque period, and the blacks and whites, sun and shadow, sharps and flats, recurring on the old church fronts, evoke what has been called the checkerboard of Tuscan medieval politics, the alternation of Guelph and Ghibelline, Pope and Emperor, Black and White. These were the terms in which the Tuscans thought and saw."

—Mary McCarthy, *The Stones of Florence*

Side Roads of Tuscany

BY MURIEL SPARK

editor's note

This piece, by one of my favorite writers, is my favorite essay in this collection. It is beautifully written, true to the spirit of Tuscany, and an inspiration.

MURIEL SPARK is the author of a number of books, including *The Prime of Miss Jean Brodie* (HarperCollins, 1999), *Reality and Dreams* (Houghton Mifflin Company, 1997), and *The Girls of Slender Means* (New Directions, 1998).

It was by chance, not choice, that I came to Tuscany five years ago, to spend several months at the house of a friend in the olive groves between Arezzo and Siena. So that I have never been properly "on tour" in Tuscany. It is a place where I work and live, visit friends or go for day trips for a special reason—to hear a concert, look at a picture or a building or a square, or to eat at a newly discovered trattoria, coming upon a small hill town or an old parish church on the way. Although Florence is not far away it is another world from rural Tuscany. Florence is Florentine. The same with Siena and all its glories. It is Sienese.

It isn't necessarily the great and famous beauty spots we fall in love with. As with people, so with places: Love is unforeseen, and we can all find ourselves affectionately attached to the minor and the less obvious. I do not have an art historian's response to places. I can discern and admire a late-Renaissance gate, a medieval street, a Romanesque church or an Etruscan wall, but my first thoughts are for the warmth of the stone or for the clouds, when they look like a 15th-century painting with a chariot or a saint zooming up into them. I notice the light and shade on buildings grouped on a hilltop, the rich skin colors and the shapes of the people around me. I love to watch people, to sit in a trattoria listening in to their talk, imagining the rest.

Nearly every evening I go somewhere in the countryside. One of my shortest drives is to the castle-hamlet of Gargonza, past the medieval market town of Monte San Savino. Dante Alighieri stopped at the castle of Gargonza for the first few days of his exile from Florence. It is an intimate fortification, well restored, with an ancient tower and an airy forest view. In this castle-village, well-equipped cottages are offered for holiday accommodation, moderately priced for families or groups. There are no shops there. The attractions are the woodland walks and the easy access by car to both Florence and Siena and their surrounding fiefdoms.

For people too busy to cook, as I am, it is easy to eat out in this region every evening; the price of a two-course meal with wine is less than $10. I often eat at the Gargonza restaurant, which has a large outdoor terrace and the advantage, always to be looked for in Italy, of being a family concern. The approach to the Gargonza is thickly wooded, and once, at sunset, I saw a wild boar—*cinghiale* in Italian—sauntering down one of the asphalt roads nearby. It was a beautiful rippling beast. It looked around as it walked like a tourist taking the air. The restaurant itself serves a good preparation of wild boar, as well as cinghiale sauce with the pasta. (Another of the specialties is a rotolo of spinach and ricotta done in butter. There is a good wine cellar, but the house wine, white or red, is good and less expensive.)

I went to the wedding of the proprietor's daughter last year; she was married in the small and lovely Romanesque church. The owner of the Gargonza estate, Count Guicciardini of historic family, was in attendance, languidly standing at the back among the peasants and artisans, friends of the family, foreigners like myself and the local doctors and lawyers. At the wedding feast, twelve courses were served—

on such occasions in Italy, one has to learn to take tiny portions of each dish. A one-man band, who also sang, enlivened the celebration.

I return again and again to Pienza, originally a medieval town that was replanned by Pius II in the 15th century. Its central square is small, enclosed by a church and three palaces, all of appropriate and elegant proportions—an attractive example of urban planning. Walking around the square of Pienza, I often have the illusion of being in a roofless temple, as in the Parthenon.

Near Pienza is Montepulciano, grandly endowed with architecture. Long ago someone gave me a relic of the cardinal-saint, Robert Bellarmine, and I was delighted to discover that this was his birthplace. It is a tourist spot, and therefore comparatively expensive.

Near Pienza, too, are several terme, or sulfur-bath resorts. Chianciano is one of the best known. For me, these towns have too much of an air of people caring greatly for their own health, and really quite healthy people at that; there are smart shops and hairdressers and luxury imports unobtainable in the rest of the region. At Bagno Vignoni, another hot-springs place near Pienza, a fountain in the piazza takes the form of an ancient bath filled with the hot curative waters.

When people come to visit me, I usually take them to see the majestic "Madonna del Parto" of Piero della Francesca. This fresco is to be found entirely on its own, in a small cemetery chapel at Monterchi. The surrounding countryside with its broad sweep of cultivated, undulating fields seems to be out of a painting of the 15th century. The picture is planned to represent a stage, the Virgin herself both dramatic protagonist and actual theater, as she undoes her dress to prepare for the historic curtain-rise of the Incarnation. In parallel action, two angels on either side hold back the curtains of the canopy beneath which she stands. Throughout this part of the Tuscan countryside, one can still see indigenous faces that resemble Piero della Francesca's famous model; there is something, too, in the setting of the head on the sturdy neck that is characteristic of many Tuscans today.

From Monterchi, it is only three miles to Sansepolcro, where Piero della Francesca was born. His stupendous fresco of the Resurrection is in the museum.

The streets of the old city are typically medieval to Renaissance. There are good hotel restaurants in Sansepolcro and, between Monterchi and Anghiari at Castello di Sorci, there is an old, capacious farmhouse where a good fixed menu of six courses, with local wine, is served at an all-inclusive price of less than $5. Here again, as in so many hidden places of Tuscany, there is a feeling of timelessness. In the ground-floor kitchens, cooks can be seen skillfully making the pasta, by hand, in different designs.

The city of Cortona is too well known, too crowded, for my comfort. For some reason, when in Tuscany, I find an abundance of English and American voices around me an irritant (this is not so in Rome, which has been cosmopolitan from its foundation). But to be in the midst of an English-speaking fraternity in this wild and natural Italy depresses me greatly. I wonder: What am I doing here? I could just as well have stayed at home. Did I come all this way to hear things like, "Why do they close the museums at the lunch hour?"—an innocent question that opens a huge cultural gulf, since the long midday meal and repose are sacred to the Italians. (Only catering establishments are absolved from the near-religious duty of going home to eat at il tocco, 1 o'clock.) And I remember an English visitor asking me, "Are you stationed out here?" Recalling this, I look out of the window and see Gino the horse farmer riding by proudly with his beasts; nobody has told him he lives "out here," and as for me, there's nothing in my life that corresponds to being stationed.

Cortona, then, is one of the places I avoid, despite its art treasures and antiquities. Even—perhaps especially—in winter, when the flocks of visitors have gone home and the streets are all the more deserted, all the more gloomy, like Edinburgh after the Festival. Better the places that never have this swarming influx.

But to me there is a fascination about Cortona: the road to it that leads south from Arezzo. This indeed is one of the classic Tuscan drives, through the rolling basin of the Valdichiana. From where I live, one comes first to Castiglion Fiorentino, a small town mainly composed of one street that rises up to the very fine municipal arcade, designed by Vasari. There is an old marketplace, from which there is an impressive view, framed by the arches.

In the picture gallery, modestly displayed, is a strange, hypnotic painting of St. Francis receiving the stigmata, beloved of Kenneth Clark, by a little-known mid-15th-century artist, Bartolomeo della Gatta. St. Francis and his companions are unusually represented in green habits in an almost cubistic formation of rocks.

Also on the way to Cortona it is worth stopping to see Montecchio, the recently restored stronghold of Sir John Hawkwood, a 14th-century English condottiere.

Cortona on its hillside is splendid in the evening light. Just outside the gate, I go to an amusing restaurant, Tonino, where a continuous dish called antipastissimo is offered. This consists of a relay of ingenious delicacies, hot and cold, no more than a mouthful of each, but perhaps as many as 40, swiftly served by several waiters. It is amazing how the nibbles mount up into a full meal—I have never been able to finish this awesome and very carefully planned feast. I appreciate good food, but it is seldom that a meal also makes me laugh: This one is positively witty. To complete the picture, Tonino's brochure is translated into joyful English, assuring you, for example, that their "fresch, comfortable cellar is a place for rediscover the old things' taste."

Up the valley of the Casentino, a grand mountain view is to be seen on the way to Camaldoli, where there is a hermitage and monastery, with a few souvenir shops and two unexceptional restaurants. The church has been much restored since its foundation in the 13th century; it is now predominantly 18th-century Baroque and contains some minor Tuscan paintings and frescoes. The main attraction for me is the old monastic pharmacy. There you can purchase such potions as amaro tonico, which is described as a neurotonic and digestive and is recommended for nervous exhaustion, for disturbances of the liver and for physical and intellectual stress. It is prepared from roots and aromatic herbs. Try it if you like; I haven't. The pure air and stillness of this great forest are enough balm for my physical and mental stress. Like so many of the vast valley and mountain scenes of Tuscany, the prospect from the heights of Camaldoli makes for a generous heart; it is one where mean thoughts are out of place, where the human spirit responds easily to the expansive benevolence of nature and its silence.

The long, shady, forest road to Vallombrosa, glorious in the leafy autumn, is another place I sally forth to. This is on the Pratomagno, a mountain ridge, and leads up to the 17th-century Benedictine abbey of Vallombrosa, quite modern for these parts (the original foundation was 11th century). Here, too, is a scene of wooded hills, canyons, crags and rivers that belongs to no century at all. A short way above Vallombrosa, on the site of a 13th-century hermitage, is a modern edifice, the Paradisino, which bears a plaque commemorating the sojourn of the supreme English poet Giovanni Milton in 1638. The inscription goes on to say that he was enamored of this forest and these skies, and one can well believe it. The view from the Paradisino has a feeling of "Paradise Lost," perhaps set to music (Wagner).

Across the highway bridge is Chianti, the vineyard country with its noble farmhouses in the midst of acre upon acre of cultivated plenty. Castellina in Chianti, Radda in Chianti are typical of many wine towns surrounded by vineyards, olive groves and thick woods.

Wine merchants offer their tastings. Castellina has a good restaurant, the Antica Trattoria la Torre. It is comparatively high priced, since in Chianti there is a more prosperous, upper-crust society than one finds near my own central zone of Arezzo. Farther west, San Gimignano, the little town with numerous towers, is a place beloved of the Grand Tourists of the last century, and the manifold tourists of this; like Cortona, it is a place where I don't go often, lest I be jostled.

Arezzo is the nearest big town to the spot where I spend part of my life. The remains of the original walls are Etruscan, it has a number of notable medieval and Renaissance churches and palazzi, but much of the town is modern. The overwhelming attractions of the city are the abundant frescoes of Piero della Francesca. In the cathedral is his fresco of Mary Magdalen, while the church of San Francesco holds his depiction of the Legend of the Holy Cross. Paintings made churchgoing a wonderful picture show for the faithful. I often think, as I look at them, how fortunate it is for us that so few people could read in those days, and were obligingly informed by these wonderful stories in pictures. The Tuscan face of the Madonna del Parto is here in other roles.

Even closer to my second home are the two hill towns I visit most for such practical purposes as shopping or eating out: Monte San Savino and Lucignano. I have grown fond of them.

Serene Lucignano has a simple main street circling the summit of a hill with a dominant collegiate church of the 13th century. It is good to approach Lucignano on a winter day, for the winter light in Tuscany is extraordinary. There are two excellent restaurants where I go on alternate days during my Tuscan visits: La Rocca and La Tavernetta, both of which are run by families rightly proud of their fine and inventive cooking.

At Monte San Savino, there is no place to eat of any account, but until last year I used to be invited to lunch every Thursday at the home of an elderly signora of that place. She was in her 80's and had wonderful and terrible stories to tell as we made our leisurely way through a meal of Tuscan rarities, cunningly prepared with the herbs and flavorings she knew were the right ones.

Thrilling and terrible were her stories. The Germans had taken her villa during the war—it still stands high on a hillside, but her house at the time I knew her was in the piazza. The Germans had shot her 19-year-old son; a street bears his name. She herself, with her daughter, had been put on a truck bound for a train connection to dreaded Germany, but one of the officers on guard, noted for his rigid toughness, nevertheless put them off in the countryside because of a mutual love and knowledge of music.

Love stories, escape stories, stories of the wars and occupations, of her youth, of provincial balls, of visits to the opera: Those Thursday lunches were unforgettable. After lunch, she would play the piano and sing romantic songs from the turn of the century. My favorite was called "Tormento," which she rendered with her whole heart. When she returned the visit, she would bring with her those things befitting a day in the country: her embroidery, her sketchbook and a book of poems by Leopardi.

Carolina died on her 90th birthday. She seemed to sum up my Tuscan experience. A whole people, the product of civilized time past, the product of the dramatic landscape, the Tuscans are also the progenitors of what one finds there. It is their spirit of endurance and rejoicing in the goodness of life that inspired the architecture, the paintings, the churches and those ancient cultures of olive groves and vineyards which are the essence of Tuscany.

Savoring the Joys of Market Day

BY NANCY HARMON JENKINS

∼

editor's note

The daily and weekly markets of Italy can be as dramatic and entertaining as a stage production. If the big markets of Florence are Broadway, the country markets are Off-Broadway: the same great quality and characters, but a little easier to find the plot.

The following two pieces highlight features that are common among all markets in Italy as well as those unique to a Tuscan market, in Camucia.

NANCY HARMON JENKINS is the author of *Flavors of Tuscany: Traditional Recipes From the Italian Countryside* (Broadway Books, 1998) and *The Mediterranean Diet Cookbook* (Bantam Books, 1994), among others. She is also a contributing editor to *Food & Wine* and writes frequently for *The New York Times*.

Nice, fresh octopus, live octopus!" cries the fishmonger from his display in a corner of the Saturday market in Monopoli, a little fishing port south of Bari, north of Brindisi, on Italy's Apulian coast. "I've got octopus!" he sings. The octopus, its pale, opalescent arms stretched seductively over a bed of crushed ice, does indeed look fresh, but the fishmonger misinterprets my hesitation.

"*Non le vuole, signora?*" he pretends to plead. "Don't you want any?"

"I can't," I say. Because I'm traveling, I don't have a stove, and much as I crave the opportunity to do a little work with some red wine and cinnamon and bay leaves on that octopus, it just isn't possible.

"It's fresh," he says again. "Try it!" And before I can turn away, he has proffered a trembling chunk of octopus flesh, raw, glistening like wet alabaster and tasting faintly of brine.

Octopus for breakfast is not to everyone's taste. But my experience in Monopoli's lively open-air market, which sprawls under awnings and tent-sized umbrellas across the town's main square each weekday morning, is a good illustration of the marvels in store for the traveler in Italy who ventures into local food markets. Good food, of course, but more than that—a sharpened sense of what folklorists call foodways, meaning how and why people grow and cook and eat the things they do. In the end, the market is the place where curious and watchful visitors begin to appreciate what it is that makes Italian food so interesting, so pleasureful.

In a lifetime of traveling, I have found that hanging out in food markets like these is one of the best ways to get inside the head, so to speak, of the town I'm visiting, to shed the artificial role of tourist and start, if only in my own head, to feel like a participant. A food market offers a way to engage in conversation, if only made up of gesture, wink and nudge. With a minimum armory of phrases ("*Quanto costa,*" "*Troppo caro*" and "*Dovè il ristorante?*" are among the most useful), you will discover such invaluable lore as how to tell the difference between handmade and machine-made mozzarella, or which eating place of the many that surround each market provides the best zuppa di pesce.

Market people, shoppers and sellers alike, are always eager to talk about food, to tell you how they grow it, how much better it is than the exact same product from two valleys away, how their grandmothers always prepared it and what they do nowadays to lower the fat content of their traditional diet. (It's true: Given half a chance, people in the most remote parts of the Italian peninsula will recount in loving detail how they are reducing the fat in their meals.)

You can learn a lot through the language of food. About seasonality, for instance: In Italian markets you will not find artichokes in August, asparagus in October or wild mushrooms in March.

About regions, too: There is still a strong sense of regional pride throughout Italy (although this sentiment is changing so fast that social scientists have a hard time keeping up). Neapolitans wouldn't know what to do with a Piedmont sausage, and Venetian cooks would look askance at the offerings of a Genovese fishmonger.

Ask a Florentine for the Mercato Centrale and you may draw a blank look. Ask for the San Lorenzo, however, and the light of understanding breaks. The great San Lorenzo market in Florence, just a short walk down the Borgo San Lorenzo from the Duomo, merits a visit for architectural reasons alone. The nineteenth-century cast-iron building is a magnificent two-story landmark—one of the largest covered markets in Europe. And as the main supplier of foodstuffs basic and esoteric for the capital of a region that takes food very, very seriously, the market is without peer. Of special interest here is the main, entry-level floor of the building, which is devoted to everything but fresh produce (that's all upstairs and well worth a visit, too)—cheeses from all over Italy, particularly the pecorino (sheep's milk) cheeses for which Tuscany is noted, fine olive oils from both famous and little-known Tuscan producers, fresh pasta and meat—lots and lots of meat, both freshly butchered and cured into an enormous variety of flavorful sausages and hams. (These can be purchased by the etto—100 grams, or just over three and a quarter ounces—for those who want a sample.)

For an American, the confrontation with a hanging carcass of lamb, pork or Chianina beef may be a little startling, yet it is instructive. Chianina, for instance, is a Tuscan breed of white cattle, originally prized as working animals and now grown primarily for their well-marbled flesh. T-bone steak from a Chianina is what makes bistecca fiorentina such a favorite in Florentine restaurants.

In the fall, the San Lorenzo meat stalls are also piled with wild and semiwild game—boar, pheasants and other birds, wild hare and other creatures that were once hunted in the country but now tend to be raised in game parks or imported from the wilder parts of Europe, such as they are.

Culinary exotica like these are not the only thing to look for in Italian markets. In the country towns of Tuscany and Umbria at this time of year, visitors will find wild mushrooms in shades from dark sienna to pale biscuit heaped in baskets, their unmistakable odor mixing the bosky and the carnal. And at any time of the year, the smell of roasting meat, garlic, fennel and rosemary permeates the air, drawing the hungry to the porchetta stands with their whole spit-roasted pigs. Market-goers line up to buy porchetta sandwiches, generous slabs of roasted meat tucked in a crisp bun with crosta (crackling) and grasso (the clean white fat, redolent of garlic and herbs). Add a bottle of local red wine, a couple of sun-ripened tomatoes, a wedge of fresh or lightly aged pecorino cheese, along with some grapes or strawberries or cherries, and you have the foundation of a splendid picnic. Ask the cheese seller or the porchetta vendor for a good picnic site, and you may be directed to a park beneath a medieval fortress, a mountaintop outcropping with a wonderful view or a clean, sandy brook known only to locals.

All Italian country markets, and many city markets, too, have extensive sections of housewares and hardware—perhaps some fine linen sheets and towels, edged with lace and cutwork, or minimally useful but nonetheless attractive kitchen gadgets like the pale-green porcelain-corked bottles for oil or vinegar that are increasingly hard to find. There are always pots and pans of earthenware or cheap aluminum, sometimes of brass and copper, and wooden cutting boards, long-handled spoons and other implements. And there are gardening tools, some of exceptionally cunning design.

In the Tuscan country markets that I frequent, my favorite objects are two: a zappa, the long-handled cast-steel hoe that is a useful tool for Tuscan farmers, and a girarrosto toscano, a clockwork spit for hearth cooking. The zappa may be a bit impractical to bring home, but the girarrosto, about $100, weighs close to 30 pounds, and if you can carry it onto the plane (I wouldn't dare put it in the cargo holds), you may be the first on your block with a genuine model.

How do you find the market in an Italian town or city? While major cities usually have daily markets (most are closed Sunday, fish markets Sunday and Monday), small towns most often have a weekly market day, which differs from town to town. In my own neighborhood in southern Tuscany, shoppers know that if it's Tuesday it must be Montepulciano, while Thursday is the big market in Camucia and on Saturday the country folk from the mountains join tourists and art students at the Cortona market. Any hotel concierge should be able to direct you to the right place. When in doubt, look for streams of shoppers overburdened with bags of provender and ask them.

Throughout Italy, food markets operate only in the morning (food shops, on the other hand, usually reopen after the long lunch break). Go early to see the place in all its fresh and pearly glory (but not too early—public markets don't usually open before 8 A.M. or so); go later, around noon, if you want to see the market in a riotous frenzy building toward the climax of the midday meal.

In the end, of course, food is what market-watching is all about. And for a traveling cook, that's the hard part, to gaze slack-jawed with wonder at all this magnificence, and know that there's no way to cook it. And no way of getting it past those cute little Department of Agriculture beagles in their green jackets when you have to confront U.S. Customs.

Picnicking on the local produce is one way to satisfy the consuming urge, renting a house with a kitchen is another. But a surprising number of food products can be brought back to this country. Forget about any pork or other cured meat product (don't even try!), but hard cheeses—if they're aged beyond ninety days, as many are—are O.K., as are other nonmeat, cured or preserved or otherwise packaged goods, such as pickles, jams, honeys, olives and olive oils, vinegars and other condiments, pasta, rice and other grains, dried beans and lentils, dried spices and dried mushrooms. You can't, alas, bring back the fragrance of basil, the sharpness of freshly squeezed blood-orange juice, the sweetness of peaches and melons and figs so ripe they are on the verge of evanescence. But that, after all, is what memories are for.

Market Day in a Tuscan Town

BY FRANCES MAYES

~

editor's note

This piece originally appeared in the travel section of *The New York Times* on July 19, 1992. Later, it became part of a chapter titled "A Long Table Under the Trees" in *Under the Tuscan Sun*. I decided to include it because it existed first as an article, and it's a wonderful depiction of one of the essential aspects of life in the Tuscan countryside. After the piece appeared in *The New York Times,* a reader wrote a letter to say that she, her husband, and two friends were inspired to visit Camucia, which she described as "an experience we all relished and continue to enjoy. It just goes to show that filing information away for future reference is worthwhile even if the article is four years old by the time we use it."

FRANCES MAYES, in addition to *Under the Tuscan Sun,* is the author of *Bella Tuscany* (Broadway Books, 1999), five books of poetry, and a college textbook. Her articles, essays, and poems have appeared in *House Beautiful, Food and Wine, Poetry, The Virginia Quarterly Review,* and *Manoa,* among others, and she teaches creative writing at San Francisco State University.

Market day is Thursday in Camucia, the lively town at the bottom of Cortona. Most tourists in Tuscany pass right through Camucia; it's just the "modern" spillover from the venerable and dominant hilltown above. But "modern" is relative. Among the frutta and verdura shops, the hardware and seed stores, you happen on a couple of Etruscan tombs. Near the butcher I like are remnants of a villa, an immense curly iron gate and swag of garden wall. Camucia, bombed in World War II, has its share of chestnut trees, photographable doors and shuttered houses.

On market day, a couple of streets are blocked to traffic. The vendors arrive an hour or so early, at about 7 A.M., unfolding what seems like whole stores or supermarket aisles from specially made trucks and wagons. One wagon sells local pecorino, the sheep's milk cheese that can be soft and almost creamy, or aged and strong as a barnyard, along with several grades of parmesan. The aged parmesan is crumbly and rich, wonderful to nibble as I walk around the market. I'm hunting and gathering food for a dinner for three new friends.

My favorite wagons belong to the two porchetta maestros. The whole pig, parsley entwined with the tail, apple—or sometimes a big mushroom—in its mouth, stretches across the cutting board. Sometimes the decapitated head sits aside at an angle, eyeing the rest of its body that has been stuffed with herbs and bits of its own ears, etc. (best not to inquire too closely), then roasted in a wood oven. You can buy a panino (a crusty roll) with nothing on it but slabs of porchetta, or you can buy pork to take home, lean or with crispy, fatty skin.

One of the lords of the porchetta wagons looks very much like his subject: little vacant eyes, glistening skin and bulbous forearms. His fingers are short and porky, with bitten-down nails. He's smiling, extolling his pig's virtues, but when he turns to his wife, he snarls. Her lips are set in a permanent tight half smile. I've bought from him before and his porchetta is delicious. This time I buy from the milder man at the next stand. I ask for extra sale (salt), which is what the indefinable stuffing is called. I like it but find myself picking through to see if there's something peculiar in it.

Though the pig is useful and tasty in all its parts and preparations, the slow-roasted porchetta must be its apogee. Before I move on to the vegetables, I spot a pair of sandals and balance my pocketbook and shopping bag while I try on one. Perfect, and less than $10. I drop them in with the porchetta and parmesan.

Scarves and tablecloths float from awnings, toilet cleaners, tapes and T-shirts are stacked in bins and on folding tables. Besides buying food, you can dress, plant a garden and stock a household from this market. There are local crafts for sale but you have to look for them. The Tuscan markets aren't like ones in Mexico, with wonderful weaving and pottery. It's a wonder these markets continue at all, given the sophistication of Italian life and the standard of living in this area.

The ironworking tradition is still somewhat in evidence. Occasionally I see good andirons and handy fireplace grills. My favorite is a holder for whole prosciutto, an iron grip with handle mounted on a board for ease in slicing; maybe someday I'll find I need that much prosciutto and buy one. One week I bought handwoven baskets made from dark supple willow twigs, perfect for the peaches and cherries.

One woman sells table and bed linens, some with thick monograms, all of which must have been gathered from farms and villas. She has three mounds of old lace. Perhaps some of it was made on the nearby island, Isola Maggiore in Lake Trasimeno. Women still sit in the doorways there, hooking lace in the afternoon light.

I find two enormous square linen pillowcases with miles of inset lace and ribbons. Ten thousand lire (about $9), same as the sandals, seems to be the magic number today. Of course I will have to have the pillows especially made. When I buy some striped linen dish towels, I notice several goatskins hanging from a hook. I have in mind that they would look terrific on the cotto, the old brick floors at my house. The four the man has are too small but he says to come back next week. He tries to convince me that his sheepskins would be better anyway, but they don't appeal to me.

I'm wending my way toward the produce, but walk up to the bar for a coffee. Actually, I stop with an excuse to stare. People from surrounding areas come not only to shop but also to greet friends, to make business arrangements.

The din around the Camucia market is a lovely swarm of voices, many of them speaking in the local Val di Chiana dialect; I don't understand most of what they're saying but I do hear one recurring habit.

They do not use the *ch* sound for *c*, but slide it into an *s* sound. "Shento," they say for "cento" (100), instead of the usual "chento." Once I heard someone say "cappushino," for "cappuccino," though the usual affectionate shortening of that is "cappuch." Their town is not "Camuchia," but "Camushea." Odd that the *c* is often the affected letter. Around Siena people substitute an *h* sound for *c*—"hasa" and "Hoca-Hola."

Whatever the local habit with *c*, they're all talking. Around the bar, groups of farmers, maybe a hundred men, mill about. Some play cards. Their wives are off in the crowd, loading their bags with tiny strawberries, basil plants with dangling roots, dried mushrooms, perhaps a fish from the one stand that sells seafood from the Adriatic. Unlike the Italians who take their thimbleful of espresso in one quick swallow, I sip the black, black coffee.

A friend says Italy is getting to be just like everywhere else, homogenized and Americanized, she says disparagingly. I want to drag her here and stand her in this doorway. The men have the look of their lives—perhaps we all do. Hard work, their faces and bodies affirm. All are lean, not a pound of extra fat anywhere. They look cured by the sun, so deeply tan they probably never go pale in winter. Their country clothes are serviceable, rough—they don't "dress," they just get dressed. They wear, as well, a natural dignity. Surely some are canny, crusty, cruel, but they look totally present, unhidden and alive.

Some are missing teeth but they smile widely without embarrassment. I look in one man's eyes and the left one is milky white with veins only, like an exploded marble. The other is black as the center of a sunflower. A retarded boy wanders among them, neither catered to nor ignored. He's just there, living his life like the rest of us.

At home I plan, though I frequently alter the menu as I shop. Here, I only begin to think when I see what's ripe this week. My impulse is to buy too much. At first I was miffed when tomatoes or peas spoiled when I got around to cooking them a few days later. Finally I caught on that what you buy today is ready to eat immediately. This also explained another puzzle; I never understood why Italian refrigerators are so minute until I realized that they don't store food the way we do. The Sub-Zero giant I have at home begins to seem almost institutional compared to the toy fridge I have here. The habit I have comes from buying produce at home that is picked before it's ripe.

This week the small purple artichokes with long stems are in. There's my first course. Steamed, stuffed with tomatoes, garlic, yesterday's bread and parsley, then doused with oil and vinegar. The slender beans are irresistible. I'll slice some fennel into them, add a few dry olives. Can I have two salads, because the beans also would be good with raw vinaigrette? Why not? I buy white peaches for a recipe with macaroons and white wine I've been meaning to try. But

for tonight's dessert, the cherries are perfect. I take a kilo, then set off to find a pitter back in the other part of the market.

Since I don't know the word I'm reduced to sign language. I do know ciliegia (cherry), which helps. I've noticed in French and Italian country desserts, the cooks don't bother to pit the cherries but I like to use the pitter when they're served in a dish. These I'll steep in Chianti with a little sugar and lemon. When I buy bread, I'll pick up some biscotti to go with them. I decide on some tiny yellow potatoes still half covered with dirt. Just a dribble of oil and some rosemary and they'll roast in the oven.

I could complete my shopping for this meal right here. I pass cages of guinea hens, ducks and chickens, as well as rabbits. If my friend Paul, a chef, were here, I know we'd be going home with some trembling creature in the trunk. Since I had a black Angora rabbit as a pet once, I can't look with cold eyes on the two spotted ones nibbling carrots in the dusty Alitalia flight bag. I intend to stop at the butcher's for a veal roast. The butcher's is bad enough. I admit it's not logical. If you eat meat, you might as well recognize where it comes from. But the drooped heads and closed eyelids of the quail and pigeon make me stop and stare. Rooster heads, chicken feet (with nails like Mrs. Ricker's, my grandmother's Rook partner), the clump of fur to show the skinned rabbit is not a cat, whole cows hanging by their feet—all these things make my stomach flip. Surely they're not going to eat those fluffy chicks. I love roast chicken. Could I ever wring a neck?

I have as much as I can carry. The other stop I'll make is at the cooperative cantina for the local red and white wine. If I had a demijohn, I could back the car up and get the wine hosed in from what looks exactly like a gasoline pump.

Near the end of the sinuous line of market stalls, a woman sells flowers from her garden. She wraps an armful of pink zinnias in newspaper and I lay them under the straps of my bag. The sun is ferocious and people are beginning to pack up for siesta. A woman who has not sold many of her striped lime and yellow towels looks weary. She dumps the dog sleeping in her folding chair and settles down for a rest before she begins to fold.

On my way out, I see a man in a sweater, despite the heat. The trunk of his minuscule Fiat is piled with black grapes that have warmed all morning in the sun. He offers me one. The hot sweetness breaks open in my mouth. I have never tasted anything so essential in my life as this grape on this morning. The flavor, older than the Etruscans and deeply fresh and pleasing, just leaves me stunned. Such richness, the big globes, the heap of dusty grapes cascading out of two baskets. I ask for un grappolo, a bunch. The taste will stay with me all summer.

From *Under the Tuscan Sun* by Frances Mayes © 1996 published by Chronicle Books, San Francisco.

This Side of Paradiso

By Jason Epstein

∿

editor's note

The dream of many a visitor is to rent a place to stay—to live, really—in Tuscany, for a week, a month, or longer. Prospective tenants will have no trouble finding a suitable property (you'll find a number of sources to contact throughout this book) as the region of Tuscany dominates the Italian vacation rental market.

This piece is one of the best I've read about "living" in Tuscany.

JASON EPSTEIN writes frequently about travel, food, and wine for a variety of magazines and is an executive editor at Random House.

Some sixty years ago, the eccentric—one might as well say insane—Italian Futurist F. T. Marinetti wanted to replace the traditional Italian diet with one that reflected the modern world of radio, fast trains, and ocean liners: a diet with a taste of steel and electricity. Above all, he wanted to abolish pasta. "We stand on the last promontory of the centuries! We will glorify war—the world's only hygiene," Marinetti had written as a young man in 1909, in his *Futurist Manifesto*. "We will destroy the museums, libraries, academies of every kind. . . . We will sing of great crowds excited by work, by pleasure, and by riot; we will sing of the multicoloured, polyphonic tides of revolution in the modern capitals; we will sing of the vibrant nightly fervour of arsenals and shipyards blazing with violent electric moons. . . . It is from Italy that we launch through the world this violently upsetting incendiary manifesto of ours. With it, today, we establish *Futurism,* because we want to free this land from its smelly gangrene of professors, archaeologists, *ciceroni,* and antiquarians. For too long Italy has been a dealer in second-hand clothes. We mean to free her from the numberless museums that cover her like so many graveyards."

In 1919, Marinetti joined the young Fascist Party, but he soon abandoned it. In 1926, when Mussolini tried to lure him back with an offer of membership in his Italian Academy, Marinetti, an anarchist and a snob, refused. Mussolini was lucky to be rid of him, for Marinetti's antics might have caused a rebellion when, four years later, he issued his manifesto of Futurist cooking. Pasta is passé, he wrote, and it makes people heavy and brutish. (Perhaps he was thinking of Mussolini himself.) He proposed instead a menu of *consumato* of roses and sunshine, roast lamb in lion sauce, and a Mediterranean "zig, zug, zag." There would be no more spaghetti, no knives and forks, no after-dinner speeches. To replace "anti-virile pastasciutta," he suggested nutritious radio waves, aerofood, and similar Dada foolishness. He wasn't joking. He apparently believed that human beings should resemble machines.

Today, Marinetti is all but forgotten by a soul-starved age that has been dispossessed by countless alienating technologies—an age, moreover, that has made a religion of noodles. I, too, had all but forgotten Marinetti until I found myself awake and restless on a flight to Italy recently and took from a pile of books I had brought a copy of his *Futurist Cookbook*, reissued by Trefoil, a London firm that specializes in the writings of such modernists as Le Corbusier, Raymond Loewy, and Buckminster Fuller. As I sat there, thinking of the pasta and other pleasures I looked forward to in Tuscany, these men seemed to me as passé as Futurism itself, and their work as old-fashioned as Saarinen's grimy and crumbling T.W.A. terminal, where I had awaited my flight three hours earlier.

It must have been the Tuscan hills on a September morning that inspired Dante's Paradiso: the pure and boundless light; the planted hillsides, with their rows of vines and silver olive trees, looking as if they had been painted; the valleys, with their fields of sunflowers, the walled towns in a blue haze cresting the hills. To see all this from the hilltop farmhouse that some friends and I rented for a few weeks is to know what Dante meant when he said that he had found, at last, all the leaves of the universe bound into one volume.

Our farmhouse, pale yellow trimmed in tan, with a classical façade, a Palladian roof, and symmetrical windows framed by shutters, turned out to be a much larger and more splendid place than we needed or had expected. It came complete with servants: Silvia, the cook; her husband, Francesco, who looked after the garden; and Ivana, the maid, who helped in the kitchen and waited on table, and who believed that if she spoke in a lilting cadence, as if addressing an infant or a cat, and shaped each word carefully with her hands, we would surely understand her fine Tuscan speech.

Some weeks earlier, I had written to the agent from whom we rented the farmhouse to say that I would like to cook some of our meals myself, and she replied that Silvia would be delighted. This turned out to be true. Silvia proved a joy to cook with and, unlike many cooks in her situation, soon found my meddling in her kitchen entertaining rather than a threat or a nuisance. By the time our stay was over, she had taught me more than I could ever have learned by deconstructing the dandified tourist dishes we were served in the half-dozen expensive Tuscan restaurants that we visited. Yet the beginning of our collaboration was difficult, for on the day of our arrival, when I accepted Silvia's invitation to come down to her spotless kitchen, with its floor of red tiles, and ran my hand along her white marble counters and admired her eight-burner stove, with its electronic pilots and enough oven space for a half-dozen pies, she could see at once that I was disappointed.

In those first, stiff moments, as we groped toward a mixture of English and Italian that would suit us both, I asked, more brusquely than I meant to, whether we couldn't buy in the market something better than the cottony, unsalted bread with a spongy crust that I found on the counter. "*Insipido*" was the tactless word I used. She said, with an apologetic shrug, "No. No one has time to bake bread at home now, and the old village bakeries are gone. This is what they sell here now." And when I asked if she had some good ripe tomatoes—round red ones rather than the pale plum tomatoes in her basket—she said, "Not in the market, but maybe Franco can find a few in his garden." But why, her puzzled expression implied, would I want red, ripe tomatoes? Then she laid a few scrawny, factory-raised chickens from Livorno on the counter for our first dinner, and I asked whether there wasn't a farmer in the neighborhood who sold plump, farm-grown chickens. "No," she said. "The *contadini* raise their chickens for themselves. Everyone else goes to the Superal and buys these." But then, sensing that my disappointment had gone too far, she said, "Look at this," and, with a confident smile, opened a big stainless-steel freezer and removed a pale-pink haunch of what looked like veal. "*Bellissimo!*" she said.

"*Vitello!*" I replied, relieved to find at last something to praise.

"*Vitello no,*" she said, holding the haunch up to the light and patting it. "*Cinghiale.* Maybe for tomorrow, if you like, or *lunedì,* if you'd rather. Wild pig. The best part." She thrust her hip out and rubbed the top of her rump to show where the meat had come from. "Shot in the forest. The best part."

"Fine," I told her. "Anytime you like." I was charmed by her good nature and by the way her face reacted instantly to each passing emotion, mine as well as her own.

At that moment, it became plain that Silvia and I were going to get along. She handed me a piece of pecorino—the straw-colored cheese made from sheep's milk—that Franco, she said, had bought from a farmer on a back road to Florence. The cheese had a slight sharpness tucked beneath its gentle surface, and it was better, I told Silvia, than the pecorino I buy on Grand Street, in Manhattan. She answered not in words but with an uplifted right shoulder, as if to say, "What else would you expect?"

But why were Silvia's bread and chickens such miserable imitations of what could be found on Grand Street and in countless other post-modern culinary enclaves in the United States? At first, I was puzzled, but soon the answer became obvious. America's appetite for what might be called retro food—authentic reproductions of classic staples, such as crusty, firm-textured bread baked in brick ovens, and well-fed poultry raised not in cramped factory cages but in airy outdoor yards—was a reaction to the mechanized American diet that accompanied the hegemony of the supermarket after the Second World War. Except for a few items, like Silvia's bread and chickens, the Tuscans had yet to suffer the full assault of this modernization, and so they felt no urgency to re-create the old forms of production. It occurred to me that this might change as the E.C. imposed its uniform agricultural standards throughout Europe and forced the Tuscans to restore their old village bakeries and poultry yards in self-defense. But this wasn't about to happen during our Tuscan holiday, and it didn't matter. The rest of Silvia's ingredients, to say nothing of her technique, were as authentic as the Tuscan hills where she had grown up and where her family had lived, as far as she knew, forever.

Silvia was in her forties, though she seemed younger; and she had two grown sons—one in the carabinieri, the other still at school. She was no longer slim, but with her dyed yellow hair, her enthusiasm, and her agility in the kitchen, she seemed to me girlish. I would have been happy spending all my time with her at the farm-house or exploring the markets at Castelfiorentino, at the base of our hill, and at Gambassi Terme, in the hills on the road to San Gimignano, some twenty kilometres to the south. But the others wanted to visit churches and look at pictures, so every morning, despite unusually hot September weather, we would set out for Volterra or Siena or Arezzo or Florence or Lucca. None of these cities were more than an hour away, on roads that twisted through the beautiful Tuscan hills, their slopes covered with neat rows of vines bearing the Sangiovese grapes from which the local Chianti gets its flavor.

Each day, after we had visited the churches and seen the pictures, we would find a place for lunch. Before lunch, I would look in the shops for some good bread, always in vain, and a ripe tomato or some good ham and local cheese. One day, in a small shop in a town called Radda, where a number of English and American vacationers rent villas for the summer, I was lucky enough to find two farm-raised chickens. As I was paying for them, it struck me that I was as eager to surprise Silvia with my discoveries as I was to provide for our own meals.

I was curious, during my trip, about what difference, if any, Italy's new right-wing government, with its Fascist and federalist allies, had made in the few months it had been in power. Were the alarming prophecies that I had heard in New York likely to come true? Were the Florentines and other Tuscans, some of whom had been defiant of Mussolini, now ready to shave their heads, buy black leather jackets, and parade through their cities, as a band of skinheads had paraded in the rich northern city of Vicenza four months earlier? Was there a new Marinetti, once more proposing to abolish Italy's corrupt and stultifying past? Was it in his spirit that the bread had been rendered tasteless and the chickens wrapped in plastic?

In Siena, at any rate, nothing seemed to have changed. The fan-shaped Piazza del Campo, its lovely brick pavement sloping down toward the 700-year-old Palazzo Pubblico, was no different from what I remembered from my last visit to Siena, thirty years ago. Except for a few Sienese on motor scooters, and the café, with its San Pellegrino umbrellas, very little can have changed—at least outwardly—since the time of Cosimo de' Medici.

To judge by the expensive shops along the narrow Gothic streets that surround the piazza, Siena's 60,000 inhabitants were evidently prospering despite Italy's widely proclaimed economic mess, including a national debt that is said to be a 120 percent of last year's GDP. The lira was very low, and the extravagant Italian pension system still took 40 percent of the national budget. There is no telling how much had been stolen by corrupt businessmen and politicians of all parties, thousands of whom, under Italy's peculiar criminal code, were now imprisoned and denied bail as they awaited trial. Though the shops selling good antique furniture, expensive hams, and the confection called *panforte,* which the Sienese have been making since the Middle Ages, were evidently aimed at the tourist trade, this could not be true of the shops selling rare wines, wild game, and fish—the fish lit theatrically from above and arranged, like jewels, upon beds of ice. These shops obviously catered to the Sienese themselves, some of whom apparently didn't mind paying the equivalent of $15 a kilo for fresh sardines and even more for red mullet.

But on our two visits to Siena we saw very few Sienese. Except for groups of tourists, with their green *Michelins* and their video cameras, the streets in September were almost empty—a phenomenon that we noticed wherever we went in Tuscany. In some of the smaller cities and towns, it was as if a neutron bomb had landed. "Everyone is still at the seashore," I was told, or people were in their houses having lunch, but these explanations seemed inadequate. I knew that Italy had the lowest birth rate in the world and was losing population, especially in the north, but this could hardly account for the empty streets. I never did find the answer, but I was grateful that in Siena the churches and the museums weren't crowded and there weren't many customers in the shops that sold autumn's first plump porcini—the apotheosis of edible mushrooms. Moreover, the price was only about 20,000 lire a kilo—$12 for nearly two and a quarter pounds, or less than a quarter of the price of porcini in New York, if they could be found there at all. Greedily, I bought an entire basket. I also bought some Treviso radicchio—the kind you toss in olive oil and grill lightly over a wood fire.

That morning, on the way to the piazza we had passed a *macelleria* that displayed in its window one side of a short loin of beef. When I crossed the narrow Via della Sapienza with my sack of porcini and stepped through the beaded curtain into the *macelleria*—it was called Cetoloni Alberto—I could see that the loin was about two-thirds the size of its American equivalent. That meant that it came from the white Chianina steers that produce the famous *fiorentina* T-bones—a local specialty that is never found outside Italy and that is now increasingly rare even in Italian restaurants. Certainly those T-bones can't often be found three inches thick, which is how I asked Signor Cetoloni to cut them for our dinner that night.

"These are the best," he told me when the steaks were wrapped and tied in a neat bundle. "*Autentico*," he added, pointing to a medallion on the wall behind him which displayed the slogan "Cinque Erre," meaning "Five R's," for the five *razze,* or breeds, of cattle raised in the region. The Chianini are descended from the white oxen that have been bred here since Etruscan times. They are traditionally butchered before they reach full growth, when they are relatively lean and their meat is tender, but Chianini don't lend themselves to large-scale industrial production, and as less expensive beef produced elsewhere in the E.C. enters the Italian market the Chianina breeders are gradually going out of business.

As I was leaving, Signor Cetoloni asked me to wait, and took from the counter behind him a large roulade of piglet, which he called a *porchetta*. "*Un tantino di questo?*" he asked, offering me a bit that he held out on the end of his knife. It was still warm from the oven, and was filled with a mixture of herbs and spices, in which I could detect black pepper, rosemary, sage, nutmeg, and probably some juniper and thyme. I bought a kilo, though I had no idea what we would do with it, since it hardly belonged with a dinner of steak and porcini and would cool off and become greasy by the time we got home. In the shop, however, it was glorious. It would have been insane not to buy some. When we got home, we gave the *porchetta* to Silvia, who took it away with her, holding it in its wrapper against her shoulder as if it were an infant. She said she would warm it later in the oven in the apartment that she and Franco share in a wing of the farmhouse.

Since two more of our fellow-tenants had arrived, and there were now six of us living in the farmhouse, which nevertheless still felt as underpopulated as Italy itself, I had bought three of the T-bones, and expected some leftovers for the next day's lunch or for Silvia, Ivana, and Franco if the *porchetta* wasn't enough. As it turned out, there were no leftovers.

By now, Silvia and I had been cooking together for several days, and she had grown used to having me in her kitchen. At first, she would stand, hands on hips, watching me work at her counter, as if I were a potentially dangerous eccentric, likely to ruin the meal and possibly even the kitchen. But soon she relaxed. At dinner on the night we arrived, I had peeled some garlic in the familiar way—by smashing the clove with the flat of a knife, so that the skin can be slipped off easily. Silvia had never seen this done before. With a quizzical look, she picked up her paring knife and began to peel a clove in her own style—by holding it close to her eye and loosening the skin with the knife, then peeling it off bit by bit. Suddenly, she tossed her head slightly, as if to say "Let's see who wins," and began to race me. I was unaware at first that a contest had begun, but, nevertheless, I won easily. "*Bravissimo*," she whispered and bowed slightly. Thereafter I felt that she had begun to trust me. I noticed, too, that as her trust increased so did our fluency in the pidgin Italian that she and I had concocted. It was by means of this odd language that I managed one afternoon to understand why Tuscans prefer their tomatoes underripe. In the south, where tomatoes are abundant, they are allowed to ripen for the table, and they are also canned and used for sauce. But in Tuscany, where the weather is cooler, tomatoes are grown mainly for the table, and are used sparingly, if at all, in sauces. For this purpose, one wants them just this side of ripe, still with a tinge of yellow, so that they will be both sharp and sweet, with a firm, almost crisp texture. In America, she said, we probably eat our tomatoes the way the Neapolitans do, soft and ripe, and in this way we miss their true flavor. She said this sympathetically, as if my American taste in tomatoes were the result of a handicap, for which I could not be held responsible.

While we were away in Siena that day, Silvia must have gone to Francesco's garden, because now on her counter were a dozen or more tomatoes, ripe and plump, as red as blood. Francesco, she said, had been thinking of using them for sauce or giving them to his goats, but if I wanted them for our dinner I could have them.

The radicchio, the porcini, and the T-bones were stacked on the counter beside the tomatoes and some basil from the garden. While Silvia cut the porcini in thin slices from top to bottom, so that each slice resembled a tiny two-dimensional umbrella, I went out to the herb garden beside the kitchen door to cut some parsley. When I returned, I found that she had already tossed the porcini in a large kettle with some chopped garlic, olive oil, and a dash of salt and pepper, and had left them to sweat over a low flame until they absorbed most of the oil. Then she added a little more water and half covered the kettle until the porcini, with their aroma of earth and heaven, were simmering. Ten minutes later, she spooned them out of the pot. They were silky and tender, having absorbed almost all the liquid in which they had simmered, leaving only enough for a fine *jus*.

On the terrace, the others were seated in semi-darkness around the table. The evening was still warm, and the candles that lit the table heated the air around them like tiny furnaces. Ivana had put the steaks on an iron grill over an olivewood fire; Silvia had brushed a few embers to one side, putting them under a smaller grill, upon which she had spread the radicchio. I had sliced half a dozen of

Francesco's tomatoes and let them sit for half an hour in oil, a little pepper and sea salt, and a touch of vinegar, and I asked Ivana to serve them as our first course, with some leaves of fresh basil on each plate. Except for a band of red turning purple behind the hills, the sun had set. I made a Martini for myself and joined our friends, confident that this would be our best meal so far in Tuscany.

My collaborations with Silvia had by this time acquired their own rhythm, and the dinners we produced harmonized her Tuscan orthodoxy with the improvisations that I had learned in my culinary wandering. I saw that we had formed one of those late marriages, devoid of illusions, in which one values the other's distinctiveness and does not attempt to impose one's will.

A few nights after our dinner of porcini and Chianina steaks, a well-known Italian politician drove up from Rome to join us for dinner. That morning, the others had driven over to San Gimignano to buy some of the good grappa that is sold there and to look at Gozzoli's seventeen frescoes of the life of St. Augustine. I had seen the Gozzolis the day before, so I went with Silvia to Castelfiorentino, the market town in the valley beneath our farmhouse. There was a large Superal in Castelfiorentino, and on the day of our visit the travelling market, which comes to each of the neighboring towns once a week, had also arrived. Silvia suggested that we get to this market early, before the best things were gone. But even here all the poultry I saw was factory-raised, and the bread was poor. We did, however, find some good ham and local cheese, which kept us going through the morning. We also bought some white-bait at one of the fish stalls and then set out for the Superal.

When I go to the market, I usually go without a list, and even when I have one I ignore it and fall instead into a sort of trance, waiting for the menu to create itself, so to speak, from what happens to be for sale. My inspiration that morning in the Superal came from a display of pink and black octopuses, their heads the size of softballs and their glistening tentacles like oiled bullwhips. The supermarket itself was dreamlike. Opposite the checkout counter was a hairdresser's shop, with half a dozen seated clients draped in long yellow clothes and staring like Medusas through fringes of wet hair. Infants were sitting on the hairdresser's floor, playing with large, odd-shaped objects made of red and yellow plastic. Expensive espresso machines were stacked in their cartons next to a display of computer programs. At the fish counter, I imagined the octopuses, cleaned and cut into segments, stewing with garlic and onions in white wine, to which I would add tomato and bay leaf and peppercorns just before tossing in some clams and mussels. Then I would add rosemary and a few lemon slices, peel and all, and just before the stew was ready for the table I would put in some cubes of blackfish, or the local equivalent, and more garlic and wine to roughen the broth a bit, and I would serve it in deep bowls with thick slices of good bread, toasted and rubbed with still more garlic. But where, I wondered, would I find the bread?

It was the bread problem that brought me out of this reverie. "Pasta," I said to myself. "That's what I'll use instead." I asked the clerk for some mussels and clams, and instead of octopus, which now seemed too coarse for what I had in mind, I asked for a kilo of the smallest squid he had. Then I went to look for Silvia. I found her at the poultry display, her chin resting on a bent index finger as she gazed warily, I thought, at the chickens in their plastic wrappers.

"*Perchè non dei piccioni?*" I suggested, holding up a plump pigeon that fitted neatly into my hand. Unlike chickens, pigeons aren't mass-produced; they're raised on farms or in coops and are fed real corn, the way chickens used to be raised. We bought a dozen and headed for home. We agreed that the whitebait, dusted in flour and tossed quickly in very hot oil, would be the hors d'oeuvre. The clams, mussels, and squid we would make into a stew with a little white wine, garlic, and hot peppers, and serve over pasta, and the pigeons we would bone, marinate in muscatel, and grill on the fire. To go with them, we could braise some fennel from the garden, and then we could slowly bake some underripe tomatoes and mix them with a touch of grilled egg-plant. For dessert, there were figs from the trees near the pool, ricotta *salata* that I had bought the day before in Volterra, and biscotti left over from the night before. The politician, I told myself as I boned the pigeons that afternoon and made a stock of their ribs and breastbones and necks, would have a good dinner. He was a man of some ampli-tude, and I was eager to feed him well.

As it turned out, he had so much to say that night that he hardly noticed what he had been served. The pasta, under its sauce of clams, squid, and mussels, with a sprinkling of diced tomato and a shower of parsley, looked like an Italian flag that had been abandoned on his plate by a fleeing army. Like so many of his colleagues from the previ-ous government, he was in legal difficulties. Unlike so many of the oth-ers, however, he was not being held without bail, so perhaps the allegations in his case were not serious. Even so, it would have been outrageous to ask where he stood with the law. By the time Ivana had removed our pasta bowls and returned with the grilled pigeons—glint-ing in the candlelight under a sheen of reduced stock flavored with rosemary—and poured some Poggio Rosso into our glasses, the conversation had become entirely his. The rest of us had faded silently into the darkness of the terrace while his large, pale face and fluttering hands bobbed in the candlelight to the rhythm of his monologue.

The electronic superhighway, he said, leaving his pigeon untouched, would transform the world, and for this reason, among others, it was a good thing that Mr. Berlusconi, the forward-looking new Prime Minister, was in office. He would know how to introduce Italy to these new technologies. Moreover, the Germans would buy Berlusconi's television companies and forge a new European network. My recollection of the politician's remarks may not do them justice, for I find such conversations impossible to follow. The future seems to me a vacuum, while the past, as one considers it, appears substantially uniform, shaped less by new technologies than by predictable human behavior, most of it discouraging. The moral world of the Divine Comedy is, after all, identical to the one we still inhabit. So is Homer's. As our guest went on about computers and the Internet, I thought, of course, of Marinetti, but said nothing. The dinner, I felt, had been fine, but the politician's prattle somewhat disrupted the illusion that on our Tuscan hilltop we had transcended the confusion of everyday life. I was reminded that our vacation was almost over.

On the following day, we drove over to San Gimignano for a final visit. By now, I understood why this town had made such an erotic impression upon E. M. Forster when he visited it as a young Cambridge graduate and chose it as the setting for *Where Angels Fear to Tread,* the novel of sexual discovery that launched his career and also a procession of imitators. San Gimignano is, of course, famous for its slab-sided towers, which when they are seen from a distance resemble the towers of lower Manhattan. These stone towers were probably erected by feuding groups of Guelphs and Ghibellines—the former owing allegiance to the popes, in Rome, and the latter to the Holy Roman emperors, on the far side of the Alps. Their quarrel was complex and has puzzled generations of historians, but perhaps it is not entirely unlike the disputes today between advocates of a strong central government and those Italians who prefer regional autonomy.

The towers and the violent legends attached to them give San Gimignano a forbidding aspect at first, but this is soon dispelled by the unmistakable erotic intensity of the place—suggested, for instance, by the twelfth-century frescoes in the Museo Civico, which show a young man and woman quite naked except for the man's hat and the woman's headband. They are sharing a bath. The woman's hand rests upon the man's shoulder, and his hand, hidden by the tub's rim, rests, perhaps, on her upper thigh. In the adjacent panel, the woman is in bed, her back to the man, who, still naked, is climbing in after her. San Gimignano's patron saint is a young woman named Fina, whose martyrdom began when a young man of the town offered her an orange. So intense was her revulsion that she took to her bed and never ate again. Some years after her anorexic martyrdom, Ghirlandaio painted for Fina's chapel the scene of her transfiguration, using as his model a pink-cheeked young beauty in excellent health, reclining on her couch, her eyes shut, her palms pressed together in a gesture whose piety seems, if not actually coy, then certainly hesitant.

On that last visit to San Gimignano, as I was standing beneath the great Ghirlandaio fresco of the Annunciation outside the Duomo, which houses Santa Fina's chapel, and was trying to imagine how this young woman's story must have struck the young Forster, I became aware of a melody coming from the grassy courtyard behind me. I turned, and saw that the source of the music was a handsome young flutist wearing a burgundy cape over a pair of jeans. His hair rose and fell as he swung his head in time with the music. He was playing, of all things, one of Grieg's Norwegian folk songs, and was creating from this grammar-school chestnut a tune so vivid that a group of tourists had put down their video cameras and gathered silently around him.

A few minutes later, under the flutist's spell, I walked back into the square to rejoin my friends, and there I glimpsed what Forster might have seen when he conceived his novel's hero. Reclining on a balustrade, his back against a pillar, his head turned to one side, a book unread in his hand, and his expression distracted or irritable, was a young man of such forbidding beauty that he dispelled any inclination to possess it, even if one were so inclined. He might have been a Della Robbia, if he were not so clearly human. Forster's young English suburbanites flung themselves incautiously at such a Tuscan beauty and never recovered their native aplomb. This was a blessing in Forster's estimation, though not nearly as great a blessing, of course, as the divine enlightenment bestowed upon Dante by Beatrice. Yet the transformation undergone by Forster's suburbanites was not entirely incompatible with Dante's, either. In Tuscany, you approach Heaven by way of the senses. Beauty is all.

I was eager to return to the farmhouse and Silvia's kitchen. Tonight was our last dinner in Tuscany. Silvia was going to make wild boar, and she said that for our farewell meal she would prefer to cook alone. The meal was sublime, but our imminent departure inspired that melancholy premonition of death typical of all leave-taking.

The following morning it rained. As we were getting ready to drive down to Rome, Silvia handed me a jar of spices that she had ground into powder, and a handwritten recipe for wild boar: three kilos of *cinghiale* rubbed with her ground spices, two chopped onions, three branches of rosemary, some parsley, a little white wine, salt, pepper. Though the chances of finding wild boar in New York City are slim, I carried Silvia's recipe in my pocket for weeks after I returned, and eventually tucked it into my copy of Forster's novel.

The Simple Secrets of Tuscany

BY ALEXANDRA FOGES

∿

editor's note

Lorenza de' Medici's Villa Table, at Badia a Coltibuono, is the most famous cooking school in Tuscany. It is also the most expensive, but students get to hobnob with someone of noble lineage, after all.

LORENZA DE' MEDICI is the author of numerous cookbooks, including *Lorenza's Antipasti* (1998) and *Lorenza's Pasta* (1996), both published by Clarkson Potter; *Italy: The Beautiful Cookbook* (Collins, 1989); and *Florentines: A Tuscan Feast* (Random House, 1992). This article originally appeared in the January 1994 issue of *Condé Nast Traveler*.

The subject on the table was *uova alla neve*. "Of course, there is only one way to tell if the egg whites are enough beaten, and that is to put them on your head." The hot Tuscan sun, filtered through louvered shutters, fell in wavy stripes across the marble counter as Lorenza de' Medici picked up the copper basin and upended its contents on her chic helmet of streaked gray hair. "*Ecco*, they never fall . . . if you have done it right." Which, of course, she had. We clapped, Lorenza took a bow, and then we turned our attention to the deep yellow yolks, which sat in the top half of a double boiler waiting patiently to be transformed into crème anglaise. "In France they call this a *bain-marie*, in Italy a *bagno maria*," Lorenza explained as she stirred the almost orange yolks with an old wooden spoon, "because as a method of cooking, it is as gentle as the Virgin herself."

Wood pigeons rustled the branches of the big magnolia tree outside as we, her disciples, scribbled furiously in our notebooks. Next, she poured a giant bag of flour onto the table and began to shape it into a volcanic cone. "Vesuvius," she proclaimed, scooping out the top and plopping a raw egg into its crater. "You have never been to Naples? Of course one would hesitate to compare their cooking with what we do in Toscana. . . ." Her voice trailed off. The volcano and its eggy lava were being kneaded together by hand, and Lorenza's diamond rings were now buried, like treasures in Pompeii, under wads of dough. "To make fresh pasta, this is all you need. Egg, flour, and two hands. That's all. Please do not think about pasta machines. They are extremely expensive and extremely useless." A pronouncement, worthy of the Luddites, that I was to hear again—and again—over the next week. What, no Cuisinart? (A sharp knife and a wooden chopping board were just as good.) No electric beater? (A wire whisk was so much more flexible.) And what about my favorite machine of all—that wonderful all-American invention, the dishwasher? (Her kitchen seemed to come with a set of smiling helpers, each equipped with two *very* flexible hands, who caused dirty dishes to fly from the table into a marble sink large enough to bathe a small child in.)

While my back was turned, Vesuvius had become a supple yellow sheet and was being coaxed through a hand-cranked contraption which, in turn, spewed tagliatelle out its rear end. The scent of fresh rosemary and olive oil escaped from the oven, where focaccia was baking for lunch. "*Andiamo!* Now we eat what *you* have cooked this morning," Lorenza said diplomatically as she swept through a set of double doors and into the mint green Rococo dining room.

What little knowledge I had of Italian food had been acquired during one summer spent as a teenager with a family who lived near Arezzo. Everything about the Brandolinis was stylish and perfect. The mother was impossibly elegant, the children were ridiculously well behaved, and the food was, naturally, quite irresistible. All the clichés, I discovered, were true: Italians *do* know how to live better than the rest of us. I managed to pick up a few words of Italian (which had been the idea behind the trip), but, far more important, I became infatuated with all things Italian, specifically with the Tuscan food produced by Celestina, their rotund and smiling (honest, she was) cook.

In Italy, I learned, simplicity should *never* be confused with lack of sophistication. Quite the contrary. The seemingly austere lines of an Armani jacket only emphasize the unerring eye of its creator, and the same may be said of Tuscan food. Its foundations, like the supple wool fabric of the jacket, lie, quite simply, in the quality of its raw materials. Start out with the best and freshest natural ingredients: the youngest (almost premature) baby beans, the ripest (almost blowsy) tomatoes, the finest (first cold-pressed) olive oil, herbs that were bushes minutes before, figs about to burst. Prepare them with elegance and their original flavor will speak clearly to you.

The Tuscans are called "*mangiafagioli,*" or "bean eaters," by other Italians. Not a compliment, apparently, but a term of (semi)abuse— *why* was never made at all clear to me. But inspired by Tuscan nationalism, Celestina used to make *fagioli all'uccelletto,* literally "beans like birds," by simmering them in a gentle oven in garlic, tomato, and sage, to give them the taste of small game. (Which it did, kind of, if you added a generous dash of your own imagination.) Speaking of game, which Tuscans are apt to do, another of her specialties was *pappardelle con la lepre:* smooth, square, eggy, fresh noodles with a ragout made of hare that has hung for at least two days.

"Traditionally, Tuscans lived off the land," Signore Brandolini explained to me, "hunting game to supplement their diet—hence the emphasis on small birds, hare, wild boar, in their cooking. Nowadays, everyone wants to return to the simple life—God alone knows why— so you see aristocratic Florentines going crazy about a meal that a peasant farmer might have eaten without comment before the war." His expression said, "So, go figure," in perfect Tuscan dialect.

Although Tuscany has never been dairy country, it is still known for its beef. Most particularly for the humpbacked white beef of

Chianina, whose most famous cut is *bistecca alla fiorentina*—a T-bone steak that is *always* simply grilled. Simple but never austere. There are even Etruscan frescoes that show these precursors of the Tuscans, grilling what looks suspiciously like a *bistecca* over a wood fire.

That summer was the first time I ever tasted radicchio and arugula, neither of which had yet reached London. Celestina's salads would usually be a patriotic echo of the Italian flag: red radicchio, deep green arugula, and albino endive bathed in olive oil. "*First Cold Pressing* are the only words you need to know," Signore Brandolini said slowly, almost spelling each letter out, "always assuming that the olive oil comes from the area near Siena, where my grandmother has her *frantoio* [olive press]. After the first cold pressing of the olives, you might as well feed what is left to the pigs," he explained, "but they go on pressing it—two, three, four times more, *with heat*—and make oil that is labeled 'pure' and 'virgin.' About as pure and virginal as a syphilitic old hooker." He snorted and turned to the subject of vinegar. "Balsamic vinegar from Modena. That is the beginning, the middle, and the end of the story." Aged in wood casks, this vinegar is as subtle and complicated as vintage wine, so soft that you can sip it from a silver spoon or pour it over strawberries still warm from the sun. And with the salad, what else but a slice of sharp, fresh pecorino cheese? Made from the (unpasteurized) milk of sheep that graze in the hills above Arezzo, shaped by hand into rounds that resemble nothing so much as a sheep's udder.

Many years after that summer in Tuscany, I was having dinner in New York with some Italian friends at a restaurant downtown. My host ordered a chianti classico that I had never come across before. Obviously I still had plenty to learn. The wine arrived at the table, the black and gold medieval insignia of the rooster at its throat and two other important clues on the label. The first was the estate: Badia a Coltibuono, which, I was told, had been producing wine since the eleventh century, when a Benedictine order first settled on this hillside about halfway between Siena and Florence. And the second was the word *Riserva,* which simply identifies those top vintages that are produced in minute quantities and then left to age for up to two years in oak casks deep in the cellar beneath the cloisters. I was beginning to catch on. Dinner was followed by tiny glasses of *vin santo,* which also happened to be from Coltibuono: a dessert wine whose saintly sweetness comes from allowing the grapes to dry while still attached to the vine by their umbilical cords, and then to ferment in the barrel for a couple of years. "But to truly understand the food of a region, you have no choice but to go there," I heard one of my friends telling me through a pleasant haze of *vin santo* and chianti and espresso. "You should stay at Badia a Coltibuono and watch the owner's wife, Lorenza, cooking. There you will learn with your hands, your eyes, your mouth, your nose, and your heart. It is the only way." And so I did.

I kept the label from the wine we drank that night in New York. It lay buried at the back of my wallet, and in mid-Atlantic, about halfway between New York and Rome, I took it out and had another look. The Romanesque church with its square campanile looked out over a wooded valley, and clustered around it were a series of buildings, a covered cloister, and a large courtyard. The ruins of a castle stood on a distant hilltop. It seemed as if the picture had been transposed from the pages of an antiquarian book or some faded old print: It did not look remotely like a place where real people might live.

The car snaked along a narrow road that was shaded by thick groves of walnut trees. After about half an hour we emerged into the sunlight and were face-to-face with . . . the picture on the label. But instead of being faded, this version was in full color. The trees were green, the stone of the buildings a pale pink terra-cotta, and the sky a Tiepolo mix of celestial blue and gauzy white clouds. A gigantic *pastore maremmano* lurched toward me and seemed to guide me, like a sheepdog (which is what this breed is used as, I later found out), onto the terrace, where iced tea was being served under a giant magnolia tree. The facade of the house was covered in overgrown jasmine, and a pergola of grapevines stretched down to the end of the formal garden. "Welcome to Coltibuono. You must meet our other guests," Lorenza de' Medici said as she led me down into the garden. There were nine of us, three couples and three women (including myself) traveling on their own. Plus John Meis, who helped Lorenza by keeping us all under control, in the nicest possible way, when we weren't elbow-deep in flour.

Mornings would be spent cooking with Lorenza in the kitchen from nine-thirty until lunchtime, when we would sit down to devour our handiwork. Afternoons were our own to loll about or swim or sleep in. Then at four we would set out on an adventure. One day it might be to a remote farm in the hills where they still made pecorino by hand, another day to a sixteenth-century villa that was closed to the public but had all its original frescoes and furniture.

A trip to Siena was set for Tuesday, and also a wine tasting at Monti, the vineyard where the Coltibuono wines are grown and made. And then dinner. This is where Lorenza's network of friends came into play. On each night a different set of neighbors would have the pleasure of our company. I never did quite figure out how you persuade your friends to have an extra ten or so garrulous Americans to dinner, but there must have been some happy quid pro quo going on here. Our hosts all beamed with delight when they saw us, served us terrifying amounts of food, filled up our glasses far too frequently, showed us around their houses (and castles and palazzi), and then expressed what certainly sounded like genuine distress when we finally waved good-bye well after midnight. I am assuming that Lorenza supplied her generous ration of quo at other times of the year.

"Now, you must be tired and want to unpack. Dinner will be at eight. We meet in the drawing room at seven." Being told what you are going to do next has many advantages, especially when the things you are expected to do are *entirely* pleasurable.

"Bread and olives—these have always been the fundamental elements in the Tuscan diet, and not so much has changed in Tuscany for hundreds of years." Lorenza was kneading the dough like a mother cat preparing a bed for her kittens. "Even now, you always find olives and bread side by side in the bakery." This was our first day in the kitchen, and the emphasis was on these Tuscan staples, with the addition of that parvenu vegetable, the *pomodoro*/golden apple/tomato that the Spanish brought back from the New World at the beginning of the sixteenth century. The three dishes we learned to cook that morning were simple, cheap, and delicious— all variations on the tomato/bread/olive theme.

I had never realized just how useful a very stale loaf of bread could be. Always assuming, as Signore Brandolini would say, that the bread was of the coarse, country variety (the flour used is a mix of grains, usually corn and wheat), that the tomatoes were at their peak of ripeness, and that the oil was First Cold Pressing.

Here's how to make the world's easiest and best appetizer, *bruschetta*:

Take three *very* ripe tomatoes, peel and chop and salt, leaving the mix to drain in a colander. Chop a handful each of fresh parsley and basil leaves, add two chopped cloves of garlic and four tablespoons of olive oil. Toast a slice of bread, brush with some oil, and then spread the tomato mixture on top. Serve *immediately* beneath a magnolia tree with a glass (or two) of Coltibuono Sangioveto '85.

The bread in this case should actually be fresh, but for *panzanella* (bread salad) make sure it is good and stale before you add tomatoes, black olives, red onions, and more olive oil and balsamic vinegar. And for *pappa al pomodoro* (tomato-bread soup) the ingredients are much the same (skip the vinegar), except that they are cooked in a light meat broth, and fresh sage and thyme are added.

"So you see," Lorenza said as she sat down at the head of her long dining room table, "in Toscana we don't waste food. The bread is always used up, and we have learned to cook every part of the animal. My American friends do not love the pancreas or calf's brains as I do. And when I tell you that a lamb's head cut in half and grilled can be absolutely wonderful, you do not believe me. But it is true." The expression on her audience's collective face was a mix of horror and skepticism, with a thin coating of polite ("Is that so?") curiosity glossed over the top. "But tonight we are going to dinner with the Barone Bettino Ricasoli at Brolio," Lorenza added. "No stale bread or lamb's heads there, I promise you."

After lunch we all escaped in different directions but were told quite firmly by John, our erudite and endlessly patient human sheepdog, to be in the main courtyard at four o'clock. The schedule was flexible—but only up to a very limited point. With ten people to get into a minivan, a side trip to the Villa de Geggiano, and then dinner at Brolio, straggling was *not* encouraged. Out of breath and with still-damp hair, I made it just in time. The giant *pastore maremmano* was finally evicted from my seat, and we set off down the walnut-shaded road.

This particular part of Tuscany has lived through the twentieth century miraculously unscathed by its worst desecrations. Ultrastrict zoning and building regulations have preserved the countryside, not as nature intended it, but in the form that human beings have imposed upon it over the past thousand years or so. Just as a use is found for every part of an animal, so every inch of arable land has been made productive: cultivated and tended and husbanded over the centuries to feed man.

Those bits of forest that still remain are hunted for small birds and game, olive trees cling to terraces where the soil is too poor to sustain other crops, and vegetables and sunflowers are squeezed into the scraps of land that surround the farmhouses. I looked out at the green and rounded hills, their curves as smooth and gratifying as those on a Titian nude, where vines and olives and fields and forest formed a landscape of sublime harmony, and tried to make some sense of this unadulterated perfection. As with physical beauty in human form, it had a mesmerizing quality, which numbed the brain and made you realize how easy it would be to fall in love forever with land like this.

At the very top of the highest hill for miles around stood a fortress of mythic proportions: Brolio, where we were headed for dinner that night. If we had thought that Badia a Coltibuono was old (and God knows I had), then what on earth was one to make of Brolio? This castle and its surrounding land had been in the Ricasoli family since the early 700s. It took a few moments for this to sink in: The eighth century is not a date that sets too many bells ringing in American history.

The Ricasolis spent several hundred years fighting their neighbors, but when their ally Cosimo de' Medici (one of Lorenza's better-known ancestors) finally defeated Siena in 1555, they were able to turn to the cultivation of their vineyards. Brolio chianti was soon being exported all over Europe—as it still is four hundred years later.

The Barone greeted us at the door and led us into a marble hallway of *Citizen Kane* proportions, through a library, across a drawing room, and out to a terrace the size of several football fields. The spires of Siena could just be seen on the horizon through the evening haze. Drinks were passed around and polite conversation followed, with talk of the weather.

"We are terribly lucky to have this little space outdoors," the Baronessa said, referring, I realized, to the football fields, "as it gets so very hot here in the summer." And food: "Our new cook is English," the Barone informed me, not noticing as my jaw dropped several inches. "She is particularly gifted with puddings, having been trained by my old governess in London." Speechless, I was saved by the summons to dinner.

The dining room was also straight out of Xanadu: As big as a New York loft, it had a twenty-foot ceiling and was "decorated" with suits of armor and carefully arranged displays of spears, swords, pikes, axes, and various other instruments of torture and death. The English dinner slipped by without comment. Tiny gilded cups of espresso were served, and then the Barone stood and asked if we would like to see the family chapel.

It was more of a statement than a question. The interior of the church was cool, there was a faint smell of wax in the air, and it was almost pitch-black. What little illumination there was came from candles, tall, thin stalks that stood in a cluster at the end of the nave, in front of a bronze crucifix, wavering in an imperceptible breeze.

We walked slowly down the aisle, until the Barone stopped us at an elaborate baroque grille set into the flagstone floor. Cautiously, I peered down, and he murmured, "They are all there, my entire family." It was a bewildering thought: Deep in the rock beneath the church were stacked not only his first wife but also his parents and sundry cousins and great-aunts and -uncles stretching back into the miasma of time. The idea of living in the same place for twelve hundred years *and* having your ancestors neatly arranged under your own private church was not an easy notion to come to grips with. We drove back to Coltibuono, struck dumb by a combination of the Brolio *vin santo* and the amazing *foreignness* of Barone Ricasoli's life.

"Today we will make risotto with lemon and that wonderful thing—I don't know the English word—that you find inside the legs of very young cows." Lorenza smiled brightly as she poked the marrow out of the core of the veal shanks and began to simmer it with onions in the melted butter. Not one millimeter of the animal was wasted. There are, I learned, only a few things to remember about risotto: *Always* use arborio rice, stir gently but constantly, and *never* keep it waiting. Like a soufflé, risotto needs to be eaten the instant it decides it is ready. On this, our next-to-last day, risotto and *tiramisù* (Lorenza made it quite clear that this dessert was a big concession to us, her American guests, since it was most definitely *not* a typical Tuscan dish) occupied the morning, with Siena our afternoon and evening adventure.

On my way to Coltibuono, I had changed planes in Rome, where I met a South African professor of malacology who was returning from Siena. He had just delivered a lecture on his special subject, snails, at the university there and told me that his Sienese colleagues had listened, rapt, as he expounded on the life cycle of the mollusk. Afterward, they had given a dinner in his honor. Long trestle tables were set up along a cobbled street, musicians wandered about like troubadours, and the entire faculty and student body turned out to feast upon a dazzling array of—what else—snails. Quantities of chianti classico accompanied the garlic-drenched mollusks, and the dancing lasted until dawn. His story made me want to be there: It seemed that the Sienese understood how life should be lived.

One of the many civilized things about Siena is the complete absence of cars. While you are there, you can forget that the internal combustion engine was ever invented. This is a medieval town, perched on the crest of three hills. Its twisted streets were created for horses and man and are scarcely wide enough for a carriage, never mind anything larger. We arrived in the late afternoon, just as the sun was turning the brick and stone of the etiolated houses around the Piazza del Campo into (appropriately enough) burnt sienna.

The shape of a cockleshell, semicircular, with a gentle dip toward its center, the piazza is Siena's secular heart. (Twice a summer it also becomes a racetrack, when the Palio drives the whole of Siena temporarily, but certifiably, insane.) The Palazzo Pubblico, which dominates the piazza, is a monument to the medieval

Republic of Siena, while the cathedral, candy-striped in dark green, white, and pink marble, stands in its own square to the west, as a reminder of the power of the Church, the other great force in Sienese history. Dinner was a good three hours away, so with our hostess's address carefully written down, and with a map and several books, I set off alone.

Siena is afflicted with what I came to think of as the Brolio complex: It is not just that it's ancient, but that it reached such a degree of artistic and political sophistication almost a thousand years ago. *This* is what is truly breathtaking. The cathedral—enormous, with a 292-foot nave—is the architectural embodiment of the almost limitless wealth and ambition of the medieval Sienese. Its pavement is tattooed with a series of gigantic "paintings" of biblical scenes, each one composed of elaborate inlaid stone and marble mosaics. The structure was begun around 1196 and completed at the end of the fourteenth century. In its library, the floors are decorated with delicate gold-and-blue crescents to commemorate Pope Pius II's victory over the Saracens during the Crusades, and hand-painted Psalters are displayed open, under glass, on shelves that line the walls.

Emerging from the cathedral, I walked toward the setting sun until I found myself in the Piazza del Duomo, one whole side of which was taken up with a ninth-century building. Its entrance was blocked by an incongruously modern looking ambulance, and as I watched, a pale, elderly man, attached to a drip, was wheeled out on a stretcher. I suddenly understood that the building was actually a hospital—and a hospital that was clearly still working hard after hundreds of years. Cathedrals that took a quarter of a millennium to build where people still worshiped, medieval buildings that were hospitals, the Crusades as an interior decorating motif . . . it took my mind awhile to get used to time-traveling on this scale.

We met that night for dinner at an old building in the center of Siena. An inspired architect had sliced off the roof and turned the entire top floor into a terrace. Rough terra-cotta tiles covered the floor, tables were set up under square white canvas umbrellas, and wild rosemary and sage bushes grew in pots along the edge of the railing. The whole of Siena lay below us, serene and inviolable.

Swallows swooped among the spires that I had first seen in the evening haze from the terrace at Brolio, and we could hear the church bells ringing, slightly mournfully, for the last time that day. Once again, it was hard to make sense of such aesthetic perfection. I was struck dumb (in both senses), but our Italian hosts, understandably, seemed to take it as a given, as part of the natural order of their lives. They nodded politely whenever we gasped in wonder, and then quickly returned to their conversations and, more important, their food.

Saucers of chartreuse-colored olive oil (from Lucca, of course) replaced butter on the table, and baskets of still-warm focaccia were passed around as we sat down. Fresh spinach gnocchi (shaped by hand into small ovals) with butter and sage (picked from the bushes that edged the terrace) came first, followed by *uccelletti alla maremmana* (small game birds grilled over a wood fire) and tiny new potatoes that had been roasted in olive oil, sea salt, and sprigs of still-green rosemary.

A Brolio Riserva '85 flowed as generously as the Arno River, and a pyramid of ripe peaches (from the cook's grandmother's orchard) was dessert. Grappa (for the brave) and *vin santo* (for the timid) were offered as the coup de grâce. This dinner summed up, for me, the essence of Tuscan food—and life. It had innate simplicity and grace: Nothing was excessive, and yet it had, at the same time, a deep generosity of spirit. Centuries of civilization had composed this meal—and the way in which these people lived. The Professor of Snails had got it: The Sienese had solved the riddle. It may be possible, I thought as I gazed out at the Duomo, to understand the food of a country in a practical, even an intellectual, sense without traveling, but it can never be the same as going there. If you really want to learn about food, you need to cross borders, and you need to have a sense of place and proportion. You have to use not just your mouth but your eyes, your nose, your ears, your hands, your head—and, of course, your heart.

Mangiamo!

Wisely not adding oven heat to Italy's summer, **Badia a Coltibuono** holds cooking classes in spring (five one-week sessions in May and June) and fall (five more in September and October). During the last spring session, when the medieval Palio *festa* races through Siena, the price goes up about $500 at Coltibuono (53013 Gaiole in Chianti, Siena; telephone: 0577.749498; fax: 0577.749235; www. chianticlassico.com/coltibuono;

in the U.S.: Judy Ebrey, Cuisine International, P.O. Box 25228, Dallas, Texas 75225; 214-373-1161; fax: -1162; e-mail: cuisineint@aol.com.

Giuliano Bugialli's Cooking in Florence is held in the Augustus & Dei Congressi Hotel—which is not reserved solely for Bugialli's students, so book early. Sessions are held in May, June, July, September, and October (fall classes are held in the chianti wine country), plus one week in December (60 Sutton Place South, #1KS, New York, New York 10022; 212-813-9552; fax: 486-5518; www.bugialli.com).

In warmer Palermo, **The World of Regaleali** classes take place in April, May, and November. The Regaleali estate provides most of the food used in the classes, which include bread-baking, cheese-making demonstrations, and winery tours (contact Anna Tasca Lanza at via Principessa Giovanna 9, Palermo 90149, Sicily, Italy; 091450.727; fax: 0921.542783).

Reading

Tuscany: The Beautiful Cookbook and *The De' Medici Kitchen* (both HarperCollins) are by Lorenza de' Medici of Coltibuono. Other recommended books include *A Taste of Tuscany* by John Meis (Abbeville Press); *Within Tuscany: Reflections on a Time and Place* by Matthew Spender (Viking); *The Food of Italy* by Waverley Root (Vintage); *Bugialli on Pasta* by Giuliano Bugialli (Simon & Schuster); *Marcella's Italian Kitchen* by Marcella Hazan (Knopf); *The Heart of Sicily* by Anna Tasca Lanza (Clarkson Potter).

Giuliani? Politics? Forget It. Give Me a Week of Cooking in Tuscany!

BY TODD S. PURDUM

∽

editor's note

Though this piece was written over a decade ago, it remains an accurate account of an experience at La Cucina al Focolare (Cooking by the Fireside). Classes are taught in a fifteenth-century villa—Fattoria Degli Usignoli—in *Donato in Fronzano*, in the countryside outside Florence. Readers will not be surprised that the most appealing aspect of this course for me is best summed up by a former student, who was grateful for the enriching experience and noted that "total immersion is hard to come by in the hustle-bustle of the nineties."

TODD PURDUM has been a staff writer for *The New York Times* for many years.

The bulging waistline is a notorious side effect of time spent along the manic smorgasbord of political campaigns. So it could have been folly to seek relief from the heartburn of covering the New York City mayoral election by retreating to cooking school in Italy, where long knives had a different meaning but eating and drinking produced equally predictable results.

Nevertheless, I began plotting just such an escape last October, too tired to think hard, yet awake enough to know I'd crave a change of venue after Election Day. A solo vacation loomed as lonely, and organized tours, cruises or trips repelled. As I pondered how to make a week of self-indulgence feel like self-improvement, inspiration dawned.

Cooking and eating have been favorite pastimes since my childhood in the care of quintessential Midwestern homecooks, and I'd fallen in love with Tuscany on an earlier family visit. A look at the bible of culinary education, the *Shaw Guide to Cooking Schools*, disclosed that two of the big mammas of Italian cuisine, Lorenza de' Medici and Marcella Hazan, had closed up shop for the season.

Then my eye fell on a more modest entry, La Cucina al Focolare (Cooking by the Fireside), a weeklong spring and fall program conducted in a converted fifteenth-century friary in the Vallombrosa Valley outside Florence by Silvia and Roberto Pincitore, who have lovingly restored what was once her family's hilltop farm into a cozy resort. I called a toll-free number in Boulder, Colorado, where Peggy Markel, a former macrobiotic cook and all-around Italophile who runs the program from the States, was immediately helpful and sent a brochure. I mailed back the deposit and counted the hours.

Yes, I gained weight—about seven pounds. But in six fat and happy November days, two more important things became clear: Everything tastes better in Italy, and everything sounds better in Italian, even in the sometimes mangled mix of Italian and English that was the lingua franca of nine American novitiates and their tutors.

As she grappled to explain the earthy serendipity that is the essence of Tuscan cooking, Signora Pincitore often seized on a literal translation of the Italian word for imagination, the quality she extolled in combining ingredients and courses.

"*Allora*," she would say—the wonderful temporizing preface that means "then," but doubles as "well" and "so" and "um"—"*Allora*, it's, ah, up your fantasy!"

Sublime Joys

That became the rallying cry of a diverse group, including an architect, computer experts, an engineering analyst, an interior designer and an editor, who ranged in age from thirty-something to just over seventy. All of us had gathered to learn how to make—and just as important it turned out, to eat—Italian food the way Italians do (at about $2,000 for the week, including meals, lodging and excursions).

The joys of the Tuscan landscape and table are at once humble and sublime: from the undulant brown hills that gave burnt sienna its name to the fog that shrouds a single valley in mist while all its neighbors bask in sun; from the soft, tangy crumble of a wedge of pecorino cheese athwart a slice of fennel salami to the unexpected union of a fizzy new Chianti and fresh roasted chestnuts for dessert.

From the moment Ms. Markel, a native Alabamian whose Southern hospitality has not diminished, met my Alitalia train from the Rome airport in Florence on a drizzly Sunday morning, I sensed I had made the right choice. Minutes later, as we drove through olive groves and vineyards to the Pincitores' Fattoria degli Usignoll (Farm of the Nightingales), that conviction strengthened. When I sat down to lunch with my new classmates in the converted wine cellar that serves as the dining room, I knew I was home.

First came a plate of typical Tuscan antipasti—roasted yellow peppers, mozzarella and tomatoes, a grilled porcini mushroom (then just finishing its season)—followed by gnocchi, their bumble-bee fuselages coated in a silken sauce of gorgonzola and asparagus. Next, slivers of rare steak grilled over a wood fire and nestled in a wreath of peppery arugula. And finally, the chestnuts and the fattoria's own six-week-old wine. And that was just lunch.

So began a cycle of observation, creation and consumption of the work of our teacher and resident chef, Fortunato Domenici, a gentle bear of a man with a voice like a pumice stone and the ready spirit of a fry-cook, whose instructions were translated (roughly) by Signora Pincitore and Ms. Markel. Our morning sessions began after breakfasts of ambrosial espresso and steamed milk and lasted about four hours, till lunch with our work as the centerpiece.

After a nap or a walk up the hill to a quaint cemetery, afternoon sessions covered lighter topics like Italian culinary terms, table settings and napkin-folding, under the droll tutelage of Aldo Settembrini, the resort's young maitre d'hôtel, who had spent a few months at Le Cirque in New York and liked to make bedroom eyes at the women and burst into ribald parodies of "That's Amore," as he served grappa at the end of a meal.

By eight o'clock each night, we would gather again for aperitifs, a leisurely four-course dinner and rambling discussions that embraced Fellini films and organic markets in Colorado. With a self-consciousness that diminished daily, we oohed and aahed and exchanged happily guilty meditations on our good fortune, and la dolce vita.

If It's Wednesday, It's Pizza

Two whole days were reserved for excursions, one to the markets and trattorias of Florence and the other to the nearby hill towns of

Siena, San Gimignano (with its medieval skyscraper towers), and Monteriggioni, a tiny walled village. In the minibus, we learned that even Italian junk food can be astonishing: On the way back from Florence our thoughtful driver ran into a convenience store and emerged with handfuls of sophisticated snack cakes—orange-scented, chocolate-covered, curaçao-laced twists on the Twinkie—that woke us up enough to let us eat again.

The classes themselves were a study in controlled chaos, with Signor Domenici and his assistants coolly working wonders while we, in aprons stenciled with the school logo, lobbed questions thick and fast. Monday was devoted to antipasti; Wednesday to pasta, pizza and soups; Thursday to meat courses and desserts.

Sometimes we gathered by the giant stove in the restaurant's modern kitchen; at others, we clustered around the open hearth of a woodfired rotisserie in the dining room. But with the exception of rolling and cutting gnocchi and ravioli, and shaping and baking paper-thin pizzas in the brick oven, there was much more watching and eating than doing, and even a middling kitchen hand like me was sometimes frustrated not to be given more actual work.

Occasionally, it seemed that too many cooks really might spoil the broth, as we jockeyed to get a better view of browning veal shanks or simmering risotto, or asked about unfamiliar ingredients or directions for recipes that were read aloud but not handed out (for reasons that became clear later). Indeed, the week sometimes boiled down to a blend of summer camp and group therapy, as nine egos, ids and agendas blended or clashed in close quarters.

Picnic Pleasures

Still, there was plenty of time for quiet reading, and the lack of rigid structure or discipline was among the week's greatest charms. Signor Domenici was no Cordon Bleu martinet. He never scolded anyone for a tough frittata or leaden biscotti, and because we did not unduly fuss over the food, our appetites were always good and it tasted marvelous.

Perhaps the pleasantest meal was the least formal: a picnic in the cantina where the Chianti was aged, in front of a roaring fire. We toasted saltless bread, smeared it with whole peeled cloves of garlic until they half melted, drizzled viscous green olive oil over the bruschetta and sprinkled it with salt. Four or five kinds of prosciutto, including one made from wild boar, cheese and raw vegetables rounded out the feast.

Now, when people ask what the adventure taught me, my stock answer is: "To go to Balducci's." What I mean is that Tuscan cooking is so basic that the quality of the ingredients—the olives and oil, the cheese, the artichokes, the meats—is vital, because there are no heavy sauces or lengthy stewing to mask inferior goods. I also learned that, the views of my health-conscious colleagues notwithstanding, there is nothing like a generous puddle of olive oil to conduct the aromas of garlic and onions and herbs through every spoonful of a simple tomato sauce, without leaving it the least bit greasy.

There were limits. I doubt I'll ever feel up to emulating Signor Domenici's adroit wrestling of three or four forbidding varieties of squid and octopus into a delicious cold seafood salad. Commercial American eggs and sugar don't taste the same as their Tuscan counterparts in tiramisu, and expensive imported Chianti and olive oil don't have half the unpretentious charm of the fattoria's house labels.

Spiritual Lessons

Still, I have found it surprisingly easy to duplicate the course's recipes at home, with some help from the well-thumbed books of Mrs. Hazan and Mrs. de' Medici. And while I can't replicate the precious family heirlooms Signora Pincitore laid out in festive table settings one afternoon, her sense of style rubbed off enough to enable me to turn out a plate of mixed antipasti that looks as lovely as any in all but the fanciest New York restaurants.

The most enduring lessons have been spiritual, memories of a time and a culture where people work to live, not vice versa. After days of heavy eating, and sodden compromises with one another's shopping and museum-hopping desires as we chased around Florence in a downpour on the final Friday, we all seemed ready for the course to end.

Yet, back in the warmth of the dining room that night, as Signor Domenici brought out plate after plate for our gala graduation dinner, we grew sentimental. One by one, Signora Pincitore called us to the fireplace to receive the final treat: a portfolio of peacock green and purple Florentine paper, bound with buckram and containing three dozen-odd recipes on parchment paper to take home. In an instant, we understood why they had been guarded all week.

But later, in my room, as I untied the cloth ribbon that sealed the folder and perused its contents, I was reminded again how hard it would be to translate the experience when I returned home. At least one recipe, for bistecca alla Florentina (Florentine steak) was decidedly inscrutable. It called for "young bovine meat, taken from a hind part of the back of the animal, which does not go further than the three ribs of the back, the rib part is called chops and can be used until the seventh rib."

For an instant, I was irked at such a useless prize. But then I realized the secrets had all been, and would remain, "up my fantasy," and that this gentle mystery had given me the perfect excuse to return.

Planning a Culinary Trip

The standard directory of culinary courses in the United States and abroad is *The Guide to Cooking Schools,* published by Shaw-Guides Inc. [see Cooking Schools in *Informazioni Practiche*]. The guide is available in cooking and travel bookshops. It lists schools in the United States and other countries, including a great number in

Italy. It also lists nearly two hundred culinary arts programs offered by community colleges and technical schools, with cross-indexes for special programs for children and rankings by tuition costs.

La Cucina al Focolare at the Fattoria degli Usignoli, in San Donato in Franzano, Italy, an hour southeast of Florence, offers twelve courses a year. All apartments are efficiency-style, with wood-beamed ceilings, tile floors, generous-size sitting and dining areas, small kitchens and multiple bedrooms.

The fifty-five-acre grounds include vineyards, stables and horse-back trails, tennis courts, swimming pool, fountains and lovely out-door fireplaces and warm-weather dining areas.

Bookings may be made through Peggy Markel, Box 54, Boulder, Colorado 80306; 800-988-2851; fax: 303-440-8598; www.cookinitaly.com.

Travelers seeking help with Italian destinations would be in good hands with Marjorie Shaw, a Brooklyn-based travel consultant who was born in Rome and lived in Italy for many years. Her service, "Insider's Italy," was a delight. For a reasonable fee, she booked me in two wonderfully situated, reasonably priced hotels and produced a custom travel portfolio full of helpful hints about everything from the names of maitre d'hôtels and concierges in her favorite establishments to obtaining Italian bus tickets, plus maps, train schedules and a list of recommended reading. Her fee is based on the number of accommodations booked: a typical package for two to four people or a family staying in four or five destinations on a two-week trip would cost about $895. (41 Schermerhorn Street, Suite 891, Brooklyn, New York 11201; 718-855-3878; fax: 855-3687; http://members.aol.com/insidersit.)

Cucina Fiorentina

BY HOLLY BRUBACH

~

editor's note
....

The Capezzana Wine and Culinary Center school is held at the Tenuta di Capezzana estate of Countess Lisa and Count Ugo Contini Bonacossi, about half an hour outside Florence. Of all the accolades the program has received, and quite apart from the estate's superb wine and olive oil, to my mind the best part about the course is that Faith Heller Willinger is included in the package. Willinger is a co-director of the school with Jean-Louis de Mori, who is also chef-owner of Locanda Veneta (and four other restaurants) in the Los Angeles area.

HOLLY BRUBACH, former style editor of *The New York Times Magazine,* is the author of *Girlfriend: Men, Women, and Drag* (Random House, 1999). She is also a fashion columnist for *The New Yorker* and a staff writer for *The Atlantic Monthly.*

On a Sunday night in mid-November, the members of the coming week's class at the Capezzana Wine & Culinary Center, which offers cooking courses in the Tuscan countryside, have convened at a restaurant in Florence. The waiters bring each table a bowl of olive oil, freshly pressed, which is to your standard, store-bought, extra-virgin variety what Technicolor is to black-and-white. For those of us who are tasting *olio nuovo* for the first time, this is an epiphany. The oil, we are told, retains its peppery tang for roughly two months after it has been pressed; by January, the flavor will have evened out and grown more subtle—more like what we Americans, who tend to buy our olive oil months after the harvest and far from the source, are accustomed to. So we seize the moment, using thick slices of bread as sponges. Naturally, the conversation turns to olive oil. "*My* best olive oil story . . ." a New

Yorker named Rosemary begins, and my heart sinks. A culinary rookie with no repertoire of olive oil anecdotes, I fear I'm out of my league.

All sixteen of my classmates seem to live and breathe food. In their spare time, they attend department-store demonstrations by famous chefs. There is Michael, an interior designer from New York; Eve, a photographers' agent from New Jersey; Barbara, a housewife from a Boston suburb; Mary and Bob, a Canadian couple and Capezzana alumni, returning this time with Bob's mother. My own cooking "technique," if that's not too big a word for it, has been limited to omelettes and baked goods; on those rare occasions when I cook for friends, it is always the same menu—chicken roasted in mustard—and this effectively prevents me from inviting the same people twice. So my excitement about the course at Capezzana is tinged with a certain amount of trepidation. What if I flunk?

As it turns out, there was no cause for worry: the chief—perhaps the only—requirement for participation in the course is not experience or skill, but enthusiasm. The school's co-director, Faith Willinger, an American who has lived in Florence for the past twenty-five years and written two books, exudes a love of food—of Italian food in particular, and of the lore surrounding it—that transcends all our disparities. In five days, she would introduce us to the artisans, the ingredients, the wines, and the recipes that make Tuscan cooking so unlike anything back home. Dressed that first evening in an oversize yellow fleece jacket, brightly patterned leggings, and red sneakers, Willinger cut a somewhat eccentric figure as we made our way back through the narrow streets to our hotel; her short, graying hair belies her vigor.

Before registering for the program, I had briefly considered enrolling in two other popular courses, one taught by a stately aristocrat, the other by an imperious cookbook author. Both of these instructors, I was warned, would take it for granted that I already knew how to make a béchamel sauce. Willinger, for her part, takes nothing for granted, and she brings to her role as teacher the patience of a saint and the humor of a stand-up comic. Her ability to put people at ease convinced me instantly that I had made the right decision.

Cooking class is my idea of "adventure travel." I work in the fashion business, among an irreversibly skewed subset of the human species that regards eating (never mind cooking) as a sin and celebrates restaurants for their "scene." "You're doing *what?*" my incredulous colleagues asked. Going on safari they could understand, but this. . . . No sooner had Donna Karan sent her final model down the runway, marking the end of the semiannual month long marathon of collections, than I, utterly exhausted, hailed a taxi to the airport.

Monday, we boarded a bus that took us to the Tenuta di Capezzana, an estate twenty-five minutes west of Florence that would be our campus. The road passed through Carmignano, the nearest town, then wound high into the hills, climbing above the early-morning fog and affording us spectacular views of the landscape rendered in countless Renaissance paintings as the backdrop for noblemen and saints. A row of cypresses along a ridge, a lone umbrella pine silhouetted against the sky, the golden light that drenches the fields all contribute to an unmistakable sense of place: this is Tuscany, still true to itself despite the encroaching sameness that seems to beset the rest of the world.

The villa at Capezzana, built in the sixteenth century for a member of the Medici family, is typical of the region, with pale yellow stucco walls and a red tile roof. There are three dining rooms, one equipped with a grill, another with a wood oven for pizza. Throughout the house, the floors are paved with terra-cotta tiles; the furniture is a hodgepodge of different periods, amassed over four generations. Capezzana is now home to Count Ugo Contini Bonacossi and his wife, Lisa. Willinger calls him "the count from central casting"—handsome, dressed in the manner of an English country squire, adept at charming the ladies. Countess Lisa, though not as gregarious, is a lesson in seemingly effortless efficiency; the night before our arrival, she had held a dinner for 300.

The house at Capezzana is also the headquarters for a thriving business in which three of the seven Contini Bonacossi children take an active part: Filippo, an agronomist, supervises the production of the olive orchards and vineyards; Beatrice (known as Bea) handles marketing; Benedetta runs tours of the estate and the cellars. Bea's two-year-old daughter, Annalu, already shows signs of an affinity for the family business. Tagging along on a tour of the *limonaio,* where grapes intended for the manufacture of *vin santo* (the local dessert wine) are drying on racks, she silenced the visitors: "Shh," she told us, putting a finger to her lips. "The grapes are sleeping."

The Contini Bonacossis seemed to take our comings and goings in stride: The seventeen of us were readily absorbed by the house and its everyday routine. The accommodations proved to be simple but comfortable, more along the lines of a dormitory (singles and doubles available) than a hotel—albeit a dormitory outfitted with antiques. A communal breakfast room also serves as a late-night lounge. The atmosphere is convivial, and apart from a jet-lag-induced nap that I stole one afternoon, I found that I spent surprisingly little time in my room.

The heart of the house is the kitchen, where everyone congregates, family and students alike, around the large central worktable. Patrizio Cirri, the resident chef, presides over preparations for lunch and dinner with an aplomb envied by those of us who still rely on recipes. He cracks an egg and deftly plops it into the center of the ring of flour he has shaped on the table's marble surface, then, with his fingers, gradually mixes a batter for biscotti. He sloshes olive oil into a pan. "How much was that?" we ask, already concerned about re-creating the dish at home. "A third of a cup? Half a cup?" Willinger estimates the quantities, which we dutifully record in our notebooks. Years of use have worn the numbers off the dials on Patrizio's oven, which for him poses no problem: he can tell the difference between 325 degrees and 350 simply by sticking his hand inside. For us, Willinger specifies the temperatures.

In addition to Willinger and the family chef, the faculty at Capezzana includes Countess Lisa, many of whose recipes have entered into the curriculum; Jean-Louis de Mori, Willinger's co-director, who teaches half of the ten sessions a year (the rest of the time, he's seeing to his restaurants in Los Angeles, including Locanda Veneta and Allegria); and assorted guest chefs. When I was at Capezzana, Johanne Killeen and George Germon, proprietors of Al Forno in Providence, Rhode Island, were in residence. Anna Tasca Lanza, a celebrated cook who offers her own course at her house in Sicily, came to pay her friend Faith a visit and stayed two days. These experts gave us the benefit of their knowledge as they answered our questions and showed us their techniques.

No two days were alike, but the agenda always included some kitchen time—a few hours prior to lunch or dinner, during which we learned to roast a guinea fowl, to clean baby artichokes, to sharpen knives. Countess Lisa's recipes for penne with leeks and lemon (which appears in Willinger's book *Red, White & Greens,* a compendium of Italian vegetable dishes) and for a cake made with olive oil instead of butter were mastered easily enough. We watched Benedetta prepare her pizza dough—a bizarre concoction incorporating honey and red wine that looks like primordial ooze at the outset and over the course of the day transforms itself, on the basis of nothing but a punching down every few hours. "The nice thing about this dough, though it does require a commitment," Willinger remarks, "is that you don't have to give it orthodonture, you don't have to send it to college."

Willinger's informal disquisitions—on balsamic vinegar, *sop-*

pressata, ribollita ("reboiled" soup, made with white beans, vegetables, and bread)—are often punctuated by priceless one-liners. She pronounces a good Pinot Nero "the kind of wine that makes a perfect substitute for psychotherapy": When you're feeling really bad, she explains, you need something really good. She says of the canned tuna caught seasonally in the Mediterranean, where the fish go to spawn: "These are tuna thinking of sex." France—to her mind, a misguided, pretentious nation where it's hard to get a good meal—is contemptuously referred to as "the *F* country."

It would be difficult to imagine a more entertaining guide to the local attractions. Off we went every day on field trips, with Willinger leading the way: to the *macelleria,* or butcher shop, in Ferruccia, where we saw how prosciutto is made (while the vegetarians among us waited outside); to the bakery in Prato, where we snacked on a bagful of the scrumptious crumbs that result when long batons of biscotti are cut into slices; to the area's leading producer of liqueur-filled chocolates, in Agliana, where we witnessed the little bottle-shaped molds being filled with *vin santo.* To say that many of these destinations are off the tourist track does not begin to convey just how inconspicuous they are. In several cases, as Willinger remarked with only a small degree of hyperbole, our arrival doubled the village's population.

Sometimes our objective was a famous local restaurant, where we were introduced to the chef and his specialties. In the town of Prato, Osvaldo Baroncelli took us into the kitchen to demonstrate his *fricassea,* a chicken dish made-to-order from the white meat, livers, and wattle. His stuffed chicken neck may not rate high on the list of recipes we plan to trot out for friends, but it certainly illustrated the frugality that pervades Tuscan cooking, even at its most elaborate. Nothing is thrown away; many recipes incorporate leftovers.

At lunch in Florence, Fabio Picchi, the proprietor of Cibrèo, reprimanded certain members of our party for tackling their polenta with spoons rather than forks; he also forbade us to share portions or to offer one another tastes. In the end, however, the food was so sublime that it won out over the severity of his welcome. "This," Willinger announced, savoring her meat course, "happens to be a lamb that read Dante."

It was no time to go on a diet. Lunches and dinners consisted of four courses, each with its own wine. I, who have always loved to eat and helped myself to seconds, suddenly discovered my appetite's outer limits. Dessert, when it arrived, was too much; breakfast was unthinkable. Three times, I managed to put myself through an hour of aerobics in my room, which was the only mitigating factor in what seemed like a week of Thanksgivings. On a visit to the Pitti Palace, where we were granted a private tour of the collection assembled by Count Ugo's grandfather—an astounding array of paintings and sculpture by Tintoretto, Della Robbia, Goya, El Greco, Bernini, and others—I found myself grateful for the respite from food.

I, for one, had underestimated the omnipresence of meat in Tuscan cooking, from the seasonal *salumi* (cured meats), served as appetizers, to the *bistecca alla fiorentina,* charcoal-grilled steak (a beloved main course). As the week wore on, several of us who had previously succeeded in rising above our carnivorous urges were confronted with a new temptation at nearly every meal. Eve stuck to her guns, but others, like Barbara and I—whose vegetarian habits were based not on moral conviction but on mere good intentions concerning our health—soon wavered in the presence of a good prosciutto.

One morning midweek, we set out for Panzano in Chianti, a sleepy town on a steep hillside, where we descended on the premises of butcher Dario Cecchini. Festooning the ceiling were garlands of garlic and red chili peppers, draped from big iron meat hooks. A bookcase housed hefty volumes on Jan Dibbets, the Dutch conceptual artist, and Renzo Piano, the contemporary architect, interspersed with reference works on *charcuterie.* There were paintings on the walls and, in the far corner, a statue of a naked woman, as fat as I felt; the work, Cecchini explained, of an artist friend living in Paris, whom he is paying in installments of prosciutto.

A handsome man in his thirties, with striking blue eyes and a short beard, Cecchini was dressed in a blood-stained white apron, a paisley scarf, and a red hat like the one Federico da Montefeltro wears in his famous portrait by Piero della Francesca. The hat was a nice touch, a theatrical flourish suggesting that this renaissance man is a Renaissance man as well. I remarked to Willinger that although there must be unattractive men working somewhere in the Tuscan food industry, she had certainly failed to find them. "I don't want to hurt my eyes," she replied.

The white-tiled room reverberated with the sound of a Beethoven string quartet. Cecchini lowered the volume so Willinger could be heard. She had reverently billed his shop as "the Vatican of meat," and now, during our two-hour audience with this debonair pope, she interviewed him on assorted subjects—among them, salt (only salt from Sicily is acceptable for Italian cooking, he decreed, and the use of salt from the Atlantic is "blasphemy"). Cecchini has become something of a celebrity in food circles and is regularly presented with opportunities to enlarge his business—to open far-flung branches, to star in a festival organized by a famous New York restaurant. He has politely refused it all. He is an artisan, in love with his craft, and his love is pure.

Cecchini's first-rate selection of meats and *salumi* is augmented by a handful of cheeses (among them, a superb young pecorino) and three types of beans, including the small, round *fagioli zolfini di Valdarno,* slightly sulfurous in taste and delicious when cooked with rosemary, then tossed with new olive oil. But in the end it was Cecchini's *profumo di Chianti*—his own blend of salt and indigenous seasonings such as rosemary, sage, bay leaves, and coriander—

that we all bought. Soon after my return to New York, a liberal sprinkling of it on some Cornish hens was all it took to persuade the friends I'd invited for dinner that I had acquired some new, hard-won culinary expertise.

And that, in fact, turns out to be not a lie but merely an exaggeration. I learned a lot. But, in keeping with one of the prime hazards of any education, I now have a much better idea of all that I don't know. What I still lack is the ability to take a recipe and make it my own—as Countess Lisa once did on an almost daily basis, when she would make olive oil cake for her children, each time flavoring it with different ingredients.

Friday—our last day—was devoted to wine. Nick Belfrage, a consultant to several vineyards in the area, provided a crash course that ranged wide, from the genesis of the new "super-Tuscans" (renegade reds that have developed outside the old standards for classification) to the local approach, in which wine is considered an adjunct to food—an attitude inconducive to the sort of wine cults that have sprung up in northern Europe, where wine is regarded as an entity unto itself.

Our graduation ceremony that evening was—what else?—a dinner, with a menu by George and Johanne, featuring as a first course their famous pizza cooked over a wood fire on the grill. Count Ugo delivered the commencement address, quoting Virgil, musing on the immortality of great books as compared to other, more ephemeral achievements. "Those of us who make wine and food," he said, "dedicate our energies to the pleasure of the moment." *Well,* I thought, *let's not overestimate the value of literature.* After all, the week's convivial delights—however fleeting—had succeeded in restoring my soul.

Then Willinger called out our names, one by one, and Countess Lisa bestowed our diplomas. "Barbara!" Faith announced. "A lapsed vegetarian. My kinda girl!"

Olive oil tastes best within a year of its production. Top producers include date of harvest on their labels.

Kale, cauliflower, broccoli, winter squash, and apples are all more flavorful after the first frost.

For making pasta and pizza dough, use American pastry flour; it has the same low-gluten, soft-wheat composition as Italian flour.

Carnaroli is the ultimate rice for making risotto: its center stays al dente, and the outside has just enough starch to create a lightly creamy sauce—without cream.

Tuscans prepare garlic bread (*fettunta*) by toasting slices of bread, rubbing garlic on the surfaces, then sprinkling on salt and extra-virgin olive oil. This is Faith Willinger's favorite dish.

Use a carrot peeler to make Parmesan cheese curls—a perfect garnish for pasta and vegetables.

A Corian cutting board chilled in the freezer can take the place of marble for making pastry.

For asparagus as sweet as the day it was picked, lop off the ends and soak the stalks for fifteen to twenty minutes in a half-inch of sugar water.

The Facts: Tuscany

The Capezzana Wine & Culinary Center offers five-day cooking classes ten times a year, conducted by food writer Faith Willinger or Los Angeles restaurateur Jean-Louis de Mori. The curriculum varies depending on season and composition of the group, which rarely exceeds fourteen. All lessons are in English—most students are American or Canadian—but even a rudimentary knowledge of Italian makes the experience more enjoyable, especially during exchanges with local chefs and on shopping excursions. Days are typically devoted to demonstrations and field trips; in the evenings, students prepare dinner from supplies they've gathered.

Fees for the week per person range from about $2,400 (for a shared room and bath) to about $3,000 (for private quarters), and include all meals and an overnight in Florence. Capezzana also offers tours to the public; the estate produces eleven types of wine and a superb olive oil, available as *olio nuovo* in November and December, immediately after the first pressing. For more information, contact Tenuta di Capezzana (100 Via Capezzana, Carmignano 50042; 055.870.6005; fax: 055.870.6673) or the estate's U.S. agent, Lili Rollins, 1607 Pearl Street, Alameda, California, 94501; Phone/fax: 510-865-8191; e-mail: lrr@prodigy.net.

Faith Willinger's Address Book

Tuscan destinations for the food-obsessed.

Artisans

Antonio Mattei, 20 Via Ricasoli, Prato; tel. 0574.25756. Most famous for biscotti, but try the scrumptious brutti buoni ("ugly but good"), chewy almond cookies.

Antica Macelleria Cecchini, 11 Via XX Luglio Panzano; tel. 055.852.020. Refinement and intellect in a butcher shop. Check out the salumi (cured meats, such as prosciutto), butcher Dario Cecchini's mix of salt and herbs, fennel pollen (delicious on salmon), and lavender (Cecchini recommends it with lamb).

Arte del Cioccolato, 378 Via Provinciale, Agliana; tel. 0574.718.506. Above his candy shop, Roberto Catinari painstakingly makes chocolates with liquid centers. Varieties include logs filled with grappa, corks with champagne, and wine bottles with Chianti. Also look for exquisite chocolates in the shape of chestnuts, acorns, and porcini mushrooms.

Macelleria Marini, 313 Via Selva, Ferruccia; 0574.718.119. Renowned producer of prosciutto Toscano, slightly saltier than the more ubiquitous San Daniele or Parma types. Perfect with unsalted Tuscan bread.

Markets (Open Monday to Saturday, unless indicated.)
San Lorenzo, Piazza del Mercato Centrale, Florence.

Mercato di Sant'Ambrogio, Piazza Ghiberti, Florence.

Santo Spirito, Piazza Santo Spirito, Florence.

Mercato di Prato, Prato (Monday mornings only).

Restaurants
Cibrèo, 8/r Via A. del Verrocchio, Florence; tel. 055.234.1100; dinner for two about $90. Superb cooking by Fabio Picchi, one of Italy's most celebrated chefs.

La Bussola, 382 Via Vecchia Fiorentina, Catena; tel. 0573.743.128; dinner for two about $68. Wonderful Tuscan specialties, including cured goose breast with *limonella,* a lemon herb, on flatbread.

Ristorante Osvaldo Baroncelli, 13 Via Fra Bartolomeo, Prato; tel. 0574.23810; dinner for two about $74. Try the *scottiglia di pollo in fricassea,* an exotic chicken and tomato stew.

Shops
Bartolini, 30/r Via dei Servi, Florence; tel. 055.211.895. A comprehensive selection of housewares, from the utilitarian to the deluxe.

Richard-Ginori, 17/r Via dei Rondinelli, Florence; tel. 055.210.041. Classic Ginori china, as well as crystal (including glasses by Riedel) and silver.

Abbigliamento da Lavoro, Alba 27/r Via dei Servi, Florence; tel. 055.287.754. Uniforms and aprons for professional cooks—and amateurs who want to look the part.

Winery
Tenuta di Bagnolo, 156 Via Montalese, Montemurlo; tel. 0574.652.439. After touring Capezzana, visit this producer of Marchesi Pancrazi, an excellent Pinot Noir. Sample the olive oil and the pecorino as well.

Oil by Mail
Capezzana's *olio nuovo* can be ordered in early December from Zingerman's in Ann Arbor (888-636-8162). A half-liter costs about $30.

On and Around Italy's Argentario

BY DOONE BEAL

editor's note

It's really due to my friend, Charles, that I went to the Argentario. He grew up in Porto Ercole and had spoken of it with much passion over the years, and, armed with the names of his childhood family friends, I really felt I had to go. As my husband was driving, I read this article aloud to him. Neither one of us is accustomed to reading the names of people we know (or, in this case, people we were to meet) in national magazines, so you can imagine our surprise to come across the names of the very people we were searching for at Marina Cala Galera.

The Coventrys proved to be exceptionally kind and funny hosts, and regaled us with stories of Charles as a young boy. At Katie's suggestion, we hiked around Monte Argentario and took a trip to Isola Giglio. But mostly, we simply enjoyed being on a section of the Italian coast where we encountered few Americans.

Although this piece was featured in July 1988, I think the statement that the Argentario "is scarcely undiscovered, but neither is it a byword among Mediterranean resorts" is still accurate. You might want to inquire locally about the restaurants mentioned here, but if too much time has passed, ask around for some recommendations. Like the author, we had a delicious meal at La Lampara, named for the light on Italian fishing boats.

DOONE BEAL lives in London and has been a frequent contributor to *Gourmet* for many years.

Speeding along the *autostrada* some 160 kilometers northwest of Rome you might notice on your left a misty but quite sizable peak lying beyond the placid stretches of a lagoon. Mount Argentario is the most striking feature of the Argentario Peninsula, moored to the mainland at Orbetello by three stringlike causeways. The area is scarcely undiscovered, but neither is it a byword among Mediterranean resorts.

Like an island in every aspect except its easy accessibility, the Argentario is a postscript to the Tuscan mainland, a geographical afterthought, echoing the same landscape of olive trees and patches of vineyards, dotted with ochre and sepia houses, terra-cotta roofs, and sentinel cypresses. It is lit in summer by shocks of indigo broom, blue thistles, scarlet poppies, and rockroses. The peninsula's western coast, washed by the Tyrrhenian Sea, is rimmed by the spectacular Strada Panoramica, which winds and switchbacks through massive gray rocks that drop sheer into ravishing dark blue coves, a-skim in summer with sails, and the odd ketch or sloop lies enviably at anchor for a picnic lunch in the lee of an offshore grotto. It is owing to this rocky coast and the resulting lack of good beaches that the Argentario has remained thus unsullied, though some of the original mule tracks now lead to (mostly) discreet cottage developments, of

which clay rooftops are the only visible evidence from afar. As for the rest of the peninsula, parts of the mountainous, maquis-shrouded interior must surely remain untrodden, even by mules.

The Argentario can claim the distinction of having been charted by Leonardo da Vinci—the original map hangs in the Vatican Museum—at the end of the six-teenth century, when Philip II of Spain, lured by the peninsula's two strategic ports, annexed it from the republic of Siena. What the Argentario represents today is a tightly packed posy of beguiling contrasts. Within a thirty-minute drive one can dip into Orbetello, the once-fortified city that lies at the lagoon; enter the big, bustling port of Santo Stefano, from where the ferries and the *aliscafi* ply to the off-shore islands of Giglio and Giannutri; and take in Porto Ercole, sheltered on the leeward coast, which, these days, is the choice residential area (including the sum-mer villa of the Dutch royal family) and draws exponents of *la bella figura*, as well as weekend trippers from Rome.

The low hills embracing the harbor at Porto Ercole are dotted with Aragonese-style forts dating back to the days of Spanish suzerainty. The old town, suspended like a ship's prow above the port, is proclaimed by a lovely sixteenth-century Sienese gate, and its flagstoned streets are linked by shallow flights of steps that descend from the parish church of Saint Erasmus to the pink-bricked Piazza Santa Barbara, which, as the local guidebook puts it, "never fails to draw a response." Picturesque it certainly is, as are the views from its balustraded balcony of the harbor and the amphitheater of slanting blue hills on the distant mainland.

This old quarter, not yet adopted by tourists, remains quite unselfconscious. The action goes on along the waterfront; that is, except on Porto Ercole's feast day, June 2, when, accompanied by a vast procession of townsfolk, including first communicants, the effigy of Saint Erasmus is carried down from the church through the streets and is finally blessed at sea, together with the entire fishing fleet, in a ceremony that culminates in a massive fireworks display. We watched some of the festivities from the waterfront terrace of La Lampara, which was even more agog than usual. This simple, family-run *trattoria* is by common consent the hub of Porto Ercole, where locals and expatriates gather for *spaghetti alle vongole*, fish, and, in the evening, bubbling crusty pizzas, all accompanied by relays of fragrant white wine.

Among the boutiques that line the waterfront, Sarciappone is a tiny treasure trove with well chosen and very fairly priced resort clothes by such designers as Bruno of Rome. All the shops, including an excellent bookstore, stay open until at least eight in the evening, and customers drift in and out between apéritifs at Kings Bar, where a wooden terrace built out over the water feels all but seaborne.

Similar animation surges around the Marina Cala Galera, just outside the old port. Here, offshoot boutiques from Florence and Rome are interspersed with ship chandlers, provision stores for mariners, and marine agencies. This is one of the best-equipped marinas along the Italian coast, berthing some 650 yachts. Should you want to charter, if only for a day or two, reliable and knowledgeable advice can be had from Katy and Robin Coventry of Covemare, who also handle car rentals.

Sailing, skin diving, and aquatic life in general are prime objectives of people in Porto Ercole. But for many others the magnet is Il Pellicano, secluded a couple of bays along the coast just off the Strada Panoramica. A member of Relais & Châteaux, this small hotel has the sophisticated simplicity and well honed comfort of a superbly staffed country villa; and such is its quality of peace and calm that the surest awakener is the dawn chorus of birdsong. A series of split-levels, all bowered with flowers, create an ambiance of privacy. Terraces cascading with geraniums and shaded by pines and cypresses lead down, past a refreshing saltwater pool, to an elaborate bathing establishment secreted among the rocks from which one plunges (or steps decorously backward down a ladder) into deliciously cool, clear depths for wonderful swimming and snorkeling.

Room service, one of the more remarkable aspects of Il Pellicano's incidental luxuries, must be some of the swiftest on record, and breakfast—orange juice, a big assortment of breads, and a crock of Bel Paese, as well as jams and honey—is delivered by a smiling juggler of a waiter. As for the décor, it is the kind one would like to wrap up and take home, from the charmingly frescoed headboards to the pots of wild flowers and the tole lamp brackets, which I coveted most of all. The rooms are decorated in variations on clear jades and peacock blues, yellows and Sienese reds; and the bathrooms are well equipped with built-in hair dryers. One caveat: Some, but not all, of the twenty-eight rooms have private terraces on which to bask in the late-afternoon sun or watch the magic of moonrise. Ours did, but it is vital to request one described in the hotel's brochure as having a "sea view." Those with a "garden view," though cheaper, afford the less attractive prospect of car park and tennis courts; "standard" means just what it says. It is also worth noting that accommodations are available as well in some immensely attractive cottages on the estate.

Piano music and Ricardo's cocktails enliven the evening scene on the lamplit deck. The culinary offerings are split between the menu and the buffet table, where platters of fish and shellfish are arrayed beside appealing antipasti. Marinated sardines and anchovies, Tuscan bean salad, and *datte del mare* (cockles) vie with all sorts of rich salads, raw vegetables, and greens, notably the astringent dandelion leaves. Grilled *spigola* (sea bass) and a split *aragosta* (lobster) are other examples of refreshing simplicity; Chef Antonio also turns out a Lucullan *risotto con tartufi*. This deserved a bottle of Lambrusco, which we finished off with *fresh* Parmesan, a revelation of flavor and texture.

Shaded by trees on a patio above the pool, festive buffet lunches are the weekend—and in high season, daily—diversion. Apart from a mosaic of different salads, enticements include *scampi,* lobster, sea bass, T-bone steaks, lamb cutlets, and gutsy local sausages, all grilled over charcoal. One of the chef's signature dishes is salmon baked in pastry; the light blanket of pastry seals in the moisture and flavor. Another specialty is the wickedly delicious almond tart, which successfully tempted me on several occasions.

Altogether, one would be hard put to find fault with what is a blissful place in which to luxuriate for a few days. But Il Pellicano's mood varies wildly from midweek to weekends and also according to season: Late May, June, and September offer more tranquillity and, inevitably, the best of the excellent service. If no rooms are available there, one might try the Hotel Don Pedro, overlooking Porto Ercole. The rooms are very pleasant, as is the staff, and there is an attractive balconied bar and restaurant.

The prettiest part of Porto Santo Stefano, located on the north coast, is Porto Vecchio, the original fishing village—as opposed to Porto Nuovo, the bigger, newer port around the headland, which contains the ferry terminals and the Cantiere Navale, or naval shipyard. The shopping in Santo Stefano is much more varied than in

Porto Ercole. In a corner of Porto Nuovo, Lo Scoglio offers an excellent range of Ken Scott prints, and on the Porto Vecchio waterfront Marieangelo carries a good selection by Missoni. La Vela stocks a worthy collection of sandals and resort clothes; and, in one of the few visible signs of changing times, Gucci has replaced the original *alimentari*. However, I was reassured to find my favorite local hairdresser, Pietro, still in business.

There is a welcome addition to the restaurant scene—Ristorante dal Greco, the terrace of which has a prime vantage point of the old harbor. Sebastiano Greco and his wife, Annamaria, run a most elegant, small establishment, with a piano bar in the evening. In contrast to the usual fish and pasta (still to be found, and of quality, at Ottavio, around the corner), true *cucina* and imagination are in evidence here with such items as *scampi,* breaded and fried sizzling crisp and presented in a huge goblet with mayonnaise and petals of *radicchio; zuppa di datte del mare,* cockles in a delicate broth infused with tomato; and *tortelli* stuffed with minced *calamari* and ricotta. Each of these was delicious, but the star was unquestionably *scampi in crosta,* shrimp in a creamy broth, flavored with scallion and *peperoncini* (pickled Tuscan peppers), topped with a Bocuse-inspired pastry crust and baked. It was exquisite. With this entirely winsome meal we drank a white Vernaccia di San Gimignano, rounding off with a glass of Pinot Frizzante Grand Bleu, which comes in an exotic blue bottle and would be equally good as an apéritif.

It would be a shame to leave Porto Santo Stefano without visiting Armando, one of the oldest and best loved Argentarian restaurants, in Porto Nuovo. The daytime sounds of drilling and grinding from the Cantiere Navale across the street make dinner (in any event, the more festive occasion here) preferable to lunch. The décor is very *navale*, with ships' lanterns and lots of canvas and polished wood, and there is a pleasant outdoor terrace. Roberto, the *padrone,* tends to stick to his basics, and so do I. For one cannot improve on anchovies and black olives with hot, crusty toast as a starter; followed by *gnocchi verdi,* made to delicate, nutmeg-scented perfection; and, finally, *scampi alla griglia,* which are scarcely more than kissed over the grill. Locals generally outnumber visitors, and the well worn conviviality of the place is all part of its appeal.

Another turn of the Argentarian kaleidoscope took us to a small rustic *trattoria,* La Fontanina di San Pietro, perched, as it was in its days as a shepherd's hut, on a pergola, overlooking the distant lagoons and Orbetello. It's the perfect place to lunch after you have made the circuit of the Strada Panoramica, or walked in the hills, or, on a clear day, driven up the coiling road to the summit of Mount Argentario, somewhat unpoetically called Monte Telegrafo, from the windy ridge of which there is a cartographer's view of the coast, the mainland hills, and the offshore islands.

But back to lunch and the pasta, a specialty of La Fontanina's family kitchens. *Tagliatelle con carciofi* (pasta with artichokes, tomato, and cream) was, for me, a new and seductive taste sensation. The *spaghetti alla pirata,* zingy with *peperoni* (peppers), garlic, and seafood, was quite different but equally toothsome. Then one could have fish, but somehow a *bistecca alla fiorentina,* grilled and served simply with an *insalata del campo* (literally, "salad of the field"), seemed more appropriate to the setting. We finished our very satisfying meal with the classic Tuscan *crostate* (crisp, semisweet cookies) and a glass of dark golden Vin Santo, a perfect combination.

Orbetello is a resolutely southern, palmy town, knotted in the lagoon from which Marshall Italo Balbo led a squadron of twenty-four flying boats, a kind of seaplane, across the Atlantic to make a dashing entry at the Chicago International Exposition of 1934 (a feat never attempted either before or since). Guarded by handsome sixteenth-century gates that were part of the original fortifications and bordered on both sides with tree-lined promenades, Orbetello exhibits both grace and character, and its very lack of tourist-oriented chic is an endearment. In order to imbibe its flavor, one should take in the lovely Romanesque doors of the cathedral, stroll the promenade, and then sit at a café in the Piazza Garibaldi to watch the swallows wheel and twitter across the early evening sky, while tots barely out of their perambulators play football. The town seems to excel in butchers, *alimentari,* hardware shops by the dozen (it was here, years ago, that I bought the best carbon-steel carving knife I ever owned), wine stores, and cheese shops.

Orbetello is the gateway to the Maremma, that narrow strip of coastal plain and its hinterland stretching up toward Viareggio. A malarial marshland until a century ago—though it was in fact known to the Etruscans—the Maremma was finally cleared and re-inhabited after World War II. As one might expect, there is some interesting food that figures largely in this region. It is famed, for example, for *cinghiale,* or wild boar, which appears in many different dishes. Fruits and vegetables, especially artichokes and grapes, as well as grains grow here in profusion. But in past days much of the population subsisted on bread rather than the pasta that is today's staple; hence two of the most celebrated dishes. *Acqua cotta* (literally, "cooked water") is a regional specialty based on celery, tomatoes, onions, and any other such odds and ends that came to hand. An egg is poached in the broth just before serving it over slices of fried bread, which are still a garnish and a makeweight for many soups prepared in local peasant fashion. A better known dish is *crostini.* This varies from one cook to another, but it is always sliced from a coarse, crusty loaf and served warm, either fried in Tuscan olive oil or toasted and drizzled with the oil.

La Taverna, a beguiling Orbetello restaurant at Via Roma, 52, specializes in *crostini.* The fried variety, topped with finely chopped tomato and basil, drew such appreciative comments from us that Piero, the *padrone,* a man who loves people who love food, came bustling out with two more variations—one spread with a wonderful wild mushroom mixture, the other with a nicely gamy chicken liver pâté. Our main dishes included potato *gnocchi* with oil-braised eggplant, garlic, and orégano, served at volcanic heat in an earthenware crock; and a firm *spigola,* perfectly grilled with oil and lemon juice. The *crema caramella* was exactly to my taste but so, too, was the *semifreddo* with spongecake soaked in wine and combined with creamy *mascarpone.* We divided the spoils.

Heading for the restaurant da Egisto, Corso Italia, 190, one evening, I was diverted by the sight and scent of beautiful leather at Assarit, at the head of the same street. The hardworking young craftsman here, his lathes still humming at half past eight in the evening, turns out some very good-looking handbags and tote bags in softest baby calf, mostly unlined but well styled and finished, at far less than the prevailing prices. Almost next door, at I Gioielli del Mare, attractive coral and *pietra dura* (semi-precious stone) jewelry is also worth investigating.

Two such unexpected discoveries in one evening went straight to my head, adding something more to our excellent meal at Egisto, an old favorite. Local friends with whom we dined reminded me of the maxim of Italian restaurants: never ask to see the menu; listen to the *padrone* as he reels off the specialties of the day. Happily for those whose Italian is less than commanding, Marino Batani, who put in a couple of years at London's Savoy, speaks English. He recommended the asparagus soup, with a generous quantity of tender stems and tips, served with the ubiquitous bread—a substantial and delicious starter. Then there was *cinghiale* treated like prosciutto, though it is gamier and more peppery, and a steaming black *risotto di seppie* (inkfish). We drank a smooth, fruity Chianti and a delicate white Colli Euganei from Padua. Egisto is thoroughly commendable (for dinner rather than lunch, at any rate in summer) but preferable in the quiet midweek to weekends, when, as we discovered on a revisit, even the best restaurateurs are run off their feet by huge family parties.

꙳

Only twenty-minutes' drive from Orbetello, yet worlds apart, is Capalbio, crowding a hill speckled with olive trees and cork oak and striped by vineyards through which runs the ravishingly lovely approach road. A tiny medieval town, girdled with two sets of defense walls, Capalbio is the main center for horse breeding in this part of Tuscany and a rallying point for wild boar hunters, who celebrate their sport and its objective the second week of September. It is famed, too, for its herbs and a myriad variety of wild mushrooms, particularly the fleshy, strong-flavored *porcini*. One *alimentari* after another stocked *salsiccia di cinghiale* (wild boar sausage), as well as preserved mushrooms and *peperoni* with herbs bottled in local olive oil. These are fruits of the earth indeed and well worth buying on the spot. As we wandered the tight, winding streets, our eyes were also caught by huge, encrusted amphorae filled with geraniums, by the faded frescoes in the Church of Saint Nicola, and by shadowy flights of steps and curly street lamps. The crenellated towers of the sixteenth-century Palazzo Collacchioni crown the summit. Just beneath it, La Torre di Carlo is an agreeable tavern with a beam and rush ceiling and nests of vine leaves embracing the lights; the local red and white wines are dispensed from two immense kegs.

The cooking is *casalinga* (home-style), and one of the house specialties is *pappardelle* with wild boar (a variation of this dish is with wild hare). Either way, one portion is enough for two: This is trencherman country, and the food is intended for the hungry *butteri* who herd the horses and cattle. After considering our choices we opted for steak and a wonderful *insalata verde,* fragrant with basil and orégano, dressed with wine vinegar and that wondrous olive oil; and *caciotta* cheese was the perfect foil to our excellent lively red wine.

A walk around the ramparts of Capalbio, the sea glinting in the distance beyond the arcadian landscape, sharpened a desire for more of the same. Our last day we set off along the Gianella Causeway through flat landscape and then abruptly came upon the contrasting hill towns of Magliano, Pereta, and Scansano. Compared to Volterra and San Gimignano (both within eighty kilometers of the Argentario) this is "lesser" Tuscany and hence much of its appeal, for it holds no lure for the sightseeing buses. Pereta, with its single tower, fortified gateway, and tiny Piazza del Mercato—alas, not in action that day— is especially pretty. In Scansano, a clocktower gate leads out of the Piazza Garibaldi into the Centro Storico, which is quite devoid of tourist trappings—or of much action of any kind—but has some lovely, old façades and overhanging eaves.

The road that links the two towns, balconied over the plains with views that made us stop every other minute, was lined with vetch and poppies, yellow daisies, newly harvested corn, cypresses, and dwarf pines. If there is a tourist magnet hereabouts it is Saturnia, famed since Roman times for its sulphur springs, which gush warm and pungent over aching backs and shoulders.

Our objective was a restaurant near Montemerano, within whose picturesque but labyrinthine streets I managed to get lost just as every house was putting up its shutters against the midday heat. All prospects of lunch began to fade as I plunged down one identical alley after another. Such are the pleasures, and/or perils, of "lesser" Tuscany. But we found our gastronomic grail at the tiny hamlet of Poderi di Montemerano a couple of kilometers farther on the road to Manciano.

Notched above the road and all too easy to miss, Locanda Laudomia is a former posting inn some hundred years old and famed among cognoscenti for the *cucina* of Clara Dettin, a third generation *padrona*. I first met Signora Clara, a pretty woman with businesslike chained spectacles, in her kitchens, seasoning, tasting, stirring, and generally masterminding her minions. There could have been little doubt of the pleasures to come. We sat outside beneath the shade of a lime tree as numerous starters were presented: *crostini, acqua cotta,* and *pappardelle con la lepre,* as well as a truly superb *zuppa di funghi,* the flavor of which I can only describe as being both rich and wild. Then came the *piatto supremo,* which I had already earmarked as it whizzed by on a platter destined for another table: *coniglio a porchetta* (rabbit, roasted and stuffed with pork liver and herbs). It was perfection, served with fried zucchini and baked sliced potatoes with grated cheese. Luscious fruit tarts with bananas and strawberries were the penultimate delight before the *crostate* and Vin Santo. Dining here can be alfresco or in the very comfortable restaurant, but, whichever you choose, Laudomia should not be missed—as much for its taste, in every sense, of the Tuscan Maremma as for its food.

The road from here opens the door to many other resolutely Italian towns, and one's inclination may be to push on and see more of them, but it may also be very hard to resist the Argentario's beckoning call to return.

Taking the Waters in Tuscany

BY WILLIAM WEAVER

❧

editor's note

Spa treatments are included in Italy's national health service, but even if they weren't, I feel certain they'd be hard to resist, by Italians and foreigners alike. Visitors seem to forget that Italy has a great number of thermal spas throughout the country, and a look at the spa brochure produced by the Italian Tourist Office reveals that Tuscany is blessed with many of them.

WILLIAM WEAVER is the editor of *Open City* (Steerforth Italia, 1999) and is the author of *A Legacy of Excellence: The Story of Villa I Tatti* (Abrams, 1997; with photographs by David Finn). He is the translator of the works of Umberto Eco, and writes frequently about Italy for *The New York Times* and other publications. Weaver is also on the languages and literature faculty of Bard College in Annandale-on-Hudson, New York.

There is a special attraction about complete idleness, especially when you are told it is good for your health. Watering places, in particular, seem to establish a tempo that becomes immediately congenial; an adagio that goes with emptying cups of more or less palatable liquid, window-shopping (Gucci, Cartier, et al. have local outlets), newspaper-scanning (foreign papers at the kiosk halfway down Viale Verdi), and an occasional anodyne card game, never for money (loss would be bad for the heart as well as the temper), but for fun, to pass the seemingly endless, undemanding time.

At Montecatini in central Tuscany, one of Italy's most famous and most popular spas, the visitor easily falls into the relaxed rhythm of the city's life. Unlike almost every other Italian town, here no obligatory sights require your attention: no museums crammed with unparalleled masterpieces, no grand churches or frescoed palaces. If you can't live without high culture, you can, of course, find plenty within easy reach (the local travel agencies offer daily afternoon excursions to nearby Pisa or Lucca or to Florence, an hour away). But you are more likely to succumb to the temptation of letting Montecatini's easy, not to say lazy pace, carry you serenely along. With a population of over 20,000, the town has a life beyond the thermal establishments. If you walk along the busy Corso Roma, you find yourself in a normal small Tuscan city, with shops and, on the side streets, quiet blocks of apartments and small villas.

Most of the visitors are here with a purpose: to improve their health. For, since the Middle Ages, Montecatini has been famous for its waters. They are mentioned in a letter, of 1387, written by Marco Datini, the famous "merchant of Prato" to a Florentine doctor: "Many people go to the bath at Monte Chatini," he says; a few years later, a local scientist and chronicler, Ugolino Simoni, wrote (in Latin) that the local water "wondrously loosens the belly and dissolves stone . . . stimulating appetite." The Medici grand duke Cosimo I took an interest in the baths, and his successor, the grand duke Pietro Leopoldo of the house of Lorraine, had new thermal buildings built (today's Terme Leopoldine commemorate his important patronage). The Palazzina Regia, built to accommodate the grand ducal family, still stands on Viale Verdi, and now houses the administration offices of the spa.

Around the end of the eighteenth century, the city began to assume its present aspect, though much of the important architecture dates from the turn of the century. The main street, Viale Verdi, was laid out, and began to be flanked by the first hotels and shops. Tree-shaded, outlined by flower beds and patches of sward, the avenue climbs gently uphill to the vast, attractive park, where the chief springs are scattered, each with its delightful, fanciful architecture, with rotundas and towers and fountains: the Leopoldina, the Regina and the elaborate Tettuccio, which has long been considered the most elegant of the establishments, the tacit gathering place of Montecatini's most distinguished guests.

As you stroll up toward the Tettuccio along the Viale Verdi, with the broad park rising and spreading out to your left, you first encounter the Excelsior, another popular establishment; its original Art Nouveau building, richly and handsomely decorated, with an open semicircular veranda and a great bow window, boasts a substantial modern addition, whose inviting cafe-bar overlooks the street, ideal for people-watching (a Montecatini sport). Behind the Excelsior, at the central Biglietteria in the park, visitors can buy a subscription allowing entrance to the various watering places during their stay. Continuing along the Viale Verdi to its upper end, you reach the Leopoldina (specializing in mineral and mud baths, and massage), then you come to the imposing facade of the Tettuccio, a long rectangle of golden stone with a glass marquee and wrought-iron gates. The hotels do not offer treatments, so the visitor can choose among the watering places as whim or cure dictates. A mineral bath at the Leopoldina can be followed by a glass of the lighter saline water at the Regina.

Though all the separate establishments are open to any paying customer, the Tettuccio is traditionally considered the most fashionable (it was the favorite of Giuseppe Verdi, who came here annually for eighteen years). It is certainly the most dressy. Nowadays, when dress codes have relaxed almost to the vanishing point in Italy as elsewhere, in the grand open foyers of the Tettuccio most of the gentlemen wear jacket and tie; and some of the ladies, hats and gloves. Conversation is conducted in low tones, and if, occasionally, a child shouts or a newcomer laughs too loudly, faces assume an expression of surprise, if not of reproach.

Taking the waters is a serious business, and the Tettuccio's patrons take it seriously. There is a one-day admission fee, and as you enter you see, on your left, a check room: there a disposable plastic cup costs about 40 cents, or you can rent a genuine glass mug for the duration of your stay.

In the main courtyard there is a long marble table with various spouts, each labeled according to the source—Regina, Torretta, Tettuccio—and you can fill your glass or cup at will. Against a side wall another jet offers warm Tamerici, from a nearby hot spring. The various waters have different qualities and are recommended for specific complaints. The mildest is the salty Tettuccio, an effective diuretic. It is also available in bottles from the local pharmacies.

Completely rebuilt in the late 1920s, the Tettuccio complex retains its Art Nouveau flavor, with grand mosaics of discreet but near-naked allegorical women holding up pitchers and pots. At the end of the main, neo-Renaissance courtyard, an arched passage leads to a Roman-style nympheum with fountain and a curving double staircase to the park above. In the court, on a columned bandstand, an orchestra plays a repertory a good deal older than the architecture, but much blander. The gems from operettas and the popular songs long out of copyright are not intended to distract anyone from firm devotion to hygiene.

Numerous signs request the patrons not to fill the empty seats with their belongings (in high season, June through September, even the ample spaces can fill up); at the same time they are asked not to throw water on the pavement (furtive emptying of a cup into the shrubbery is not unknown). It would take a very crass patron to defile—even with water—the lovely tile-and-marble composition that is the floor.

The atmosphere is that of a sober, somewhat old-fashioned club, particularly in the dark-paneled writing room, where desks and tables are occupied by readers as well as writers (postcards are for sale). The staid hall also provides a counter for changing money; and the bookstores have obvious best sellers, and, perhaps not surprisingly, books on massage, sex, and (for the pessimistic) on the beyond.

Those who want to read their morning papers often go to the cafe for a breakfast of coffee and brioches (ideally, you take your first waters of the day on an empty stomach). Others occupy the chairs in the park facing the tactful entrance to the extensive and well-attended toilets.

Many choose to wander, glass in hand, along the gently curving paths, beneath the huge trees probably planted in the days of the grand dukes. A pharmacy is available, with nonprescription diet aids as well as normal medicines. And there are a few fancy shops (Marcella Borghese occupies a prominent position with her ecological beauty aids).

A handsome plaque commemorates the visit, in August 1918, of the Nobel laureate Marie Curie, who "measured the radioactivity of the waters." The results of her measuring are not vouchsafed, but in 1918 radioactivity was generally considered a good thing.

Around the time of her visit, just after World War I, the grand Town Hall was just being completed. It is an impressive late Art Nouveau palace halfway down Viale Verdi, also housing the main post office. It rewards a visit, with its fastidiously detailed, ornate architecture, its stained glass skylights and many frescoes, including some by the Tuscan artist Galileo Chini, who designed Puccini's "Chinese" opera *Turandot* and, at one point in his career, decorated the royal palace in Bangkok. Chini's work can also be seen at the Tettuccio and (a ceramic mural) the Tamerici, whose spaces are often used for the medical conferences that are a long-established and closely followed feature of Montecatini.

Even a short visit to Montecatini is restful, enjoyable. You can sip some of the water in the morning and feel you have given your intestines a good cleansing, then prolong this self-congratulatory mood with golf at the 18-hole course at La Picvaccia, about five miles from town in an incomparable setting, or tennis. Within the park in town is the Circolo Tennis, with seven courts; many hotels have their own pools.

To get a good look at the town from above you can buy a round trip on the funicular. For almost a century the little car has been jerking and jolting its way up to Montecatini Alto, the upper town, whose fortress once dominated the lower slopes and the plain, where the spa now extends. Ascending through stands of acacia, chestnut and alder, the funicular affords glimpses of olive groves and cultivated fields. Then, from the little largely medieval town at the top, belvederes invite contemplation of the poetic Val di Nievole to the north; there are also several inviting restaurants and cafes, for a cup of tea in a traffic-free little square.

At night, some Montecatini visitors, exhausted by a day of doing practically nothing, retire early; but all the hotels provide a room with a few green-baize tables for games of bridge or canasta, spiced by the gossip that is a part of spa life. During the season—from early May to the end of October—there are regular events in the outdoor theater in the park and in other spaces. Concerts, often by local artists, are a part of the city's summer life. After all, Montecatini was a preferred haunt not only of the elderly Verdi but also of his younger followers, Giacomo Puccini, Pietro Mascagni, Umberto Giordano and Ruggero Leoncavallo, composer of *Pagliacci,* who spent the last part of his life in the city, which has duly named a street after him.

Getting There

Montecatini Terme is just off the Florence-to-Mare superhighway, half-an-hour's drive from Florence or from the coast. Frequent trains between Florence and Pisa airport stop at Montecatini (some require a change at Lucca). Buy a second-class ticket; the little trains often do not have a first-class car or, if they do, it is likely to be packed.

The Costs

For many Italians, a two-week or three-week stay at Montecatini is a part of their medical year, like a checkup or an eye examination or a visit to the dentist. Their regular doctor prescribes the cure and often recommends a consultation with one of the medical staff of the spa, to decide on a choice of waters, the amounts to be consumed and at what hours, or on one or more of the several other cures such as the mud baths or the hydromassage.

A medical examination is recommended but not required. One can also buy a subscription good for one year, allowing admission to the four main establishments (Tettuccio, Excelsior, Tamerici, and Torretta).

There are less expensive subscriptions for three weeks or for twelve days, the cost varying with the season. Special cures, baths at the Excelsior or Leopoldina, inhalations, facials, intestinal irrigation at the Excelsior, physical therapy at the Tamerici have a broad price range.

More Information

The Excelsior is open all year. Most of the others are open from May to October.

Information and advice about the spas is available from the Direzione Generale delle Terme, 41 Viale Verdi, 51016 Montecatini Terme, Italy; telephone: 0572.7781; fax: 0572.778444.

Tourist information can be obtained from Azienda di Promozione Turistica, 66 Viale Verdi, 51016 Montecatini Terme; 0572.772244; fax: 0572.70109.

Hotels

There are hundreds of hotels in Montecatini (the tourist board calculates 15,000 beds), ranging from the splendid, tasteful luxury of the 150-room **Grand Hotel & La Pace,** one of Italy's finest, to the dozens of convenient mom-and-pop establishments that line the peaceful, shady side streets of the center of town. Rates are for a double without breakfast because many visitors take their first waters on an empty stomach.

If money is no object, **La Pace,** 1A Via della Torretta, Monte-catini Terme, 51016 Italy, 0572.75801; fax: 0572.78451, is certainly the first choice. In business since 1870, it has been recently renewed (but not spoiled), and the standard of comfort and service has remained impeccable. Prices range from about $195 to $300.

At a somewhat less grand, but extremely comfortable and always agreeable level is the 108-room **Nizza et Suisse,** 72 Via Verdi; 0572.79691; fax: 0572.74324. This is where I stayed, and although my good-sized single room did not have a lot of character, the service and the friendly staff were a pleasure. Rates from about $110 to $150.

On a quiet side street, parallel to Viale Verdi, the 89-room **Imperial Garden,** 20 Via Puccini, 0572.910862; fax: 0572.910863, has a pleasant Victorian flavor, with a shaded terrace and a garden. Rates about $100 all year.

Farther down Via Puccini, at No. 15, the **Hotel Trieste,** 0572.79427; fax: 0572.910866, is small, family-run, inexpensive, friendly, with few frills (though TV and minibars are included). Rates about $75 to $100.

Coming Home to Chianti

BY GINI ALHADEFF

❧

editor's note

GINI ALHADEFF is the author of *The Sun at Midday: Tales of a Mediterranean Family* (Pantheon, 1997, hardcover; The Ecco Press, 1998, paperback) and is currently at work on a new book. She is also a contributing editor at *Travel & Leisure*.

It was in Tokyo, at the terrible age of thirteen, that I first heard of Strada in Chianti. What I heard came in the form of stories. They were told to us by a genuine Tuscan called Franco Innocenti. My father was then working for Olivetti, and Franco, a surrealist painter in his spare time, had come to train some young Japanese in the art of selling typewriters. He was far from home, and from his American wife and two children, and he came to dinner often. There was only one Italian restaurant in Tokyo then, Antonio's, and an Italian could easily have felt homesick. "Poor thing," my father would say, "he doesn't know anyone here." But we were the "poor things," starved as we were for any news of our faraway country, for any particulars that could make the abstraction of our Italian nationality less abstract.

Franco lived in Strada in Chianti, a small town fifteen minutes from Florence, set among the hills that produce Chianti wine and the best olive oil in Italy. The town began as four houses built in the 1500s on either side of the old Via Chiantigiana, hence its name, which means a "street in Chianti." Along the rectangular piazza, one finds Roberto's car repair shop, a pharmacy, a newsstand, and the carabinieri. About 3,000 people live here, most of whom know each other, as their parents and their parents' parents did before them, and there is usually one person, and no more than three, for every profession—an electrician, a plumber, a builder, three butchers, three greengrocers (if one includes Gastone, who sells his vegetables door-to-door from a van). The one supermarket is the size of a shoebox, and so is the latteria, which sells dairy products. The town is not picturesque, like Greve some twenty kilometers away, or Radda or Gaiole, but the landscape is.

The first story Franco told of Strada was of a family friend, an Englishwoman, who had arrived to spend a fortnight. She was very round, milky-skinned, and pink-cheeked, with stocky legs, and Mario, the fattore—the man who tended the vines and olive groves—on the Innocentis' land, said, sizing her up in admiration, "What lovely legs the signorina has, lovely as a pig's." It was a compliment, of course. Franco himself painted a picture in which a slice of prosciutto crudo was unfurled on a pole like a proud flag in the wind.

Years later Mario's brother Terzilio came to work for us, when my parents bought a piece of land in Strada between two castles, neither medieval, one pompous, one pretty, the pretty one imposing from a distance but a one-room affair close-up. The land had a ruined farmhouse on it—a casa colonica with a lovely big arched entrance and a Madonna nestled in a sky-blue niche above it—some rows of vines and ancient twisted olive trees, and a great deal of dry stony earth. All around was the silvery green of olive trees, spiky dark points of cypresses, hills combed with rows of vines, a barn here and there, and the idea of Florence nearby: on the horizon, on crisp evenings, the city's sprinkling of lights cast a rosy yellowish haze on the sky. The house was known as La Casa Nova, and that is the name it has kept.

What better place to write about the Chianti region than from a kitchen, in Chianti, where I am sitting at a long wooden table. Some thirty years ago, when this house was converted from a farm for animals to a house, my brothers and I were instructed to "weather" the kitchen table by denting the surface here and there with a hammer so it wouldn't look so new. A few real dents have been added to those first impatient ones. On the table is a bottle containing a green, somewhat cloudy, olive oil, from the very olives grown on this small property, and a bottle of our 1992 Chianti La Casa Nova—fermented, bottled, and labeled in the garage and stored in the cellar beneath the kitchen. Farther down the table is a mound of hand-cut ribbons of pasta made this morning and laid out to dry by a woman who could have stepped out of a Piero della Francesca painting: Peppina has vivid black eyes, a round face, curly black hair that seems to want to escape from her scalp and into the heavens, a voice that travels on gusts of air making its way triumphantly from the lungs through the vocal chords into the surrounding countryside, with every hard "c" Tuscanized into an "h" so that "casa" becomes "hassa."

Strada in Chianti is a place of voices such as hers, of opinions fit to be spoken out loud, unequivocally. In the haze of jet lag, when eight in the morning is two A.M. for me and I struggle with the injustice of the hours lost during the journey from New York, voices tell me I have arrived in Strada—the voice of Peppina when she comes in and those of Franca and Bruno who live in a house next to ours. They have always made their living as they do now: he takes care of the land, tends the olive trees, the vines, the orchard, and the animals, makes the wine and the olive oil; she cooks. Before coming here, they worked at one of the larger wineries in the region belonging to the Frescobaldis, then, on a remote estate five times the size of ours. Even so, Bruno took care of all the vines and olive trees himself. Their daughter, Marilla, studies at the Liceo Classico in Florence. Emilio, their eldest child, works at a Ford dealership in a nearby town. It seems unlikely that either will want to apply what they may have learned from their father about the making of wine and oil. It is unlikely they will even live here: this place is not exotic to them as it is to me, who lives so far from it and misses it.

For years, even after La Casa Nova was restored and the vines and olive trees had had the earth dug up around their roots and more fertile earth deposited on them, the place looked quite barren. In three decades, the three pines on the front lawn have grown so tall that their branches intertwine on top to form a single cloud of fragrant shade under which the dogs like to lie on summer mornings and crack pinecones between their teeth. The larch, the magnolia, and the horse chestnut are at least twenty times the size they were when they were planted.

At the end of the garden, by the vines, there is a coop, with chickens, guinea hens, ducks, and rabbits, and a cement sty with a green roof on it where pigs used to be kept—two a year, till none of us could stand to see them led to slaughter anymore. Still, as Count Niccolò Capponi intoned when I visited his family estate, Calcinaia, "The pig is fundamental to the countryside. As they say around here," he added, "a pig is like a woman: you throw none of it away." He proceeded to enumerate the animal's various uses: "The bristles are used for brushes, the flesh for cured meats—salame, prosciutto, bacon, sausage . . ." He mentioned the uses of the snout, too, and of the hoofs, but now I forget what they were. We dove into a passageway and emerged, festooned in cobwebs, in Bluebeard's locked chamber, only with the pig as victim: from the ceiling hung four whole hams, myriad salami and finocchione (soft salami with fennel seeds), and many hunks of bacon, all of which were encrusted with grains of pepper, salt, and dust.

Since we gave up keeping pigs, we buy the meat and make our own salame in the cellar. Most people in Chianti have a cellar, or know someone who does who will sell them good unadulterated wine and olive oil—though the latter is harder to find, and few can really tell the difference between average and excellent oil. But it's a far cry from our cellar, where the wine vats compete for space with the Fiat and the garden furniture, and the Capponis' high-vaulted cellar, with its rows of gleaming oak barrels from Slavonia where the only creature you might encounter is a toad. And though our respective wines might taste quite different, they are both good. With small quantities it's possible to add only a small amount of sulfites compared with more commercial wines which have to endure storage, changes of temperature, and transport. Every town in Chianti has an enoteca, a store that sells wines from the surrounding estates. The thing to do is to taste a few wines there, choose one, then buy a supply directly from the vineyard's retail outlet, usually located at the entrance to the winery or not far down the road.

I'll take any pretext to get into the car and drive into one of the nearby towns. The choice is between Strada in Chianti, the smallest, Impruneta, the most impersonal, or Greve, the farthest from us—though it takes only twenty minutes to get there—but my favorite. During the ritual of morning coffee around the kitchen table, the day's menu is discussed. The contents of the freezer—chickens, ducks, guinea fowl—are taken into consideration, as is what the garden has to offer: in the summer, tomatoes, eggplant, radicchio (which in Tuscany is a dark green bitter lettuce that is sliced like cabbage), string beans, zucchini. The chickens lay eggs, too, bless them. But if there are no white beans to go with the bistecca or black cabbage to make ribollita (a vegetable soup ladled over slices of bread) or mushrooms to go into the sauce for the tagliatelle, I take off. Going shopping is the peculiar form of sightseeing I have developed here.

It is a visit to stories and conversations I have heard, to the people who have told them to me and who tell me new ones every time I see them. I take the breathtakingly pretty Chiantigiana that winds its way from Florence to Siena, through the hills and vineyards of Chianti, to the town of Greve. It doesn't matter how many times I've driven through it. I'm always thrilled when I go up a steep incline and come upon a certain stretch of fields and farms, always amused to see the hedges in front of the church at Giobbole which the eccentric priest has clipped in the shape of swans and doves. I always remember, too, the sermon I heard him give, about a girl possessed by demons who spoke Greek though she was Italian—a proof of her possession, he said. A Tuscan is incapable of telling a story without adding salt to it; something unsalted is "sciocco"—stupid. No transaction, no matter how trivial, takes place without words leaping about on the flat field of the everyday. Everything is made funny.

The piazza at Greve, which began to be built in the 1400s to serve as a marketplace, is like a triangular stage, with arcades of shops on two sides, where one feels that one's every move is for the entertainment of an audience who sit on their terraces above the arches and survey the action through fronds of pink and red geraniums. I have never seen a single outsider, let alone a foreigner, among them. Sometimes they appear not to be looking and set the table for lunch under a beach umbrella or go about hanging laundry on the clothesline. They themselves are on a stage enacting their own curiosity and their everyday existence.

The piazza, which is dedicated to Verrazzano, has all one needs: La Formicola, the bookstore, which also stocks books in English, a newsstand, food shops, an enoteca, real estate offices, an information center, and, as in all self-respecting Italian piazzas, two competing cafés—La Loggetta, for a glass of wine, and the Caffè Lepanto (also known as Caffè Centrale), for ice cream and a complete view of the square. At the entrance to Falorni, the butcher, there is a farouche stuffed boar that bears a marked resemblance to the one I almost collided with one evening while driving down a road through the woods. The preservation of boars has been so successful, certain areas are overrun with them—the property of a woman who did not allow boar hunting is ravaged by hoof marks. Chiantigiani do not approve of this form of preservation, and they mind, too, when they are not hired to cultivate lands they have always known and now see lying fallow. One palpable instance of an ecological conscience is in the signs lining most roads which say optimistically, "This is a denuclearized zone"—in intention, that is, if nothing else.

Politics is nobody's pastime anymore. Just over a year ago a loudspeaker on the roof of an Italian Socialist Party van cruising through the piazza incited the inhabitants to gather on the following Sunday evening at seven. A punctiliously dressed old contadino in a gray suit, white shirt, and black felt hat was heard to comment acidly, "That's when they give us all our money back." Until recently, most farmers in the area were Socialist or Communist, and those who were known to have been active Fascists—such as the now defunct carpenter of Strada, who, it was rumored, forced cod liver oil down the throats of partisans from whom he wanted information—were shunned. But since the corruption scandal that involved political parties in Italy two years ago and brought down, first and foremost, the Socialist Party for accepting millions in bribes, people have been scouring the newspapers for the names of the latest victims of their bloodless revolution. In the evening, after supper, Bruno dons wide beige cotton trousers and a short-sleeved shirt with a blue-and-white diamond pattern, gets into his pewter-colored Fiat Uno, and rides off to Strada to play bocce at the Christian Democrat court. He doesn't care what party the court belongs to, he says, as long as it is properly maintained.

One Tuesday morning I went with him and his daughter to the market in Strada; the goal of our expedition was to buy canvas shoes and anchovies. On the way, at the crossing in Martellina, where there is a grocery with good pecorino and a restaurant overlooking the hills, Bruno caught sight of the mailwoman—a gaunt young creature in blue overalls straddling a bicycle, a black mailbag slung across her chest. "There's my little treasure!" Bruno exclaimed, putting on the brakes.

There was another postina before her who had asked to be transferred. Bruno said that a German shepherd had pinched her—in Tuscan "pinching" means biting; it is something that snakes, bees, dogs, mosquitoes do. When the wisteria was in bloom by our front gate, in May, the new postina complained to Bruno of the bumblebees, afraid she'd get bitten. Bruno confided that he had told her, "The calabroni won't touch you, but I will, I'll give you pollen." From the backseat, his daughter, who is experiencing the first stirrings of a feminist conscience, implored, "Papà!" An American feminist might encounter many instances of apparent "sexual harassment," but in Chianti the harassment, if it can be termed that, is reciprocal and a way of giving an edge to an otherwise uniform social climate: one would have to go all the way to Florence or Siena to meet a stranger.

Bruno carries on verbal courtships with attached and unattached women of spirit, but only those who are an equal match. He asks Beppina news of her husband, for instance, and inquires whether old age has impaired his performance. This is an ongoing skit: Beppina's husband, Giotto (so nicknamed because he worked as a house-painter for a while), is Bruno's best friend and a peer. Beppina's repartee is always something along the lines of, "You'll keep still when the rats start gnawing on you." The exchange usually takes place in the presence of Bruno's wife. Here, as everywhere, there is real adultery, too. But because no one has a pied-à-terre or knows of a hotel that isn't owned by someone's relative, it's usually carried out in the fields, often in daylight, and so doesn't remain clandestine for long. I am sorry to return to the subject of sex so often, but it is pertinent to the spirit of the region, where women are described in the same language used for wine—harsh when too young, perfect in their prime, and known to be affected by the moon. The people of Chianti generally have a low opinion of physical exertion for its own sake. Once when Bruno and I were driving up from Florence, we saw a group of runners carrying flags and Bruno remarked that youthful energy—something he stressed he no longer had—should not be wasted this way but lavished on a ragazza under a tree.

At the Strada market, we looked for the acciughino, the anchovy man, also known as "povero Marchino," poor little Mark, because he shouts, comically, "Come buy anchovies, I need money to get married." We immediately ran into Giotto, almost as all-knowing as his wife when it comes to the affairs of the region, who told us "povero Marchino" hadn't come because he was actually getting married, at last. We bought the anchovies instead from a shop called Bussotti, on the square at Strada, and they came out of a vat-size tin: coarse, silvery, beheaded, and a bit larger than one would have wished, but Bruno eyed them approvingly. One of his favorite dishes consists of anchovies mixed with chopped red onions, oil, and pepper. This is for initiates. I understand him better when he talks about his passion for bread and figs, a combination he indulges in at sunrise sitting by himself in the shade of one of the three fig trees in our garden.

As we drive back over the Chiantigiana I am reminded of a story told to me by Tebaldo, the mechanic and taxi driver of Strada, who has now retired and been replaced by his son. He had taken an Englishwoman on a drive to see the countryside, which the English call Chiantishire, and at every turn in the road she gasped, "We have nothing like this in England!" They passed Castellina and reached Radda, and there, too, she exclaimed, "We have nothing like this in England!" They drove to Passignano, had lunch below an abbey set in an oval clump of cypresses as in a Renaissance landscape, and she repeated, "We have nothing like this in England!" Finally, Tebaldo, who had been to England once in his life, saw her point; he confided thinking to himself, "But is it fair that we should have everything and the others nothing?" He had nothing to be modest about.

The Chianti Region

A sixty-five-square-mile stretch of vineyards and hill towns between Florence and Siena, Chianti is an ideal area to rent a villa or a room in a farmhouse hotel and revel in the pleasures of the Tuscan countryside. Days can revolve around visits to markets, piazzas, and wineries; hiking and biking trips; and pilgrimages to historic sites— the romantic Badia a Coltibuono (the abbey of San Lorenzo), the fortified town of Montefioralle—and museums (Florence's Uffizi is about a fifteen-minute drive from Strada in Chianti). Eating and sleeping are also respected as serious pursuits in these parts.

The easiest way to get to Chianti is by flying to Florence and renting a car at the airport. You can also fly to Pisa or Rome and take an Alitalia train from either airport to Santa Maria Novella station in Florence.

Chianti is prettiest in spring and summer. Even on the hottest days a breeze floats in by afternoon. And the hills are always cooler than the streets of Florence. The big draw in September and October is the grape and olive harvest.

Hotels

Since agriculture rather than tourism is the mainstay of the region, there are more lodgings in the vicinity of Siena or Florence than in the heart of the wine country. The following hotels, however, are well situated for travelers who want to see—and taste—Chianti.

Hotel Villa La Montagnola, 110–12 Via della Montagnola, Strada in Chianti; tel. 0550.858.485. No-frills accommodations in a prime location.

Il Cenobio Villa Vignamaggio, Greve in Chianti; tel. 0550.853.007; doubles, villa apartments, house for two, cottage for four. The setting for Kenneth Branagh's *Much Ado About Nothing,* this estate has guest rooms and apartments in the villa, as well as two small houses and a cottage on the grounds. There's a tennis court, a pool, and a glorious garden.

Villa Le Barone, 19 Via San Leolino, Panzano in Chianti; tel. 0550.852.621. A sixteenth-century villa surrounded by parkland, olive groves, and vineyards. Pool on the grounds and tennis and golf nearby. Breakfast is served on a terrace.

Villa San Giovese, 5 Piazza Bucciarelli, Panzano in Chianti; tel. 0550.852.461; fax: 550.852.463. A Swiss-German couple, who have lived in Italy for fifteen years, run this simple shipshape hotel with terra-cotta tiled floors and beds under beamed ceilings. An Italian cook is in residence, and tables are set on an enclosed courtyard during the summer.

Romantic Hotel Tenuta Di Ricavo, Castellina in Chianti; tel. 0577.740.221. Lovely gardens and two swimming pools at a farmstead inn, with pleasant walks in the area. The restaurant is a good place to sample regional wines and dishes, such as ribollita, a thick vegetable soup served over slices of toasted bread.

Castello Di Spaltenna, Gaiole in Chianti; tel. 0577.749.483. A twenty-one-room hotel and restaurant on the premises of a thirteenth-century monastery. Local gourmets flock here for sophisticated Tuscan cuisine. Breakfast and drinks are served by a well in the cloister garden.

Hotel Villa Belvedere, Colle di Val d'Elsa; tel. 0577.299. A seventeenth-century villa, with fifteen rooms, overlooking a formal Italian garden. The food extends beyond the Tuscan basics, and in summer, meals are served in the garden with views of San Gimignano. Lake fishing, riding, and tennis in the vicinity.

Villa Scacciapensieri, 24 Via di Scacciapensieri, Siena; tel. 0577.41.441. Located in the countryside just north of Siena, this eighteenth-century villa has formal gardens with clipped hedges, a pool, and tennis court.

Villas

The following agencies advise Americans seeking a house or apartment rental in Italy. Most are affiliated with Italian companies and issue catalogues of properties that range from cottages to estates. Rates are approximately $400–$13,500 a week, but decrease by as much as 45 percent during off-season. Radda in Chianti, Castellina in Chianti, and Gaiole in Chianti are particularly charming locales.

Vacanza Bella, 2443 Fillmore St., Suite 228, San Francisco, CA 94115; 415-554-0234.

At Home Abroad, 405 E. 56th St., New York, NY 10022; 212-421-9165; Fax: 212-752-1591.

Italian Rentals, 3801 Ingomar St. NW, Washington, D.C. 20015; 202-244-5345; fax: 202-362-0520.

Vacanze in Italia, 22 Railroad St., Great Barrington, MA 01230; 800-533-5405 or 413-528-6610; fax: 413-528-6222.

Restaurants

Da Padellina, 54 Corso del Popolo, Strada in Chianti; tel. 0550.858.388. The dining room may be uninspiring, but the kitchen turns out wonderful Chianti cuisine: charbroiled T-bone steak, white beans, ribollita, and pappa al pomodoro (a summer soup).

Borgo Antico, 115 Via Case Sparse, Lucolena; tel. 0550.851.024. Fresh pasta is the thing to order here. There's also satisfying grilled pork and chicken.

Badia a Coltibuono, Gaiole in Chianti; tel. 0577.749.498. This first-rate trattoria has wonderful views of the abbey of San Lorenzo. During the summer, tables are set up in a courtyard. The excellent wine is from the nearby estate of Badia a Coltibuono.

Il Papavero, Barbischio; tel. 0577.749.063. No credit cards. One of the few restaurants where you won't be expected to order a three-course meal. This is a nice spot for a light evening meal of panzanella (a tomato-based soup made with bread) and a salame sandwich.

Da Antonio, 40 Via Fiorita, Castelnuovo Berardenga; tel. 0577.355.321. The place in Chianti for fresh fish. Everything is impeccably prepared, from the seafood hors d'oeuvres to the charbroiled red snapper.

Cafés

Bar Italia, Piazza Buondelmonti, Impruneta; tel. 0550.201.1046. This is a classic stand-up coffee bar. In the summer there are a few tables on the sidewalk. The gelato is especially good (the hazelnut and the coffee are favorites); so is the tiramisù.

Caffè Le Logge, Piazza Matteotti, Greve in Chianti; tel. 0550.853.038. A café, with wooden benches and marble tables, where locals go for a cappuccino or a glass of wine and a sandwich.

Caffè Lepanto, Piazza Matteotti, Greve in Chianti; tel. 0550.853.040. The other café in Greve attracts tourists, who come for the views of the square, and children, who come for the staggering selection of gelato. The newsstand next door carries the area's largest assortment of foreign-language newspapers, magazines, and guidebooks.

Shopping

If you're planning to spend some time in the area, here's where to stock your kitchen, Chiantigiana style.

Groceries

La Martellina, 39 Via della Montagnola, Martellina; tel. 0550.858.051. On the main road between Impruneta and Strada in Chianti, this general food store is notable for its cold cuts, such as finocchiona (a soft salame flavored with fennel seeds), pecorino cheese, and breads. The restaurant in back has a terrace overlooking the hills.

Alimentari Piccini, Via Mazzini, Impruneta. Recommended for basic staples, as well as olives, fresh pasta (including potato gnocchi), and cheeses. Piccini's delicious locally made ricotta should be mixed with black currant jam and eaten as a dessert.

Markets

Fruit and vegetables, canvas shoes, cotton sheets and tablecloths, and vats of anchovies. Hours: about 8 A.M.–2 P.M. **Impruneta,** Piazza Buondelmonti, Saturday. **Strada in Chianti,** Piazza del

Mercato, Tuesday. **Greve in Chianti,** on the piazza, Saturday. All of these markets are open year-round.

Meat

Secci, 1 Borgo Baldassare Paoli, Strada in Chianti; tel. 0550.858.039. Like his father before him, Pier Francesco Secci is the best butcher in the area, especially for Florentine T-bone steak and rabbit.

Antica Macelleria Falorni, 69 Piazza Matteotti, Greve in Chianti; tel. 0550.858.039. A renowned establishment, grander and more commercial than Secci. A highlight is the array of prosciuttos: crudo dolce comes from the north and is sweet; crudo nostrano, the salty hard local variety, goes well with unsalted Tuscan bread. Falorni also has perfect round thin slivers of bresâola, a sliced dried beef which, like carpaccio, is served with oil, lemon, and pepper.

Bread

Falciani, 245 Via Cassia, Falciani; tel. 0550.202.0091. This bakery makes traditional thick-crusted Tuscan bread, which Chiantigiani prefer to eat when it's a day old. In August and September, look for schiacciata di uva, a sort of sweet focaccia covered with grapes.

Vegetables

Donatella, Strada in Chianti. Next to Secci, the butcher, this Strada shop sells verza (the Savoy cabbage for making ribollita), tomatoes, white beans, and zucchini flowers, which, dipped in batter and lightly sautéed, make a wonderful appetizer. Fresh porcini mushrooms are always in supply after a rain.

Terra-Cotta

Chianti is famous for its pots, tiles, and olive oil urns. These shops sell pieces straight from the kiln.

La Fornace Manetti, 50A Via del Ferrone, Impruneta; tel. 550.850.631.
Urbano Fontana E Figlio, Castellina in Chianti; tel. 0577.740.340.

Wine and Oil
Most towns in Chianti have an *enoteca*—a liquor store stocked with local wines (which can be sampled) and olive oil. Take note: Vineyards sell their own products at 30 to 40 percent less than enoteca prices.

Best Books

Cadogan Guides: Tuscany and Umbria by Dana Facaros and Michael Pauls (Globe Pequot Press). An exceptional combination of sightseeing and practical information. Detailed maps, paths to hidden cultural treasures, and tips on finding local delicacies round out the best book on the region.

Philip's Travel Guides: Tuscany by Jonathan Keates, photographs by Charlie Waite (George Philip, London). Dazzling color images capture the attractions of the area while the text explores its culture and past.

The House of Medici: Its Rise and Fall by Christopher Hibbert (William Morrow). This chronicle of the Florentine banking family from obscurity to preeminence as art patrons and power brokers, and then its inglorious descent, exemplifies the best in popular history.

On Screen

Much Ado About Nothing. The Chianti countryside never looked lovelier than in Kenneth Branagh's enchanting version of Shakespeare's comedy.

Lucca: A Tuscan Treasure

BY LORRAINE ALEXANDER

〜

editor's note

....

Lucca is not always included in visitors' grand tour of Tuscany, which I suppose is because it has no real art masterpieces or famous museums. The town itself makes Lucca worth a detour, and I would indeed refer to it as a treasure.

Recently a friend from out of town was staying with me for a couple of days and began leafing through a book of photographs of Lucca. "Now this," she said with sudden feeling, "looks exactly the way Italy is *supposed* to look."

If there is something inherently convincing about going straight to the center of an issue, then Lucca's nomination as Italy-writ-small is only bolstered by its location in a quiet corner of Tuscany, the country's geographic and historic bull's-eye. Meanwhile Lucca itself is so self-effacingly off-center that tourists, wearing the topsoil thin between Florence and Siena, barely know it exists. (Opera lovers may be the exception, for Lucca was Giacomo Puccini's native city.) Taken as a whole, this ironic situation is, for the resident and traveler alike, equivalent to having your *torta* and eating it, too.

Lucca has never eluded attention entirely, of course. With the sea to the west and mountains to the north, it was Julius Caesar's favorite winter resort (marshland to the south toward Pisa—which is why the Leaning Tower leans—made it undesirable in summer). One of Tolstoy's characters in *War and Peace* mentions Lucca, however briefly ("Eh bien, mon prince, so Genoa and Lucca are now no more than private estates of the Bonaparte family"). The writer who really "discovered" Lucca, though, was the brilliant, eccentric art critic and social reformer John Ruskin, initially traveling there in 1845. He would return a half dozen times, but it was this first trip that set his course.

> Here in Lucca I found myself suddenly in the presence of twelfth-century buildings . . . so incorruptible that, after 600 years of sunshine and rain, a lancet could not now be put between their joins . . . I took the simplest of façades for analysis . . . and thereon literally began the study of architecture.

Ruskin eventually became associated more with Venice than with Lucca, just as Henry James, who admired Lucca's "charming mixture of antique character and modern inconsequence," wrote mostly about Rome and Florence in his *Italian Hours*. Still, even James fell under her spell: "I remember saying to myself . . . that no brown-and-gold Tuscan city could *be* as happy as Lucca looked . . . [seeming] fairly to laugh."

Not that the city hasn't had to withstand difficult times in the usual way of history. Her advantage was really that during the Middle Ages, when the growing pains of Tuscany's other city-states were ending in seizures of villainy and violence, Lucca concentrated on trade with northern Europe and used her wealth wisely, once purchasing ninety years of peace from the pope's functionaries for 2,000 gold pieces. Profits from silk, wool, and banking financed expansion of Lucca's defensive wall and employment for stonemasons and sculptors as they built—or rebuilt on ancient sites—her finest churches.

By the time Napoleon arrived in 1805, Lucca was edging up to her "modern inconsequence," and the new emperor, his attention fixed more in the vicinity of Lord Nelson, gave the city to his sister Elisa, who set about widening the streets and adding neoclassical touches to Piazza Napoleone. When Marie Louise de Bourbon was given Lucca by the Congress of Vienna, she, perhaps not to be outdone, planted double rows of horse-chestnut trees along its wall, creating two and a half miles of what James called a "circular lounging-place of a splendid dignity." Today the wall's garden path is where the fortunate Lucchesi take their evening *passeggiata,* and the churches where they worship and make *musica lirica* comprise one of Italy's great concentrations of Romanesque architecture.

The handful of hotels inside the city wall are relentlessly ordinary, perhaps because Lucca is so precisely not on the tourist track, and for this reason visitors often prefer to make their base in the near countryside. To the west, on the way to Puccini's villa at Torre del Lago and the popular beach resort of Viareggio, is Villa Casanova, the chief attributes of which are the view from its tree-shaded terrace of Castello di Nozzano's crenellated tower; the modest price; and the main house itself, "roomy and stony, as an Italian villa should be," in the words of James. In the converted fieldworkers' dwellings, rooms are smaller, sparer, but equally—and not unpleasantly—evocative of past centuries' rural life. Do have dinner elsewhere, however; this is not the Tuscan table to write home about.

To the south of town is a cluster of grander houses converted to hotels. The newest and prettiest by far is the ten-room Principessa Elisa, a mauve and white villa that, glimpsed through its surrounding greenery, looks like a debutante who's strayed from the ballroom into the conservatory. The rooms are cocoons of sumptuous fabrics, and the elegant glassed-in Gazebo restaurant brings the garden indoors to complement chef Antonio Sanna's cuisine, the most refined of the region.

Across from the Elisa is the parent Villa La Principessa, an impressive house, with loggias giving into parkland, that was originally built by the general who saved Lucca from the Pisans in the fourteenth century (and, some say, was Machiavelli's model prince). The main salon is ornate—coffered ceiling, enormous stone fireplace, and handsome circa 1750 console made in Lucca—but it can seem a battlefield of dueling decoration as the plaid carpet squares off against the floral wallcovering. The unusual décor takes another twist in the guest rooms; ours was spacious, comfortable, and electric blue from bedspread to baseboard.

Villa San Michele once belonged to a Luccan prior, and if you imagine him as I did—with a weakness for intrigue and old *vin santo*—the rococo reception room looks the perfect setpiece. Our room was a tight fit (the one to try for, number 109, has a baldacchino bed and a window aimed straight at Lucca's medieval towers), but from its tiny balcony I could see the sun rise to wake the swallows and filter through the villa's somewhat neglected olive grove, at that hour still touched by a silvery dignity.

Other countryside options for lodging, ones that bring opportunities for a closer experience of both people and place, are Fattoria Villa Maionchi and Tenuta di Valgiano, both *agriturismi* (farms with tourist lodgings) in the beautiful olive- and vine-planted hills to Lucca's northeast. The owners live in the "big house," while guests stay in the former fieldworkers' stone quarters, which come with kitchens and most of the comforts and quirks of home. Maria Maionchi and Roberto Palagi offer, in addition, umbrellaed garden tables and tubs of flowers, the charms of their pet donkey (an enchantment for children), and a friendliness that is at the heart of "farm vacations." The excellent Maionchi wines and olive oil can, of course, be purchased by guests and passersby alike. This is the case, too, at Valgiano, where Laura di Collobiano and Moreno Petrini rent out the four apartments that sit atop their wine cellars. Spread over the estate's 260 acres are 3,000 olive trees, their rows stitching the hillsides, and up near the guests' lodgings a swimming pool has been added. When I visited, Laura, Moreno, and winemaker Saverio Petrilli were bottling their white Giallo dei Muri '94, and last fall Valgiano's was one of only three Tuscan olive oils honored by the World Olive Conference from a field of a hundred.

The one night I spent in town, to attend a late jazz concert in

Lucca's Roman-era *amfiteatro,* I chose the Universo, where, having read that Ruskin had favored it, I hoped to find an art-historical cobweb or two. Only the reception area hinted nostalgically at the long ago, but here-and-now amenities included CNN, wake-up calls, and a porter who was not someone's grandmother. Location is a plus, too: across from the Teatro del Giglio, where Rossini's *William Tell Overture* premiered in 1831 and Lucca's opera season unfolds each September; and one piazza away from San Martino, the city's cathedral.

As you enter Lucca's narrow streets, you will find yourself tracing a pleasant grid (the Roman plan survives) of cobblestoned streets broadening here and there into piazzas, most of which are named for the churches that dominate them. Roman columns (removed from the amphitheater) punctuate San Frediano's nave, though nothing inside compares, for effect, with the magnificent gold-grounded Ascension mosaic spread over the top third of the twelfth-century church's otherwise plain façade. Unless, that is, you count the mummified remains of Saint Zita, patron saint of servants, which nearly sent me spinning for the exit. But, as creepy as her glass cubicle is, her legend of food smuggled to the poor and miraculously transformed into flowers so that she might escape detection by her masters is touchingly evoked each April 26, when flowers are brought to fill the piazza in her honor.

At Piazza San Giusto you can stop by the café across from the church for housemade frozen yogurt or, on Saturday mornings, rummage through the crafts/flea market, which leads around San Giusto to tables of books and finally, facing Via Beccheria, a permanent stall of Pucciniana: sheet music, libretti, and sepia photos of the maestro. For me this cache was irresistible, especially the glimpses of Puccini-at-play, debonair in his roadster, at the wheel of a speedboat, and hoisted on the shoulders of his hunting pals.

Reminders of Puccini are around every corner, nowhere more so than at San Martino. Appointment as cathedral organist was an honor handed down in an unbroken line from Giacomo, Sr. (1722–81) to "our" Giacomo (1858–1924), when he was six, and held for him in trust by an uncle. The church's façade, a masterpiece of carved marble; a strikingly Mannerist *Last Supper* by Tintoretto; even the relic of the Holy Countenance, supposedly modeled by Nicodemus immediately after the Crucifixion, though this one is an eleventh-century copy, are no more significant to many Lucchesi than the double organ on which those generations of Puccinis played. The sole exception might be the exquisite tomb of Ilaria del Carretto, sculpted by the Sienese Jacopo della Quercia, which Ruskin called "the loveliest Christian tomb in Italy." On my last visit it was *in restauro*, but perhaps you'll be luckier, for this is no formulaic sepulchral stone; seek it out for Ilaria's serene beauty, and for the adoring dog at her feet.

The church in Lucca I return to first and last is inevitably San Michele in Foro (its adjacent piazza was the site of the Roman forum), at the very center of town now, as then. This fact alone is worth a moment's pause, used as we are to ever-altering urban plans. In Lucca, though, the wall has kept things orderly—and growth outside its bounds—so that when present-day Lucchesi buy flowers at the piazza's stalls or step into Farmacia Massagli for a sip of *china* (pronounced *kee*-na, the Italian word for quinine), the city's specialty herbal liqueur, they are walking with similar purpose literally in the footsteps of their ancestors.

San Michele, begun in 1070, is most famous for its remarkable façade, the base a strictly Romanesque series of rounded blind arches, above which rise four levels of intricately carved pillared galleries. This delicate elaboration distinguishes the church (and its contemporary, San Martino) as Pisan-Romanesque, after the cathedral complex only twenty miles south, which embodies so gloriously the late-medieval Tuscan desire to balance weight with grace and decorative innovation. By the time Ruskin happened upon San Michele the marble sculptures and intarsia were "in such a state of abandon that I felt obliged to draw them if only for fear that they would soon disappear." Restoration began in the 1860s, with heroes of the Risorgimento, including the anticlerical Garibaldi, replacing the antique elements that are now displayed at Lucca's Museo Nazionale at Villa Guinigi.

San Michele's interior is as somber as the exterior is joyous. There is a beautiful painting of four saints by Filippino Lippi and a Madonna and Child medallion by Andrea della Robbia. But, if you must choose between inside and out, consider spending a quiet half-hour before that magnificent façade—perhaps to sketch as Ruskin did, or just to imagine Giacomo Puccini, as a boy, making his way down Via di Poggio to choir practice there and then, years later, composing the choirboys' Te Deum for *Tosca*.

The obvious next step is to accompany young Giacomo back along that single block from San Michele to his childhood home, today's Casa Puccini museum. Here you will find the family tree of Lucca's great musical dynasty; letters and original scores; photographs and portraits (including one of an ancestor who surely married for love and not the name when she became Angela Maria Piccinini Puccini); and drawings of costumes and sets. There is also the Steinway on which Puccini composed *Turandot,* his final opera—unfinished at the time of his death, in fact, but completed by one of his pupils.

Anyone as intrigued as I was by the Casa will want to make the detour to nearby Torre del Lago, where Puccini's lakeside villa was built after his first popular success, *Manon Lescaut* (1893), mainly to indulge his passion for duck hunting. The house contains some Liberty touches, thanks to Puccini's friendship with Galileo Chini, who was Italy's leading exponent of Art Nouveau—and later designed the exotic sets for *Turandot*. The mosaic floor and fireplace tiles in the sitting room are Chini's work, and when sun shines through the colored glass of the doors and windows the room fairly glows. Its focal point is the simple upright piano on which Puccini wrote the music for nine of his twelve operas, among them *La Bohème, Tosca, Madama Butterfly,* and *Turandot.* Preferring to spend his days hunting on the lake and socializing in Lucca or Viareggio, he composed through the night, having fitted the piano with dampers to avoid disturbing his household.

In some ways, though, as our guide recounted with spirited affection, the family was quite regularly disturbed, in particular by Puccini's (inordinate, in his wife's view) love of women. Puccini's life does seem to have been marked by tragic overtones worthy of, well, grand opera. Restless after years of living with Elvira—mother of his only child but still married to someone else—the composer was about to run away with a singer when he wrecked his car on the road to Lucca and was taken home ("Where *else* can you go when you're not well?" pleaded our guide, every syllable weighted with the subtext of destiny) to Elvira . . . whose husband had died that very day, freeing her to marry the stunned maestro. Which is what happened.

We were all hanging on our guide's every word by now, but the most dramatic hush descended when he moved to his next subject: "The big problem of Puccini was without doubt [not his love life but] his smoking—sixty to seventy cigarettes a day." He died at sixty-six, before anyone knew the dangers, of course, from throat cancer.

Finally came the moment just before the curtain is lowered. Did any of us know, we were asked, Puccini's last words, scribbled in pencil on a scrap of paper (and displayed at the villa)? It was as if Butterfly were about to disappear behind her screen, as if we could hear Scarpia's firing squad climbing the castle steps. "*Elvira, povera donna, finita.*" (Elvira, poor lady, it's finished.) Nothing could be more affecting, and, though the visit is conducted in Italian, it may hardly matter if you don't speak the language—you will understand a great deal by simply walking through the villa's rooms and catching your guide's inflections.

A half-day at Torre del Lago can be completed by an excursion on Lake Massaciuccoli or a *gelato* at Ristorante Antonio, where Antonio's brother, Sergio, has his own Puccini collection. I discovered this quite by accident when I noticed, above the bar, the program for the New York premiere of *Madama Butterfly*, February 11, 1907, with Enrico Caruso as Pinkerton. "If you wish, I have more about Puccini," said Sergio somewhat timidly before showing me to a back dining room where, lovingly preserved, were drawings of the costumes from *Manon Lescaut*, among other memorabilia. Before leaving Torre, you may want to consult the program for July's Puccini Festival, part of which takes place at Torre's open-air theater.

Lucca's charms do not exist in isolation, and striking out in any direction inevitably means stumbling upon some treasure. A short drive northeast into the hills toward Tofori is Villa Torrigiani, once the home of Lucca's ambassador to the court of Louis XIV. Restored in the Baroque style beginning in the 1660s, the villa boasts fine frescoes and furnishings but is most famous for its Lenôtre-designed gardens and, not least, the fountains' water games, which have become a tradition and which the present count still delights in setting in motion—just as he did as a child when the Duke of Windsor came to call . . . and, startled by a sudden spouting, landed, linen suit and all, in the mud. The villa's façade is as busy as its owner, but with statues rather than pranks, as if an entire house party decided long ago to stay on, perpetually roaming the balustrades and ducking into the niches.

To prolong a pleasant day in the country, a particularly satisfying plan might include a meal at La Mora, where Angela Brunicardi and her mother-in-law, Assunta, cook such local fare as citrus-sauced salmon trout (fresh from the Serchio, which flows nearby) and lamb chops with artichokes. Fattoria Maionchi's luscious red Cintello, a blend of Sangiovese and Canaiolo grapes aged in Luccan chestnut, accompanies both the fish and meat perfectly.

If you haven't a car or simply prefer to inhabit the spell within Lucca's wall, try not to miss Palazzo Mansi's frescoed ballroom and sumptuous "bridal chamber," every inch covered in golden Luccan silk. Or you may choose to sip something cool and people-watch in late-afternoon sun at the café across from San Paolino, where Puccini's first composition, Mass in Four Voices, premiered in 1881. Should you stop by Panificio Chifenti, on the same street, for a slice of Lucca's specialty vegetable tart with "birds' beaks" (for the pastry points decorating the crust), you'll recognize the two owners, sisters with silver hair in shining marcelle waves, as the *nonne* of your dreams.

And finally—or firstly—there is Lucca's astonishing Guinigi Tower. Broad, shallow steps lead to its roof garden, a shaded nest beneath which the city extends: plains of tile roofs, stonemasons' plots cultivated nearly a millennium ago; ancient streets, dark as old mortar; the massive wall, proud and blossoming; and, at every turn, Lucca herself, still laughing.

Dining Within Lucca's Wall

Lucca lies in a fertile plain, reclaimed centuries ago from swampland and given over to the cultivation of *cereali* (grains). Within the city's wall the best menus reflect this, and none more authentically than Da Giulio in Pelleria, on the site of a former tannery, where first-course pastas and *ribollita,* the bread soup found elsewhere in

Tuscany, are supplanted by thick, grain-based dishes. Such characteristic, unfussy food is exemplified by this popular restaurant's hearty, delicious *farinata* (cornmeal cooked with vegetables).

For excellent seafood in sophisticated surroundings, lunch might be scheduled at Puccini, across from Casa Puccini. The *fritto misto alla retina* ("from the fisherman's net") is noteworthy not only for its shrimp and mullet but also for the light-as-air batter. *Branzino al cartoccio* (sea bass in a foil envelope), boned at table, is perfection for the purist. For such exemplary fish a wine equal to the task was Fattoria del Buonamico's Vasario '93, named for the author of *Lives of the Artists*.

Too-strong salt cod at the Buca di Sant'Antonio was, on the other hand, disappointing, but the *farro,* combining spelt, vegetables, and cranberry beans; salmon trout "Carpaccio" on arugula with only salt, pepper, and Lucca's renowned olive oil; and *tordelli lucchesi* (meat-stuffed and -sauced pasta) were splendid, especially with Fattoria Maionchi's 1994 red. Such dishes and the cozy atmosphere—copper hung from the ceiling, lamps and bouquets on the tables—make this restaurant a favorite among Lucchesi for special occasions, and you may well see a wedding or confirmation party convening here, as it is only steps from San Michele.

On the street behind San Michele, by the way, is the Antica Botega di Prospero—sacks of rice, beans, and pastas propped against the walls; dried mushrooms and figs, nuts and oils, on the shelves—a shop that is a window into Lucca's agricultural and culinary life. Also nearby, on Via Fillungo, the main shopping street, is Caffè di Simo, an Art Nouveau gem. This, Puccini's preferred café, was before and after him a gathering place for artists and litterati, among them the Nobel-honored poets Carducci and Quasimodo.

Other possibilities for casual meals—with greater selection—are Gli Orti di Via Elisa and Il Tabarro, the former a cheery neighborhood place near Via del Fosso (what remains of the Roman moat).

Lunch offerings include a salad bar, especially good *polpette* (meatballs, called *porpette* in Lucca), a cold plate of fava beans with shrimp, and a "Tuscan milk shake" of *gelato*, red fruits, and grappa. Il Tabarro, named for a lesser-known Puccini opera, is a restaurant-pizzeria at Piazza del Giglio, where students stand around en masse on Friday nights. When we asked what the draw was, the chef said good-naturedly, "They come to the piazza to talk, just to talk. That's what we do in Italy," and, with that and a gesture worthy of the Giglio theater's stage, he ushered us inside for the best spaghetti (*al raddicchio*) of our trip.

Finally, a restaurant actually *on* Lucca's wall is the Antico Caffè delle Mura, a monument to the Belle Epoque good life. Salads here are noteworthy, and the calf's liver in red-wine sauce with pears was excellent, but the most memorable dish of all was *tordelli scuri* (meat-filled pasta made with unsweetened cocoa—an idea as old as the Renaissance—in cream sauce). A *dolce* worth scaling the wall for is *panna cotta al caffè*, a coffee custard under a delicately crisp glaze.

Hotels

Fattoria Villa Maionchi, Località Tofori, 55012 San Gennaro (Lucca); 0583.978194; fax: 0583.978345.

Principessa Elisa, Via Nuova per Pisa, 55050 Massa Pisana (Lucca); 0583.379737; fax: 0583.379019.

Tenuta di Valgiano, Via di Valigano, 7, 55010 Valgiano (Lucca); tel./fax: 0583.402271.

Villa Casanova, 55050 Balbano (Lucca); 0583.548429; fax: 0583.368955.

Villa La Principessa, Via Nuova per Pisa, 55050 Massa Pisana (Lucca); 0583.370037; fax: 0583.379136.

Villa San Michele, Via di San Michele in Escheto, 55050 Massa Pisana (Lucca); 0583.370276; fax: 0583.370277.

Universo, Piazza del Giglio, 55100 Lucca; 0583.493678; fax: 0583.954854.

Restaurants

Antico Caffè delle Mura, Piazzale Vittorio Emanuele, 2; 0583.47962.

Buca di Sant'Antonio, Via della Cervia, 3; 0583.312199.

Da Giulio in Pelleria, Via delle Conce, 45, Piazza San Donato; 0583.55948.

Il Gazebo (*see* Principessa Elisa).

La Mora, Via Sesto di Moriano, 1748, Ponte a Moriano (Lucca); 0583.406402.

Siena in Three Acts

BY WILLIAM ZINSSER

∽

editor's note

"I had always believed, and continue to believe, really, that there is no more beautiful square in the world than the one in Siena." Those are the words of Gabriel García Márquez, from his work *Watching the Rain in Galicia,* and the fact that he continued on to say that the only place that made him doubt that statement was the plaza in Santiago de Compostela is irrelevant: One is allowed to feel that more than one public place is not only beautiful but extraordinary, as I believe Siena's Piazza del Campo to be.

Only a little over an hour from Florence, Siena is perceived by some visitors as merely a day trip. I think this is a mistake, as Siena and its surrounding countryside are worthy of much more than a day (walking around the Campo and looking at the paintings by Ambrogio Lorenzetti and Simone Martini in the Museo Civico easily occupy a full day for me). It is unlikely that many of us can claim as personal an odyssey with Siena as the author of this piece, but many of us can at least claim that Siena is one of the most exceptional places in the world.

Writer, editor, and teacher WILLIAM ZINSSER is the author of two widely used books about writing, *On Writing Well* (HarperReference, 1998, sixth revised edition) and *Writing to Learn* (HarperCollins, 1989). He joined the staff of the New York *Herald Tribune* after serving in the army during World War II and became a freelance writer in 1959. Zinsser has contributed to dozens of national magazines and was general editor of the Book-of-the-Month Club for eight years. In 1998, his papers, which cover his career of over fifty years, were donated to the Fales Library at New York University.

In early May of 1945 my army unit was stationed in an Italian seaside town south of Leghorn. World War II was ebbing to a close, and talk of Germany's surrender was in the air. For GIs like us, far behind the lines, there was nothing to do. I remember that we played a lot of baseball. I also remember that I kept hearing about a town called Siena, two or three hours' drive away. It was one of those names that travelers listen for, like Kyoto or Fez, and I persuaded three of my friends—we were all sergeants—that we should try to go see it. We got permission to take a company jeep for one day, and on the morning of May 7 we set out.

The gravel road left the coast and climbed across a landscape of hills and farms and brought us to Volterra, an old Etruscan town, hunched like a fortress on a hilltop. It was famous for its alabaster, and with the fervor of all tourists coming upon a local specialty of unsuspected beauty, we bought alabaster cigarette boxes and ashtrays for our unsuspecting families back home. The ancient city held us with its power, and it was midday before we pushed on.

Later, far off to the left, we saw a sight so fanciful, an illustration from a child's fairy tale, that I thought if I blinked it would go away. It was a cluster of stone towers rising out of a village on a hill. After the war I would learn that it was San Gimignano, a relic of the many Tuscan towns that once had such towers, built for defense and long since fallen down. But on that afternoon it was only a teasing apparition; there was no time to go chasing mirages.

If San Gimignano was the perfect miniature, Siena was the master painting. Announcing itself to us from a distance, it looked both proud and playful, arrayed across three hills and sprawling down the sides, all contained within a medieval wall. Bestriding the city from its highest ridge was an immense white cathedral. Inside, I was struck by the city's remarkable harmony. The prevailing color was pale red brick, the prevailing architecture was Gothic, and the geometry was uniformly random: all curves and inclines. Yet such was Siena's gravitational logic that the streets from all three hills funneled down into one large public square, the Piazza del Campo.

It was the most beautiful square I had ever seen, partly because it wasn't square; it was shaped like an open fan. Anchoring the Campo was the handsome Palazzo Pubblico, or city hall, built around 1300, which had a bell tower so slender and audacious, so much taller than anyone would expect, that it set a tone of high civic enjoyment. The square sloped upward, and all the buildings around its rim were consistent in their height and sensibility. It was a collective work of art, and we sat at an outdoor cafe and had lunch, our goal achieved, hardly believing our good luck.

The square had the serenity of well-proportioned space, but it was also alive with people; obviously it had always been the emotional center of Sienese life. At that time I hadn't even heard of its most famous event, the horse race called the Palio, held every summer since 1659 amid much medieval pageantry and hysteria. The nags that clomp around the perimeter of the Campo represent

Siena's contentious political districts, and the event takes its passion from the fact that it's much more than a horse race. It's a ritual acting out of an arcane system of municipal governance by seventeen highly territorial tribes.

After lunch we walked up to the cathedral, which, along with a jaunty striped campanile, regally occupied the city's high ground. But nothing about the exterior of the church prepared me for its interior. All I could think when I stepped inside was "How wonderful!" I was amazed that an isolated Italian town in the early 1200s had found the energy to raise such an exuberant house of God. The nave was a fantasia of zebra stripes—alternating bands of black and white marble that formed not only the walls of the church but two rows of massive columns, which supported two rows of Romanesque arches, which supported two higher rows of Gothic arches and windows, which in turn supported a blue ceiling with gold stars and a vaulted dome. Other wonders gradually revealed themselves: a mosaic floor that covered the entire area of the church, a superb marble pulpit by Nicola Pisano, a haunting *Saint John the Baptist* by Donatello, and a profusion of other works tucked into every niche. From there we went next door to a small museum, where Siena sprang its final marvel on me: Duccio's group of small paintings of the life of Christ that had been part of the duomo's original altarpiece.

All those Duccios completed our crash course in Sienese art, and we began to think about heading back. Just then we noticed a stone stairway that a guard said would take us to a panoramic view. The museum, it turned out, was housed within the walls of a new nave that the city started adding to the cathedral in 1339 but had to abandon, and our stairs, spiraling up and up, deposited us on top of its unfinished facade. From that catwalk we could look down on the entire city. The time was around 4:20. I remember that it wasn't on the hour or the half-hour, because we were startled when the bells in the campanile began to ring. It was a jubilant, spread-the-news kind of ringing, and suddenly it dawned on us what news was being spread. The war was over!

Below us the city exploded into life. Men and women and children came running from every direction down the streets that emptied into the Campo. We scrambled down to join them. The square was a shifting sea of happy people, and it already had an air of pageantry—heraldic banners were hanging from the windows of the Palazzo Pubblico. We seemed to be the only Allied soldiers there; Siena had been skirted by the retreating and pursuing armies, and whatever troops may have once been stationed in the city were gone. Later it occurred to me that all four of us had German names: Helmuth Gerbich, Herbert Myers, William Schramm and William Zinsser.

Now, seeing four GIs, the people of Siena hugged us and shouted "*Viva America!*" and lifted us onto their shoulders and carried us around the square. We didn't feel like conquering heroes—none of us had seen combat. But we had lived with the smashed towns and smashed lives that were the residue of that bloody campaign up the Italian peninsula, and on behalf of its real heroes we acted as happy as we felt, bobbing above the crowd. Darkness had fallen by the time we got back to our jeep. But we weren't allowed to leave; little bands of musicians and revelers kept falling in ahead of us and behind us as we inched our way through the crowded streets. Finally we broke away, reached a gate through the wall, and found our road to the coast.

The night was black and the countryside was asleep. But the villages were awake, and when the people heard our jeep they ran out to shout "*Viva la pace!*" One old man handed a bottle of Chianti into our jeep and we all joined him in a drink. At one point we saw a bonfire on a hill far ahead. Eventually our road took us past that bonfire, which was being tended by some farmers, and from there we could see another bonfire on another hill, and when we reached that bonfire we saw still another one, far away. Only after three or four bonfires did we make the connection: the country people were spreading the news. Many hills later, around midnight, we got back to our base. The next morning we learned that nobody else had been allowed off the base. When the end of the war was announced on Armed Forces Radio, all passes were suspended.

But that wasn't the end of Siena in my life. After V-E Day the army faced the problem of keeping its men occupied, not having enough troopships to bring us home. As one solution, it started a college in Florence, recruiting its faculty from officers and enlisted men who had been teachers in civilian life. My unit had moved back to a dismal region of southern Italy; months of tedium stretched out ahead of us. One day I saw in *The Stars and Stripes* an item announcing the new college. Only one man per unit would be admitted. Being whisked off to Florence was the ultimate fairy godmother's intervention, and I ran to the adjutant to be the first to apply. My lifelong newspaper-reading habit was rewarded, and on the first of July I went off to college.

Our campus was a former Italian air corps academy just outside Florence. My dormitory window had a perfectly framed view across the red tile roofs to Brunelleschi's soaring cathedral dome and Giotto's campanile. I decided to sign up for art history courses, never having taken any, and they became my passport into the Renaissance. In the morning I could look at slides of Ghiberti's baptistery doors and then go see the doors on my own; our afternoons were free, and we were the only tourists in town. The city had just begun to bring its masterpieces out of hiding, and sometimes I caught one of them being hauled through the streets or hoisted back onto its pedestal—I looked Cellini's Perseus in the eye. That summer was a re-Renaissance—art again belonged to the Florentine people, as it had when the statues were first put up. By September the city was in my bones. I found myself dropping in on statues and paintings that had become old friends, or hiking across the Ponte Vecchio—every other bridge across the Arno had been blown up— and climbing up to my favorite church, San Miniato, and my favorite view of Florence, lying below me in the palm of my hand.

When the summer was over I reported to an embarkation depot at Naples to wait for a troopship to take me home. There I had plenty of time to think about returning to civilian life. Everything depended on whether I would have to go back to college. When I left Princeton to enlist in the army I had a grab-bag of wartime credits that almost added up to a B.A. degree. Now I had three more credits, which Princeton granted just for serving in the armed forces, plus some certificates for the courses I took at Florence. Originally I had thought I would want to go back to Princeton to round out my fragmented college years. Now I only wanted to get on with whatever I was going to do next.

In November a troopship finally brought me home, and I went to Princeton for an interview. I was nervous as I walked toward Nassau Hall, its walls clothed in 200 years of historic ivy; the army certificates I was clutching suddenly looked crude. Worst of all, I learned that my interview would be with Dean Root. Robert K.

Root, dean of Princeton's faculty and guardian of its academic honor, was then in his late sixties, the prototype old professor: stern and dry and dour. As a sophomore I had taken his lecture course in eighteenth-century English literature and had listened, week after week, as he rained on our unappreciative heads the pearls of his life-long scholarship, excavating with dry precision the buried ironies of Jonathan Swift and the unsuspected jests of Alexander Pope, which even then we continued not to suspect. It never occurred to me that he and I would ever meet, and I was appalled to be meeting him now. He looked just as stern up close.

Dean Root studied my Princeton transcript and then looked at my army certificates. He said he had never seen anything like them; my impression was that he didn't think I had spent the summer at Oxford. He examined my Princeton transcript again and took another look at the certificates and made some notes. I could see that he was adding up my credits and that they weren't coming out right. He went over his figures one more time. Finally he shook his head and mumbled that I seemed to be a little short. I told myself I was a dead duck.

Then, abruptly, I was no longer being interviewed by a dean. A real person was sitting across from me, his features not unkindly, and he was asking me what I had done during the war. I found myself talking to him about my year in North Africa and how it had opened my eyes to the Arab world. I told him about my trips to Rome, and about seeing *La Bohême* in the Naples opera house, and about my Renaissance summer in Florence, and about the weekend jaunts I made to Pisa and Lucca and Siena. A clouded look came over Dean Root's face.

"Tell me," he said, "I suppose Siena was mostly destroyed during the war." I realized that I was the first returning veteran to bring him news of the city. Suddenly I understood what Siena would mean to this quintessential humanist; probably he had first visited Siena as a young man himself. Suddenly it was possible to understand that

Dean Root had once been a young man. I told him that Siena hadn't been touched by the war and that the great duomo was still there on the crest of the hill.

Dean Root smiled fleetingly and saw me to the door. He said Princeton would inform me of its decision soon. Two weeks later he wrote to say that I had met Princeton's requirements for a B.A. degree and that I could receive my diploma at a special winter graduation for returning servicemen. I was quite sure he had waived one or two credits to make the total add up. In the middle of my interview, I think, he decided to stop counting. Numbers weren't as important to him as learning, and he freed me to get on with my life. But I also think that if Siena had been destroyed I would have had to go back to college for one more term.

In the fall of 1992 I watched the steady approach of my seventieth birthday and wondered how to contend with it when it arrived. Then one day I knew what I wanted to do. "Let's go to Siena for my birthday," I said to Caroline. I would celebrate the day by going back to the place where I spent the most celebratory day of my life. I didn't want to re-live that distant moment; I just wanted to make a connection with its emotions—to borrow its essential joy. Whether such emotions were transferable across the decades I wouldn't know until I made the journey.

Over the years I had been back to Tuscany several times, but always as part of a longer trip, not as a destination, and always in summer. Florence was then so swollen with tourists that I could hardly find the city I remembered. But now it was fall, and I made a one-week itinerary that would take Caroline and me to Siena by way of Florence, starting in Rome. There was no question of starting anywhere else. My Italy begins and ends in Rome—and has since I was a schoolboy, when my Latin teacher kept plaster statues of the Roman gods on his desk. He knew that the icons that inhabit the classrooms of our youth can exert a lifelong spell, and in my case he was right. As soon as the war landed me in Italy I fidgeted to see Rome, though I was stationed in far-off Brindisi, in Italy's heel. When I finally wangled a five-day pass I hitchhiked to Rome in a truck, over the Apennines in midwinter, taking two days to get there and two to get back. But the day in between was one I've never forgotten.

Since then I've stopped off in Rome whenever I could. I go to Rome the way other people go to the Bahamas and lie in the sun—to be renewed. Friends try to warn me; the traffic, they say, is "impossible." But it's never any more impossible than it was the last time, and it wasn't impossible when Caroline and I arrived there on a Friday morning in October of 1992. After twenty-four hours of walking all over the city I felt young again.

On Saturday afternoon we took a train to Florence and headed out into the streets to get reacquainted. I was wary, recalling my earlier sense of loss. But the summer hordes were gone, and Florence was no longer their captive. The city had a mercantile bustle, going about its old business. Money was still its lubricant—the shops were elegant and expensive—and the Medicis were still around every corner. I had forgotten what a serious face Florence presents to the world, its color relentlessly brown, its grid flat and rectilinear, its buildings massive in their stonework—just the opposite of gay, red, undulating Siena. No wonder the two medieval city-states, so unalike in temperament, were such enemies for so many centuries.

Now, rediscovering Florence, I felt fresh respect for the city. If it was serious, as many serious people are admirable without necessarily being much fun, it insisted that I take it seriously, and I did. It had the earnest familiarity of an old college roommate. So did the other guests at our hotel: professorial men and tweed-skirted women ensconced under reading lamps. They looked as if they had been coming there every year since the 1920s—sent by, or perhaps invented by, E. M. Forster.

On Sunday my feet took me all over Florence; they still knew the way. Ghiberti's baptistery doors were still "worthy to be the gates of paradise," as Michelangelo described them. His own statue of David in the Galleria dell'Accademia and Giotto's frescoes in the church of Santa Croce were no less worthy, and Fra Angelico's frescoes in the convent of San Marco had lost none of their unassailable purity. Caroline let me follow my inner compass, and when it pointed to San Miniato I warned her that we were in for a climb. Walking across the Ponte Vecchio, I was back in my army boots: left along the Arno, then a right turn, then through the old wall, then up the long penitential steps. San Miniato was waiting for me at the top.

I remembered the church as being so likable, almost toy-like in its gaiety and in the daring of its split-level nave—it was begun in 1013—that I was afraid my older self would find it too likable, too ingratiating; my naive soldier self had undoubtedly been seduced by it. But that fear evaporated as soon as I walked in, and when my art-wise wife pronounced it a gem and my guidebook pronounced it "one of the finest Romanesque churches in Italy" I felt that my pilgrimage to Florence was complete, the circle full.

On Monday we rented a car and headed south for Siena, first stopping at San Gimignano, whose phantom towers had hailed me so long ago. It turned out to be real, a medieval jewel. Beyond it I found the country road my friends and I had taken on the day the war ended, and I followed it toward the coast. But the road hadn't improved much since 1945, and I decided to turn south to Siena.

"I thought this was a return trip," Caroline said. "Keep going to Volterra." I told her that Volterra was quite a push. "I want to see it," she said, and after quite a push we sighted it in the distance, silhouetted on a hill behind its armament of walls. The brooding city held me again, and I was glad I had come—another memory nailed down. When at last we did head for Siena we ran out of daylight and ended up driving in the dark. No bonfires kept us company; in 1992 any news worth spreading would be spread by television. But otherwise I imagined life on those Tuscan farms to be not much different. For the grandchildren of the villagers who cheered our jeep through the night with bottles of Chianti it was probably still 1945.

At Siena our hotel was outside the wall, as most of Siena's hotels are, and we spent Tuesday visiting some of the hill towns, like Pienza and Montepulciano, that give the region its distinctive flavor. I was saving Siena for my birthday, and the next morning Caroline and I went into town. We entered by the Porta Romana and walked up a meandering street that I had no doubt would bring us to the Campo. When it did, the square looked exactly as I remembered it; nothing had changed. I felt a surge of gratitude that such a place existed in my life, always available, no appointment necessary. I strolled over to the restaurant where I wanted to have lunch and reserved an outdoor table for four. Just before leaving New York I had run into old friends, Rosa and Al Silverman. They happened to mention that they would be vacationing in Perugia, and I asked if they would drive over to Siena on October 7 to help us celebrate. They said they would, and we set a rendezvous for 1:30 at the restaurant.

Caroline and I lingered in the Campo, but I could feel the cathedral pulling me up the hill, and I didn't resist. As soon as I stepped inside I thought "How wonderful!" It, too, was unchanged. We spent an hour marveling and then went to the museum next door to see the Duccios. But I also kept an eye out for my stairway, and when I found it I knew what I had to do. At the summit my view was intact—no postwar buildings, as in London or Paris, impinged on a remembered skyline. Far below, the Campo spread its fan, and I mentally filled it with crowds pouring into it from every direction. Except for the vertigo I felt terrific.

By then it was almost 1:30, and we made our way back down to the Campo. Rosa and Al were there, and the four of us settled down to an unhurried lunch. As the October sun moved across the sky, the buildings around the Campo turned in subtle gradations from red to rose to pink. In the square, people came and went, meeting and separating. Toddlers played, mothers watched, teenagers lounged, old men and women gossiped. Watching the reality of the Campo, I was struck by how much it meant to me to be with good friends from my own real life. None of us talked about tourist things— where we had been or what sights we had seen. We talked about the same things everyone in the square was talking about: children and grandchildren, food and drink, work and play. Things got said that we hadn't known about each other.

Ordinarily I seek change—it has always been a tonic to me. But on that October 7 in Siena I was at ease, slipping over into my next decade without regret. The connection I had hoped to make was made; the joyful emotions of May 7, 1945, did turn out to be transferable. But mainly I was contented because I was in a place where values that are important to me had endured for a thousand years: the humanity of urban space, the integrity of architecture, the magnificence of Christian art.

Dean Root's rueful question came back to me. The thought that Siena might have been destroyed seemed unthinkable now, as it hadn't when the dean was old and I was young, home from the war that destroyed so much. Now the continuity of the city mattered just as deeply to me. Siena had survived, and so had I.

The Palio

BY LIS HARRIS

editor's note

Allow me to state that I have never had the opportunity to attend the Palio. But I still think Leslie Forbes has it right in her book, *A Taste of Tuscany,* when she wrote that "To say that it is just a horse race is like saying that Everest is just a mountain. The Palio is not an event that occurs twice a year at Siena. It *is* Siena."

LIS HARRIS, a staff writer at *The New Yorker* for many years, is a professor at the Graduate School of the Arts, writing division, at Columbia University. She is also the author of *Holy Days: The World of a Hasidic Family* (MacMillan, 1995) and *Rules of Engagement* (Touchstone, 1996).

In 1924, Aldous Huxley paid a visit to Siena on the day of the Palio, a violent bareback horse race that has existed in its present form for more than three hundred years and has its roots in the city's ancient past. The Palio is run twice every summer—once in July and once in August—in the Piazza del Campo, the city's magnificent main square. Ten of the city's seventeen *contrade,* or wards, compete in the race, which is dedicated to the Virgin, and the winner receives a painted silk banner, called the Palio (the name is used for both the event and the prize), bearing her image. Huxley enjoyed the Palio but disapproved of the emotions associated with it. He noted in his journal that the course's two dangerously sharp curves and its uneven topography probably made it "the most dangerous flat-race in the world," and added that "it is made the more dangerous by the excessive patriotism of the rival *contrade.*"

The wards of Siena function like small independent city-states; each has its own constitution, seat of government, hymn, motto, insignia, flag, church, museum, and patron saint, and enmities and friendships among the wards have evolved over hundreds of years. Huxley particularly admired the authenticity of the pre-race procession, in which representatives of the *contrade* and of various other civic institutions past and present march in luxurious costumes faithfully copied from Renaissance paintings. He contrasted it favorably with various English pageants he had attended, usually in the rain. "The Palio is just a show, having no 'meaning' in particular," he wrote, "but by the mere fact of being traditional and still alive signifying infinitely more than the dead-born English affairs." In fact, as I was to discover last summer when I arrived in Siena, a short time before the August Palio, there is scarcely an aspect of the race that is not rife with meaning, and the "excessive patriotism" that Huxley disapproved of is the city's most vital expression of a unique capacity for cultural self-preservation.

Initially, when a European friend who summers near Siena suggested that I attend the race, I resisted the idea. I know less than nothing about horse races, and, in general, civic manifestations make me feel gloomy. My mind was changed by a book entitled *La Terra in Piazza*, written by two cultural anthropologists—Alan Dundes, an American, and Alessandro Falassi, a Sienese. In the preface the authors mention a few aspects of the Palio that distinguish it from all other horse races. They point out, for example, that "before the race, each horse is taken inside a church to be solemnly blessed," that "although thousands of dollars change hands, there is no betting," that "during the days immediately before the race, the jockeys are guarded night and day and they are not permitted to speak to anyone except to and through their bodyguards," that "during the race, the jockeys beat each other and their horses with whips made from calf phalluses," that "the winner of the race receives a silk banner as a prize but he must spend a small fortune to pay for the victory," that "the losers receive money but they are sad at the disgrace of having lost," that "the traditional enemy of the winner is considered to have also lost the race even if he did not actually race as one of the ten participants," and that "after the race, the winner sucks pacifiers, while the losers take a purge." Dundes and Falassi also make it clear that although the race itself occupies no more than a minute and a half, the animating rivalries of the Palio are never far from the thoughts of the average Sienese 365 days a year.

I arrived in Siena on Tuesday, August 9th, exactly a week before the race. That evening, along with what seemed to be a respectable majority of Siena's population of 60,000, I took a walk along one of many narrow cobbled lanes that flow from all directions of the city to converge on the Piazza del Campo. At daybreak the next morning, workmen would begin bringing truckloads of Siena's distinctive golden earth from a storage hangar in the neighboring countryside of Cerchiaia, and the beautiful medieval Piazza would be transformed into a beautiful medieval Piazza-cum-racetrack. But this evening the normal swarm of peanut venders, souvenir hawkers, shoppers, students with backpacks, dog-walkers, priests, and elderly ladies strolling arm in arm were out and about. A few of the small shops facing the square were already partly blocked by six-tiered wooden bleachers that would eventually ring the Piazza for the race. Tourists crowded the shops and cafés or lined up to ascend the slender, soaring Mangia Tower of the Palazzo Pubblico—the town hall—which dominates the eastern end of the square. The vivacity of the scene, which, give or take a few donkeys and market stalls, could not have been much different in the days when the Piazza was a swarming medieval marketplace, set off to great effect the cool Gothic grandeur of the dark battlements, old balconies, and mullioned windows of the surrounding palazzi.

The ancient upheavals that produced Siena's topography left

few flat surfaces, and the Piazza del Campo is no exception. It is sloping and scallop-shaped (older Sienese like to describe it as the cloak of the Madonna spread out to protect them), and its concavity plays strange tricks with perspective: people walking away from you seem to diminish quickly in size, as if they had traversed a vast distance, though they have walked only a few hundred feet. The Piazza's well-worn rosy brick pavement had no sooner been restored to a state of immaculate cleanliness by the street-sweepers at sunup on Wednesday than a large red dump truck filled with earth began to discharge its load at the downward-sloping San Martino corner—so called because it stands at the entrance to the Via San Martino, to the left of the Palazzo Pubblico. San Martino is one of the Palio's two murderous curves; the other, which slopes upward and is slightly less steep, is called Casato, because it is at the entrance to the Via del Casato di Sotto. In all the years that the Palio has been run, there has rarely been a race in which a jockey or a horse, and sometimes a whole clutch of both, has not run afoul of the San Martino corner. Before 1721, when the city ruled that only ten wards could run in any one Palio, the track was so crowded that the pileups of jockeys and steeds at San Martino became truly horrific. Nowadays, mattresses are put up to cushion the impact of the crashes.

Not every fall at the corner is an accident. Jockeys have frequently been known to deliberately fall from their horses at San Martino, in order to let another ward's horse pass them. This seemingly perverse behavior becomes intelligible only when you understand that it is an accepted part of the complicated deals made before the race is run. The jockeys cheat and are cheated. On July 2, 1855, a jockey named Francesco Santini but known as Gobbo (Hunchback), who had won the Palio fifteen times, for seven different wards, "went to San Martino," as the saying goes, and lost the race, although he had been mounted on one of the best horses running. Confronted by enraged members of the ward for which he had ridden, he reportedly burst out, "But why should I have won for you skinflints who were giving me a hundred and forty lire, when I got a hundred and seventy out of it?" This unusual candor concerning one of the most commonly known, if least publicly discussed, aspects of the Palio set Gobbo back several hundred lire in court costs and scarcely even begins to suggest the complexity of the pre-race arrangements.

After each truckload of earth fell onto the cobblestones of the Piazza's perimeter, a steamroller flattened it, and five relaxed-looking workmen, chatting and smoking as they walked along, patted it smooth with shovels and wooden tampers, and hosed it down. As the morning went on, the red dump truck was joined by a blue and then a green one, and many people passing on their way to work or market stopped briefly to gaze approvingly at the earth. A few pressed their hands to it—an act that, according to Dundes and Falassi, has near-mystical meaning to a Sienese, reaffirming both his bond to the land and the fact that "the past has returned and a future event, the Palio, is about to become present." Curiously, for all the trouble being taken to lay a smooth course, and for all the obvious respect, not to say veneration, for the earth, no effort was made to keep people away from it. Everyone walked calmly across the track as soon as it went down, and though hundreds of tiny heel marks and scattered cigarette butts soon began to deface it, no one—not even the workmen—seemed to find this behavior dismaying, or at all odd. Throughout the week, the commercial and social life of the Piazza would go on as before, providing a placid counterpoint to the fervent emotions focused on the racecourse. The shops behind the bleachers would continue to sell olive oil, *panforte,* and hardware. In the center of the Piazza, where most of the 60,000 to 70,000 expected spectators would stand, gratis, to watch the procession and the race, the hawkers and venders would continue to ply their trade, and the cafés and restaurants would push their umbrella-shaded tables and wooden chairs directly onto the track, pulling them back only for the preliminary trials and the Palio itself.

On Tuesday night, I had been introduced to a number of local citizens, of whom one, as luck would have it, was Alessandro Falassi. Professor Falassi, an affable bearded man, told me that he spent half the academic year at the University of California at Los Angeles and the other half at Siena's Scuola di Lingua e Cultura Italiana per Stranieri. This arrangement was satisfying, he said, because, like most Sienese, he found the idea of permanently leaving the city unsupportable. Sienese who live elsewhere will go to almost any lengths to return to their *contrade* each year for the Palio. Even the most hidebound Italian bureaucracies, like the military, understand the Palio's significance. Unofficially, it is considered the right (and certainly the need) of any Sienese serving in the armed forces to be granted a pass so as not to miss the event.

Most Sienese take a great deal of pride in the beauty and valiant history (real and imagined) of their city and regard it as indisputably superior to any other, but the true center of their lives is the ward. For a Sienese, the ward plays an emotional role more central even than the family—which in Italy is saying quite a lot. No one knows exactly how the wards originated, but they have verifiable roots in two sources: the military companies of the Middle Ages, which provided soldiers to defend the city, and the independent civic and religious associations that kept the wheels of Sienese society turning in the city's darkest and most chaotic hours. Each of the seventeen wards bears the name of its symbol, usually an animal, and the symbol and the traditional colors of each ward are displayed on its flags, shields, and costumes. The seventeen wards are Aquila (Eagle), Bruco (Caterpillar), Chiocciola (Snail), Civetta (Owl), Drago (Dragon), Giraffa (Giraffe), Istrice (Porcupine),

Leocorno (Unicorn), Lupa (She-Wolf), Nicchio (Shell), Oca (Goose), Onda (Wave), Pantera (Panther), Selva (Forest), Tartuca (Turtle), Torre (Tower), and Valdimontone (Ram).

Within the city's medieval walls, the Sienese do not refer to themselves as Sienese. They say "I am of the Goose" or "of the Snail," or "I am a little Porcupine" or "a Unicorn." Scholars have pointed out the virtually totemic relationship between the *contradaioli* and their symbol, and countless anecdotes attest to this central fact of Sienese life, such as the story about the cavalryman from Dragon who refused to accept a medal because it was engraved with an image of St. George slaying the dragon. There may once have been as many as eighty wards, but by the middle of the fourteenth century wars and plagues had reduced their number to forty-two; by the beginning of the eighteenth century, there were only seventeen. Over the years, disputes concerning ward boundaries erupted so frequently into public brawls that in 1729 the *governatrice* of Siena, Beatrice Violante of Bavaria, issued a decree fixing the exact territorial delineations of each ward and freezing the number at seventeen in perpetuity. The *governatrice* issued the decree, she said, in the (alas, vain) hope of "putting a stop to the dangerous and costly wrangles that have arisen between the inhabitants." Although the boundaries remain unchanged, the rivalries and antagonisms engendered by ancient disputes have continued to arouse violent passions.

Ward rivalries and alliances have shifted over the centuries; friends have become enemies, and enemies have (less frequently) become friends. Some wards have even been enemyless for a while, as is the case today with Dragon and Forest. Dragon and She-Wolf used to be enemies, but peace descended—largely, it is said, because She-Wolf's more virulent rivalry with Porcupine left little room for another enemy. Forest has had no enemies since it made peace with Panther, nearly 200 years ago. The city's two strongest rivals are

Goose (where women are still not allowed to vote in *contrada* elections) and Tower—neighboring wards that are both densely populated and predominantly working class. Goose has won many Palios, the latest of them in 1985, whereas Tower has not won a Palio since 1961, and although it is still not the *nonna* (grandmother)—the term for the ward that has gone the longest without winning, a distinction that belongs to Caterpillar—its long losing streak inspires countless local jokes that do little to diminish the antagonism between the two wards. In 1949, when the Australian writer Alan Moorehead attended a Palio and described it for this magazine, the ward that had won the most Palios over the years was Goose. It still is. Its jockey, Andrea Degortes, called Aceto (Vinegar), is considered one of the three greatest Palio jockeys of the twentieth century, and its museum and oratory are crammed with the bounty that the ward's sixty victories have brought it from grateful *contradaioli*. (The wards' claims to various items in their treasuries have sometimes caused terrible strife. In 1600, for example, when Goose separated from the Company of St. Catherine, the schism engendered a violent dispute with the Dominicans, who were closely associated with the Saint, over the matter of ownership of Catherine's head. The disagreement simmered for years and eventually boiled over at a May Day procession in 1609, during which the Geese tried to wrest the sacred relic from the Dominicans by force.) Of dozens of stories illustrating the depth of the hatred between Goose and Tower, perhaps the best known is about an old priest from Goose who was compelled to miss a Palio in order to conduct a funeral service for one of his parishioners. It happened that the priest was intoning prayers at the grave site at the very moment that the cannon report signalling the start of the race sounded. As the deceased was being interred, the priest walked over to the coffin, where the dead man's relatives were standing. The family assumed that he was about to whisper some words of comfort to them. Instead, as the coffin was lowered the priest addressed the deceased: "Holy soul, who is certainly going to Heaven, tell the Lord not to let Tower win!"

Siena's charming, chain-smoking, Socialist mayor, Vittorio Mazzoni della Stella, warns visitors not to misinterpret the Palio hostilities. "The race is an annual explosion," he told me shortly after my arrival, as we sat across from each other at an elaborately carved table in his elegant sixteenth-century office in the Palazzo Pubblico. "No one ever uses sticks or weapons, and when the Palio is over so is the violence. We have hardly any crime in Siena, you know. Our last murder occurred thirty-five years ago, and even a small robbery here is considered a scandal. What's wrong with acknowledging these passions in ourselves once a year? As far as I can tell, the rest of the world is doing the same thing surreptitiously, and far more violently, all year long."

I asked the Mayor why he thought the Palio had endured in his city, while similar festivals in other cities had died out.

"Originally, when Florence defeated Siena, in 1555, it encouraged festivals of this kind, to redirect the energy formerly expended in warfare," he replied. "It hoped to mummify Siena, so that the city would cease to have a sense of its own vigor and would pose no threat. Instead, Siena's Palio has become a revitalizing institution, while others, all over Italy, either have died out or live on only as tourist attractions. Why? Because the *contrade* have remained strong and meaningful, and powerfully attached to the ancient rituals."

"Including all the scheming and plotting?"

"Well," he said, from behind a plume of cigarette smoke, "since as far as the Palio is concerned a man is considered guilty until he is proven innocent, there is absolutely no way that the so-called crimes perpetrated by *contrade*, or by jockeys, can be prevented, so everybody acts accordingly. But it would be a mistake to judge these things too harshly. The Palio is like an artichoke. You must peel away the coarse outer layers to get to the heart."

Eager to visit some of the wards, I had enlisted the help of Professor Falassi in finding a guide, and he had introduced me to his assistant, Lucia Filippeschi, a beautiful olive-skinned young woman in her early twenties dressed in a Snoopy T-shirt and a miniskirt, who offered to show me around on Wednesday afternoon. We met near the Campo at the appointed hour, Lucia pulling up on her motor scooter, and decided to visit Wave first, since it was situated just behind the Palazzo Pubblico. (I had suggested that we lunch together, but Lucia politely excused herself, explaining that she ate the midday meal with her family every day—miniskirt and Vespa notwithstanding.) We could hear from all parts of the city the low drumrolls of the *tamburini,* or drummers, who were practicing for the Renaissance pageant that precedes the Palio. At first, these rhythms all sound the same, but after a while the distinctive dum-da-dee-dums and tum-tee-tum-tums associated with the different wards become recognizable.

Lucia said we would visit Wave's *società,* which she translated as "social club"—a term I associate with dimly lit storefronts, mangy dogs, and late-night police raids. But the Wave *società* was a busy, cheerful clubhouse, with a bar, many tables, and a bright, flower-filled terrace. According to Armando Santini, Wave's *priore,* or elected head, the ward *società* functions as both a mutual-aid society and a community center. While small children wearing the bright sky-blue-and-white wave-patterned scarves of the ward played hide-and-seek nearby, Signor Santini told me that each ward raised money from dues, from wealthy patrons, from property it owns within its territory, from its bar, which is manned by volunteers, and from special fund-raising events. The money raised is used not only for the Palio—which, he said, can cost anywhere from 150 million lire (about $100,000) to the stars—but for the everyday needs of members in financial distress. Signor Santini, a tall, mustachioed man with pale-blue eyes, asked me to look around the room and tell him what I saw. I reported that I saw men and women of all ages chatting, drinking, playing cards, and looking as if they were having a good time. He laughed, and said it must be because I was an American that I didn't notice that there were people of all classes socializing together. Like virtually all the ward officers I met, he spoke with considerable pride about the democratic tradition of the *contrade*. In a society where class differences are still openly acknowledged, he said, the classlessness of the Sienese *contrade* was unique: "Everybody calls everyone '*tu*' here, and we are all united in our efforts to defeat Tower, our common enemy, in the Palio."

"How did Tower become your enemy?" I asked.

"Well, most of these antagonisms are centuries old," he replied. "We have been enemies since the sixteen-hundreds. Tower is our neighbor, and it has never been a good neighbor. There used to be great violence, but nowadays almost all the antagonism is limited to the time of the Palio."

Did that mean that the rest of the year he looked upon the Tower members more benignly? For example, did he count any of them among his friends?

He stroked his mustache for a second or two, then smiled slyly. "Well, not friends, perhaps," he said. "But acquaintances, certainly."

Santini's vagueness about the source of his ward's rivalry proved to be typical of most *contradaioli*. The origins of the antagonisms seem to be far less important than their depth and resonance. Actually, Wave is not "officially" considered Tower's enemy, and the people of Tower make a great show of publicly ignoring Wave. All their derisive songs are directed against Goose. The records show, however, that Wave and Tower have long tried hard to prevent each other from winning the Palio, and that there have been many bloody clashes between them. In the early eighteen-seventies, Frances Eliot, an Englishwoman travelling in Italy, who considered the Palio a race run by "medieval blockheads," wrote in her diary that "an offence was lately given by the Wave to the Tower," and that a gang of Tower members laid an ambush near a "dark and filthy alley— ready, should a Wave surge up on the common shore of the Piazza, to strike it down then and there."

On the way to Wave, Lucia had told me that a jockey from Sardinia known as Cianchino (Shortshanks) usually rode for the ward. (Most of the Palio jockeys come from outside the city, many of them from Sardinia.) In 1978, Cianchino's horse ran the fastest Palio on record: 1:14:5. I asked Santini if Cianchino would be riding for Wave the following week. "Perhaps," he said, with an enigmatic smile. "That depends. Anyway, he's with us for the moment."

Later, I asked Lucia if she knew what Santini had meant when he said that his jockey was with them "for the moment."

"The jockeys get traded a lot," she said. "The horse that each *contrada* gets for the Palio is decided by lot, and the *contradaioli* have no control over that. They are in the hands of fate. But they can manipulate fate when it comes to the jockeys. Suppose Wave gets a bad horse—one that can't possibly win. It will give its *fantino*"—its jockey—"to whichever ally has the best chance of winning, or whichever ally with a good horse it may owe favors to. The main thing is to defeat your enemy. If you can't win, you still feel happy if your enemy loses and you know you have played a role in his defeat."

One ward that wanted very much to win was Shell, a neighborhood in the southeastern part of the city. Shell had won the July Palio, and if it won the August one as well it would become only the second ward to win two Palios in one year since the century began.

The term for such a double victory is *cappotto* (literally, "a cloak with a hood"), and though there were several *cappotti* in the nineteenth century, only Turtle, which won both 1933 Palios, had achieved this distinction in the twentieth. On Thursday morning, walking around the Shell ward, I heard my first *contrada* song, and the power of the melody stopped me in my tracks. In the days preceding the Palio, groups of *contradaioli* sing countless variations on this melody, with lyrics rich in self-praise and insults to their enemies. At all hours of the day and night—as I found out early the following morning, in my hotel bed—young men and women stroll along the streets singing the songs at the top of their lungs.

Throughout the city, ward flags were more and more in evidence. On the Via dei Pispini, Shell's main street, old (silk and hand-printed) and new (polyester and factory-made) versions of Shell's blue-red-and-yellow flag, which is emblazoned with a large cream-colored seashell surmounted by a crown, were displayed on balconies and in shopwindows, and beautiful *contrada* scarves were sported as neckerchiefs or draped around women's hips. Outside Shell's *società*, its bars, and its pizzeria, people talked of this and that, but eventually most conversations led to Shell's glorious showing in the July Palio, Shell's excellent young jockey, Massimo Coghe—referred to universally as Massimino—and the ward's prospects in the coming race.

Lucia arrived in the neighborhood not long after I did, and introduced me to Dr. Franco Filippini, a soft-spoken man with wire-rimmed glasses and a gentle manner, who is Shell's *priore* and, in his non-*contrada* life, a surgeon and laser therapist. Dr. Filippini offered to take me on a tour of Shell's museum, which was filled with the riches amassed by the ward over the years: Palios from past victories, beautifully embroidered silk chasubles, silver altar cloths into which the arms of the *contrada* had been woven, lace cassocks, and silver chalices. Dr. Filippini was particularly proud of the

Palios, which were mounted in glass cases; in this century alone, he told me, Shell had won the Palio fifteen times. Across the street from the museum was the oratory, a small church built in the Sienese baroque style. In earlier times, the often profane and occasionally violent ward assemblies took place in the oratories, and the local clergy would cover the religious statues and paintings with cloth in anticipation of the blasphemies that would be uttered in their presence. Today, the oratories are used only for special occasions, such as weddings, funerals, baptisms, and the blessing of the horses before the Palio. The day-to-day worship of the parishioners takes place in another church. Every member of a ward must be baptized in the ward's baptismal font, and it is the *priore,* not the local priest, who officiates. Like the admission of the Palio horse to the oratory, this suspiciously pagan-sounding ritual is routinely accepted by local Church officials as one of the ineluctable rights of the Sienese. Children are baptized twice—once by a priest, and once by their *priore.* The spirit of give-and-take that exists between the Sienese clergy and local civic interests has its roots in the Middle Ages, when the power of the Church was curtailed and the idea of a partnership of two interdependent governments, one spiritual and one temporal, began to be articulated. Two saints, Catherine and Bernardine, came from Siena, and the citizens, Communist or not, celebrate the feast days of both and rejoice in the rituals of the Church no less than in those of their *contrada.*

Next to the oratory's altar stood the July Palio. Like all Palios since 1906, when the iconography of the banners was fixed, it bore the image of the Madonna, but—somewhat to my surprise—it also depicted a black child and a white child embracing and the American and Russian flags. Dr. Filippini explained that the July race had been designated a "Peace Palio"—the second race to have peace as its theme. "The previous one was in 1945, to celebrate the end of the war," he said. The sexton, who was showing us around the oratory, whispered something in his ear, and Filippini laughed. "I have been reminded that the first one was not so peaceful," he said as we stepped out of the oratory into the dazzling light of afternoon. "Dragon won the race, but Caterpillar disputed its victory. There was a terrible fight. Other *contrade* joined in. The flag—the Palio of Peace, it was called—was torn to shreds. Caterpillar had to pay for a new one."

Over small glasses of delicious coffee provided by the *società* bar, Filippini told me that his duties occupied many hours of every week but that even on days when he was exhausted from his medical practice he looked forward to his work at the *contrada*. It was, he said, like being the father of a very large and complex family. These days, though, he was more like a benevolent uncle. For most of the year, he and the other *priori* run the wards, but for the period of the Palio they step aside and are under the orders of a *capitano,* who is virtually an absolute ruler. The *capitano* is responsible for everything concerning the Palio. It is he who calls upon old allies, negotiates deals with new ones, and dispenses whatever funds are necessary to gain a victory— or, at least, defeat a rival. Since all negotiations are carried on in secret, the *capitano* more or less has carte blanche to do what he can on behalf of his fellow-*contradaioli*.

Shell's traditional enemy, Ram, was not running in the August Palio, and I assumed that Shell didn't have to worry about Ram until next year. Not so. Ram had an excellent young jockey under its protection, Dr. Filippini said, and it would give him to "whichever *contrada* has the best chance of beating us."

I asked him if his position as *priore* made it hard for him to have cordial relations with the members of Ram.

He grimaced and shrugged his shoulders. "Well, the bitter truth is that my wife is from Ram," he said. "We survive by never discussing the Palio. During the time of the Palio, I go home only to sleep—otherwise it would be impossible."

"And your children?"

"They are little Shells. They were born here. Originally, that was the sole criterion. You belonged to the *contrada* you were born in, and though you might change the place where you lived you belonged to that *contrada* forever. That is still largely true. But things began to get complicated when more and more babies were delivered in hospitals. In order to keep the child symbolically in the *contrada*, the family would drag a bucket of *contrada* soil to the hospital and spread it beneath the delivery table, or put the *contrada* flag beneath the newborn. Nowadays simply being the son or daughter of a member is considered a sufficient basis for belonging to a *contrada*, and even outsiders with strong ties may be allowed to join."

Despite the wards' vaunted democratic foundations, the official names of a number of them include what seem to be aristocratic titles, belying their populist spirit. The phrase "*Nobil Contrada del Nicchio*," for example, was worked into many of the artifacts I had just seen in Shell's museum and oratory. Eventually, I learned that the sources of the ward titles were sometimes imperial, sometimes royalist, sometimes republican, and sometimes even revolutionary. Shell's title and the crown over the shell in its insignia were given to it in 1680, as a reward for its good showing in important battles in Siena's history—particularly the Battle of Montaperti, in 1260, in which Siena, against all odds, managed to defeat Florence, its formidable Goliath of an enemy. Eagle earned a *Nobil* by paying homage to the Emperor Charles V; Caterpillar was made noble in 1841, for the role its military companies had played in expelling Emperor Charles IV of Bohemia at the Battle of Croce del Travaglio, in 1369; and Goose became noble in 1846, as a reward for courageous action during the sixteenth-century war with the Florentines. Giraffe, which calls itself *Imperiale*, was given that title for its victory in Mussolini's Palio of the Empire, run in July of 1936. Like most of their fellow-Sienese, the people of Giraffe were unenthusiastic about Fascism and today regularly vote Communist or Socialist. They have retained the *Imperiale* not out of any nostalgia for Fascism but because they like the way it sounds.

At 6:30 that evening, the *drappellone* (another name for the Palio banner) was officially presented in the Cortile del Podestà, the small, many-pillared inner courtyard of the Palazzo Pubblico. Mayor Mazzoni della Stella made a brief welcoming speech, and then, after a flourish of trumpets and the presentation of Siena's own black-and-white flag, a standard-bearer dressed in a Renaissance costume of fur-trimmed green-and-blue velvet presented the new Palio. At once, a great "Ooh!" and "Ah!" filled the courtyard, followed by many shouted bravos and some applause. There were also a few gasps and catcalls, and more than a few rude sotto-voce comments about the quality of the painting: a bright-colored, vaguely Cubist three-eyed Virgin cradling a three-eyed baby Jesus swaddled in gray, above a sinuous tangle of horses' heads, and flanked by crudely depicted insignia of the wards. Famous artists are often commissioned to paint the *drappellone,* and this August's banner had been created by Bruno Cassinari, an elderly artist from Piacenza. In an article in the next day's *Corriere di Siena* Cassinari explained that the three eyes of the Madonna symbolized her "powerful, all-encompassing vision," and that the gray swaddling used for the child was a symbol of poverty. But most Sienese did not see poverty in the child, did not like the serpentine horses, and did not understand the reason for the three eyes. What annoyed them most, though—according to the paper—was that the ward insignia were not clearly identifiable.

At 9:30 in the evening, I paid a brief visit to Unicorn, Lucia's *contrada,* which is a small ward of only about six hundred members. Lucia was waiting for me in the Piazzetta Grassi, in front of the ward's headquarters, along with a cluster of young men standing protectively around a robust fellow who turned out to be Vittorio Ceciarelli, Unicorn's jockey. The jockeys in the Palio tend to be larger than conventional jockeys, since in the absence of saddle and stirrups arm strength counts heavily in controlling the horse, and (not incidentally) in wielding the whip. Palio jockeys have nearly always been male. The exceptions are La Fanciulla Virginia, a fourteen-year-old peasant girl who rode for Dragon and came in third in the August Palio in 1581, and Rosanna Bonelli, known as Diavola, who rode for Eagle in 1957 but fell at San Martino.

Ceciarelli had never raced in a Palio, Lucia told me, but the Unicorn *contradaioli* thought he showed promise, so they were going to use him—unless, she added matter-of-factly, they got a good horse: "Then, of course, we'll go for a more experienced *fantino*." I exchanged a few amenities with Ceciarelli under the watchful eye of his *guardia fantino,* the official entrusted with the job of guarding him (a *guardia fantino* actually sleeps in the same room as his charge) before the Palio, to keep him from making any secret deals. It was unlikely that an untested young jockey like Ceciarelli would be lured away by another ward, but Unicorn's enemy, Owl, might well offer him a considerable sum of money—more, at any rate, than Unicorn was able to pay him—just to insure his losing.

Over coffee at Unicorn's *società,* its *priore,* a grandfatherly man named Graziano Bari, discussed some of the economic realities of the Palio with us. A small and rather poor ward like Unicorn had a harder time than other wards, he said. It was difficult to engage the best jockeys, or to enlist the "help" it needed from other *contrade.* All jockeys are paid a nominal fee (a minimum of ten million lire) for racing in the Palio, but this represents only a pittance of what they actually receive. Signor Bari declined to discuss specific sums of money, but it is said that the under-the-table remuneration of the average *fantino* ranges from twenty million to forty million lire, and that top jockeys fetch as much as sixty million. The previous year, Silvano (Bastiano) Vigni, a jockey who had won the Palio three times, reportedly asked for 100 million if he won again, and got it. Traditionally, these and other Palio deals, which are called *partiti* (literally, "agreements"), are worked out by the interested parties in various preestablished rendezvous around the city in the days before the Palio, and most particularly on the Palio eve. The secrecy is necessary because *partiti* are explicitly forbidden by Article 89 of the official Palio rules. Nonetheless, everyone knows that these arrangements are made and, further, that in the very unlikely event that Article 89 should ever be enforced much of the participants' pleasure in the Palio would be spoiled. *Partiti* are made between one ward and the jockey of another with the knowledge of the jockey's ward; they are made without the knowledge of the jockey's ward; and sometimes they are made privately between jockeys.

I asked Signor Bari why Article 89 was not simply dropped from the regulations.

"Drop it!" he exclaimed, as if he had been asked an extremely bizarre question. "Why? It's good to have rules. I don't see why it should be dropped."

Every Palio has its own complex set of negotiations. Foreigners stopping off in Siena for the Palio have a hard time understanding this game and have tended to judge the Sienese harshly for their machinations. ("Short, brutal, and crooked" is how the Palio was described by even as generous and temperate an observer as the travel writer Kate Simon.) The Sienese insist that it is wrong to see the *partiti* as signs of cynicism and corruption, and point out that the city's survival over many centuries depended on the elaborate military, commercial, and diplomatic negotiations it made with often unreliable neighbors. In truth, Siena would probably never have achieved its glory days of democratic self-government in the late Middle Ages if its citizens had not found a way to circumvent the inept royal and feudal bureaucracies of the time by secretly negotiating among themselves and forming their own rebel magistracies. The magistracies evolved into the Siena Commune—a political entity, with elected officials, in which the complicated needs of a diverse population of merchants, bankers, peasants, craftsmen, and landowners were addressed. The well-known fierce independence of the Sienese may not have its noblest expression in the *partiti,* but the considerable joy they afford the *contradaioli* is surely linked to all the little and big deals that have given them a sense of controlling their fate.

It was past midnight when I left Unicorn, a time when on most nights the crowds have left the Campo and only a few knots of people remain in front of the closing cafés. That night, however, there were still a lot of people about, because at two in the morning the unofficial *prova di notte,* a semisecret nighttime trial, was due to begin. This trial is held in order to accustom the animals to the perilous track before the formal trials; it also gives jockeys and *contradaioli* a closer look at the horses and their habits. At this point, nobody knew which horses would be running in the Palio. On Saturday, the captains of the ten participating wards would pick ten of the horses, in a preliminary event called the *tratta* (trade). The *tratta* eliminates horses thought to be either too bad or too good, so that all participants are—theoretically—given an even chance. Some of the horses under consideration have run in previous Palios, some have been observed at their farms during the year by emissaries from the wards, some have been watched in the spring races, and some are new. Almost all are half-breed geldings or mares; thoroughbreds sometimes run, but in general they are considered too nervous for the course.

As the city became quieter, the mood of the people in the Piazza grew more and more buoyant. Many teenagers were on hand, obviously delighted with the opportunity to stay up all night. A few stood ostentatiously on the outer edge of the track, and no one asked them to move, even after the first horse—a splendid chestnut-colored mare—appeared out of the blackness around 2:30 and nearly skidded into them. They just shrieked, backed off, and returned to the same spot. A few minutes later, a roan and a dapple gray joined the chestnut, and the three cantered slowly around the Piazza a few times, then broke into a full gallop, their manes flying—creating the only discernible air currents in the sultry night.

By 4:30, about ten horses were racing around the track in groups of three or four. So many had come and gone that it was hard to keep count of them. A rider with long golden hair, whom I recognized from newspaper photographs as an aspiring young jockey named Claudio Bandini, entered the Campo at around five and kept his horse, a spirited-looking chestnut, back for a while, allowing it to be passed by the five horses then on the track. After a few minutes, all six, as if responding to a pistol shot, began to race furiously around the course. Bandini's horse was apparently unprepared for this burst of speed. It whinnied in protest when it neared San Martino, came to an abrupt halt, turned sidewise, and refused to budge—much to the chagrin of its jockey. Bandini ultimately gave up, dismounted, and led it away. Soon the stars began to disappear, and the sky turned a soft cerulean blue. A slight breeze came up, causing the sleepy-looking spectators to pull sweaters and wraps around their shoulders. Only three horses were left on the track, and fewer than a hundred people remained in the bleachers. Then, just as the show appeared to be over, Bandini reappeared, this time on a dark-brown horse, which, possibly in an attempt to undo his earlier embarrassment, he rode hell-for-leather around and around the Campo. On one of these circuits, he took the San Martino curve so sharply that he fell halfway off his horse, but, holding fast to the reins, he managed to slow the horse down and remount without actually hitting the ground—a maneuver that was accompanied by a tremendous cheer from the spectators.

In the Palio itself, the first horse to cross the finish line wins, even if it is riderless. Occasionally, local authorities have stepped in to rule otherwise, as in the July Palio of 1664, when His Serene Highness Prince Mattias ruled that the winner was Owl, which came in second, and not She-Wolf, whose riderless horse arrived at the finish line first. Popular irritation at this decision was summed up by a contemporary chronicler, who remarked that Owl "had the Palio by the decision of the imbecile Prince Mattias, although by commonsense, the Horse wins and not the Jockey."

The sky was now a pale gray-blue, and only two horses remained, so I decided to leave. As I mounted a stone stairway leading away from the Campo, I turned for a last look and was struck by the incongruity of the scene: the sweating horses galloping around the placid Gothic square, with thin barriers at the corners all that prevented the animals from barrelling into the elegant shops behind them. The mock though often bloody battles fought there in medieval times with wooden swords and lances, the bullfights and races on buffalo-back in the Renaissance, even the Etruscan bas-relief found in Siena showing horses ridden by men wearing cone-shaped helmets and brandishing riding crops—all were evoked by the ghostliness of the spectacle. Except for a few street-sweepers, the streets were deserted as I headed for my hotel, about a five-minute walk from the Campo. Shutters were closed, iron grilles locked, ancient wooden doors bolted. Dark alleyways loomed everywhere. But from behind the stone façade of house after house came the sweet fragrance of oleander growing in the inner court-yard, and here and there the comforting smell of baking bread.

In 1721, when the understandably alarmed officials of Siena decided to reduce the number of accidents in the Palio by limiting the number of participants, they also established a procedure for selecting them that is followed to this day. The event takes place in the Palazzo Pubblico on a Sunday several weeks before the Palio. The seven wards that did not run in the previous year's Palio of that month run "by right" in the current one, and lots are cast to choose the three others. The drawing also determines the order in which the participating wards will march in the parade, the order in which they will be listed in official communications, and the order in which their flags will fly from the Palazzo Pubblico during the preliminary trials.

If the drawing of lots is the event that gets the Palio engine revved up, the *tratta* is the one that puts it in high gear. The *tratta* is held in the Campo three days before the Palio; in it some thirty quadruped hopefuls run three circuits of the track, and the ten who are selected are assigned to the wards by another drawing of lots. Just after dawn on Saturday, the city veterinarians began to examine this Palio's thirty-two candidates, which had been temporarily stabled in the Cortile, the pillars of which were serving as tethering posts. The veterinarians must certify that the horses are in good health, so that no ward can complain that it was assigned a sick horse. Once a horse is assigned to a ward, it cannot be exchanged, even if it becomes sick and dies. The horses, like the jockeys, are closely guarded before the Palio, and one reason is that many "sicknesses" have been induced by ill-wishing *contradaioli*. All Sienese have stories to tell about horses that developed mysterious illnesses or became nearly comatose from sneak injections of soporific drugs. In one famous case, mares' vaginal extract was sprayed on the Cortile pillar of a previously calm horse, who soon became wildly uncontrollable. If a horse should die during the trials, the unlucky ward marches in the Palio procession in mourning, with the hooves of the deceased carried on a silver tray by a page.

Since Friday, when hardly a man, woman, or child ventured out without a ward scarf and the full complement of ward flags were unfurled, the streets of the city had been a field of brilliant color. The *Corriere di Siena* had focused on several of the more promising horses running in the *tratta*. Among others, it mentioned a six-year-old black gelding named Galleggiante, who some thought might be "psychologically unstable"; a seven-year-old bay gelding named Figaro, who was nicknamed Il Culturista (the Bodybuilder), because of his splendid appearance and boundless energy; and a fiery seven-year-old bay mare named Dominique, who showed great promise as "a horse of the Piazza."

By noon, all the horses had been examined and divided into groups of six or seven, which would run in five separate heats. I had been told that I would easily find a seat in the bleachers for the *tratta* at the last moment, but this proved untrue. As a phalanx of local police cleared the track by circling it arm in arm, I just managed to slip behind the inner barricade into the large central area—known as the "dog bleachers"—where some 2,000 spectators stood waiting for the *tratta* to begin.

To novice Palio spectators trying to get a grip on things, the *tratta* and the preliminary trials are terribly confusing events, owing to their surprising lack of fire and comparatively sluggish pace. At the *tratta,* the ten *capitani,* who will select the horses, look for good starts, intelligence, and obedience, so there is no particular pressure to win. Even the ward rivalries seem in abeyance, since the jockeys ride not in the colors of their wards but in which livery, with the black-and-white caps of the City of Siena.

My spot behind the inner barrier was at the San Martino corner, and so close to the galloping horses that showers of dirt kicked up by their hooves fell on me and everyone around me each time they took the turn. The heat was overwhelming. Many of the spectators were holding small scorecards—provided as inserts by the Sienese papers—to help them follow the day's events, and quite a few people were using them as fans. Jockeys fell off their horses as they rounded the sharp curves, and horses stumbled. One horse lost a shoe. Between the second and third rounds, a small girl fainted from the heat, and the *tratta* was temporarily suspended to let her parents carry her through the throng of spectators and across the track to a first-aid truck at the San Martino corner.

During a break of about an hour, the cafés and trattorias buzzed with speculation about the likely choices. Then everyone came back to the Campo, where the Mayor, the ten *capitani,* and two young costumed pages were standing on a platform in front of the Palazzo Pubblico. Next to the platform, like contestants in a beauty contest, stood the ten selected horses, all of which now sported ear numbers. On each side of the platform were two crank-turned urns, one containing the ear numbers of the horses and the other the names of the ten participating wards. For all the talk about selecting evenly matched animals, there were obviously strong and weak contenders, and as the urns were cranked and a large scoreboard showed everyone which ward got which horse, cries of joy and loud laments went up from the crowd. It was clear from the wild shouts of glee from Owl and the groans of despair from its enemy, Unicorn, that the horse that Owl had drawn—the spirited and possibly unhinged Galleggiante—was considered a potential winner. The disappointment of the Unicorn members increased when they learned that they had drawn Euro, an eight-year-old bay gelding of little or no distinction.

Even before the results went up on the scoreboard, you could tell what sort of horse a ward had drawn if you were standing close enough to the platform—as I was—to hear the Mayor read out the pairings and see the reactions of the liveried grooms. Eagle's groom, for example, threw his cap high in the air and jumped up and down ecstatically the instant his ward was paired with the much lauded Figaro; Wave's did a little dance (albeit a less abandoned one) upon hearing that his ward would get a horse named Fogarizzu; and

Shell's looked at least content with the drawing of a seven-year-old pureblood bay stallion named Odeon. Immediately after a horse was assigned, it was led away from the Campo by its groom, followed by a large delegation of *contradaioli*. Some left joyfully singing their ward songs; some left in silence; some, including Unicorn, trudged off like mourners in a funeral cortège.

Later that afternoon, Lucia and I paid a visit to Professor Anna Maria Befani, an immunologist at Siena's Polyclinical Hospital and the recently retired three-term captain of Ram. You would have to be deaf and blind to miss the fact that the Palio and the institutions associated with it are male-dominated, and, needless to say, only a handful of women have served as captains. Professor Befani is said to have been a much loved and admired leader; she brought her ward two Palio victories, with the help of a talented young rider named Giuseppe Pes, who has been Ram's jockey for the past few years, and with whom she has a warm and nurturing relationship. Several wards were rumored to be deeply interested in procuring the services of Pes for the coming Palio, and there was much speculation as to which of them Ram would release him to.

Professor Befani, a plump, intelligent-looking woman in her mid-sixties, with a crown of white-blond hair, received us in her comfortable old house on the outskirts of the city with an apology. Indicating a room full of men engaged in sober conversation which we passed on the way to her living room, she said that she had only a little time to spare from "an important meeting" on a subject she was "not free to disclose." Over cool drinks and cookies, she showed us photographs of past Ram victories and of the jockeys and officials who had played crucial roles in them, and various mementos and plaques that had been given to her by her devoted *contradaioli*. The Palios she described sounded different from others I had heard about—more like madcap family outings than like wars—and she reminisced about the years of her captaincy with evident gusto. I asked her if being a woman in a male-dominated tradition had greatly influenced her leadership.

"In some ways, yes. In others, no," she said. "I am a professional woman, and, until my father died, I lived here with him all my life. I've led a fairly independent existence, and on my own terms. They elected me captain because they thought I'd do a good job, and I don't think they were disappointed. Some women thought I should encourage more women jockeys, but I found that women jockeys didn't have enough strength in their arms. For a Sienese, to be a captain is the best experience there is! I never hated Shell very much, though. In fact, I proposed that we make peace, and we talked about it. They decided not to make peace, but they sent me flowers afterward. I also didn't do as much making and unmaking of *partiti* as some do. My policy was to make a *partito* and keep it. But, when you think of it, if there were no more enemies and no *partiti* the light of the Palio would be extinguished."

A worried-looking fellow appeared at the door. After whispering a few words to him, Professor Befani told us she was sorry but she had to return to her meeting. As she showed us out, we once again passed the room full of men. The door was now closed, but the man who had just spoken to her opened it to tell the others that she would soon be there, and we could see the relief on their faces.

The first trial was held at a quarter past seven that evening. Dr. Filippini had invited me to watch the trials in a section of the Shell bleachers, near the San Martino corner. As it happened, the section where we were to meet was reserved for men, though one or two women were seated there. Unfortunately, Dr. Filippini had not yet arrived when I slid onto a narrow wooden bench at the appointed place, and I soon found myself engaged in a futile effort to convince the Nicchiaioli that one of their seats could be occupied by someone who was not only not a man, not from their ward, and not

Sienese but not even Italian. Luckily, the *priore* soon showed up, and I was thenceforth ignored by my neighbors.

Every ward marched into the Campo behind its horse and jockey, carrying its flag, singing its songs. A few groups marched with arms uplifted and fists clenched, and when the members of Eagle marched by in this posture, behind a startlingly Teutonic-looking banner of black double eagles on a yellow field, ugly visions of Second World War newsreels flashed through my head—though Eagle's eagles are in fact Roman in origin. Long after everyone had been seated, threats, jeers, and melodious insults wafted back and forth across the Campo, bringing the emotional temper of the crowd to full throttle. At one point, an enthusiastic section of angelic-looking Tower children concluded their anti-Goose songs with a collective obscene gesture toward the principal Goose section of the Campo—a sight that would have amazed me if I had not learned from Dundes and Falassi that, while Sienese parents expect their children to be polite and mannerly most of the time, rudeness in relation to one's enemy is tolerated, even encouraged.

Just before the start of the trial, a hush fell, and the ten captains, who until then had been with their jockeys and horses in the Cortile, walked slowly across the track to their seats. The jockeys are watched especially carefully in the Cortile (the only place where they can possibly meet each other) and as they take their places at the start for any behavior or gesture that might be interpreted as a secret sign. Ward members sit in different spots around the Campo to insure thorough surveillance of their jockeys from all sections of the track. Some wards have gone as far as to have observers proficient in lipreading posted at various places, so that all exchanges between jockeys can be observed and conveyed to ward officials. Since even jockeys associated with specific wards are often lent to other wards in order to help defeat an enemy, they have formed their own opinions about their employers and, like the mercenaries they are often compared to, have frequently offered their services to the highest bidder. They make these arrangements at their peril, however; enraged *contradaioli* who learn that their hirelings have "gone to San Martino" or betrayed them in some other way have been known to assault them viciously, even to attempt to set them on fire. Double-crossing jockeys sometimes try to flee the Piazza as soon as the race is over. After the August Palio in 1877, She-Wolf's jockey fled at full gallop and did not stop until he reached open country—an act he repeated under similar circumstances in 1885. Eleven years later, another treacherous jockey so feared for his life that he begged for asylum in the middle of the night from the Frati dell'Osservanza. He had ridden for Tower and was still wearing its burgundy livery. According to a contemporary account, the flustered friar who opened the door of the monastery was moved to call out, "There's a man who wants to sleep here—he looks like a stick of sealing wax!" More recently, in 1961, a veteran Palio jockey named Giuseppe Gentile and known as Longshanks was racing for Goose on a superior horse and allowed Tower's horse to graze his horse, slip by, and career on to victory. Later, he explained what had happened by saying that the other jockey had "made my horse swerve"—a phrase that has ever since been a synonym for *fantino* treachery in popular Sienese parlance. The people of Goose nearly lynched Longshanks. He was out of commission for more than six months, his photograph was removed from the Goose Hall of Victories, and he was banned from riding in the Palio for five years. Jockeys may be "reprimanded," "admonished," or "disqualified" for their conduct, and it is the rare jockey who has not had many reprimands and admonitions and at least a few disqualifications. Good jockeys will always push the rules to the limit to win; in fact, it is regarded as being to a jockey's credit if he wins by doing something that earns some kind of official reproof. In the records of recent jockeys I could find only one winner—Primo Arzilli, nicknamed Il Biondo (the Blond), a fastidious horseman who ran in thirty-five

Palios and won five—who was never disqualified, never reprimanded, never even admonished.

The first trial, run in 1:22:05, was "won" by Turtle, but the members of Shell seemed deliriously happy and left the Piazza singing at the top of their voices. Massimino, their dark-skinned, bright-eyed young jockey, was surrounded by admirers, who clapped him on the back and ruffled his hair. Odeon had finished somewhere in the middle, having been checked by Massimino for most of the heat. I asked a kindly-looking gentleman sitting near me in the Shell bleachers what the source of this happiness was.

"Didn't you notice?" he said. "Odeon came out first from the starting rope. At the Palio, the start is everything. It's at the rope that most of the maneuvering and fighting for position occurs, and if you can get yourself into a good post position you have a good chance of winning."

"But I thought the post positions were fixed," I said.

"They are, but . . . things happen. Massimino was just trying to find out what he had between his legs. You know, until this year they never even timed the trials, because the time isn't what counts."

The nervous excitement and bellicosity of the crowd mounted over the next few days as the trial heats were run, although the real drama was taking place not on the track but behind closed doors all around the city, as each participating ward tried its hardest to get—or keep—the best jockey for its horse and equally hard to make sure that its rival did not end up with a good jockey. The talk of the cafés and trattorias on Sunday night, after the second and third trials had been run, was not about who won them but about the fact that Ram had given its excellent jockey, Pes, to Tower, thereby infuriating Goose—which took the gesture as a slap in the face from a theretofore friendly ward—and considerably reducing Shell's chances of gaining a *cappotto*. Goose had a poor horse and, giving up the Palio for lost, retaliated by lending the veteran jockey Aceto to Owl, which had drawn Galleggiante. When Unicorn learned that Owl, its enemy, would have the services of Aceto, it dumped Vittorio Ceciarelli and hired Francesco Ticci, nicknamed Tredici (Thirteen), who had ridden in two previous Palios. She-Wolf, which had a good horse, also sent its jockey packing, in favor of the celebrated Bastiano.

Between the second and third trials, all Siena had come out either to watch or to participate in the 800-year-old Corteo dei Ceri e dei Censi (procession of candles and tributes), in which ward members, in full Renaissance costume despite a temperature of well over 100 degrees, wound their way slowly through the streets from the Campo to Siena's handsome black-and-white Gothic Romanesque cathedral. On the simplest level, the procession serves as an official escort of the *drappellone* from the Palazzo Pubblico to the Duomo, where, after being blessed by the Archbishop, it will remain until the day of the race. But, more important, it serves as a (considerably diluted) historical reenactment of the Siena Commune's annual petition to have its earthly power sanctioned by its heavenly patron, the Blessed Virgin. In the thirteenth century, this procession also involved an annual act of homage: every town and village that the Commune had conquered, every castle and monastery with which it had made an alliance, sent emissaries to the city, who marched to the Duomo to repeat the oath of allegiance to the Commune. Ferdinand Schevill, in his history of the Commune, describes the scene:

> In that procession were the proud descendants of the ancient counts of the city, mitred abbots or their mandataries, the representatives of villages and towns; and in their hands they bore, in honor of the Virgin, each one a lighted candle. Through dense and exultant crowds they made their way up the marble steps of the cathedral until they stood within the portal, before the desk of a secretary of the commune. To the

humble scrivener, seated before a solemn ledger, they consigned their offerings . . . of candle-wax, or banners of brocade, or money, according to the articles of submission.

Nowadays wax offerings are presented by a few representatives from each ward, a ten-foot candle is offered by the Palazzo Pubblico, and the lighted tapers are carried by children. Nonetheless, when each ward entered the church and joyfully gave its cheer ("O-O-Onda!" "Lu-Lu-Lupa!" "Ni-Ni-Nicchio!"), when the *drappellone,* which brings up the rear of the procession, was carried down the aisle to the altar to be blessed and everyone tried to touch it for luck, when the *contrada* flags were thrown high in the cathedral nave to the accompaniment of loud drumbeating, the exultant pride of Siena's age of glory seemed very much alive. In fact, with the ward flags and scarves waving wildly back and forth and trumpets blasting and roll after roll of drumbeats resounding and everybody wildly shouting, the event seemed more like a siege than like a procession.

On Sunday night, when the third trial was held, tourists and expatriate Sienese returning for the Palio had more or less doubled the population around the Campo. Each ward entered singing twice as lustily as before, and its handsomest, most muscle-bound young men, wearing sleeveless undershirts to show off their biceps, were in the front ranks. The kindly gentleman I had spoken to after the first trial sat next to me at the third. He introduced himself as Celso Rossi, a Sienese who had lived in England ever since the Second World War, when he had been a prisoner of war and had fallen in love with and married an Englishwoman. He returned every year for the Palio, he said, and in the years when Shell won it he usually managed to go back for the victory dinner in the fall. A good-humored man with a toothy, mischievous smile, Signor Rossi seemed to know half the people in the Piazza and all the people in his ward. He joined enthusiastically in a series of jeering songs that

Shell directed at Ram. Since the songs included sentiments such as "We bought their jockey last July," "They stink like the toilet," and "If you touch a Shell, it's dangerous, you might get killed," I was somewhat surprised to see him get up from his seat immediately afterward and heartily embrace an elderly man who had just walked over to the Shell bleachers wearing the yellow-red-and-white rosette of Ram. "Ha-ha, old friend, how have you been? Ugh, don't make me touch that thing!" Rossi exclaimed, drawing back from the embrace and rolling his eyes dramatically at his friend's rosette.

The next day, after the fourth trial, I bumped into Signor Rossi and some of his cronies at a little bar called Diacceto, not far from the Campo. Rossi introduced his friends as "fellow-graduates of the University of Rastrelli," which turned out to be an allusion to a big hole in the ground on the Via Rastrelli where they had all played as children. The hole had been dug for the foundation of the Jolly Hotel, which today is a fancy modern hostelry. The usual dyadic rivalries seemed to have been suspended. Though rosettes of fierce rivals were plainly visible on their lapels, the men, who were mostly late-middle-aged or older, were obviously enjoying a pleasant reunion over glasses of strong red Tuscan wine. The group included a tall, deeply tanned man named Umberto Piazzesi, who makes the Palio *nerbi* (whips) and had one with him; a small, shy man, whom the others called "little mouse"; and a slightly sinister-looking fellow wearing dark glasses, who quoted Tacitus and was introduced to me as a former paratrooper.

"You know what we call Celso, don't you?" Signor Piazzesi asked. "*Bocca di leone,* because he talks so much."

"Well, I might as well earn my name," Signor Rossi said. "I heard that Tower paid 120 million lire to get Pes." At this, his friends whistled softly, clucked, and shook their heads.

I asked Signor Rossi about the evident lapse of *contrada* enmity at Diacceto.

"Well, we all go back a long way," he explained. "There are times for rivalry and times to forget it. That's true even for the most violent archrivals. In 1983, Artemio Franchi, who was the captain of Tower and also the president of the Italian Soccer Federation, was on his way to a dinner party when he was killed in an accident. Well, Goose and Tower are enemies, as you know, but Goose put up posters all over town which said '*Nemici nel Campo, amici nel dolore*'—enemies in the square, friends in sadness."

At the fifth trial, on Monday night, the eve of the Palio, the jeers and insults became more and more insistent, the scarf-waving became more and more frantic, and the faces of the young hotheads became redder and redder. Having recently adjusted to the idea that ward enmities might not be so virulent, or even so "real," after all if old enemies could schmooze amicably together in a bar, I was shocked when, immediately after the trial, the most terrifying mass fight I'd ever witnessed broke out. It seemed to come from nowhere. As the horses and jockeys were being led out of the Campo, a member of Goose confronted a member of Tower and objected to the quantity and flavor of the insults hurled at his ward during the trial. One of the two—each side later claimed it was the other—pushed his opponent slightly, and within seconds hundreds of enraged Towers and Geese swarmed from the bleachers and began punching, kicking, and bloodying each other with such ferocity that it seemed certain that a number of them would not live to see another Palio. No class or age group, except young children, went unrepresented in the melee. The police arrived within minutes and broke it up, and a Misericordia di Siena ambulance whisked away the wounded. The jockeys of both wards had already been hustled out of the Piazza to safety, but several horses had been trapped inside and were now led out, followed, as usual, by their wards. Unfortunately, Shell and Ram happened to converge at the San Martino exit, and though it was clearly impossible for the two contingents to squeeze into the narrow street at the same time, neither side would yield ground, and another fight broke out—this one squelched immediately by the police. Once the two wards got around the corner and somewhat out of range of the police, however, they began hurling themselves at each other again with terrible abandon.

I watched these developments from the highest bench of the Shell bleachers, with a gentle, magnificently unaggressive Nicchiaiolo called Sandro Luzzi, whom Signor Rossi had introduced me to during the trial. Signor Luzzi was wearing his *contrada* scarf, but though several battle-primed Ram foot soldiers cruised by and gazed balefully up at him, they did not bother him. I asked him why they left him alone. "You don't have to fight," he replied, shrugging, "but you have to look as though you could take care of yourself if you had to"—a credo I first heard articulated when I was a student at P.S. 46 in the Bronx, and one that would surely be on New York City's coat of arms if it had one.

Of all the pre-Palio events, perhaps the most enjoyable for the Sienese are the ward good-luck banquets, which take place on the eve of the race. They are held alfresco, with cloth-covered makeshift tables lining the central street or streets of each ward. Strangers can buy tickets for these events, but by and large the participants are ward members, out in force if the ward has a good horse and any chance of winning. I had been invited to eat with the members of Shell, who, with Massimino as their jockey, and the possibility of a *cappotto,* were there in great numbers. Some 1,600 people were seated at tables that ran along the Via dell'Oliviera and the Via dei Pispini, forming a V around the Shell oratory and converging in front of a dias that had been set up near the entrance of the *società.* On the dais were the *capitano,* several of his assistants, Dr. Filippini, and Massimino, who was trying his best not to look uncomfortable—a nearly impossible task when you are simultaneously the object of wildly exalted hopes and the darkest suspicions. Between several superb courses of hearty Tuscan food prepared and served by ward members, the *capitano* and the *priore* delivered impassioned, optimistic speeches, and Massimino made a more modest and decidedly more cautious one, in which he promised that he would do his best. Black eyes, bruises, and bandages were everywhere in evidence, and those who bore them were the objects of numerous good-natured pinches and pats.

Shortly after dessert, the *capitano* excused himself and departed, announcing that he and his assistants "had something to take care of." Since all present knew they were going out to meet their counterparts in other wards to make the final *partiti*—or, as one guidebook euphemistically puts it, to "survey the development of all formalities connected with the Palio"—everyone smiled knowingly and shouted words of encouragement. Dr. Filippini then made another speech, which Celso Rossi, who was sitting at a table near mine, characterized as a bit too cocksure about Shell's chances of victory. Signor Rossi's son, who had accompanied him from England, told us he had heard that the members of Tower were so wound up that they had been fighting among themselves, and the police had been called on to intervene. The banquet would go on until the small hours of the morning. At midnight, when I left, Massimino was looking on complacently as the ward serenaded him. The songs varied, but most had refrains such as "Our Massimino, who comes from Sardinia, we'll teach you how to win, and we're going up your ass," and "You are ours, Massimino, bring us the *cappotto,* and we shall celebrate, and we're going up your ass."

On my way back to the hotel, I passed several brightly lit, boisterous banquets. The members of Unicorn seemed inexplicably merry, considering their glum prospects, and Owl, well hidden behind a border of potted bushes, sounded even merrier. Around the corner from the hotel, someone had drawn a fairly faithful chalk copy of July's Peace Palio on the street. Nearby, two large groups of neatly dressed teen-age boys and girls wearing the scarves of Goose and Tower were trading ferocious insults.

The sun shone with particular intensity on Tuesday, the day of the Palio. Even at 7:00 in the morning, the handful of spectators who had come to a small open-air chapel at the foot of the Mangia Tower to attend the ritual Mass for the jockeys were making frequent use of small paper fans. In the center of the Piazza, raggedy piles of backpacks and sleeping bags marked the places of students who had spent the night there in order to be sure of having a good view of the race.

At 7:30, the jockeys, dressed in jeans and sports shirts, began straggling sleepily into the chapel. The ceremony itself, which was totally obscured by television cameras and technicians, took place around eight, when the Archbishop arrived, resplendent in vestments of rose-pink and white. His Excellency counted noses, shrugged, whispered a few words to the Mayor, who had also just arrived, and bestowed his blessing upon the jockeys. Massimino arrived late, but not too late to be blessed. Aceto never showed up. True to his name, he has refused year after year to participate in this ceremony, and no amount of pleading from *contradaioli* has ever swayed him.

As the Archbishop was intoning the last words of the Mass, the horses were led into the Campo for the final pre-Palio trial, which was scheduled for 9:00. This final trial is little more than a walk-through. The jockeys try mainly to conserve the horses' energy and prevent any calamitous last-minute accidents—much to the observable perplexity of visitors who have just arrived in Siena primed for hot-blooded derring-do on the track. The trial does, however, present one last opportunity for the jockeys to make or unmake private deals. Thus, as Massimino, Aceto, Tredici, Pes, Bastiano, and their fellow-jockeys left the Cortile, their every shrug, twitch, or pleasantry was the object of the keenest scrutiny. Tower "won" the trial, but only a few tourists cheered.

By 3:00, the streets surrounding the oratories of the participating wards were completely packed. Inside each church, the ward horse was led to the altar rail to be blessed. The jockey was on hand and would also receive a blessing, but, as everyone knew, this was really the horse's show. In the tiny Shell oratory, every inch of space was taken up by *contradaioli* straining to see the priest sprinkle holy water on the horse as he prayed, "Let this animal receive Thy blessing, O Lord, whereby it may be preserved in body and freed from every harm by the intercession of the blessed Anthony, through Jesus Christ, Our Lord, Amen."

I was unable to see anything but a small patch of Odeon's hindquarters, which, however, turned out to be an object of universal interest, since it is deemed a sign of great good luck if the horse defecates on the floor of the church. Odeon, alas, left the church as clean as he found it. After the priest finished the benediction, he shouted, "Go! And return victorious!" (this exhortation is omitted from printed versions of the ceremony), and the assembled worshippers brought the ritual to an end by yelling the *contrada* cheer. Before the ceremony, the members of the *comparsa*—the ward delegation that would march in the Palio parade—had donned their exquisite, handmade, carefully maintained fur-and-velvet costumes, and as soon as everyone came out of the oratory they gave a spirited flag-throwing and drumrolling performance for the benefit of those who were too old or too ill to take part in the *comparsa* march through the city.

At some point after the blessing and before the start of the race, the horses may be given a stimulant, locally known as a *beverone* (drench) or a *bomba* (bomb)—the administration of stimulants being yet another of the Palio's open secrets. In earlier times, every ward had its own concoction, which drew upon the exotic pharmacopoeia of herbalists, alchemists, and folk wisdom; coffee, grappa, Marsala, pepper, ginger, tarragon, and eggs were often among the ingredients. In modern times, the stimulant is usually administered by injection and consists of some mixture of vitamins, Methedrine, and glucose. It is crucial to neither overdose a horse nor mistime a dosage. An overdosed horse will be impossible to handle in the pre-Palio procession and will probably be lathered in sweat before the race begins. A horse might also recover from the drug too early and be useless for the race. Animal-protection groups have long decried this aspect of the Palio—as a matter of fact, there is virtually no aspect of the Palio that they do not abominate—but so far the city has not undertaken to conduct any formal tests of the horses, either before or after the race.

As a courtesy to a foreign reporter, the Monte dei Paschi bank had at the last minute given me a ticket entitling me to watch the Palio from a balcony of the Palazzo Sansedoni, an elegant building that the bank owns and that stands approximately halfway between the start and the San Martino corner. Seats of any kind are hard to obtain in the week before the Palio, and would-be spectators are turned away from the entrance to the Campo on Palio day by the thousands every year, so I was happy to have the ticket. I did not realize until I had begun inching my way behind a row of chairs which took up virtually the whole width of the blazingly hot little balcony that (a) the palazzo would remain in full sun for most of the afternoon, and (b) my ticket was carefully stamped, in minute letters, "*In Piedi*" ("Standing"). It was 4:00. The procession was scheduled to begin at 4:45 and the race itself at seven. The floor of the balcony was ridged, and its heat penetrated the soles of my espadrilles. I envisioned grille marks appearing on my feet over the next four hours, like the ticktacktoe patterns on barbecued hamburgers. Happily, there were a few no-shows, and I was permitted to fry seated.

The Piazza and the surrounding balconies and windows and rooftops slowly began to fill and flower with the riotous colors of the ward flags, rosettes, and scarves. The ward entrances this afternoon were rather low-key, in contrast to the pandemonium that had characterized the trials; the mood, now that the actual day of the race had arrived, was positively subdued. There was little singing or shouting, and hardly any outright bellicosity. You could not characterize the atmosphere as calm; it was more like a mass inhalation.

Whether by accident or intention, the historical procession, which takes two hours, succeeds in slowing time even more by its stately, measured pace. Just before the parade began, the *mortaretto*—a small cannon, which also signals the beginning and the end of the race—was fired, and the track was cleared by the usual laconic white-suited policemen. Three ranks of mounted carabinieri, armed with swords and wearing three-cornered cockaded hats and nineteenth-century uniforms, rode slowly around the Campo and then, at a signal from their captain, began to gallop, swords drawn, in a dangerous-looking cavalry charge. They exited at full gallop. As soon as they departed, the bell of the Mangia Tower began a slow, ghostly, and oddly unreverberating toll (it would sound without cease until just before the horses came out of the Cortile for the race), signaling the start of the procession.

It may have been the heat or the rhythmic tolling of the bell, or perhaps the steady beat of wave after wave of solemn drummers, but I found myself pulled easily into the pageant's theatrical evocation of Siena's past. The procession entered from the Via del Casato. The first contingent, some of its members mounted, some on foot, represented the Old Republic of Siena and all the former principalities, towns, castles, and manors that owed it allegiance.

First came the mounted standard-bearer of the Commune, followed by four commanders-in-chief, a groom, six mace-bearers, twelve trumpeters wearing turbanlike hats and playing silver instruments that flashed in the sun, eighteen musicians playing assorted Renaissance instruments, and thirty-six flag-bearers, carrying the flags of the old Renaissance dependencies and led by the representative of Montalcino, the city-state that offered sanctuary to the Sienese fleeing their disastrous war with Florence in 1555. After them came the "captain of the people," followed by a page, a groom, and three powerful-looking centurions—in suits of armor and mounted on elaborately armored and draped horses—representing the three ancient geographical divisions of the city. Participation in the Palio procession is considered an honor, and despite the brutal heat each bewigged, armored, cloaked marcher, every drummer encased in parti-colored hose and a doublet slashed with bright contrasting colors marched erect. There was no mugging at the spectators. Having only a few days before, in the Palazzo Pubblico, seen Lorenzetti's famous and beautiful fresco *Allegory of Good and Bad Government,* I was fascinated by the transformation of the Sienese into perfect replicas of their long-suffering forebears. But, of course, many—probably most—of them were the descendants of the burghers, bankers, and peasants who marched in the procession hundreds of years ago, and who gaze down upon us still from the walls of the city hall and the picture gallery of the Duomo.

The second group in the procession consisted of the representatives of the old guilds associated with the various wards, carrying the symbols of their craft, and the third was made up of the *comparse* of the ten participating wards, each one led by a drummer and followed by the ward's two best *alfieri* (flag-wavers), who executed graceful passes and tosses at strategic locations around the Campo; an armored *duce* (picked for heft and virile good looks), who is the delegation's symbolic leader; two armored men-at-arms; three pages carrying standards; the richly caparisoned Palio horse, which is led unmounted, to save its strength; and, last, the jockey, riding a parade horse, which was theoretically being led by a footman, though many of the nervous, hot, and heavily draped horses needed a fair degree of steadying from their riders. As the last ward was finishing its tour of the Campo and its members were hastening to their seats in a section of the bleachers in front of the Palazzo Pubblico reserved for the *comparse,* there appeared one of the most charming groups in the procession: two ranks of little boys in Renaissance costumes, festooned with a long laurel garland draped so that the boys' arms seemed to be made of leaves. Behind them came seven horsemen representing the nonparticipating wards, and then six spectacularly eerie armored riders with closed visors, who were mounted on masked horses. These sepulchral figures represented six of the many "dead," or suppressed, wards that no longer ride in the Palio: Cock, Lion, Bear, Oak, Strong Sword, and Viper.

The hush that accompanied the dead wards on their circuit of the Campo was followed by a great waving of scarves as an ox-drawn triumphal chariot entered bearing the Palio. The chariot also bore four elderly men, representing the ruling financial council of Siena during the heyday of the Republic; seven trumpeters from the Palazzo Pubblico; and a little boy ringing the *martinella,* a bell that had been sounding along with the one in the Mangia Tower throughout the procession and that would continue to sound until it ended. While the Palio was being placed in the judges' stand, near the starting rope, the *alfieri* lined up in front of the Palazzo Pubblico and executed a final act of homage to Siena. The police then closed a small entrance to the right of the Palazzo Pubblico which had been left open so that a steady trickle of latecomers could come in and attempt to find a spare inch in the Piazza. Now no one could enter. At five minutes to seven, a loud burst of the *mortaretto* signalled the clearing of the track, and after the captains left the Cortile and walked to their seats another loud report announced the emergence of the horses onto the track.

Moments before the jockeys had mounted, they had been solemnly instructed by the starter to abide faithfully by the Palio rules, though all present knew that they would try their utmost to bend and break them; they had splashed water on their pants (from individual buckets, because the common bucket that was formerly used was deemed to have been a site for cabals), to give them a better grip on their horses; and they had been frisked by the police, to make sure that they were carrying no weapons. As the horses entered the track, each jockey was handed a whip. These are often used to hit an enemy jockey, and many *partiti* specify such blows, with a particular sum guaranteed for each one administered. In earlier centuries, the whips were longer, and sometimes had lethal iron tips or braided-leather lashes. Today's regulation-issue, calf's-phallus *nerbo* (described euphemistically in the Palio rule book as a "*tendine di bue,*" or ox sinew) dates from 1701, when the local authorities forbade the use of any whips other than those it would provide, in order to prevent the bloody debacles that many Palios had become. But even today the jockeys wear metal helmets, painted in their wards' colors, to protect themselves from the sharp, painful blows of the *nerbo*.

The jockeys turned their horses toward the Palazzo Pubblico and raised the whips in salute. As they began their slow approach to the start, they still did not know their post positions. The positions are determined by a mechanical device in the judges' stand; it is not set in motion until the horses come out on the track, nor are the results disclosed until the horses are halfway to the start. Nine of the ten horses would be behind one rope and the tenth, a length in back of them, at the inside position behind a second rope. When the starter gives the signal, the tenth horse is to charge forward and begin the race. Before this happens, those who have received positions on the outside of the track try to sneak close to the infield. Often, when the jockey in tenth position sees that his allies have found favorable places, he will force the start of the race by charging forward and thereby setting everything in motion. The starter calls everyone back when this happens, and declares it a false start.

The crowd could not hear the starter read out the post positions (there is no public-address system), so people watched avidly, roaring their approval or displeasure as each horse called moved into its place at the rope, since the pre-Palio arrangements depend in part on the position of the horses. At conventional horse races, the horses line up at the gate and are soon off and running. Not at the Palio. The order in which the entries were supposed to line up (low numbers inside) were (1) Tower, (2) Giraffe, (3) She-Wolf, (4) Unicorn, (5) Owl, (6) Turtle, (7) Eagle, (8) Goose, (9) Shell, and, standing behind the others, (10) Wave. Theoretically, all the horses simply had to line up in that way and run. This is called a good *mossa*, or start, but, practically speaking, it is extremely difficult to achieve. After hours of parading, or waiting around to parade, in the heat, many of the horses were nervous. For reasons that have already been suggested, the jockeys were also nervous, and their nervousness added to the nervousness of their mounts. Pressing for advantage in the highly charged disarray of the lineup, jockeys will frequently *pretend* that their horses are nervous, in order to push aside a rival or sneak into a more favorable spot.

When the horses got to the start, there was a good deal of jostling, shoving, and confusion. Giraffe's horse steadfastly faced in the wrong direction and left its choice No. 2 spot open. Since Tower, Wave's enemy, had the most desirable spot, Cianchino, Wave's jockey, did his best to turn his horse and force a delay, so that jockeys with good horses could maneuver toward the space left by Giraffe. There were five false starts: twice the horses pressed so hard against the rope that the starter felt he had to lower it; twice it seemed as if all the horses were ready, but they were not; and once there were so many horses in the wrong positions that the starter brought them all back. But at last, with a tremendous roar from the crowd, the race began.

With a little help from his friends, Eagle's jockey, Bucefalo, in brilliant yellow-and-black silks, had managed to get Figaro past Tower's horse into the No. 1 position, and he came out like lightning. In the subsequent flash of horseflesh and ward colors one could see that Wave was concentrating on blocking Tower, and that Unicorn's jockey, Tredici, was after Aceto, who was racing for Owl. As the horses rounded the San Martino corner on the first of the three laps, She-Wolf's horse stumbled, bringing Giraffe's horse and Tower's horse down with him. Pes, Tower's jockey, looked as if he had been badly hurt, but he managed to stumble off the track. The impact of the crash brought several of the protective mattresses down, and they remained in the middle of the track for the rest of the race. Galleggiante had also stumbled at San Martino, but Aceto kept his seat and urged him on in an effort to catch up to Figaro, who had pulled far ahead. Unicorn's Euro, who was widely thought to be a lemon, was surprising everyone by seriously threatening Galleggiante. On the second lap, Turtle's horse fell at San Martino, and Galleggiante stumbled there again, whereupon Tredici brought Euro alongside him and performed what the next day's *Corriere di Siena* called "a real masterpiece" by pressing Aceto against the barrier at the Casato corner. There the two jockeys engaged in a "spectacular" (*Corriere di Siena* again) exchange of *nerbo* blows, and, to Aceto's deep humiliation, he was slowed enough so that Euro could pull well ahead. On the third lap, Eagle's Figaro, putting on a burst of speed, had the field pretty much to himself.

As Eagle passed the finish line, followed by Unicorn, Shell, and Wave, a loud report from the *mortaretto* signaled the end of the race. Instantly, thousands of laughing, shouting, jumping, weeping

Eagles tumbled from their seats to kiss Bucefalo and Figaro, to hug and kiss each other, and to storm the judge's stand to claim their twenty-third Palio. The exultant *contrada* called for the banner with cries of "*Drappellone! Drappellone!*" and "*Dàccelo!*" ("Give it to us!"), the traditional victory cry of the Palio, which Dundes and Falassi suggest is symbolically addressed either to "a woman yielding her virginity, the Madonna giving her cloak, a mother offering her breast, or a father figure (the Commune) handing down the *asta*"—the pole that holds the Palio up—"as a symbol of male virility." Dundes and Falassi's classically Freudian reading of much of the symbolism of the Palio caused many raised eyebrows when their book first appeared, but considering the preponderance of oral, anal, and genital language associated with the event it is difficult to see how such an interpretation could have been avoided. As the Palio flag was passed to the eager members of Eagle, every ward but Panther, Eagle's enemy, waved its flag in homage. "*È morto un bischero!*" a young Eagle shouted exultantly, pointing to a group of grim-looking Panthers in the middle distance: "A prick has died!"

There are other losers in the Palio besides the winner's enemy. Normally, they include the ward that came in second, any ward that had a good horse but did not make a good showing, and any ward that had a good lead and lost it. This year, since it was Eagle's horse more or less all the way, there were no front-runners that fell behind and no suspicion of major betrayals. Though Unicorn's horse came in second, its young jockey, Tredici, had made the ward happy by overtaking Owl's horse and humiliating Aceto. The Tower members were mortified, because neither their good horse, their good jockey, nor their good starting position had been a match for the maneuvers of their enemies—particularly Wave, their unofficial enemy. And the Shells were disappointed that Massimino didn't make a better showing and that they failed to achieve a *cappotto*—though their disadvantageous starting position combined with a less than perfect horse was later viewed as an insuperable obstacle.

After marching with the Palio to the Duomo to sing a Te Deum, the members of Eagle escorted the banner to their oratory. There it was put on display and admired by throngs of Sienese—in between frequent victory processions around the city, which went on intermittently all night. Many of the marchers plastered their faces with shaving cream in honor of their horse, Figaro—a name associated in the minds of most Italians with "The Barber of Seville." Many others had rubber pacifiers hanging from cords around their necks, and some carried small bottles of castor oil symbolizing the purgatives that may or may not have actually been sent to a select number of their enemy. Small children banging little drums and sombrely waving yellow-and-black flags added considerably to the charm of these triumphal processions. Around midnight, among the thousands of well-wishers from friendly wards who visited Eagle's headquarters were a number of captains, accompanied by their assistants, who had come to have the terms of whatever arrangements they had made with the winner honored.

The next morning, the street that marked the entrance to the Panthers' ward was draped with a black curtain made from trash bags, and in the adjoining ward their victorious enemies were offering free shaves and haircuts at a small table covered with yellow flowers, near the Eagle baptismal font. In the Campo, Eagle's yellow-and-black flag was flying from the Palazzo Pubblico. All the bleachers and about half the earth had been removed, and ten small children were galloping on invisible horses around the Cortile and hitting each other with rolled-up newspapers.

Lucia told me that Unicorn and Owl had had a fight a little before midnight, in the Piazza Tolomei—one of several "traditional" fighting sites in the city—and that some Tower members had attacked Goose and their own jockey, Pes, and that Goose had counterattacked. Later, I learned that Shell, Ram, and Wave had been disqualified from next July's Palio, because of various brushes with the police. But according to the local papers there had been no big fights on the day of the Palio and people had been no more excited than they usually were. Only a few had been injured: three people had been overcome by heat and treated at the first-aid station, someone had been kicked by a horse, and the man in charge of the mattresses had got dirt in his eye and missed the end of the race because officials had insisted that he receive immediate treatment. He was furious. As anticipated, the pickpockets had cashed in on the day. Professor Falassi and two hotel clerks had warned me about the pickpockets—not Sienese, they assured me emphatically, but outsiders, who came to take advantage of the large crowds. Five were arrested. Three were foreigners, and two were well-known Italian purse-snatchers.

Members of the Union for Animals had demonstrated in Querce Grossa, a nearby town, complaining, much to the disgust of the Sienese, that the horses were made to run too fast in the middle of "a cacophony of disturbing voices, music, and cries, which causes psychological distress," and decrying the fact that inevitably some horses got hurt—although for the first time in the history of the Palio a vehicle equipped for surgery was present in the Piazza, so that serious attempts could be made to save badly injured horses instead of shooting them. Rejecting the view of the Palio as—to quote a guidebook—"the moment of consciousness and liberation, of immense gratification and recovery of the roots and traditions of an inimitable people," the Union for Animals in effect echoed the sentiments of Henry James, who wrote in *Italian Hours,* a book of travel essays, that the Palio was a distressing memory that "smudges that special sojourn as with the big thumb-mark of a slightly soiled and decidedly ensanguined hand."

The city returned to its normal routines with impressive rapidity on the day after the race. I was strolling its streets and enjoying its aura of quiet orderliness when there suddenly appeared, amid a great blasting of trumpets and banging of drums, *mirabile dictu,* an even bigger and more elaborate version of the previous night's victory parade. Twice as many flags, costumed men, women, and children, old people with faded ward scarves tied around their necks, and priests and nuns with the ward colors draped around their clerical robes were taking part in a victory tour of the city. Figaro was in this procession, too, and as he moved into a patch of sunlight in front of me I was struck by his transformation from Il Culturista, the energetic Palio hopeful, into mythological beast. His bay coat glowed, his mane and tail had been braided, his hooves had been gilded, and "23" had been artfully painted on both hindquarters—a testament to Eagle's victories.

A strange-looking, dishevelled man stood near Figaro distributing a broadsheet to onlookers. I had seen him wandering listlessly around the Piazza all week, and again the night before, marching with the Eagles in their victory procession. I had inquired about him at the restaurant where I usually ate. The waiter knew right away whom I was talking about. "A lost soul," he said. The poor man didn't even know which ward he belonged to, so at the end of every Palio he usually donned the colors of the winner and insinuated himself into its celebrations and processions. Nobody minded, and it seemed to make him happy. His eyes were vacant as he handed me a boldly printed yellow-and-black handbill, but he presented it with a flourish. It proved to be a sonnet that the Aquilini had composed in honor of their victory. Loosely translated, it read:

The Noble Contrada of Eagle

ON THE OCCASION OF THE SPLENDID VICTORY IN THE PALIO OF AUGUST 16TH 1988 WON BY THE FABULOUS

HORSE FIGARO AND THE GREAT JOCKEY MAUREZIO FARNETANI, CALLED BUCEFALO, WITH CAPTAIN RENATO ROMEI, TRUSTEES FABIO MARCHETTI, GIROLAMO BRANDOLINI D'ADDA, MASSIMO MARCHETTI, AND PRIORE ADINOLFO BRANDOLINI D'ADDA, THE FOLLOWING SONNET IS OFFERED TO POSTERITY:

Forgive us if we are late
In coming to you with the banner of the Casato.
No disrespect was intended.
We took the first train we could.

In fact, Figaro, like a locomotive,
Took off and arrived right on time,
Led in an admirable race

By a truly extraordinary Bucefalo.

And Eagle again rejoices,
The Color Yellow again enters history!
And the crowd in our church,

While singing the praises of the Mother,
Proclaims that what really inspires us
Is an indomitable yearning for victory!

Biblioteca

A Small Place in Italy, Eric Newby, first published by HarperCollins, 1994; U.S. edition published by Lonely Planet Publications, 1998. I'm a big fan of the Lonely Planet travel guide series, and when I learned the publisher was introducing a new line of travel writing—Lonely Planet Journeys—I knew it would be worthwhile. *A Small Place in Italy* is one of the wonderful volumes in this series. There are now so many Tuscan memoirs, by this or that expatriate, that readers might reasonably inquire, "Do we really need another?" I don't believe we do, but I do believe Newby's memoir is the best of the lot, and if you're going to read only one, make it this one. He and his wife, Wanda, bought I Castagni—near the villages of Fosdinovo and Caniparola in northwest Tuscany, the closest town of any real size being La Spezia in Liguria—in 1967, and they remained absentee owners until 1991. Most of the farm buildings and houses in these foothill villages are painted *sangue di bue* (ox-blood), "which grows paler and paler as the years pass until it ends up a very pale pink." I was impressed that the folks at Lonely Planet selected this same shade for the cover of the book and featured a photograph of a crumbling farmhouse wall, also in this unusual color. At the time the Newbys arrived, they were the first foreigners to ever live in the area. Fortunately, they each spoke Italian well enough; Eric was a prisoner of war in Italy from 1942 to 1945, and Wanda, originally from Slovenia, was relocated to a village near Parma when she was of high-school age. Though this memoir is filled with the Newbys' funny and frustrating experiences—with Italian bureaucracy, joining their neighbors in harvesting grapes and hunting for mushrooms, and repairing and restoring their farmhouse—what sets it apart, to me, is Eric's enormous respect for the *contadini* (country people, usually peasants) and his gratitude to them, especially the men, women, and children who helped hide and feed him during the war. He and Wanda continued to visit these families over the years. Read Newby's *Love and War in the Appenines* for a more thorough description of the mountain villagers and the life they led. In fact, you really must read both books.

Within Tuscany: Reflections on a Time and Place, Matthew Spender, Penguin Books, 1993; first published by Viking Press, 1992. Sculptor Matthew Spender and his wife went to Tuscany over twenty years ago to ostensibly escape for a while from the London weather. They ended up moving there, and had two children along the way, and might still live there as far as I know. This memoir is not like any of the others you might read. Spender is obsessively interested in all aspects of Italian history and manages to blend historical details with his personal observations to create a portrait of the "ordinary" Tuscans he has encountered. This book is much more about *people* than other memoirs and is thoroughly engaging. With sixteen pages of black-and-white photos.

Under the Tuscan Sun: At Home in Italy, Frances Mayes, Chronicle Books, 1996, hardcover; Broadway Books, 1997, paperback. I had read articles Frances Mayes wrote for *The New York Times* travel section for a number of years before she became a bestselling author, and I remember thinking at the time that here was a writer who really seemed to understand the Italians—Tuscans, at least—and seemed to revel in the details of everyday life that matter. So I wasn't surprised when this book touched so many people. Granted, Mayes did not invent the genre of combining narrative with recipes (M. F. K. Fisher, Laura Esquivel, and Elizabeth Romer are a few writers who successfully tried their hand at it previously), but the book is a joy to read, and if you somehow happen to be among the few who has *not* read it yet, it's not too late to remedy this situation. You'll enjoy it very much indeed. (There's plenty of Umbria in the book, too.)

Bella Tuscany: The Sweet Life in Italy, Frances Mayes, Broadway Books, 1999. Okay, I admit I didn't enjoy this *quite* as much as *Tuscan Sun;* still, I eagerly read it—no, devoured it—because the journey was continuing, and I wanted to be part of it. I was glad Mayes ventured beyond the Tuscan border: All of Italy is *bella,* not just its heart, but she is really in her element when writing about Tuscany. In response to the question of why she is so smitten with this corner of the world, Mayes answers with some of the best remarks I've ever read about why life is different in Italy, why we have much to admire in the Italians. She notes that despite such ills as prostitution, pollution, and strikes, the Italians have generally managed the twentieth century better than Americans. "Everyday life in Tuscany is good," she writes. "There's very little violent crime, people have manners, the food is so much better and we all know the Italians have more fun." Mayes elaborates that her expatriate friends, most of whom have lived in Tuscany longer, talk of how much Cortona has changed. "But," she adds, "the changes were rapid—and needed—after the war. Now they have slowed. The life of the town is intact, they've taken the right measures to protect the countryside, the cultural life of this tiny town puts to shame most good-sized American cities. I think of the younger generation . . . bringing along all the good traditions. When our adored Rita retired from her *frutta e verdura* last year, a young man took over. Unlike many rural towns, this one hasn't lost its young to the cities."

A Tuscan Childhood, Kinta Beevor, originally published in Great Britain by Viking, a division of Penguin Books, 1993; American edition published by Pantheon Books, 1999, hardcover; Vintage, 2000, paperback. Ordinarily, I would have included this memoir in the *I Personaggi* section, but since I had, regrettably, never heard of Kinta Beevor before I read this, and as it is really more of a memoir about Tuscany in a specific time period rather than a story of her entire life, I thought it more properly belonged here. As a five-year-old, Beevor, with her father (painter Aubrey Waterfield) and her mother (writer

Lina Duff Gordon), moved to the Tuscan village of Aulla (way up in the northwest corner of the region, closer to La Spezia in Liguria than any other large Tuscan town). Life there, and at the fourteenth-century villa Poggio Gherardo outside Florence, between the wars is wonderfully evoked. Much of that life is long gone, except in extremely rural corners of Italy, which is what makes this book not only interesting but valuable. Many personalities of the day—D. H. Lawrence, Bernard Berenson, Rex Whistler, Kenneth Clark, Iris Origo, Virginia Woolf—figure into the narrative, and the twenty-four pages of black-and-white photos, some reproductions of Waterfield's canvases, add much to this engaging, bittersweet story.

The Hills of Tuscany: A New Life in an Old Land, Ferenc Máté, Albatross, distributed by W. W. Norton, 1998. I know I mentioned above that I didn't think we needed any more Tuscan memoirs, and now this one is the fifth listed here. I meant what I said, but there *is* room for this one. I can't exactly say what it is that makes this one *different* necessarily, only that I started it one night and didn't—couldn't—put it down until I was nearly done, finishing it the next morning. Perhaps because it reads like a dream, a dream of moving to Tuscany (even if only temporarily). Also, I appreciated Máté's honesty: "When I started this memoir I swore I would not clutter it with dissertations about food, but I soon realized that writing about Tuscany without talking about food is like writing about the *Titanic* without mentioning that it sunk."

Songbirds, Truffles, and Wolves: An American Naturalist in Italy, Gary Paul Nabhan, Pantheon, 1993. Nabhan is also the author of another favorite book of mine, *The Desert Smells Like Rain* (North Point Press, 1987), which is about the southwestern part of the U.S., but in this work he sets out on a walk across the Tuscan and Umbrian countryside to *really look* at the land and the people who use it, learn from it, and depend upon it. Accompanying him is a friend, Ginger Harmon, who co-authored *Hiking Europe From Top to Bottom* with Susanne Margolis (Sierra Club Books, 1986). Nabhan writes of Harmon, a number of years his senior, that she "continues to outwalk me and most other postpuberty males." He was in good company, in more ways than one, and using Saint Francis as a guide, the walk became a spiritual quest and ethnobotanical field trip. In talking with farmers, bakers, truffle dealers, etc., he discovers what still has merit for us today in the old ways of working the land. A beautiful, original work.

Tuscany, photographs by Sonja Bullaty and Angelo Lomeo, Abbeville Press, 1995. Of the multitude of titles we've come to refer to as coffee-table books, on Tuscany, I like this one the best. The pages are irresistible to turn, so perhaps it *is* best kept on a coffee table for frequent peeks. I especially like the way the book is organized, with chapter headings such as "The Land," "Springtime and Gardens," "Trees and Vineyards," "Faces," "Marble," and "Windows and

Doors," with both the text and the images capturing those details we see and remember the most.

The Hill Towns of Italy, photographs by Richard Kauffman, text by Carol Field, originally published by Dutton, 1983; Chronicle Books, 1997. The title of this lovely and interesting book is a bit misleading as it actually only refers to the hill towns of Tuscany and Umbria, and a single volume on "the heart-stopping beauty of this part of Italy" is a welcome addition. Carol Field is the respected cookbook author of *The Italian Baker, Focaccia, Celebrating Italy,* and others, and she has long been one of my personal favorites. Whether she's writing about food or history or an architectural detail, she is a contemporary authority on all things Italian. The towns featured in this volume include Siena, San Gimignano, Montepulciano, Pienza, Volterra, Cortona, Arezzo, Perugia, Assisi, Orvieto, Todi, Spoleto, and Gubbio. The accompanying photos are beautiful, some among the most unique I've ever seen of two much-photographed regions.

Escape to Tuscany: The Definitive Collection of One-of-a-Kind Travel Experiences, photography by Antonio Sferlazzo, text by Candice Gianetti, Fodor's Travel Publications, 1999. With this new line, Fodor's has tried to strike a perfect balance between detailed, nitty-gritty information for visitors and evocative pictures. This small hardcover features twenty-six special aspects or places of Tuscany, some of which are La Torciata San Giuseppe, the island of Giglio, Carnevale in Viareggio, the quarries of Carrara, Terme di Saturnia, Hotel La Cisterna in San Gimignano, the villas of the Luccan hills, and the Palio. At the back of the book are two maps plus all the practical information.

The Most Beautiful Villages of Tuscany, James Bentley, with photographs by Hugh Palmer, Thames & Hudson, 1997. One volume in the impressive "Most Beautiful Villages" series, and, like the other editions, turning the pages of this one makes you want to reserve a seat on a plane *rapidamente*. A traveler's guide and map to thirty-six villages make it a practical trip planner, too.

Hidden Tuscany: Unusual Destinations and Secret Places, Massimo Listri and Cesare M. Cunaccia, Rizzoli, 1999. This is both a beautiful and practical book detailing a variety of gardens, country churches, studios, villas, museums, etc., off the beaten path. Six chapters with gorgeous photographs and a high price tag—but lovers of Tuscany will consider it a must-have.

Architectural Guides for Travelers: Medieval Tuscany and Umbria, Anthony Osler McIntyre, Chronicle Books, 1997. The focus of this slender paperback, which packs easily, is indeed the medieval period; but the author reminds us that this book is selective: "Every century has left us works of high quality, from the pre-Roman Etruscans to the Renaissance and right into our own century. It would take a determined individual to walk the streets of Florence and see only medieval buildings, or to drive through Umbria and not be deeply impressed by the landscape." He implores us to use this book as a magnifying glass to study the particular details of a country at a particular point in history. I applaud his themelike approach—it's merely one of many ways to look and learn about a place. Buildings are presented so that their appearance in the text corresponds to convenient road routes. With dozens of black-and-white photographs, a glossary, chronology, and bibliography.

Villas and Gardens of Tuscany, Sophie Bajard and Raffaello Bencini, Editions Pierre Terrail, Paris, 1992. To quote from the historical outline, "Today, the Tuscan villa remains faithful to its fourteenth century image as a place of rest, tranquility and privacy . . . only if you have an adventurous spirit will you be able to discover its jealously-guarded secrets." These "secrets" include addresses or phone numbers, which the authors do not provide, but with the help of the Italian tourist office you should be able to contact the owners. Still, I think this is a good book for travelers who want to visit some of these secluded villas near Florence, Siena, and Lucca. Some villas require an advance request and are not generally open to the public, and those selected for this volume collectively present an extensive survey of Tuscan art from the fourteenth to seventeenth centuries. The photographs are excellent, by one of the most talented photographers of Italian art, and the text informs readers of each property's special features.

Discovering Tuscany: A Wine Lover's Guide to the Best Restaurants, Trattorias, Hotels and Wineries to Visit; special issue of *Wine Spectator,* May 15, 2000. To order a copy (it's great), call (800) 761-4099 or write to M. Shanker Communications, P.O. Box 55676, Boulder, CO 80322. Back issues are $7, which includes shipping and handling.

L'Umbria

(Umbria)

"Mild-tempered, isolated from outside influences—Umbria is the only Italian region that neither touches the sea nor shares a frontier with another country—the Umbrians tend to be complacent in their cocoon and conservative in their ways, refusing even to improve the recipe for the medieval paving stones they insist on calling bread. But for many this basic lack of interest in the outside world, combined with Umbria's gentle beauty, makes the region an ideal retreat for the spirit. St. Francis of Assisi's doctrine of mystical love for all creation seems to come out of the soft bluish-green hills of Umbria, which has proved a fertile land for saints, producing a bumper crop, not only St. Francis and St. Clare, but St. Benedict, the founder of monasticism; St. Rita, the saint of impossibilities; and St. Valentine, the patron of lovers. Umbrians go to visit their relics the way we would call on a fond uncle or aunt."

—Dana Facaros, Michael Pauls,
Cadogan Guide: Italy

Second Honeymoon

BY JAMES TRAUB

editor's note

....

This piece and the following one offer different accounts of staying in Umbria, and each emphasizes the best reasons for going.

Umbria is sometimes spoken of in a way that insinuates we should have pity on it as it exists in the shadow of its admittedly more glamorous neighbor, Tuscany. I suppose it's all in how you view that glass, half-empty or half-full, but I don't believe the Umbrians care a whit about being "less fashionable" than the Tuscans. They have their own art treasures to look after and their own delicious food and drink to imbibe. When people talk about what they expect to find in Tuscany, I think they don't realize they're talking about attributes that haven't defined Tuscany in about 20 years but that still do define Umbria.

JAMES TRAUB is a staff writer for *The New Yorker* and a freelance contributor to a number of publications.

Why travel to a country with bad food when you can go to Italy? The first time I ever traveled with my wife, the Buff, we went to Tuscany. The very first evening, in Pisa, I was bent low over a plate of mozzarella, basil, and oil, and the Buff looked at me hard and said, "You're crying!" And it was true. It was the first time she had ever seen me crying, and I was embarrassed—not only because of the man thing but because my education had predisposed me to believe that I should be moved by frescoes, not by antipasto. The Buff, who is a museum curator, loves Italy for the high-minded reasons as well as the visceral ones. I'm mostly stuck in the viscera, although owing to the dictates of my conscience I try to persuade myself otherwise. For our honeymoon we went to the Greek islands: the ruins were admirable, of course, but the bread tasted like soap and even the grilled fish came lapped in oil. The Buff practically kissed the ground when we reached Paris. And so, for our tenth anniversary, this past June, we decided to create the trip that we wish had been our honeymoon—not to Tuscany this time, but to Umbria, the region just next door.

Umbria is a quiet, gracious, and rather isolated area of Italy. The hilltop fastnesses of Todi, Gubbio, Assisi, Spello, and Spoleto were outposts under the Roman Empire and free *comuni*—in effect, city-states—as early as the twelfth century; but the Renaissance largely passed them by, and later ages left little behind beyond bad restoration. They're small towns with ancient memories. One morning, when the Buff and I ducked into a bar to get out of a rainstorm in Spello, we watched the town's chief Rotarians gather to chat at the counter—the policeman, the druggist, the mailman, and a man of affairs in a shirt and tie. The rain abated, and everyone returned to their respective posts.

Nothing in Italy is all that far from Rome. By doing as the Romans do, which is to say about eighty to eighty-five miles per hour, we made it to our first stop, Orvieto, in about an hour and a half. Most Americans know of Orvieto for its wine, which, like Umbrian wine in general, is undistinguished save for its low price. Orvieto itself is a quiet town built on a steep cliff, with one of the great medieval churches in Italy. You can see minute biblical history in stone on the fourteenth-century façade of the Duomo. In one panel near ground level, God can be seen delicately withdrawing a rib from a lip-shaped opening he's made in Adam's chest; in the next, he holds Eve gently by the neck as he extrudes her through the slot, her feet still lodged in Adam's torso. Even God, one feels, is human.

Orvieto has several other fine churches, including the Romanesque San Giovenale, where, if you show even a passing acquaintance with Italian, a kindly, toothless old gentleman in a blue smock will recite the history of the church and the city. You will also find, conveniently located midway between the Duomo and San Giovenale, the *gelateria* Il Sant'Andrea. In a country where you do not dine before 8:30 unless you want to look like a total hick, the midday snack is not an indulgence but a necessity. Il Sant'Andrea is located on a quiet piazza overlooking a church; many minutes can pass without a sign of a car or even a waiter. I bestirred myself and ordered a cone with chocolate and *nocciola* (hazelnut). The cone was foamlike, but the gelato was pure velvet. You would have to go to Florence or Rome for better.

The following morning we cruised off toward Todi, performing a dogleg left around the glassy Lake Corbara. The sun was brilliant. Peace reigned. "I can't *believe* we're in Italy," said the Buff, who thinks that good fortune is evanescent and that its gods must be propitiated with signs of genuine gratitude. It was already her fourth or fifth iteration of the phrase since we had reached Italy, two days before, the previous one having been a few hours earlier when we had awakened to birdsong in our room in La Badia, a converted twelfth-century abbey on a hillside beneath Orvieto. After about half an hour, Todi loomed up before us, a triangular silhouette with a campanile poking up like a smokestack, the whole mass loaded on top of a steep hill.

We started the morning with a *cappuccino freddo* on the piazza—the midmorning equivalent of the midday gelato. A two-year-old boy in blue-jeans overalls chased a pigeon across the worn cobblestones with a child's inexhaustible patience. People criss-crossed the piazza, going about their lives. From the steps of the Duomo we looked across the square at the Palazzo dei Priori, with its austere white façade and lopped-off campanile, and the Buff said, "One church, one palazzo, one café, one child, one pigeon—it's perfect."

It was in Todi that we had our first transcendent food experience. We walked down a narrow lane that ran downhill from the

Piazza del Popolo to a weathered stone house with a small sign that read, "Umbria." A bicycle leaned against the wall. We passed through several dark dining rooms and emerged onto a dazzling terrace covered by a rough arbor of plaited branches and muslin. The retaining wall was lined with boxes of fat red geraniums, and beyond the geraniums was the thin air, for the Umbria is located at the edge of the massif upon which Todi sits. We gazed out over checkerboard fields of brown and green, farmhouses with faded-shingle roofs, and the chalky ribbons of local roads. We made inarticulate little noises of deep happiness. We had grilled trout; it was aromatic, tender, crisp. I had a half bottle of the light and faintly fizzy local white wine. I was feeling light and faintly fizzy myself.

The Umbria is not a great restaurant, but it is a wonderful restaurant. Herein lies a critical difference between eating in Italy and eating in France. The Italians cherish food, but they don't fetishize it. Italian cuisine has the virtue of nonchalance—*sprezzatura,* as Castiglione called it. And what one is consuming is, in part, that very nonchalance. When Italians cook, they talk and they drink and they chop something up and throw it in a pan with olive oil and they shoo away the cat and they throw in the pasta and the next thing you know you're sitting in front of something wonderful. The integrity of the products and the simplicity of the process exalt even the humblest offering. It's very hard to eat badly in Italy.

The day after our moment of bliss in Todi, the Buff and I found ourselves trudging uphill in Assisi; one is always trudging uphill in Umbria. There were swarms of tourists, but Assisi seemed to be going about its essential spiritual business undisturbed. Here was a monk in his brown robe and black sandals hefting a box of copier paper across a crowded piazza. Here were nuns singing vespers in their gray and black habits. There's something fundamentally unself-conscious about Assisi. The restaurant we were hoping to go to happened to be closed, so we stopped at an establishment whose sign read, like those of half the places in town, "Ristorante Medioevo." The restaurant was in the basement. A flushed, middle-aged woman appeared from the kitchen and offered a choice of three kinds of pasta. A few minutes later our cook-waitress-proprietor emerged with two metal bowls, from which she scooped our pasta onto our plates. It wasn't great, but it was, in its own, small way, perfect.

Every good trip needs a bummer, and we had ours that night at Lo Spedalicchio, a very attractive converted palazzo on the road between Perugia and Assisi. A preprandial walk in the neighborhood proved completely depressing: the town consisted almost entirely of drab three-family houses, and no one save the snarling guard dogs was outside. At dinner the waiter recommended the duck breast, which turned out to be inedible. At a nearby table, three Italian children spent the entire evening yelling at the top of their lungs. We escaped for coffee at a nearby bar and asked the owner what time in the morning the campanile just outside our window started tolling. "At 7," he said. "And then at 7:30"—here he grinned fiendishly—"it gets much louder." And he wasn't joking. We were bonged awake at the stroke of 7 and practically knocked out of our bed half an hour later, with the call for mass. Don't stay at Lo Spedalicchio on a Saturday night.

Still, we got a very early start toward Gubbio, one of the oldest of the Umbrian hill towns. Over the centuries Gubbio retreated farther and farther up its steep hill. Now it feels like Umbria in its most concentrated form—stony, proud, and almost wholly free of the marks of modern life. The houses along the narrow, vertiginous lanes seem to lean together until they almost join overhead. Parallel to Gubbio's main street is the tiny, hidden Via Galeotti, whose paving stones roll up and down as if on waves. Shattered wooden double doors are secured by old chains; a cat darts into a dark alleyway. And then, suddenly, there's a stairway with pots of roses climbing up each side toward the stone house on top. You might have taken the same walk and witnessed the same scene half a millennium ago.

Something went slightly wrong in Gubbio. The Buff, who does not believe in walking for walking's sake, somehow kept us from seeing most of the recommended sights in town and, in an unprecedented reversal of roles, argued me out of buying so much as a single specimen of Gubbio's charming ceramics. As we left town I was feeling unfulfilled and grouchy, and I insisted on having lunch at Taverna del Lupo, a restaurant whose name commemorates the story that Saint Francis pacified a wolf—shook his paw, in fact—that had been terrorizing Gubbio.

The taverna turned out to be an extremely elegant restaurant hidden inside a medieval house with stone walls and a barrel-vaulted ceiling. The waiter more or less insisted that we order the typical Gubbio antipasti. He brought a plate with a thin slice of what might have been veal, with balsamic vinegar, shaved Parmesan, and arugula, a *bruschetta* of liver pâté, and a triangle of prosciutto sitting on a wedge of what may or may not have been fried polenta. Whatever it was, it was astoundingly light and layered and crisp; and when the waiter saw how transported we were, he brought us another. And then he brought yet another plate, and we explained that we had ordered a different entree. No; it was the *rest* of the antipasti—scrambled eggs with shaved white truffle, a tiny tart of porcini, a mozzarella *in carrozza*. And then came the mixed Umbrian grill, with baby pork and veal and a plump sausage. I had a bottle of a local red to wash it down. Somewhere in here—the wine has fogged my memory—a tear dropped onto my plate. And the Buff caught me at it again.

That evening we stayed at the Villa Roncalli, a lovely country house situated in a garden on the edge of Foligno, just south of Assisi. An Italian friend had told us that Maria Luisa Scolastra, whose family owns the villa, was the finest chef in Umbria. I began to get performance anxiety. There are people, I know, who can go from a great lunch to a great dinner. I can't; I don't have the constitution. I took a long walk through the neighboring town of San Eraclio. Here was the small-town Italian life one imagines: tiny gardens with olive trees; harmless little dogs; a boy, sitting with his mother, who shouted, "*Buona sera!*" as I walked by.

It was a great walk, but it didn't help. Maria Luisa began by sending out—as a gift, an *amuse-gueule*—a vegetable soup surrounding a delicately cinched crepe filled with minced eggplant. It was a groan-with-joy moment; but, alas, even this little offering taxed my capacities. The food was so beautiful and the high-ceilinged Renaissance dining room so luxurious that it was all I could do to cover myself with apologies and promise to return. The next morning, Maria Luisa was cooking breakfast, and the waitress, no doubt her sister or cousin, brought out a warm nut bread and then croissants filled with cream and apricot jam and then a crumb cake. All we had to do to reciprocate Maria Luisa's act of dedication was eat—a classic Italian transaction, after all.

The Buff and I were ready to swear off restaurants. All we wanted was a simple picnic. At that point, however, it started raining. We spent an eerie morning in Bevagna, a tiny town just west of Foligno that peaked 1,700 years ago. It was a Monday, and everything was closed—stores, restaurants, even churches. The streets were empty. It was as if we were invading Bevagna's stony privacy. Even the people in the tourist office wouldn't talk to us. The only open restaurant in town, Da Nina, was deserted, though the glasses and silverware shone at every table. The lone waitress was eating a salad when we came in. She stood at our table and recited the menu in a rapid Italian monotone, looking furious. She was so intimidating that I ordered the last dish she described because I was afraid to ask her to repeat the others. When the pasta came, the Buff asked for pepper. The waitress looked at her contemptuously and said, "No."

"There's no pepper?" the Buff asked, rather cheekily, I thought. "No," the woman said. "The pasta is fine without it."

That night, exhausted and depleted, we finally had our picnic. It was our last night, and we were staying not at a converted abbey or a converted palazzo but at a converted mill, the Vecchio Molino, near Spoleto. In Umbria you never need stay in a place built as a hotel, or for that matter built fewer than 400 years ago. The fifteenth-century Vecchio Molino is situated about twenty feet below a major road and 100 yards from the railroad tracks, and yet it feels like an enclosed garden. Swans float along the canal beside the old mill, paddling up to strangers, hoping to cadge some bread. There are gravel walkways, clipped hedges, benches set on little bridges. At a round table we had the picnic that we had harvested in Spoleto—sausage, prosciutto, a local sweet ricotta, buffalo mozzarella, tomatoes, and a fine bottle of Antinori. Every once in a while a train roared by or a car squealed, reminding us that our pastoral setting was a contrivance. But it was a beautiful contrivance. And by and by the sun set, the noise dropped away, and it was just the Buff and me and our sausage and tomato and bread and wine. And that, too, was perfect.

Exploring the Hill Towns

Umbria is compact enough that you can rent a villa in a central locale, say, near Perugia or Assisi or Foligno, and take a series of day trips. Or, you might want to plant yourself in one of the hill towns and feel time gently drip away. Spoleto, even without its summer festival, is the most sophisticated and varied; Todi, to my mind, is the most beautiful; Gubbio is the most remote. You should not miss the tiny places: Montefalco, with the Gozzoli frescoes of the life of Saint Francis in the Church of St. Francis; and Bevagna, with its Romanesque churches and tiled Roman bath (don't go on a Monday; almost everything is closed).

Many of Umbria's most delightful accommodations were once palaces, mills, or convents—some that are now five or six centuries old. Thanks to a relatively weak lira and the humbleness of the region, you need never spend more than $200 a night for lodging.

Perhaps the most majestic of the inns is **La Badia,** a twelfth-century abbey near Orvieto. La Badia has cloisters and battlements and a twelve-sided campanile where crows swoop in and out all day; there's also a pool, air-conditioning, and a very satisfactory grill (8 Località La Badia; 0763.90.359; about $175–$300 including breakfast). Of the many converted palazzi in Umbria, one of the most luxurious is the **Le Tre Vaselle,** a seventeenth-century town house in Torgiano that has been a bit too ruthlessly modernized. Le Tre Vaselle is owned by the Lungarotti family, the great vinters of the region, and what make the stay worth the price are the refined cuisine and the remarkable wine museum across the street (48 Via Giuseppe Garibaldi; 075.988.0447; about $190–$275).

Lo Spedalicchio, just north of Assisi, in Ospedalicchio, is a palazzo that has been left intact. The rooms are spacious and the lobby charming; it would be perfect if it weren't situated between a highway and a bell tower (3 Piazza Bruno Buoni; 075.801.0323; about $85–$100). Just outside the old Roman town of Foligno is the **Villa Roncalli,** another marvelous palazzo, run by the admirable though non-English-speaking Scolastra family. And the cuisine is sensational—*cucina nuova* with a strong regional bias (25 Via Roma; 0742.391091; about $75). Spoleto has a number of fine hotels; nobody seems to stay at the **Vecchio Molino** (Old Mill), just north of the city in Campello Clitunno. But with its canals and its swans, its winding staircases and odd landings, the Vecchio Molino turns out to be a rather romantic spot (34 Via del Tempio; 0743.521.122; about $130–$175, including breakfast).

Umbria has only a few really grandiose restaurants, those at the Villa Roncalli and Le Tre Vaselle being among them. Few of the others charge more than $25 a person, and usually they charge much less. I would, however, return to Umbria solely for the chance to indulge once more in the antipasto at **Taverna del Lupo,** in Gubbio (21 Via Giovanni Ansidei; 075.927.4368; about $40–$100). I would be deeply happy to try the mixed grill on the terrace of the **Umbria,** in Todi (13 Via San Bonaventura; 075.894.390; about $50). I deeply regret not having arrived in Montefalco in time for lunch at **Il Coccorone,** which is famous for its risotto made with the local Sagrantino wine (Largo Tempestivi; 0742.379.535; about $50).

Italian for a Week

BY POPE BROCK

∽

editor's note

POPE BROCK is a freelance journalist who has contributed to *Esquire, GQ, Rolling Stone, Life,* and a number of other publications. His first book was *Indiana Gothic,* a nonfiction novel, published in 1999 by Nan A. Talese Books/Doubleday.

I threw open the shutters and let in a big rectangle of Umbrian morning. From the bedroom window I could see over the top of a fig tree across the whole sun-dusted Vale of Umbria to the far-off town of Santa Maria degli Angeli—its ghostly basilica etched in the morning haze—and on and on across central Italy to the blue humpbacked Apennine mountains some fifty miles away. The golden light slanting in gave the villa's dark red floor tiles and rounded archways a romantic, almost decadent air.

Certainly, I wasn't the first American to be seduced by those cinematic images of the Italian countryside: narrow roads winding through the olive-green hills, misty valleys lined with silver-gray cypresses, tumblers of fruity young wine and plates of fresh-cut pasta. After all, if you love Italy and you've already checked off the Uffizi, the Pantheon, and the Doge's Palace, what you really want is to live there—if only for a week at a time. And the best way to do that, to get a lasting taste of the *campagna,* is renting a villa. Along with all the practical advantages of doing this—saving money, cooking your own Italian meals, getting peacefully drunk on the atmosphere—comes the promise of really getting to know some Italians, and not just waiters and hotel clerks. The only cloud on my particular horizon was that I don't speak any Italian, apart from *ciao, bella* and *arrivederci,* but—as I sat leafing through stacks of brochures on a rainy March morning back in the States—this seemed like a welcome challenge, a chance to prove I could overcome any language barrier, and not feel like an outsider looking in, nose pressed to the glass.

Fall clearly seemed the time to go. The September light turns the hills a bright gold, the summer heat is slowly ebbing, and rental rates drop with the temperatures. Dozens of U.S.-based companies act as brokers for thousands of vacation properties throughout Italy (many of their listings overlap somewhat); these range from smallish apartments carved out of unused farm buildings to huge mansions that sleep two dozen guests, and the prices can run anywhere from $500 to $20,000. At $925 a week in September, the villa I rented was nothing too fancy—a simply furnished living/dining room and a kitchen and, upstairs, two bedrooms with private bathrooms—but it was airy, with a porch wrapping halfway around the house. And though built only about five years ago, it had the same timeless stucco walls and red tiled roof I saw on the farmhouses on either side.

One reason I chose Umbria was that it's quite easy to get to—an hour north by train from Rome to Perugia, where I picked up a rental car for the twenty-minute drive to the villa. A more compelling factor, though, was that Umbria's still very rural: a landscape of olive groves, vineyards, and little family vegetable plots. Though there are other vacation rentals in and around the village of Sterpeto, where my villa was located, the roadside sprawl of the twentieth century hasn't taken over. Much of Umbria is mountain and hills, with ancient towns the color of rust and walnut shells spilling over their slopes. The whole region has a rugged, uncluttered feel, especially compared to neighboring Tuscany. And while people go to Tuscan cities like Florence and Siena to revel in the Renaissance, the glories of Umbrian art and architecture are mostly late medieval. True, some of these treasures—the luminous marble facade of Orvieto's cathedral, the hill towns of Gubbio and Spoleto, and, most notoriously, the Giotto frescoes in Assisi—have become mandatory stops on the art lover's pilgrimage, but you can still escape the tour buses and crowds that trek up and down those well-beaten paths.

Along with art, Umbria has also produced saints, scores of them over the centuries, which has given the place a mystical, almost eerie reputation. In the fifth century, St. Benedict was born here; it was he who founded a string of monasteries that eventually spread across Europe, forming civilization's strongest cable during the big sleep of the Dark Ages. (He was always a friend to travelers, too, unless a guest got out of hand. Then, wrote St. Benedict, "it shall be said to him, honestly, that he must depart. If he does not go, let two stout monks, in the name of God, explain the matter to him.") In the following centuries religious hermits were practically fighting for space in Umbria's caves. Then came St. Francis, born in Assisi in 1182, the most famous and enduring saint of all. Abandoning a big inheritance, he lived from hand to mouth, trying by simple force of example to give Christianity a human face.

Assisi itself, though, has turned the memory of this patron saint of poverty into a cash cow. Even before last September's earthquakes, which damaged frescoes in the basilica and sent residents fleeing, Assisi had become a depleted place, stripped of its atmosphere and much of its native population. After walking streets that were gantlets of kitsch, I soaked up the Giottos and fled.

Straight into the arms of my landlords and new best friends, the Pampanoni family. The patriarch, Tarcisio, who's in the banking supply business, and his wife, Anna Maria, have left the villa's management to the next generation, so it was the Pampanoni sons—Francesco, an accountant in his twenties, and Paolo, a college student—who stopped by to introduce themselves. That didn't surprise me, but I wasn't at all prepared for the way the Pampanonis swept me into their hearts. It turns out that even with the twenty-first century seeping in, the old world hangs on here. The Pampanonis have stayed close to their roots and to one another. For a stranger, it's like being pulled through the door to join the party.

On my first Saturday night Francesco (who speaks English fluently), Paolo, and a few friends took me to something called a *sagra,* which is the Umbrian equivalent of a Texas-style barbecue. There are a lot of different kinds around here in late summer—a wild-boar *sagra,* a grape *sagra,* you name it—but this was a Festa della Cipolla, or onion *sagra.* Under outdoor canopies in the tiny medieval town of Cannara, hundreds of people were leaning over long tables having a big community feed. We joined in, working our way through a menu that included onion pizza, onion soup, onions parmigiana, lamb in onion sauce, and so forth, topped off with onion cake and *aragoste,* lobster-shaped pastries filled with sweet onion cream. Afterward we strolled through the winding streets, wreaths and garlands of onions hanging over the doorways of the shops, and red and pink *bella di notte* foaming from the window boxes, on into the main square where the local orchestra was playing "Goldfinger." Francesco gave me a mint. "You'll be tasting onions for a couple of days," he said. "Don't worry. It's normal."

And then there was what happened after I came back from my expedition to Gubbio, triumphantly carrying the makings of a fabulous salad: tomatoes, bell peppers, radicchio, basil, porcini mushrooms. When I realized, upon unpacking the car, that I'd forgotten to buy oil and vinegar.

After looking up how to say "do you have any . . ." in my little phrase book, and then rehearsing for a while, I did what anybody living there would do. I went next door, a few minutes' walk down the winding road, to borrow some.

I found an old woman, a farmer's wife, skinning a rabbit in her yard. She was just working the last of the fur off. On the grass below, kittens were romping, blood-spattered and greedy. Their mother was there, too, along with a few chickens.

It wasn't easy, but finally I managed to convey what I was asking for. Mopping off her knife, she hurried into the house and came back with a bottle of olive oil the size of a magnum of Champagne. She pointed to the olive trees a few yards away, then at the bottle; she'd made it herself. Meanwhile her neighbor had gotten into the act, and came bustling out with about a year's supply of vinegar. I staggered away with my haul.

Later, salad-sated, I sat on the porch, watching the evening light melting on the hills. I exploded a black grape against the roof of my mouth. Okay, so life in Italy wasn't quite like the movies. It was more complicated, and sometimes a little hard for an outsider to navigate—but it was real.

Although I found that it's always helpful to have a good phrase book and an Italian/English dictionary on hand, and that there are times when a talent for charades and reading people's body language is really all you need, sooner or later you run into situations when those props just aren't enough. One bright, cool morning I drove to Gubbio, the nearest big town, to pick up ingredients for dinner. The outdoor market there, held in a covered colonnade smelling of vegetables and old, damp stone, wasn't the collection of individual stalls that I'd expected, but a kind of farmers' clearinghouse staffed by a lone sales clerk who always seemed to have three or four transactions going at once, spinning in the air like plates at a carnival. The customers, those ageless grandmothers you see all over Italy, their heads covered with kerchiefs and their arms laden with bulging string bags, peppered him with questions and sparred good-naturedly with one another. If shopping is a sport, this would be touch football—aggressive but still friendly. All this I could guess from watching, but when it came to speaking, I found it hard enough just to find out what exactly I was buying or whether it was ripe, let alone join the complex cat's cradle of bargaining and banter.

But such struggles paled next to the unexpected dip into real local life. (Somehow, since this was Italy, they all seemed to revolve around food.) There was dinner at the home of the Sfornas, Francesco's in-laws: tomatoes drying in the eighteenth-century hallway, the dining room crowded with sculptures and oil paintings, and eight or nine of us altogether having a high old time over the *signora*'s homemade pizza Margherita—sliced tomatoes, strips of basil, and fresh mozzarella. Besides myself, only Francesco spoke English, but somehow we all swapped stories and even got into a raucous philosophical debate over the nature of beauty. At least, I think that's what we were arguing about.

If you like being totally taken care of, renting a villa is probably not for you. But if you want to combine high-end living with a touch of the pioneer spirit, it's ideal. Dollar for dollar, you're likely to get far more space in a rental than you would in a hotel. Cooking your own meals also saves on restaurants.

Rule one for villa-renting: Book early. If you wait till the spring to reserve a property for the summer, you may still be able to find something, but your choices will be drastically reduced.

Ask your rental agent lots of questions. Take nothing for granted. Is there a washer/dryer? A view? A telephone? (Some rentals either have no phone or you're restricted to incoming calls.) Most important, ask for photos of the location.

Be aware, too, that booking a villa or farmhouse is a more serious commitment than booking a hotel room. There can be stiff penalties for canceling.

Here are some of the organizations that can help you live the dream.

I rented my villa through Barclay International (800-845-6636 or 212-832-3777). They feature several hundred rentals in Umbria (and many others elsewhere), from lower-priced apartments to villas and farmhouses. Interhome USA (973-882-6864), a Swiss-owned company, also lists several hundred Umbria rentals, divided between houses and apartments. Grand Luxe International (800-319-4555 or 201-327-2333) has about thirty-five mostly higher-end Umbria listings. Eurovillas (800-767-0275) has twenty to twenty-five listings in Umbria, from small apartments to large villas housing eighteen to twenty, all in the countryside.

Umbria: Out of This World

BY STEFANO BONILLI

∽

editor's note

Umbria is not in the path of Italy's north-south Autostrada or its major train lines, and it doesn't have the equivalent of Michelangelo's *David* to bring crowds the size of those going to Florence. "But the very causes for Umbria's neglect," as stated in Gambero Rosso's introduction to this piece, "have become the sources of its growing success. More sophisticated travelers are anxious to escape the crowds, explore the back roads, find quiet towns, sleepy museums, and honest tasty meals. They are discovering that Umbria has magnificent art works, beautiful architecture, a lovely landscape and excellent food and wine."

Would you like to get to know the real Umbria? We have to start with names, each one the key to a kingdom's worth of artistic and architectural glory.

Perugia, Orvieto, Assisi, Todi, Spello, Norcia . . . and the list doesn't end here because we've skipped Trevi and Gubbio, Città della Pieve and Narni. This is the Umbria—a region in the heart of the peninsula—that embodies all that is most spectacular in Italy's culture. Here, in town after town, we come across beautifully preserved medieval and Renaissance buildings, frescoes, and paintings. In the Basilica of San Francesco in Assisi we can see the glowing frescoes of Cimabue, Giotto, Simone Martini, and Pietro Lorenzetti, the key revolutionaries of late thirteenth and early fourteenth century art. In this one church is a panorama of the paintings that led the flat and static Byzantine style into the spacious, plastic creativity of the Renaissance. But Assisi, the rose-colored stone city of both St. Francis and St. Clare, draws crowds of visitors all year round, so you may prefer nearby Spello. With just a handful of other travelers, you can see the Church of Santa Maria Maggiore and the Baglioni Chapel, completely frescoed by Pinturicchio around 1500. The brilliant colors of the Annunciation and the exuberant sixteenth-century ceramics from Deruta on the floor of the chapel will make your heart sing on the dreariest winter day. And if you see the frescoes in June, on the Corpus Domini weekend when the narrow streets of Spello are densely carpeted with flower petals, joy is a pale word for describing the feeling.

Would you like to taste the real Umbria? Then start with its extra vergine olive oil. There's one from Trevi with an emerald green color, light grassy fragrance, and a delicate almondy flavor: a delicious, special oil. Umbria is also cured pork products from Norcia, a town whose traditions in this art go back to the Middle Ages. Taste prosciutto from Norcia, or, if you enjoy strong flavors, *mazzafegati,* sausages made from liver, or Umbrian mortadella made in the village of Preci, or *budellacci,* fashioned from smoked pork organ meats. The taste of Umbria is also in truffles, a fundamental ingredient in the region's cuisine. Black truffles come from Norcia, Spoleto and Monte Subasio. White truffles that hold their own against the more famous ones from Alba in Piedmont come from around Gubbio, from the Val Tiberina, and Città di Castello.

Umbria is also the great new enological zone, destined to achieve stardom with its hundred million liter production capacity, its excellent quality and competitive prices. To grasp the importance that wine has for Umbrian culture, and in general for Italy, visit the Museo del Vino in Torgiano, a few kilometers from Perugia. It is one of the most important wine museums in the world. Its exhibits help visitors understand how ancient and mysterious wine's origins are, tracing its history back to pre-Roman times, to the lost world of the Etruscans, a people whose alphabet we have still not been able to decipher. In Orvieto we can see a microcosm of the rest of Italy. Its history is interwoven with the church and with religious orders, their culture and traditions. Perhaps this influence is even more important in Umbria because when the land was still harsh and savage, it became the home of Franciscans and Benedictines. Little towns, churches and convents sprang up and were enriched by hundreds of works of art, painted and sculpted to order. Umbria has remained one of the most verdant regions in the country. Its art works are among the best preserved, and its little medieval towns have survived intact. Today it is one of Italy's most livable regions, a place where past and present live in comfortable equilibrium.

Orvieto: The City That Fell Out of Time

BY MASSIMO COLONNA

～

You've been in Rome, you've visited churches, museums, monuments, and you are full to the brim with beauty. One of your stops was at the Sistine Chapel to see Michelangelo's *Last Judgment*, unveiled after restoration that continued for ten years. And like most travelers to Italy, you are planning Florence as your next stop. Change your plans. Stop in Orvieto. An hour north of Rome, and perched high on an imposing tufa cliff, it is a captivating city, and little-known precisely because it is so close to the capital.

Stop in Orvieto because you have to visit one of the masterpieces of Italian Gothic architecture, the Duomo. In any mental architectural glamour contest, this cathedral would be among the top ten. Built in celebration of a religious miracle (the holy relic is housed inside in a cathedral-shaped box), the facade was gradually fashioned over the course of centuries, beginning in the thirteenth and mostly completed in the sixteenth. Architect Lorenzo Maitani designed the facade and executed some of the delicate bas reliefs on the pilasters between the doors. But many hands added to the glorious confusion, from Andrea Orcagna who created a rose window in the fourteenth century to Emilio Greco who designed a bronze portal in the mid-twentieth. Somehow the thousands of decorative details and the much-restored mosaics blend into a glittering, hypnotizing whole, especially on a sunny day. The shimmering facade catches the light and is visible from miles and miles away. It must have seemed like a promise of paradise to weary travelers.

Tear yourself away from the showy, gluttonous feast of the facade and go inside, making your way to the Cappella Nuova to see the *Last Judgment*. It is one of the benchmarks of the Renaissance, and was begun in 1447 by Fra Angelico, who painted *Christ the Judge and the Prophets*. Then the work was halted for decades and begun again by an aging Luca Signorelli in 1499, who was commissioned to finish the frescoes, a project that took him five years. A powerful series of scenes make up the cycle: *Preaching of the Antichrist, End of the World, Paradise, Inferno, Resurrection of the Dead*. Michelangelo studied the immense work before he began his own Sistine ceiling. This *Last Judgment* is rea-

son enough to visit Orvieto, both for its own beauty and for its role as a predecessor of Michelangelo's chapel.

For a change of scene, leave the Duomo and the piazza, walking to the extreme eastern limit of the city, to the edge of the rock that looks out over the newer part of town and the plain below. Here is the Pozzo di San Patrizio, Saint Patrick's Well, a deep, deep opening that leads straight down into the rock to the water supply below. It is almost forty feet wide and a hundred and eighty feet deep (fifteen stories) with seventy-two low windows. Its unusual feature is that two independent but parallel spiral staircases, one for descending and the other for ascending, fill the space. The 248 steps are shallow, wide, dimly lit, and cold, designed primarily for use by donkeys carrying casks. The work was constructed between 1527 and 1537. Its purpose was to provide the city with an enormous water reservoir in case of attack. Another thousand grottoes under the tufa cliff were dug out for use as water cisterns, but were later abandoned. Now where? If you are curious about the Etruscans, the Museo Archeologico and the Palazzo Faina both have collections of pieces that come from the local excavations that honeycomb the area. The Etruscan necropolis itself is just outside the city. Or perhaps you choose a stroll to the church of San Giovanni, across Via Loggia dei Mercanti. Walk along the quiet street that runs next to the outside edge of the cliff until you reach the eighteenth-century Porta Romana gate; there is a pretty view of the medieval rooftops of the city.

Orvieto is a good place to live. It is divided into two parts: the historic city center and the newer sections below the tufa cliff, on the flat land, nearer roads and railroad station. The countryside is densely farmed and wine production of the classic Orvieto white has always been important. Tourism is growing. Orvieto is one of the sites of Umbria Jazz, a very important music festival. Concerts take place in various cities in the region during both summer and winter sessions.

Orvieto's long exclusion from the standard Italian grand tour, partly due to a lack of autostrade and major railroad lines, partly because of the overbearing nearness of Rome, has made this one of the most unspoiled cities on the peninsula. Umbria's isolation, which goes back centuries, has had a beneficial effect both on this city and on the region in general. Orvieto can leap into the twenty-first century with an intact architectural heritage.

Although Orvieto is well-governed, of course it has its problems, but a visitor can enjoy the sensation of being in a dreamlike medieval town. Walk around the car-free narrow streets and alleyways late at night: everything is silent, peaceful, the only sound your feet on the cobblestones. The Saturday morning market voices may wake you early, but a cappuccino and the shiny baroque piles of cucumbers and tomatoes on the stands may help you accept your fate. Ancient customs and well-preserved architectural beauty struggle with the need to be part of the modern world.

Hotels

Fattoria di Titignano, S.S. 79 bis, località Titignano 7; tel: 0763.308322. An ancient castle belonging to the noble Corsini family, on Lake Corbara, about thirty kilometers (eighteen miles) from Todi, with beautiful frescoed rooms. This is an *agriturismo,* that is, part of a working farm that accepts paying guests. The rooms, all with baths, are simple but comfortable. The farm produces oil, cheese, wine and jam. The restaurant provides tasty food, and welcomes outside guests, but they must reserve ahead. Cost: about $25 per person, without wine; 6 rooms; about $50 a person, half pension; breakfast included; credit cards: no.

Italia, via di Piazza, del Popolo, 13; tel: 0763.342065; fax: 0763.342066. A recently restored nineteenth-century palazzo in the center of the old part of the city. Spacious lobby, flowered couches, breakfast room with antique furniture. Breakfast is buffet style and includes home-made sweets, cold cuts, cheese. Classic bedrooms, pleasantly soft colors. The ones on the courtyard are quieter. 45 rooms; double: about $75–95; breakfast: $10; credit cards: AE, Visa.

Maitani, via L. Maitani, 5; tel: 0763.342011; fax: 0763.660209. A venerable palazzo in the heart of town, right near the Duomo, with a tranquil, restful atmosphere. Large lobby with flowered couches and armchairs that blend nicely with the more modern parts. Comfortable rooms and well-appointed bathrooms with good quality towels. Continental breakfast served in the restaurant, with cold cuts and cheese on request. Closed in January; 49 rooms; double: about $125; breakfast: $10; credit cards: all.

Restaurants

Fattoria di Titignano, località Titignano, S.S. 79 bis; tel: 0765.308322; trattoria. Many spiffy changes in this splendid farm belonging to the Corsini princes. The kitchen itself is more spacious and functional, the dining rooms have been painted and the food is worthy of a great family name. Monica Gori is in charge and offers a dazzling antipasto (marvelous pizza prepared by Alba, crostini, ricotta, cheeses) followed by pappardelle in goose sauce, lasagna with porcini mushrooms, capon cooked in red wine, guinea hen, sausages, grilled pork chops, wild boar in olive sauce. The farm women prepare the cakes; the olive oil and wine are home-grown. Closed: never (call ahead); cost per person: about $25 (without wine); credit cards: no; reservations necessary.

Osteria dell'Angelo, corso Cavour, 166; tel: 0763.341805; restaurant. A simple and very pleasant place. Sandro Zavattaro will bring you excellent and original dishes and can satisfy all your wine desires. A farmhouse menu: eggplant flan, goose breast with goat cheese and olive sauce, liver loaf, duck carpaccio with mint sauce and pecorino cheese, guinea hen aspic with egg and truffle sauce, smoked tuna served on a purée of beans and chives. That's only antipasto. Afterwards, choose from tagliolini with truffles, barley soup with beans and squid, bean soup with pasta and porcini mushrooms. Then the choice is between a perfect duck breast with truffles or a fragrant pork fillet with aromatic herbs. The desserts were a revelation: lemon mousse with raspberry sauce, chestnut charlotte, or a chocolate and cream cake. The wine list is worth a good long look. Closed: Monday and part of March; cost per person: about $30 (without wine); credit cards: AE, Visa.

I Sette Consoli, piazza S. Angelo, 1/a; tel: 0763.343911; restaurant. This is one of the pleasantest places in town. The restaurant is comfortable and welcoming, with a lovely garden for warm-weather dining. The service is courteous and considerate. A fine choice of wine, served by the glass as well. Tasting menus at very fair prices. Antipasto of game salami, eggplant flan with tomato coulis, farro soup, squab with Vinsanto (a sweet Tuscan wine), guinea hen with olives. For dessert a bitter almond biscuit mousse. An excellent choice of Italian and French cheeses. Closed: Wednesday; cost per person: about $30 (without wine); credit cards: all.

La Volpe e l'Uva, via Ripa Corsica, 1; tel: 0763.341612; restaurant. Don't try to come without a reservation because this charming, enticing restaurant is very popular with the locals. It unfailingly provides good food and wine at fair prices. On our last visit we tasted lard with puréed fava beans, a selection of salumi (cold cuts), pasta with egg, pancetta and asparagus or with meat sauce, tiny gnocchi with olive oil, pepper and grated pecorino, eggs scrambled with tomatoes and fava beans, roast pork with herbs, an excellent choice of cheeses and honey, ricotta pudding, and bitter chocolate mousse. Exhaustive wine list. Closed: Monday and mid July–mid August; cost per person: about $25 (without wine); credit cards: AE, Visa.

Norcia: Of Saints and Butchers

BY ANTONIO PAOLINI

～

Norcia is rarely mentioned in guidebooks, but it is of particular interest to food-enthusiasts. The inhabitants were known for their skill as hog butchers and the excellence of their cured pork products, so much so that the word *norcineria* is still commonly used in central Italy to mean a shop where pork and pork products are sold. Eating salami in Norcia is like sampling cheese in Roquefort or Gruyère. You are at the source, and food becomes a good excuse to explore the surrounding countryside. Today Norcia, 1,800 feet above sea level and near the Sibillini mountains, is also visited by skiers. There is a lift only thirteen miles away.

The heavy hand of frequent earthquakes has been the major urban planner in this prosperous, ancient country town. Despite its dangers—Norcia is in the heart of a seismic zone—this site has been occupied since neolithic times. Only one of the town's thirty original towers remains standing, but its fourteenth-century walls, complete with seven gates, have survived unscathed. They enclose a population of about 5,000 inhabitants. The town's centuries-old houses are mostly two stories high, and never more than three.

In the central piazza, named for native son Saint Benedict (San Benedetto, born here in 480 A.D.) is the impressive Castellina, a robust palace fortress built in 1554 by renowned architect Vignola. Almost every country town in Italy has at least one truly noteworthy building, and modest Norcia is no exception. A walk around town reveals a number of different neighborhoods, each with a piazza, a fountain, and a coat of arms. Some are more countrified, with remnants of stables and barns; others are more bourgeois, their buildings recently restored. Walk back to the central piazza through the Porta Romana. To the left is a surreal slice of building left after the widening of the present-day Corso. It is said that the mayor of the time went bankrupt by paying for the work from his own pocket; no kickbacks in those days. At the feet of the statue of Saint Benedict are a series of Masonic symbols donated by the Masons during a centennial of his birth; they seem to have made him, posthumously, one of their own. Look for the rings that hold the flags of the various neighborhoods on the day of the Palio, a competition similar to the world-famous one held in Siena. Under a portico to the left, the sixteenth-century hollow stones used to measure grain have survived intact. A little further on is a small fresco that was restored with funds raised through an interesting enterprise: "A Picture, a Restoration," run by a local association, auctioned paintings donated by famous contemporary artists and used the money to restore the work of their colleagues of centuries before.

There are a number of lovely buildings to visit: the fourteenth-century church of San Benedetto, the Duomo, Vignola's Castellina, and the Museo Civico, which has an interesting collection of Umbrian wooden sculptures. Two sacred sites deserve special mention here because they are kept under lock and key. The keys for the first one are easy to come by; just ask for Don Dario at the Duomo, or cathedral. L'Oratorio di Sant'Agostinuccio has a handsome wooden ceiling and the Chiesa al Cimitero is richly frescoed. One of its paintings is particularly strange. It shows San Benedetto and his twin sister Santa Scolastica standing next to each other, but painted in different centuries. A few years ago, a puzzling wall inscription encouraged a group of researchers to gently scrape at the surface in search of hidden treasures. In two separate explorations, Santa Scolastica was unveiled, and so rejoined her beloved brother, painted some centuries later. To visit the church, you must stop by the *Scuola Media,* or middle school, and ask for Professor Giorgio Ursu, the principal and also honorary superintendent of monuments.

Less spiritual pleasures are displayed in the appetizing windows of the town's food shops, especially in Ansuini, right behind the church of San Benedetto. But in the convent of the church, both body and soul can be satisfied. A new building has been constructed alongside the ancient one, destroyed in the 1979 earthquake and only partially restored. The sisters now run a hostel-hotel, with comfortable if somewhat spartan rooms but truly charitable prices. What is astonishing, though, is the quality of the food offered in the hostel's restaurant. The sisters prepare handmade tagliatelle, homemade cured pork products from their own five pigs (the limit, according to their own ancient rules) and vegetables from their own sizable garden. A little pleading, and you may be able to buy some to take away with you.

The sisters also make wonderful honey. They told us that they were once asked to sell, under their own name, honey produced elsewhere. They sent a sample out to be analyzed and, not 100 percent satisfied by the results, they gently refused. We were comforted to think that the Benedictine sisters chose safeguarding us, the consumers, over increasing their profit.

Stroncone: The Tavern Beneath the Convent

BY LAURA MANTOVANO

∽

Stroncone is a medieval hamlet with its original gates, arches, and winding alleyways intact. After a hearty Sunday lunch somewhere else, it was the perfect place to go for a stroll. An Enchanted Kingdom where a spell seemed to have fallen over all. Visitors love to happen upon these magical places, but for the young of the village, escape was the goal. Dull, industrial Terni beckoned with work in its steel refineries.

Davide Menesto had other ideas, and seven years ago he took over the Taverna de Porta Nova, and woke up the drowsy town. Upstairs lived the six Franciscan nuns that ran the nursery school.

Downstairs, in the cellars of the convent, the floors were terracotta, and the original wooden beams, brick arches and fireplace had survived the centuries. Davide's dream was to turn the tavern into a trattoria and offer visitors the chance to enjoy the cooking that he had grown up with in this country town.

He joined forces with his wife, Milly, her sister Elisa, and brother-in-law Enzo Iapadre. They opened their doors three days a week—Friday, Saturday and Sunday—helped by an old cook of the town who still remembered all the traditional recipes. The sisters learned the secrets of homemade pasta, gnocchi, and soup while Davide specialized in fireplace cooking. He became expert at *pizza sotto lu focu,* pizza cooked under ashes on a flat stone in the fireplace and then stuffed with vegetables, cheese or sausage. Enzo became the food buyer and looked after the antipasto: prosciutto, grilled eggplant and peppers, seasoned chickpeas and beans and toasted olive or nut bread. If you reserve, you'll find a welcoming assortment ready at the table when you arrive.

Suor Anita, the Mother Superior at the nursery school, began reminiscing about food one day when Davide came by to pick up his daughter. She described a wonderful dish that was the daily fare of the Franciscan brothers: soup served in a bowl made of bread. Intrigued by the idea of recovering this old-fashioned flavor, Davide determined to find a way. The trick was to find a baker in the neighborhood who could make the right sort of bread container. A search turned up one near Rieti, in the tiny town of Colle di Lugnola, who was willing to try. Little by little, neighbors began to give the new enterprise a hand, but it wasn't easy.

In the town of Stroncone, each family lives in a self-sufficient autonomous unit. Each has a little vegetable garden and raises a pig and a few chickens. No one was terribly interested in a neighborhood restaurant. For a while. But Milly, Elisa, Enzo and Davide got everyone into the act. They found wonderful produce right in their own backyard: mushrooms, chestnuts, lentils, farro, and an array of naturally-grown vegetables. The olive mill was proud to find an audience for its excellent light oil, made from a variety of tree that grows best on rocky soil and produces a taste similar to the world-famous olive oil of Liguria. The *norcineria* (pork butcher) in Colle di Lugnola furnished flavorful meat, sausages, and prosciutto. Giovanni, the shepherd, was delighted to see Davide serving his cheese, lightly grilled in the fireplace, to grateful guests. The Taverna de Porta Nova is now a going concern. Open six evenings a week and for lunch on Sundays and holidays, the family pulls together (Davide and Milly's parents have joined in, as well) to serve a hundred guests at a sitting. Enzo and Davide have taken a sommelier course, and the wine cellar always has something interesting to offer. Stroncone is lively until one in the morning now, and Davide Menesto's little idea has awakened the Sleeping Beauty.

Wine and olive oil: Vascigliano di Stroncone, Azienda Agricola La Palazzola-Grilli; tel.: 0744.607735.

Sausages, prosciutto, meat: Stroncone, Butcher-Norcineria, Giulia Contessa, frazione Colle; 4; tel.: 0744.607285.

Bakery: Configni (Rieti), L'Antico Pane, colli di Lugnola; tel.: 0764.672082.

Handicrafts in wood and wrought iron: Stroncone, Officina Vittori, viale Lanzi; tel.: 0744.60144.

Where to Go

Outdoors: a walk in the meadows near Stroncone, altitude 3,000 feet, or else a stroll along the Franciscans' paths.

Festival: the last week in June there are performers in every piazza, singing, playing, juggling, miming for the Festival degli Artisti.

Fair: during August, painting shows, local artisans' work, and performances every evening.

Walk: the four most important sections of Stroncone—Aguzzo, Coppe, Finocchietto, and Vasciano—have preserved their medieval look.

Perugia, Spoleto, and Todi are hill towns with pretty hotels, authentic local food, and intriguing shops.

Perugia

Hotels

Locanda della Posta, corso Vannucci, 97; tel.: 075.5728925; fax: 075.5722413. Near the imposing Palazzo dei Priori, the hotel has retained the charm of its eighteenth-century past as an inn where the post horses were changed or rested and travelers could spend the night. In 1990 it was very elegantly restored, and the old and the new integrated with intelligence and taste. The furniture in the rooms is modern, but fabric on the walls and elegant lighting create a cozy ambiance. The bathrooms are large, with lovely marble and ceramic details. A big buffet breakfast is served in a frescoed room of the original inn. 40 rooms; double: about $135–$200; breakfast included; credit cards: all.

Priori, via dei Priori; tel.: 075.5723378; fax: 075.5723213. Right in the middle of town. The lobby is furnished with flowered couches and armchairs, the rooms in the old Umbrian style with terra-cotta floors and flowered upholstery. Bathrooms have showers and courtesy kits. In the summer, breakfast is served on the splendid terrace that overlooks Perugia's rooftops. 50 rooms; double: about $85; breakfast included; credit cards: no.

Sangallo Palace, via Masi, 9; tel.: 075.5730202; fax: 075.5730068. A tastefully restored building in the historic center of the city. Lobby elegantly furnished with rose-colored upholstery and couches. The bedrooms and suite have a sober Renaissance flavor with Perugino and Pinturicchio reproductions on the walls. Some bathrooms have sauna and Jacuzzi tubs. Pleasant breakfast with hot rolls and homemade sweets. Particularly courteous personnel. 93 rooms; double: about $130–$180; breakfast: $10; credit cards: all.

Villa Ada, strada Forcella, 35, località Cenerente; tel.: 075.690125; fax: 075.690666. In a pretty valley far from trafficky roads, this hotel is in a nineteenth-century home surrounded by lush vegetation and gardens. Its lovely facade is in the style of old country villas. Elegantly furnished bedrooms respect traditional Umbrian taste in the choice of flooring, linens, and fabric. Handsome, well-appointed bathrooms. A buffet breakfast is served. 21 rooms; double: about $140; breakfast included; credit cards: all.

Restaurants

Da Apparo, località San Marco, viale Cappuccini, 2; tel.: 075.690177; trattoria. A family-owned place for generations, the food is honest and simple, the wine list brief. *Torta al testo,* a thin, round bread cooked on a terra-cotta dish, is served with a generous portion of home-cured prosciutto and salami as antipasto. Then comes an unusual version of *panzanella* (a Tuscan tomato, bread, and basil salad), homemade tagliatelle, gnocchi in meat sauce, pasta and fagioli, or *umbrichelli,* an Umbrian pasta. The meat courses change daily: rabbit cooked with wild fennel, charcoal grilled pork or lamb, and sometimes lamb *pajata*, organ meats considered a delicacy by many. Delicious homemade desserts. Closed: Tuesday and August; cost per person: about $25 (without wine); credit cards: no.

Osteria del Bartolo, via Bartolo, 30; tel.: 075.5731561; restaurant. Walter Passeri takes the time to pay loving attention to the clients of his small but elegant restaurant. The bread is homemade, as is the lightly salted butter, the pasta, and the desserts (raspberry parfait, Floating Island, rum crêpes). Many traditional Umbrian flavors are on the menu including mixed bean soup, onion pancakes, aged ricotta, and truffles. The fish is even better: pasta with scallops, fresh pasta with shrimps, turbot with fennel, skate with mushrooms. A varied wine list. Closed: Sunday, most of January; cost per person: about $50 (without wine); credit cards: all.

Shops

Caffè and pastry shop: Sandri, corso Vannucci, 32; tel.: 075.5724112. Not to be missed. The street, named for Renaissance painter Pietro Vannucci (Perugino), is the scene of the town's late-afternoon stroll and window-shopping ritual. Sandri, although it changed hands some time ago, has survived unblemished. The ambiance and the sweets are as they have been for 150 years. Outdoors the view is of Perugia's splendid piazza, the gothic cathedral, and a medieval fountain.

Wine shop: Enoteca Provinciale, di Perugla, via Ulisse Rocchi, 18; tel.: 075.5724824. A look around Leonardo Raggiotti's shop, just behind the cathedral and the Fontana Maggiore by Pisano, will give you a complete overview of Umbrian wines. He carries major top-quality labels as well as more ordinary commercial wines and examples from little-known, up-and-coming producers. Closed: Monday, open Sunday morning.

Dried foods, household goods: Spezieria Bavicchi, piazza Matteotti, 32; tel.: 075.5731752. Even if you aren't likely to buy anything, take a look. This type of store is rapidly disappearing as Italian housekeeping habits come to resemble American ones. The store's philosophy seems to be, "If you don't see it, ask." A glance around will reveal grains and legumes of every imaginable shape and color, flour made from rice, chick peas, chestnut, corn, rye, and almonds. A dizzying variety of teas and spices. closed: Thursday afternoon

Spoleto

Hotels

Aurora, via Apollinare, 3; tel.: 0743.220315; fax: 0743.221885. This small hotel in the center of Spoleto offers simple but comfortable rooms with pleasant bathrooms, and above all, a very good restaurant, Apollinare. A chance to eat Umbrian food at its traditional but updated best. The owner and personnel treat guests with winning graciousness. 15 rooms; double: about $60–$75; breakfast: $5; credit cards: all.

Charleston, piazza Collicola, 10; tel.: 0743.220052; fax: 0743.222010. An eighteenth-century building in the heart of town, and a happy marriage of classical and modern. Spacious and soberly decorated lobby. Bright, light, and prettily furnished rooms with both modern and antique furniture. Well-appointed bathrooms. Continental breakfast is served on a little terrace in the summer. 18 rooms; doubles: about $80–$110; breakfast included; credit cards: AE, DC, Visa.

Clarici, piazza della Vittoria, 32; tel.: 0743.223311; fax: 0743.222010. Located just at the edge of the city, this hotel is a convenient jumping off place for a visit to Spoleto. The rooms have all the necessary comforts although no color TV, but essentials like air conditioning, minibar, and pristine bathrooms have not been overlooked. 24 rooms; double: about $80–$110; breakfast included; credit cards: all.

Nuovo Clitunno, piazza Sordini, 6; tel.: 0743.223340; fax: 0743.222663. This recently renovated family-run hotel near the Duomo is a pleasant blend of old and new. The lobby and the bedrooms have terracotta floors and pastel, color-coordinated decor. Some rooms have wrought-iron beds, wood-beamed ceilings, and Persian carpets on parquet floors. Comfortable bathrooms. Buffet breakfast. Pleasant personnel. Closed in February; 38 rooms; double: about $80–$100; breakfast included; credit cards: AE, DC, Visa.

Restaurants

Pecchiarda, vicolo San Giovanni, 1; tel.: 0743.221009; trattoria. A great favorite with the actors and singers who come to perform at the Spoleto Festival, this simple trattoria serves home-style food cordially and attentively and presents an affordable, honest bill at the end of the meal. In summer, tables are outdoors under a pleasant pergola. Ricotta gnocchi, pork fillet, wild boar, lentils with sausages, stuffed chicken, braised fava beans. Desserts and wine are homemade. Closed: Thursday; cost per person: about $25 (without wine); credit cards: no.

Il Tartufo, piazza Garibaldi, 24; tel.: 0743.40236; restaurant. Emilio Di Marco tends toward the traditional. His son Paolo pushes for innovation. The results are interesting, the food is excellent, and the service courteous. We ordered the tasting menu ($45): mushroom fricassee with truffles, liver and truffle torte, chickpea purée with *baccalà* (salt cod), fettuccine made with rye flour and truffles. Homemade cookies and cakes. Good choice of wine. Closed: Wednesday, part of July and August; cost per person: about $50 (without wine); credit cards: all.

Shops

Specialty foods: Padrichelli, via Arco di Druso, 22; tel.: 0743.46617. Spoleto's oldest *salumeria,* right near piazza del Mercato, stocks a vast assortment of artisanal cured pork products from the Valnerina zone: boar, truffle, and home-style salamis, prosciutto, and sausages. Buy bread baked in a wood-burning oven, and choose from an inviting assortment of cheeses (pecorino studded with white and black truffles, fresh goat cheese, salted ricotta covered with bran, and fresh ricotta, among others). There are truffles in every form, fresh or worked in pasta, sauces, or oil, and an array of intriguing legumes. Closed: Sunday afternoon.

Bread: Santini, vicolo del Forno, 2; tel.: 0743.223359. Alessandro Santini and his wife, Rita, have had this bakery for twenty-two years. They use only the best-quality flour, and all the breads—made with olives, walnuts, soy, or whole wheat—are baked in their wood-burning oven. Closed: Sunday.

Todi

Fonte Cesia, via L. Leonj, 3; tel.: 075.8943737; fax: 075.8944677. This splendid palazzo in the center of Todi, just a few steps from piazza del Popolo, still has all the trappings of its aristocratic past: vaulted ceilings, granite floors, French upholstery, and antique furniture. Bedrooms and bathrooms are spacious, comfortable, and modern. There is a lovely terrace with deck chairs and a view over Todi's rooftops. Ample breakfast with fresh rolls, local cakes, juices, cereal, and fruit. A convention hall is available in the deconsecrated church of San Benedetto. 36 rooms; double: about $175; breakfast included; credit cards: all.

Restaurants

Lucaroni, viale A. Cortesi, 57; tel.: 075.887370; restaurant. A few steps from the Porta Romana. Try the puréed fava beans as antipasto. Among the first courses, walnut ravioli and risotto made with radicchio and Sagrantino, a powerful red wine. Meat dishes include lamb with truffles, wild boar, and charcoal-grilled steaks and chops. Homemade desserts. Umbrian wine. Closed: Tuesday; cost per person: about $30 (without wine); credit cards: all.

La Mulinella, via Pontenaia, 29, frazione Vasciano; tel.: 075.8944779; trattoria. Cordial, informal service. Pasta is made on the premises, and the bread is baked in woodburning ovens. Try crostini made with game meats, tagliatelle with mushrooms, roasted guinea hen, savory meat and vegetable pies. *Panpepato* (a firm mixture of nuts, candied fruit, chocolate, flour, honey) and pine nut cake, two typical sweets, are on the dessert menu. Mostly local wines. Closed: Wednesday; cost per person: about $30 (without wine); credit cards: no.

Preserves: Principi, piazza del Popolo, 1; tel.: 075.8942313. Floro Principi's handsome store facing Todi's breathtaking piazza del Popolo has at least thirty types of sauce for rice or pasta (truffles, arugula, walnut, etc.) and a variety of spreads (black and green olive, artichoke, eggplant, etc.) to use on crackers, crostini, or as a vegetable dip. Closed: Thursday afternoon, July.

Pastry: Del Papa, via G. Cocchi, 11; tel.: 075.8944254. Tucked into one of the streets near piazza del Popolo, this little shop is full of Todi's delightful pastry specialties. Forty years of experience are behind the traditional holiday sweets, and there's at least one for every occasion. All year round you can munch on cannoli, meringues with whipped cream, and a variety of typical rustic Umbrian cookies. Closed: Thursday.

This piece, composed of four separate articles featuring different aspects of Umbria, originally appeared in *Gambero Rosso*. Copyright © 1997. Reprinted with permission.

Burning the Candle at Both Ends at Gubbio's Mad, Medieval Festa dei Ceri

BY DAVID DOWNIE

༼

editor's note

I have never had the pleasure of being in Gubbio for the Festa dei Ceri, but I'm going to plan my next visit to Umbria around it.

DAVID DOWNIE lives in Paris but studied, lived, and worked in Italy for several years before moving there. He holds undergraduate and Master's degrees in Italian literature, and is the author of *Enchanted Liguria: A Celebration of the Culture, Lifestyle and Food of the Italian Riviera* (Rizzoli, 1997).

At precisely 1:45 in the afternoon on May 15th, 1997, Sant'Ubaldo floated by my second-floor window at the Hotel Tre Ceri. The bearded, benign-looking saint nodded at me. Then his golden-cloaked effigy vanished around a cobbled meander into the center of moody, medieval Gubbio—among the mountainous Umbria region's most startling hilltowns.

A dream?

I leapt from my napping place. Drums rolled and a trumpet sounded. I blinked at another improbable sight: the arcing trajectory of four scarlet-shirted men about 200 feet aloft. Back and forth they swung, higher and higher: they were rough-riding the immense, booming bell of the crenellated Palazzo dei Consoli's campanile.

As I wove through thronging roisterers towards the palazzo—Gubbio's main monument, housing its municipal museum—up went a wild cheer. A marching band blared in the warren of stony streets. People danced, sang, ate. Unlike me, these merrymakers seemed unfazed by a sleepless night's feasting and—above all—quaffing of the local red San Giovese-Trebbiano wine. It flows unabated at the dozens of taverns that sprout on street corners the evening of May 14th, the Bacchanalian eve of Gubbio's riotous annual Festa dei Ceri.

Ubaldo supposedly saved the town in 1155 from destruction by invading German Emperor Frederick Barbarossa, and the festa has honored him as patron saint ever since. But the two-day extravaganza of parades, processions, races and feasting is as profane as it is sacred, and may be even older than Sant'Ubaldo. Apparently it resembles the pagan rites of spring celebrated hereabouts by the Etruscans and ancient Romans.

The festa centers around three portable floats called *ceri*. Centuries old, made of wood and fabric and standing about fifteen feet high, they are intended to represent gigantic bundles of votive candles (in Italian *cero* means "large candle"). To me, though, they looked more like a cross between a ballistic missile and a two-tiered Chinese lantern. On top of each cero perches the effigy of a saint, representing the town's three parishes of Sant'Ubaldo, San Giorgio and Sant'Antonio. The base is pinned to a wooden chassis carried on the shoulders of *ceraioli* (bearers). They sport white pants and a red kerchief, and wear shirts color-coded by parish: yellow for Sant'Ubaldo, blue for San Giorgio and black for Sant'Antonio.

At about 11:30 on the morning of the fifteenth, in front of the Palazzo dei Consoli, three teams of kaleidoscopically costumed ceraioli hefted the teetering, 800-pound candlesticks and alternately sprinted or strolled behind two mounted *capitani* (team captains) and a single trumpeter. Carried aloft, the saints then "visited" homes where someone had died, been born or married since the last festa.

The real action started at about six, though, once the ceraioli had recovered from their earlier exertions. By then Gubbio was throbbing with nearly 100,000 spectators. Amid deafening shouts the ceri flew at breakneck speed clockwise around town, covering about three miles at a gallop. Because of the load's weight and unwieldiness, anywhere from twenty to forty bearers carried each cero. Even Herculean ceraioli lasted only about a hundred yards, so there was a constant swarming as they spelled each other in rapid motion.

As evening fell this surreal, multicolored blur corkscrewed through the city walls and up the staggeringly steep switchbacks 1,400 vertical feet to the basilica of Sant'Ubaldo that crowns Monte Ingino above town—a 2.3-mile climb. Sprinting in relay, the ceraioli covered the distance in a seemingly impossible nine minutes, twenty-two seconds. It took me twice that, unloaded, at a run.

How did they do it? A mystery. Some say it's religious ecstasy. Others swear it's the local wine, possibly the same kind of robust red that fuelled Gubbio's pagan rites of spring 2,000 years ago.

Mass Appeal

BY JAN MORRIS

∾

editor's note

Here are two pieces on the popular Umbrian hilltown of Assisi, this one written eight years before the 1997 earthquake, the other one year after it.

The earthquake might have made Assisi more popular than it ever was, but even before the tragedy, its streets and monuments could often be crowded with tourists. However, as noted in this piece, rising early ensures you will encounter fewer tourists at churches and basilicas (this is true throughout Italy). If the thirteenth-century Basilica di Santa Chiara is no longer under scaffolding when you visit, try to see it late in the day, when its pink-and-beige-striped stone façade is remarkably beautiful.

JAN MORRIS is the author of over twenty books, including *Fifty Years of Europe* (Villard, 1997), *Destinations* (Oxford University Press, 1982), *The World of Venice* (Harvest/Harcourt Brace, 1995), *Hong Kong: Epilogue to an Empire* (Vintage, 1997), and *Among the Cities* (Oxford University Press, 1985).

It is a travelers' truism that the holiness of holy places is cumulative—the more people think them holy, the holier they become. A few places, however, are so absolutely sacred that they depend not at all upon the faith of their pilgrims. Among these supremely God-graced places unquestionably stands Assisi, home of that Saint Francis whose message of kindness and simplicity transcends all religious dogma.

Assisi is a classic hill town of central Italy, backed by the 4,000-foot Monte Subasio, crowned with a castle and surrounded by a venerable eight-gated rampart. It houses some 6,000 people within the walls, another 18,000 outside, and it is by no means immune to the world's corrosions. The wide plain that faces the town, crossed by the adolescent Tiber, is littered with those peculiarly ugly constructions for which modern Italy has a special aptitude. The streets of Assisi itself are loud and hideous with cars. The full blast of mass tourism is let loose each year upon the memory of Il Poverello (the Little Poor One), upon the sites associated with his life and upon the marvelous works of art that attend them. Organized religion has done its worst to swamp the Franciscan values with grandeur and gigantism.

Many another place of pilgrimage has been utterly degraded by such influences; I don't mean to sound sententious when I say that in Assisi a sort of miracle really has happened: the presence of Saint Francis easily survives it all, to touch the heart of nearly everyone who visits his happy town.

Take the Porziuncola, the chapel where, in 1206, the young Francis entered upon his saintly career by founding his own brotherhood. Look for it where it should be, a couple of miles out of town on the plain, and you find it inside a mighty, baroque church, Santa Maria degli Angeli, erected in the sixteenth century and aggrandized in the 1920s with a properly Mussolini-style plaza. A town of its own has arisen all around, vivid with cafés, traffic cops and picture-postcard stands. Your heart may sink when, at the start of your own Assisi pilgrimage, you enter the vast facade of the church, built in 1927 in Renaissance (but still fairly fascist) style.

Cheer up, as Il Poverello himself would doubtless say: deep

within the echoing interior of the building there stands to this day, like an enchanted cottage in a fairytale, the actual first little chapel of the Franciscans. They have stuck an unsuitable baroque ornament on top of it and faced it with an unnecessary fresco, but inside, the chapel is still innocent and charming as ever. To see a group of foreign pilgrims celebrating Mass there—in German, perhaps, or French or English—while the candlelight shines on the rough stone walls, and the gigantic structure of Santa Maria degli Angeli looms forestlike all around, is still to capture something of the original Franciscan magic.

At the other end of the saint's story is his tomb, and there is no pretending that this is always inspiring. When Francis died in 1226, they erected as his mausoleum the enormous Basilica di San Francesco—two basilicas, really, one above the other—beneath which is a stone sepulchre, rediscovered only in 1818, where the saint's body lies. So stupendously embellished is this place with works of genius, so universal is the reputation of Saint Francis, that on an average afternoon the building is a nightmare of jostling tour groups, booming lecturers, flashlight beams illuminating frescoes and schoolchildren scrambling in and out of a souvenir shop that is conveniently located between the upper and lower churches.

But I went there very early one rainy morning (the basilica opens at 6:30) and had the place almost to myself. Down in the crypt, two or three early worshipers were kneeling before the saint's sarcophagus. In the transept up above, the marble floors gleamed in the early light and the prodigiously painted ceilings glimmered mysteriously. I was entirely alone when I came face-to-face with the most famous of all images of the saint: Cimabue's haunting picture of him, looking back at me grave, unshaven, wry-eyed, at the beginning of another long day.

Between these two symbolic landmarks, the first church and the last resting place, Saint Francis has left his physical mark all over Assisi, and a visit to the town is necessarily a tour of his associations. Here, during twenty years of leadership, he built up the order that was to become not only one of the great forces of Christendom but also a profound influence on art, literature and philosophy. Scarcely an alley or hillslope of Assisi does not recall the saint, and if fact does not make the connection plain, legend has long sufficed.

Here in a niche in the Chiesa Nuova is the stable in which Francis, though the son of a well-off merchant, is alleged, Christlike, to have been born. Here is the font of his baptism, here the very stone closet in which his father once imprisoned him for unfilial behavior. ("It was nothing," said a resident friar when I expressed my utter horror at this kind of punishment. "Every father did it in those days.")

In the church of Santa Chiara is the Byzantine crucifix that once told Francis, in the voice of God, "rebuild my house." In the church of Santa Maria di Rivotorto is preserved the crude stone structure, not at all unlike a pigsty, that Francis himself called the hovel, in which he lived for three years with his eleven original companions. Far up a gully on Monte Subasio perches the hermitage of the Carceri, to which Francis from time to time withdrew for penitence and meditation. It is everyone's idea of a hermitage, all jumbled and nooky in the flank of the mountains, up narrow steps, through dark passages, with an old, old olive tree—held precariously together with clamps and struts—that certainly remembers the days when Il Poverello came up here himself.

And out on the plain stands the garden where Francis preached to the birds in the most famous Franciscan tale of all—a proper place of dedication for anyone, of whatever faith, who cares about the essential order of things.

The garden is unfortunately flanked nowadays by a chicken farm on one side and a row of pigeon coops on the other, but when

I was out there one morning, thinking rather morosely about this irony, I chanced to look up and to the north. There, framed by cypress trees, reclining languidly on its hillside, was Assisi itself. It was a sight of exquisite beauty, like an ideal city of romance, its pinkish mass so perfectly proportioned, so elegantly punctuated with flowers and domes, its emphasis so tactfully balanced between the ruined fortress at the top and the basilica with its monastery at the bottom.

Plenty of places, like plenty of people, are good without being likable. Saint Francis was evidently both, and so is his little city. If the flat land in front is indeed tarnished with insensitive concrete and birdcages, the hills behind, and the fertile flanks of Subasio, are precisely the delectable landscapes so beloved of the old Italian painters: rolling wooded landscapes speckled with towers and hilltop farms, hatched with vineyards, spiked with cypresses and marked everywhere, as in allegory, with white roads winding toward infinity.

The town itself is a charmer, too. Besides its plethora of churches—Romanesque, Gothic, Renaissance—it possesses an enchanting labyrinth of steep cobbled lanes and one of the most agreeable small city squares in Italy, the Piazza del Comune, whose modest medievalism is set off astonishingly by the facade of a genuine Roman temple with six Corinthian columns, dedicated to Minerva but long since given Christian meaning.

It is a very amiable place, its streets habitually crowded with noisy and high-spirited young people, laughing and shouting and larking about. Assisi is also highly serendipitous.

All sorts of unexpected pleasant things happen here. At the end of April you can find yourself hilariously caught up in the town's world-famous Feast of Calendimaggio, a three-day phantasmagoria of charade and display, but at any other time of the year you might be just as happily surprised. Out of the blue, perhaps, you will find yourself dancing at a disco in a medieval mansion, or listening to

Bach among the Giotto frescoes of the basilica, or talking to a lutemaker in his workshop, or bumping into a scarecrow, a pony and a couple of geese in the shadow of the city walls, or being whisked from the parking lot to the Porta Nuova not on donkey-back but on a new, covered escalator.

For an extra miracle of Assisi is this: besides being holy, as it unmistakably is, and beautiful by art and nature, and kindly as one might expect the city of Saint Francis to be, it is lots of fun.

Resurrection in Assisi

BY MANUELA HOELTERHOFF

editor's note

MANUELA HOELTERHOFF, former book review editor of *The Wall Street Journal,* is the author of *Cinderella & Company: Backstage at the Opera with Cecilia Bartoli* (Random House, 1998, hardcover; Vintage, 1999, paperback).

Over a quiet breakfast in the shady garden restaurant of the Hôtel Subasio, where basil grows in pots and waiters out-number guests, I look out across the plains below, past sunflower fields and recently reaped wheat toward the banal immensity of Santa Maria degli Angeli. Begun in the late sixteenth century, it's undistinguished except for the rustic little house that happens to be inside it and goes by the name of Porziuncola.

Meaning "tiny land parcel." Saint Francis himself is said to have helped finish its roof, and the chapel served as headquarters for the Franciscan community. And it was here that he died in 1226, after an exhausting life filled with travels (he spent months on pilgrimage in the Holy Land), many miracles, and many friends. A medieval green man, he called the sun his brother and the moon his sister, and he brought a cheerful, open approach to his dealings with God, men and women, beasts and birds. Not for him the gloom and doom of the desiccated mystic for whom life was just a meaningless passage to the hereafter.

He would probably cry into his cowl at the sight of Santa Maria, for he liked architecture to be humble. So I suppose he might also object to the great church that bears his name and holds his bones: the Basilica of St. Francis.

But for the rest of us, this awe-inspiring complex is one of the greatest monuments in Western civilization, a remarkable amalgam of faith, art, and engineering. Started in 1228, the basilica consists, most unusually, of two churches built double-decker-style and rising thrillingly on a bluff overlooking the Umbrian plain. Amply funded by the Papacy, Saint Francis's church turned into a showcase at the pivotal moment when the ethereal, otherworldly visions of medieval art were losing ground to new and convincing ways of representing the real world. While the old-fashioned Cimabue slaved mightily on his frescoes decorating the apse and transepts of the Upper Church, the younger Giotto would show off his storytelling genius in the St. Francis cycle two decades later.

Both artists also worked in the Lower Church, where the dim lighting creates an air of mystery and awe that is temporarily lifted by the charming St. Martin cycle by Simone Martini, who cheerfully transformed the French saint's Francis-like life of privation into a fairy-tale fashion parade. In stark contrast are the scenes from the Passion of Christ by Pietro Lorenzetti, who took a less varnished view of life. His *Last Supper* shows the kitchen help scraping plates by the fire, attentively observed by a small white dog and a large gray cat. Across the nave is Cimabue's posthumous portrait of Francis in a pose of quiet resolve, showing his stigmata, eyes like embers, and all-weather robe. (The saint's moth-eaten, much-patched tunic and wide winter slippers may be viewed in the reliquary museum.)

Even though I know what happened here on September 26, 1997, the sight gives me goose bumps as I climb from the hotel to the basilica. The facade of the Upper Church has a red and green rubble tube running out of its gable. Scaffolding covers the south transept, facade, and bell tower. It's like visiting a friend in intensive care.

The first quake hit in the early morning hours and rained fresco fragments from the ceiling of the Upper Church. Then, just before noon, came the second, far more violent quake. In a matter of seconds, two of the nave's three elaborately frescoed vaults partially collapsed, ripping large gaps in the ceiling and burying two friars and two restoration experts. While the walls held firm, several saints by Giotto and Cimabue fell from the vaults and disintegrated on impact into thousands of fragments. Although the undamaged Lower Church speedily reopened its portals to the diminished multitudes, the Upper Church has been closed since the quake. But with the jubilee year just around the corner, the race is on to open the doors in time for the millions of pilgrims expected in Assisi in December 1999.

That date has to be pressing down like stones on the teams of restorers toiling inside the Upper Church and, below ground, in the under-air-conditioned laboratory newly installed inside the mammoth stable of Sixtus IV, a fifteenth-century pope who kept an apartment in the complex attached to the basilica. Giuseppe Basile, a slender man in jeans and glasses, heads up the art-historical flank of the complex restoration effort that involves architects, engineers, conservators, and officials from the Church, federal ministries, and the regional power base in Perugia. He is showing me around.

At one end of the laboratory, experts are hovering over computers, looking to match up the thousands of fresco chips that dropped to the floor in a confusing heap. Long tables occupy the other half of the room, topped off with full-size color reproductions of saints who are no longer attached to the archivolt of the inner facade above the portal. Lunch trays filled with fresco remains of the saints suggest the difficulties of reassembling images that are now in pieces often not much larger than a fingernail. Saint Rufinus's eyes peer up at me from one table.

The vault section with Saint Matthew by Cimabue was a ghostly wreck even when in one piece. Basile opens a door and walks into a smaller storage area stacked high with pull-out boxes filled with fresco pieces. "There are eight hundred boxes marked C for Cimabue," he says simply. What he doesn't say is that the ghost is gone forever.

There's a better prognosis for some of the larger, festively banded chunks that edged the vaults. Basile points to a restorer who is sitting on a little stool, holding a syringe with a consolidating liquid that will prevent further chipping. The sections will eventually be returned to the ceiling, although how the vaults will finally look is unclear. Where the losses are too severe, should restorers leave the areas blank or sketch them in to deceive the eye from twenty yards below? Should a Cimabue copy be placed in the vault that the original once graced? Basile says these decisions are still in the future.

We leave the lab for the church, which is sealed off by a construction fence. Inside, the immense nave has sprouted a forest of silver scaffolding with golden joints all the way up to the ceiling. Leave it to the Italians to have the most elegant scaffolds in the world. I step behind the poles near the entrance for a glimpse of the St. Francis cycle on the walls. There are twenty-eight paintings in all, showing such significant moments in the saint's life as his sermon to the birds. These have a plainspoken directness that reflects the saint, an ardent popularizer who delivered sermons in conversational Italian and avoided the pomp and circumstance of the Papacy. How many of the images Giotto actually limned himself has kept scholars beetle-browed for some time. Given the likely dates for the cycle, Giotto, who was born around 1277, would have been painting astonishingly mature works in his early twenties, since the frescoes precede his epochal decorations for the Arena Chapel in Padua, where he worked from 1305 to 1306. The Italian sage Federico Zeri, for instance, likes to credit the Roman Pietro Cavallini, making his case through a comparison of figure types and saints' sizes, an exercise that many other historians find interesting but unconvincing.

"Giotto and workshop" is still generally accepted for both the St. Francis cycle and the Magdalen Chapel in the Lower Church, which was painted after Giotto returned to Assisi as the big star of Italian painting (and a future benchmark for the fat: "Round like the *o* in Giotto" is the Italian version of "calorie-challenged").

"It is a miracle not more was damaged," says Sergio Fusetti, the church's conservator for twenty-five years, who is standing by the entrance watching his crew climb down the scaffolding for lunch, all dressed in white, and virtually all about to light a cigarette. No doubt the story of the photographer Ghigo Roli's fortunate addiction has only encouraged local smoking. During the morning of September 26, 1997, Roli was helping to inspect the damage of a fairly minor quake during the night when he stepped outside for a cigarette. He heard a growling sound, turned around, and saw the smoking rubble from the collapsing vaults.

"I myself was buried with the altar, where the second vault collapsed," says Fusetti, who crawled away with three broken ribs. "But never mind that," he continues. "A few more seconds and the entire ceiling could have come down." He explains what made the crash so lethal, giving me a quick course in construction techniques. A vaulted ceiling is hung on a system of interconnected ribs that are attached to the roof; the pressure on the walls is contained by external buttresses, typical of pointy-arched Gothic buildings. To add further stability, builders typically stuffed the empty spaces between the roof and the vaults with rubble, a construction technique used in earlier Romanesque structures. But the pressure points on a round Romanesque arch and a pointed arch are different. While the fill strengthened the keystone in Romanesque arches, it only added destructive weight to the basilica's Gothic vaults.

When the quake bounced the church around, the loose rubble moved and pushed against the vaulting, which could not sustain the pressure. Those sections broke, raining down some two tons of plaster, bricks, and rubble along with the frescoes. Fusetti figures 1,200 more tons remained after the quake, all of which had to be removed.

Fusetti picks up his files and follows his conservators out the door, passing underneath the miraculously unharmed rose window, as I stay behind, thinking of the trays, boxes, tables, and storage rooms filled with remnants, and wondering if anything short of levitating saints can lift the bits and pieces back to the starry vault. Then again, if thirteenth-century masons could put up a large church in a matter of years, perhaps fixing it will not be beyond the capacities of their millennial descendants.

And so I leave, hope-filled, stepping into the blazing sun on a day so hot that cooked pigeons could fall out of the sky—another Italian saying, perhaps not very sensitive to this special place, but very apt. Hope is not a mood likely to be shared by the thousands in such out-of-the-way towns and hamlets as Gualdo Tadino or Nocera Umbra, whose inhabitants pass hardscrabble lives without ever seeing a tour bus.

Some of these places in the umbra of Assisi are now so quiet that you can hear chickens scratching a block away: Life in the last year has changed immeasurably, and perhaps forever.

A policeman and a sweaty fireman in flame-resistant pants stop me at Nocera Umbra's portal that afternoon. The fireman tells me that the city was declared unsafe after the quake and sealed within its medieval walls. He points into the valley, where the landscape now features a new village of "containers"—prefab structures for which the Italian language has no equivalent. (The prefab church with gabled roof and aluminum siding that the government provided to the larger container communities is thus called Madonna dei Containers.) In the small park outside Nocera's gate, people have put up hand-lettered posters that vent their frustration with hot containers and slow bureaucrats.

No legendary monuments distinguish Nocera Umbra, but these little places are the humble background against which Assisi sparkles. Even before the quakes their populations were dwindling, and whether the will and the funds exist to rebuild is very much in question, although some places have shown great spirit in adversity. In Bevagna, half an hour away, the mayor, a chunky optimist named Bruno Bini, tells me that he ordered exterior scaffolding removed as quickly as was safely possible, to restore a sense of confidence within the community. He banned container housing, found empty apartments for the displaced, and bought his first tuxedo. "No, not to cheer myself up," he grins, looking up from his truffled *strangozzi,* a local specialty. "To meet the Prince of Wales." The British chapter of the World Monuments Fund is helping to restore Bevagna's San Silvestro; prince and mayor shook hands at the fund-raising gala in London last June. Bini can't wait to hang the official photograph inside the ovenlike trailer that serves as the temporary city hall.

Even more endangered are the tiny *pievi*—rural churches modest enough to please Saint Francis, yet often embellished with the carved beasts and pale frescoes that excite the most exacting art historian. In sleepy Castel Ritaldi, the Friends of Assisi, a group of New Yorkers who summer in and around Todi, have adopted the *pieve* of San Gregorio, a medieval church with a beautifully carved facade dating back to 1141. After several quakes, the last this April, the facade began lifting away from the masonry wall and the church was closed, dispersing an active congregation. Just $200,000 will restore the church to its people and posterity.

In the area of Sellano, where tiny hamlets cling to gruff escarpments linked by dusty roads, the devastation is worse. Walking through Montesanto, a one-street town overlooking a peaceful valley, the only sounds I hear are chirping birds and cicadas echoing like 747s in the ghostly quiet. Flowerpots sprout weeds, and lizards skitter up cracked walls and across abandoned patios.

"I don't think I will ever see it open again," an old peasant woman says, giving me a start as I creep out from underneath the plywood buttress. She has suddenly materialized on the stony path in the company of a tabby.

"He's *vecchio* [old], like me," she says by way of introduction, swinging her feed bucket in the cat's direction. He appeared from somewhere after the quake looking hungry, she says, and is now her companion on her daily peregrinations between her container and her coop of guinea hens. As they walk away, I hear one mewling, the other muttering. It isn't quite the sermon of the birds, but the spirit is right.

After the Earthquakes

Assisi and Beyond

While the 1997 earthquakes and aftershocks damaged several thousand private and public buildings (mostly churches) in Umbria—as well as in the neighboring province of The Marches—few major sites are closed. "What earthquake?" a New Jersey couple ask, pondering the nun huddling at a table and collecting alms for "quake repair" underneath a visibly cracked ceiling in the Basilica of Santa Chiara— Saint Clare—who headed up the women's wing of the Franciscan movement. American visitors in particular seem to expect that large numbers of Italy's monuments spend years draped in drop cloths.

If you are willing to help with the reconstruction and preservation efforts, contact the World Monuments Fund/Friends of Assisi (949 Park Avenue, New York, N.Y. 10028; 212-517-9367; fax: 9494).

Assisi

Main sights: The Basilica of St. Francis, Santa Chiara, San Damiano, Eremo delle Carceri (avian sermon site, a few miles outside the walls), and Santa Maria degli Angeli (containing the Porziuncola). **Condition:** The Upper Church is closed for repairs at least until Christmas 1999. The Lower Church and Crypt, which contains the bones of Saint Francis, are open and unscaffolded. The cracks in the Porziuncola have been repaired; Santa Chiara is open but heavily scaffolded. San Damiano, the convent where Saint Clare lived, suffered minor damage but is open; the Eremo, or hermitage, suffered none at all, although the fabled oak tree will surely collapse underneath the next sparrow.

Bevagna

Main sights: The Roman theater recycled into medieval housing; the hushed piazza with two Romanesque churches. **Condition:** Speedy emergency repairs have restored the town's quiet charm, although the extensively damaged churches will remain closed for years.

Foligno

Main sight: The richly decorated, long-suffering Palazzo Trinci, a rare surviving example of a patrician residence at the dawn of the

Renaissance. Shook up by the area's 1832 earthquake and World War II bombing; the major monument in a town short on charm. **Condition:** Lucky this time, the Trinci is open to the public after many years of restoration and stabilization. The less fortunate bell tower on the town hall swayed and finally crumpled in front of TV cameras in October 1997 as three aftershocks hit the area.

Gubbio

Main sights: The Piazza della Signoria, with the Palazzo dei Consoli and picture gallery and, for Francis fans, San Francesco, which includes parts of the house in which he resided while negotiating the peace settlement with Gubbio's hungry wolf. **Condition:** Unharmed.

Montefalco

Main sight: The church-museum of San Francesco, with scenes of the saint's life by Benozzo Gozzoli, an underappreciated painter with a flair for footwear and fine hats. **Condition:** The church is open, despite damage to the apse; the Gozzolis are partly draped for nontraumatic damage.

Orvieto

Main sight: The zebra-striped duomo towering festively over the piazza —breathtaking, from the bronze doors to the recently restored chapel by Luca Signorelli, whose vision of Hell and damnation thrilled Michelangelo, if not the painter's fickle girlfriend (she appears as the prostitute companion of the Antichrist). **Condition:** Extremely minor damage was caused to the duomo, but none to the chapel, which is open to the pious (no faking—the guard checks for bowed heads and closed eyes), although heathens may visit at certain times with a ticket from the tourist agency across the piazza.

Perugia

Main sights: The thirteenth-century town square, with fountain, cathedral, and immense Palazzo dei Priori. **Condition:** The fountain is unharmed, there is very minor damage to the cathedral, and the palace is undergoing consolidation and is partly scaffolded.

Spello

Main sights: The town itself, with its narrow streets, covered passageways, tiny hidden squares, chapel painted by Pinturicchio, and examples of the *porta del morto*—a raised secondary entrance designed to deflect intruders and extrude corpses onto the street. **Condition:** Excellent. The Pinturicchios in Santa Maria Maggiore are as fresh as the water flowing past the tiny fisherman and village idiot sitting in the background of *The Adoration of the Shepherds*.

Spoleto

Main sight: The duomo, with *Life of the Virgin* frescoes by Fra Filippo Lippi, who spent his days painting chaste Madonnas and his nights with a nun he'd abducted from a convent where he was saying Mass. (They later married and were so popular that when Lippi died, the Spoletini refused to part with his corpse, claiming they were short on famous dead people, and buried him right in the church, in a nice casket ordered up by Lorenzo de' Medici.) **Condition:** There are minor repairs to the duomo, but the Lippi paintings are unharmed and can be visited.

Todi

Main sights: The Piazza del Popolo, with Ivanhoe-era buildings and, outside the walls, Santa Maria della Consolazione—its bulbous beauty peculiarly suggestive of St. Peter's and *gelato misto*. **Condition:** Unharmed.

Pilgrimage to Assisi

"Have a room for two pilgrims?" we asked the round-faced, somber manager of the Hôtel Subasio in Assisi at 9 P.M. one evening last summer.

He looked up from his book and said, "I think we can accommodate you."

And the next dozen people who come wandering in unannounced. Hotels, even parking places, are easy to come by throughout Umbria and The Marches in the aftermath of last year's earthquakes.

Lodging and Dining

In Assisi, we left the car alongside the colonnade leading to the basilica, which towered over us as the sky turned dove blue and mauve. Hôtel Subasio is just a few vertiginous steps away, a nineteenth-century hotel whose grand days have faded a bit since the huge guest book recorded the visits of the ceaselessly traveling king of Belgium, the moneybags art historian Bernard Berenson, and Bette Davis (!). Decorative additions to the lobby include framed reproductions of Peter Paul Rubens' fleshy *Three Graces,* of which just one would have sent Saint Francis into cardiac arrest. But room No. 42, meanwhile, had *three* narrow balconies overlooking Santa Maria degli Angeli as well as the west side of the basilica. It would not have been available without a reservation at the same time last year. "Right after the quake, we just closed down for three months. Nobody came," said Lucio Trappelli, the day manager. He'd been behind the desk on September 26 and had watched as the door to the bar swung sideways and then up and down. He ran outside and saw smoke belching out of the cathedral's entrance—actually the dust from the collapsing vault (075.812206; fax: 075.816691; doubles, about $175).

It was twenty minutes north of Assisi, however, where we found the ideal mixture of the sybaritic and the saintly. Le Silve di Armenzano is a small country hotel with a swimming pool, a fine restaurant, and a spectacular site overlooking a countryside not all that changed since the days of the first Franciscan. Carefully planned by its Roman owner to incorporate medieval buildings, it is part of a working farm inside a large regional park. Breakfast was on a terrace facing the sunrise and a valley filled with the owner's curious deer herd. during dinner we watched the sun set on Le Silve's cows, every one of them outfitted with appealing bells (075.8019000; fax: 075.8019005; doubles about $175).

Farther south, outside Foligno, is the coolly spectacular Relais II Canalicchio, inserted into a bird's nest of a *borgo,* or hamlet. Equipped with a stunningly sited pool and a panoramic restaurant, the hotel has an isolated splendor very different from the more casually run Le Silve, whose front desk signora puts on an apron come dinner time (075.8707325; fax: 075.8707296; doubles, about $115–$150.

In Bevagna, which has a medieval festival in June, lunch started with a memorable black truffle frittata at the L'orto degli Angeli, underneath a hanging garden that connects two scenic palaces. Both belong to Francesco Mongalli, a silver-haired aristocrat who returned to his long-shuttered family home to open an elegantly low-key hotel and restaurant inside its historic walls. Then came the quake. Signor Mongalli and his excellent cook wouldn't mind welcoming a few more tourists to Bevagna (0742.360130; fax: 0742. 361756; doubles, about $120–$145).

Reading

The Britishly wry Rough Guide to *Tuscany & Umbria* proved reliable and amusingly informative. The Cadogan guide to *Tuscany, Umbria & The Marches* was no less well written and filled with the kind of eccentric stuff that lingers in the mind, as in: "The traditional way of cooking *fagioli* (white beans) was to put olive oil, herbs, beans and a little water inside an empty Chianti bottle (with the straw wrapping removed) and leave them to cook for several hours beside or above the embers of a charcoal fire." Alas, the bottle is no longer what it was—so best use a casserole. Passport's *Umbria, The Marches & San Marino* is more literary but useless as a practical guide.

The Basilica of St. Francis of Assisi: Glory and Destruction (Abrams) includes the hair-raising account by photographer Ghigo Roli, who was fortunately a smoker. He had just stepped outside the basilica for a cigarette when the vaults fell. *Assisi: The Frescoes in the Basilica of St. Francis* (Rizzoli), another picture book, is less about the earthquake than it is about the basilica as a whole, including both Upper and Lower churches.

Biblioteca

Umbria: Italy's Timeless Heart, Paul Hofmann, Henry Holt and Company, 1998. There is hardly a better companion to Umbria than Hofmann, also author of *Cento Città, That Fine Italian Hand*, and *The Seasons of Rome*. In addition to Hofmann's personal observations, there is an appendix on each town with specifics on altitude (this might seem odd, but remember that the terrain is hilly), hotels, restaurants, sights to see, and directions. *Essenziale*.

A Valley in Italy: The Many Seasons of a Villa in Umbria, Lisa St. Aubin de Teran, HarperCollins, 1994 (hardcover); HarperPerennial, 1995 (paperback). Besides being the only memoir—by an Italian *or* an expatriate—I've read about living in Umbria, this is a really delightful account of life at Villa Orsola. A great companion read. You'll wish for more when you reach the end.

La Bella Vita
(Good Things, Favorite Places)

"Wherever I go, I am surrounded by these beautiful objects . . . and all is Italian; not a house, not a shed, not a field that the eye can for a moment imagine to be American."
—Ralph Waldo Emerson (European tour, 1832)

GRANTED, IT'S QUITE PERSONAL, but this is my list, in no particular order, and subject to change on any day of the week, of some favorite things to see, do, and buy. A note about stores: I have a particular knack for "discovering" shops that a year or so later end up in books and articles; therefore, I have tried not to be redundant, and only list retailers that also appear in *Made in Italy* (see Shopping/I Ricordi, below) if I have something different to say about them.

~**Corridoio Vasariano** (Vasari Corridor): I've always been impressed by Cosimo de' Medici's plan to construct a covered passageway connecting the Galleria degli Uffizi on the north bank of the Arno to the Palazzo Pitti on the south bank, via the Ponte Vecchio. It was a brilliant idea, and it was brilliantly designed by architect Giorgio Vasari. The corridor might be difficult to visualize if you've never seen it before, and in that case I direct you to a nifty book called *Bridges: A History of the World's Most Famous and Important Spans* (by Judith Dupre, introduction by Frank Gehry; Black Dog & Leventhal, 1997), which is published in a horizontal format measuring 18″ by 8″, allowing for the best possible presentation of bridges. The double-page spread photograph of the Ponte Vecchio reveals its ingenious design, and the accompanying text provides interesting details and construction facts. To visit the corridor, check with the tourist office as hours are sporadic after bomb damage in 1993.

~**Giulio Giannini & Figlio** (Piazza Pitti 36–37/r): Founded in 1856, this is Florence's oldest marbled-paper shop, just across the street from the Palazzo Pitti. Marbled paper probably originated in

Japan or Persia and flourished in Turkey in the fifteenth century. It made its way to Europe via Venice, a natural point of entry as it has always looked eastward; but today most marbled paper is made in Florence. The sheets of paper, paper products, and hand-tooled leather book bindings are beautiful gifts, for yourself included. Other shops I like for fine paper products are Il Torchio (via dei Bardi 17), Il Papiro (Piazza Duomo 24/r), Il Parione (Via Parione 10/r), and Pineider (Piazza della Signoria 13/r and Via de' Tornabuoni 76/r).

~**Aldo Giorgi** (Piazza Santa Croce 32/r, Florence): An old workshop for painted wooden boxes, trays, furniture, mirrors, etc.

~**Battistero** (baptistry) doors of San Giovanni (Florence): Designed and executed from 1425 to 1452 by Lorenzo Ghiberti, the carved doors are magnificent. Note that the originals underwent serious restoration work in 1989, and, after six years, were moved to the museum indoors. The doors you see outside are copies.

~**Officina Profumo-Farmaceutica di Santa Maria Novella** (via della Scala 16, Florence): This farmaceutica/erborista is now quite famous, but when I first walked inside, in 1990, it was quite by accident and it was not mentioned in any guidebooks. The Officina is the most beautiful retail shop I have ever been in in my life and is worth visiting just to see the interior; but I doubt you'll be able to leave empty-handed. All the lotions, potions, soaps, and scents—for men and women—are made from herbs and plants that grow in the hills of Tuscany. The potpourri is unbelievably wonderful. Thank God there is an Officina boutique in New York in the Takashimaya Building (693 Fifth Avenue, New York, New York 10022; 212-350-0100) that also fills mail orders. Prices are only slightly higher.

~**The Uffizi,** every inch of it. *Uffizi* means offices as the building was originally the administrative headquarters for the Medici princes. I don't believe there is any better place in the world to look at Italian Renaissance paintings.

Sandro Botticelli's *Prima-vera, in the Uffizi*. For his book, *Greatest Works of Art of Western Civilization*, Thomas Hoving (former director of the Metropolitan Museum of Art in New York) included Sandro Botticelli's *Prima-vera*. He said of this magnificent painting that "among the thousands of works of Western art that depict floral motifs—the most popular of subjects—this triumphant burst of creative energy is by far the most subtle and luminous. It is as if every element in the image is made of or enveloped in flowers. Primavera is the best antidote I know of for the gloom of winter." Some works of art, when you encounter them, make you gasp. Primavera is one of them.

~**Madova** (via Guicciardini 1/r, Florence): Beautiful leather gloves can be purchased many places in Florence, but I think Madova is the best for selection, quality, size, and color. You can even be added to its mailing list and receive a catalog at home.

~**Brancacci Cappella, Santa Maria del Carmine** (Piazza del Carmine 14, Florence). A fire in the main portion of Santa Maria del Carmine in 1771 permanently darkened Masaccio's frescoes in the Brancacci chapel, but it wasn't until 1981 that restoration work began, not to be completed until June 1990. The fanfare surrounding their unveiling was justified: They are truly stunning and unusual, and if you doubt me, here's what Leonardo da Vinci had to say about them in 1550 in his *Treatise on Painting:* "After Giotto, art declined, because all artists imitated other paintings, and continued to decline, until Tomaso Fiorentino, known as Masaccio, showed with perfect work how all others who chose a maestro other than nature, maestro of maestros, labored in vain."

~**Gelato,** anywhere, but especially at Vivoli (via Isola della Stinche 7, near Santa Croce in Florence).

~**Pizza,** especially the kind with thinly sliced potatoes and rosemary on top.

~**Menegatti** (piazza del Pesce 2/r, Florence, just across from the Ponte Vecchio): A wonderful (although expensive) ceramics shop with beautiful examples of *maioliche tradizionali.* The staff also arranges for shipping.

~**Museo di Firenze com'Era** (Florence as it Was, Via del Oriuolo 24): The history of Florence presented in old maps, plans, and watercolor views. Fascinating and never crowded.

~**Fiesole,** about a half hour up the hill from Florence. This beautiful, ancient suburb—which provides awesome panoramic views of Florence—is probably not on itineraries of first-time visitors. I admit it's difficult to convince someone to add another item to an already too-long list of things to see in Florence, but I would make an enthusiastic effort, even if that visitor came up the hill for just a few hours.

~**Piazza del Popolo,** Todi, "the finest small square in Italy": Even if I had not read this superlative I would have arrived at the same conclusion.

~**Terra di Siena** (piazza San Giovanni 14–15) and **Zina Provvedi** (Via di Citta, 96): Two wonderful ceramic shops in Siena, neither of which is possible to leave empty-handed.

~**Baskets of dried** *porcini* set out on counters in the most unpretentious shops, for about half the price of what they sell for in the U.S.

~**The walls of Lucca,** which I think are *almost* as impressive as the walls of Dubrovnik. They're 39' high, 98' thick, and 2½ miles long, and you can walk along the top for one of the best views anywhere in the world.

~The evening passegiata. Every Mediterranean country has a word for the evening walk, which is always before dinner and which serves as a way to see friends and relatives, put on fine clothes, and meet potential boyfriends or girlfriends. It is typically a family affair, including young children and the elderly, and is a wonderful tradition to witness. I also believe it's healthy and surely contributes to the scarcity of overweight people one sees in Italy.

~The landscape, no matter where you are. I am repeatedly reminded of an observation by Edith Wharton: "Travellers accustomed to the marked silhouette of Italian cities . . . often find the old French provincial towns lacking in physiognomy. Each Italian city, whether of the mountain or the plain, has an outline easily recognisable after individual details have faded, and it is, obviously, much easier to keep separate one's memories of Siena and Orvieto than of Bourges and Chartres." (*Edith Wharton Abroad: Selected Travel Writings, 1888–1920*, St. Martin's Press, 1995, 1996).

~Enotechi (wine bars), especially the Enoteca Italiana Permanente in Siena, Italy's largest.

~Driving around the countryside, anywhere. But be forewarned: You'll probably get lost at some point. I have a memory (and a photograph) of driving somewhere in the vicinity of Montespertoli with my husband, trying to find the house some family relatives had rented that summer. We came upon a T in the road. There was no indication at all of what roads we had actually come upon, or even what road we had been driving on. Only signs pointing in every direction for pizza. (P.S.: We never did find the house.)

Biblioteca—Companion Reading

....

Italy in Mind, edited and with an introduction by Alice Leccese Powers, Vintage
Departures, 1997. Book excerpts from works by Homer Bigart, Harold
Brodkey, Elizabeth Barrett Browning, Lord Byron, Eleanor Clark, Lawrence
Durrell, Mary Morris, William Murray, Tim Parks, John Ruskin, Bernard
Malamud, Susan Sontag, R.W.B. Lewis, Mark Twain, etc. Five of the passages
are about Florence or Tuscany.

Desiring Italy: Women Writers Celebrate the Passions of a Country and Culture,
edited by Susan Cahill, Fawcett Columbine, 1997. A very fine anthology of
book excerpts by women writers, including Barbara Grizzuti Harrision, Edith
Wharton, Mary McCarthy, Shirley Hazzard, Rose Macaulay, Mary Taylor
Simeti, Kate Simon, Iris Origo, Jan Morris, Muriel Spark, and Francine Prose,
among others. There are six pieces representing Tuscany and Umbria.

Edith Wharton Abroad: Selected Travel Writings, 1888–1920, edited by Sarah
Bird Wright with a preface by Shari Benstock, St. Martin's Press, 1995, 1996.
Included in this selection of seven of Wharton's travel pieces are two essays on
Italy: "Italian Villas and Their Gardens" and "Italian Backgrounds." Wharton
traveled widely in the years before World War I, and the other essays in this
collection are on Algiers, Tunis, Greece, Turkey, France, and Morocco. With
twenty black-and-white photos and illustrations and a glossary of foreign
words and phrases used throughout the text.

Just Visiting, George Grant and Karen Grant, Cumberland House Publishing,
Inc., Nashville, Tennessee, 1999. An unusual collection, which brings together
quotations, poems, remarks, and even recipes that emphasize the affect some of
the world's greatest cities—in this case, London, Edinburgh, Paris, Venice,
Florence, Vienna, New York, Washington, Jerusalem, and Rome—have had on
some of the best writers, observers, and leaders throughout history. More
importantly, the Grants share a view of travel that is so akin to my own that I
include it here enthusiastically and highly recommend this edition. Travel, they
write in the introduction, "has always been a component part of a well-rounded
education. The banal prejudice and narrow presumption that inevitably accompany all unexposed, inexperienced, and undiscerning existence can often be
ameliorated only by the disclosure of the habits, lifestyles, rituals, celebrations,
and aspirations of the peoples beyond the confines of our limited parochialism.
The great Dutch patriot Groen van Prinsterer aptly commented to his students,
'See the world and you'll see it altogether differently.'" They also share a quotation by a noted nineteenth-century Scottish architect, James Ferguson, who

penned that "Travel is more than a visitor seeing sights; it is the profound changing—the deep and permanent changing—of that visitor's perspective of the world, and of his own place in it." Very much worth reading.

Ceramics

Deruta: A Tradition of Italian Ceramics, Elizabeth Helman Minchilli, photographs by Susie Cushner and David Hamilton, in collaboration with Melanie Doherty, Chronicle Books, 1998. "Those familiar with Italian ceramics will have already heard of Deruta." So begins the text for this beautiful book relating the history and tradition of the brilliantly glazed pottery known as majolica. Deruta might be the best-known brand of Italian ceramics; it is certainly the oldest, having been produced for over six centuries without interruption. The town of Deruta has also become inseparable from its ceramics. Visitors can hardly escape—not that they would want to—their presence in the hilltop town, nor really anywhere else in Umbria or Tuscany. This work is a portrait of both the craft and the town, and it also contains a helpful directory of sources where the pottery can be purchased in Italy, the U.S., and Canada, as well as museums and churches worldwide that hold Deruta ceramics in their collections.

"Italys Majolica Road" (Irwin Glusker, *Gourmet,* September 1997) is a great article to read with a thorough description of this popular earthenware and recommendations for places to stay, eat, and visit.

Classics

Italo Calvino, in his thoughtful book *Why Read the Classics?* (Pantheon, 1999), notes that "Classics are books which, the more we think we know them through hearsay, the more original, unexpected, and innovative we find them when we actually read them." Don't postpone joy, then! Here's a selection to choose from, to read or reread, poetry included. These are available in several different publishing series (Modern Library, Plume, etc.) in both hardcover and paperback. The choice is yours.

The Decameron, Giovanni Boccaccio
The Divine Comedy, Dante Alighiere
The Prince, Niccolo Machiavelli

Fiction and Poetry

All Our Yesterdays, Natalia Ginzburg, published in the U.S. by Arcade Publishing, Little, Brown Company, by arrangement with Seaver Books, 1989; originally published in Italy under the title *Tutti I Nostri Ieri,* © 1952 by Giulio Einaudi editore s.p.a.; translation © 1956 by Martin Secker & Warburg, Ltd.

The English Patient, Michael Ondaatje, Alfred A. Knopf, 1997, hardcover; Vintage, 1998, paperback.

Italian Fever, Valerie Martin, Alfred A. Knopf, 1999.

Italian Folktales, selected and retold by Italo Calvino, Pantheon, 1992; original © 1956 by Giulio Einaudi editore, s.p.a.; English translation © 1980 by Harcourt Brace Jovanovich, Inc.

The Little Virtues, Natalia Ginzburg © 1962 by Giulio Einaudi editore s.p.a., translation © 1985 by Dick Davis; originally published in Italy under the title *Le Piccole Virtu*; first Arcade paperback edition 1989.

Partisan Wedding, Renata Viganò, University of Missouri, 1999. Though this story collection is fiction, it is based on the true efforts of women who were members of the Italian resistance in World War II, the author included.

Poets in a Landscape, Gilbert Highet, A Common Reader Edition published by The Akadine Press, Inc., 1996; original © 1957. A very original and beautiful book, presenting Italy as the home and inspiration of seven of the greatest Roman poets: Catullus, Vergil, Propertius, Horace, Tibullus, Ovid, and Juvenal. Umbria is featured in the chapter on Propertius.

Rat King, Michael Dibdin, Faber & Faber.

A Rich Full Death, Michael Dibdin, Vintage.

The Road to San Giovanni, Italo Calvino, Vintage International, 1994; translated from the Italian by Tim Parks.

A Room With a View, E. M. Forster, published by several different publishers.

The Secret Book of Grazia dei Rossi, Jacqueline Park, Simon & Schuster, 1997.

The Things We Used to Say, Natalia Ginzburg, translated from the Italian and introduced by Judith Woolf, originally published in Italian under the title *Lessico Famigliare* © 1963 by Giulio Einaudi s.p.a.; translation © 1997 by Judith Woolf. Ginzburg asked that this be read as a novel, but it is actually autobiographical, and she makes the single best short observation about World War II in Italy that I've ever read: "We thought that the war would immediately turn everyone's lives upside down. Instead, for years many people remained undisturbed in their own homes and went on doing the things they had always done. Then just when everyone thought that in fact they had got off lightly and that there would not be any devastations after all, nor houses destroyed nor flights nor persecutions, then all of a sudden bombs and shells exploded everywhere and houses collapsed and the streets were full of rubble and soldiers and refugees. And there was no longer a single person who could pretend that nothing was happening and close their eyes and stop their ears and bury their head under the pillow, not one. That is what the war was like in Italy."

Where Angels Fear to Tread, E. M. Forster, published separately as well as in Forster collections.

~I must make special mention of a new book imprint, Steerforth Italia, which has embarked upon a mission to introduce American readers to fine books by Italians and about Italy. "The Italians," to quote from the Steerforth catalog, "have created one of the great national literatures of the twentieth century. . . . Above all the Italians have created a great literature of witness to the central struggle of the century between democracy and Fascism. Ignazio Silone and Natalia Ginzburg described the onset of Fascist authoritarianism under Benito Mussolini before the Second World War. Giorgio Bassani related the terrible fate of the Italian Jews in the Holocaust. Elsa Morante chronicled the everyday hardships of life during the war, and Carlo Levi recreated the heartbreaking chaos of a shattered Italian society when the war was finally over." At the time this book was nearing completion, the titles Steerforth had published thus far were not specifically Tuscan or Umbrian in theme or characters or plot; but this is no reason not to read them, and I share them with you most enthusiastically. Not only is each book a superb literary work, but each is beautifully printed: *The Conformist*, Alberto Moravia; *Journey to the Land of the Flies and Other Travels*, Aldo Buzzi; *Open City: Seven Writers and Rome*, edited and with an introduction by William Weaver; *The Watch*, Carlo Levi; and *The Woman of Rome*, Alberto Moravia.

Italian Style and Decorating

Italia: The Art of Living Italian Style, Edmund Howard with photographs by Oliver Benn, first published in Great Britain, 1996; published in the U.S. by St. Martin's Press, 1997. Although encompassing all of *Italia*, there is enough material in this beautiful book on Florence, Perugia, Pisa, Pistoia, San Gimignano, Siena, Spoleto, Arezzo, Assisi, Gubbio, Orvieto, Lucca, and Montepulciano to make it worth consulting even if you never travel to other parts of Italy. Chapters are organized by themes, such as Interiors, Gardens, Details, etc., and there is a visitor's guide at the back of the book, plus a bibliography.

Tuscany Interiors, Paolo Rinaldi, edited by Angelika Taschen, Taschen, 1998. One of the gorgeous editions in the Taschen "Interiors" series (other titles feature New York, Paris, Provence, Morocco, and India). Beautiful and creative interiors in six areas of Tuscany are presented in full color, with text in three languages: English, French, and German. The opening essay, "Tuscany: A Journey Into Harmony," is excellent.

Bringing Italy Home: Creating the Feeling of Italy in Your Home Room by Room, Cheryl MacLachlan, photographs by Bardo Fabiani, Clarkson Potter, 1995.

Italian Country, Clarkson Potter, 1988.

Shopping/I Ricordi

I am not much into shopping as a general rule, but I enjoy buying gifts for other people, especially when I'm traveling. Most of what I purchase, even for myself, falls into the food and wine category, and I have found that even Italian supermarkets sell beautifully packaged items of yummy stuff that in the U.S. is hard to find, expensive, or both. Occasionally, I look for other types of singular gifts, so I've enjoyed consulting *Made in Italy: A Shopper's Guide to Florence, Milan, Rome & Venice* (Annie Brody and Patricia Schultz, Workman Publishing Company, 1988). I know this book is over ten years old, but I still recommend it if you are at all interested in discovering some unique shops, bargains, workshops, and manufacturers' outlets. In the first place, many of the establishments listed are not only still in business but thriving. And in the second place, this book is much more than a shopping guide; it includes a very good—and still applicable—"Shopping With Know-How" section, covering things such as money matters, size chart, symbols for reading labels, shipping services, and a glossary of words for shops, food stores, store signs, etc. Short essays are provided for local specialties, such as Ferragamo, factory outlets, Gucci, the erboristeria, international antiques fair, and extra-virgin olive oil. ~Another good book with not quite as much information is *Frommer's Born to Shop—Italy: The Ultimate Guide for Travelers Who Love to Shop* (Suzy Gershman, 1999). One of the best things about this paperback is its size, which is so slender it will fit in any bag or a large pocket. There is a separate chapter on Florence. ~Customer service as we know it in the States is an unknown concept in Italy. Customers are almost never right, and you should not expect to return anything you've purchased, for any reason. ~If you're buying packaged foods, look for the expiration date (*data di scadenza*). Dried mushrooms in particular, of any variety, can and do go bad and shouldn't be stored over hot summer months. Pasta, rice, and polenta can be purchased vacuum-packed, and even though these packages are rather lumpy to pack in your bag, they're better for traveling. ~Useful vocabulary: *prezzi fissi* (fixed prices).

Hands-On Renaissance

BY LEIGH NEWMAN

~

editor's note

Short of donating money to help preserve Italy's art works, the next best thing is to participate in a restoration project, and this piece details some unique opportunities for visitors to do so.

LEIGH NEWMAN is a contributing editor of *Travel Holiday,* where this piece originally appeared.

A marble head, a hand, an elbow, and a chunk of torso lie scattered on a paint-flecked table. On the wall behind them hangs a black-and-white photograph of a little boy sculpted from that same stone. Yellow grease-pencil arrows criss-cross the photograph, pointing to the boy's arm, head, and any other place where the jigsaw of body parts he is now might possibly fit together. "The biggest problem is," says Castello Isidoro, a restorer for the Opificio delle Pietre Dure, "we don't know the bends of his arms."

All Castello and his team have to guide them is this photograph— the only one in existence—and the nine or ten pieces left from the original figure Michelangelo created. The workshop air is thick with dust and ammonia. Machines whine in the background. Across the room, a laser flashes, zipping patches of centuries-old soot off another sculpture. Castello shows me the reconstructed base of the sculpture, where the boy's muscular legs stand torso-less, each texturized with a marble *chiaroscuro*. He only shakes his head at the photograph when I ask him how long it will take to finish this job. "When the marble sings," one of his co-workers says, pulling off his goggles. He is at work on a Donatello angel relief; he claims the "the color, the sound, the ring," of the marble help him find where to remove the grime and where to leave the stone untouched.

With a single photograph, with the sound of the stone, or with methods as scientific as solvents, CAT scans, and X-rays, Florence is restoring its Renaissance art—and history. As I walk out of the Opificio and down slatelike *pietra serena* sidewalks too narrow to negotiate except in single file, it seems as though everything in sight is either covered in scaffolding or crowded with visitors here to see the newly cleaned Botticelli or Giotto. Florence, best known for its adherence to tradition and its conservative spirit, is buzzing with new energy as masterwork after masterwork—from the simple frescoes in a family villa to the grandeurs of the Pitti palace—is rescued and refurbished. And as the scaffolding comes down and the artwork returns to its place in the gallery, you can't help but see the city and its treasures afresh. Perhaps for this reason, perhaps only to find out if marble does sing, I decide to go undercover, to join forces with the restorers saving the art that once saved Europe from the Dark Ages.

Past Palettes

Not surprisingly, Florence is the center for restoration technique as well as for the work itself. Though Rome too has a strong restoration community, Florence's enormous stores of Medici-funded art and its long tradition of skilled artisans, who repaired everything from gold to gilt frames for that same banking elite, have made it and restoration synonymous. Almost every school here has a restoration department—from the University of Florence to the state-run Opificio delle Pietre Dure (which accepts only a handful of students a year) to private programs such as Istituto per l'Arte e il Restauro Palazzo to the English-speaking Studio Art Centers International (or SACCI), where I enroll for a monthlong crash course.

"A painting is like a patient" says Roberta Lapucci, "Every one has different symptoms." Lapucci, wearing a white lab coat over her skirt, does resemble a doctor more than what she is: a specialist on Caravaggio's painting styles and a SACCI professor. Evidently, the typical image of a restorer, palette in hand, looking up at a painting and touching a brush to it here and there, is mostly fantasy. As Lapucci explains, you begin where the painting needs support, usually on the back, to clean and reinforce it. Often, the wooden frame needs replacing and the canvas re-stretching. Then, grime and dirt must be cleaned off the surface of the painting itself and any holes or missing paint must be filled in with applications of gesso (a plaster of paris-like paste).

Finally the restorer uses *trattegio,* a technique that creates an impressionistic patch of neutral colors on the gesso spots so they won't distract your eye from the actual painting. To practice this, I apply a layer of brush strokes to a cardboard mock-up—a square with a paper reproduction of Da Vinci's *Annunciation* attached to it.

Like many restoration techniques, *trattegio* doesn't require you to be an artist, or even be artistic. You only have to develop the skills, eye, and patience to build up layer after layer of watercolor until it matches one of the colors that exists in the original painting. These colors help to camouflage the *trattegio* patch. You also must master the brushwork—thin, delicate strokes, curved at the end— that distinguishes your work from the artist's, even in places where the *trattegio* is painted to mimic a missing section of the painting.

Though my struggles range from having too much water in my brush to having too much pigment in it, it's matching my *trattegio* colors to the mock-up's that turns out to be the most difficult— and the most illuminating—task. As I build up layers of brush strokes from eight to nine to ten, I realize that this brown, made of ochre and red and green and yellow, is the same brown that Da Vinci mixed and used. Almost any action in restoration—whether it's choosing between pasta or fish glue for the back of the canvas or deciding on the number of layers of gesso used to prime it—

requires you to re-create the same process as a Renaissance master. And that's an amazing, even chilling feeling. But at the same time, you must always remember to keep some distance. "The closer you stick to the original," Roberta Lapucci says, "the longer the painting will last."

Most students will end their course helping to restore a real painting, like the one at the front of the class: a fifteenth-century oil-on-wood panel that glistens with dark green trees and chiffon-colored nymphs. Like many you see in art restoration schools, this one is from a private collection, usually lent by a family in exchange for free restoration work. The sheer amount of art in Florence—and art old enough to be damaged—gives most students, even beginners, the opportunity to work on actual Renaissance pieces.

Dueling Paintbrushes

Inevitably, as I progress, the question comes up: Where is the line—figuratively and literally—drawn between the artist and the restorer. For the world, this question arose during the restoration of the Vatican's Sistine Chapel—a project completed under the glare of television cameras and the news media. Many critics challenged the results, claiming that Michelangelo's shadows and perspective had been cleaned off, ruining the frescoes in the process.

In contrast, Florence's most famous project remained shielded from such direct attacks—partly because the restoration was done in typical Florentine fashion, under wraps (as opposed to the southern Italian-style drama of the Sistine project), and partly because of the project site itself, the Brancacci Chapel. Nicknamed the Sistine Chapel of the North, the Brancacci has always more of a quiet masterpiece, a painters' painting hidden inside the unassuming brick facade of the Santa Maria del Carmine church.

Just off Via di Santo Spirito, where artisan *botteghe* or workshops continue the mosiac, gilt, and marble work of their Renaissance predecessors, the chapel's walls display daily life in this city-state at its zenith. In a cycle of twelve panels, three consecutive artists—Masaaccio, Masolino, and Filippino Lippi—painted the stories of the Old and New Testaments, but in the clothes, architecture, and manners of Renaissance Florence. The rich merchants that pass Saint Peter healing the lame wear the intricate brocades of the Florentine cloth merchants' guild. Piazzas, arches, and terra-cotta tile roofs fill each panel.

The restoration took more than nine years. There is even a false window that exactly replicates the original (including the movement of a fake sun though it) that was removed because it allowed too much pollution into the chapel. However, what you notice most is the color, cleaned of damage caused years of humidity, pollution, and the overzealous work of restorers in the past, blazing out in luminous pinks and greens and blues.

As you stand in front of one of these panels such as Adam and Eve's expulsion from Eden, where the genius of Masaccio is rubbed into every feature of their grieving faces as they walk toward a life in exile, it's easy to forget the controversy that surrounds this work. Critics charge that restorers cleaned the fresco with too heavy a hand. All the leaves on the trees, freshened up with new paint over the years, were removed in an effort to get the frescos as close to their original appearance as possible. Now the trunks stand sticklike, oddly bare. Even Adam's fig leaf was removed (though that decision was praised by many). Most disturbing is the loss of shadows that critics claim destroyed the innovations of perspective and *chiaroscuro* that made the fresco so revolutionary in its day.

Seeing Is Believing

However, as with any restoration project, no one can know exactly how these frescoes looked 600 years ago. Seventeen years ago, though, when the restorations began, they were clouded with dark films of milk and bread (historically used for cleaning), layers of candle smoke, and actual smoke stains from a fire in the eighteenth century. So many Florentines and visitors alike feel that no matter what was lost in the process, the restoration of the Brancacci Chapel ultimately brought the painting back to life just by letting people see it again. At any rate, it seems that controversy is as impossible to avoid in restoration as it is in Italian politics. Taking sides is part of the game, no surprise in Florence—a city founded by two feuding factions, the Guelfs and the Ghibellines, who left a legacy of Medici power struggles and intrigues.

Heading back over the Ponte Vecchio, I remember what Andrea Papi, a director of the Palazzo Spinelli Institute of Restoration, warned me about cleaning a painting. "What you take off," he said, "is gone forever." Perhaps, he, like every Florentine, was forced to learn that lesson too well. In the fall of 1966 the Arno that I'm now crossing overflowed its stone banks, inundating almost every museum and church in the city, even ripping five of Ghiberti's bronze panels off the Baptistery doors.

Santa Croce, the resting place of Dante and Michelangelo, reveals how much that flood cost Florence. I walk through the quiet cloisters under a loggia of stone arches where Cimabue's famous crucifix is mounted. A dramatic, emaciated Christ hangs from a wooden cross, all rib and hip and elbow against a blue and gold background. I try to imagine this figure as it was discovered in 1966, floating in floodwater and swollen to twice its size. It took restorers more than a year just to shrink the wood. Experts declared the piece was close to 70 percent damaged. But as restorers flocked to Florence to save it, later establishing new schools, techniques, and workshops, Cimabue's masterpiece became a kind of talisman for the repair of the entire city.

At first glance, the crucifix today seems to be just a simple wooden figure, its gold made more brilliant by the white wall behind. But where the thin line of blood drips down, Christ's foot is missing,

Instead, there's a putty colored splotch that contrasts with Cimabue's gold and greens. That blemish, along with many like it, seems like a catastrophe on such a masterpiece. But as I get closer, I can make out a rippled quality to the putty-color from the application of layer upon layers of watercolor, *trattegio*-style. If I lean my head to one side, I can make out the difference in the brush strokes. There—in the contrast between the original and the restoration—the genius of Cimabue's line and iridescent color is finally revealed. I begin to understand the real artistry hiding in this disfigured icon. I see what the artist might have painted for us to see—the patient, downcast man suffering in his beauty and his humanity.

Most of the restoration schools in Florence are two- to three-year programs, designed for students who want to become professional restorers. However, a few run one- to two-month courses in the spring, summer, and fall. You learn the basic techniques of saving both the front and back of a painting, as well as *trattegio* retouching. Most courses will put you to work on paintings that are about 300 years old, which the schools restore for private collectors.

Because it's the only school with English-speaking instructors, the best choice for Americans is probably Studio Art Centers International, or SACI, which runs monthlong programs in art conservation in the late spring or summer. Field trips to major restoration sites, workshops, and museums in Florence are included. (In Florence, call 055.48.61.64. In the U.S., call the Institute of International Education at 212-984-5548. Tuition: about $3,000). Another school, considered one of the best in Florence, is the Istituto per l'Arte e il Restauro, Palazzo Spinelli. In July, August, and September it offers two- to four-week courses in everything from painting restoration to gilding to wood and paper conservation—many of them held in a sixteenth-century palace. Courses in Italian are offered to help get foreigners up to speed (Spinelli's head office is located on Borgo Santa Croce, 10; 055.24.60.01; tuition is about $800 to $1,250 per course).

If you're interested in restoration but not a hands-on experience, there are a number of places to visit in Florence. For the next two years, Cellini's famous statue of Perseus, which used to stand outside the Palazzo Vecchio, is being restored behind a wall of glass. You can observe restorers removing the mineral deposits under his eyes, take a multimedia tour of Renaissance Florence on a computer, or watch a short film that explains the process of making the statue and saving it (Perseo Benvenuto nel Futuro, Live and On-Line, Galleria degli Uffizi, 10 A.M. to 5 P.M., Wednesday–Sunday, free). The Opificio delle Pietre Dure, the state-run professional school of restoration and the most prestigious, has its own museum, Museo dell'Opificio delle Pietre Dure (Via degli Alfani, 78; 055.29.41.15). Though most of the displays focus on mosaic work, the school's original function, the museum still gives you a glimpse into the world of the craftsman, a world to which Florentine restorers consider themselves the heirs.

If you're looking for a dose of the Renaissance while you sleep, try Loggiato dei Serviti (Piazza Santissima Annunziata, 3; 055.28.95.92; doubles start at about $185). Not only can you see the dramatic bronze sculptures on the cobblestoned piazza outside your window, but the rooms will give you a feel for the age when they were sculpted. Vaulted ceilings in parchment colors, tasseled key rings, and regal, drapery-covered headboards evoke the past without overwhelming you with flounces and musty clutter.

Additional Credits

Informazioni Pratiche: From *Time Out Guide: Florence & Tuscany.* Penguin Books, 1997 edition.

La Cronaca Mondana: Carol Field, *Celebrating Italy,* William Morrow, 1990, hardcover; Harper Perennial, 1997, paperback.

La Cucina Italiana: David Leavitt, Mark Mitchell, from "Flavor" *Italian Pleasures,* Chronicle Books, 1996.

Firenze: Mark Twain, *The Innocents Abroad,* originally published in 1868.

Piazze, Giardini, e Monumenti: D. H. Lawrence, *Aaron's Rod,* Martin Secker, London, 1922.

A Tavola!: Burton Anderson, from the introduction to *Treasures of the Italian Table: Italy's Celebrated Foods and the Artisans Who Make Them,* William Morrow, 1994.

I Personaggi: E.M. Forster, *Where Angels Fear to Tread,* originally published by William Blackwood & Sons, Edinburgh, 1905; first U.S. edition by Alfred A. Knopf, 1920. Sonja Bullaty and Angelo Lomeo, *Tuscany,* Abbeville Press, 1995. Text copyright © 1995 Marie-Ange Guillaume, photographs © 1995 Sonja Bullaty and Angelo Lomeo. English translation and compilation © 1995 Abbeville Press.

La Toscana: Sonja Bullaty and Angelo Lomeo, from the preface to *Tuscany,* Abbeville Press, 1995. Text copyright © 1995 Marie-Ange Guillaume, photographs © 1995 Sonja Bullaty and Angelo Lomeo. English translation and compilation © 1995 Abbeville Press. Mary McCarthy, *The Stones of Florence,* Harcourt Brace Jovanovich, 1959.

L' Umbria: Dana Facaros, Michael Pauls, *Cadogan Guide: Italy,* 1994 edition.

La Bella Vita: Ralph Waldo Emerson, from various editions of Emerson's collected essays and writings.